CELEBRATION HYMNAL FOR EVERYONE

PEOPLE'S EDITION

WITH SUPPLEMENT
1 – 1009

McCrimmons
Great Wakering, Essex, England

Celebration Hymnal for Everyone with Supplement was first published
in United Kingdom in 2005 by
McCRIMMON PUBLISHING COMPANY LIMITED.

10–12 High Street, Great Wakering, Essex SS3 0EQ, England.
Telephone: 01702–218956 Fax: 01702–216082
info@mccrimmons.com www.mccrimmons.com

CELEBRATION HYMNAL FOR EVERYONE	– WITH SUPPLEMENT (1 - 1009)		*McCrimmon Order reference*
People's edition	**(Plastic/PVC)**	**ISBN 978-0-85597 6-75-0**	**MB6756**
People's – Large Print edition	(Softback)	ISBN 978-0-85597 5-37-1	MB5377
Melody/Guitar edition	(Softback)	ISBN 978-0-85597 6-83-5	MB6837
CELEBRATION HYMNAL FOR EVERYONE	– WITHOUT SUPPLEMENT		
Full Music edition (1-856)	(Hardback)	ISBN 978-0-85597 5-36-4	MB5369
CELEBRATION HYMNAL FOR EVERYONE	– SUPPLEMENT ONLY		
People's edition (857-1009)	(Softback)	ISBN 978-0-85597 6-77-4	MB6772
Full Music edition (857-1009)	(Hardback)	ISBN 978-0-85597 6-78-1	MB6780

Revised by Jane Porter and Joan McCrimmon
Supplement edited by Tony Charlier

Cover design: Nick Snode
Typeset in Times 10/11.5pt and Optima 18pt and 7pt
Printed on 70gsm white woodfree
Printed in China

A/0G

Contents

1 Gregory Norbet, OSB

A child is born for us today, alleluia.
He is our Saviour and our God, alleluia.

1 Let our hearts resound with joy
and sing a song of gladness
for the Lord, our brother,
is come and we are redeemed.

2 Tell the world of our good news:
Jesus the Christ is among us,
and his presence we celebrate
offering peace and our joy to all.

3 Christ is born, the Christ has come!
Sing everyone 'Alleluia!'
Caught in wonder at this birth
we worship God become man for us.

4 Glory to God, born today
of the Virgin Mary,
in a cave at Bethlehem:
is there room in our lives for him?

5 His name shall be 'Emmanuel':
'God–who–lives–among–us',
angels sing and shepherds cry:
'Born is the saviour, our Lord!'

6 The magi went and worshipped him
with gifts so precious and costly.
In the fervour of their faith
they sought the child who is Lord and
King.

7 The Lord will make integrity
and peace to grow in our times.
A covenant he offers us:
lasting joy will be ours to share.

8 Arise! Shine out, Jerusalem!
The glory of Yahweh* has come to you.
Lift up your eyes and look around!
Radiant is your salvation!

* *Instead of 'Yahweh' you may prefer to substitute 'God'*

Final Refrain

A child is born for us today, alleluia.
He is our Saviour and our God, alleluia.
Alleluia, alleluia.

2 Latin, 14th century, tr. Ralph Wright, OSB

1 A child is born in Bethlehem, alleluia:
so leap with joy Jerusalem,
alleluia, alleluia.

A new song let us sing for Christ is born
let us adore and let our gladness ring.

2 Through Gabriel the Word has come,
alleluia:
the Virgin will conceive a son,
alleluia, alleluia.

3 Within a manger now he lies,
alleluia:
who reigns on high beyond the skies,
alleluia, alleluia.

4 The shepherds hear the angel's word,
alleluia:
this child is truly Christ the Lord,
alleluia, alleluia.

5 From Saba, from the rising sun,
alleluia:
with incense, gold, and myrrh they come,
alleluia, alleluia.

6 Till with their gifts they enter in,
alleluia:
and kings adore the new–born King,
alleluia, alleluia.

7 From virgin's womb this child is born,
alleluia:
the Light from Light who brings the dawn,
alleluia, alleluia.

8 He comes to free us from our strife,
alleluia:
and share with us the Father's life,
alleluia, alleluia.

9 At this the coming of the Word,
alleluia;
O come, let us adore the Lord,
alleluia, alleluia.

10 To Father, Son, and Spirit praise,
alleluia:
from all his creatures all their days,
alleluia, alleluia.

3 *Martin Luther (1483–1546), tr. Honor Mary Thwaites*

1 A mighty stronghold is our God,
a sure defence and weapon.
He'll help us out of every need
whatever now may happen.
The ancient evil fiend
has deadly ill in mind;
great power and craft are his,
his armour gruesome is;
on earth is not his equal.

2 With our own strength is nothing done
soon we are lost, dejected;
but for us fights the rightful Man
whom God himself elected.
You ask: Who may this be?
Christ Jesus it is he,
the Lord Sabaoth's Son,
our God, and he alone
shall hold the field victorious.

3 And though the world were full of fiends
all lurking to devour us,
we tremble not nor fear their bands,
they shall not overpower us.
The prince of this world's ill
may scowl upon us still,
he cannot do us harm,
to judgement he has come;
one word can swiftly fell him.

4 The Word they must allow to stand –
for this they win no merit;
upon the field, so near at hand,
he gives to us his Spirit.
And though they take our life,
goods, honour, child, and wife,
though we must let all go,
they will not profit so:
to us remains the Kingdom.

4 *Anonymous, based on John 13:34–35*

A new commandment I give unto you,
that you love one another as I have loved you,
that you love one another as I have loved you.
By this shall all men know that you are my disciples,
if you have love one for another.
By this shall all men know that you are my disciples,
if you have love one for another.

5 *German, 15th century, tr. Anthony G Petti*

1 A noble flow'r of Juda
from tender roots has sprung,
a rose from stem of Jesse,
as prophets long had sung;
a blossom fair and bright,
that in the midst of winter
will change to dawn our night.

2 The rose of grace and beauty
of which Isaiah sings
is Mary, virgin mother,
and Christ the flow'r she brings.
By God's divine decree
she bore our loving Saviour
who died to set us free.

3 To Mary, dearest mother,
with fervent hearts we pray:
grant that your tender infant
will cast our sins away,
and guide us with his love
that we shall ever serve him
and live with him above.

6 *James Quinn, SJ*

1 A sign is seen in heaven,
a maiden–mother fair;
her mantle is the sunlight,
and stars adorn her hair.
The maiden's name is Mary;
in love she brings to birth
the Lord of all the ages,
the King of all the earth.

2 Like moonlight on the hilltops
she shines on all below,
like sunlight on the mountains
her Child outshines the snow.
O Mary, Queen of mothers,
still smile on young and old;

bless hearth and home and harvest,
bless farm and field and fold.

3 Pray, Mother, Queen in glory,
before the Father's throne;
praise God's eternal Wisdom,
the Child who is your own;
rejoice in God the Spirit,
whose power let you conceive
the Child of Eden's promise,
O new and sinless Eve.

7 *Carey Landry*

Abba, Abba, Father, you are the potter,
we are the clay, the work of your hands.

1 Mould us, mould us and fashion us
into the image of Jesus, your Son,
of Jesus, your Son. *(2)*

2 Father, may we be one in you
as he is in you,
and you are in him. *(2)*

3 Glory, glory and praise to you,
glory and praise to you for ever. Amen.
For ever. Amen. *(2)*

8 *Ginny Vissing*

1 Abba, Father, send your Spirit.
Glory, Jesus Christ. *(2)*
Glory hallelujah, glory, Jesus Christ. *(2)*

2 I will give you living water …

3 If you seek me you will find me …

4 If you listen you will hear me …

5 Come, my children, I will teach you …

6 I'm your shepherd, I will lead you …

7 Peace I leave you, peace I give you …

8 I'm your life and resurrection …

9 Glory Father, glory Spirit …

Other words from Scripture may be substituted according to the occasion or the season. For example, in Advent:

1 Come, Lord Jesus, Light of nations …

2 Come, Lord Jesus, born of Mary …

3 Come, and show the Father's glory …

9 *Henry Francis Lyte (1793–1847)*

1 Abide with me, fast falls the eventide;
the darkness deepens, Lord, with me abide!
When other helpers fail, and comforts flee,
help of the helpless, O abide with me.

2 Swift to its close ebbs out life's little day;
earth's joys grow dim, its glories pass away;
change and decay in all around I see;
O thou who changest not, abide with me.

3 I need thy presence every passing hour;
what but thy grace can foil the tempter's power?
Who like thyself my guide and stay can be?
Through cloud and sunshine, O abide with me.

4 I fear no foe with thee at hand to bless;
ills have no weight and tears no bitterness.
Where is death's sting? Where, grave, thy victory?
I triumph still, if thou abide with me.

5 Hold thou thy Cross before my closing eyes;
shine through the gloom, and point me to the skies;
heaven's morning breaks, and earth's vain shadows flee:
in life, in death, O Lord, abide with me!

10 *Denis E. Hurley*

1 Across the years there echoes still
the Baptist's bold assertion:
the call of God to change of heart,
repentance and conversion.

2 The word that John more boldly spoke
in dying, than in living,
now Christ takes up, as he proclaims
a Father all–forgiving.

3 The erring son he welcomes home
when all is spent and squandered.
He lovingly pursues the sheep
that from the flock has wandered.

4 Forgive us, Lord, all we have done
to you and one another.
So often we have gone our way,
forgetful of each other.

5 Forgetful of the cross they bear
of hunger, want, oppression –
grant, Lord, that we may make amends,
who humbly make confession.

11

Jacques Berthier

A
B
(hum)
A- do- ra- mus te Do- mi- ne.

12

Attributed to St Thomas à Kempis (c 1380–1471)
tr. John Mason Neale (1818–66) and others

1 Again the Lord's own day is here,
the day to Christian people dear,
as week by week it bids them tell
how Jesus rose from death and hell.

2 For by his flock the Lord declared
his resurrection should be shared;
and we who trust in him to save
with him are risen from the grave.

3 We, one and all, of him possessed,
are with exceeding treasures blest;
for all he did and all he bore
is shared by us for evermore.

4 Eternal glory, rest on high,
a blessèd immortality,
true peace and gladness, and a throne,
are all his gifts and all our own.

5 And therefore unto thee we sing,
O Lord of peace, eternal King;
thy love we praise, thy name adore,
both on this day and evermore.

13

Johann H Heermann (1585–1647)
based on 11th century Latin
tr. Robert S Bridges (1844–1930)

1 Ah, holy Jesus, how hast thou offended,
that men to judge thee have in hate
pretended?
By foes derided, by thine own rejected,
O most afflicted.

2 Lo, the good Shepherd for the sheep is
offered;
the slave hath sinnèd, and the Son hath
suffered;
for our atonement, while he nothing
heedeth,
God intercedeth.

3 For me, kind Jesus, was thy incarnation,
thy mortal sorrow, and thy life's oblation;
thy death of anguish and thy bitter passion,
for my salvation.

4 Therefore, kind Jesus, since I cannot pay
thee,
I do adore thee, and will ever pray thee;
think on thy pity and thy love unswerving,
not my deserving.

14 *Hayward Osborne*

1 All creation, bless the Lord.
Earth and heaven, bless the Lord.
Spirits, powers bless the Lord.
Praise God for ever.
Sun and moon, bless the Lord.
Stars and planets, bless the Lord.
Dews and showers, bless the Lord.
Praise Him for ever.

2 Winds and breezes, bless the Lord.
Spring and Autumn, bless the Lord.
Winter, Summer, bless the Lord.
Praise God for ever.
Fire and heat, bless the Lord.
Frost and cold, bless the Lord.
Ice and snow, bless the Lord.
Praise Him for ever.

3 Night and daytime, bless the Lord.
Light and darkness, bless the Lord.
Clouds and lightning, bless the Lord.
Praise God for ever.
All the earth, bless the Lord.
Hills and mountains, bless the Lord.
Trees and flowers, bless the Lord.
Praise Him for ever.

4 Springs and rivers, bless the Lord.
Seas and oceans, bless the Lord.
Whales and fishes, bless the Lord.
Praise God for ever.
Birds and insects, bless the Lord.
Beasts and cattle, bless the Lord.
Let all creatures bless the Lord.
Praise Him for ever.

5 Let God's people bless the Lord.
Men and women, bless the Lord.
All creation, bless the Lord.
Praise God for ever.
Let God's people bless the Lord.
Men and women, bless the Lord.
All creation, bless the Lord.
Praise Him for ever.

15 *William Henry Draper (1855–1933) based on St. Francis of Assisi's 'Cantico di Frate Sole'*

1 All creatures of our God and King,
lift up your voice and with us sing
alleluia, alleluia!
Thou burning sun with golden beam,
thou silver moon with softer gleam:

O praise him, O praise him,
alleluia, alleluia, alleluia.

2 Thou rushing wind that art so strong,
ye clouds that sail in heaven along,
O praise him, alleluia!
Thou rising morn, in praise rejoice,
ye lights of evening, find a voice:

3 Thou flowing water, pure and clear,
make music for thy Lord to hear,
alleluia, alleluia!
Thou fire so masterful and bright,
that givest us both warmth and light:

4 Dear mother earth, who day by day
unfoldest blessings on our way,
O praise him, alleluia!
The flowers and fruits that in thee grow
let them his glory also show.

5 And all who are of tender heart,
forgiving others, take your part,
O sing ye, alleluia!
Ye who long pain and sorrow bear,
praise God and on him cast your care.

6 And thou, most kind and gentle death,
waiting to hush our latest breath,
O praise him, alleluia!
Thou leadest home the child of God,
and Christ our Lord the way hath trod:

7 Let all things their Creator bless,
and worship him in humbleness,
O praise him, alleluia!
Praise, praise the Father, praise the Son,
and praise the Spirit, Three in One.

16 W. J. Sparrow-Simpson (1859–1952)

1 All for Jesus, all for Jesus,
this our song shall ever be;
for we have no hope, nor Saviour,
if we have not hope in thee.

2 All for Jesus, thou wilt give us
strength to serve thee, hour by hour;
none can move us from thy presence,
while we trust thy love and power.

3 All for Jesus, at thine altar
thou wilt give us sweet content;
there, dear Lord, we shall receive thee
in the solemn sacrament.

4 All for Jesus, thou hast loved us;
all for Jesus, thou hast died;
all for Jesus, thou art with us;
all for Jesus crucified.

5 All for Jesus, all for Jesus,
this the Church's song must be;
till, at last, her sons are gathered
one in love and one in thee.

17 St Theodulph of Orleans (d 821) tr. John Mason Neale (1818–66)

All glory, laud and honour,
to thee, Redeemer King,
to whom the lips of children
made sweet hosannas ring.

1 Thou art the King of Israel,
thou David's royal Son,
who in the Lord's name comest,
the King and blessed one.

2 The company of angels
are praising thee on high,
and mortal folk, with all things
created, make reply.

3 The people of the Hebrews
with palms before thee went:
our praise and prayer and anthems
before thee we present.

4 To thee before thy passion
they sang their hymns of praise;
to thee now high exalted
our melody we raise.

5 Thou didst accept their praises,
accept the prayers we bring,
who in all good delightest,
thou good and gracious king.

18 Dave Bilbrough

All hail the Lamb, enthroned on high;
His praise shall be our battle cry;
He reigns victorious, forever glorious,
His name is Jesus, He is the Lord.

19 Edward Perronet (1726–92) and others

1 All hail the pow'r of Jesus' name!
let angels prostrate fall;
bring forth the royal diadem

To crown him, crown him,
crown him,
crown him Lord of all.

2 Crown him, ye martyrs of your God,
who from his altar call;
praise him whose way of pain ye trod,
and crown him Lord of all.

3 Ye prophets who our freedom won,
ye searchers, great and small,
by whom the work of truth is done,
now crown him Lord of all.

4 Sinners, whose love can ne'er forget
the wormwood and the gall,
go spread your trophies at his feet,
and crown him Lord of all.

5 Bless him, each poor oppressèd race
that Christ did upward call;
his hand in each achievement trace,
and crown him Lord of all.

6 Let every tribe and every tongue
to him their hearts enthral:
lift high the universal song,
and crown him Lord of all.

20 *Noel and Tricia Richards*

1 All heaven declares
the glory of the risen Lord;
who can compare
with the beauty of the Lord?
For ever He will be
the Lamb upon the throne;
I gladly bow the knee,
and worship Him alone.

2 I will proclaim
the glory of the risen Lord,
who once was slain
to reconcile man to God.
For ever You will be
the Lamb upon the throne;
I gladly bow the knee,
and worship You alone.

21 *Robert S Bridges (1844–1930) based on 'Mein Hoffnung stehet feste' by Joachim Neander (1650–80)*

1 All my hope on God is founded;
he doth still my trust renew.
Me through change and chance he guideth,
only good and only true.
God unknown, he alone
calls my heart to be his own.

2 Pride of man and earthly glory,
sword and crown betray God's trust;
what with lavish care man buildeth,
tower and temple, fall to dust.
But God's power, hour by hour,
is my temple and my tower.

3 God's great goodness ay endureth,
deep his wisdom, passing thought:
splendour, light and life attend him,
beauty springeth out of nought.
Evermore, from his store
new–born worlds rise and adore.

4 Still from man to God eternal
sacrifice of praise be done,
high above all praises praising
for the gift of Christ his Son.
Christ doth call one and all;
ye who follow shall not fall.

22 *Verses 1–4: William Keithe (d 1594), from 'Day's Psalter'(1560–61). Verse 5: 19th century adaptation of a doxology in Tate and Brady's 'New Version' (1696), altered*

1 All people that on earth do dwell,
sing to the Lord with cheerful voice;
him serve with fear, his praise forth tell,
come ye before him and rejoice.

2 The Lord, ye know, is God indeed,
without our aid he did us make;
we are his folk, he doth us feed
and for his sheep he doth us take.

3 O enter then his gates with praise,
approach with joy his courts unto,
praise, laud, and bless his name always,
for it is seemly so to do.

4 For why? The Lord our God is good:
his mercy is for ever sure;
his truth at all times firmly stood,
and shall from age to age endure.

5 To Father, Son and Holy Ghost,
the God whom heaven and earth adore,
from men and from the angel–host
be praise and glory evermore.

23 *Sebastian Temple*

1 All that I am, all that I do,
all that I'll ever have, I offer now to you.
Take and sanctify these gifts
for your honour, Lord.
Knowing that I love and serve you
is enough reward.
All that I am, all that I do,
all that I'll ever have I offer now to you.

2 All that I dream, all that I pray,
all that I'll ever make, I give to you today.
Take and sanctify these gifts
for your honour, Lord.
Knowing that I love and serve you
is enough reward.
All that I am, all that I do,
all that I'll ever have I offer now to you.

24 Lucien Deiss, based on Psalm 100 (99)

All the earth proclaim the Lord,
sing your praise to God.

1 Serve you the Lord, hearts filled with gladness.
Come into his presence, singing for joy!

2 Know that the Lord is our creator.
Yes he is our Father; we are his sons.

3 We are the sheep of his green pasture,
for we are his people; he is our God.

4 Enter his gates bringing thanksgiving,
O enter his courts while singing his praise.

5 Our Lord is good, his love enduring,
his word is abiding now with all men.

6 Honour and praise be to the Father,
the Son, and the Spirit, world without end.

25 Adapted by David Haas and Marty Haugen

All the ends of the earth
have seen the power of God;
All the ends of the earth
have seen the power of God.

1 Sing to the Lord a new song,
for he has done wondrous deeds;
his right hand has won the vict'ry for him,
his holy arm.

2 The Lord has made his salvation known,
his justice revealed to all.
Remembered his kindness and faithfulness
to Israel.

3 All of the ends of earth have seen
salvation by our God.
Joyfully sing out all you lands,
break forth in song.

4 Sing to the Lord with harp and song,
with trumpet and with horn.
Sing in your joy before the king,
the king, our Lord.

26 Michael Cockett

All the nations of the earth,
praise the Lord who brings to birth
the greatest star, the smallest flower.
Alleluia.

1 Let the heavens praise the Lord. *Alleluia.*
Moon and stars, praise the Lord. *Alleluia.*

2 Snow–capped mountains, praise the Lord.
Rolling hills, praise the Lord.

3 Deep sea water, praise the Lord.
Gentle rain, praise the Lord.

4 Roaring lion, praise the Lord.
Singing birds, praise the Lord.

5 Kings and princes, praise the Lord.
Young and old, praise the Lord.

27 Mrs Cecil Frances Alexander (1818–95)

All things bright and beautiful,
all creatures great and small,
all things wise and wonderful,
the Lord God made them all.

1 Each little flower that opens,
each little bird that sings,
he made their glowing colours,
he made their tiny wings.

2 The purple–headed mountain,
the river running by,
the sunset and the morning,
that brightens up the sky.

3 The cold wind in the winter,
the pleasant summer sun,
the ripe fruits in the garden,
he made them every one.

4 The tall trees in the greenwood,
the meadows for our play,
the rushes by the water,
to gather every day.

5 He gave us eyes to see them,
and lips that we may tell
how great is God Almighty,
who has made all things well.

28 *Willard F. Jabusch*

1 All this world belongs to Jesus,
ev'rything is his by right;
all on the land, all in the sea;
ev'rything is his by right.

2 Shining stars in all their beauty
are outnumbered by his gifts.
Sand on the shore, stars in the sky,
are outnumbered by his gifts.

3 Ev'ry foot that starts a–dancing
taps a rhythm full of hope;
full of his joy, full of his hope,
taps a rhythm full of hope.

4 All that's good reflects his goodness;
may it lead us back to him.
All that is good, all that is true,
may it lead us back to him.

5 So give thanks for what he's given;
touch and taste, and feet to dance;
eyes for the lights, ears for the sound,
for the wonders of our Lord.

29 *Verses 1–3: Vincent Stanley Stratton Coles (1845–1929), altered Verse 4: Patrick Geary*

1 All who claim the faith of Jesus
sing the wonders that were done,
when the love of God the Father
o'er our sin the victory won,
when he made the Virgin Mary
Mother of his only Son.

2 Blessed were the chosen people
out of whom the Lord did come,
blessed was the land of promise
fashioned for his earthly home;
but more blessed far the mother
she who bore him in her womb.

3 Therefore let all faithful people
sing the honour of her name,
let the Church in her foreshadowed
part in her thanksgiving claim;
what Christ's mother sang in gladness
let Christ's people sing the same:

4 How my soul proclaims God's greatness!
God, for me, great things has done:
scattering the proud and haughty,
lifting those who are cast down.
Merciful throughout the ages
God protects us as his own.

30 *Lucien Deiss, based on Psalm 66 (65)*

All you nations,
sing out your joy in the Lord:
Alleluia, alleluia!

1 Joyfully shout, all you on earth,
give praise to the glory of God;
and with a hymn,
sing out his glorious praise:
Alleluia!

2 Lift up your hearts, sing to your God:
tremendous his deeds to behold!
Vanquished your foes,
struck down by power and might:
Alleluia!

3 Let all the earth kneel in his sight,
extolling his marvellous fame;
honour his name,
in highest heaven give praise:
Alleluia!

4 Come forth and see all the great works
that God has brought forth by his might;
fall on your knees
before his glorious throne:
Alleluia!

5 Parting the seas with might and pow'r,
he rescued his people from shame;
let us give thanks
for all his merciful deeds:
Alleluia!

6 His eyes keep watch on all the earth,
his strength is forever renewed;
and let no–one
rebel against his commands;
Alleluia!

7 Tested are we by God the Lord,
as silver is tested by fire;
burdened with pain,
we fall ensnared in our sins:
Alleluia!

8 Over our heads wicked men rode,
we passed through the fire and the flood;
then, Lord, you brought
your people into your peace:
All you nations,
Alleluia!

9 Glory and thanks be to the Father;
honour and praise to the Son;
and to the Spirit,
source of life and of love:
Alleluia!

31 *18th century, tr. Edward Caswall (1814–78)*

1 All ye who seek a comfort sure
in trouble and distress,
whatever sorrow vex the mind,
or guilt the soul oppress:

2 Jesus, who gave himself for you
upon the cross to die,
opens to you his sacred heart;
oh, to that heart draw nigh.

3 Ye hear how kindly he invites;
ye hear his words so blest:
'all ye that labour come to me,
and I will give you rest.'

4 Jesus, thou joy of saints on high,
thou hope of sinners here,
attracted by those loving words
to thee I lift my prayer.

5 Wash thou my wounds in that dear blood,
which forth from thee doth flow;
new grace, new hope inspire, a new
and better heart bestow.

32 *Don Fishel*

Alleluia, alleluia,
give thanks to the risen Lord.
Alleluia, alleluia,
give praise to his name.

1 Jesus is Lord of all the earth.
He is the King of creation.

2 Spread the good news o'er all the earth.
Jesus has died and has risen.

3 We have been crucified with Christ.
Now we shall live for ever.

4 God has proclaimed the just reward.
Life for all men, alleluia.

5 Come, let us praise the living God,
joyfully sing to our Saviour.

33 *Michael Cockett*

Alleluia, alleluia!
I will praise the Father for all of my life.
I will sing to my God as long as I live,
alleluia, alleluia, alleluia!

1 Do not place all your trust
in a woman or man:
they cannot save.
Their schemes will all perish
when they yield up their breath
at the end of their days.

2 But so happy are those
who will trust in their God:
they will find help.
For God is the maker
of the heavens and earth
and of all that these hold.

3 All the searchers for justice,
for freedom, for love,
God will fulfil.
The widow, the orphan,
and the blind and the lame
in his love are restored.

34 *Patrick G Fitzpatrick*

Alleluia, alleluia!

1 Salvation and glory and pow'r belong to
our God, *alleluia!*
His judgements are true and just.

2 Praise our God, all you his servants,
alleluia!
You, who fear him, great and small.

3 The Lord, our God, the almighty, reigns,
alleluia!
Let us rejoice and exult and give him the glory.

4 The marriage of the Lamb has come,
alleluia!
And his Bride has made herself ready.

35 Christopher Walker

PREMANANDA ALLELUIA

Alleluia, alleluia!

36 Traditional

1 Alleluia *(8 times)*

2 Jesus is Lord, …

3 And I love him, …

4 Christ is risen, …

37 W. Chatterton Dix (1837–98)

1 Alleluia, sing to Jesus,
his the sceptre, his the throne,
alleluia, his the triumph,
his the victory alone:
hark! the songs of peaceful Sion
thunder like a mighty flood;
Jesus, out of every nation,
hath redeemed us by his blood.

2 Alleluia, not as orphans
are we left in sorrow now;
alleluia, he is near us,
faith believes, nor questions how;
though the cloud from sight received him
when the forty days were o'er,
shall our hearts forget his promise,
'I am with you evermore'?

3 Alleluia, Bread of Angels,
thou on earth our food, our stay;
alleluia, here the sinful
flee to thee from day to day;
intercessor, friend of sinners,
earth's Redeemer, plead for me,
where the songs of all the sinless
sweep across the crystal sea.

4 Alleluia, King eternal,
thee the Lord of lords we own;
alleluia, born of Mary,
earth thy footstool, heaven thy throne;
thou within the veil hast entered,
robed in flesh, our great High Priest;
thou on earth both priest and victim
in the Eucharistic Feast.

38 Marty Haugen

Alleluia! (8 times)

1 This is the day the Lord has made,
let us rejoice, be glad, and sing!
Thanks and praise be to our God,
for his mercy endures for evermore!

2 The right hand of God has come with power,
the Lord, our God, is lifted high!
I shall not die, but I shall live
and rejoice in the works of the Lord.

3 The stone which the builders once denied
now has become the cornerstone.
By the Lord has this been done,
it has brought wonder to our eyes!

39 Vincent Stuckley Stratton Coles (1845–1929)

1 Almighty Father, Lord most high,
who madest all, who fillest all,
thy name we praise and magnify,
for all our needs on thee we call.

2 We offer to thee of thine own
ourselves and all that we can bring,
in bread and cup before thee shown,
our universal offering.

3 All that we have we bring to thee,
yet all is naught when all is done,
save that in it thy love can see
the sacrifice of thy dear Son.

4 By his command in bread and cup,
his body and his blood we plead;
what on the cross he offer'd up
is here our sacrifice indeed.

5 For all thy gifts of life and grace,
here we thy servants humbly pray
that thou would'st look upon the face
of thine anointed Son today.

40 *John Newton (1725–1807)*

1 Amazing grace! How sweet the sound
that saved a wretch like me.
I once was lost but now I'm found,
was blind, but now I see.

2 'Twas grace that taught my heart to fear,
and grace my fears relieved.
How precious did that grace appear
the hour I first believed.

3 Through many dangers, toils and snares
I have already come.
'Tis grace hath brought me safe thus far,
and grace will lead me home.

4 The Lord has promised good to me;
his word my hope secures.
He will my shield and portion be
as long as life endures.

41 *AMERICAN EUCHARIST Sandra Joan Billington*

LORD, HAVE MERCY

Lord, have mercy. Lord, have mercy,
on your servants, Lord, have mercy.
God Almighty, just and faithful,
Lord have mercy. Lord, have mercy.

Christ, have mercy. Christ, have mercy,
gift from heaven, Christ have mercy.
Light of truth, and light of justice,
Christ, have mercy. Christ have mercy.

Lord, have mercy. Lord, have mercy,
on your servants, Lord, have mercy.
God almighty, just and faithful,
Lord, have mercy. Lord, have mercy.

HOLY, HOLY, HOLY

Holy, holy, holy, holy,
Lord of hosts. You fill with glory
all the earth and all the heavens.
Sing hosanna, sing hosanna.

Blest and holy, blest and holy
he who comes now in the Lord's name.
In the highest sing hosanna,
in the highest sing hosanna.

LAMB OF GOD

Jesus, Lamb of God, have mercy
bearer of our sins, have mercy.
Jesus, Lamb of God, have mercy,
bearer of our sins, have mercy.

Saviour of the world, Lord Jesus,
may your peace be with us always.
Saviour of the world, Lord Jesus,
may your peace be with us always.

42 *Fred Pratt Green*

1 An upper room did our Lord prepare
for those he loved until the end:
and his disciples still gather there,
to celebrate their Risen Friend.

2 A lasting gift Jesus gave his own:
to share his bread, his loving cup.
Whatever burdens may bow us down,
he by his cross shall lift us up.

3 And after Supper he washed their feet,
for service, too, is sacrament.
In him our joy shall be made complete –
sent out to serve, as he was sent.

4 No end there is! We depart in peace.
He loves beyond our uttermost:
in every room in our Father's house
he will be there, as Lord and Host.

43 *Charles Wesley (1707–88)*

1 And can it be that I should gain
an interest in the Saviour's blood?
Died he for me, who caused his pain;
for me, who him to death pursued?
Amazing love! – How can it be
that thou, my God, shouldst die for me?

2 'Tis mystery all! – The Immortal dies –
who can explore His strange design?
In vain the first–born seraph tries
to sound the depths of love divine!
'Tis mercy all! – Let earth adore,
Let angel minds inquire no more.

3 He left his Father's throne above,
So free, so infinite his grace;
emptied himself of all but love,
and bled for Adam's helpless race.
'Tis mercy all, immense and free;
for, O my God, it found out me.

4 Long my imprisoned spirit lay
fast bound in sin and nature's night:
thine eye diffused a quickening ray;
I woke – the dungeon flamed with light.
My chains fell off, my heart was free;
I rose, went forth, and followed thee.

5 No condemnation now I dread;
Jesus, and all in him, is mine!
Alive in Him, my living Head,
and clothed in righteousness divine,
bold I approach the eternal throne,
and claim the crown through Christ my
own.

44 *William Blake (1757–1827)*

1 And did those feet in ancient time
walk upon England's mountains green?
And was the holy Lamb of God
on England's pleasant pastures seen?
And did the countenance divine
shine forth upon our clouded hills?
And was Jerusalem buildèd here
among those dark satanic mills?

2 Bring me my bow of burning gold!
Bring me my arrows of desire!
Bring me my spear! O clouds, unfold!
Bring me my chariot of fire!
I will not cease from mental fight,
nor shall my sword sleep in my hand,
till we have built Jerusalem
in England's green and pleasant land.

45 *Francis Pott (1832–1909)*

1 Angel–voices ever singing
round thy throne of light,
angel–harps, for ever ringing,
rest not day nor night;
thousands only live to bless thee
and confess thee Lord of might.

2 Thou who art beyond the farthest
mortal eye can see,
God almighty, thou regardest
all our song to thee;
and we know that thou art near us,
and wilt hear our ev'ry plea.

3 Yes, we know that thou rejoicest
o'er each work of thine;
thou didst ears and hands and voices
for thy praise design;
craftsman's art and music's measure
for thy pleasure all combine.

4 In thy house, great God, we offer
of thine own to thee;
and for thine acceptance proffer,
all unworthily,
hearts and minds and hands and voices
in our choicest psalmody.

5 Honour, glory, might and merit
thine shall ever be,
Father, Son and Holy Spirit,
Blessed Trinity!
Of the best that thou hast given
earth and heaven render thee.

46 *'Quem Pastores Laudavere' (German, 15th century)*

1 Angel voices richly blending,
shepherds to the manger sending,
sing of peace from heav'n descending!
Shepherds, greet your Shepherd King.

2 Lo! a star is brightly glowing!
Eastern Kings their gifts are showing
to the King whose gifts pass knowing!
Gentiles, greet the Gentiles' King!

3 To the manger come adoring,
hearts in thankfulness outpouring
to the child, true peace restoring,
Mary's Son, our God and King!

47 *James Chadwick (1813–82)*

1 Angels we have heard in heaven
sweetly singing o'er our plains,
and the mountain tops in answer
echoing their joyous strains.

Gloria in excelsis Deo.
Gloria in excelsis Deo.

2 Shepherds, why this exultation?
Why your rapturous strain prolong?
Tell us of the gladsome tidings,
which inspire your joyous song.

3 Come to Bethlehem, and see him
o'er whose birth the angels sing,
come, adore, devoutly kneeling,
Christ the Lord, the new–born king.

4 See him in a manger lying
whom the choir of angels praise!
Mary, Joseph, come to aid us
while our hearts in love we raise.

48 *James Chadwick (1813–82)*

1 Angels we have heard on high
sweetly singing o'er our plains,
and the mountains in reply
echo still their joyous strains.

Gloria in excelsis Deo.
Gloria in excelsis Deo.

2 Shepherds, why this jubilee?
Why your rapturous strain prolong?
Say, what may your tidings be,
which inspire your heavenly song.

3 Come to Bethlehem and see
him whose birth the angels sing:
come, adore on bended knee
the infant Christ, the new–born King.

4 See within a manger laid,
Jesus, Lord of heaven and earth!
Mary, Joseph, lend your aid
to celebrate our Saviour's birth.

49 *The Iona Community*

1 Among us and before us, Lord you stand
with arms outstretched and bread and
wine at hand.
Confronting those unworthy of a crumb,
you ask that to your table we should come.

2 Who dare say No, when such is your
resolve
our worst to witness, suffer and absolve,
our best to raise in lives by God forgiven,
our souls to fill on earth with food from
heaven?

3 Who dare say No, when such is your intent
to love the selves we famish and resent,
to cradle our uncertainties and fear,
to kindle hope as you in faith draw near?

4 Who dare say No, when such is your
request
that each around your table should be
guest,
that hear the ancient word should live as
new
'take, eat and drink – all this is meant for
you'?

5 No more we hesitate and wonder why;
no more we stand indifferent, scared or shy.
Your invitation leads us to say Yes,
to meet you where you nourish, heal and
bless.

50 *Versified by Marty Haugen*

As a tree planted
by streams of water,
is the one who delights
in the word of the Lord.

1 Blessed are the poor in spirit,
theirs is the Kingdom of heaven;
blessed are the ones who mourn,
for they shall be comforted.

2 Blessed are the meek and lowly,
they shall inherit the earth;
blessed are those who thirst for good,
for they shall be satisfied.

3 Blessed are the merciful, for
they shall have mercy shown them;
blessed are the pure in heart,
for they shall see their God.

4 Blessed are the peaceful hearts, for
they shall be called God's children;
bless'd those suff'ring for righteousness,
the Kingdom of heaven is theirs.

51 *Steven Jones*

1 As we come before you now,
Mary, hear us as we call;
take our prayers to Christ the Lord,
O Mother of us all.

Ave Maria, gratia plena,
Dominus tecum,
benedicta tu.

2 You who heard the angel's voice,
you who hastened to obey,
show us how to serve the Lord
and walk in heaven's way.

3 You who cared for God's own Son,
you who played the mother's part:
show us how to welcome Christ
and hold him in our heart.

4 You whose heart was pierced with grief,
you who saw your Son in pain,
teach us not to flinch from fight
but strive the prize to gain.

5 You who saw Christ ris'n again,
you who felt the Spirit's flame:
teach us how to raise our voice
and praise God's holy name.

6 You whom God raised up on high,
first to taste Redemption's joy,
be for us a sign of hope
that fear cannot destroy.

7 Pray with us poor sinners now
help us follow your dear Son:
so that when our hour has come
we find the battle won.

52 *John L. Bell and Graham Maule*

1 As if you were not there,
the skies ignite and thunder,
rivers tear their banks asunder,
thieves and nature storm and plunder:
all beware,
as if you were not there.

2 As if you were not there,
famine and flood together
usher death, disease and terror;
stricken mothers wonder whether
God heeds prayer,
as if you were not there.

3 As if you were not there,
we televise the dying,
watch the helpless victims crying,
salve our consciences by sighing
'Life's unfair!'
As if you were not there.

4 As if you were not there,
your Son, when faith defied him,
faced a crowd which crucified him,
leaving friends who had denied him
in despair,
as if you were not there.

5 Because he rose again
and showed God's love is vaster
than the ultimate disaster,
we entreat you now to master
strife and pain,
because he rose again.

53 *Bob Hurd*

As the deer longs for running streams,
so I long, so I long, so I long for you.

1 Athirst my soul for you
the God who is my life!
When shall I see, when shall I see,
see the face of God?

2 Echoes meet as deep
is calling unto deep,
over my head, all your mighty waters,
sweeping over me.

3 Continually the foe
delights in taunting me:
'Where is God, where is your God?'
Where, O, where, are you?

4 Defend me, God,
send forth your light and your truth,
they will lead me to your holy mountain,
to your dwelling place.

5 Then I shall go
unto the altar of my God.
Praising you, O my joy and gladness,
I shall praise your name.

54 *Martin Nystrom*

1 As the deer pants for the water,
so my soul longs after You.
You alone are my heart's desire
and I long to worship You.

You alone are my strength, my shield,
to You alone may my spirit yield.
You alone are my heart's desire
and I long to worship You.

2 I want You more than gold or silver,
only You can satisfy.
You alone are the real joy–giver
and the apple of my eye.

3 You're my Friend and You're my Brother,
even though You are a king.
I love You more than any other,
so much more than anything.

55 *William Chatterton Dix (1837–98)*

1 As with gladness men of old
did the guiding star behold,
as with joy they hailed its light,
leading onward, beaming bright,
so, most gracious God, may we
evermore be led to thee.

2 As with joyful steps they sped,
to that lowly manger–bed,
there to bend the knee before
him whom heaven and earth adore,
so may we with willing feet
ever seek thy mercy–seat.

3 As they offered gifts most rare
at that manger rude and bare,
so may we with holy joy,
pure, and free from sin's alloy,
all our costliest treasures bring,
Christ, to thee, our heavenly King.

4 Holy Jesus, every day
keep us in the narrow way;
and, when earthly things are past,
bring our ransomed souls at last
where they need no star to guide,
where no clouds thy glory hide.

5 In the heavenly country bright
need they no created light,
thou its Light, its Joy, its Crown,
thou its Sun which goes not down;
there for ever may we sing
alleluias to our King.

56 *Nunc Dimittis Luke 2:29–32 tr. The Grail*

Guard us, O Lord, while we sleep and
keep us in peace.

or:

My eyes have seen your salvation:
the light of all peoples.

1 At last, all powerful Master,
you give leave to your servant to go
in peace, according to your promise.

2 For my eyes have seen your salvation
which you have prepared for all nations
the light to enlighten the Gentiles
and give glory to Israel, your people.

3 Give praise to the Father almighty,
to his Son, Jesus Christ, the Lord,
to the Spirit, who dwells in our hearts,
both now and forever. Amen.

57 *STABAT MATER*

Ascribed to Jacopone da Todi (d 1306)
tr. Edward Caswall (1814–78)

1 At the cross her station keeping
stood the mournful mother weeping,
close to Jesus to the last;

2 Through her heart his sorrow sharing,
all his bitter anguish bearing,
now at length the sword has pass'd.

3 Oh, how sad and sore distress'd
was that mother highly blest,
of the sole–begotten One.

4 Christ above in torment hangs;
she beneath beholds the pangs
of her dying glorious Son.

5 Is there one who would not weep,
'whelm'd in miseries so deep,
Christ's dear mother to behold?

6 Can the human heart refrain
from partaking in her pain,
in that mother's pain untold?

7 Bruised, derided, cursed, defiled,
she beheld her tender child,
all with bloody scourges rent;

8 For the sins of his own nation,
saw him hang in desolation,
till his spirit forth he sent.

9 O thou mother! Fount of love!
Touch my spirit from above,
make my heart with thine accord:

10 Make me feel as thou hast felt;
make my soul to glow and melt
with the love of Christ my Lord.

11 Holy Mother, pierce me through,
in my heart each wound renew
of my Saviour crucified.

12 Let me share with thee his pain
who for all my sins was slain,
who for me in torments died.

13 Let me mingle tears with thee,
mourning him who mourn'd for me,
all the days that I may live:

14 By the cross with thee to stay,
there with thee to weep and pray,
is all I ask of thee to give.

15 Virgin of all virgins best,
listen to my fond request:
let me share thy grief divine;

16 Let me, to my latest breath,
in my body bear the death
of that dying son of thine.

17 Wounded with his every wound
steep my soul till it hath swoon'd
in his very blood away.

18 Be to me, O Virgin, nigh,
lest in flames I burn and die,
in his awful judgement day.

19 Christ, when thou shalt call me hence,
be thy mother my defence,
be thy cross my victory.

20 While my body here decays,
may my soul thy goodness praise,
safe in paradise with thee.

58

Anonymous, 7th century,
tr. Robert Campbell (1814–68)

1 At the Lamb's high feast we sing
praise to our victorious king,
who hath washed us in the tide
flowing from his piercèd side.
Praise we him whose love divine
gives the guests his blood for wine,
gives his body for the feast,
love the victim, love the priest.

2 Where the paschal blood is poured
Death's dark angel sheathes his sword;
Israel's hosts triumphant go
through the wave that drowns the foe.
Christ the Lamb, whose blood was shed.
Paschal victim, paschal bread;
with sincerity and love
eat we manna from above.

3 Mighty victim from the sky,
powers of hell beneath thee lie;
death is conquered in the fight;
thou has brought us life and light.
Now thy banner thou dost wave;
vanquished Satan and the grave;
angels join his praise to tell –
see o'erthrown the prince of hell.

4 Paschal triumph, paschal joy,
only sin can this destroy;
from the death of sin set free
souls re–born, dear Lord, in thee.
Hymns of glory, songs of praise,
Father, unto thee we raise.
Risen Lord, all praise to thee,
ever with the Spirit be.

59 *Caroline Maria Noel (1817–77)*

1 At the name of Jesus
every knee shall bow,
every tongue confess him
King of glory now;
'tis the Father's pleasure
we should call him Lord,
who from the beginning
was the mighty Word.

2 At his voice creation
sprang at once to sight,
all the Angel faces,
all the hosts of light,
thrones and dominations,
stars upon their way,
all the heavenly orders,
in their great array.

3 Humbled for a season,
to receive a name
from the lips of sinners
unto whom he came,
faithfully he bore it
spotless to the last,
brought it back victorious
when from death he passed.

4 Bore it up triumphant
with its human light
through all ranks of creatures,
to the central height,
to the throne of Godhead,
to the Father's breast,
filled it with the glory
of that perfect rest.

5 Name him, Christians, name him,
with love as strong as death;
but with awe and wonder,
and with bated breath.
He is God the Saviour,
he is Christ the Lord,
ever to be worshipped,
trusted, and adored.

6 In your hearts enthrone him;
there let him subdue
all that is not holy,
all that is not true;
crown him as your captain,
in temptation's hour
let his will enfold you
in its light and power.

7 Christians, this Lord Jesus
shall return again,
with his Father's glory,
with his angel train,
for all wreaths of empire
meet upon his brow,
and our hearts confess him
King of glory now.

60 *Roger Ruston*

1 Attend and keep this happy fast
I preach to you this day.
Is this the fast that pleases me
that takes your joy away?
Do I delight in sorrow's dress,
says God, who reigns above,
the hanging head, the dismal look,
will they attract my love?

2 But is this not the fast I choose,
that shares the heavy load;
that seeks to bring the poor man in
who's weary of the road;
that gives the hungry bread to eat,
to strangers gives a home;
that does not let you hide your face
from your own flesh and bone?

3 Then like the dawn your light will break,
to life you will be raised.
And all will praise the Lord for you;
be happy in your days.
The glory of the Lord will shine,
and in your steps his grace.
And when you call he'll answer you;
he will not hide his face.

61 *Estelle White*

1 Autumn days when the grass is jewelled
and the silk inside a chestnut shell,
jet planes meeting in the air to be refuelled,
all these things I love so well.

So I mustn't forget. No, I mustn't forget,
to say a great big thank you,
I mustn't forget.

2 Clouds that look like familiar faces,
and a winter's moon with frosty rings,
smell of bacon as I fasten up my laces
and the song the milkman sings.

3 Whipped up spray that is rainbow–scattered,
and a swallow curving in the sky.
Shoes so comfy, though they're worn–
out and they're battered,
and the taste of apple–pie.

4 Scent of gardens when the rain's been
falling,
and a minnow darting down a stream,
picked–up engine that's been stuttering
and stalling,
and a win for my home team.

62 *'Sister M'*

1 Ave Maria, O Maiden, O Mother,
fondly thy children are calling on thee;
thine are the graces unclaimed by another,
sinless and beautiful Star of the sea.

Mater amabilis, ora pro nobis,
pray for thy children who call upon thee;
Ave Sanctissima, Ave Purissima,
sinless and beautiful Star of the sea.

2 Ave Maria, the night shades are falling,
softly our voices arise unto thee;
earth's lonely exiles for succour are calling,
sinless and beautiful Star of the sea.

3 Ave Maria, thy children are kneeling,
words of endearment are murmured to thee;
softly thy spirit upon us is stealing,
sinless and beautiful Star of the sea.

63 *Marty Haugen*

1 Awake! awake, and greet the new morn,
for angels herald its dawning,
sing out your joy, for now he is born,
Behold! the Child of our longing.
Come as a baby weak and poor,
to bring all hearts together,
he opens wide the heav'nly door
and lives now inside us for ever.

2 To us, to all in sorrow and fear,
Emmanuel comes a–singing,
his humble song is quiet and near,
yet fills the earth with its ringing;
music to heal the broken soul
and hymns of loving kindness,
the thunder of his anthems roll
to shatter all hatred and blindness.

3 In darkest night his coming shall be,
when all the earth is despairing,
as morning light so quiet and free,
so warm and gentle and caring.
Then shall the mute break forth in song,
the lame shall leap in wonder,
the weak be raised above the strong,
and weapons be broken asunder.

4 Rejoice, rejoice, take heart in the night,
though dark the winter and cheerless,
the rising sun shall crown you with light,
be strong and loving and fearless;

love be our song and love our prayer,
and love, our endless story,
may God fill every day we share,
and bring us at last into glory.

64 *J.R. Peacey (1896–1971)*

1 Awake, awake: fling off the night!
For God has sent his glorious light;
and we who live in Christ's new day
must works of darkness put away.

2 Awake and rise, like people renewed,
and with the Spirit's power endued,
the light of life in us will glow,
and fruits of truth and goodness show.

3 Let in the light; all sin expose
to Christ, whose life no darkness knows.
Before his cross for guidance kneel;
his light will judge and, judging, heal.

4 Awake, and rise up from the dead,
and Christ his light on you will shed.
Its power will wrong desires destroy,
and your whole nature fill with joy.

5 Then sing for joy, and use each day;
give thanks for everything alway.
Lift up your hearts; with one accord
praise God through Jesus Christ our Lord.

65 *Daniel L. Schutte, SJ*

1 Awake from your slumber! Arise from
your sleep!
A new day is dawning for all those
who weep.
The people in darkness have seen a
great light.
The Lord of our longing has conquered
the night.

Let us build the city of God.
May our tears be turned into dancing!
For the Lord, our light and our Love,
has turned the night into day!

2 We are sons of the morning;
we are daughters of day.
The One who has loved us
has brightened our way.
The Lord of all kindness has called us to be
a light for his people to set their hearts free.

3 God is light; in him there is no darkness.
Let us walk in his light, his children,
one and all.
O comfort my people; make gentle your
words.
Proclaim to my city the day of her birth.

4 O city of gladness, now lift up your voice!
Proclaim the good tidings that all may
rejoice!

66 *Verses 1 and 2 Anonymous; verse 3 J.T. McFarland (1851–1913)*

1 Away in a manger, no crib for a bed,
the little Lord Jesus laid down his sweet
head,
the stars in the bright sky looked down
where he lay,
the little Lord Jesus asleep on the hay.

2 The cattle are lowing, the baby awakes,
but little Lord Jesus no crying he makes.
I love thee, Lord Jesus! Look down from
the sky,
and stay by my side until morning is nigh.

3 Be near me, Lord Jesus; I ask thee to stay
close by me for ever, and love me, I pray.
Bless all the dear children in thy tender
care,
and fit us for heaven, to live with thee
there.

67 *Michael A Saward*

1 Baptised in water, sealed by the Spirit,
cleansed by the blood of Christ our King:
trusting his promise, heirs of salvation,
faithfully now God's praises we sing.

2 Baptised in water, sealed by the Spirit,
dead in the tomb with Christ our King:
one with his rising, freed and forgiven,
thankfully now God's praises we sing.

3 Baptised in water, sealed by the Spirit,
marked with the sign of Christ our King:
born of one Father, we are his children,
joyfully now God's praises we sing.

68 *Simphonia Sirenum (1695) tr. Ronald Arbuthnott Knox (1888–1957)*

1 Battle is o'er, hell's armies flee:
raise we the cry of victory
with abounding joy resounding,
alleluia, alleluia.

2 Christ who endured the shameful tree,
o'er death triumphant welcome we,
our adoring praise outpouring,
alleluia, alleluia.

3 On the third morn from death rose he,
clothed with what light in heaven shall be,
our unswerving faith deserving,
alleluia, alleluia.

4 Hell's gloomy gates yield up their key,
paradise door thrown wide we see;
never–tiring be our choiring,
alleluia, alleluia.

5 Lord, by the stripes they laid on thee,
grant us to live from death set free,
this our greeting still repeating,
alleluia, alleluia.

69 *Anne Scott (née Conway)*

1 Be still, and know I am with you,
be still, I am the Lord.
I will not leave you orphans.
I leave with you my world. Be one.

2 You fear the light may be fading,
you fear to lose your way.
Be still, and know I am near you.
I'll lead you to the day and the sun.

3 Be glad the day you have sorrow,
be glad, for then you live.
The stars shine only in darkness,
and in your need I give my peace.

70 *John L. Bell and Graham Maule*

1 Be still and know that I am God,
And there is none beside me.
Be still and know that I am God,
And there is none beside me.

2 I am the one who calls you my friends,

3 I am the one whose love never fails,

4 I am the one who says 'Follow me',

5 Be still and know that I am God,

71 *Anonymous*

1 Be still and know that I am God, *(3)*

2 I am the Lord that healeth thee, *(3)*

3 In thee, O Lord, I put my trust, *(3)*

72 *David J. Evans*

1 Be still, for the presence of the Lord,
the Holy One, is here.
Come, bow before Him now,
with reverence and fear.
In Him no sin is found,
we stand on holy ground.
Be still, for the presence of the Lord,
the Holy One, is here.

2 Be still, for the glory of the Lord
is shining all around;
He burns with holy fire,
with splendour He is crowned.
How awesome is the sight,
our radiant King of light!
Be still, for the glory of the Lord
is shining all around.

3 Be still, for the power of the Lord
is moving in this place,
He comes to cleanse and heal,
to minister His grace.
No work too hard for Him,
in faith receive from Him;
Be still, for the power of the Lord
is moving in this place.

73

Katharina von Schlegel, tr. Jane L. Borthwick (1813–1897)

1 Be still, my soul: the Lord is on your side;
bear patiently the cross of grief and pain;
leave to your God to order and provide;
in every change he faithful will remain.
Be still my soul: your best, your heavenly friend,
through thorny ways, leads to a joyful end.

2 Be still, my soul: your God will undertake
to guide the future as he has the past.
Your hope, your confidence let nothing shake,
all now mysterious shall be clear at last.
Be still, my soul: the tempests still obey
his voice, who ruled them once on Galilee.

3 Be still, my soul: the hour is hastening on
when we shall be for ever with the Lord,
when disappointment, grief and fear are gone,
sorrow forgotten, love's pure joy restored.
Be still, my soul: when change and tears are past,
all safe and blessed we shall meet at last.

74

Irish (8th century), tr. Mary Byrne (1881–1931), versified by Eleanor Hull (1860–1935), and others, adapted

1 Be thou my vision, O Lord of my heart,
naught be all else to me save that thou art;
thou my best thought in the day and night,
waking or sleeping, thy presence my light.

2 Be thou my wisdom, be thou my true Word;
I ever with thee, and thou with me, Lord;
thou my great Father, and I thy true son;
thou in me dwelling, and I with thee one.

3 Be thou my breast–plate, my sword for the fight;
be thou my armour, and be thou my might,
thou my soul's shelter, and thou my high tower,
raise thou me heavenward, O Power of my power.

4 Riches I heed not, nor man's empty praise,
thou mine inheritance through all my days;
thou, and thou only, the first in my heart,
high King of heaven, my treasure thou art!

5 High King of heaven, when battle is done,
grant heaven's joy to me, O bright heaven's sun;
Christ of my own heart, whatever befall,
still be my vision, O Ruler of all.

75

Anacrusic version
Irish (8th century), tr. Mary Byrne (1881–1931), versified by Eleanor Hull (1860–1935), and others

1 Be thou my vision, O Lord of my heart,
be all else but naught to me save that thou art;
be thou my best thought in the day and the night,
both waking and sleeping, thy presence my light.

2 Be thou my wisdom, be thou my true Word;
be thou ever with me, and I with thee, Lord;
thou my great Father, a true child make me;
be thou in me dwelling, and I one with thee.

3 Be thou my breastplate, my sword for the fight;
be thou my whole armour, be thou my true might,
be thou my soul's shelter, and thou my high tower,
O raise thou me heavenward, great Power of my power.

4 Riches I heed not, nor meaningless praise,
be thou mine inheritance now and always;
be thou, and thou only, the first in my heart,
O Sovereign of heaven, my treasure thou art!

5 High King of heaven, thou heaven's bright Sun,
O grant me its joys, after vict'ry is won;
Great heart of my own heart, whatever befall,
still be thou my vision, O Ruler of all.

76 *Michael Joncas*

Be with me, Lord; be with me, Lord
when I am in trouble and need.

1 You who dwell in the shelter of God
most high,
who abide in Almighty's shade,
say to the Lord: 'My refuge, my fortress,
my God, in whom I trust.'

2 Evil shall never befall you,
nor affliction come near to your tent.
Unto his angels he's given command
to guard you in all your ways.

3 On their hands the angels will bear you up,
lest you dash your foot 'gainst a stone.
Lion or viper might strike at your life
but you will not come to harm.

4 Cling to the Lord and he'll surely deliver
you:
He raises up all who call on his name.
He will bring joy to your hearts
and bless you with peace in all your days.

77 *Christopher Walker*

1 Because the Lord is my shepherd,
I have ev'rything I need.
He lets me rest in the meadow
and leads me to the quiet streams.
He restores my soul and he leads me
in the paths that are right:

Lord, you are my shepherd, you are my
friend.
I want to follow you always, just to
follow my friend.

2 And when the road leads to darkness,
I shall walk there unafraid.
Even when death is close
I have courage for your help is there.
You are close beside me with comfort,
you are guiding my way:

3 In love you make me a banquet
for my enemies to see.
You make me welcome, pouring down
honour from your mighty hand;
and this joy fills me with gladness,
it is too much to bear:

4 Your goodness always is with me
and your mercy I know.
Your loving kindness strengthens me
always as I go through life.
I shall dwell in your presence forever,
giving praise to your name:

78 *John L. Bell and Graham Maule*

Behold the Lamb of God,
behold the Lamb of God.
He takes away the sin,
the sin of the world.

79 *Aurelius Prudentius (348–413), tr. E. Caswall (1814–78)*

1 Bethlehem! of noblest cities
none can once with thee compare;
thou alone the Lord from heaven
didst for us incarnate bear.

2 Fairer than the sun at morning
was the star that told his birth,
to the lands their God announcing,
hid beneath a form of earth.

3 By its lambent beauty guided,
see the eastern kings appear;
see them bend, their gifts to offer –
gifts of incense, gold and myrrh.

4 Solemn things of mystic meaning!
Incense doth the God disclose;
gold a royal child proclaimeth;
myrrh a future tomb foreshows.

5 Holy Jesu, in thy brightness
to the gentile world display'd,
with the Father and the Spirit,
endless praise to thee be paid.

80 Bob Gillman

Bind us together, Lord,
bind us together with cords
that cannot be broken.
Bind us together, Lord,
bind us together,
bind us together with love.

1 There is only one God.
there is only one King.
there is only one Body.
that is why we sing:

2 Made for the glory of God,
purchased by his precious Son,
born with the right to be free,
for Jesus the victory has won.

3 You are the family of God,
you are the promise divine,
you are God's chosen desire,
you are the glorious new wine.

81 Verses from 'The Psalms, A New Translation' (The Grail) Response from Taizé.

♩ = 76
p
Bless the Lord my soul and bless God's ho - ly name.
Bless the Lord my soul, who leads me in - to life.

1 It is God who forgives all your guilt,
who heals ev'ry one of your ills,
who redeems your life from the grave,
who crowns you with love and compassion.

2 The Lord is compassion and love,
slow to anger and rich in mercy.
God does not treat us according to our sins
nor repay us according to our faults.

3 As a Father has compassion on his children,
the Lord has pity on those who fear him;
for he knows of what we are made,
he remembers that we are dust.

82 Edward Walker

Bless the Lord, O my soul,
let all that is within me bless his holy name.

1 For you are my glory, my Saviour and Shield,
deliver me from my distress. And raise me higher
than heaven from earth, in your goodness rescue my life.

2 A Father of tender compassionate love,
you take all my sins away.
And hurl them farther than east is from west,
where you hold their mem'ry no more.

3 For you are my Shepherd who keeps me from need,
sustainer of all that I am.
And in your merciful love, like an eagle in spring,
my youth you renew.

83 The Beatitudes

Blessed are they who follow God's law
and walk in his way; the Kingdom is theirs.

The chorus is sung continuously.
The cantor sings verses as required.
When the cantor is singing, the people hum with closed lips.

1 Blest the poor in spirit,
for theirs is the kingdom of Heaven.

2 Blest the gentle,
for they shall inherit the earth.

3 Blest those who mourn,
for they shall be comforted.

4 Blest those who hunger and thirst for justice,
for they shall be satisfied.

5 Blest the merciful
for they shall have mercy shown them.

6 Blest the pure in heart,
for they shall see God.

7 Blest the peacemakers
for they shall be called sons of God.

8 Blest those who suffer for righteousness,
for theirs is the kingdom of Heaven.

84 Fanny Crosby (née Frances van Alstyne 1820–1915)

1 Blessed assurance, Jesus is mine:
O what a foretaste of glory divine!
Heir of salvation, purchase of God;
born of His Spirit, washed in His blood.

This is my story, this is my song,
praising my Saviour all the day long;
this is my story, this is my song,
praising my Saviour all the day long.

2 Perfect submission, perfect delight,
visions of rapture burst on my sight;
angels descending, bring from above
echoes of mercy, whispers of love.

3 Perfect submission, all is at rest,
I in my Saviour am happy and blest;
watching and waiting, looking above,
filled with His goodness, lost in His love.

85 David Haas

Repeat each line of the refrain after the cantor

Blessed be God! O Blessed be God

Who calls you by name!

Holy and chosen one!

1 Come, and return to the Lord!
Live by the Word of God,
who calls you by name! *(2)*

2 Seek to be children of light!
Live in the love of God,
who calls you by name! *(2)*

3 Sing now with all your heart!
Praise and glory be to our God,
who calls you by name! *(2)*

86 *The Benedictus, The Grail*

Blessed be the Lord, the God of Israel!
He has visited his people and redeemed them.

He has raised up for us a mighty saviour
in the house of David his servant,
as he promised by the lips of holy men,
those who were his prophets from of old.

A saviour who would free us from our foes,
from the hands of all who hate us.
So his love for our fathers is fulfilled
and his holy covenant remembered.

He swore to Abraham our father to grant us,
that free from fear, and saved from the hands of our foes,
we might serve him in holiness and justice
all the days of our life in his presence.

As for you, little child, you shall be called
a prophet of God, the Most High.
You shall go ahead of the Lord
to prepare his ways before him.

To make known to his people their salvation
through forgiveness of all their sins,
the loving–kindness of the heart of our God
who visits us like the dawn from on high.

He will give light to those in darkness
those who dwell in the shadow of death,
and guide us into the way of peace.

Glory be to the Father, and to the Son,
and to the Holy Spirit,
as it was in the beginning, is now and ever shall be,
world without end, Amen.

87 *T. Clausnitzer (1619–84) tr. Catherine Winkworth (1827–78), and others.*

1 Blessèd Jesus, at thy word
we are gathered all to hear thee;
let our hearts and minds be stirred
now to seek and love and fear thee;
by thy teachings true and holy
drawn from earth to love thee solely.

2 All our knowledge, sense and sight
lie in deepest darkness shrouded,
till thy Spirit breaks our night
with the beams of truth unclouded;
thou alone to God canst win us,
thou must work all good within us.

3 Glorious Lord, thyself impart,
light of light, from God proceeding,
open thou each mind and heart,
help us by thy Spirit's pleading;
hear the cry thy Church now raises,
Lord, accept our prayers and praises.

88 *Verses 1 and 3 by John Keble (1792–1866), verses 2 and 4 from W. J. Hall's Psalms and Hymns (1836)*

1 Blest are the pure in heart,
for they shall see our God;
the secret of the Lord is theirs,
their soul is Christ's abode.

2 The Lord who left the heavens
our life and peace to bring,
to dwell in lowliness with men,
their pattern and their king.

3 Still to the lowly soul
he doth himself impart
and for his dwelling and his throne
chooseth the pure in heart.

4 Lord, we thy presence seek;
may ours this blessing be:
give us a pure and lowly heart,
a temple meet for thee.

89 *David Haas*

1 Blest are they, the poor in spirit,
theirs is the kingdom of God.
Blest are they, full of sorrow,
they shall be consoled.

Rejoice! and be glad!
Blessed are you, holy are you.
Rejoice! and be glad!
Yours is the kingdom of God!

2 Blest are they, the lowly ones,
they shall inherit the earth.
Blest are they who hunger and thirst;
they shall have their fill.

3 Blest are they who show mercy,
mercy shall be theirs.
Blest are they, the pure of heart,
they shall see God!

4 Blest are they who seek peace;
they are the children of God.
Blest are they who suffer in faith,
the glory of God is theirs.

5 Blest are you who suffer hate,
all because of me.
Rejoice and be glad, yours is the
kingdom;
shine for all to see.

The refrain is sung twice at the end.

90 Aniceto Nazareth

1 Blest are you, Lord, God of all creation,
thanks to your goodness this bread we
offer:
fruit of the earth, work of our hands,
it will become the bread of life.

Blessed be God! Blessed be God!
Blessed be God forever! Amen!
Blessed be God! Blessed be God!
Blessed be God forever! Amen!

2 Blest are you, Lord, God of all creation,
thanks to your goodness this wine we
offer:
fruit of the earth, work of our hands,
it will become the cup of life.

91 Daniel L. Schutte, SJ

Blest be the Lord; blest be the Lord,
the God of mercy, the God who saves.
I shall not fear the dark of night,
nor the arrow that flies by day.

1 He will release me from the nets
of all my foes.
He will protect me from their
wicked hands.
Beneath the shadow of His wings
I will rejoice
to find a dwelling place secure.

2 I need not shrink before the terrors
of the night,
nor stand alone before the light of day.
No harm shall come to me,
no arrow strike me down,
no evil settle in my soul.

3 Although a thousand strong have
fallen at my side,
I'll not be shaken with the Lord at hand.
His faithful love is all the armour
that I need
to wage my battle with the foe.

92 Bernadette Farrell

Bread for the world: a world of hunger,
wine for all peoples: people who thirst.
May we who eat be bread for others.
May we who drink pour out our love.

1 Lord Jesus Christ, you are the bread of life,
broken to reach and heal the wounds
of human pain.
Where we divide your people you are
waiting there
on bended knee to wash our feet
with endless care.

2 Lord Jesus Christ, you are the wine of
peace,
poured into hearts once broken and
where dryness sleeps.
Where we are tired and weary you are
waiting there
to be the way which beckons us beyond
despair.

3 Lord Jesus Christ, you call us to your feast,
at which the rich and pow'rful have
become the least.
Where we survive on others in our
human greed
you walk among us begging for your
ev'ry need.

93 Christopher Walker

Bread for the world broken;
wine for us all shed;
word in flesh spoken;
God in love made manifest,
God in love made manifest.

1 Love on the road that's lonely,
love in our minds as guide,
love speaking words of wisdom,
love walking by our side. *(Refrain)*

2 Love on our lips for praising,
love in our eyes to care,
love on our hands for healing,
love in our hearts to share. *(Refrain)*

3 Love feeds our starving brother,
love heals our sister's pain,
love is a light in darkness,
love soon will rise again. *(Refrain)*

4 Love redeems all creation,
love is the only way,
love is our song forever,
so with the world we say:

You are the love broken;
yours is the blood shed;
you are the word spoken;
you are love made manifest,
you are love made manifest.

94 Christopher Walker

Christmas Version

Bread for the world broken;
wine for us all shed;
word in flesh spoken;
God in love made manifest,
God in love made manifest.

1 Love has come down from heaven,
love blessing all the earth,
love of our God is given,
love here in human birth. *(Refrain)*

2 Love in the eyes of shepherds,
love in the Virgin's joy,
love in a lowly stable,
love for a holy boy. *(Refrain)*

3 Love on my lips to praise him,
love in my eyes to care,
love on his hands for healing,
love in his heart to share. *(Refrain)*

4 Love redeems all creation,
love is the only way,
love is our song forever,
so with the world we say:

You are the love broken;
yours is the blood shed;
you are the word spoken;
you are love made manifest,
you are love made manifest.

95 Bernadette Farrell

Bread of life, hope of the world,
Jesus Christ, our brother:
feed us now, give us life,
lead us to one another.

1 As we proclaim your death,
as we recall your life,
we remember your promise
to return again. *(Refrain)*

2 This bread we break and share
was scattered once as grain:
just as now it is gathered,
make your people one. *(Refrain)*

3 We eat this living bread,
we drink this saving cup:
sign of hope in our broken world,
source of lasting love. *(Refrain)*

4 Hold us in unity,
in love for all to see;
that the world may believe in you,
God of all who live. *(Refrain)*

5 You are the bread of peace,
you are the wine of joy,
broken now for your people,
poured in endless love.

96 *Bernadette Farrell*

Christmas Version

Bread of life, hope of the world,
Jesus Christ, our brother:
feed us now, give us life,
lead us to one another.

1 A child is born for us,
a son is given to us,
in our midst, Christ, our Lord and God
comes as one who serves. *(Refrain)*

2 With our own eyes we see,
with our own ears we hear
the salvation of all the world,
God's incarnate Word. *(Refrain)*

3 You are the hope of all,
our promise and our call,
radiant light in our darkness,
truth to set us free. *(Refrain)*

97 *Reginald Heber (1783–1826)*

Bread of the world in mercy broken,
wine of the soul in mercy shed,
by whom the words of life were spoken,
and in whose death our sins are dead.
Look on the heart by sorrow broken,
look on the tears by sinners shed;
and be your feast to us the token
that by your grace our souls are fed.

98 *Edwin Hatch (1835–89)*

1 Breathe on me, Breath of God,
fill me with life anew,
that I may love what thou dost love,
and do what thou wouldst do.

2 Breathe on me, Breath of God,
until my heart is pure:
until with thee I have one will
to do and to endure.

3 Breathe on me, Breath of God.
till I am wholly thine,
until this earthly part of me
glows with thy fire divine.

4 Breathe on me, Breath of God,
so shall I never die,
but live with thee the perfect life
of thine Eternity.

99 *Reginald Heber (1783–1826)*

1 Brightest and best of the sons of the
morning,
dawn on our darkness, and lend us
thine aid;
star of the east, the horizon adorning,
guide where our infant Redeemer is laid.

2 Cold on his cradle the dew–drops are
shining;
low lies his head with the beasts of
the stall:
angels adore him in slumber reclining,
Maker and Monarch, and Saviour of all.

3 Say, shall we yield him, in costly devotion,
odours of Edom, and offerings divine?
Gems of the mountain and pearls of the
ocean,
myrrh from the forest and gold from the
mine?

4 Vainly we offer each ample oblation,
vainly with gifts would his favour secure;
richer by far is the heart's adoration;
dearer to God are the prayers of the poor.

5 Brightest and best of the sons of the
morning,
dawn on our darkness, and lend us
thine aid;
star of the east, the horizon adorning,
guide where our infant Redeemer is laid.

100 *Wipo (11th century), tr. Walter Kirkham Blount*

1 Bring, all ye dear–bought nations, bring
your richest praises to your king,
alleluia, alleluia,
that spotless Lamb, who more than due,
paid for his sheep, and those sheep you,
Alleluia.

2 That guiltless Son, who bought your peace,
and made his father's anger cease,
then, life and death together fought,
each to a strange extreme were brought.

3 Life died, but soon revived again,
and even death by it was slain.
Say, happy Magdalen, oh say,
what didst thou see there by the way?

4 'I saw the tomb of my dear Lord,
I saw himself and him adored,
I saw the napkin and the sheet,
that bound his head and wrapped his feet.'

5 'I heard the angels witness bear,
Jesus is ris'n; he is not here;
go, tell his followers they shall see,
thine and their hope in Galilee.'

6 We, Lord, with faithful hearts and voice,
on this thy rising day rejoice.
O thou, whose power o'ercame the grave,
by grace and love us sinners save.

101 *Anonymous*

1 Bring flowers of the rarest,
bring blossoms the fairest,
from garden and woodland
and hillside and dale;
our full hearts are swelling,
our glad voices telling
the praise of the loveliest
flower of the vale.

O Mary we crown thee with blossoms today,
Queen of the Angels and Queen of
the May. (2)

2 Their lady they name thee,
their mistress proclaim thee.
Oh, grant that thy children
on earth be as true,
as long as the bowers
are radiant with flowers
as long as the azure
shall keep its bright hue.

3 Sing gaily in chorus,
the bright angels o'er us
re–echo the strains we begin upon earth;
their harps are repeating
the notes of our greeting,
for Mary herself is the cause of our mirth.

102 *St Francis of Assisi, adapted by Donovan*

1 Brother Sun and Sister Moon,
I seldom hear you, seldom hear your tune.
Preoccupied with selfish misery.

2 Brother Wind and Sister Air,
open my eyes to visions pure and fair
that I may see the glory around me.

I am God's creature, of him I am part.
I feel his love awakening my heart.

3 Brother Sun and Sister Moon,
now do I see you, I can hear your tune,
so much in love with all I survey.

103 *Beverlee Paine*

1 But I say unto you, love your enemies
and pray for those who hurt you.
Give to those who ask, don't turn away.

And be like your Father in heaven above
who causes his sun to shine on evil and
good,
and sends down his rain to quench all
our thirst.
In him we live and move and have our
being.

2 If you forgive each other,
so will God forgive you.
Do not judge lest
you be judg'd yourselves.

3 When you see the hungry,
feed them from your table.
For the poor and weary,
be their wat'ring place.

104 *James G. Johnston*

Called to be servants, called to be sons,
called to be daughters, we're called to be one.
Called into service, called to be free;
you are called to be you, and I'm called to be me.

1 Children, come, with wide open eyes.
Look at the water; you have been baptised.
You're free from the slav'ry that bound you to sin,
so live now as children in the kingdom of heav'n.

2 We are saints! Forgiveness is sure
not of ourselves, but the cross Christ endured.
We're free from the Law that said 'You must provide!'
We're free to be servants; we're called; we're baptised.

3 Jesus closed the dark pit of death.
He has breathed on us with his holy breath.
He gives us the faith to respond to his News.
We're free to show mercy, to love, to be bruised.

105 *Mary Macdonald (1789–1872), tr. Lachlan MacBean (1853–1931)*

1 Child in the manger, infant of Mary;
outcast and stranger, Lord of all;
child who inherits all our transgressions,
all our demerits on him fall.

2 Once the most holy child of salvation
gently and lowly lived below;
now as our glorious mighty Redeemer,
see him victorious o'er each foe.

3 Prophets foretold him, infant of wonder;
angels behold him on his throne:
worthy our Saviour of all their praises;
happy for ever are his own.

106 *Adapted from 'St Patrick's Breastplate' by James Quinn, SJ*

1 Christ be beside me, Christ be before me,
Christ be behind me, King of my heart.
Christ be within me, Christ be below me,
Christ be above me, never to part.

2 Christ on my right hand, Christ on my left hand,
Christ all around me, shield in the strife.
Christ in my sleeping, Christ in my sitting,
Christ in my rising, light of my life.

3 Christ be in all hearts thinking about me,
Christ be in all tongues telling of me.
Christ be the vision in eyes that see me,
in ears that hear me, Christ ever be.

107 *Pamela Stotter*

1 Christ is alive, with joy we sing;
we celebrate our risen Lord,
praising the glory of his name.
Alleluia, alleluia, alleluia.

2 He is the grain of wheat that died;
sown in distress and reaped in joy,
yielding a harvest of new life.

3 He is the sun which brings the dawn:
he is the light of all the world,
setting us free from death and sin.

4 He is the vine set in the earth,
sharing our life, becoming man,
that we might share in God's own life.

5 Christ is alive, with joy we sing;
we celebrate our risen Lord,
praising the glory of his name.

108 *Ivor J. E. Daniel (1883–1967)*

1 Christ is King of earth and heaven!
Let his subjects all proclaim,
in the splendour of his temple,
honour to his holy name.

2 Christ is King! No soul created
can refuse to bend the knee
to the God made man who reigneth
as 'twas promised, from the tree.

3 Christ is King! Let humble sorrow
for our past neglect atone,
for the lack of faithful service
to the Master whom we own.

4 Christ is King! Let joy and gladness
greet him; let his courts resound
with the praise of faithful subjects
to his love in honour bound.

5 Christ is King! In health and sickness,
till we breathe our latest breath,
till we greet in highest heaven,
Christ the victor over death.

109 *Latin 7th or 8th century, tr. J .M. Neale (1818–66) alt.*

1 Christ is made the sure foundation,
Christ the head and corner–stone,
chosen of the Lord, and precious,
binding all the Church in one,
holy Sion's help for ever,
and her confidence alone.

2 All that dedicated city,
dearly loved of God on high,
in exultant jubilation
pours perpetual melody,
God the One in Three adoring
in glad hymns eternally.

3 To this temple where we call you
come, O Lord of Hosts, today;
with your wonted loving kindness
hear your people as they pray,
and your fullest benediction
shed within its walls alway.

4 Here vouchsafe to all your servants
what they ask of you to gain,
what they gain of you forever
with the blessed to retain,
and hereafter in your glory
evermore with you to reign.

5 Praise and honour to the Father,
praise and honour to the Son,
praise and honour to the Spirit,
ever Three and ever One,
consubstantial, co-eternal,
while unending ages run.

110 *Estelle White*

Christ is our king, let the whole world rejoice!
May all the nations sing out with one voice!
Light of the world, you have helped us to see
that all men are brothers and all men one day will be free.

1 He came to open the eyes of the blind,
letting the sunlight pour into their minds.
Vision is waiting for those who have hope.
He is the light of the world.

2 He came to speak tender words to the poor,
he is the gateway and he is the door.
Riches are waiting for all those who hope.
He is the light of the world.

3 He came to open the doors of the gaol,
he came to help the downtrodden and frail.
Freedom is waiting for all those who hope.
He is the light of the world.

4 He came to open the lips of the mute,
letting them speak out with courage and truth.
His words are uttered by all those who hope.
He is the light of the world.

5 He came to heal all the crippled and lame,
sickness took flight at the sound of his name.
Vigour is waiting for all those who hope.
He is the light of the world.

6 He came to love everyone on this earth
and through his Spirit he promised rebirth.
New life is waiting for all those who hope.
He is the light of the world.

111 *Fred Pratt Green*

1 Christ is the world's light, he and no other;
born in our darkness, he became our brother.
If we have seen him, we have seen the Father:
Glory to God on high.

2 Christ is the world's peace, he and no other;
no–one can serve him and despise another.
Who else unites us, one in God the Father?

3 Christ is the world's life, he and no other,
sold once for silver, murdered here, our brother,
he who redeems us, reigns with God the Father:

4 Give God the glory, God and no other;
give God the glory, Spirit, Son and Father;
give God the glory, God in man, my brother:

112 *Wipo 11th century, tr. Jane Elizabeth Leeson (1809–1881)*

1 Christ the Lord is risen today!
Christians, haste your vows to pay,
offer ye your praises meet
at the paschal victim's feet;
for the sheep the Lamb hath bled,
sinless in the sinner's stead.
Christ the Lord is ris'n on high;
now he lives, no more to die.

2 Christ, the victim undefiled,
all to God hath reconciled
when in strange and awful strife
met together death and life;
Christians, on this happy day
haste with joy your vows to pay.
Christ the Lord is ris'n on high;
Now he lives, no more to die.

3 Say, O wond'ring Mary, say
what thou sawest on thy way.
'I beheld, where Christ had lain,
empty tomb and angels twain,
I beheld the glory bright
of the rising Lord of light;
Christ my hope is ris'n again;
now he lives, and lives to reign.'

4 Christ, who once for sinners bled,
now the first–born from the dead,
throned in endless might and power,
lives and reigns for evermore.
Hail, eternal hope on high!
Hail, thou king of victory!
Hail, thou Prince of life adored!
Help and save us, gracious Lord.

113 *Michael Saward*

1 Christ triumphant ever–reigning,
Saviour, Master, King,
Lord of heav'n, our lives sustaining,
hear us as we sing.

Yours the glory and the crown,
the high renown,
the eternal name.

2 Word incarnate, truth revealing,
Son of Man on earth!
Power and majesty concealing
by your humble birth:

3 Suffering servant, scorned, ill–treated,
victim crucified!
Death is through the cross defeated,
sinners justified:

4 Priestly King, enthroned for ever
high in heaven above!
Sin and death and hell shall never
stifle hymns of love:

5 So, our hearts and voices raising
through the ages long,
ceaselessly upon you gazing,
this shall be our song:

114 *Christopher Idle*

1 Christ's church shall glory in his power
and grow to his perfection;
He is our rock, our mighty tower,
our life, our resurrection.
So by his skilful hand
the church of Christ shall stand;
the master–builder's plan
he works, as he began,
and soon will crown with splendour.

2 Christ's people serve his wayward world
to whom he seems a stranger;
he knows its welcome from of old,
he shares our joy, our danger.
So strong, and yet so weak,

the church of Christ shall speak;
his cross our greatest need,
his word the vital seed
that brings a fruitful harvest.

3 Christ's living lamp shall brightly burn,
and to our earthly city
forgotten beauty shall return,
and purify and pity.
To give the oppressed their right
the church of Christ shall fight;
and though the years seem long
God is our strength and song,
and God is our salvation.

4 Christ's body triumphs in his name;
one Father, sovereign giver,
one Spirit, with his love aflame,
one Lord, the same for ever.
To you, O God our prize,
the church of Christ shall rise
beyond all measured height
to that eternal light,
where Christ shall reign all–holy.

115 *John L. Bell and Graham Maule*

1 Christ's is the world in which we move,
Christ's are the folk we're summoned to love,
Christ's is the voice which calls us to care,
and Christ is the one who meets us here.

To the lost Christ shows his face;
to the unloved he gives his embrace;
to those who cry in pain or disgrace,
Christ makes, with his friends,
a touching place.

2 Feel for the people we most avoid,
strange or bereaved or never employed;
feel for the women, and feel for the men
who fear that their living is all in vain.

3 Feel for the parents who've lost their child,
feel for the women whom men have defiled,
feel for the baby for whom there's no breast,
and feel for the weary who find no rest.

4 Feel for the lives by life confused,
riddled with doubt, in loving abused;
feel for the lonely heart, conscious of sin,
which longs to be pure but fears to begin.

116 *Christus Vincit, 9th century*

Christus vincit: Christus regnat:
Christus imperat.
Christus vincit: Christus regnat:
Christus imperat.
Exaudi Christe: *Exaudi Christe.*
Summo Pontifici et universali Papae: *Vita.*
Salvator mundi: *tu illum adjuva.*
Sancta Maria: *tu illum adjuva.*
Sancte Petre: *tu illum adjuva.*
Sancte Paule: *tu illum adjuva.*
Sancte Gregori: *tu illum adjuva.*
Christus vincit: Christus regnat:
Christus imperat.
Rex regnum! *Christus vincit.*
Rex noster! *Christus regnat.*
Gloria nostra! *Christus imperat.*
Ipsi soli imperium
gloria et potestas,
per immortalia saecula saeculorum.
Amen.
Christus vincit: Christus regnat:
Christus imperat.

117 *Samuel Johnson (1822–82)*

1 City of God, how broad and far
outspread thy walls sublime!
The true thy chartered freemen are,
of every age and clime.

2 One holy Church, one army strong,
one steadfast, high intent;
one working band, one harvest song
one King Omnipotent.

3 How purely hath thy speech come down
from our primeval youth!
How grandly hath thine empire grown,
of freedom, love and truth!

4 How gleam thy watch–fires through the night
with never–fainting ray!

How rise thy towers, serene and bright,
to meet the dawning day!

5 In vain the surge's angry shock,
in vain the drifting sands:
unharmed upon the eternal Rock
the eternal City stands.

118 *Sue McClellan, John Paculabo and Keith Rycroft*

1 Colours of day dawn into the mind,
the sun has come up, the night is behind.
Go down in the city, into the street,
and let's give the message to the people
we meet.

So light up the fire and let the flame burn,
open the door, let Jesus return.
Take seeds of his Spirit, let the fruit grow,
tell the people of Jesus, let his love show.

2 Go through the park, on into the town;
the sun still shines on, it never goes down.
The light of the world is risen again;
the people of darkness are needing our
friend.

3 Open your eyes, look into the sky,
the darkness has come, the sun came to die.
The evening draws on, the sun disappears,
but Jesus is living, and his Spirit is near.

119 *St Thomas Aquinas (1227–74) tr. James Quinn, SJ*

1 Come, adore this wondrous presence,
bow to Christ, the source of grace.
Here is kept the ancient promise
of God's earthly dwelling–place.
Sight is blind before God's glory,
faith alone may see his face.

2 Glory be to God the Father,
praise to his co–equal Son,
adoration to the Spirit,
bond of love, in Godhead one.
Blest be God by all creation
joyously while ages run.

120 *David Haas*

Come and be light for our eyes;
be the air we breathe,
be the voice we speak!
Come be the song we sing,
be the path we seek!

1 Your life was given; food for all people,
body and blood, new life in our midst!
Death is no longer, life is our future,
Jesus, Messiah; name of all names!

2 We hold your presence; risen for ever!
Your name now names us people of God!
Filled with your vision, people of mission,
healing, forgiving; light for the world!

3 Lead us to justice, light in the darkness;
singing, proclaiming Jesus is Lord!
Teach us to speak, and help us to listen
for when your truth and our dreams
embrace!

121 *Traditional; unknown*

1 Come and praise the Lord our King,
alleluia.
Come and praise the Lord our King.
Alleluia!

2 Christ was born in Bethlehem, alleluia.
Son of God and Son of Man. Alleluia!

3 He grew up an earthly child, alleluia.
in the world, but undefiled. Alleluia!

4 He who died at Calvary, alleluia.
rose again triumphantly. Alleluia!

5 He will cleanse us from our sin, alleluia.
if we live by faith in him. Alleluia!

6 Come and praise the Lord our King,
alleluia.
Come and praise the Lord our King.
Alleluia!

122 *Gregory Norbet, OSB (based on Hosea)*

1 Come back to me with all your heart.
Don't let fear keep us apart.
Trees do bend, though straight and tall;
so must we to others' call.

Long have I waited
for your coming home to me
and living deeply our new life.

2 The wilderness will lead you
to your heart, where I will speak.
Integrity and justice
with tenderness you shall know.

3 You shall sleep secure with peace;
faithfulness will be your joy.
Long have I waited for your coming
home to me
and living deeply our new life.

4 Come back to me with all your heart.
Don't let fear keep us apart.
Trees do bend, though straight and tall;
so must we to others' call.

123 *John Glynn*

1 Come, Christian people, take heed what
I say:
here, in this stable, your King was born
today.

Star of wisdom, child of gladness,
tell him all your troubles.
Mary's boy has banished sadness,
why be sorrowful now?

2 Not much to look at – simply straw
and hay –
yet on that carpet your King was laid today.

3 Say, are you listening? Take heed what
I say:
here on this planet your King still lives
today.

124 *Anonymous*

Come, come, come to the manger,
children, come to the children's King:
sing, sing, chorus of Angels,
stars of morning o'er Bethlehem sing.

1 He lies 'mid the beasts of the stall,
who is Maker and Lord of us all;
the wintry wind blows cold and dreary,
see, he weeps, the world is weary;
Lord, have pity and mercy on me!

2 He leaves all his glory behind;
to be born and to die for mankind.
With grateful beasts his cradle chooses,
thankless man his love refuses;
Lord, have pity and mercy on me!

3 To the manger of Bethlehem come,
to the Saviour Emmanuel's home;
the heav'nly hosts above are singing,
set the Christmas bells a–ringing;
Lord, have pity and mercy on me!

125 *Bianco da Siena (d. 1434), tr. Richard Frederick Littledale*

1 Come down, O love divine,
seek thou this soul of mine,
and visit it with thine own ardour glowing;
O comforter, draw near, within my heart
appear,
and kindle it, thy holy flame bestowing.

2 O let it freely burn,
till earthly passions turn
to dust and ashes in its heat consuming;
and let thy glorious light shine ever on
my sight,
and clothe me round, the while my path
illuming.

3 Let holy charity
mine outward vesture be,
and lowliness become mine inner clothing;
true lowliness of heart, which takes the
humbler part,
and o'er its own shortcomings weeps
with loathing.

4 And so the yearning strong,
with which the soul will long,
shall far outpass the power of human
telling,
for none can guess its grace,
till he become the place
wherein the Holy Spirit makes his dwelling.

126 *Ascribed to Rabanus Maurus (776–856) tr. Anonymous*

1 Come, Holy Ghost, Creator, come
from thy bright heavenly throne,
come, take possession of our souls,
and make them all thine own.

2 Thou who art called the Paraclete,
best gift of God above,
the living spring, the living fire,
sweet unction and true love.

3 Thou who are sev'nfold in thy grace,
finger of God's right hand;
his promise, teaching little ones
to speak and understand.

4 O guide our minds with thy blest light,
with love our hearts inflame;
and with thy strength, which ne'er decays,
confirm our mortal frame.

5 Far from us drive our deadly foe;
true peace unto us bring;
and through all perils lead us safe
beneath thy sacred wing.

6 Through thee may we the Father know,
through thee th'eternal Son,
and thee the Spirit of them both,
thrice–blessed Three in One.

7 All glory to the Father be,
with his co–equal Son:
the same to thee, great Paraclete,
while endless ages run.

127 *David Haas*

1 Come! Live in the light!
Shine with the joy and the love of the
Lord!
We are called to be light for the kingdom
to live in the freedom of the city of God!

*We are called to act with justice,
we are called to love tenderly,
we are called to serve one another;
to walk humbly with God!*

2 Come! Open your heart!
Show your mercy to all those in fear!
We are called to be hope for the hopeless
so all hatred and blindness will be no more!

3 Sing! Sing a new song!
Sing of that great day when all will be one!
God will reign, and we'll walk with
each other
as sisters and brothers united in love!

128 *Kevin Mayhew*

1 Come, Lord Jesus, come.
Come, take my hands, take them for
your work.
Take them for your service, Lord.
Take them for your glory, Lord,
Come, Lord Jesus, come.
Come, Lord Jesus, take my hands.

2 Come, Lord Jesus, come.
Come, take my eyes, may they shine
with joy.
Take them for your service, Lord.
Take them for your glory, Lord.
Come, Lord Jesus, come.
Come, Lord Jesus, take my eyes.

3 Come, Lord Jesus, come.
Come, take my lips, may they speak
your truth.
Take them for your service, Lord.
Take them for your glory, Lord.
Come, Lord Jesus, come.
Come, Lord Jesus, take my lips.

4 Come, Lord Jesus, come.
Come take my feet, may they walk
your path.
Take them for your service, Lord.
Take them for your glory, Lord.
Come, Lord Jesus, come.
Come, Lord Jesus, take my feet.

5 Come, Lord Jesus, come.
Come, take my heart, fill it with
your love.
Take it for your service, Lord.
Take it for your glory, Lord.
Come, Lord Jesus, come.
Come, Lord Jesus, take my heart.

6 Come, Lord Jesus, come.
Come, take my life, take it for your own.
Take it for your service, Lord.
Take it for your glory, Lord.
Come, Lord Jesus, come.
Come, Lord Jesus, take my life.

129 *French 18th century, tr. Sr. Mary of St Phillip*

1 Come, O divine Messiah!
The world in silence waits the day
when hope shall sing its triumph,
and sadness flee away.

Sweet Saviour, haste; come, come to earth:
dispel the night, and show Thy face,
and bid us hail the dawn of grace.
Come, O divine Messiah!
The world in silence waits the day
when hope shall sing its triumph,
and sadness flee away.

2 O Thou, whom nations sighed for,
whom priests and prophets long foretold,
wilt break the captive fetters,
redeem the long–lost fold.

3 Shalt come in peace and meekness,
and lowly will thy cradle be:
all clothed in human weakness
shall we thy Godhead see.

130 *Marty Haugen*

1 Come, O God of all the earth:
come to us, O Righteous one;
come, and bring our love to birth:
in the glory of your Son.

Sing out, earth and skies!
Sing of the God who loves you!
Raise your joyful cries!
Dance to the life around you!

2 Come, O God of wind and flame:
fill the earth with righteousness;
teach us all to sing your name:
may our lives your love confess.

3 Come, O God of flashing light:
twinkling star and burning sun;
God of day and God of night:
in your light we all are one.

4 Come, O God of snow and rain:
shower down upon the earth;
Come, O God of joy and pain:
God of sorrow, God of mirth.

5 Come, O Justice, come, O Peace:
come and shape our hearts anew;
come and make oppression cease:
bring us all to life in you.

131 *Versified by James Quinn, SJ*

1 Come, praise the Lord, the almighty,
the King of all nations!
Tell forth his fame, O ye peoples,
with loud acclamations!
His love is sure;
faithful his word shall endure,
steadfast through all generations!

2 Praise to the Father most gracious,
the Lord of creation!
Praise to his Son, the Redeemer who
wrought our salvation!
O heav'nly Dove,
praise to thee, fruit of their love.
Giver of all consolation!

132 *Rorate Caeli, Anonymous, tr. Luke Connaughton (1919–1979)*

Come Saviour, come like dew on the grass;
break through the clouds like gentle rain.

1 Be angry, Lord, no more with us;
remember no longer our transgression.
See the city of God laid waste and desolate:
Zion is turned to wilderness,
Jerusalem, ravaged and ruined,
your dwelling place and the Holy of holies,
the house of your glory; silent are those
voices now
that once proclaimed your praise.

2 We have gone astray;
in the multitude of our sins
we have been made unclean,
fallen, fallen,
stricken as the leaves of autumn.
The stormwind carries us away,
the tempest of our evil deeds;
you have turned away from us
the face of your mercy,
and our iniquity has crushed us
like a potter's vessel.

3 O Lord our God, look upon your people
in their affliction:
be mindful of your promises.
Send us the Lamb who will
set up his dominion
from the Rock of the Wilderness
to Zion
throned on her mountain.
There is no other whose power
can break our chains and set us free.

4 Be comforted, be comforted,
take heart, my people:
you shall quickly see your salvation.
Why do you waste yourself with grief,
though you have walked so long
with sorrow?
I am your Saviour, be afraid no more.
For am I not God,
the Lord your God whom you worship,
the Holy One of Israel,
come to redeem you?

Alternative response

Rorate caeli desuper
et nubes pluant justum.

133 *Charles Wesley (1707–88)*

1 Come, thou long–expected Jesus,
born to set thy people free,
from our fears and sins release us,
let us find our rest in thee.

2 Israel's strength and consolation,
hope of all the earth thou art;
dear desire of every nation,
joy of every longing heart.

3 Born thy people to deliver,
born a child and yet a king,
born to reign in us for ever,
now thy gracious kingdom bring.

4 By thine own eternal Spirit
rule in all our hearts alone;
by thine all–sufficient merit
raise us to thy glorious throne.

134 *Gregory Norbet, OSB & Mary David Callahan, OSB*

Come to me, all who labour
and are heavy burdened,
and I shall give you rest.
Take up my yoke and learn from me,
for I am meek and humble of heart.
And you'll find rest for your souls.
Yes, my yoke is easy and my burden is light.

The Lord is my shepherd,
I shall never be in need.
Fresh and green are the meadows
where he gives me rest.

135 Bernadette Farrell

Come to set us free,
come to make us your own.
Come to show the way
to your people, your chosen.
Open our lives to the
light of your promise.
Come to our hearts with healing,
come to our minds with power,
come to us and bring us your life.

1 You are light which shines in darkness,
Morning Star which never sets.
Open our eyes which only dimly see
the truth which sets us free.

2 You are hope which brings us courage,
you are strength which never fails.
Open our minds to ways we do not know,
but where your Spirit grows.

3 You are promise of salvation,
you are God in human form.
Bring to our world of emptiness and fear
the word we long to hear.

136 Henry Alford (1810–71)

1 Come, ye thankful people, come,
raise the song of harvest–home!
All be safely gathered in,
ere the winter storms begin;
God, our maker, doth provide
for our wants to be supplied;
come to God's own temple, come;
raise the song of harvest–home!

2 We ourselves are God's own field,
fruit unto his praise to yield;
wheat and tares together sown,
unto joy or sorrow grown;
first the blade and then the ear,
then the full corn shall appear:
grant, O harvest Lord, that we
wholesome grain and pure may be.

3 For the Lord our God shall come,
and shall take his harvest home;
from his field shall purge away
all that doth offend, that day,
give his angels charge at last
in the fire the tares to cast,
but the fruitful ears to store
in his garner evermore.

4 Then, thou Church triumphant, come,
raise the song of harvest–home;
all be safely gathered in,
free from sorrow, free from sin,
there for ever purified
in God's garner to abide;
come, ten thousand angels, come,
raise the glorious harvest–home!

---

137 Taizé chant, from Psalms 105 (106) and 117 (118)

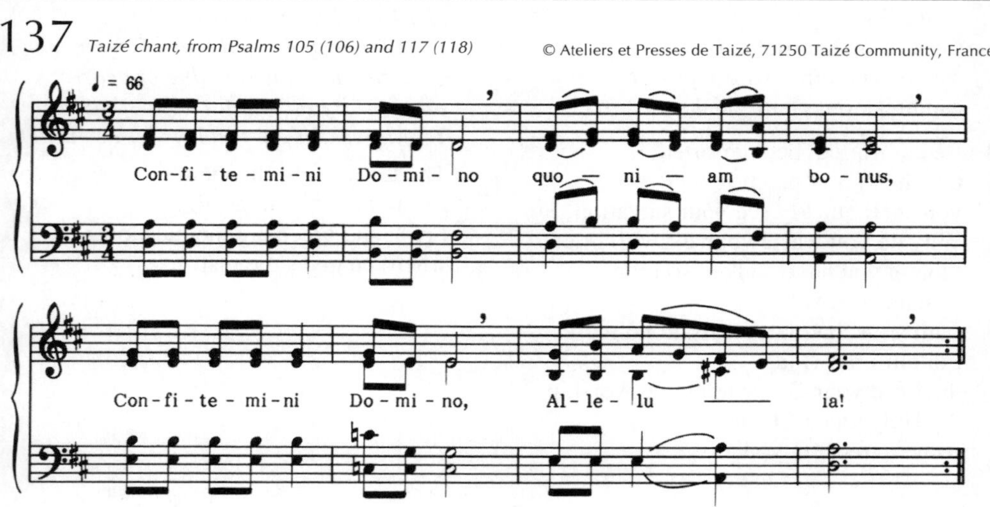
♩ = 66
Con-fi - te - mi - ni Do - mi - no quo — ni — am bo - nus,
Con-fi - te - mi - ni Do - mi - no, Al - le - lu ia!

138 *7th century, tr. J.M. Neale (1818–1866), and others*

1 Creator of the stars of night,
your people's everlasting light,
Jesus, redeemer of us all,
O hear your servants when they call.

2 Now grieving at the helpless cry
of all creation doomed to die,
You came to save our fallen race
by healing gifts of heavenly grace.

3 When earth was near its evening hour
you came in love's redeeming power.
Like bridegrooms from their chambers come,
you sprang forth from the Virgin's womb.

4 At your great name, exalted now,
all knees in lowly homage bow;
all things in heav'n and earth adore
and own you King for evermore.

5 Great judge of all, in that last day,
be present then with us, we pray.
Preserve us, while we dwell below
from all the menace of our foe.

6 To God the Father, God the Son,
and Holy Spirit, three in one,
praise, honour, might and glory be
from age to age eternally.

139 *Matthew Bridges (1800–94)*

1 Crown him with many crowns,
the Lamb upon his throne;
hark, how the heav'nly anthem drowns
all music but its own:
awake, my soul, and sing
of him who died for thee,
and hail him as thy matchless King
through all eternity.

2 Crown him the Virgin's Son,
the God incarnate born,
whose arm those crimson trophies won,
which now his brow adorn;
fruit of the mystic rose,
as of that rose the stem,
the root, whence mercy ever flows,
the babe of Bethlehem.

3 Crown him the Lord of love;
behold his hands and side,
rich wounds, yet visible above,
in beauty glorified:
no angel in the sky
can fully bear that sight,
but downward bends his burning eye
at mysteries so bright.

4 Crown him the Lord of peace,
whose power a sceptre sways,
from pole to pole, that wars may cease,
absorbed in prayer and praise:
his reign shall know no end,
and round his piercèd feet
fair flowers of Paradise extend
their fragrance ever sweet.

5 Crown him the Lord of heaven,
one with the Father known,
and the blest Spirit through him given
from yonder triune throne:
all hail, Redeemer, hail,
for thou hast died for me;
thy praise shall never, never fail
throughout eternity.

140 *Ascribed to St. Bernard of Cluny (12th century), tr. Henry Bittleston (1818–1886)*

1 Daily, daily, sing to Mary,
sing my soul, her praises due;
all her feasts, her actions honour,
with the heart's devotion true.
Lost in wond'ring contemplation
be her majesty confessed:
call her Mother, call her Virgin,
happy Mother, Virgin blest.

2 Sing, my tongue, the Virgin's trophies,
who for us her Maker bore;
for the curse of old inflicted,
peace and blessings to restore.
Sing in songs of praise unending,
sing the world's majestic Queen;
weary not nor faint in telling
all the gifts she gives to men.

3 All my senses, heart, affections,
strive to sound her glory forth;
spread abroad the sweet memorials,

of the Virgin's priceless worth,
where the voice of music thrilling,
where the tongues of eloquence,
that can utter hymns beseeming
all her matchless excellence?

4 All our joys do flow from Mary,
all then join her praise to sing;
trembling sing the Virgin Mother,
Mother of our Lord and King,
while we sing her awful glory,
far above our fancy's reach,
let our hearts be quick to offer
love the heart alone can teach.

141 *Pamela Stotter*

1 Day and night the heav'ns are telling
the glory which with us is dwelling,
the works of God to us made known.
Dawn and dusk are still with wonder.
The wind cries out, the waters thunder,
displaying his almighty power.
Our God is great indeed,
and knows our constant need, our creator.
So with creation we proclaim
his goodness as we praise his name.

2 Lord, we stand in awe before you,
your people coming to adore you,
so cleanse our hearts, renew our minds.
See us now in shadows dwelling,
and come like sun, the clouds dispelling,
enlighten, heal us, Lord of love.
Your Spirit in us prays.
He teaches us your ways, as we listen.
Touch once again with living flame
your people gathered in your name.

142 *James Quinn, SJ*

1 Day is done, but Love unfailing
dwells ever here;
shadows fall, but hope, prevailing,
calms every fear.
Loving Father, none forsaking,
take our hearts, of Love's own making,
watch our sleeping, guard our waking,
be always near!

2 Dark descends, but Light unending
shines through our night;
you are with us, ever lending
new strength to sight;
one in love, your truth confessing,
one in hope of heaven's blessing,
may we see, in love's possessing,
love's endless light!

3 Eyes will close, but you, unsleeping,
watch by our side;
death may come: in love's safe keeping
still we abide.
God of love, all evil quelling,
sin forgiving, fear dispelling,
stay with us, our hearts indwelling,
this eventide!

143 *John Greenleaf Whittier (1807–92)*

1 Dear Lord and Father of mankind,
forgive our foolish ways!
Re–clothe us in our rightful mind,
in purer lives thy service find,
in deeper reverence praise, *(2)*

2 In simple trust like theirs who heard,
beside the Syrian sea,
the gracious calling of the Lord,
let us, like them, without a word,
rise up and follow thee, *(2)*

3 O Sabbath rest by Galilee!
O calm of hills above,
where Jesus knelt to share with thee
the silence of eternity,
interpreted by love! *(2)*

4 Drop thy still dews of quietness,
till all our strivings cease;
take from our souls the strain and stress,
and let our ordered lives confess
the beauty of thy peace. *(2)*

5 Breathe through the heats of our desire
thy coolness and thy balm;
let sense be dumb, let flesh retire;
speak through the earthquake, wind
and fire,
O still small voice of calm! *(2)*

144 *Based on the Irish of Tadhg Gaelach Ó Suilleabhain by James Quinn, SJ,*

1 Dear love of my heart, O heart of Christ, my Lord,
what treasure you leave within my heart, O Guest!
You come to my heart O heart on fire with love,
and leave me your heart, O how my heart is blest!

2 My heart cannot tell, O King of angel hosts,
how great was that pain you bore upon the cross:
so small is my heart, so deep your wounds of love,
so precious the crown of those you save from loss!

3 Your death has restored your likeness in my heart,
your cross in my shield your loving heart my gain!
How sad is my heart when I recall my sins!
How could I have loved what gave your heart such pain?

4 O King of all bliss, all glory set aside,
what heart could have known the pain within your breast?
The wound in your side laid bare your burning love,
and opened for all the heart where all find rest!

145 *David Haas*

Deep within I will plant my law,
not on stone, but in your heart.
Follow me, I will bring you back,
you will be my own,
and I will be your God.

1 I will give you a new heart, a new spirit within you,
for I will be your strength.

2 Seek my face, and see your God,
for I will be your hope.

3 Return to me, with all your heart,
and I will bring you back.

146 *George Ratcliffe Woodward (1848–1934)*

1 Ding dong! Merrily on high
in heav'n the bells are ringing,
ding dong! Verily the sky
is riv'n with angels singing.

Gloria, hosanna in excelsis!

2 E'en so here below, below,
let steeple bells be swungen,
and io, io, io,
by priest and people sungen.

3 Pray you, dutifully prime
your matin chime, ye ringers;
may you beautifully rime
your evetime song, ye singers.

Footnote: 'io' is pronounced 'ee–o'

147 *Gerald Markland*

Do not be afraid, for I have redeemed you.
I have called you by your name; you are mine.

1 When you walk through the waters I'll be with you.
You will never sink beneath the waves.

2 When the fire is burning all around you,
you will never be consumed by the flames.

3 When the fear of loneliness is looming,
then remember I am at your side.

4 When you dwell in the exile of the stranger,
remember you are precious in my eyes.

5 You are mine, O my child, I am your Father,
and I love you with a perfect love.

148 Sebastian Temple

Do not worry over what to eat,
what to wear or put upon your feet.
Trust and pray, go do your best today,
then leave it in the hands of the Lord.
Leave it in the hands of the Lord.

1 The lilies of the field, they do not spin or weave,
yet Solomon was not arrayed like one of these.
The birds of the air, they do not sow or reap,
but God tends to them, like a shepherd tends his sheep.

2 The Lord will guide you in his hidden way,
show you what to do and tell you what to say.
When you pray for rain, go build a dam to store
ev'ry drop of water you have asked him for.

3 The Lord knows all your needs before you ask.
Only trust in God; the Lord will do the task
of bringing in your life whatever you must know,
and lead you through the darkness wherever you must go.

149 Anonymous

1 Dona nobis pacem, pacem.
Dona nobis pacem. *(3)*

150 From the Antiphonary of Bennchar (7th century) tr. J. M. Neale (1818–66)

1 Draw nigh, and take the body of our Lord,
and drink the holy blood for you outpoured;
saved by that body, hallowed by that blood,
whereby refreshed we render thanks to God.

2 Salvation's giver, Christ the only Son,
by that his cross and blood the victory won,
offered was he for greatest and for least;
himself the victim, and himself the priest.

3 Victims were offered by the law of old,
that, in a type, celestial mysteries told.
He, ransomer from death and light from shade,
giveth his holy grace his saints to aid.

4 Approach ye then with faithful hearts sincere,
and take the safeguard of salvation here,
he that in this world rules his saints and shields,
to all believers life eternal yields.

5 With heav'nly bread makes them that hunger whole,
gives living waters to the thirsty soul,
Alpha and Omega, to whom shall bow
all nations at the doom, is with us now.

152 W. Whiting (1825–78)

1 Eternal Father, strong to save,
whose arm doth bind the restless wave,
who bidd'st the mighty ocean deep,
its own appointed limits keep:
O hear us when we cry to thee
for those in peril on the sea.

2 O Saviour, whose almighty word
the winds and waves submissive heard,
who walkedst on the foaming deep
and calm amid its rage didst sleep:
O hear us when we cry to thee
for those in peril on the sea.

3 O sacred Spirit, who didst brood
upon the waters dark and rude,
and bid their angry tumult cease,
and give, for wild confusion, peace:
O hear us when we cry to thee
for those in peril on the sea.

4 O Trinity of love and power,
our brethren shield in danger's hour.
From rock and tempest, fire and foe,
protect them wheresoe'er they go,
and ever let there rise to thee
glad hymns of praise from land and sea.

151 *Jacques Berthier*

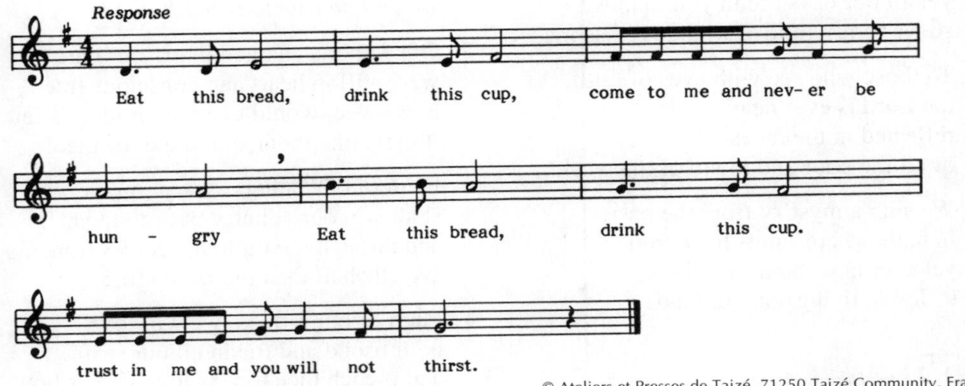
Response
Eat this bread, drink this cup, come to me and nev- er be
hun - gry Eat this bread, drink this cup.
trust in me and you will not thirst.

1 I am the bread of life,
the true bread sent from the Father.

2 Your ancestors ate manna in the desert,
but this is the bread come down from
heaven.

3 Eat my flesh and drink my blood,
and I will raise you up on the last day.

4 Anyone who eats this bread,
will live for ever.

5 If you believe and eat this bread,
you will have eternal life.

---

153 *Sydney Carter*

1 Ev'ry star shall sing a carol;
ev'ry creature, high or low,
come and praise the King of heaven
by whatever name you know:

God above, man below,
holy is the name I know.

2 When the King of all creation
had a cradle on the earth,
holy was the human body,
holy was the human birth:

3 Who can tell what other cradle,
high above the Milky Way,
still may rock the King of heaven
on another Christmas Day?

4 Who can count how many crosses,
still to come or long ago,
crucify the King of heaven?
Holy is the name I know:

5 Who can tell what other body
He will hallow for his own!
I will praise the son of Mary,
brother of my blood and bone:

6 Every star and every planet,
every creature, high and low,
come and praise the King of heaven
by whatever name you know:

154 *Marty Haugen*

Eye has not seen, ear has not heard
what God has ready for those who love him;
spirit of love, come give us
the mind of Jesus,
teach us the wisdom of God.

1 When pain and sorrow weigh us down,
be near to us, oh Lord,
forgive the weakness of our faith,
and bear us up within your peaceful word.

2 Our lives are but a single breath,
we flower and we fade,
yet all our days are in your hands,
so we return in love what love has made.

3 To those who see with eyes of faith,
the Lord is ever near,
reflected in the faces
of all the poor and lowly of the world.

4 We sing a myst'ry from the past,
in halls where saints have trod,
yet ever new the music rings,
to Jesus, living song of God.

155 *Bob Hurd*

Flow, river, flow, flow over me.
O living water, poured out for free.
O living water, flow over me.

1 You will be mine
and I will be your God,
for I will wash you clean.
And a new heart,
a heart of flesh and feeling,
I will place within you
for your heart of stone.

2 The blind shall see,
the mute shall find a voice,
the lame shall leap for joy.
Rivers will flow
into dry and barren desert;
flowers bloom in splendour,
glory fills the land.

3 Whoever drinks
the water I will give
will never thirst again.
The drink I give
is an ever–flowing river,
welling up within you
to give eternal life.

156 *Frederick William Faber (1814–63)*

1 Faith of our fathers! living still
in spite of dungeon, fire and sword;
oh, how our hearts beat high with joy
whene'er we hear that glorious word!

Faith of our fathers! Holy Faith!
We will be true to thee till death,
we will be true to thee till death.

2 Our fathers, chained in prisons dark,
were still in heart and conscious free;
how sweet would be their children's fate,
if they, like them, could die for thee!

3 Faith of our fathers, Mary's prayers
shall win our country back to thee;
and through the truth,that comes from God
We all shall then indeed be free.

4 Faith of our fathers, we will love
both friend and foe in all our strife,
and preach thee too, as love knows how,
by kindly words and virtuous life.

157 *A.J. Newman (adapted)*

1 Father and life–giver, grace of Christ
impart;
he, the Word incarnate – food for mind
and heart.
Children of the promise, homage now we
pay;
sacrificial banquet cheers the desert way.

2 Wine and bread the symbols – love and
life convey,
offered by your people, work and joy
portray.
All we own consigning, nothing is retained;
tokens of our service, gifts and song
contain.

3 Transformation wondrous – water into
wine;
mingled in the Godhead we are made
divine.
Birth into his body brought us life anew,
total consecration – fruit from grafting true.

4 Christ, the head and members living now
as one,
offered to the Father by this holy Son;
and our adoration will be purified,
by the Holy Spirit breathing through our
lives.

158 *Love Maria Willis (1824–1908), and others*

1 Father, hear the prayer we offer:
not for ease that prayer shall be,
but for strength that we may ever
live our lives courageously.

2 Not for ever in green pastures
do we ask our way to be;
but the steep and rugged pathway
may we tread rejoicingly.

3 Not for ever by still waters
would we idly rest and stay;
but would smite the living fountains
from the rocks along the way.

4 Be our strength in hours of weakness,
in our wanderings be our guide;
through endeavour, failure, danger,
Father, be there at our side.

159 *J. Hewer*

1 Father, I place into your hands
the things I cannot do.
Father, I place into your hands
the things that I've been through.
Father, I place into your hands
the way that I should go,
for I know I always can trust you.

2 Father, I place into your hands
my friends and family.
Father, I place into your hands
the things that trouble me.
Father, I place into your hands
the person I would be,
for I know I always can trust you.

3 Father, we love to see your face,
we love to hear your voice.
Father, we love to sing your praise
and in your name rejoice.
Father, we love to walk with you
and in your presence rest,
for we know we always can trust you.

4 Father, I want to be with you
and do the things you do.
Father, I want to speak the words
that you are speaking too.
Father, I want to love the ones
that you will draw to you,
for I know that I am one with you.

160 *Frank Anderson, MSC,*

1 Father, in my life I see,
you are God, who walks with me.
You hold my life in your hands:
close beside you I will stand.
I give all my life to you:
help me, Father, to be true.

2 Jesus, in my life I see …

3 Spirit, in my life I see …

161 *Stewart Cross*

1 Father, Lord of all creation,
ground of being, life and love;
height and depth beyond description
only life in you can prove:
you are mortal life's dependence:
thought, speech, sight are ours by grace;
yours is every hour's existence,
Sovereign Lord of time and space.

2 Jesus Christ, the man for others,
we, your people, make our prayer:
give us grace to love as brothers
all whose burdens we can share.
Where your name binds us together
you, Lord Christ, will surely be;
where no selfishness can sever
there your love may all men see.

3 Holy Spirit, rushing, burning
wind and flame of Pentecost,
fire our hearts afresh with yearning
to regain what we have lost.
May your love unite our action,
nevermore to speak alone:
God, in us abolish faction,
God, through us your love make known.

162 *10th century, tr. A. E. Alston*

1 Father most holy, merciful and loving,
Jesu, redeemer, ever to be worshipped,
life–giving Spirit, comforter most gracious,
God everlasting.

2 Three in a wondrous unity unbroken,
one perfect Godhead, love that never faileth,
light of the angels, succour of the needy,
hope of all living.

3 All thy creation serveth its creator,
thee every creature praiseth without ceasing,
we too would sing the psalms of true devotion:
hear, we beseech thee.

4 Lord God almighty unto thee be glory,
one in three persons, over all exalted.
Thine, as is meet, be honour, praise and blessing
now and forever.

163 *E. Cooper (1770–1833)*

1 Father of heav'n, whose love profound
a ransom for our souls hath found,
before thy throne we sinners bend,
to us thy pard'ning love extend.

2 Almighty Son, incarnate Word,
our prophet, priest, Redeemer, Lord,
before thy throne we sinners bend,
to us thy saving grace extend.

3 Eternal Spirit, by whose breath
the soul is raised from sin and death,
before thy throne we sinners bend,
to us thy quickening power extend.

4 Thrice Holy Father, Spirit, Son;
mysterious Godhead, Three in One,
before thy throne we sinners bend,
grace, pardon, life to us extend.

164 *Terry Coelho*

1 Father, we adore You,
lay our lives before You,
how we love You.

2 Jesus, we adore You …

3 Spirit, we adore You …

165 *Based on the book of Ruth, by Anthony Sharpe*

1 Father, we come in prayer
to witness to your love,
to make two hearts as one.
Father, we give ourselves to you,
we give our lives anew for all time.

Wherever you must go
I'll be always at your side.
Wherever you live you'll find me there,
for your God is mine.

2 Jesus, we ask your help
to conquer for all time
the darkness in our land.
Jesus, where we live you live too,
unite our hearts with you in your love.

3 Spirit, we feel your pow'r
your presence in our hearts:
be with us in each day,
Spirit, may we be one in you,
make all we say and do give you praise.

166 *James Walsh, OSB*

Cantors

Father, we come to you,
God of all power and might.
Show us your glory: give us your life.

All

Father, we come to you,
God of all power and might.
Show us your glory: give us your life.

Cantors

You have united us,
bound us in love and peace:
God in the midst of us, holy, unseen.

All

Blessed is he who comes,
piercing the night of sin.
Open your hearts to him.
Great is his name.

Cantors

Bread of life shared with us,
body of Christ the Lord,
broken and died for us: life for the world.

All

Father, we come to you,
God of all power and might.
Show us your glory: give us your life.
Blessed is he who comes
piercing our night of sin.
Open our hearts to you: great is your name.
Open our hearts to you: great is your name!

167 Donna Adkins

1 Father, we love You,
we worship and adore You,
glorify Your name in all the earth.
Glorify Your name, glorify Your name,
glorify Your name in all the earth.

2 Jesus, we love You …

3 Spirit, we love You …

168 St Gregory the Great (540-604) tr. Percy Dearmer (1867–1936), slightly altered

1 Father, we praise you now the night is
over;
active and watchful, stand we all before you;
singing, we offer pray'r and meditation:
thus we adore you.

2 Monarch of all things, fit us for your
kingdom;
banish our weakness, health and
wholeness sending;
bring us to heaven, where your saints united
joy without ending.

3 All holy Father, Son and equal Spirit,
Trinity blessèd, send us your salvation;
yours is the glory gleaming and resounding
through all creation.

169 Priscilla Wright Porter

Fear not, rejoice and be glad,
the Lord hath done a great thing;
hath poured out his Spirit on humankind,
on those who confess his name.

1 The fig tree is budding, the vine beareth
fruit,
the wheat fields are golden with grain.
Thrust in the sickle, the harvest is ripe,
the Lord has given us rain.

2 Ye shall eat in plenty and be satisfied,
the mountains will drip with sweet wine.
My children shall drink of the fountain of
life,
my children will know they are mine.

3 My people shall know that I am the Lord,
their shame I have taken away.
My Spirit will lead them together again,
my Spirit will show them the way.

4 My children shall dwell in a body of love,
a light to the world they will be.
Life shall come forth from the Father above,
my body will set mankind free.

170 Charles A. Buffham (altered)

1 'Feed my lambs, my son, feed my sheep;
if you love me, do not sleep.
In the fields, my son, work and weep;
feed my lambs, my son, feed my sheep.'

2 To the servant girl first he lied:
'You were with him!' this she cried.
But the Master he denied;
on the following day, Jesus died.

3 Someone questioned him quietly,
'Aren't you Peter of Galilee?
I can tell you by your speech, you see.'
Peter swore and said, 'It's not me!'

4 Peter heard the cock when it crew;
as he left, he wept – and he knew!
Ev'ry one of us is guilty too;
yet Christ died for us, me and you.

5 Feed my lambs, my son, feed my sheep;
if you love me, do not sleep.
In the fields, my son, work and weep;
feed my lambs, my son, feed my sheep.

171 *J. S. B. Monsell (1811–75)*

1 Fight the good fight with all thy might,
Christ is thy strength, and Christ thy right;
lay hold on life and it shall be
thy joy and crown eternally.

2 Run the straight race through God's good grace,
lift up thine eyes and seek his face;
life with its way before us lies,
Christ is the path, and Christ the prize.

3 Cast care aside, upon thy Guide
lean, and his mercy will provide;
lean, and the trusting soul shall prove
Christ is its life, and Christ its love.

4 Faint not nor fear, his arms are near,
he changeth not, and thou art dear;
only believe, and thou shalt see
that Christ is all in all to thee.

172 *Peter Kearney*

1 Fill my house unto the fullest.
Eat my bread and drink my wine.
The love I bear is held from no–one.

All I own and all I do
I give to you.

2 Take my time unto the fullest.
Find in me the trust you seek,
and take my hands to you outreaching.

3 Christ our Lord with love enormous
from the cross his lesson taught
– to love all men as I have loved you.

4 Join with me as one in Christ–love.
May our hearts all beat as one,
and may we give ourselves completely.

173 *John Henry Newman (1801–90)*

1 Firmly I believe and truly
God is three, and God is one,
and I next acknowledge duly
manhood taken by the Son.

2 And I trust and hope most fully
in that manhood crucified;
and each thought and deed unruly
do to death, as he has died.

3 Simply to his grace and wholly
light and life and strength belong;
and I love supremely, solely,
him the holy, him the strong.

4 And I hold in veneration,
for the love of him alone,
Holy Church, as his creation,
and her teachings, as his own.

5 Adoration aye be given,
with and through th' angelic host,
to the God of earth and heaven,
Father, Son and Holy Ghost.

174 *Dave Richards*

For I'm building a people of power
and I'm making a people of praise,
that will move thro' this land by My Spirit,
and will glorify My precious Name.
Build Your Church, Lord,
make us strong, Lord,
join our hearts, Lord, through Your Son.
Make us one, Lord,
in Your Body,
in the Kingdom of Your Son.

175 *Michael Cockett*

Follow me, follow me,
leave your home and family,
leave your fishing nets and boats upon the shore.
Leave the seed that you have sown,
leave the crops that you've grown,
leave the people you have known and follow me.

1 The foxes have their holes
and the swallows have their nests,
but the Son of man has no place to lay down.
I do not offer comfort, I do not offer wealth,
but in me will all happiness be found.

2 If you would follow me,
you must leave old ways behind.
You must take my cross and follow on
my path.
You may be far from loved ones,
you may be far from home
but my Father will welcome you at last.

3 Although I go away
you will never be alone,
for the Spirit will be there to comfort you.
Though all of you may scatter,
each follow his own path,
still the Spirit of love will lead you home.

176 *William Walsham How (1823–97)*

1 For all the saints who from their labours
rest,
who thee by faith before the world confest,
thy name, O Jesus, be for ever blest.

Alleluia! Alleluia!

2 Thou wast their rock, their fortress, and
their might;
thou, Lord, their captain in the
well–fought fight;
thou in the darkness drear their one
true light.

3 O may thy soldiers, faithful, true
and bold,
fight as the saints who nobly fought of old,
and win, with them, the victor's crown
of gold.

4 O blest communion! Fellowship divine!
We feebly struggle, they in glory shine;
yet all are one in thee, for all are thine.

5 And when the strife is fierce, the warfare
long,
steals on the ear the distant triumph-song,
and hearts are brave again, and arms are
strong.

6 The golden evening brightens in the west;
soon, soon to faithful warriors cometh rest:
sweet is the calm of paradise the blest.

7 But lo! There breaks a yet more glorious
day;
the saints triumphant rise in bright array:
the king of glory passes on his way.

8 From earth's wide bounds, from ocean's
farthest coast,
through gates of pearl streams in the
countless host,
singing to Father, Son and Holy Ghost.

177 *F.S. Pierpoint (1835–1917)*

1 For the beauty of the earth,
for the beauty of the skies,
for the love which from our birth
over and around us lies,
Christ our God, to you we raise
this our sacrifice of praise.

2 For the beauty of each hour
of the day and of the night,
hill and vale, and tree and flower,
sun and moon and stars of light.
Christ our God, to you we raise
this our sacrifice of praise.

3 For the joy of ear and eye,
for the heart and mind's delight,
for the mystic harmony
linking sense to sound and sight.
Christ our God, to you we raise
this our sacrifice of praise.

4 For the joy of human love,
brother, sister, parent, child,
friends on earth and friends above,
pleasures pure and undefiled,
Christ our God, to you we raise
this our sacrifice of praise.

5 For each perfect gift divine
to our race so freely given,
joys bestowed by love's design,
flowers of earth and fruits of heaven,
Christ our God, to you we raise
this our sacrifice of praise.

178 *Fred Pratt Green*

1 For the fruits of his creation,
thanks be to God;
for his gifts to every nation,
thanks be to God;
for the ploughing, sowing, reaping,
silent growth while men are sleeping,
future needs in earth's safe keeping,
thanks be to God.

2 In the just reward of labour,
God's will is done;
in the help we give our neighbour,
God's will is done;
in our world–wide task of caring
for the hungry and despairing,
in the harvests men are sharing,
God's will is done.

3 For the harvests of his Spirit,
thanks be to God;
for the good all men inherit,
thanks be to God;
for the wonders that astound us,
for the truths that still confound us,
most of all, that love has found us,
thanks be to God.

179 *Fred Kaan*

1 For the healing of the nations,
Lord, we pray with one accord,
for a just and equal sharing
of the things that earth affords.
To a life of love in action
help us rise and pledge our word.

2 Lead us, father, into freedom,
from despair your world release,
that, redeemed from war and hatred,
men may come and go in peace.
Show us how through care and goodness
fear will die and hope increase.

3 All that kills abundant living,
let it from the earth be banned;
pride of status, race or schooling,
dogmas keeping man from man.
In our common quest for justice
may we hallow life's brief span.

4 You, creator–God, have written
your great name on all mankind;
for our growing in your likeness
bring the life of Christ to mind;
that by our response and service
earth its destiny may find.

180 *Based on Isaiah 9:6*

For unto us a child is born,
unto us a son is given;
and the government
shall be upon his shoulder
and his name shall be called
'wonderful–counsellor',
'the Mighty–God',
'the everlasting Father',
and 'the Prince of Peace' is he.

181 *Based on the 'O' Antiphons, by Marty Haugen*

For You, O Lord, my soul in stillness waits,
truly my hope is in you.

1 O Lord of Light, our only hope of glory,
your radiance shines in all who look to you,
come, light the hearts of all in dark and
shadow.

2 O Spring of Joy, rain down upon our spirits,
our thirsty hearts are yearning for
Your Word,
come, make us whole, be comfort to our
hearts.

3 O Root of Life, implant your seed within us,
and in Your advent, draw us all to you,
our hope reborn in dying and in rising.

4 O Key of Knowledge, guide us in our
pilgrimage,
we ever seek, yet unfulfilled remain,
open to us the pathway of Your peace.

5 Come, let us bow before the God
who made us,
let ev'ry heart be opened to the Lord,
for we are all the people of His hand.

6 Here we shall meet the Maker
of the heavens,
Creator of the mountains and the seas,
Lord of the stars, and present to us now.

182 *Rosamond Herklots*

1 'Forgive our sins as we forgive,'
you taught us, Lord, to pray,
but you alone can grant us grace
to live the words we say.

2 How can your pardon reach and bless
the unforgiving heart
that broods on wrongs and will not let
old bitterness depart?

3 In blazing light your Cross reveals
the truth we dimly knew:
what trivial debts are owed to us,
how great our debt to you!

4 Lord, cleanse the depths within our souls
and bid resentment cease.
Then, bound to all in bonds of love,
our lives will spread your peace.

183 *James Quinn, S.J.*

1 Forth in the peace of Christ we go;
Christ to the world with joy we bring;
Christ in our minds, Christ on our lips,
Christ in our hearts, the world's true King.

2 King of our hearts, Christ makes us kings;
kingship with him his servants gain;
with Christ, the Servant–Lord of all,
Christ's world we serve to share Christ's
reign.

3 Priests of the world, Christ sends us forth
the world of time to consecrate,
the world of sin by grace to heal,
Christ's world in Christ to recreate.

4 Prophets of Christ, we hear his word:
he claims our minds, to search his ways,
he claims our lips, to speak his truth,
he claims our hearts, to sing his praise.

5 We are the Church; he makes us one:
here is one hearth for all to find,
here is one flock, one Shepherd–King,
here is one faith, one heart, one mind.

184 *Charles Wesley (1707–88)*

1 Forth in thy name, O Lord, I go,
my daily labour to pursue;
thee, only thee, resolved to know,
in all I think or speak or do.

2 The task thy wisdom hath assigned
O let me cheerfully fulfil;
in all my works thy presence find,
and prove thy good and perfect will.

3 Thee may I set at my right hand,
whose eyes my inmost substance see,
and labour on at thy command,
and offer all my works to thee.

4 Give me to bear thy easy yoke,
and every moment watch and pray,
and still to things eternal look,
and hasten to thy glorious day;

5 For thee delightfully employ
whate'er thy bounteous grace hath given,
and run my course with even joy,
and closely walk with thee to heaven.

185 *George Hunt Smyttan (1822–70) and Francis Pott (1832–1909)*

1 Forty days and forty nights
thou wast fasting in the wild;
forty days and forty nights
tempted still, yet unbeguiled:

2 Sunbeams scorching all the day,
chilly dew–drops nightly shed,
prowling beasts about thy way,
stones thy pillow, earth thy bed.

3 Let us thy endurance share
and from earthly greed abstain
with thee watching unto prayer,
with thee strong to suffer pain.

4 Then if evil on us press,
flesh or spirit to assail,
victor in the wilderness,
help us not to swerve or fail!

5 So shall peace divine be ours;
holier gladness ours shall be,
come to us angelic powers,
such as ministered to thee.

6 Keep, O keep us, Saviour dear,
ever constant by thy side,
that with thee we may appear
at the eternal Eastertide.

186 *J. Garrity*

Freely, I give to you the gift of a child,
my own,
in hope that you will receive the life that
he gives for your own.

1 Call him Emmanuel for your God is with
you this day.
He'll be by your side sharing your joy
and pain.

2 Call him Jesus, for Yahweh saves his own.
For he is the shepherd who will guide his
flock safely home.

3 Call him Lamb of God for he has died
for your sins
and all will be saved and truly belong
to him.

187 *Graham Kendrick*

1 From heaven You came, helpless babe,
entered our world, Your glory veiled,
not to be served but to serve,
and give Your life that we might live.

This is our God, the Servant King,
He calls us now to follow Him,
to bring our lives as a daily offering
of worship to the Servant King.

2 There in the garden of tears
my heavy load He chose to bear;
His heart with sorrow was torn,
'Yet not my will but yours,' He said.

3 Come see His hands and His feet,
the scars that speak of sacrifice,
hands that flung stars into space
to cruel nails surrendered.

4 So let us learn how to serve
and in our lives enthrone Him,
each other's needs to prefer,
for it is Christ we're serving.

188 *Willard F. Jabusch*

1 From the depths of sin and sadness
I have called unto the Lord;
be not deaf to my poor pleading,
in your mercy, hear my voice.
Be not deaf to my poor pleading,
in your mercy, hear my voice.

2 If you, Lord, record our sinning
who could then before you stand?
But with you there is forgiveness;
you shall ever be revered.
But with you there is forgiveness;
you shall ever be revered.

3 For the Lord my heart is waiting,
for his word I hope and wait.
More than watchmen wait for sunrise
I am waiting for the Lord.
More than watchmen wait for sunrise
I am waiting for the Lord.

4 Hope, O people, in your Saviour,
he will save you from your sin.
Jesus from his cross is praying,
'Father, forgive them,
they know not what they do.'
Jesus from his cross is praying,
'Father, forgive them,
they know not what they do.'

189 *Henry Smith*

Give thanks with a grateful heart.
Give thanks to the Holy One.
Give thanks because He's given Jesus
Christ, His Son. *(Repeat)*

And now let the weak say 'I am strong',
let the poor say 'I am rich',
because of what the Lord has done for us.
And now let the weak say 'I am strong',
let the poor say 'I am rich',
because of what the Lord has done for us.
(last time) Give thanks.

190 *Traditional*

1 Give me joy in my heart, keep me praising,
give me joy in my heart, I pray.
Give me joy in my heart, keep me praising.
Keep me praising till the end of day.

Sing hosanna! Sing hosanna!
Sing hosanna to the King of Kings!
Sing hosanna! Sing hosanna!
Sing hosanna to the King!

2 Give me peace in my heart, keep me resting,
give me peace in my heart, I pray.
Give me peace in my heart, keep me resting.
Keep me resting till the end of day.

3 Give me love in my heart, keep me serving,
give me love in my heart, I pray.
Give me love in my heart, keep me serving,
keep me serving 'till the end of day.

4 Give me oil in my lamp, keep me burning,
give me oil in my lamp, I pray,
Give me oil in my lamp, keep me burning,
keep me burning to the end of day.

191 *Estelle White*

1 Give me peace, O Lord, I pray,
in my work and in my play,
and inside my heart and mind,
Lord, give me peace.

2 Give peace to the world, I pray,
let all quarrels cease today.
May we spread your light and love.
Lord, give us peace.

192 *Estelle White*

1 Give me yourself O Jesus Christ my brother,
give me yourself O Jesus Christ my Lord.

2 Give me your peace, …

3 Give me your love, …

4 Give me your heart, …

193 *Lucien Deiss*

1 Give praise to the Lord, one and all, *alleluia!*
O praise the name of the Lord, *alleluia!*
Bless'd be the name of the Lord, *alleluia, alleluia!*

2 Now and evermore.
From dawn to the close of day.
Bless'd be the name of the Lord.

3 On high, above the earth is the Lord.
His glory above the sky.
There is none like the Lord our God.

4 Enthroned in heaven on high.
He views the earth and the sky.
To those in need he gives his help.

5 From the dust he raises the poor.
He makes them sit among kings.
Among the kings of the earth.

6 Behold the barren wife.
Now abides in her home.
As the happy mother of sons.

7 Let us sing to the Lord.
Singing glory and praise.
Both now and evermore, Amen.

194 *Sebastian Temple*

1 Glorious God, King of creation,
we praise you, we bless you, we worship you in song.
Glorious God, in adoration,
at your feet we belong.

Lord of life, Father almighty,
Lord of hearts, Christ the King.
Lord of love, Holy Spirit,
to whom we homage bring.

2 Glorious God, magnificent, holy,
we love you, adore you, and come to you in pray'r.
Glorious God, mighty, eternal,
we sing your praise ev'rywhere.

195 *John Newton (1725–1807)*

1 Glorious things of you are spoken,
Sion, city of our God:
he whose word cannot be broken
formed you for his own abode.
On the Rock of Ages founded,
what can shake your sure repose?
With salvation's walls surrounded,
you may smile at all your foes.

2 See, the streams of living waters,
springing from eternal love,
well supply your sons and daughters
and all fear of want remove:
who can faint, while such a river
ever flows their thirst to assuage –
grace, which like the Lord, the giver,
never fails from age to age?

3 Blest inhabitants of Sion,
washed in their Redeemer's blood:
Jesus, whom their souls rely on,
makes them Kings and priests to God.
'Tis his love his people raises
over self to reign as kings,
and, as priests, his solemn praises
each for a thank–offering brings.

4 Saviour, since of Sion's city
I, through grace, a member am,
let the world deride or pity,
I will glory in your name:
fading is the worldling's pleasure,
all his boasted pomp and show;
solid joys and lasting treasure
none but Sion's children know.

196 *Daniel L. Schutte, SJ*

Glory and praise to our God,
who alone gives light to our days.
Many are the blessings he bears
to those who trust in his ways.

1 We, the daughters and sons of God
who built the valleys and plains,
praise the wonders our God has done
in ev'ry heart that sings.

2 In his wisdom he strengthens us,
like gold that's tested in fire,
though the power of sin prevails,
our God is there to save.

3 Ev'ry moment of ev'ry day
our God is waiting to save,
always ready to seek the lost,
to answer those who pray.

4 God has watered our barren land
and spent His merciful rain.
Now the rivers of life run full
for anyone to drink.

197 *Italian18th century, tr. Edward Caswall (1814–78)*

1 Glory be to Jesus, who in bitter pains
poured for me the life–blood from his
sacred veins.

2 Grace and life eternal in that blood I find:
blest be his compassion, infinitely kind.

3 Blest through endless ages be the
precious streams,
which from endless torment doth the
world redeem.

4 There the fainting spirit drinks of life her
fill;
there as in a fountain laves herself at will.

5 Abel's blood for vengeance pleaded to
the skies,
but the blood of Jesus for our pardon cries.

6 Oft as it is sprinkled on our guilty hearts,
Satan in confusion terror–struck departs.

7 Oft as earth exulting wafts its praise on
high,
hell with horror trembles; heaven is filled
with joy.

8 Lift ye, then, your voices; swell the
mighty flood;
louder still and louder, praise the
precious blood.

198 *Traditional Peruvian*

1 Glory to God, glory to God,
glory to the Father. *(2)*
To him be glory for ever. *(2)*
Alleluia, amen. *(4)*

2 Glory to God, glory to God,
Son of the Father. *(2)*
To him be glory for ever. *(2)*
Alleluia, amen. *(4)*

3 Glory to God, glory to God,
glory to the Spirit. *(2)*
To God be glory for ever. *(2)*
Alleluia, amen. *(4)*

199 *John Greally*

1 Glory to thee, Lord God!
In faith and hope we sing.
Through this completed sacrifice
our love and praise we bring.
We give thee for our sins
a price beyond all worth,
which none could ever fitly pay
but this thy Son on earth.

2 Here is the Lord of all,
to thee in glory slain;
of worthless givers, worthy gift,
a victim without stain.
Through him we give thee thanks,
with him we bend the knee,
in him be all our life, who is
our one true way to thee.

3 So may this sacrifice
we offer here this day
be joined with our poor lives in all
we think and do and say.
By living true to grace,
for thee and thee alone,
our sorrows, labours, and our joys
will be his very own.

200 *T. Ken (1637–1711)*

1 Glory to thee, my God, this night
for all the blessings of the light;
keep me, O keep me, King of kings,
beneath thy own almighty wings.

2 Forgive me, Lord, for thy dear Son,
the ill that I this day have done,
that with the world, myself and thee,
I, ere I sleep, at peace may be.

3 Teach me to live, that I may dread
the grave as little as my bed;
teach me to die, that so I may
rise glorious at the aweful day.

4 O may my soul on thee repose
and with sweet sleep mine eyelids close,
sleep that may me more vigorous make
to serve my God when I awake.

5 Praise God, from whom all blessings flow;
praise him, all creatures here below;
praise him above, ye heavenly host;
praise Father, Son, and Holy Ghost.

201 *Mark 16:15*

[1]Go out to the [2]whole world,
[3]proclaim the [4]Good News.

202 *Traditional*

Go, tell it on the mountain,
over the hills and ev'rywhere.
Go, tell it on the mountain
that Jesus Christ is born.

1 While shepherds kept their watching
o'er wand'ring flocks by night,
behold from out of heaven
there shone a holy light.

2 And lo, when they had seen it,
they all bowed down and prayed,
they travelled on together
to where the Babe was laid.

3 When I was a seeker,
I sought both night and day:
I asked my Lord to help me
and he showed me the way.

4 He made me a watchman
upon the city wall,
And if I am a Christian,
I am the least of all.

203 *Sister Marie Lydia Pereira*

1 Go, the Mass is ended,
children of the Lord.
Take God's Word to others
as you've heard it spoken to you.
Go, the Mass is ended,
go and tell the world
the Lord is good, the Lord is kind,
and loves us ev'ry one.

2 Go, the Mass is ended,
take God's love to all.
Gladden all who meet you,
fill their hearts with hope and courage.
Go, the Mass is ended,
fill the world with love,
and give to all what you've received
– the peace and joy of Christ.

3 Go, the Mass is ended,
strengthened in the Lord,
lighten ev'ry burden,
spread the joy of Christ around you.
Go, the Mass is ended,
take God's peace to all.
This day is yours to change the world
– to make God known and loved.

204 *Denis E. Hurley*

1 God, at creation's dawn,
over a world unborn,
your Spirit soared.
By word and water deign
that this same Spirit reign
in those now born again,
through Christ our Lord.

2 We, who in Adam fell,
are, as the Scriptures tell,
saved and restored.
For, when these rites are done,
dying we are made one,
rising we overcome,
with Christ our Lord.

3 Hear us, your Church, rejoice,
singing with grateful voice,
Father adored;
telling our faith anew,
greeting with welcome true
children new born to you,
in Christ our Lord.

205 *Horae Diurnae BVM, Sarum (1514)*

1 God be in my head, and in my
understanding;
God be in mine eyes, and in my looking;
God be in my mouth, and in my speaking;
God be in my heart, and in my thinking;
God be at mine end, and at my departing.

206 *J.E. Rankin (1828–1904)*

1 God be with you till we meet again;
by his counsels guide, uphold you,
with his sheep securely fold you:
God be with you till we meet again.

2 God be with you till we meet again;
'neath his wings protecting hide you,
daily manna still provide you:
God be with you till we meet again.

3 God be with you till we meet again;
when life's perils thick confound you,
put his arm unfailing round you:
God be with you till we meet again.

4 God be with you till we meet again;
keep love's banner floating o'er you,
smite death's threatening wave before you:
God be with you till we meet again.

207 *Bernadette Farrell*

1 God, beyond our dreams,
you have stirred in us a mem'ry;
you have placed your pow'rful spirit
in the hearts of humankind.

All around us we have known you,
all creation lives to hold you.
In our living and our dying
we are bringing you to birth.

2 God, beyond all names,
you have made us in your image;
we are like you, we reflect you;
we are woman, we are man.

3 God, beyond all words,
all creation tells your story;
you have shaken with our laughter,
you have trembled with our tears.

4 God, beyond all time,
you are labouring within us;
we are moving, we are changing
in your spirit ever new.

5 God of tender care,
you have cradled us in goodness,
you have mothered us in wholeness,
you have loved us into birth.

208 *Harold Riley*

1 God everlasting, wonderful, and holy,
Father most gracious, we who stand
before thee
here at thine altar, as thy Son has taught us,
come to adore thee.

2 Countless the mercies thou hast lavished
on us,
source of all blessing to all creatures
living;
to thee we render, for thy love o'erflowing,
humble thanksgiving.

3 Now in remembrance of our great
redeemer,
dying on Calvary, rising and ascending,
through him we offer what he ever offers,
sinners befriending.

4 Strength to the living, rest to the departed,
grant, Holy Father, through this pure
oblation:
may the life–giving bread for ever bring us
health and salvation.

209 *Carol Owens*

1 God forgave my sin in Jesus' name;
I've been born again in Jesus' name;
and in Jesus' name I come to you
to share his love as he told me to.

He said:
'Freely, freely, you have received;
freely, freely give.
Go, in my name,
and because you believe,
others will know that I live.'

2 All pow'r is giv'n in Jesus' name,
in earth and heav'n in Jesus' name;
and in Jesus' name I come to you
to share his pow'r as he told me to.

3 God gives us life in Jesus' name,
he lives in us in Jesus' name;
and in Jesus' name I come to you
to share his peace as he told me to.

210 *Medical Mission Sisters*

1 God gives his people strength.
If we believe in his way.
he's swift to repay all those
who bear the burden of the day.
God gives his people strength.

2 God gives his people hope.
If we but trust in his word,
our prayers are always heard.
He warmly welcomes anyone who's erred.
God gives his people hope.

3 God gives his people love.
If we but open wide our heart,
he's sure to do his part;
he's always the first to make a start.
God gives his people strength.

4 God gives his people peace.
When sorrow fills us to the brim,
and courage grows dim,
he lays to rest our restlessness in him.
God gives his people peace.

211 *Steven Jones adapted from Sarah Betts Rhodes, 1870*

1 God who made the earth, the sky, the sea,
who gave light its birth,
careth for me.
God who made the grass, the flower,
the tree,
day and night to pass,
careth for me.

Come to me when you have gone astray
and I will give you faith. (Repeat)

2 God who made the sun, the moon,
the stars,
who when skies are grey
careth for me.
God who made all things, on earth, in sea,
through the seasons he
careth for me.

Come to me when you have lost your way
and I will give you hope (Repeat)

3 God who sent his Son to Calvary
if I lean on him
careth for me.
When at last in heaven I hope to be
I will sing out loud
'God cared for me.'

Come to me when you are dying
and I will give you love. (Repeat)

212 *Bernadette Farrell*

1 God has chosen me, *(2)*
to bring good news to the poor.
God has chosen me, *(2)*
to bring new sight to those searching for
light:
God has chosen me, chosen me:

And to tell the world that God's kingdom
is near,
to remove oppression and break down fear,
yes, God's time is near,
God's time is near, (2)

2 God has chosen me, *(2)*
to set alight a new fire.
God has chosen me, *(2)*
to bring to birth a new kingdom on earth:
God has chosen me, chosen me:

3 God is calling me, *(2)*
in all whose cry is unheard.
God is calling me, *(2)*
to raise up the voice with no power or
choice:
God is calling me, calling me:

213 *Tom Conry, based on Psalm 23*

God alone may lead my spirit
far away from want and fear,
for the Lord is my true shepherd
and I know the Lord is near.

1 I am led beside God's peaceful water
and I sleep in the arms of the earth.
Who guides me along paths of honour?
Who refreshes my life from my birth?

2 Though I wander the valley of dying,
I shall know that I walk in your sight,
with your staff that is ever before me
and your rod to guard at my right.

3 You have spread your banquet before me
in the unbroken sight of my foes,
while my head is anointed with kindness
and the cup of my life overflows.

4 Only mercy and goodness pursue me
while that breath and that justice endure.
And I'll dwell in the house of God's
keeping
who has opened the mouths of the poor.

214 *Ubi Caritas, versified by James Quinn, SJ*

God is love, and where true love is
God himself is there.

1 Here in Christ we gather, love of Christ
our calling.
Christ, our love, is with us, gladness be
his greeting.
Let us love and serve him, God of all
the ages.
Let us love sincerely, seeing Christ in
others.

2 When we Christians gather, members of one Body,
Christ, our God, be present, loving and beloved.
Let there be no discord, banished every quarrel.
Let there be one Spirit, bond of peace among us.

3 Grant us love's fulfilment, joy with all the blessed,
when we see your glory, risen Lord and Saviour,
bathe us in your splendour, Light of all creation,
be our bliss forever as we sing your praises.

215 *Percy Dearmer (1867–1936), altered*

1 God is love: his the care,
tending each, everywhere.
God is love, all is there!
Jesus came to show him,
that we all might know him!

Sing aloud, loud, loud!
Sing aloud, loud, loud!
God is good!
God is truth! God is beauty!
Praise him!

2 None can see God above;
humankind we can love;
thus may we Godward move,
finding God in others,
sisters all, and brothers:

3 Jesus lived here for all:
strove and died, rose once more,
rules our hearts evermore;
for he came to save us
by the truth he gave us:

4 To our Lord praise we sing,
light and life, friend and king,
coming down love to bring,
pattern for our duty,
showing God in beauty:

216 *Timothy Dudley-Smith*

1 God is my great desire,
his face I seek the first;
to him my heart and soul aspire,
for him I thirst.
As one in desert lands,
whose very flesh is flame,
in burning love I lift my hands
and bless his name.

2 God is my true delight,
my richest feast his praise,
through silent watches of the night,
through all my days.
To him my spirit clings,
on him my soul is cast;
beneath the shadow of his wings
he holds me fast.

3 God is my strong defence
in ev'ry evil hour;
in him I face with confidence
the tempter's power.
I trust his mercy sure,
with truth and triumph crowned:
my hope and joy for evermore
in him are found.

217 *A. C. Ainger (1841–1919)*

1 God is working his purpose out
as year succeeds to year,
God is working his purpose out
and the time is drawing near;
nearer and nearer draws the time,
the time that shall surely be,
when the earth shall be filled with the glory of God as the waters cover the sea.

2 From utmost east to utmost west
where human foot hath trod,
by the mouth of many messengers
goes forth the voice of God.
'Give ear to me, ye continents,
ye isles give ear to me,
that the earth may be filled with the glory of God as the waters cover the sea.'

3 What can we do to work God's work,
to prosper and increase
the friendship of all humankind,
the reign of the Prince of Peace?
What can we do to hasten the time,
the time that shall surely be,
when the earth shall be filled with the
glory of God as the waters cover the sea?

4 March we forth in the strength of God
with the banner of Christ unfurled,
that the light of the glorious Gospel of
truth may shine throughout the world.
Fight we the fight with sorrow and sin,
to set their captives free,
that the earth may be filled with the
glory of God as the waters cover the sea.

5 All we can do is nothing worth
unless God blesses the deed;
vainly we hope for the harvest–tide
till God gives life to the seed;
yet nearer and nearer draws the time,
the time that shall surely be,
when the earth shall be filled with the
glory of God as the waters cover the sea.

218 *Marty Haugen*

1 God of day and God of darkness,
now we stand before the night;
as the shadows stretch and deepen,
come and make our darkness bright.
All creation still is groaning
for the dawning of your might,
when the Sun of peace and justice
fills the earth with radiant light.

2 Still the nations curse the darkness,
still the rich oppress the poor;
still the earth is bruised and broken
by the ones who still want more.
Come and wake us from our sleeping,
so our hearts cannot ignore,
all your people lost and broken,
all your children at our door.

3 Show us Christ in one another,
make us servants strong and true;
give us all your love of justice,
so we do what you would do.
Let us call all people holy,
let us pledge our lives anew,
make us one with all the lowly,
let us all be one in you.

4 You shall be the path that guides us,
you the light that in us burns;
shining deep within all people,
yours the love that we must learn
for our hearts shall wander restless
'til they safe to you return;
finding you in one another,
we shall all your face discern.

5 Gentle Father, Loving Mother,
Jesus: Brother, Saviour, Friend:
spirit of all grace and power,
may we praise you without end.
Grant us all a peaceful resting,
let each mind and body mend,
so we rise refreshed tomorrow,
hearts renewed to kingdom tend.

219 *E. Vaughan (1827–1908)*

1 God of mercy and compassion,
look with pity upon me;
Father, let me call thee Father,
'tis thy child returns to thee.

Jesus Lord, I ask for mercy;
let me not implore in vain:
all my sins I now detest them,
never will I sin again.

2 By my sins I have deservèd
death and endless misery,
hell with all its pain and torments,
and for all eternity.

3 By my sins I have abandon'd
right and claim to heaven above,
where the saints rejoice for ever,
in a boundless sea of love.

4 See our Saviour, bleeding, dying,
on the cross of Calvary;
to that cross my sins have nail'd him,
yet he bleeds and dies for me.

220 *David Shore*

God of tender mercy, God of love,
God of glorious light from heav'n above;
in your light we see light, in your love we feel love:
Light eternal, love which never ends.

1 Living God, creator of all life,
heav'n and earth proclaim your mighty pow'r.
Man and woman you have fashioned
in your loving kindness,
setting them to prosper and to grow.

2 Word of God, inviting us to trust,
bidding us to pledge our hope–filled vow,
son and daughter by your grace
in one flesh now united,
called to live the sacrament of love.

3 Spirit of our God and bond of peace,
day by day you call us to be one.
Hopes and fears we bring to you
in sorrow and rejoicing,
strengthened by the promise of your love.

4 Age to age shall raise its voice in song,
as your Church rejoices in your name:
singing to the God of life
and source of ev'ry blessing:
praise and glory now and evermore!

221 *Christopher Walker*

God our fountain of salvation,
renew the spring of your life in us.
In living water wash away our sin,
that we may come to you in holiness,
God, our fountain of salvation.
God, our fountain of salvation.

1 Truly now God is my Saviour.
I have trust, I will not fear.
God my song, God my salvation.
God alone my pow'r and strength!

2 Draw with joy from wells of salvation.
Praise the Lord, call on God's name.
What God does, tell all the nations:
God has done great things for us!

3 Sing out loud praise for God's wonders,
let the whole world hear the news.
Shout and sing people of Zion:
God the holy, God with us!

222 *Denis E. Hurley*

1 God, our maker, mighty Father,
all creation sings your praise,
sun and stars in all their splendour,
moon in ev'ry changing phase,
earth with all its trees and grasses,
sparkling rivers, ocean blue,
all unite to pay you homage,
singing joyously to you.

2 Provident and wise creator,
as your mighty plan unfurled,
man you made to share your labour
in the building of the world.
Man and woman you created,
that united, heart and home,
they might work and strive together
till your endless kingdom come.

3 God of truth and love unbounded,
further still your mercy went,
when uniting earth with heaven,
your incarnate Son you sent:
first–born of your vast creation,
holding all in unity,
leading all in power and wisdom
to a glorious destiny.

223 *English Traditional Carol*

1 God rest you merry, gentlemen,
let nothing you dismay,
remember Christ our Saviour
was born on Christmas Day,
to save us all from Satan's pow'r
when we were gone astray;

O tidings of comfort and joy,
comfort and joy,
O tidings of comfort and joy.

2 In Bethlehem, in Judah,
this blessed Babe was born,
and laid within a manger,
upon this blessed morn;
the which his Mother Mary
did nothing take in scorn.

3 From God our heavenly Father,
a blessed angel came;
and unto certain shepherds
brought tidings of the same;
how that in Bethlehem was born
the Son of God by name:

4 'Fear not then,' said the angel,
'Let nothing you affright,
this day is born a Saviour
of a pure virgin bright,
to free all those who trust in him
from Satan's power and might.'

5 The shepherds at those tidings
rejoicèd much in mind,
and left their flocks a–feeding
in tempest, storm and wind;
and went to Bethlehem straightway
the Son of God to find.

6 And when they came to Bethlehem
where our dear Saviour lay,
they found him in a manger,
where oxen feed on hay;
his mother Mary kneeling down
unto the Lord did pray.

7 Now to the Lord sing praises,
all you within this place,
and with true love and friendship
each other now embrace;
this holy tide of Christmas
all other doth deface.

224 *The Iona Community*

1 God the Creator, You in love made me
who once was nothing but now have
grown.
I bring the best of all my life offers;
for you I share whatever I own.

2 O Christ the Saviour, You in love called me
who once was no–one lost and alone.
I pledge to go wherever you summon,
making your will and purpose my own.

3 O God the Spirit, You in love move me
who once was nowhere and felt unknown.
I know my need of you for companion:
all things can change when not on my own.

4 And with the people summoned together
to be the Church in which faith is sown.
I make my promise to live for Jesus
and let the world know all are his own.

225 *Stanbrook Abbey*

1 God, who made the earth and sky
and the changing sea,
clothed his glory in our flesh:
one with us to be.

2 Mary, Virgin filled with light,
chosen from our race,
bore the Father's only Son
by the Spirit's grace.

3 He whom nothing can contain
no one can compel,
bound his timeless Godhead here,
in our time to dwell.

4 God, our Father, Lord of days
and his only Son,
with the Holy Spirit praise:
Trinity in one.

226 *vv. Didier Rimaud, tr. Brian Wren* *Refrain tr. Ronald Johnson*

God, your glory we have seen
in your Son,
full of truth, full of heavenly grace;
in Christ make us live,
his love shine on our face,
and the nations will see in us
the triumph you have won.

1 In the fields of this world
his good news he has sown,
and sends us out to reap
till the harvest is done.

2 In his love like a fire
that consumes he passed by:
the flame has touched our lips;
let us shout: 'Here am I!'

3 He was broken for us,
God–forsaken his cry,
and still the bread he breaks:
to ourselves we must die:

4 He has trampled the grapes
of new life on his Cross;
now drink the cup and live:
he has filled it for us:

5 He has founded a kingdom
that none shall destroy;
the corner–stone is laid:
Go to work, build with joy!

227 *Alan Dale*

1 God's spirit is in my heart,
who has called me and set me apart.
This is what I have to do,
what I have to do.

He sent me to give the Good News to the poor,
tell prisoners that they are prisoners no more,
tell blind people that they can see,
and set the downtrodden free,
and go tell ev'ryone
the news that the Kingdom of God has come,
and go tell ev'ryone
the news that God's kingdom has come.

2 Just as the Father sent me,
so I'm sending you out to be
my witnesses throughout the world,
the whole of the world.

3 Don't carry a load in your pack,
you don't need two shirts on your back.
A workman can earn his own keep,
can earn his own keep.

4 Don't worry what you have to say,
don't worry because on that day
God's spirit will speak in your heart,
will speak in your heart.

228 *Ascribed to St. Thomas Aquinas (1227–74), tr. Gerard Manley Hopkins (1844–89)*

1 Godhead here in hiding, whom I do adore,
masked by these bare shadows, shape and nothing more,
see, Lord, at thy service low lies here a heart
lost, all lost in wonder at the God thou art.

2 Seeing, touching, tasting are in thee deceived;
how says trusty hearing? That shall be believed;
what God's Son hath told me, take for truth I do;
truth himself speaks truly, or there's nothing true.

3 On the cross thy Godhead made no sign to men;
here thy very manhood steals from human ken;
both are my confession, both are my belief;
and I pray the prayer of the dying thief.

4 I am not like Thomas, wounds I cannot see,
but can plainly call thee Lord and God as he;
this faith each day deeper be my holding of,
daily make me harder hope and dearer love.

5 O thou our reminder of Christ crucified,
living Bread, the life of us for whom he died,
lend this life to me then; feed and feast my mind,
there be thou the sweetness man was meant to find.

6 Jesu, whom I look at shrouded here below,
I beseech thee send me what I long for so,
some day to gaze on thee face to face in light
and be blest for ever with thy glory's sight.

229 *John Mason Neale (1818–66)*

1 Good Christians all, rejoice
with heart and soul and voice;
give ye heed to what we say:
Jesus Christ is born today;

ox and ass before him bow,
and He is in the manger now:
Christ is born today,
Christ is born today!

2 Good Christians all, rejoice
with heart and soul and voice!
Now ye hear of endless bliss:
Jesus Christ was born for this.
He hath opened heaven's door,
and we are blest for evermore:
Christ was born for this,
Christ was born for this.

3 Good Christians all, rejoice
with heart and soul and voice!
Now ye need not fear the grave:
Jesus Christ was born to save;
calls you one, and calls you all,
to gain His everlasting hall:
Christ was born to save,
Christ was born to save.

230 *C. A. Alington (1872–1955)*

1 Good Christians all, rejoice and sing!
Now is the triumph of our King!
To all the world glad news we bring:
Alleluia! (3)

2 The Lord of Life is risen for ay:
bring flowers of song to strew his way;
all humankind rejoice and say.

3 Praise we in songs of victory
that Love, that Life, which cannot die,
and sing with hearts uplifted high.

4 Thy name we bless, O risen Lord,
and sing today with one accord
the life laid down, the life restored.

231 *The Magnificat, versified by Paul Inwood*

1 Great is the Lord my soul proclaims,
in him my spirit sings for joy;
for he who saves has looked on me
with boundless love to raise me high.

2 Ages to come shall know that I
am blessed and favoured by the Lord:
his name is holy, mighty God;
his wondrous power on me is poured.

3 All those who fear him find his love,
in every age, in every land.
His strong right arm puts down the proud,
disperses them like grains of sand.

4 Down from their thrones he casts the strong,
and raises up the meek of heart.
He gives the hungry choicest food;
in emptiness the rich depart.

5 Israel his servant knows his help,
in keeping with the promise sworn
to Abraham and all his race:
God's love will never be withdrawn.

6 Glory to God: the Father, Son,
and Spirit – Trinity sublime.
All honour, thanks and praise be theirs
across the spans of endless time.

232 *Frederick Oakeley (1802–80)*

1 Great Saint Andrew, friend of Jesus,
lover of his glorious cross,
early by his voice effective
called from ease to pain and loss,
strong Saint Andrew, Simon's brother,
who with haste fraternal flew,
fain with him to share the treasure
which, at Jesus' lips, he drew.

2 Blest Saint Andrew, Jesus' herald,
true apostle, martyr bold,
who, by deeds his words confirming,
sealed with blood the truth he told.
Ne'er to king was crown so beauteous,
ne'er was prize to heart so dear,
as to him the cross of Jesus
when its promised joys drew near.

3 Loved Saint Andrew, Scotland's patron,
watch thy land with heedful eye,
rally round the cross of Jesus
all her storied chivalry!
To the Father, Son, and Spirit,
fount of sanctity and love,
give we glory, now and ever,
with the saints who reign above.

233 *W. Williams (1717–91), tr. P. and W. Williams*

1 Guide me, O thou great Redeemer,
pilgrim through this barren land;
I am weak, but thou art mighty,
hold me with thy pow'rful hand:
bread of heaven, bread of heaven,
feed me till I want no more. *(2)*

2 Open now the crystal fountain,
whence the healing stream doth flow;
let the fire and cloudy pillar
lead me all my journey through;
strong Deliverer, strong Deliverer,
be thou still my strength and shield. *(2)*

3 When I tread the verge of Jordan,
bid my anxious fears subside,
death of death, and hell's destruction,
land me safe on Canaan's side;
songs of praises, songs of praises
I will ever give to thee. *(2)*

234 *Sister Agnes*

1 Hail, glorious Saint Patrick, dear saint of our isle,
on us thy poor children bestow a sweet smile;
and now thou art high in the mansions above,
on Erin's green valleys look down in thy love.

On Erin's green valleys, on Erin's green valleys,
on Erin's green valleys look down in thy love.

2 Hail, glorious Saint Patrick! Thy words were once strong
against Satan's wiles and an infidel throng;
not less is thy might where in heaven thou art;
O, come to our aid, in our battle take part.

3 In the war against sin, in the fight for the faith,
dear saint, may thy children resist unto death;
may their strength be in meekness, in penance, in prayer,
their banner the Cross which they glory to bear.

4 Thy people, now exiles on many a shore,
shall love and revere thee till time be no more;
and the fire thou hast kindled shall ever burn bright,
its warmth undiminished, undying its light.

5 Ever bless and defend the sweet land of our birth,
where the shamrock still blooms as when thou wert on earth,
and our hearts shall yet burn, wheresoever we roam,
for God and Saint Patrick, and our native home.

235 *Frederick William Faber (1814–1863)*

1 Hail, holy Joseph, hail!
Husband of Mary, hail!
Chaste as the lily flower
in Eden's peaceful vale.

2 Hail, holy Joseph, hail!
Father of Christ esteemed,
Father be thou to those
thy foster Son redeemed.

3 Hail, holy Joseph, hail!
Prince of the house of God,
may his blest graces be
by thy pure hands bestowed.

4 Hail, holy Joseph, hail!
Comrade of angels, hail:
cheer thou the hearts that faint,
and guide the steps that fail.

5 Hail, holy Joseph, hail!
God's choice wert thou alone;
to thee the Word made flesh
was subject as a Son.

6 Mother of Jesus, bless,
and bless, ye saints on high,
all meek and simple souls
that to Saint Joseph cry.

236 *Carey Landry*

Hail Mary, full of grace,
the Lord is with you.
Blessed are you among women,
and blest is the fruit of your womb, Jesus.
Holy Mary, Mother of God,
pray for us sinners
now and at the hour of death. Amen.

Gentle woman, quiet light,
morning star, so strong and bright,
gentle mother, peaceful dove,
teach us wisdom; teach us love.

1 You were chosen by the Father;
you were chosen for the Son.
You were chosen from all women,
and for women, shining one.

2 Blessed are you, among women.
Blest in turn all women too.
Blessèd they with peaceful spirits.
Blessèd they with gentle hearts.

237 *Willard F. Jabusch*

1 Hail Mary, mother of our God,
a lamp that always burns;
for you the angels keep a feast,
from you all evil turns,
from you all evil turns.

2 It's thanks to you God's only Son
in darkness shed his light;
it's thanks to you that sinful man
rejoiced to know what's right,
rejoiced to know what's right.

3 You gave a place within your womb
to him who knows no bound;
a virgin yet a mother too,
in you his home he found,
in you his home he found.

4 It's thanks to you creation came
to know what's good and true;
God calls his servant 'mother' now –
no other maid but you,
no other maid but you!

238 *John Lingard (1771–1851)*

1 Hail, Queen of heav'n, the ocean star!
Guide of the wand'rer here below!
Thrown on life's surge, we claim thy care;
save us from peril and from woe.
Mother of Christ, star of the sea,
pray for the wanderer, pray for me.

2 O gentle, chaste and spotless maid,
we sinners make our prayers through thee;
remind thy son that he has paid
the price of our iniquity.
Virgin most pure, star of the sea,
pray for the sinner, pray for me.

3 Sojourners in this vale of tears,
to thee, blest advocate, we cry;
pity our sorrows, calm our fears,
and soothe with hope our misery.
Refuge in grief, star of the sea,
pray for the mourner, pray for me.

4 And while to him who reigns above,
in Godhead One, in Persons Three,
the source of life, of grace, of love,
homage we pay on bended knee,
do thou, bright Queen, star of the sea,
pray for thy children, pray for me.

239 *Patrick Brennan C.Ss.R., (1877–1952)*

1 Hail, Redeemer, King divine!
Priest and Lamb, the throne is thine,
King, whose reign shall never cease,
Prince of everlasting peace.

Angels saints and nations sing:
'Praised be Jesus Christ, our King;
Lord of life, earth, sky and sea,
King of love on Calvary.'

2 King whose name creation thrills,
rule our minds, our hearts, our wills,
till in peace each nation rings
with thy praises, King of kings.

3 King most holy, King of truth,
guide the lowly, guide the youth;
Christ thou King of glory bright,
be to us eternal light.

4 Shepherd–King, o'er mountains steep,
homeward bring the wandering sheep,
shelter in one royal fold
states and kingdoms, new and old.

240 *Charles Wesley (1707–88), Thomas Cotterill (1779–1823), and others*

1 Hail the day that sees him rise, *alleluia!*
To his throne above the skies; *alleluia!*
Christ, the Lamb for sinners given,
alleluia!
Enters now the highest heaven, *alleluia!*

2 There for him high triumph waits;
lift your heads, eternal gates!
He hath conquered death and sin;
take the king of glory in!

3 Circled round with angel–powers,
their triumphant Lord and ours;
wide unfold the radiant scene,
take the king of glory in!

4 Lo, the heaven its Lord receives,
yet he loves the earth he leaves;
though returning to his throne,
he calls humankind his own.

5 See! He lifts his hands above.
See! He shows the prints of love;
hark! His gracious lips bestow,
blessings on his Church below.

6 Still for us he intercedes,
his prevailing death he pleads;
near himself prepares our place,
he the first–fruit of our race.

7 Lord, though parted from our sight,
far above the starry height,
grant our hearts may thither rise,
seeking thee above the skies.

8 Ever upward let us move,
wafted on the wings of love;
looking when our Lord shall come,
longing, sighing after home.

241 *James Montgomery (1771–1854)*

1 Hail to the Lord's anointed!
Great David's greater son!
Hail, in the time appointed,
his reign on earth begun!
He comes to break oppression,
to set the captive free;
to take away transgression,
and rule in equity.

2 He shall come down like showers
upon the fruitful earth,
and love, joy, hope, like flowers,
spring in his path to birth:
before him on the mountains
shall peace the herald go;
and righteousness in fountains
from hill to valley flow.

3 Kings shall fall down before him,
and gold and incense bring;
all nations shall adore him,
his praise all people sing;
to him shall prayer unceasing
and daily vows ascend;
his kingdom still increasing
a kingdom without end.

4 O'er every foe victorious,
he on his throne shall rest,
from age to age more glorious,
all–blessing and all–blest;
the tide of time shall never
his covenant remove;
his name shall stand for ever;
that name to us is love.

242 *Sebastian Temple*

Happy the man who wanders with the Lord.
Happy the man who knows how to live.
Happy the man who never seeks reward,
giving because he loves to give.
He seeks no gold, he wants no gain.
He knows those things are all in vain.
He needs no praise nor honour, too.
His only motto: 'To your own self be true.'
Happy the man who learned how to pray.
Happy the man who has a burning goal.
Happy the man whose service needs no pay.
This man has found his own soul.
Happy the man,
happy the man of the Lord.

243 *6th century, tr. Edward Caswall (1814–78)*

1 Hark! A herald voice is calling:
'Christ is nigh' it seems to say;
'cast away the dreams of darkness,
O ye children of the day!'

2 Startled at the solemn warning,
let the earth–bound soul arise;
Christ, her sun, all sloth dispelling,
shines upon the morning skies.

3 Lo! the Lamb, so long expected,
comes with pardon down from heaven;
let us haste, with tears of sorrow,
one and all to be forgiven.

4 So when next he comes with glory,
wrapping all the earth in fear,
may he then as our defender
on the clouds of heaven appear.

5 Honour, glory, virtue, merit,
to the Father and the Son,
with the co–eternal Spirit,
while unending ages run.

244 *Charles Wesley (1743), George Whitefield (1753), Martin Madan (1760), and others*

1 Hark, the herald angels sing,
glory to the new–born King;
peace on earth and mercy mild,
God and sinners reconciled:
joyful all ye nations rise,
join the triumph of the skies,
with the angelic host proclaim,
Christ is born in Bethlehem.

Hark, the herald Angels sing,
glory to the new–born King.

2 Christ, by highest heaven adored,
Christ, the everlasting Lord,
late in time behold him come,
offspring of a Virgin's womb!
Veiled in flesh the Godhead see,
hail the incarnate Deity!
Pleased as man with man to dwell,
Jesus, our Emmanuel.

3 Hail the heaven–born Prince of Peace!
Hail the Son of righteousness!
Light and life to all he brings,
risen with healing in his wings;
mild he lays his glory by,
born that man no more may die,
born to raise the sons of earth,
born to give them second birth.

245 *The Iona Community*

He became poor that we may be rich
loving the world and leaving his throne;
King of all Kings and Lord of all Lords,
flesh of our flesh and bone of our bone.

246 *Anonymous*

1 He is Lord, he is Lord.
He is risen from the dead and he is Lord.
Ev'ry knee shall bow, ev'ry tongue confess
that Jesus Christ is Lord.

2 He is King, he is King.
He is risen from the dead and he is King.
Ev'ry knee shall bow, ev'ry tongue confess
that Jesus Christ is King.

3 He is love, he is love.
He is risen from the dead and he is love.
Ev'ry knee shall bow, ev'ry tongue confess
that Jesus Christ is love.

247 *From The Grail, by Willard F. Jabusch*

1 He is risen, tell the story
to the nations of the night;
from their sin and from their blindness,
let them walk in Easter light.
Now begins a new creation,
now has come our true salvation.
Jesus Christ, the Son of God!

2 Mary goes to tell the others
of the wonders she has seen;
John and Peter come a'running
what can all this truly mean?
O Rabboni, Master holy,
to appear to one so lowly!
Jesus Christ, the Son of God!

3 He has cut down death and evil,
he has conquered all despair;
he has lifted from our shoulders,
all the weight of anxious care.
Risen Brother, now before you,
we will worship and adore you.
Jesus Christ, the Son of God!

4 Now get busy, bring the message,
so that all may come to know
there is hope for saint and sinner,
for our God has loved us so.
Ev'ry church bell is a'ringing,
ev'ry Christian now is singing.
Jesus Christ, the Son of God!

248 *Percy Dearmer (1867–1936), after John Bunyan (1628–88)*

1 He who would valiant be 'gainst all disaster,
let him in constancy follow the Master
there's no discouragement
shall make him once relent
his first avowed intent to be a pilgrim.

2 Who so beset him round with dismal stories,
do but themselves confound: his strength the more is.
No foes shall stay his might though he with giants fight;
he will make good his right to be a pilgrim.

3 Since, Lord, thou dost defend us with thy Spirit,
we know we at the end shall life inherit.
Then fancies flee away! I'll fear not what they say,
I'll labour night and day to be a pilgrim.

249 *Traditional*

1 He's got the whole world in his hand. *(4)*

2 He's got you and me, brother …

3 He's got you and me, sister …

4 He's got everybody here …

5 He's got the whole world …

250 *Anthony Sharpe*

Hear my cry, O God, listen to my prayer.
In despair and far from home I call to you.

1 Take me to a resting place, for you are my protector;
my strong defence against my enemies.

2 Let me live in your temple for all my life;
let me find safety under your wings.

3 You have heard my promise to follow you,
and so you will give me my heritage.

4 So I will always sing praises to you;
following you day by day.

251 *Attende Domine, (10th century), tr. Ralph Wright, OSB*

Hear us, almighty Lord,
show us your mercy,
sinners we stand here before you.

1 Jesus our Saviour, Lord of all the nations,
Christ our Redeemer, hear the prayers we offer,
Spare us and save us, comfort us in sorrow.

2 Word of the Father, keystone of God's building,
source of our gladness, gateway to the Kingdom,
free us in mercy from the sins that bind us.

3 God of compassion, Lord of might and splendour,
graciously listen, hear our cries of anguish,
touch us and heal us where our sins have wounded.

4 Humbly confessing that we have offended,
stripped of illusions, naked in our sorrow,
pardon, Lord Jesus, those your blood has ransomed.

5 Innocent captive, you were led to slaughter,
sentenced by sinners when they brought false witness.
Keep from damnation those your death has rescued.

Alternative response
Attende Domine et miserere
quia peccavimus tibi.

252 *John Henry Newman (1801–90)*

1 Help, Lord, the souls that thou hast made,
the souls to thee so dear,
in prison for the debt unpaid
of sin committed here.

2 These holy souls, they suffer on,
resigned in heart and will,
until thy high behest is done,
and justice has its fill.

3 For daily falls, for pardoned crime
they joy to undergo
the shadow of thy cross sublime,
the remnant of thy woe.

4 Oh, by their patience of delay,
their hope amid their pain,
their sacred zeal to burn away
disfigurement and stain.

5 Oh, by their fire of love, not less
in keenness than the flame;
oh, by their very helplessness,
oh, by thy own great name.

6 Good Jesus, help! Sweet Jesus, aid
the souls to thee most dear,
in prison for the debt unpaid
of sins committed here.

253 *Marty Haugen*

1 Here in this place, new light is streaming,
now is the darkness vanished away,
see, in this space, our fears and our
dreamings,
brought here to you in the light of this day.
Gather us in the lost and forsaken,
gather us in the blind and the lame;
call to us now, and we shall awaken,
we shall arise at the sound of our name.

2 We are the young – our lives are a mystery,
we are the old – who yearn for your face,
we have been sung throughout all of
history,
called to be light to the whole human race.
Gather us in the rich and the haughty,
gather us in the proud and the strong;
give us a heart so meek and so lowly,
give us the courage to enter the song.

3 Here we will take the wine and the water,
here we will take the bread of new birth,
here you shall call your sons and your
daughters,
call us anew to be salt for the earth.
Give us to drink the wine of compassion,
give us to eat the bread that is you;
nourish us well, and teach us to fashion
lives that are holy and hearts that are true.

4 Not in the dark of buildings confining,
not in some heaven, light years away,
but here in this place, the new light is
shining,
now is the Kingdom, now is the day.
Gather us in and hold us for ever,
gather us in and make us your own;
gather us in all peoples together,
fire of love in our flesh and our bone.

254 *Estelle White*

1 Here's a child for you, O Lord,
we shall cherish, we shall care.
We'll be faithful to your Word
for we want this child to share
your lovelight.

2 May he hold his head up high,
graceful, joyful, strong of limb.
May his eyes be clear and bright,
seeing beauty in all things
that you've made.

3 We were young ourselves, O Lord,
we were eager, we were fresh
like the opening buds of spring,
and we wanted happiness
in your way.

4 Then, at times, we went astray,
we were foolish, we were weak,
and the innocence we had
vanished like the trace of feet
when snow melts.

5 But we come, O Lord and king,
at your bidding, and we pray

that the precious gift we bring
will grow stronger every day
in your love.

6 By the water poured out here
and our promise, we believe,
he will master every fear,
and at last will come to see
your Godhead.

** Change he to she and him to her, according to circumstance.*

255 *C.E. Oakley (1832–65)*

1 Hills of the north, rejoice;
river and mountain–spring,
hark to the advent voice;
valley and lowland, sing:
though absent long, your Lord is nigh;
he judgement brings and victory.

2 Isles of the southern seas,
deep in your coral caves
pent be each warring breeze,
lulled be your restless waves:
he comes to reign with boundless sway,
and makes your wastes his great highway.

3 Lands of the east, awake,
soon shall your sons be free;
the sleep of ages break,
and rise to liberty.
On your far hills, long cold and grey,
has dawned the everlasting day.

4 Shores of the utmost west,
ye that have waited long,
unvisited, unblest,
break forth to swelling song;
high raise the note, that Jesus died,
yet lives and reigns, the Crucified.

5 Shout, while ye journey home;
songs be in every mouth;
lo, from the north we come,
from east and west and south.
City of God, the bonds are free,
we come to live and reign in thee!

256 *Anonymous*

1 Holy Father, God of might,
throned amid the hosts of light,
take our life, our strength, our love,
King of earth and heaven above.

2 Hear the songs your people raise,
songs of joyful thanks and praise,
calling all created things
to adore you, King of kings.

3 Christ, be with us as we go,
let this blind world see and know,
burning in our lives, the sight
of its only saving light.

4 So, all people bless your name,
and your kingship all proclaim,
praising with the heavenly host
Father, Son and Holy Ghost.

257 *C. A. Walworth (1820–1900)*

1 Holy God, we praise thy name;
Lord of all, we bow before thee!
All on earth thy sceptre own,
all in heaven above adore thee.
Infinite thy vast domain,
everlasting is thy reign.

2 Hark! the loud celestial hymn,
angel choirs above are raising;
cherubim and seraphim,
in unceasing chorus praising,
fill the heavens with sweet accord,
holy, holy, holy Lord.

3 Holy Father, holy Son,
Holy Spirit, three we name thee,
while in essence only one
undivided God we claim thee;
and, adoring, bend the knee
while we own the mystery.

4 Spare thy people, Lord, we pray,
by a thousand snares surrounded;
keep us without sin today;
never let us be confounded.
Lo, I put my trust in thee,
never, Lord, abandon me.

258 *Jimmy Owens*

1 Holy, holy, holy, holy.
Holy, holy, holy, Lord God almighty!
And we lift our hearts before you as a
token of our love:
holy, holy, holy, holy.

2 Gracious Father, gracious Father,
we are glad to be your children,
gracious Father.
And we lift our heads before you as a
token of our love,
gracious Father, gracious Father.

3 Precious Jesus, precious Jesus,
we are glad you have redeemed us,
precious Jesus.
And we lift our hands before you as a
token of our love,
precious Jesus, precious Jesus.

4 Holy Spirit, Holy Spirit,
come and fill our hearts anew, Holy Spirit.
And we lift our voice before you as a
token of our love,
Holy Spirit, Holy Spirit.

5 Hallelujah, hallelujah,
hallelujah, hallelujah, hallelujah.
And we lift our hearts before you as a
token of our love,
hallelujah, hallelujah.

259 *Reginald Heber (1783–1875)*

1 Holy, holy, holy! Lord God almighty!
Early in the morning our song shall rise
to thee;
holy, holy, holy! Merciful and mighty!
God in three persons, blessed Trinity!

2 Holy, holy, holy! All the saints adore thee,
casting down their golden crowns
around the glassy sea;
cherubim and seraphim falling down
before thee,
which wert, and art, and evermore shall be.

3 Holy, holy, holy! Though the darkness
hide thee,
though the eye made blind by sin thy
glory may not see;
only thou art holy, there is none beside thee
perfect in power, in love and purity.

4 Holy, holy, holy! Lord God almighty!
All thy works shall praise thy name,
in earth, and sky and sea;
holy, holy, holy! merciful and mighty!
God in three persons, blessed Trinity!

260 *W H Parker (1845–1929)*

1 Holy Spirit, hear us; help us while we sing;
breathe into the music of the praise we
bring.

2 Holy Spirit, prompt us when we kneel to
pray;
nearer come, and teach us what we ought
to say.

3 Holy Spirit, shine thou on the book we read;
gild its holy pages with the light we need.

4 Holy Spirit, give us each a lowly mind;
make us more like Jesus, gentle, pure and
kind.

5 Holy Spirit, help us daily by thy might,
what is wrong to conquer, and to choose
the right.

261 *Ascribed to Stephen Langton (d. 1228)*
tr. Edward Caswall (1814–78)

1 Holy Spirit, Lord of light,
from the clear celestial height,
thy pure beaming radiance give;
come, thou Father of the poor,
come with treasures which endure;
come, thou Light of all that live!

2 Thou, of all consolers best,
thou, the soul's delightsome guest,
dost refreshing peace bestow:
thou in toil art comfort sweet,
pleasant coolness in the heat,
solace in the midst of woe.

3 Light immortal, light divine,
visit thou these hearts of thine,
and our inmost being fill:

if thou take thy grace away,
nothing pure in us will stay;
all his good is turned to ill.

4 Heal our wounds, our strength renew;
on our dryness pour thy dew;
wash the stains of guilt away:
Bend the stubborn heart and will;
melt the frozen, warm the chill;
guide the steps that go astray.

5 Thou, on those who evermore
thee confess and thee adore,
in thy sevenfold gifts descend:
Give them comfort when they die;
give them life with thee on high;
give them joys that never end.

262 *John Glynn*

1 Holy Spirit of fire,
flame everlasting, so bright and clear,
speak this day in our hearts.
Lighten our darkness and purge us of fear,
Holy Spirit of fire.

The wind can blow or be still,
or water be parched by the sun.
A fire can die into dust:
but here the eternal Spirit of God
tells us a new world's begun.

2 Holy Spirit of love,
strong are the faithful who trust your pow'r.
Love who conquers our will,
teach us the words of the gospel of peace,
Holy Spirit of love.

3 Holy Spirit of God,
flame everlasting, so bright and clear,
spark this day in our hearts.
Lighten our darkness and purge us of fear,
Holy Spirit of God.

263 *J. P. Lécot, tr. W. Raymond Lawrence*

1 Holy Virgin, by God's decree,
you were called eternally;
that he could give his Son to our race.
Mary, we praise you, hail full of grace.

Ave, ave, ave, Maria.

2 By your faith and loving accord,
as the handmaid of the Lord,
you undertook God's plan to embrace.
Mary, we thank you, hail full of grace.

3 Refuge for your children so weak,
sure protection all can seek.
Problems of life you help us to face.
Mary, we trust you, hail full of grace.

4 To our needy world of today
love and beauty you portray,
showing the path to Christ we must trace.
Mary, our mother, hail, full of grace.

264 *David Haas*

Hosanna, hosanna, hosanna!
Hosanna, hosanna!

1 Blessed is he, blessed is he
who comes in the name of the Lord!
Blessed is he, blessed is he
who comes in the name of the Lord!

2 Blessed is the reign
of our father David!
Blessed is the reign
of our father David to come!

265 *Jennette Threlfall (1821–80)*

1 Hosanna, loud Hosanna,
the little children sang;
through pillared court and temple
the joyful anthem rang;
to Jesus, who had blessed them
close folded to his breast
the children sang their praises,
the simplest and the best.

2 From Olivet they followed,
'mid an exultant crowd,
the victor palm–branch waving,
and chanting clear and loud;
bright angels joined in chorus,
beyond the cloudless sky:
'Hosanna in the highest!
Glory to God on high!'

3 Fair leaves of silvery olive
they strew upon the ground
while Salem's circling mountains
echoed the joyful sound;
the Lord of saints and angels
rode on in lowly state,
nor scorned that lowly children
should on his bidding wait.

4 'Hosanna in the highest!'
that ancient song we sing,
for Christ is our redeemer,
the Lord of heaven, our King.
O may we ever praise him
with heart and life and voice,
and in his blissful presence
eternally rejoice.

266 *Philipp Nicolai (1556–1608)*

1 How brightly beams the morning star!
What sudden radiance from afar
aglow with grace and mercy!
Of Jacob's race, King David's Son,
our Lord and master, you have won
our hearts to serve you only!
Lowly, holy! Great and glorious,
all victorious, rich in blessing!
Rule and might o'er all possessing!

2 Come, heav'nly bridegroom, light divine,
and deep within our hearts now shine;
there light a flame undying!
In your one body let us be
as living branches of a tree,
your life our lives supplying.
Now, though daily Earth's deep sadness
may perplex us and distress us,
yet with heav'nly joy you bless us.

3 O let the harps break forth in sound!
Our joy be all with music crowned,
our voices richly blending!
For Christ goes with us all the way
today, tomorrow, ev'ry day!
His love is never ending! Sing out!
Ring out!
Jubilation! Exultation! Tell the story!
Great is he, the King of glory!

267 *Michael Cockett*

1 How dark was the stable where Jesus
was born?
How dark was the stable that was his
first home?
It was dark as the sky on a black winter's
night,
when the stars will not shine and the
moon gives no light.

2 How cold was the stable where Jesus
was born?
How cold was the stable that was his
first home?
It was cold as the frost on a white
window pane;
it was cold as a heart that has known
no love.

3 How light was the stable when Jesus
was born?
How light was the stable he made his
first home?
It was light as the star that was shining
that night;
it was light as an angel in splendour and
might.

4 How warm was the stable when Jesus
was born?
How warm was the stable he made his
first home?
It was warm as the love of the first
Christmas morn;
it was warm as our hearts in which Jesus
is born.

268 *Leonard E. Smith Jnr*

1 How lovely on the mountains
are the feet of him
who brings good news, good news,
announcing peace,
proclaiming news of happiness:

Our God reigns (6)

2 You watchmen, lift your voices joyfully
as one,
shout for your king, your king!
See eye to eye, the Lord restoring Sion:
Our God reigns …

3 Wasteplaces of Jerusalem,
break forth with joy!
We are redeemed, redeemed,
the Lord has saved
and comforted his people.
Our God reigns …

4 Ends of the earth, see
the salvation of our God!
Jesus is Lord, is Lord!
Before the nations
he has bared his holy arm.
Our God reigns …

269 *Michael Perry*

1 How shall they hear the Word of God
unless his truth is told?
How shall the sinful be set free,
the sorrowful consoled?
To all who speak the truth today
impart your Spirit, Lord, we pray.

2 How shall they call to God for help
unless they have believed?
How shall the poor be given hope,
the prisoner reprieved?
To those who help the blind to see
give light and love and clarity.

3 How shall the gospel be proclaimed
if heralds are not sent?
How shall the world find peace at last
if we are negligent?
So send us, Lord, for we rejoice
to speak of Christ with life and voice.

270 *Dave Bilbrough*

I am a new creation,
no more in condemnation,
here in the grace of God I stand.
My heart is overflowing,
my love just keeps on growing,
here in the grace of God I stand.
And I will praise You Lord,
yes I will praise You, Lord,
and I will sing of all that You have done.
A joy that knows no limit,
a lightness in my spirit,
here in the grace of God I stand.

271 *David Konstant*

1 I am the bread of life.
He who comes to me will never be hungry.
I will raise him up. I will raise him up.
I will raise him up to eternal life.
I am the bread of life.

2 I am the spring of life.
He who hopes in me will never be thirsty.
I will raise him up. *(2)*
I will raise him up to eternal life.
I am the spring of life.

3 I am the way of life.
He who follows me will never be lonely.
I will raise him up. *(2)*
I will raise him up to eternal life.
I am the way of life.

4 I am the truth of life.
He who looks for me will never seek
blindly.
I will raise him up. *(2)*
I will raise him up to eternal life.
I am the truth of life.

5 I am the life of life.
He who dies with me will never die vainly.
I will raise him up. *(2)*
I will raise him up to eternal life.
I am the life of life.

272 Suzanne Toolan

1 I am the Bread of life.
You who come to me shall not hunger;
and who believe in me shall not thirst.
No–one can come to me
unless the Father draw him.

And I will raise you up,
and I will raise you up,
and I will raise you up on the last day.

2 The bread that I will give
is my flesh for the life of the world,
and if you eat of this bread,
you shall live for ever,
you shall live for ever.

3 Unless you eat
of the flesh of the Son of Man,
and drink of his blood,
and drink of his blood,
you shall not have life within you.

4 I am the Resurrection,
I am the life.
If you believe in me,
even though you die,
you shall live for ever.

5 Yes, Lord, I believe,
that you are the Christ,
the Son of God,
who have come
into the world.

273 John Glynn

1 I am the vine, you are the branches:
no–one can live apart from me.
Cut off from me you can do nothing:
yet joined with me, all things are yours.

2 You are the fruit borne by my Father,
who tends and cares for every limb.
Be not afraid: he will not harm you.
Your fear he'll prune, and set you free.

3 Remain in me: keep my commandments.
My love for you led me to die.
Hold fast to me: I'll never leave you,
in life, in death, I'll love you still.

274 Attributed to St Patrick (c. 386–c.460), tr. Cecil Frances Alexander (1818–95)

1 I bind unto myself today
the strong name of the Trinity
by invocation of the same,
the Three in One, and One in Three.

2 I bind this day to me forever,
by power of faith, Christ's incarnation;
his baptism in the Jordan river;
his death on cross for my salvation;
his bursting from the spicèd tomb;
his riding up the heavenly way;
his coming at the day of doom;
I bind unto myself today.

3 I bind unto myself today
the virtues of the starlit heaven,
the glorious sun's life–giving ray,
the whiteness of the moon at even,
the flashing of the lightning free,
the whirling wind's tempestuous shocks,
the stable earth, the deep salt sea
around the old eternal rocks.

4 I bind unto myself today
the power of God to hold and lead,
his eye to watch, his might to stay,
his ear to hearken to my need,
the wisdom of my God to teach,
his hand to guide, his shield to ward,
the word of God to give me speech,
his heavenly host to be my guard.

5 Christ be with me, Christ within me,
Christ behind me, Christ before me,
Christ beside me, Christ to win me,
Christ to comfort and restore me,
Christ beneath me, Christ above me,
Christ in quiet, Christ in danger,
Christ in hearts of all that love me,
Christ in mouth of friend and stranger.

6 I bind unto myself the name,
the strong name of the Trinity,
by invocation of the same,
the Three in One, and One in Three,
of whom all nature hath creation,
eternal Father, Spirit, Word.
Praise to the Lord of my salvation:
salvation is of Christ the Lord. Amen.

275 *Sydney Carter*

1 I danced in the morning
when the world was begun,
and I danced in the moon
and the stars and the sun,
and I came down from heaven
and I danced on the earth –
at Bethlehem I had my birth.

Dance, then, wherever you may be,
I am the Lord of the Dance, said he.
And I'll lead you all, wherever you may be,
and I'll lead you all in the dance, said he.

2 I danced for the scribe
and the pharisee
but they would not dance
and they wouldn't follow me,
I danced for the fishermen,
for James and John –
they came with me
and the dance went on.

3 I danced on the Sabbath
and I cured the lame.
The holy people
said it was a shame.
They whipped and they stripped
and they hung me high,
and they left me there
on the cross to die.

4 I danced on a Friday
when the sky turned black –
it's hard to dance
with the devil on your back;
they buried my body
and they thought I'd gone –
but I am the dance
and I still go on.

5 They cut me down
and I leapt up high –
I am the life
that'll never, never die
I'll live in you
if you'll live in me.
I am the Lord
of the Dance, said he.

276 *Michael Joncas*

I have loved you with an everlasting love,
I have called you and you are mine;
I have loved you with an everlasting love,
I have called you and you are mine.

1 Seek the face of the Lord and long for him:
he will bring you his light and his peace.

2 Seek the face of the Lord and long for him:
he will bring you his joy and his hope.

3 Seek the face of the Lord and long for him:
he will bring you his care and his love.

277 *Gregory Norbet, OSB*

1 I lift my eyes to the mountains;
from where shall come my help?
My help shall come from the Lord, Yahweh;
it is he who made heaven and earth.

2 May he never allow you to stumble,
let him sleep not, your guard.
No, he sleeps not, nor slumbers,
the Lord, Israel's guard.

3 The Lord is your guard and your shade,
at your right hand he stands.
By day the sun shall not smite you,
nor the moon in the night.

4 The Lord will guard you from evil,
he will guard your soul.
The Lord will guard your coming and
your going,
both now and for evermore.
The Lord will guard your coming and
your going,
both now and for evermore.

278 *Huub Oosterhuis, tr. Tony Barr*

Antiphon

I lift up my eyes to the mountain,
is anyone there to help me?

Response

Yes, my God comes to help me,
the Lord who made both heaven and earth.

1 He will not allow you to stumble,
he never sleeps but stands watch over you.
The Lord who made both heaven and earth.

No, he will not sleep nor slumber,
he stands watch over all his people.
Yes, my God comes to help me,
the Lord who made both heaven and earth.

2 Our God keeps watch;
like a shadow he covers you.
The Lord who made both heaven and earth.

In the daytime the sun shall not strike you;
by night the moon shall not harm you.
Yes, my God comes to help me,
the Lord who made both heaven and earth.

3 He keeps evil away from you;
he takes you under his protection.
The Lord who made both heaven and earth.

Whether you are coming or going,
God looks after you for ever.
Yes, my God comes to help me,
the Lord who made both heaven and earth.

Note: After verse 3 and its Response, the Psalm ends with the Antiphon and Response once more.

279 *Eric A. Thorn*

1 I met you at the cross,
Jesus my Lord;
I heard you from that cross:
my name you called –
asked me to follow you all of my days,
asked me for evermore your name to praise.

2 I saw you on the cross
dying for me;
I put you on that cross:
but your one plea –
would I now follow you all of my days
and would I evermore your great name
praise?

3 Jesus, my Lord and King,
Saviour of all,
Jesus the King of kings,
you heard my call –
that I would follow you all of my days,
and that for evermore your name I'd praise.

280 *Anonymous*

I received the living God,
and my heart is full of joy.
I received the living God,
and my heart is full of joy.

1 He has said: I am the Bread
kneaded long to give you life;
you who will partake of me
need not ever fear to die.

2 He has said: I am the Way,
and my Father longs for you;
so I come to bring you home
to be one with him anew.

3 He has said: I am the Truth;
if you follow close to me,
you will know me in your heart,
and my word shall make you free.

4 He has said: I am the Life
far from whom no thing can grow,
but receive this living bread,
and my Spirit you shall know.

281 *The Grail*

I rejoiced when I heard them say
'Let us go to the house of the Lord,'
I rejoiced when I heard them say
'Let us go to the house of the Lord!'

1 I rejoiced when I heard them say,
'Let us go to God's house,'
and now our feet are standing
in your gates, O Jerusalem.

2 Jerusalem is built
as a city, strongly compact.
It is there that the tribes go up,
the tribes of the Lord!

3 For Israel's law it is
there to praise the Lord's name.
There were set the thrones of judgement
of the house of Israel.

282 Joan McCrimmon

1 I saw a star up high above the heavens.
I heard the angels singing in the sky.
I watched the shepherds coming from the sheepfold.
I even thought I heard a baby cry.
No one there would listen to my story,
and no one seemed to care about the child;
but he was beautiful,
the baby born to save us,
as in his mother's arms he gently lay.

2 I saw the star shine down upon the stable.
I watched the kings with gifts go riding by.
I crept up close and looked into the manger
and it was then I heard a baby cry.
but ...

3 I hurried home and there I met the townsfolk.
I wandered in the hills and all around.
I tried to tell my friends about the story
of angels, shepherds, kings and babe I'd found.

But all alone I knelt before that manger,
with sheep and cows and oxen standing by;
and he was beautiful –
the baby born to save us,
as in his mother's arms he gently lay.
Yes, he was beautiful,
the baby who was born on Christmas Day.

283 Estelle White

1 I saw the grass, I saw the trees
and the boats along the shore.
I saw the shapes of many things
I had only sensed before.
And I saw the faces of men more clearly
than if I had never been blind,
the lines of envy around their lips
and the greed and the hate in their eyes.
And I turned away, yes, I turned away,
for I had seen the perfect face of a real and proper man,
the man who brought me from the dark
into light, where life began.

2 I hurried then away from town
to a quiet, lonely place.
I found a clear, unruffled pool
and I gazed upon my face.
And I saw the image of me more clearly
than if I had never been blind.
The lines of envy around the lips
and the greed and the hate in the eyes.
And I turned away, yes, I turned away,
for I had seen the perfect face of a real and proper man,
the man who'd brought me from the dark
into light, where life began.

3 I made my way into the town,
to the busy, crowded streets,
the shops and stalls and alley-ways,
to the squalor and the heat.
And I saw the faces of men more clearly
than if I had never been blind,
the lines of sorrow around their lips
and the child looking out from their eyes,
and I turned to them, yes, I turned to them,
remembering the perfect face of a real and proper man,
the man who'd brought me from the dark
into light, where life began.

284 Richard Beaumont

I sing a song to you, Lord,
a song of love and praise.
All glory be to you, Lord,
through everlasting days.

1 Holy, holy, holy,
mighty Lord and God.
He who was and is now,
and who is to come.

I sing a song to you, Lord,
a song of love and praise.
All glory be to you, Lord,
through everlasting days.

2 Worthy is the slain Lamb,
honour him and praise.
We rejoice with gladness,
sing our love today.

3 He has used his power,
has begun his reign.
So rejoice, you heavens,
and proclaim his name.

4 Shine your light on us, Lord,
let us know your way.
Be our guide for ever,
make us yours today.

285 *Daniel L. Schutte, SJ*

1 I, the Lord of sea and sky,
I have heard my people cry.
All who dwell in dark and sin
my hand will save.
I who made the stars of night,
I will make their darkness bright.
Who will bear my light to them?
Whom shall I send?

Here I am, Lord. Is it I, Lord?
I have heard you calling in the night.
I will go, Lord, if you lead me.
I will hold your people in my heart.

2 I, the Lord of snow and rain,
I have borne my people's pain.
I have wept for love of them.
They turn away.
I will break their hearts of stone,
give them hearts for love alone.
I will speak my word to them.
Whom shall I send?

3 I, the Lord of wind and flame,
I will tend the poor and lame.
I will set a feast for them.
My hand will save.
Finest bread I will provide
till their hearts be satisfied.
I will give my life to them.
Whom shall I send?

286 *Sir Cecil Spring–Rice*

1 I vow to thee, my country, all earthly things above,
entire and whole and perfect, the service of my love:
the love that asks no questions, the love that stands the test,
that lays upon the altar the dearest and the best;
the love that never falters, the love that pays the price,
the love that makes undaunted the final sacrifice.

2 And there's another country, I've heard of long ago,
most dear to them that love her, most great to them that know;
we may not count her armies, we may not see her King;
her fortress is a faithful heart, her pride is suffering;
and soul by soul and silently her shining bounds increase,
and her ways are ways of gentleness and all her paths are peace.

287 *John Glynn*

1 I was born before creation,
when the world was yet to be.
From the dawn of time uncounted
I have sung God's melody.

I am Wisdom, his companion,
ever at his side to be;
I delight in his creating,
never ending, ever free.

2 Ev'ry sea and ev'ry river
I have seen them come to birth;
for the hills and for the mountains
seen him raise the virgin earth.

3 There were stars hung in the heavens,
and the clouds were in his plan;
but the time I'll ever cherish
was the day he formed a man.

4 Never has he ceased creating,
and I'm with him to this day;
so I'm glad to see his image
in the people of today.

288 *John Glynn*

1 I watch the sunrise
lighting the sky,
casting its shadows near.
And on this morning
bright though it be,
I feel those shadows near me.

But you are always close to me
following all my ways.
May I be always close to you
following all your ways, Lord.

2 I watch the sunlight
shine through the clouds,
warming the earth below.
And at the mid–day life seems to say:
'I feel your brightness near me.'

For you are always ...

3 I watch the sunset
fading away,
lighting the clouds with sleep.
And as the evening closes its eyes
I feel your presence near me.

For you are always ...

4 I watch the moonlight
guarding the night,
waiting till morning comes.
The air is silent, earth is at rest
only your peace is near me.

Yes, you are always ...

289 *Gerald Markland*

I will be with you wherever you go.
Go now throughout the world!
I will be with you in all that you say.
Go now and spread my word!

1 Come, walk with me on stormy waters.
Why fear? Reach out, and I'll be there.

2 And you, my friend, will you now leave me,
or do you know me as your Lord?

3 Your life will be transformed with power
by living truly in my name.

4 And if you say: 'Yes, Lord I love you,'
then feed my lambs and feed my sheep.

290 *Carey Landry, SJ*

1 I will never forget you, my people,
I have carved you on the palm of my hand.
I will never forget you;
I will not leave your orphaned.
I will never forget my own.

2 Does a mother forget her baby?
Or a woman the child within her womb?
Yet, even if these forget,
yes, even if these forget,
I will never forget my own.

Repeat Verse 1

291 *Max Dyer*

1 I will sing, I will sing a song unto the
Lord. *(3)*
Alleluia, glory to the Lord.

Allelu, alleluia, glory to the Lord, (3)
alleluia, glory to the Lord.

2 We will come, we will come as one
before the Lord. *(3)*
Alleluia, glory to the Lord.

3 If the Son, if the Son shall make you
free, *(3)*
you shall be free indeed.

Allelu, alleluia, glory to the Lord, (3)
alleluia, glory to the Lord.

4 They that sow in tears shall reap in joy. *(3)*
Alleluia, glory to the Lord.

5 Ev'ry knee shall bow and ev'ry tongue confess *(3)*
that Jesus Christ is Lord.

6 In his name, in his name we have the victory. *(3)*
Alleluia, glory to the Lord.

292 *Traditional*

1 I wonder as I wander out under the sky,
how Jesus the Saviour did come for to die
for poor ord'n'ry people like you and like I.
I wonder as I wander out under the sky.

2 When Mary birthed Jesus, 'twas in a cow's stall
with wise men and farmers and shepherds and all.
But high from God's heaven a star's light did fall,
and the promise of ages it did then recall.

3 If Jesus had wanted for any wee thing,
a star in the sky, or a bird on the wing,
or all of God's angels in heav'n for to sing,
he surely could have it, 'cause he was the king.

293 *John Wyse (1825–98)*

1 I'll sing a hymn to Mary,
the Mother of my God,
the Virgin of all virgins,
of David's royal blood.
O teach me, holy Mary,
a loving song to frame,
O may I imitate thee
and magnify God's name.

2 O noble Tower of David,
of gold and ivory,
the Ark of God's own presence,
the gate of heav'n to me,
to live and not to love thee,
would fill my soul with shame;
O may I imitate thee
and magnify God's name.

3 The Saints are high in glory,
with golden crowns so bright;
but brighter far is Mary,
upon her throne of light.
O that which God did give thee,
let mortal ne'er disclaim;
O may I imitate thee
and magnify God's name.

4 But in the crown of Mary,
there lies a wondrous gem,
as Queen of all the Angels,
which Mary shares with them:
no sin hath e'er defiled thee,
so doth our faith proclaim;
O may I imitate thee
and magnify God's name.

294 *Aniceto Nazareth*

I'll sing God's praises,
now and evermore. (2)

1 He is my guide and my shepherd,
now and evermore.
He gives me rest in green pastures,
now and evermore.

2 Near restful waters he leads me,
now and evermore.
Along the right path he keeps me,
now and evermore.

3 His rod and crook are my comfort,
now and evermore.
With oil my head is anointed,
now and evermore.

4 His loving favours pursue me,
now and evermore.
His house, my dwelling for ever,
now and evermore.

295 John B. Foley, SJ

If God is for us, who can be against,
if the Spirit of God has set us free? (2)

1 I know that nothing in this world
can ever take us from his love.

2 Nothing can take us from his love,
poured out in Jesus, the Lord.

3 And nothing present or to come
can ever take us from his love.

4 I know that neither death nor life
can ever take us from his love.

296 Denis E. Hurley

1 If God is our defender,
who will th'accuser be?
His only Son he spared not,
but gave him graciously.
When God himself grants pardon,
who ventures to condemn?
Will Jesus Christ, the Saviour,
who died and rose for men?

2 Can anything divide us
from that most loving Lord?
Can pain, or tribulation?
Can famine, peril, sword?
No, none of these can cause us
from his great love to fall;
for, by the strength he gave us,
we triumph over all.

3 Of this we can be certain,
and sing with every breath:
that nought that is, or will be,
and neither life nor death,
and nothing in creation,
below us or above,
can tear us from Christ Jesus,
and from his Father's love.

297 Huub Oosterhuis, tr. Tony Barr

If God should lead us home from our exile,
what wondrous dream–world!
If God should lead us home from our exile,
what wondrous dream–world!

1 We will be singing, laughing and revelling;
then let the world say: 'Their God works
wonders.'
Yes, you work wonders, God here among us,
you, our gladness.

2 Then lead us home, restore us to life,
just as the rivers in the desert,
as the new rains fall, start flowing again.
Sowing in sorrow, reaping in gladness!
A man sets out in tears for the sowing,
back he comes singing, sheaves on his
shoulder!

If God should lead us home from our exile,
what wondrous dream–world!
If God should lead us home from our exile,
what wondrous dream–world!

298 Brian Howard

1 If I were a butterfly
I'd thank you, Lord, for giving me wings,
and if I were a robin in a tree
I'd thank you, Lord, that I could sing,
and if I were a fish in the sea
I'd wiggle my tail and I'd giggle with glee,
but I just thank you, Father, for making
me me.

For you gave me a heart and you gave
me a smile,
you gave me Jesus and you made
me your child,
and I just thank you, Father, for making
me me.

2 If I were an elephant
I'd thank you, Lord, by raising my trunk,
and if I were a kangaroo
you know I'd hop right up to you,
and if I were an octopus
I'd thank you, Lord, for my fine looks,
but I just thank you, Father, for making
me me.

For you gave me a heart and you gave me a smile,
you gave me Jesus and you made me your child,
and I just thank you, Father, for making me me.

3 If I were a wiggily worm
I'd thank you, Lord, that I could squirm,
and if I were a billy goat
I'd thank you, Lord, for my strong throat,
and if I were a fuzzy wuzzy bear
I'd thank you, Lord, for my fuzzy wuzzy hair,
but I just thank you, Father, for making me me.

299 *Bernadette Farrell*

1 If you would follow me,
follow where life will lead;
do not look for me among the dead,
for I am hidden in pain,
risen in love;
there is no harvest without sowing of grain.

All that is hidden will be made clear.
All that is dark now will be revealed.
What you have heard in the dark
proclaim in the light;
what you hear in whispers
proclaim from the house–tops.

2 If you would honour me,
honour the least of these:
you will not find me dressed in finery.
My Word cries out to be heard;
breaks through the world:
my Word is on your lips and lives in your heart.

3 If you would speak of me
live all your life in me:
my ways are not the ways that you would choose;
my thoughts are far beyond yours,
as heaven from earth:
if you believe in me my voice will be heard.

4 If you would rise with me,
rise through your destiny:
do not refuse the death
which brings you life,
for as the grain in the earth
must die for re–birth,
so I have planted your life deep within mine.

300 *Anonymous*

1 Immaculate Mary!
Our hearts are on fire,
that title so wondrous
fills all our desire.

Ave, ave, ave Maria!
Ave, ave, ave Maria!

2 We pray for God's glory,
may his kingdom come!
We pray for his vicar,
our father, and Rome.

3 We pray for our mother
the church upon earth,
and bless, sweetest Lady,
the land of our birth.

4 For poor, sick, afflicted
thy mercy we crave;
and comfort the dying,
thou light of the grave.

5 There is no need, Mary,
nor ever has been,
which thou canst not succour,
Immaculate Queen.

6 In grief and temptation,
in joy or in pain,
we'll ask thee, our mother,
nor seek thee in vain.

7 O bless us, dear Lady,
with blessings from heaven.
And to our petitions
let answer be given.

8 In death's solemn moment,
our mother, be nigh;
as children of Mary –
help us when we die.

9 And crown thy sweet mercy
with this special grace,
to behold soon in heaven
God's ravishing face.

10 To God be all glory
and worship for aye,
and to God's virgin mother
an endless Ave.

301 *W. Chalmers Smith (1825–1908)*

1 Immortal, invisible, God only wise,
in light inaccessible hid from our eyes,
most blessed, most glorious, the
Ancient of Days,
almighty, victorious, thy great name we
praise.

2 Unresting, unhasting, and silent as light;
nor wanting, nor wasting, thou rulest in
might –
thy justice like mountains high–soaring
above
thy clouds which are fountains of
goodness and love.

3 To all life thou givest, to both great and
small;
in all life thou livest, the true life of all;
we blossom and flourish as leaves on the
tree,
and wither and perish; but naught
changeth thee.

4 Great Father of glory, pure Father of light,
thine angels adore thee, all veiling their
sight;
all laud we would render: O help us to see
'tis only the splendour of light hideth thee.

302 *Kevin Nichols*

1 In bread we bring you, Lord, our bodies'
labour.
In wine we offer you our spirits' grief.
We do not ask you, Lord, who is my
neighbour?
But stand united now, one in belief.
Oh, we have gladly heard your Word,
your holy Word,
and now in answer, Lord, our gifts
we bring.
Our selfish hearts make true, our failing
faith renew,
our lives belong to you, our Lord and King.

2 The bread we offer you is blessed and
broken,
and it becomes for us our spirits' food.
Over the cup we bring your Word is spoken;
make it your gift to us your healing blood.
Take all that daily toil plants in our
heart's poor soil,
take all we start and spoil, each hopeful
dream,
the chances we have missed, the graces
we resist,
Lord, in thy Eucharist, take and redeem.

303 *John Oxenham (1852–1941)*

1 In Christ there is no east or west,
in him no south or north,
but one great fellowship of love
throughout the whole wide earth.

2 In him shall true hearts ev'rywhere
their high communion find.
His service is the golden cord
close–binding all mankind.

3 Join hands, then, brothers of the faith,
whate'er your race may be.
Who serves my Father as a son
is surely kin to me.

4 In Christ now meet both east and west,
in him meet south and north.
All Christly souls are one in him
throughout the whole wide earth.

304 *Owen Alstott*

In the abundance of your compassion
wash my sins away.
Show me your mercy, O God,
and cleansed in the water of your salvation,
I shall be whiter than snow.

1 Put a new heart in me, O God,
and give me again a constant spirit.

2 We cannot live unless we die,
unless we are born of water and spirit.

3 Trust in the Lord for he is good,
His mercy endures, his love is unending.

305 *Christina G. Rossetti (1830–94)*

1 In the bleak midwinter,
frosty wind made moan,
earth stood hard as iron,
water like a stone;
snow had fallen, snow on snow,
snow on snow,
in the bleak midwinter long ago.

2 Our God, heaven cannot hold him
nor earth sustain;
Heaven and earth shall flee away,
when he comes to reign.
In the bleak midwinter
a stable–place sufficed –
the Lord God Almighty, Jesus Christ.

3 Enough for him, whom Cherubim
worship night and day,
a breastful of milk,
and a mangerful of hay:
enough for him, whom angels
fall down before,
the ox and ass and camel which adore.

4 Angels and archangels
may have gathered there,
Cherubim and Seraphim
thronged the air.
But only his mother in her maiden bliss
worshipped the beloved with a kiss.

5 What can I give him,
poor as I am?
If I were a shepherd
I would bring a lamb;
if I were a wise man I would do my part;
yet what I can I give him – give my heart.

306 *Estelle White*

1 In the earth the small seed is hidden and
lies unseen until it is bidden by
springtime stirrings up to the sunlight and
summer ripening.
Golden is the harvest and precious the
bread that you are, and give to us, Lord.

2 In the vineyard branches are cut away
so that fresh young shoots may, with
ev'ry day,
bend beneath the fruit as it ripens and
fills with promise.
Golden is the harvest and precious the
wine that you are and give to us, Lord.

3 In me, Oh my Lord, plant the seed of love
nourished by your body and by your blood.
May my soul take wings and rise
upward to
new awakenings!
Golden is the light of your Godhead that
by love you have, and give to us, Lord.

307 *Mike Lynch*

In the land there is a hunger,
in the land there is a need
not for the taste of water,
not for the taste of bread.
In the land there is a hunger,
in the land there is a need
for the sound of the word of God
upon every word we feed.

1 Hear O Lord my cry,
Day and night I call.
My soul is thirsting
for you, my God.

2 Your word O Lord
is spirit and life.
You have the words, Lord,
of everlasting life.

3 Only in God
is my soul at rest.
He is my rock
and my salvation.

308 *Jacques Berthier, Taizé chant*

In the Lord I'll be ev - er thank - ful, in the Lord I will re -
- joice! Look to him, do not be a - fraid; in him re - joic - ing: the Lord is
near, in him re — joic — ing: the Lord is near. In the

Alternative text *tr. Paul Inwood*

In the Lord is my true salvation,
in the Lord my lasting joy.
He became my strength and my song:
I trust in him and I shall not fear,
I trust in him and I shall not fear.

---

309 *Psalm 24 (25)* *Adapted by Chris O'Hara*

In your love remember me,
in your love remember me,
in your great goodness, O Lord,
remember me.

1 Lord, make me know your ways,
Lord, teach me your paths.
Make me walk in your truth and teach me,
for you are God my Saviour.

2 Remember your mercy, Lord,
your eternal love.
In your mercy I ask forgiveness:
in your love remember me.

3 His way is faithfulness,
faithfulness and love.
To the humble he shows the right path,
teaches the way of poverty.

310 *From a Polish Carol, tr. E. M. G. Reed (1885–1933)*

1 Infant holy, infant lowly,
for His bed a cattle stall;
oxen lowing, little knowing
Christ the babe is Lord of all.
Swift are winging angels singing,
nowells rings, tidings bringing:
Christ the babe is Lord of all;
Christ the babe is Lord of all!

2 Flocks were sleeping,
shepherds keeping
vigil till the morning new,
saw the glory, heard the story
tidings of a gospel true.
Thus rejoicing, free from sorrow,
praises voicing, greet the morrow:
Christ the babe was born for you;
Christ the babe was born for you!

311 *John L. Bell and Graham Maule*

1 Inspired by love and anger,
disturbed by need and pain,
informed of God's own bias,
we ask him once again:
'How long must some folk suffer?
How long can few folk mind?
How long dare vain self interest
turn prayer and pity blind?'

2 From those, forever victims
of heartless human greed,
their cruel plight compose a litany of need:
'Where are the fruits of justice?
Where are the signs of peace?
When is the day when prisoners and dreams
find their release?'

3 From those forever shackled
to what their wealth can buy,
the fear of lost advantage
provokes the bitter cry,
'Don't query our position!
Don't criticise our wealth!
Don't mention those exploited
by politics and stealth!'

4 To God, who through the prophets
proclaimed a different age,
we offer earth's indifference,
its agony and rage:
'When will the wronged be righted?
When will the kingdom come?
When will the world be generous
to all instead of some?'

5 God asks, 'Who will go for me?
Who will extend my reach?
And who, when few will listen,
will prophesy and preach?
And who, when few bid welcome,
will offer all they know?
And who, when few dare follow,
will walk the road I show?'

6 Amused in someone's kitchen,
asleep in someone's boat,
attuned to what the ancients exposed,
proclaimed and wrote,
a saviour without safety,
a tradesman without tools
has come to tip the balance
with fishermen and fools.

312 *Adapted from 'Ubi Caritas et Amor' by Michael Cockett*

1 Into one we all are gathered through the love of Christ.
Let us then rejoice with gladness. In him we find love.
Let us fear and love the living God,
and love and cherish all mankind.

Where charity and love are, there is God.

2 Therefore, when we are together in the love of Christ,
let our minds know no division, strife or bitterness,
may the Christ our God be in our midst.
Through Christ our Lord all love is found.

3 May we see your face in glory, Christ our loving God.
With the blessed saints of heaven give us lasting joy.
We will then possess true happiness,
and love for all eternity.

313 *ISRAELI MASS, Anthony Hamson*

LORD, HAVE MERCY

Lord, have mercy. Lord, have mercy.
Lord, have mercy on us all.
Lord, have mercy. Lord, have mercy.
Lord, have mercy on us all.

Christ, have mercy. Christ, have mercy.
Christ, have mercy on us all.
Christ, have mercy. Christ, have mercy.
Christ, have mercy on us all.

Lord, have mercy. Lord, have mercy.
Lord, have mercy on us all.
Lord, have mercy. Lord, have mercy.
Lord, have mercy on us all.

HOLY, HOLY, HOLY

Holy, holy, holy, holy
Lord of power, Lord of might.
Heav'n and earth are filled with glory.
Sing hosanna evermore.

Blest and holy, blest and holy
he who comes from God on high.
Raise your voices, sing his glory,
praise his name for evermore.

LAMB OF GOD

Lamb of God, you take away the sin,
the sin of all the world.
Give us mercy, give us mercy,
give us mercy, Lamb of God. *(Repeat)*

Lamb of God, you take away the sin,
the sin of all the world.
Grant us peace, Lord, grant us peace, Lord,
grant us peace, O Lamb of God.

314 *E. H. Sears (1810–76)*

1 It came upon the midnight clear,
that glorious song of old,
from angels bending near the earth
to touch their harps of gold;
'Peace on the earth, good will to men,
from heaven's all gracious King!'
The world in solemn stillness lay
to hear the angels sing.

2 Yet with the woes of sin and strife
the world has suffered long;
beneath the angel–strain have rolled
two thousand years of wrong;
and man, at war with man, hears not
the love song which they bring:
O hush the noise, ye men of strife,
and hear the angels sing!

3 For lo, the days are hastening on,
by prophets seen of old,
when with the ever–circling years
shall come the time foretold,
when the new heaven and earth shall own
the prince of peace their king,
and all the world send back the song
which now the angels sing.

315 *Versified by Anthony Sharpe*

It is good to give thanks to your name,
O Lord,
and to honour your ways.
It is good to give glory to you,
Most High,
so we lift our voices in your praise.

1 We proclaim your love from daybreak,
from the first light of the sun.
Faithfully you guard your people
all through the night.

2 Praise your name for all creation,
for your deeds we give you thanks.
Great and true, your wondrous
achievements
by your own right hand.

3 All of our days we sing your praises
your great wisdom we acclaim.
Deep your thoughts, the fool cannot
know them.
Praise your Holy Name.

4 In your house, to give you glory,
forever we will sing:
to proclaim that Yahweh is faithful
our God, our King.

316 *Afro–American Spiritual*

It's me, it's me, it's me, O Lord,
standin' in the need of pray'r. (2)

1 Not my brother or my sister, but
it's me, O Lord,
standin' in the need of prayer.
Not my brother or my sister, but
it's me, O Lord,
standin' in the need of pray'r.

2 Not my mother or my father, but
it's me, O Lord,
standin' in the need of prayer.
Not my mother or my father, but
it's me, O Lord,
standin' in the need of pray'r.

3 Not the stranger or my neighbour, but
it's me, O Lord,
standin' in the need of prayer.
Not the stranger or my neighbour, but
it's me, O Lord,
standin' in the need of pray'r.

317 *From 'De Contemptu Mundi', St Bernard of Cluny (12th century), tr. J. M. Neale (1818–66)*

1 Jerusalem the golden,
with milk and honey blest,
beneath thy contemplation
sink heart and voice oppressed.
I know not, ah, I know not
what joys await us there,
what radiancy of glory,
what bliss beyond compare.

2 They stand, those halls of Sion,
all jubilant with song,
and bright with many an angel,
and all the martyr throng;
the prince is ever in them,
the daylight is serene;
the pastures of the blessed
are decked in glorious sheen.

3 There is the throne of David;
and there, from care released,
the shout of them that triumph,
the song of them that feast;
and they, who with their leader
have conquered in the fight,
for ever and for ever
are clad in robes of white.

4 O sweet and blessed country,
the home of God's elect!
O sweet and blessed country
that eager hearts expect!
Jesus, in mercy bring us
to that dear land of rest;
who art, with God the Father
and Spirit, ever blest.

318 *Ghana folk song, adapted by Tom Colvin*

Jesu, Jesu, fill us with your love,
show us how to serve the neighbours we
have from you.

1 Kneels at the feet of his friends,
silently washes their feet,
Master who pours out himself for them.

2 Neighbours are rich folk and poor,
neighbours are black folk and white,
neighbours are nearby and far away.

3 These are the ones we should serve,
these are the ones we should love,
all these are neighbours to us and you.

4 Kneel at the feet of our friends,
silently washing their feet,
this is the way we should live with you.

319 *Charles Wesley (1707–88)*

1 Jesu, lover of my soul!
Let me to thy bosom fly,
while the nearer waters roll,
while the tempest still is high;
hide me, O my Saviour, hide,
till the storm of life is past;
safe into the haven guide,
O receive my soul at last.

2 Other refuge have I none;
hangs my helpless soul on thee;
leave, ah! leave me not alone,
still support and comfort me.

All my trust on thee is stayed,
all my help from thee I bring;
cover my defenceless head
with the shadow of thy wing.

3 Thou, O Christ, art all I want,
more than all in thee I find.
Raise the fallen, cheer the faint,
heal the sick and lead the blind.
Just and holy is thy name,
I am all unrighteousness;
false and full of sin I am,
thou art full of truth and grace.

4 Plenteous grace with thee is found,
grace to cover all my sin;
let the healing streams abound,
make and keep me pure within.
Thou of life the fountain art,
freely let me take of thee;
spring thou up within my heart,
rise to all eternity.

320 *A. H. Collins (1827–1919)*

1 Jesu, meek and lowly,
Saviour, pure and holy,
on thy love relying,
come I to thee flying.

2 Prince of life and power,
my salvation's tower,
on the cross I view thee,
calling sinners to thee.

3 There behold me gazing
at the sight amazing;
bending low before thee,
helpless I adore thee.

4 See the red wounds streaming,
with Christ's life blood gleaming,
blood for sinners flowing,
pardon free bestowing.

5 Fountains rich in blessing,
Christ's fond love expressing,
thou my aching sadness
turnest into gladness.

6 Lord in mercy guide me,
be thou e'er beside me;
in thy wings direct me,
'neath thy wings protect me.

321 *11th century, tr. Edward Caswall (1814–78)*

1 Jesu, the very thought of thee
with sweetness fills my breast;
but sweeter far thy face to see,
and in thy presence rest.

2 Nor voice can sing, nor heart can frame,
nor can the memory find
a sweeter sound than thy blest name,
O Saviour of mankind.

3 O hope of every contrite heart,
O joy of all the meek,
to those who fall, how kind thou art,
how good to those who seek!

4 But what to those who find? Ah, this
nor tongue nor pen can show;
the love of Jesus, what it is
none but his lovers know.

5 Jesu, our only joy be thou,
as thou our prize wilt be;
Jesu, be thou our glory now,
and through eternity.

322 *Lyra Davidica (1708) and the Supplement (1816). Based partly on 'Surrexit Christus hodie'. (14th century)*

1 Jesus Christ is ris'n today, alleluia!
Our triumphant holy day, alleluia!
Who did once, upon the cross, alleluia!
Suffer to redeem our loss, alleluia!

2 Hymns of praise then let us sing, alleluia!
Unto Christ, our heavenly king, alleluia!
Who endured the cross and grave, alleluia!
Sinners to redeem and save, alleluia!

3 But the pains that he endured, alleluia!
Our salvation have procured; alleluia!
Now above the sky he's king, alleluia!
Where the angels ever sing, alleluia!

323 *John L. Bell and Graham Maule*

1 Jesus Christ is waiting, waiting in the
streets;
no-one is his neighbour, all alone he eats.
Listen, Lord Jesus, I am lonely too.
Make me, friend or stranger, fit to wait
on you.

2 Jesus Christ is raging, raging in the streets,
where injustice spirals and real hope
retreats.
Listen, Lord Jesus, I am angry too.
In the Kingdom's causes let me rage with
you.

3 Jesus Christ is healing, healing in the streets;
curing those who suffer, touching those
he greets.
Listen, Lord Jesus, I have pity too.
Let my care be active, healing just like you.

4 Jesus Christ is dancing, dancing in the
streets,
where each sign of hatred He, with love,
defeats.
Listen, Lord Jesus, I should triumph too.
On suspicion's graveyard let me dance
with you.

5 Jesus Christ is calling, calling in the
streets,
'Who will join my journey? I will guide
their feet.'
Listen, Lord Jesus, let my fears be few.
Walk one step before me; I will follow you.

324 Roger Humphrey

1 Jesus Christ, little Lord,
God and Saviour he,
born into this sinful world
to set the people free.

2 Sing, Jesus come to us
and teach us how to pray;
we will share your joy and love
and peace this Christmas Day.

325 Frederick William Faber (1814–63)

1 Jesus, gentlest Saviour,
God of might and power,
thou thyself art dwelling
in us at this hour.
Nature cannot hold thee,
heav'n is all too strait
for thine endless glory,
and thy royal state.

2 Yet the hearts of children
hold what worlds cannot,
and the God of wonders
loves the lowly spot.
Jesus, gentlest Saviour,
thou art in us now,
fill us full of goodness
till our hearts o'erflow.

3 Pray the prayer within us
that to heaven shall rise;
sing the song that angels
sing above the skies;
multiply our graces,
chiefly love and fear;
and, dear Lord, the chiefest,
grace to persevere.

326 D.J. Mansell

1 Jesus is Lord! Creation's voice
proclaims it,
for by his power each tree and flower
was planned and made.
Jesus is Lord! The universe declares it –
sun, moon and stars in heaven cry:
'Jesus is Lord!'

Jesus is Lord, Jesus is Lord!
Praise him with alleluias,
for Jesus is Lord.

2 Jesus is Lord! Yet from his throne eternal
in flesh he came to die in pain on
Calvary's tree.
Jesus is Lord! From him all life
proceeding –
yet gave his life a ransom thus setting us
free.

3 Jesus is Lord! O'er sin the mighty
conqueror;
from death he rose and all his foes shall
own his name.
Jesus is Lord! God sends his Holy Spirit
to show by works of power that Jesus is
Lord.

327 *Nicholas von Zinzendorf (1700–60), tr. Jane Borthwick, (1813–97) alt.*

1 Jesus, lead the way
through our life's long day,
when at times the way is cheerless,
help us follow, calm and fearless;
guide us by your hand
to the promised land.

2 Jesus be our light
in the midst of night,
let not faithless fear o'er–take us,
let not faith and hope forsake us;
may we feel you near
as we worship here.

3 When in deepest grief,
strengthen our belief.
When temptations come alluring,
make us patient and enduring;
Lord we seek your grace
in this holy place.

4 Jesus, still lead on
till our rest be won:
if you lead us through rough places,
grant us your redeeming graces.
When our course is o'er,
open heaven's door.

328 *Briege O'Hare*

1 Jesus, Lord, I'll sing a song
that's soft and low for you,
so you can join with me and sing it too.
You have said that when we pray,
then you are praying too,
and when your Father hears us,
he hears you.

Our Father, who art in heaven,
hallowed be thy name,
hallowed be thy name.

2 I believe that you are here
with me and praying too.
Your Father loves me because I love you.
Jesus, Lord, I'll sing a song that's
soft and low for you,
so you can join with me
and sing it too.

329 *Frederick William Faber (1814–63), altered*

1 Jesus, my Lord, my God, my all,
how can I love thee as I ought?
And how revere this wondrous gift
so far surpassing hope or thought?

Sweet Sacrament, we thee adore;
Oh, make us love thee more and more.

2 Had I but Mary's sinless heart
to love thee with, my dearest King,
Oh, with what bursts of fervent praise
thy goodness, Jesus, would I sing!

3 Ah, see! Within a creature's hand
the vast Creator deigns to be,
reposing, infant–like, as though
on Joseph's arm, or Mary's knee.

4 Thy body, soul, and Godhead, all;
O mystery of love divine!
I cannot compass all I have,
for all thou hast and art are mine.

5 Come now ye angels to our aid,
sound, sound God's praises higher still;
'tis God, whose power created us,
and in whose praise creation thrills.

330 *Briege O'Hare*

Jesus, the holy Lamb of God
carried the cross for me.
Jesus, the holy Lamb of God
died that I might be free.

1 He who is God made himself low:
a servant, and humbler yet,
He bowed his head as he was led
obedient unto his death.

2 Therefore has God raised him on high
and named him our Saviour and Lord:
all knees will bend in praise without end
to Jesus for ever adored.

331 *Paraphrased by Keith D. Pearson*

1 Jesus the Word has lived among us,
sharing his fullness, truth and grace,
God's only Son, the Father's loved one

reveals him to the human race.
Jesus the Word has lived among us
sharing his fullness, truth and grace.

2 He was with God from the beginning
and through him all things came to be.
He lightens darkness, conquers evil,
gives life for living, glad and free.
He was with God from the beginning
and through him all things came to be.

3 Sing praise to God who sent Christ Jesus
to be his sign of endless love;
sent him to live his life among us,
lifting our hearts to things above.
Sing praise to God who sent Christ Jesus
to be his sign of endless love!

332 *'S.N.D.'*

1 Jesus, thou art coming, holy as thou art,
thou, the God who made me,
to my sinful heart.
Jesus, I believe it, on thy only word;
kneeling, I adore thee, as my king and Lord.

2 Who am I, my Jesus, that thou com'st to me?
I have sinned against thee,
often grievously;
I am very sorry I have caused thee pain.
I will never, never, wound thy heart again.

3 Put thy kind arms round me, feeble as I am;
thou art my Good Shepherd,
I, thy little lamb;
since thou comest, Jesus, now to be my guest,
I can trust thee always, Lord, for all the rest.

4 Dearest Lord, I love thee, with my whole heart,
not for what thou givest, but for what thou art.
Come, oh, come, sweet Saviour!
Come to me, and stay,
for I want thee, Jesus, more than I can say.

5 Ah! What gift or present, Jesus, can I bring?
I have nothing worthy of my God and King;
but thou art my shepherd: I, thy little lamb,
take myself, dear Jesus, all I have and am.

6 Take my body, Jesus, eyes, and ears and tongue;
never let them, Jesus, help to do thee wrong.
Take my heart, and fill it full of love for thee;
all I have I give thee, give thyself to me.

333 *Dan Schutte*

Join in the dance of the earth's jubilation!
This is the feast of the love of God.
Shout from the heights to the end of creation:
Jesus the Saviour is risen from the grave!

1 Wake, O people; sleep no longer:
greet the breaking day!
Christ, Redeemer, Lamb and Lion,
turns the night away!

2 All creation, like a mother,
labours to give birth.
Soon the pain will be forgotten,
joy for all the earth!

3 Now our shame becomes our glory
on this holy tree.
Now the reign of death is ended;
now we are set free!

4 None on earth, no prince or power,
neither death nor life,
nothing now can ever part us
from the love of Christ!

5 Love's triumphant day of vict'ry
heaven opens wide.
On the tree of hope and glory
death itself has died!

6 Christ for ever, Lord of ages,
Love beyond our dreams:
Christ, our hope of heaven's glory
all that yet will be!

334 *Michael Lynch*

1 Jesus, you're the one I love;
you're the one I know.
You're the one who makes me strong,
Spirit in my soul.
From the clouds of yesterday,
through the night of pain,

teach me, Lord, to know your way,
know it once again.

Bread, blessed and broken for us all,
symbol of your love from the grain so tall.
Bread, blessed and broken for us all,
bread of life you give to us,
bread of life for all.

2 May the bread we break today,
may the cup we share
lift the burdens of our hearts,
lift them ev'rywhere.
Passing on to each of us
a measure of your love,
love to make us whole again,
as we share your Word.

3 Jesus, you're the one I love;
you're the one I know.
You're the one who makes me strong,
Spirit in my soul.

335 *Isaac Watts (1674–1748)*

1 Joy to the world, the Lord has come!
Let earth receive her King;
let every heart prepare Him room
and heaven and nature sing,
and heaven and nature sing,
and heaven, and heaven and nature sing!

2 Joy to the earth, the Saviour reigns!
Your sweetest songs employ
while fields and streams and hills and plains
repeat the sounding joy,
repeat the sounding joy,
repeat, repeat the sounding joy.

3 He rules the world with truth and grace,
and makes the nations prove
the glories of His righteousness,
the wonders of His love,
the wonders of His love,
the wonders, wonders of His love.

336

Canon – (2 Voices)
A
B
Ju-bi-la-te ...
Ju-bi-la-te De-o omnis ter-ra. Ser-vi-te Do-mi-no
in lae-ti-ti-a. Al-le-lu-ia, al-le-lu-ia, in lae-ti-ti-
in lae-ti-ti-
a. Al-le-lu-ia, al-le-lu-ia, in lae-ti-ti-a!
D.C.
Guitar

D G A

337 *Michael Praetorius (1571–1621)*

A B C D E F
Ju-bi-la-te De-o, Ju-bi-la-te De-o, A-le-lu-ia.

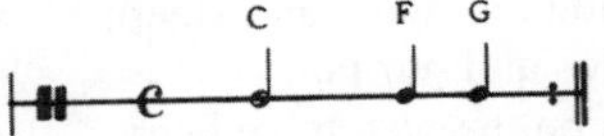
C F G

338 *Fred Dunn (1907–1979)*

Jubilate, ev'rybody,
serve the Lord in all your ways, and
come before his presence singing;
enter now his courts with praise.
For the Lord our God is gracious,
and his mercy everlasting.
Jubilate, jubilate, jubilate Deo!

339 *Charlotte Elliott (1789–1871)* *Alternate words: Marianne Farningham (1834–1909)*

1 Just as I am, without one plea,
but that thy blood was shed for me,
and that thou bidd'st me come to thee,
O Lamb of God, I come!

2 Just as I am, though tossed about
with many a conflict, many a doubt,
fighting within, and fears without,
O Lamb of God, I come!

3 Just as I am, poor, wretched, blind;
sight, riches, healing of the mind,
yea, all I need, in thee to find,
O Lamb of God, I come!

4 Just as I am, thou wilt receive,
wilt welcome, pardon, cleanse, relieve:
because thy promise I believe,
O Lamb of God, I come!

5 Just as I am (thy love unknown
hath broken every barrier down),
now, to be thine, yea, thine alone,
O Lamb of God, I come!

6 Just as I am, of that free love
the breadth, length, depth, and height
to prove,
here for a season, then above,
O Lamb of God, I come.

ALTERNATIVE WORDS FOR YOUNG PEOPLE/CONFIRMATION

7 Just as I am, thine own to be,
friend of the young, who lovest me,
to consecrate myself to thee,
O Jesus Christ, I come.

8 In the glad morning of my day,
my life to give, my vows to pay,
with no reserve and no delay,
with all my heart I come.

9 I would live ever in the light,
I would work ever for the right,
I would serve thee with all my might,
therefore to thee I come.

10 Just as I am, young, strong and free,
to be the best that I can be
for truth and righteousness, and thee,
Lord of my life, I come.

340 *Lucien Deiss*

Keep in mind that Jesus Christ has died for us
and is risen from the dead.
He is our saving Lord,
he is joy for all ages.

1 If we die with the Lord, we shall live with the Lord.

2 If we endure with the Lord, we shall reign with the Lord.

3 In him all our sorrow, in him all our joy.

4 In him hope of glory, in him all our love.

5 In him our redemption, in him all our grace.

6 In him our salvation, in him all our grace.

341 *St Gregory the Great (540 –604)* *tr. R.A. Knox (1888–1957)*

1 Keep we the fast our ancestors
learned from on high in mystic ways,
till yonder sun hath duly told
his hallowed tale of forty days.

2 This covenant, long since revealed
to patriarchs and ardent seers,
Christ by his own example sealed,
author of time, and Lord of years.

3 More wisely therefore let us walk,
sparing of food and wine and sleep;
over our trifles and our talk
more jealous be the watch we keep.

4 Still by our sins, O Lord, we grieve
thy love, so full of pardon free:
author of mercy, still reprieve
the souls that turn again to thee.

5 Remember whence our fashion came,
frail creatures, yet thy creatures still,
crush, for the glory of thy name,
the murm'rings of our stubborn will.

6 The guilt that dooms us put away,
with larger grace our prayers requite,
at last, and ever from this day,
teach us to live as in thy sight.

7 Hear us, O Trinity sublime,
and undivided unity;
so let this consecrated time
bring forth thy fruits abundantly.

342 *John L. Bell and Graham Maule*

Kindle a flame to lighten the dark
and take all fear away.

343 *George Herbert (1593–1633)*

1 King of glory, king of peace,
I will love thee;
and that love may never cease,
I will move thee.
Thou hast granted my request,
thou hast heard me;
thou didst note my working breast,
thou hast spared me.

2 Wherefore with my utmost art,
I will sing thee,
and the cream of all my heart
I will bring thee.
Though my sins against me cried,
thou didst clear me;
and alone, when they replied,
thou didst hear me.

3 Seven whole days, not one in seven,
I will praise thee;
in my heart, though not in heaven,
I can raise thee.
Small it is, in this poor sort
to enrol thee:
e'en eternity's too short
to extol thee.

344 *Spiritual*

1 Kum ba yah, my Lord, kum ba yah, *(3)*
O Lord, kum ba yah.

2 Someone's crying, Lord, kum ba yah, …

3 Someone's singing, Lord, kum ba yah, …

4 Someone's praying, Lord, kum ba yah, …

345 *Chris Bowater*

Lamb of God, Holy One,
Jesus Christ, Son of God,
lifted up willingly to die;
that I the guilty one may know
the blood once shed still freely flowing,
still cleansing, still healing.

I exalt You Jesus, my sacrifice,
I exalt You my Redeemer and my Lord.
I exalt You, worthy Lamb of God,
and in honour I bow down before Your throne.

346 *LAUDATE DOMINUM* *Jacques Berthier*

Laudate Dominum,
Laudate Dominum omnes gentes.
Alleluia.

1 Praise the Lord, all you nations,
praise him all you peoples. Alleluia.

2 Strong is his love and mercy,
he is faithful for ever. Alleluia.

3 Let ev'rything living give praise to the Lord.
Alleluia, alleluia.

4 Let ev'rything living give praise to the Lord.
Alleluia, praise to the Lord.

347 *Carey Landry*

Lay your hands gently upon us,
let their touch render your peace;
let them bring your forgiveness and healing,
lay your hands, gently lay your hands.

1 You were sent to free the broken hearted.
You were sent to give sight to the blind.
You desire to heal all our illness.
Lay your hands, gently lay your hands.

2 Lord, we come to you through one another.
Lord, we come to you in all our need.
Lord, we come to you seeking wholeness.
Lay your hands, gently lay your hands.

348 *John Henry Newman (1801–90)*

1 Lead, kindly light, amid th' encircling gloom,
lead thou me on;
the night is dark, and I am far from home,
lead thou me on.
Keep thou my feet; I do not ask to see
the distant scene; one step enough for me.

2 I was not ever thus, nor prayed that thou
shouldst lead me on;
I loved to choose and see my path; but now
lead thou me on.
I loved the garish day, and, spite of fears,
pride ruled my will; remember not past years.

3 So long thy power hath blest me, sure it still
will lead me on
o'er moor and fen, o'er crag and torrent, till
the night is gone,
and with the morn those angels faces smile
which I have loved long since, and lost awhile.

349 *Peter Skinner*

Lead me, guide me along life's way.
If I should stumble, Lord, send a helping hand.
Love me, lead me through the trials of life;
and with my friends, Lord, teach us to understand
that you have all things in your mighty hands.
Take me and fold me in your loving arms,
on the day when I come home.
Take me and fold me in your loving arms
then I shall be yours for ever.

350 *Verses: Marty Haugen, Refrain: Anonymous*

Lead us from death to life,
from falsehood to truth,
from despair to hope,
from fear to trust,
lead us from hate to love,
from war to peace;
let peace fill our hearts,
let peace fill our world,
let peace fill our universe.

1 Still all the angry cries, still all the angry guns,
still now your people die, earth's sons and daughters.
Let justice roll, let mercy pour down,
come and teach us your way of compassion.

2 So many lonely hearts, so many broken lives,
longing for love to break into their darkness.
Come, teach us love, come, teach us peace,
come and teach us your way of compassion.

3 Let justice ever roll, let mercy fill the earth,
let us begin to grow into your people.
We can be love, we can bring peace,
we can still be your way of compassion.

351 *J. Edmeston (1791–1867)*

1 Lead us, heav'nly Father, lead us
o'er the world's tempestuous sea:
guard us, guide us, keep us, feed us,
for we have no help but thee;
yet possessing ev'ry blessing
if our God our Father be.

2 Saviour, breathe forgiveness o'er us,
all our weakness thou dost know,
thou didst tread this earth before us,
thou didst feel its keenest woe;
lone and dreary, faint and weary,
through the desert thou didst go.

3 Spirit of our God, descending,
fill our hearts with heavenly joy,
love with every passion blending,
pleasure that can never cloy;
thus provided, pardoned, guided,
nothing can our peace destroy.

352 *Joseph W. Reeks (1849–1900)*

1 Leader now on earth no longer,
soldier of th'eternal king,
victor in the fight for heaven,
we thy loving praises sing.

Great Saint George,
our patron, help us,
in the conflict be thou nigh;
help us in that daily battle,
where each one must win or die.

2 Praise him who in deadly battle
never shrank from foeman's sword,
proof against all earthly weapon,
gave his life for Christ the Lord.

3 Who, when earthly war was over,
fought, but not for earth's renown;
fought, and won a nobler glory,
won the martyr's purple crown.

4 Help us when temptation presses,
we have still our crown to win,
help us when our soul is weary
fighting with the powers of sin.

5 Clothe us in thy shining armour,
place thy good sword in our hand;
teach us how to wield it, fighting
onward towards the heavenly land.

6 Onward, till, our striving over,
on life's battlefield we fall,
resting then, but ever ready,
waiting for the angel's call.

353 *Tim Manion*

Leaping the mountains, bounding the hills,
see how our God has come to meet us.
His voice is lifted; his face is joy.
Now is the season to sing our song on high.

1 Come, then, O Lord of glory, show us
your face.
Speak for we know your words are life.

2 He pastures his flock among the wild
flow'rs
and leads them to the mountain of his love.

3 All through the day, all through the night,
seek for the Lord and sing his love.

354 *Willard F. Jabusch*

Leave your country and your people,
leave your fam'ly and your friends.
Travel to the land he'll show you;
God will bless the ones he sends.

1 Go like Abraham before you,
when he heard the Father's call,
walking forth in faith and trusting;
God is master of us all.

2 Sometimes God's Word is demanding,
leave security you know,
breaking ties and bonds that hold you,
when the voice of God says: 'Go'.

3 Take the path into the desert,
barren seems the rock and sand.
God will lead you through the desert
when you follow his command.

4 Go with courage up the mountain,
climb the narrow, rocky ledge,
leave behind all things that hinder,
go with only God as pledge.

355 *Liturgy of St. James, tr. G. Moultrie (1829–85)*

1 Let all mortal flesh keep silence,
and with fear and trembling stand;
ponder nothing earthly-minded:
for with blessing in his hand,
Christ our God to earth descendeth,
our full homage to demand.

2 King of kings, yet born of Mary,
as of old on earth he stood,
Lord of lords, in human vesture –
in the Body and the Blood.
He will give to all the faithful
his own Self for heavenly Food.

3 Rank on rank the host of heaven
spreads its vanguard on the way,
as the Light of Light descendeth
from the realms of endless day,
that the powers of hell may vanish
as the darkness clears away.

4 At his feet the six–winged Seraph;
Cherubim with sleepless eye,
veil their faces to the Presence,
as with ceaseless voice they cry,
alleluia, alleluia,
alleluia, Lord most high.

356 *Traditional*

1 Let all that is within me cry holy.
Let all that is within me cry holy.
Holy, holy, holy is the Lamb that was slain.

2 Let all that is within me cry mighty …

3 Let all that is within me cry worthy …

4 Let all that is within me cry blessed …

5 Let all that is within me cry Jesus …

357 *George Herbert (1593–1633)*

1 Let all the world in every corner sing,
my God and King!
The heav'ns are not too high,
God's praise may thither fly;
the earth is not too low,
God's praises there may grow.
Let all the world in every corner sing,
my God and King!

2 Let all the world in every corner sing,
my God and King!
The church with psalms must shout,
no door can keep them out;
but, above all, the heart
must bear the longest part.
Let all the world in every corner sing,
my God and King!

358 *Dave Bilbrough*

Let there be love shared among us,
let there be love in our eyes,
may now your love sweep this nation,
cause us O Lord to arise.
Give us a fresh understanding
filled with your love that is real,
let there be love shared among us,
let there be love.

359 *Traditional*

1 Let us break bread together on our knees.
Let us break bread together on our knees.
When I fall on my knees with my face to the rising sun,
Oh Lord, have mercy on me.

2 Let us drink wine together …

3 Let us praise God together …

360 *Estelle White*

[1]Let us go forth into the world
[2]with the good news, spreading his word, for we're
[3]Easter people, saved by Christ.

361 *Fred Kaan & Mary Lu Walker*

1 Let us talents and tongues employ,
reaching out with a shout of joy:
bread is broken, the wine is poured,
Christ is spoken and seen and heard.

Jesus lives again,
earth can breathe again,
pass the Word around:
loaves abound!

2 Christ is able to make us one,
at his table he sets the tone,
teaching people to live to bless,
love in word and in deed express.

3 Jesus calls us in, sends us out
bearing fruit in a world of doubt,
gives us love to tell, bread to share:
God–Immanuel everywhere!

362 *John Milton (1608–75) based on Psalm 136 (135)*

1 Let us, with a gladsome mind,
praise the Lord, for he is kind:

For his mercies aye endure,
ever faithful, ever sure.

2 Let us blaze his name abroad,
for of gods he is the God;

3 He, with all–commanding might,
filled the new–made world with light;

4 He the golden–tressèd sun
caused all day his course to run:

5 And the horned moon at night,
'mid her spangled sisters bright:

6 All things living he doth feed,
his full hand supplies their need:

7 Let us, with a gladsome mind,
praise the Lord, for he is kind.

363 *G.W. Kitchin (1827–1912) and M.R. Newbolt (1874–1956)*

1 Lift high the cross, the Love of Christ
proclaim
till all the world adore his sacred name.

2 Come, Christians, follow where our
Captain trod,
our King victorious, Christ the Son of God:

3 Led on their way by this triumphant sign,
the hosts of God in conquering ranks
combine:

4 All new–born soldiers of the Crucified
bear on their brows the seal of him who
died:

5 This is the sign which Satan's legions
fear,
and angels veil their faces to revere:

6 Saved by this cross whereon the Lord
was slain,
the children of Adam their lost home regain:

7 From north and south, from east and west
they raise
in growing unison their song of praise:

8 O Lord, once lifted on the glorious tree,
as thou hast promised, draw us all to thee:

9 Let every race and every language tell
of him who saves our souls from death
and hell:

10 From farthest regions let them homage
bring,
and on his cross adore their sacred King:

11 Set up thy throne, that earth's despair
may cease
beneath the shadow of his healing peace:

12 For thy blest cross which doth
for all atone,
creation's praises rise before thy throne:

364 *tr. Catherine Winkworth (1827–1878), alt*

1 Lift up your heads, O mighty gates;
behold the King of glory waits!
The King of kings is drawing near;
the Saviour of the world is here.

2 O blest the land, the city blest,
where Christ the ruler is confest!
O happy hearts and happy homes
to whom this king of triumph comes!

3 Fling wide the portals of your heart;
make it a temple, set apart
from earthly use for heav'n's employ,
adorned with prayer and love and joy.

4 Come, Saviour, come with us abide;
our hearts to you we open wide:
your Holy Spirit guide us on,
until our glorious goal is won.

365 *Richard Connolly*

1 Light of our darkness, Word of God,
sent to illumine our earthly night,
you we salute with singing hearts,
bathed in the splendour of your light.

2 Sword that can pierce the inmost soul,
stripping whatever thoughts are there,
cut to the marrow of our minds,
enter our hearts and lay them bare.

3 Vessel of God's abundant life,
bearer of truth that sets us free,
breaking the deadly grasp of sin,
work in our hearts your mystery.

4 Word that has overcome the world,
seed of immortal destiny,
grow in our hearts, that we may live
sharing your deathless victory.

366 *Mary Lu Walker*

1 Light the Advent candle one.
Now the waiting has begun,
we have started on our way:
time to think of Christmas day.

Candle, candle, burning bright,
shining in the cold winter night.
Candle, candle, burning bright,
fill our hearts with Christmas light.

2 Light the Advent candle two.
Think of humble shepherds who
filled with wonder at the sight
of the child on Christmas night.

3 Light the Advent candle three.
Think of heav'nly harmony:
angels singing 'Peace on earth'
at the blessed Saviour's birth.

4 Light the Advent candle four.
Think of joy for evermore:
Christ–child in a stable born,
gift of love that Christmas morn.

5 Light the Christmas candles now!
Sing of donkey, sheep and cow.
Birthday candles for the King –
let the 'Alleluias' ring!

367 *Michael Perry*

1 Like a mighty river flowing,
like a flower in beauty growing,
far beyond all human knowing
is the perfect peace of God.

2 Like the hills serene and even,
like the coursing clouds of heaven,
like the heart that's been forgiven
is the perfect peace of God.

3 Like the summer breezes playing,
like the tall trees softly swaying,
like the lips of silent praying
is the perfect peace of God.

4 Like the morning sun ascended,
like the scents of evening blended,
like a friendship never ended
is the perfect peace of God.

5 Like the azure ocean swelling,
like the jewel all–excelling,
far beyond our human telling
is the perfect peace of God.

368 *Estelle White*

1 Like a sea without a shore
love divine is boundless.
Time is now and evermore
and his love surrounds us.

Maranatha! Maranatha!
Maranatha! Come, Lord Jesus, come!

2 So that we could all be free
he appeared among us,
blest are those who have not seen,
yet believe his promise.

3 All our visions, all our dreams,
are but ghostly shadows
of the radiant clarity
waiting at life's close.

4 Death where is your victory?
Death where is your sting?
Closer than the air we breathe
is our risen King.

369 *Bob Dufford, SJ*

Like a shepherd he feeds his flock
and gathers the lambs in his arms,
holding them carefully close to his heart,
leading them home.

1 Say to the cities of Judah:
'Prepare the way of the Lord.'
Go to the mountain–top, lift your voice:
Jerusalem, here is your God.

2 I myself will shepherd them,
for others have led them astray.
The lost I will rescue and heal their wounds
and pasture them, giving them rest.

3 Come unto me
if you are heavily burdened,
and take my yoke upon your shoulders.
I will give you rest.

370 *Response tr. Charles Watson, OSB* *Verses from 'The Psalms: A New Translation' (The Grail)*

Like as the deer that yearns for flowing
waters,
so longs my soul for God, the living God.

1 Like the deer that yearns for flowing waters:
so my soul is yearning for you my God.

2 My soul is thirsting for God, the God of
my life:
when can I enter and see the face of God?

3 These things will I remember as I pour
out my soul:
how I would lead the rejoicing crowd
into the house of God.

4 Send forth your light and your truth,
let these be my guide:
let them bring me to your holy mountain,
to the place where you dwell.

371 *Anonymous*

1 Like the dawning of the morning
on the mountains' golden heights,
like the breaking of the moonbeams
on the gloom of cloudy nights,
like a secret told by angels,
getting known upon the earth,
is the Mother's expectation
of Messiah's speedy birth.

2 Thou wert happy, blessed Mother,
with the very bliss of Heaven,
since the angel's salutation
in thy raptured ear was given;
since the Ave of the midnight
when thou wert anointed Queen,
like a river overflowing
hath the grace within thee been.

3 Thou hast waited, Child of David!
and thy waiting now is o'er!
Thou hast seen Him, Blessed Mother!
and wilt see Him evermore!
O, His human face and features
they were passing sweet to see:
thou beholdest them this moment,
Mother, show them now to me!

372 *Traditional Czech, tr. O.B.C..*

1 Little Jesus, sweetly sleep, do not stir;
we will lend a coat of fur,
we will rock you, rock you, rock you,
we will rock you, rock you, rock you,
see the fur to keep you warm
snugly round your tiny form.

2 Mary's little baby sleep, sweetly sleep,
sleep in comfort, slumber deep;
we will rock you, rock you, rock you,
we will rock you, rock you, rock you,
we will serve you all we can,
darling, darling little man.

373 *Charles Wesley (1707–1788)*

1 Lo, He comes with clouds descending,
once for favour'd sinners slain;
thousand thousand saints attending
swell the triumph of His train:
Alleluia! Alleluia! Alleluia!
God appears on earth to reign.

2 Every eye shall now behold Him
robed in glorious majesty;

those who set at naught and sold Him,
pierced and nailed Him to the tree,
deeply wailing, deeply wailing, deeply
wailing,
shall their true Messiah see.

3 Those dear tokens of His passion
still His dazzling body bears,
cause of endless exultation
to His ransomed worshippers:
with what rapture, with what rapture,
with what rapture,
gaze we on those glorious scars!

4 Yea, Amen, let all adore Thee,
high on Thine eternal throne;
Saviour, take the power and glory,
claim the kingdom for Thine own:
come, Lord Jesus! come, Lord Jesus!
come, Lord Jesus!
Everlasting God, come down!

374 *Ian Sharp*

1 Long ago in Bethlehem,
you were lying in a manger
in the midst of human danger,
at your mother's knee.
Hosanna, alleluia, *(3)*
at your mother's knee.

2 Now as King we hail the baby,
living faith proclaims the story
of that humble manger glory,
stabled in the hay.
Hosanna, alleluia, *(3)*
Christ is King today.

375 *Fred Pratt Green*

1 Long ago, prophets knew
Christ would come, born a Jew,
come to make all things new,
bear his people's burden,
freely love and pardon.

Ring, bells, ring, ring, ring!
Sing, choirs, sing, sing, sing!
When he comes, when he comes,
who will make him welcome?

2 God in time, God in man,
this is God's timeless plan:
he will come, as a man,
born himself of woman,
God divinely human:

3 Mary, hail! Though afraid,
she believed, she obeyed.
In her womb God is laid,
till the time expected,
nurtured and protected:

4 Journey ends: where afar
Bethlem shines, like a star,
stable door stands ajar.
Unborn Son of Mary,
Saviour, do not tarry.

Ring, bells, ring, ring, ring!
Sing, choirs, sing, sing, sing!
Jesus comes, Jesus comes:
we will make him welcome.

376 *Jodi Page Clark*

1 'Look around you, can you see?
Times are troubled, people grieve.
See the violence, feel the hardness;
all my people, weep with me.'

Kyrie eleison,
Christe eleison,
Kyrie eleison.

2 'Walk among them, I'll go with you.
Reach out to them with my hands.
Suffer with me, and together we will
serve them,
help them stand.'

3 Forgive us, Father; hear our prayer.
We would walk with you anywhere,
through your suff'ring, with forgiveness;
take your life into the world.

377 *Sister M. Teresine*

1 Lord accept the gifts we offer
at this Eucharistic feast;
bread and wine to be transformed now
through the action of thy priest.
Take us too, Lord, and transform us,
be thy grace in us increased.

2 May our souls be pure and spotless
as the host of wheat so fine;
may all stain of sin be crushed out,
like the grape that forms the wine,
as we, too, become partakers
in this sacrifice divine.

3 Take our gifts, almighty Father,
living God, eternal, true,
which we give through Christ, our Saviour,
pleading here for us anew.
Grant salvation to all present,
and our faith and love renew.

378 *Patrick Lee*

1 Lord, accept the praise now given
in the pledge this man and wife
make to worship, in each other,
you, the author of all life:
marriage wine, Christ's first sign,
promised sharing life divine.

2 Build the house which here is founded,
raise the walls, defend the gate,
make the love of Christ its hearthstone,
ground it on the rock of faith;
set secure, Lord, ensure
honour, trust and love endure.

3 Send him health and strength to husband
her, now standing by his side;
may she, like the vine be fruitful,
Holy Spirit be their guide:
love and praise, joy always
grace their hearts and light their days.

4 Grant their children grow to goodness,
strong as sturdy olive trees;
let their children's children gather
joyfully about their knees;
life prolong, fill with song,
Israel's peace with them belong.

379 *G.H. Bourne (1840–1925)*

1 Lord, enthroned in heavenly splendour,
first begotten from the dead,
thou alone, our strong defender,
liftest up thy people's head.
Alleluia, alleluia,
Jesus, true and living bread!

2 Prince of life, for us thou livest,
by thy body souls are healed;
Prince of peace, thy peace thou givest,
by thy blood is pardon sealed;
alleluia, alleluia,
Word of God, in flesh revealed.

3 Paschal Lamb! thine offering, finished
once for all when thou wast slain,
in its fullness undiminished
shall for evermore remain,
alleluia, alleluia,
cleansing souls from every stain.

4 Great high priest of our profession,
through the veil thou enteredest in;
by thy mighty intercession
grace and mercy thou canst win:
alleluia, alleluia,
only sacrifice for sin.

5 Life–imparting heavenly manna,
stricken rock, with streaming side,
heaven and earth with loud hosanna
worship thee, the Lamb who died;
alleluia, alleluia,
risen, ascended, glorified!

380 *Sister M. Xavier*

1 Lord, for tomorrow and its needs
I do not pray;
keep me, my God, from stain of sin,
just for today.

2 Let me both diligently work
and duly pray;
let me be kind in word and deed,
just for today.

3 Let me be slow to do my will,
prompt to obey;
help me to mortify my flesh,
just for today.

4 Let me no wrong or idle word
unthinking say;
set thou a seal upon my lips,
just for today.

5 Let me in season, Lord, be grave,
in season, gay;
let me be faithful to thy grace,
just for today.

6 And if today my tide of life
should ebb away,
give me thy sacraments divine,
sweet Lord, today.

7 So, for tomorrow and its needs
I do not pray;
but keep me, guide me, love me, Lord,
just for today.

381 *Patrick Appleford*

1 Lord, in everything I do
let me always follow you;
let the moments of my days
overflow with endless praise;
take my hands and let them move
at the impulse of your love;
every move that I shall make,
Lord, direct the steps I take.

2 Lord, with all your people here
you invite me to draw near;
Lord, accept the gifts I bring,
Lord, accept the praise I sing.
Take my lips and let them speak
of your goodness through the week;
let me echo this refrain
till I come to you again.

3 As I listen to your call,
Lord, I want to give my all;
take my heart and mind and use
every power you shall choose;
all I have has come from you
and I offer back to you
only what was yours before:
take my life for evermore.

382 *John L. Bell and Graham Maule*

1 Lord Jesus Christ, shall I stand still
and stare at you hung on the tree;
or shall I move to where you move
and die and live again for me?
Shall I to sin and failure cling,
consorting with the guilt I hate;
or on your shoulders shall I fling
the wrong I breed and contemplate?

2 Shall I your story read and tell
to note your mark on history;
or shall I make your story mine
and live by faith and mystery?
Shall I embrace the love you show
and covet this sweet, holy thing:
or of that love shall my heart speak,
my hands relate, my being sing?

3 Shall I retreat from where you fall
and seek a safer path through life;
or shall I meet you in the world
where peace is scarce, injustice rife?
Lord Jesus Christ, the God who lives
to love and die and rise again,
make me the who, and you the why,
your way the how, and now the when.

383 *Patrick Appleford*

1 Lord, Jesus Christ,
you have come to us,
you are one with us, Mary's son.
Cleansing our souls from all their sin,
pouring your love and goodness in,
Jesus our love for you we sing,
living Lord.

2 Lord Jesus Christ,
now and ev'ry day
teach us how to pray, Son of God.
You have commanded us to do
this in remembrance, Lord, of you:
into our lives your pow'r breaks through,
living Lord.

3 Lord Jesus Christ,
you have come to us,
born as one of us, Mary's Son.
Led out to die on Calvary,
risen from death to set us free,
living Lord Jesus, help us see
you are Lord.

4 Lord Jesus Christ,
I would come to you,
live my life for you, Son of God.
All your commands I know are true,
your many gifts will make me new,
into my life your pow'r breaks through,
living Lord.

384 *Bishop Synesius (375–430) tr. A. W. Chatfield (1808–96)*

1 Lord Jesus, think on me,
and purge away my sin;
from earthborn passions set me free,
and make me pure within.

2 Lord Jesus, think on me,
with care and woe oppressed;
let me thy loving servant be,
and taste thy promised rest.

3 Lord Jesus, think on me
amid the battle's strife;
in all my pain and misery
be thou my health and life.

4 Lord Jesus, think on me,
nor let me go astray;
through darkness and perplexity
point thou the heavenly way.

5 Lord Jesus, think on me,
when flows the tempest high:
when on doth rush the enemy,
O Saviour, be thou nigh.

6 Lord Jesus, think on me,
that, when the flood is past,
I may the eternal brightness see,
and share thy joy at last.

385 *Based on St Francis of Assisi*

Lord, make me an instrument of thy peace.

1 Where there is hatred, let me sow love,
where there is injury, pardon.

2 Where there is doubt, let me bring faith,
where there's despair, hope.

3 Where there is darkness, let me bring light,
where there is sadness, joy.

4 Grant I may not seek to be consoled as to
console;
not seek to be understood as to understand;
to be loved as to love.

5 For it is in giving that we receive,
in pardoning that we are pardoned;
and it is in dying that we are born to
eternal life.

386 *Jan Struther (1901–53)*

1 Lord of all hopefulness,
Lord of all joy,
whose trust, ever child-like,
no cares could destroy,
be there at our waking,
and give us, we pray,
your bliss in our hearts, Lord,
at the break of the day.

2 Lord of all eagerness,
Lord of all faith,
whose strong hands were skilled
at the plane and the lathe,
be there at our labours
and give us, we pray,
your strength in our hearts, Lord,
at the noon of the day.

3 Lord of all kindliness,
Lord of all grace,
your hands swift to welcome,
your arms to embrace,
be there at our homing
and give us, we pray,
your love in our hearts, Lord,
at the eve of the day.

4 Lord of all gentleness,
Lord of all calm,
whose voice is contentment,
whose presence is balm,
be there at our sleeping
and give us, we pray,
your peace in our hearts, Lord,
at the end of the day.

387 *Averil Norton*

1 Lord of all loving, we stand before you,
asking your blessing on us today,
love in our union this day beginning,
life–long communion every new day.

2 Lord of our living, grant in good measure
grace for forgiving each fault we find,
holding together in time of trouble
strength for each other, loving and kind.

3 Lord of salvation, daily we offer
fresh consecration, blessing and praise.
Find you in work–life, friends for our
sharing,
joy in our home–life through all our days.

4 Lord of all power, joy is our crowning,
faith is our strong tower, hope is our peace.
Love is the promise golden before us,
grant that our gladness never may cease.

388 *Graham Kendrick*

1 Lord, the light of Your love is shining
in the midst of the darkness, shining;
Jesus, Light of the World, shine upon us,
set us free by the truth You now bring us,
shine on me, shine on me.

Shine, Jesus, shine,
fill this land with the Father's glory;
blaze, Spirit, blaze,
set our hearts on fire.
Flow, river, flow,
flood the nations with grace and mercy;
send forth Your word, Lord,
and let there be light.

2 Lord, I come to Your awesome presence,
from the shadows into Your radiance;
by the blood I may enter Your brightness,
search me, try me, consume all my darkness.
Shine on me, shine on me.

3 As we gaze on Your kingly brightness
so our faces display Your likeness,
ever changing from glory to glory,
mirrored here may our lives tell Your story.
Shine on me, shine on me.

389 *Denis E. Hurley*

1 Lord, this paschal time reminds us
how you came back from the dead.
Firm and true the faith that binds us
to our glorious, risen Head.
Alleluia, alleluia,
you have risen as you said.

2 'Neath the burden of our labour,
'mid our joy and pain and strife,
in our trying to be neighbour,
to be parent, husband, wife;
alleluia, alleluia,
be to us the source of life.

3 Make us true to our vocation
with the strength that comes from you;
make our life a dedication
with the love that you imbue.
Alleluia, alleluia,
grace and peace in us renew.

4 Hold this vision, Lord, before us;
in this hope our faith sustain:
that to life you will restore us
when at last you come again.
Alleluia, alleluia,
make us worthy of your reign.

390 *H.W. Baker (1875–1959)*

1 Lord, thy word abideth,
and our footsteps guideth;
who its truth believeth
light and joy receiveth.

2 When our foes are near us,
then thy word doth cheer us,
word of consolation,
message of salvation.

3 When the storms are o'er us,
and dark clouds before us,
then its light directeth,
and our way protecteth.

4 Word of mercy, giving
courage to the living;
word of life, supplying
comfort to the dying!

5 O that we discerning
its most holy learning,
Lord, may love and fear thee,
evermore be near thee.

391 *Sebastian Temple*

1 Lord, we pray for golden peace,
peace all over the land,
may people dwell in liberty,
all walking hand in hand.

Banish fear and ignorance,
hunger, thirst and pain.
Banish hate and poverty,
let no–one live in vain,
let no–one live in vain.

2 Keep us all for ever one,
one in love and in grace.
And wipe away all war and strife,
give freedom to each race.

3 Let your justice reign supreme.
Righteousness always done.
Let goodness rule the hearts of all
and evil overcome.

392 *Claudia Frances Hernaman (1838–98)*

1 Lord, who throughout these forty days
for us didst fast and pray,
teach us with thee to mourn our sins,
and at thy side to stay.

2 As thou with Satan didst contend,
and didst the victory win,
O give us strength in thee to fight,
in thee to conquer sin.

3 As thirst and hunger thou didst bear,
so teach us, gracious Lord,
to die to self, and daily live
by thy most holy word.

4 And through these days of penitence,
and through thy Passiontide,
yea, evermore, in life and death,
Lord Christ, with us abide.

393 *Graham Kendrick*

1 Lord, You are so precious to me,
Lord, You are so precious to me
and I love You, yes I love You
because You first loved me.

2 Lord, You are so gracious to me,
Lord, You are so gracious to me
and I love You, yes, I love You
because You first loved me.

394 *Jeffrey Rowthorn*

1 Lord, you give the great commission:
'Heal the sick and preach the word.'
Lest the Church neglect its mission,
and the Gospel go unheard,
help us witness to your purpose
with renewed integrity;

With the Spirit's gifts empower us
for the work of ministry.

2 Lord, you call us to your service:
'In my name baptise and teach.'
That the world may trust your promise,
life abundant meant for each,
give us all new fervour, draw us
closer in community;

3 Lord, you make the common holy:
'This my body, this my blood.'
Let us all, for earth's true glory,
daily lift life heavenward,
asking that the world around us
share your children's liberty;

4 Lord, you show us love's true measure;
'Father, what they do, forgive.'
Yet we hoard as private treasure

all that you so freely give.
May your care and mercy lead us
to a just society;

With the Spirit's gifts empower us
for the work of ministry.

5 Lord, you bless with words assuring:
'I am with you to the end.'
Faith and hope and love restoring,
may we serve as you intend,
and, amid the cares that claim us,
hold in mind eternity;

395 *C. Gabarain, tr. Robert C. Trupia*

1 Lord, you have come to the lakeside,
seeking neither wealthy nor wise folk,
you only ask, Lord, that I should love you.

With love you have looked in my eyes, Lord,
smiling gently, you called me by name;
and I left my boat by the lakeside,
now with you I will seek other shores.

2 Lord, you well know that I carry
in my boat no treasure nor weapon.
I bring you only my willing labour.

3 Lord, you have need of my hands;
I shall labour that others may rest;
and from my love, Lord, may others love
you.

4 Lord, other seas call me onward;
hope eternal for hearts that are searching;
and love will bind us as friends for ever.

396 *Stephen Dean*

Lord, your love has drawn us near,
perfect love which casts out fear,
love has sought us, homeward brought us,
joined us in communion here.

1 How can I repay the Lord,
who feeds us with his word,
with bread and wine?
Sing in homage all your days,
a sacrifice of praise
will be our sign.

2 He who calls us to be here,
who calms us in our fear,
will guide our way;
He who gave his very life,
who conquered in the strife,
will light our day.

3 Every creature that God feeds,
praise him who fills your needs,
lift up your voice;
every creature that has breath,
praise him who conquered death,
and still rejoice!

397 *Christina Rossetti (1830–94), altered*

1 Love came down at Christmas,
love all lovely, love divine:
love was born at Christmas,
star and angels gave the sign.

(Sing Nowell, Sing Nowell, Sing Nowell.)

2 Worship we the Godhead,
love incarnate, love divine;
worship we our Jesus:
but wherewith for sacred sign?

(Sing Nowell, Sing Nowell, Sing Nowell.)

3 Love shall be our token,
love be yours and love be mine,
love to God and all the world,
love for plea and gift and sign.

(Sing Nowell, Sing Nowell, Sing Nowell.)

The refrain is not sung when the tune Gartan is sung.

398 *Charles Wesley (1707–88)*

1 Love divine, all loves excelling,
joy of heav'n, to earth come down,
fix in us thy humble dwelling,
all thy faithful mercies crown.

2 Jesus, thou art all compassion,
pure unbounded love thou art;
visit us with thy salvation,
enter every trembling heart.

3 Come, almighty to deliver,
let us all thy life receive;
suddenly return, and never,
never more thy temples leave.

4 Thee we would be always blessing,
serve thee as thy hosts above;
pray, and praise thee without ceasing,
glory in thy perfect love.

5 Finish then thy new creation,
pure and sinless let us be;
let us see thy great salvation
perfectly restored in thee.

6 Changed from glory into glory,
till in heaven we take our place,
till we cast our crowns before thee,
lost in wonder, love, and praise.

399 *Luke Connaughton (1919–79)*

1 Love is his word, love is his way,
feasting with men, fasting alone,
living and dying, rising again,
love, only love, is his way.

Richer than gold is the love of my Lord:
better than splendour and wealth.

2 Love is his way, love is his mark,
sharing his last Passover feast,
Christ at his table, host to the Twelve,
love, only love, is his mark.

3 Love is his mark, love is his sign,
bread for our strength, wine for our joy,
'This is my body, this is my blood,'
love, only love, is his sign.

4 Love is his sign, love is his news,
'Do this,' he said, 'lest you forget
all my deep sorrow, all my dear blood,'
love, only love, is his news.

5 Love is his news, love is his name,
we are his own, chosen and called,
family, brethren, cousins and kin.
Love, only love, is his name.

6 Love is his name, love is his law.
Hear his command, all who are his:
'Love one another, I have loved you.'
Love, only love, is his law.

7 Love is his law, love is his word:
love of the Lord, Father and Word,
love of the Spirit, God ever one,
love, only love, is his word.

400 Grant to us, O Lord, a heart renewed

Lucien Deiss

Grant to us, O Lord, a heart re- newed; re- cre-ate in

us your own spi - rit, Lord! 1.Be- hold, the days are co - ming,

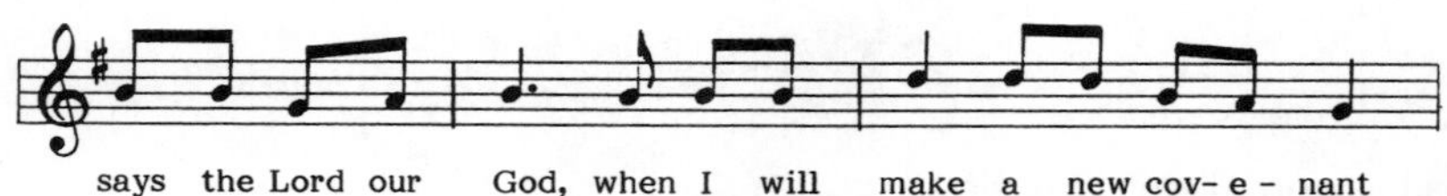
says the Lord our God, when I will make a new cov- e - nant

with the house of___ Is - ra - el. 2. Deep wi - thin their be- ing

I will im- plant my__ law; I will write it in their hearts.

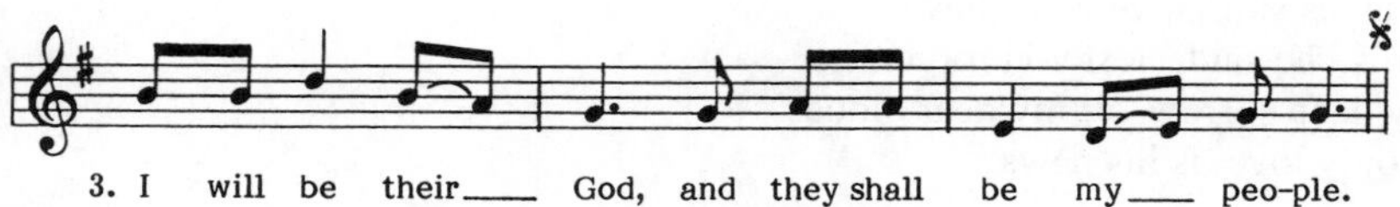
3. I will be their___ God, and they shall be my___ peo-ple.

4. And for all their faults I will grant for - give - ness; ne- ver

more will I re - mem- ber their sins.

401 Water of life

Stephen Dean

Rite of Blessing of Water

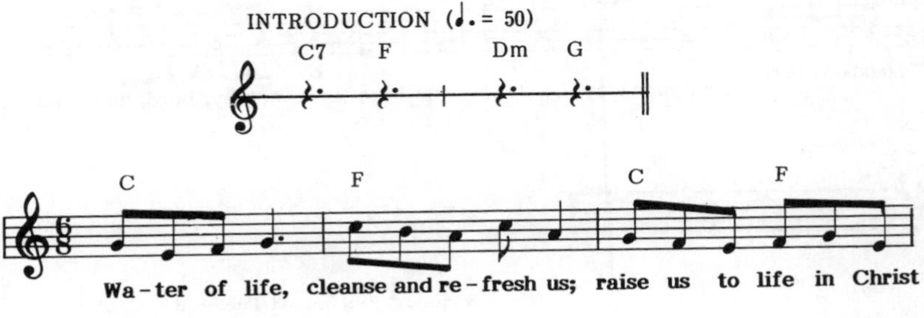
INTRODUCTION (♩. = 50)
C7 F Dm G
C F C F
Wa - ter of life, cleanse and re - fresh us; raise us to life in Christ

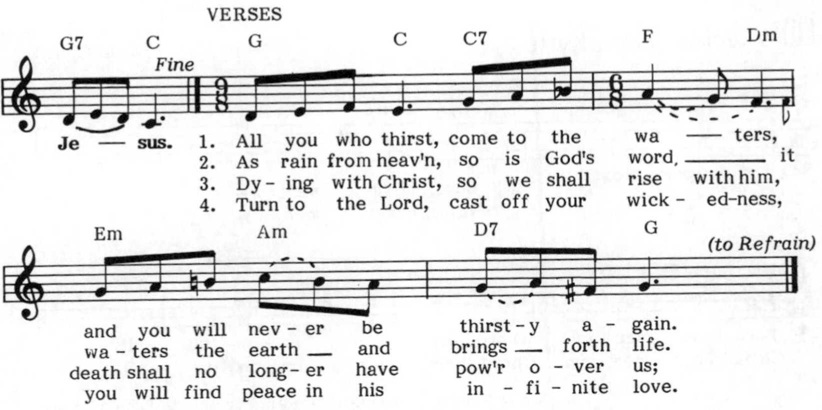
VERSES
G7 C G C C7 F Dm
Fine
Je — sus.
1. All you who thirst, come to the wa — ters,
2. As rain from heav'n, so is God's word, — it
3. Dy - ing with Christ, so we shall rise with him,
4. Turn to the Lord, cast off your wick - ed-ness,
Em Am D7 G
(to Refrain)
and you will nev - er be thirst - y a - gain.
wa - ters the earth — and brings — forth life.
death shall no long - er have pow'r o - ver us;
you will find peace in his in - fi - nite love.

402 Penitential Litany

Paul Inwood

Cantor
♩ = c.48
(spoken text....)
Have mer- cy, Lord have mer -

All
cy; Have mer-cy, Lord, have mer- cy.
(spoken text.....)

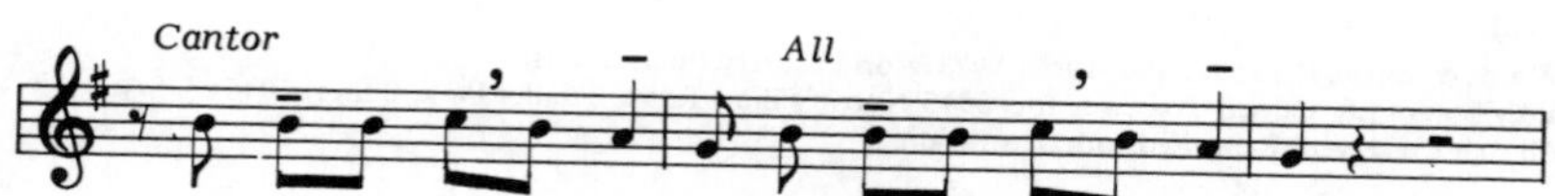
Cantor
All
Have mer-cy, Christ have mer-cy;Have mercy,Christ have mercy.

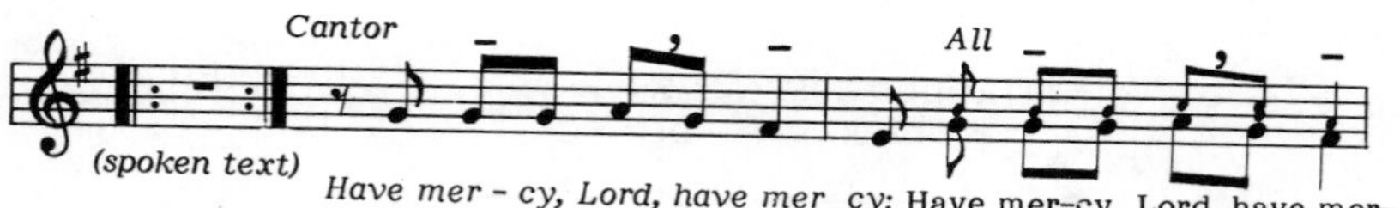
Cantor
All
(spoken text)
Have mer - cy, Lord, have mer cy; Have mer-cy, Lord, have mer-

cy.

403 White Light Kyrie

David Ogden

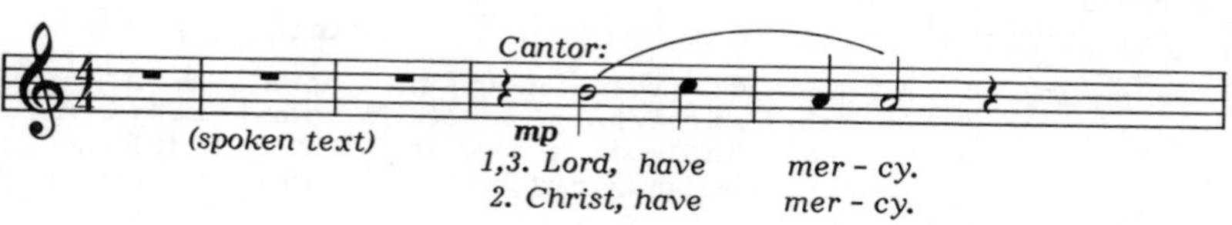
Cantor:
(spoken text)
mp
1,3. Lord, have mer - cy.
2. Christ, have mer - cy.

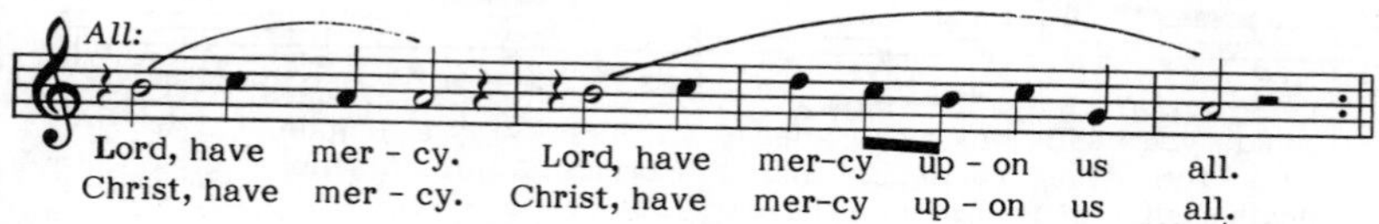
All:
Lord, have mer - cy. Lord, have mer-cy up - on us all.
Christ, have mer - cy. Christ, have mer-cy up - on us all.

404 Lord, have mercy (Mass of Peace)

Seoirse Bodley

Andante
Lord, have mer–cy. Christ, have mer–cy. Lord, have mer–cy. A — men.

405 Glory to God (Mass of Peace)

Seoirse Bodley

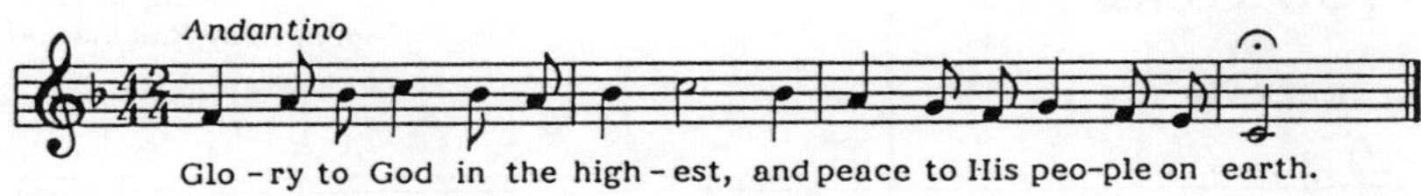
Andantino
Glo - ry to God in the high - est, and peace to His peo-ple on earth.

Lord God, hea-ven-ly King,_ Al - migh - ty_ God and_ Fa - ther, we

wor - ship_ you,_ we give you_ thanks,_ we praise you for your_ glo-ry.

*very softly
Lord Je - sus_ Christ, on-ly Son of the Fa-ther, Lord God Lamb of God, you

take a —way the_ sin_ of the world, have mer-cy on us. You are

sea - ted at the right hand of the Fa - ther, re - ceive our prayer. For

You a - lone are the Ho - ly One. You a - lone are the Lord,_

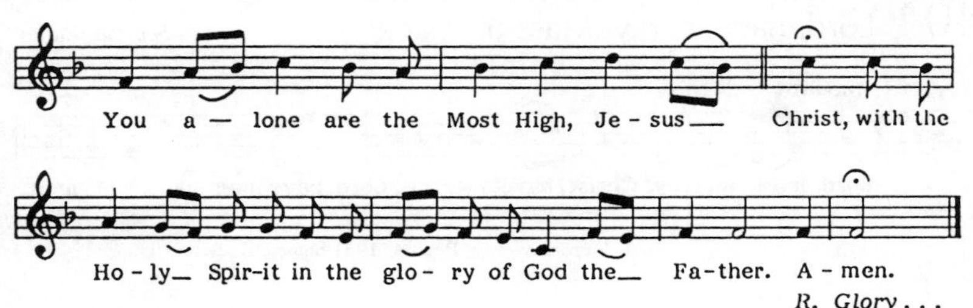
You a — lone are the Most High, Je - sus — Christ, with the
Ho - ly — Spir-it in the glo - ry of God the — Fa-ther. A - men.
R. Glory . . .

406 Gloria!

George Salazar
Arranged by Paul Inwood

REFRAIN

¡Glo – ria! ¡Glo – ria! ¡Glo– ria al Se – ñor.
Glo – ry! Glo – ry! Glo – ry to God!
¡Glo – ria! ¡Glo – ria! ¡Glo– ria! a mi Dios.
Glo – ry! Glo – ry! Glo – ry to God!

VERSES

Cue size notes in v.3

1. Glo - ry to God in the heights of the hea - vens.
2. Son - of the Fa - ther, all glo - ry and wor - ship;
3. You take a - way___ the sin of the world;___
4. Sea - ted in pow'r at the right of the Fa - ther,
5. And with the Spi - rit of love e - ver - las - ting,

Peace to God's peo - ple, all peo - ple on earth.
praise and thanks-gi - ving to you. Lamb of God.
have mer - cy on us, re - ceive___ our prayer.
Je - sus a - lone is the Lord, the Most High.
reig - ning in glo - ry for e - ver. A - men.

407 Coventry Gloria

Peter Jones

REFRAIN 1: Cantor/All repeat

Glo–ry to God, glo–ry in the high–est. Peace to his peo–ple, peace on earth.

Cantor: Lord God, heavenly King, almighty God and Father. **(Refrain 1)**

Cantor: We worship you. **(Refrain 2)**

REFRAIN 2: All

glo - ry in the high - est.

Cantor: Give you thanks, **(Refrain 2)**

Cantor: Praise you for your glory. **(Refrain 1)**

Cantor: Lord Jesus Christ, only Son of the Father, Lord God, Lamb of God, you take away the sin of the world; have mercy on us **(Refrain 3)**

REFRAIN 3: All

have mer - cy on us;

Cantor: You are seated at the right hand of the Father: receive our prayer, **(Refrain 4)**

REFRAIN 4: All

re - ceive our___ prayer.

Cantor: Glory to God, glory in the highest. Peace to his people, peace on earth. **(Refrain 1)**

Cantor: For you alone are the Holy one, you alone are the Lord, you alone are the most high, Jesus Christ, with the Holy Spirit, in the glory of God, the glory of God the Father. **(Refrain 1)**

Cantor: Amen. Amen.

408 Gloria, gloria, in excelsis Deo (Anderson)

Mike Anderson

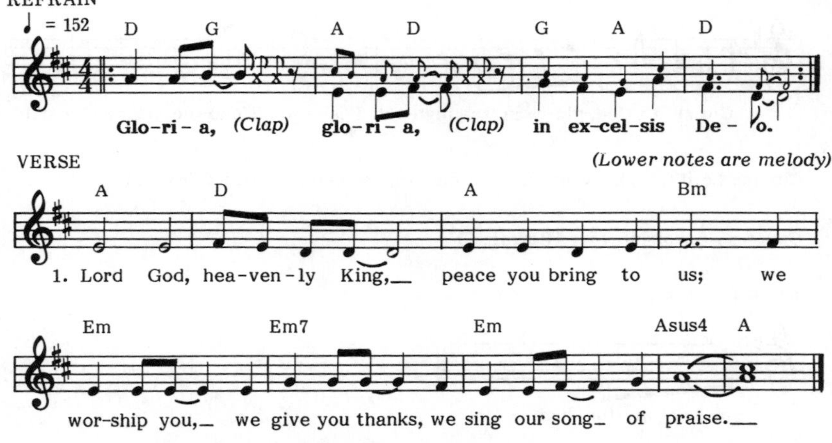
REFRAIN
♩ = 152
D G A D G A D
Glo-ri - a, (Clap) glo-ri - a, (Clap) in ex-cel-sis De - o.
VERSE
(Lower notes are melody)
A D A Bm
1. Lord God, hea-ven-ly King, peace you bring to us; we
Em Em7 Em Asus4 A
wor-ship you, we give you thanks, we sing our song of praise.

2. Jesus, Saviour of all, Lord God, Lamb of God
you take away our sins, Oh Lord, have mercy on us all.

3. At the Father's right hand, Lord receive our prayer,
for you alone are the Holy One, and you alone are Lord.

4. Glory Father and Son, Glory Holy Spirit,
to you we raise our hands up high, we glorify your name.

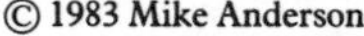

409 Gloria

Francis Duffy

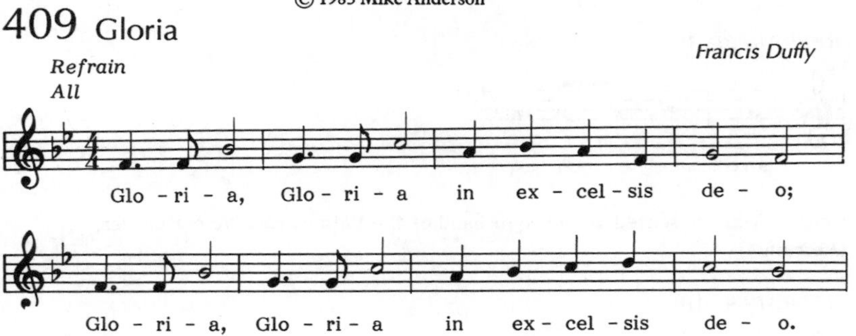
Refrain
All
Glo - ri - a, Glo - ri - a in ex - cel - sis de - o;
Glo - ri - a, Glo - ri - a in ex - cel - sis de - o.

1 Glory to God in the highest and peace to his people on earth.
Lord God, heavenly King, almighty God and Father,
we worship you, we give you thanks we praise you for your glory. *Refrain*

2 Lord Jesus Christ, only Son of the Father, Lord God, Lamb of God,
you take away the sins of the world; have mercy on us;
you are seated at the right hand of the Father; receive our prayer. *Refrain*

3 For you alone are the Holy One, you alone are the Lord,
you alone are the Most High, Jesus Christ,
with the Holy Spirit, in the glory of God the Father. *Refrain*

410 Celtic Alleluia

Christopher Walker and Fintan P O'Carroll

REFRAIN:

Al - le - lu - ia, al - le - lu - ia!

Fine
Al - le - lu - ia, al - le - lu - ia!

VERSES

1. Fa - ther we praise you as Lord, all of the
2. Bless - ed a - pos - tles sing praise; proph - ets and
3. You are the Christ ev - er - last - ing, born for us
4. Help those you saved by your blood, raise them to

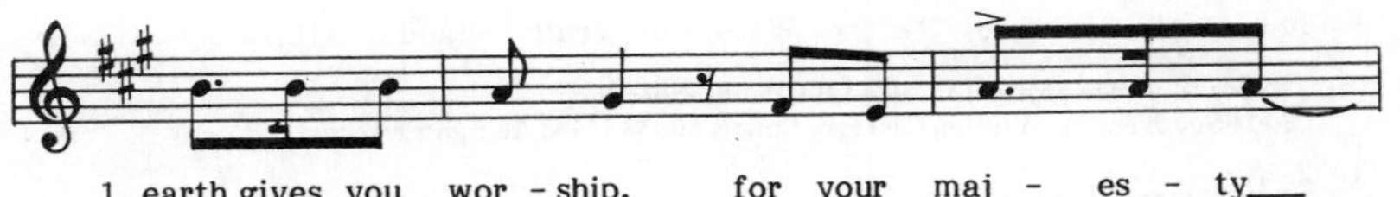
1. earth gives you wor - ship, for your maj - es - ty___
2. mar - tyrs give glo - ry; "For your maj - es - ty___
3. all of a Vir - gin, you have con - quered death,_
4. life with your mar - tyrs. Save your peo - ple, Lord,_

1. ____fills the heav - ens, fills the earth. (to Refrain)
2. ____praise the Spir - it, praise the Son!" (to Refrain)
3. _____ o - pened heav - en to all be - liev - ers. (to Refrain)
4. _____as their rul - er raise them up. (to Refrain)

Alternate verses for Easter

1 Give thanks to the Lord for he is good.
The love of the Lord knows no ending.
Sons of Israel, say:
'His love has no end.' *(Refrain)*

2 The right hand of God raised me up.
The hand of the Lord has triumphed.
I shall never die – I shall live
telling his deeds. *(Refrain)*

3 The stone which the builders rejected
becomes the conerstone chosen.
Praise the work of God for this
marvel in our eyes! *(Refrain)*

Verses for Going forth (Recessional)

1 Now with the strength of your Word,
send us to be your disciples,
to bring all the world
to the joy of your kingdom.

2 Now we are called to go forth
filled with the power of your Spirit,
to serve everyone
in the name of the Lord.

Christopher Walker

411 Gospel Acclamation (Mass of Creation)

Marty Haugen

Cantor:

1.,5. Praise the God of all cre - a - tion, God of mer - cy and com - pas - sion:
2. Tree of life and end - less wis - dom, be our root, our growth and glo - ry:
3. Liv - ing Wa - ter, we are thirst - ing for the life that you have prom - ised:
4. Come, O Spir - it, kin - dle fi - re in the hearts of all your peo - ple:

Assembly: Al - le - lu - ia! Al - le - lu - ia! *final time rit.* Praise the Word of Truth and Life!

412 Salisbury Alleluia

Christopher Walker

refrain:

Al - le-lu-ia, al- le - lu -ia, al- le- lu- ia. al- le- lu - ia.

413 Alleluia VII (Taizé)

Jacques Berthier

Mixed voices
Light and lively ♩ = 116
Al - le - lu - ia, al - le - lu - ia, al - le - lu -
ia. Al - le - lu - ia, al - le - lu - ia, al - le - lu -

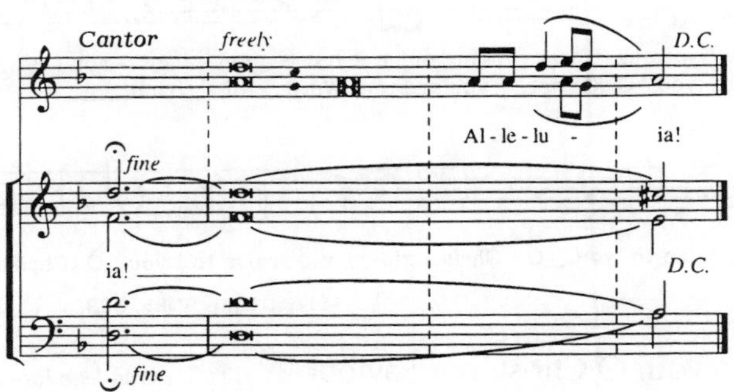
Cantor
freely
D.C.
Al - le - lu - ia!
fine
ia!
D.C.
fine

414 Glory and praise to you

Chris O'Hara

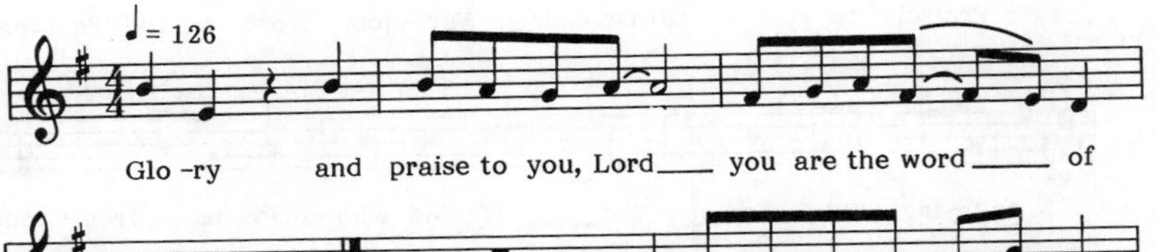

♩ = 126

Glo -ry and praise to you, Lord you are the word of life.

verse: "I am the light of the world", says the Lord.

"An - y- one who fol - lows me will have the light of life."

D.C.

415 Praise to you, O Christ, King of eternal glory

James Walsh

Praise__ to you O Christ, king of e - ter - nal glo - ry!
or: Glo - ry to you O Christ, you are the Word__ of God!____
or: Glo-ry and praise to you,_O Christ; glo-ry and praise to you,_O Christ!
Music © James Walsh, OSB.
416 Praise to you, O Christ, our Saviour
Bernadette Farrell
REFRAIN:
Praise__ to you, O Christ, our___ Sav - iour, Word of the Fa - ther,
call - ing us to life;___ Son____ of God who leads us to free - dom:
glo - ry to you, Lord Je- sus Christ!
1-4 to Verses
Final Fine
Christ!
1. You are the Word who calls us out of dark - ness; you are the
2. You are the one whom proph-ets hoped and longed for; you are the
3. You are the Word who calls us to be ser - vants; you are the
4. You are the Word who binds us and u - nites us; you are the

1. Word who leads us in - to light;_____ you are the Word who
2. one who speaks to us to - day;_____ you are the one who
3. Word whose on - ly law is love;_____ you are the Word made
4. Word who calls us to be one;_____ you are the Word who

D.C.

1. brings us through the des -ert: glo- ry to you, Lord Je - sus Christ!
2. leads us to our fu- ture: glo- ry to you, Lord Je - sus Christ!
3. flesh who lives a-mong us: glo- ry to you, Lord Je - sus Christ!
4. teach- es us for-give-ness: glo- ry to you, Lord Je - sus Christ!

417 We believe

Christopher Walker

REFRAIN
♩ = 108

We be-lieve in one__ God.

Fine

We be-lieve in one Lord. We be-lieve in one Spi - rit.____

VERSES

1 We believe in God the Father almighty,
creator of heaven and earth.

2 We believe in Jesus, his Son our Lord,
who was born of the Virgin Mary.

3 Who was crucified on a cross,
and for us he suffered death.

4 We believe he rose from the dead,
and is seated at the Father's right hand.

5 And in the Holy Spirit, the holy catholic church,
the communion of saints.

6 And the forgiveness of sins,the resurrection
and life for evermore!

Christopher Walker

418 Come, Lord Jesus, maranatha!

Christopher Walker

Cantor: Come, Lord Je - sus, ma - ra - na - tha!

All & choir Come, Lord Je - sus, ma - ra - na - tha!
S
A
T
B

419 Lord, in your mercy, hear our prayer

Paul Inwood

cantor: Lord, in your mer - cy. all: Hear our prayer.

420 In our need, we pray to the Lord

Patrick Geary

♩ = 108
CANTOR
In our need we pray to the Lord.
PEOPLE
Hear us, O Lord, and ans - wer our prayer.

421 Through our lives

The Iona Community

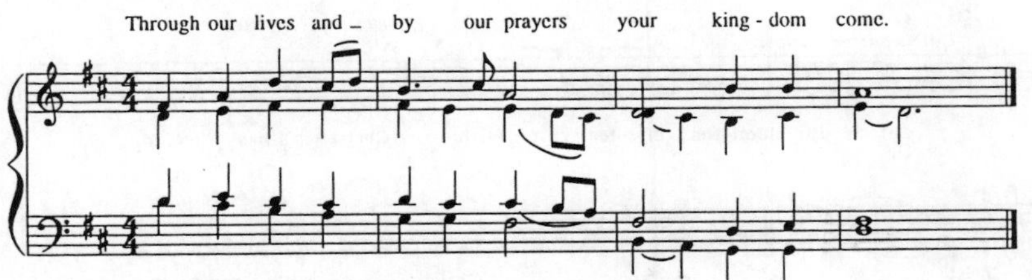
Through our lives and — by our prayers your king - dom come.

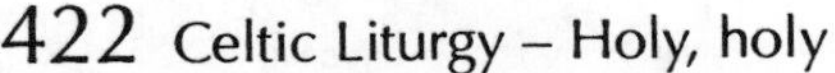

422 Celtic Liturgy – Holy, holy

Christopher Walker

HOLY, HOLY, HOLY

All
Ho — ly, ho - ly, ho — ly Lord, God of po - wer and

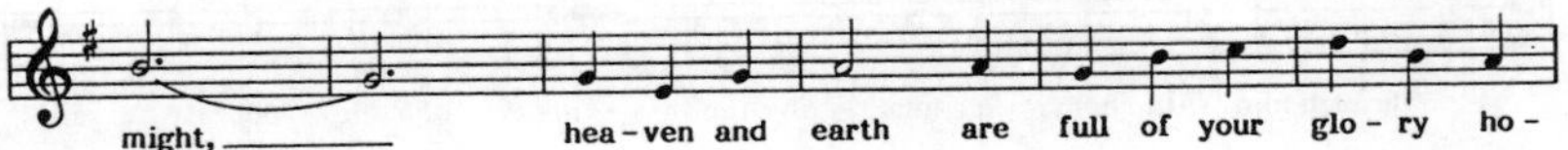
might, hea - ven and earth are full of your glo - ry ho -

- san - na, ho — san - na in the high - est.

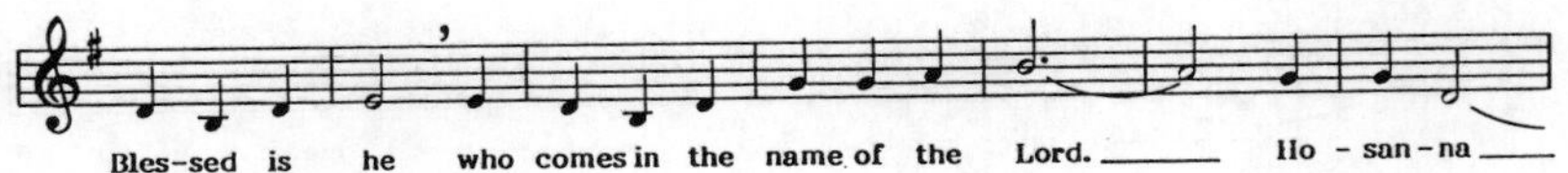
Bles - sed is he who comes in the name of the Lord. Ho - san - na

in the high - est, ho - san - na in the high - est.

423 Celtic Liturgy – Memorial Acclamation A

Christopher Walker

Celebrant or Deacon
Descant (2nd time)
All
Let us pro-claim the mys-ter-y of faith: Christ has died,
Christ is ri-sen, Christ will come a-
come a - gain.
-gain, Christ will come a - gain.

424 Celtic Liturgy – Great Amen

Christopher Walker

Celebrant
Through him, with him, in him, in the u-ni-ty of the Spi-rit all

glo-ry and ho-nour is yours, al-might-y Fa-ther, for e - ver and e - ver.

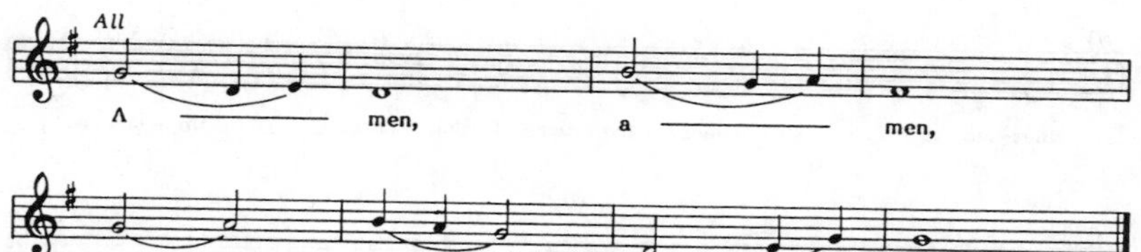
All
A men, a men,
a men, a men.

425 Coventry Eucharistic Acclamations – Holy, holy

All
Paul Inwood
Ho-ly, ho — ly, ho-ly Lord, God of
power and God of might, heav'n and earth are full heav'n and

earth are full heav'n and earth are full__ of your glo - ry. Ho -
- san - na, ho - san - na, ho - san - na__ in the high - est: ho -
3
- san - na, ho - san - na, ho - san - na__ in the high - est.
Blest is he who comes, blest is he who comes
in the name of the Lord. Ho -

(Repeat Hosannas as above)

426 Coventry Acclamations – Memorial Acclamation A

Paul Inwood

Christ has died, al - le - lu - ia! Christ is ris'n, al - le - lu - ia! Christ will
come a - gain__ in__ glo - ry! Ho -

(Repeat Hosannas as in Holy, Holy)

427 Coventry Eucharistic Acclamations – Great Amen

Paul Inwood

A —— men, a —— men, a —— men!

428 Eucharistic Acclamations (Farrell) – Holy, holy

INTRODUCTION
(♩. = c.56)
Bernadette Farrell
Melody
Ho - ly, ho - ly, ho - ly,
cresc.
Lord God of pow'r, Lord God of might, Lord God of pow'r and might.
mf
Heav'n and earth are full of your glo - ry. Ho - san - na
in the high - est. Ho - san — na, ho - san — na, ho -
- san - na in the high - est.
p
Bless - ed,
bless - ed, bless - ed, bless - ed is he who comes in the name, who comes in the
cresc.
Lord's own name.
Ho - san — na, ho - san — na, ho -
- san - na in the high — est. Ho - san — na, ho -
- san — na, ho - san - na in the high - est.

429 Eucharistic Acclamations (Farrell) – Acclamation A

Bernadette Farrell

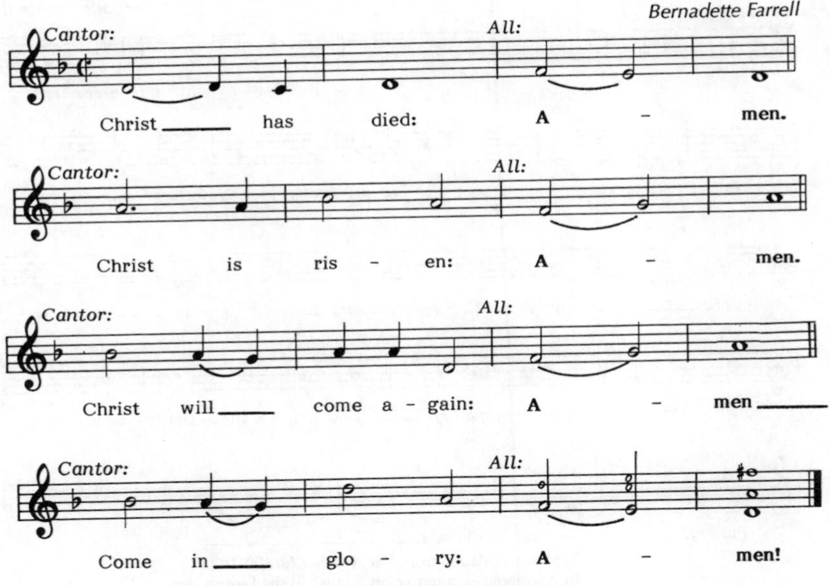
Cantor:
All:
Christ has died: A - men.
Cantor:
All:
Christ is ris - en: A - men.
Cantor:
All:
Christ will come a - gain: A - men
Cantor:
All:
Come in glo - ry: A - men!

430 Eucharistic Acclamations (Farrell) – Acclamation B

Bernadette Farrell

Dy - ing you de - stroyed our death,
ris - ing you re - stored our life. Lord Je–
sus, come, come in glo ry.

431 Eucharistic Acclamations (Farrell) – Acclamation C
INTRODUCTION
(𝅗𝅥 = c.56)
Bernadette Farrell
Melody
When we eat this bread and
drink this cup, we pro-claim your death, Lord Je — sus
Christ, un — til you come in glo-ry. un-
-til you come in glo-ry, un — til you come in
glo-ry, Je — sus Christ!
English translation from The Roman Missal © 1973
International Committee on English in the Liturgy, Inc (ICEL).
Music © 1985 Bernadette Farrell. Published by OCP.
432 Eucharistic Acclamations (Farrell) – Great Amen
INTRODUCTION
(𝅗𝅥 = c.56)
Bernadette Farrell
Presider
Melody
Through him, with him, in him,
in the u-ni-ty of the Ho-ly Spir-it all
glo-ry and hon-our is yours, al-might-y Fa — ther, for
All
Presider
ev — er, A — men, for ev — er, A —
Presider
All
men, for ev — er, A — men.
© 1985 Bernadette Farrell. Published by OCP.

433 Gathering Mass – Holy, holy

Paul Inwood

4
Ho - ly, ho - ly, ho - ly Lord,
God___ of pow'r___ and God___ of might: heav-en and
earth, heav-en and earth are full of your glo- ry, your
pow'r___ and might. Ho- san - na, ho - san - na, ho-
1
2
Fine
san - na in the high - est heav'ns. Ho - high - est heav'ns.
4
Bless-ed, bless-ed is he___ who comes, bless-ed,
bless-ed is he___ who comes; bless-ed is he, bless-ed is
D.S. al Fine
he who comes in the name of the Lord. ______ Ho -

434 Gathering Mass – Memorial Acclamation A

Paul Inwood

Let us pro - claim___ the mys-t'ry of faith: Christ___ has
died, Christ___ is ris'n, Je - sus Christ will
come___ a - gain Ho - san - na, ho - san -
Fine
na, ho - san - na in the high - est heav'ns!
Let us pro- claim___the mys-t'ry of faith: Dy - ing you___ de-
stroyed__our death, ris - ing you___ re - stored___our life.
Lord Je-sus, come Lord Je-sus come; Lord Je - sus come___in
glo - ry. Ho - san - na, ho - san - na, ho-

435 Gathering Mass – Memorial Acclamation B

Paul Inwood

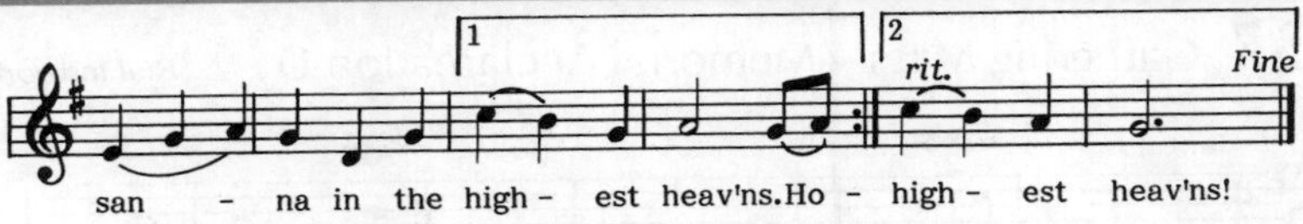

1 2 *rit.* *Fine*

san - na in the high - est heav'ns. Ho - high - est heav'ns!

436 Gathering Mass – Memorial Acclamation C

Paul Inwood

Cantor: All:

Let us pro- claim __ the mys-t'ry of faith: When we eat __ this

liv - ing bread, when we drink __ this sav - ing cup,

we __ pro-claim your death, __ Lord Je- sus, un - til __ you come - in

glo - ry. Ho - san - na, ho - san - na, ho-

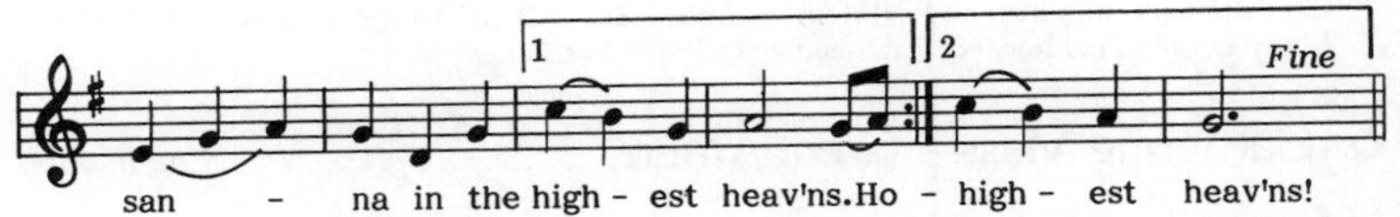
1
2
Fine
san - na in the high - est heav'ns. Ho - high - est heav'ns!

437 Gathering Mass – Memorial Acclamation D

Paul Inwood

Cantor:
All:
Let us pro-claim ___ the mys-t'ry of faith: Lord,by your cross,

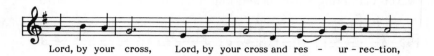

Lord, by your cross, Lord, by your cross and res - ur - rec-tion,

you ___ have set ___ your peo - ple free. You are the Sav-iour ___

___ of the world.Ho - san - na, ho - san - na, ho-

1
2
Fine
san - na in the high - est heav'ns.Ho - high - est heav'ns!

438 Gathering Mass – Great Amen

Paul Inwood

rit.
Fine
A - men. A - men.

439 Mass of Creation – Holy, holy

Marty Haugen

4
Ho - ly, ho - ly, ho - ly Lord,

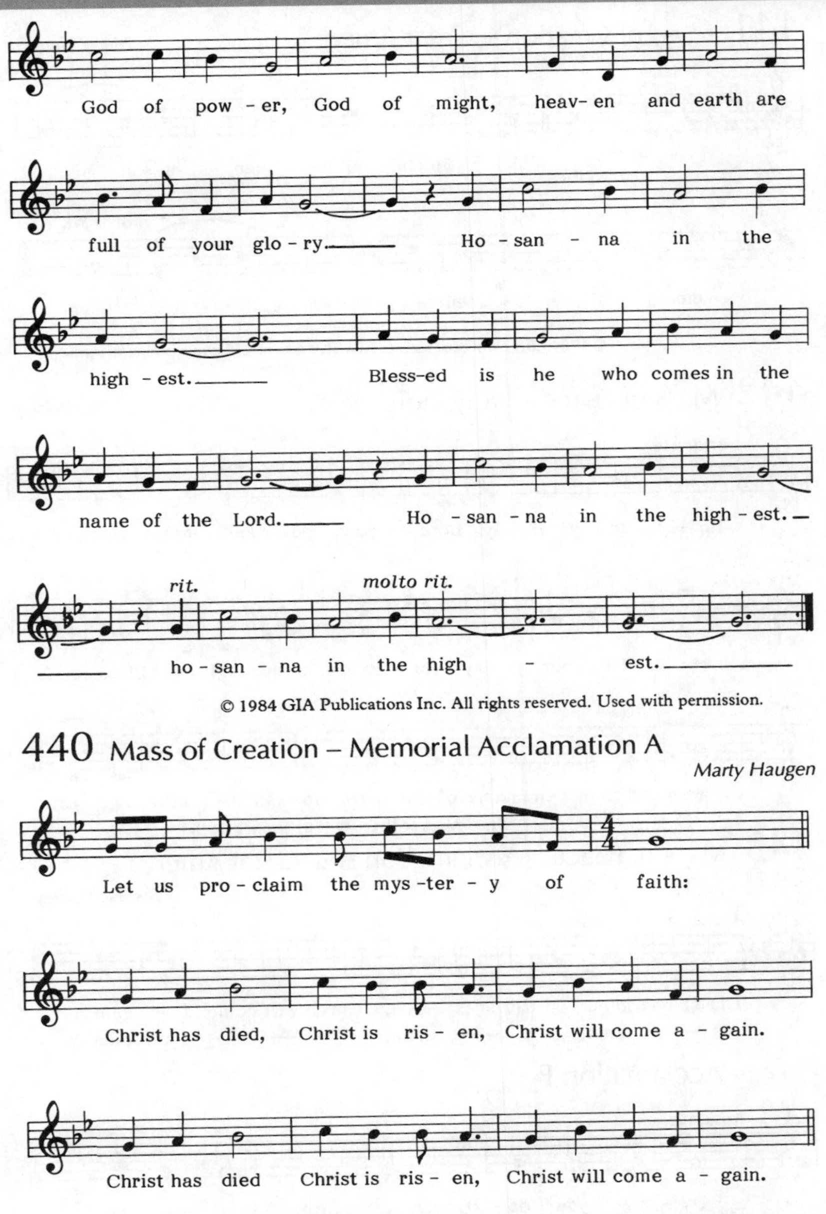
God of pow - er, God of might, heav- en and earth are
full of your glo - ry. Ho - san - na in the
high - est. Bless-ed is he who comes in the
name of the Lord. Ho - san - na in the high - est.
rit.
molto rit.
ho - san - na in the high - est.
© 1984 GIA Publications Inc. All rights reserved. Used with permission.
440 Mass of Creation – Memorial Acclamation A
Marty Haugen
Let us pro - claim the mys - ter - y of faith:
Christ has died, Christ is ris - en, Christ will come a - gain.
Christ has died Christ is ris - en, Christ will come a - gain.

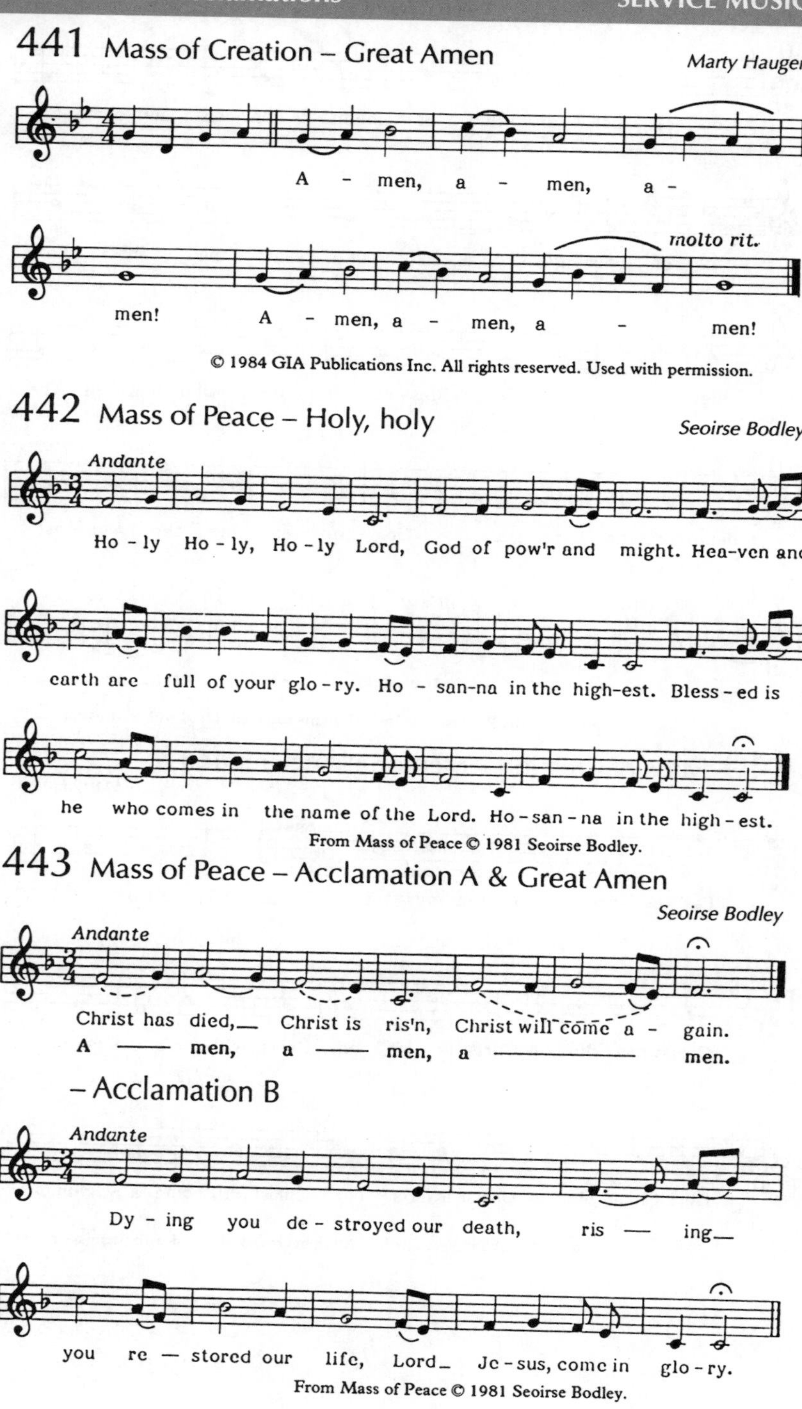
441 Mass of Creation – Great Amen
Marty Haugen
A - men, a - men, a - men! A - men, a - men, a - men!
molto rit.
© 1984 GIA Publications Inc. All rights reserved. Used with permission.
442 Mass of Peace – Holy, holy
Seoirse Bodley
Andante
Ho - ly Ho - ly, Ho - ly Lord, God of pow'r and might. Hea-ven and
earth are full of your glo - ry. Ho - san-na in the high-est. Bless - ed is
he who comes in the name of the Lord. Ho - san - na in the high - est.
From Mass of Peace © 1981 Seoirse Bodley.
443 Mass of Peace – Acclamation A & Great Amen
Seoirse Bodley
Andante
Christ has died,__ Christ is ris'n, Christ will come a - gain.
A —— men, a —— men, a —————— men.
– Acclamation B
Andante
Dy - ing you de - stroyed our death, ris — ing__
you re — stored our life, Lord__ Je - sus, come in glo - ry.
From Mass of Peace © 1981 Seoirse Bodley.

444 Saint Andrew Eucharistic Acclamations – Holy, holy

Stephen Dean

Dm Gm
Ho — ly, ho — ly, ho — ly, —

F Gm Gm C Dm A7 Dm/F
Lord, God of pow-er and might! Heav'n and earth are full of your

Gm A7 Dm Gm C F Gm A7 Dm
glo — ry. Ho - san — na, ho - san — na, ho -

A7 Dm/F G A7 Dm D
- san - na in the high - est, ho - san — na. Blest is he who

D7 Gm D Gm C
comes in the name of the Lord. Blest is he who comes in the

F G A A7 Gm C F Gm A7
name of the Lord. Ho - san — na, ho - san —

Dm Dm A7 Dm/F G A7 D
- na, ho - san - na in the high - est, ho - san — na.

445 Saint Andrew Acclamations – Acclamation A

Stephen Dean

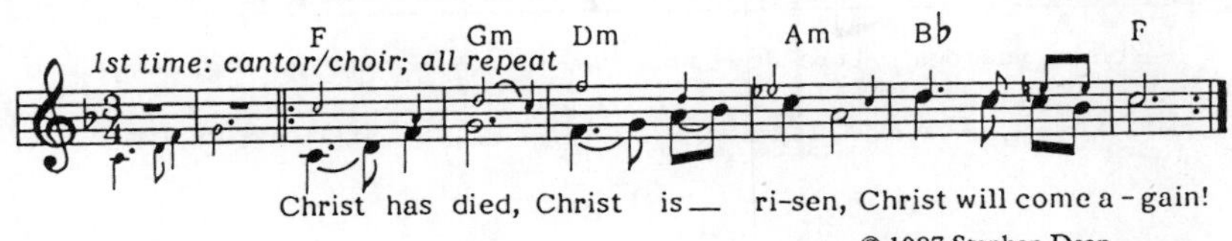
1st time: cantor/choir; all repeat
F Gm Dm Am B♭ F
Christ has died, Christ is — ri-sen, Christ will come a - gain!

446 Acclamation A (in Eastertide)

Stephen Dean

1st time: cantor/choir; all repeat
F Am C F
Christ has died, al-le - lu - ia, Christ is ris-en, al - le -
Gm C F Gm D7 Gm C F B♭ C F
lu - ia, Christ will come — a — gain, al - le - lu - ia, al - le - lu - ia.
© 1987 Stephen Dean.
447 Saint Andrew Acclamations – Acclamation B
Stephen Dean
F C F
Dy - ing you de-stroyed our death, ri - sing you re -
G7 C B♭ C Dm C
- stored our life. Lord Je - sus come, Lord Jesus come, Lord Jesus come_ in_
F B♭ C Dm C F
Lord Je - sus, Lord Je - sus,__ come ___ in glo - ry!
glo - ry. Lord Jesus come, Lord Jesus come, Lord Jesus come in_ glo - ry!
© 1987 Stephen Dean.
448 Saint Andrew Acclamations – Acclamation C
Stephen Dean
When we eat this bread, when we drink this cup, we pro -
- claim your death, Lord Je - sus, un - til you come in glo - ry!

449 Saint Andrew Acclamations – Great Amen

Stephen Dean

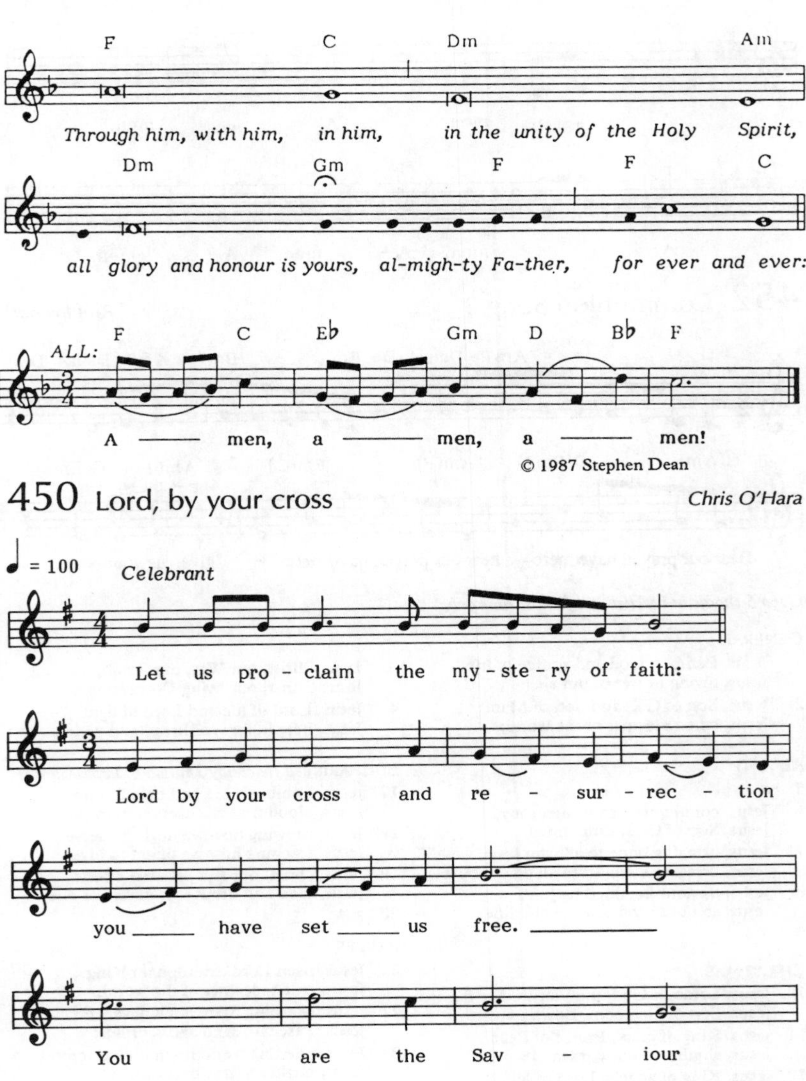
F C Dm Am
Through him, with him, in him, in the unity of the Holy Spirit,
Dm Gm F F C
all glory and honour is yours, al-migh-ty Fa-ther, for ever and ever:
ALL:
F C Eb Gm D Bb F
A — men, a — men, a — men!
© 1987 Stephen Dean
450 Lord, by your cross
Chris O'Hara
= 100
Celebrant
Let us pro - claim the my - ste - ry of faith:
Lord by your cross and re - sur - rec - tion
you have set us free.
You are the Sav - iour
of the world.

451 Amen

Traditional

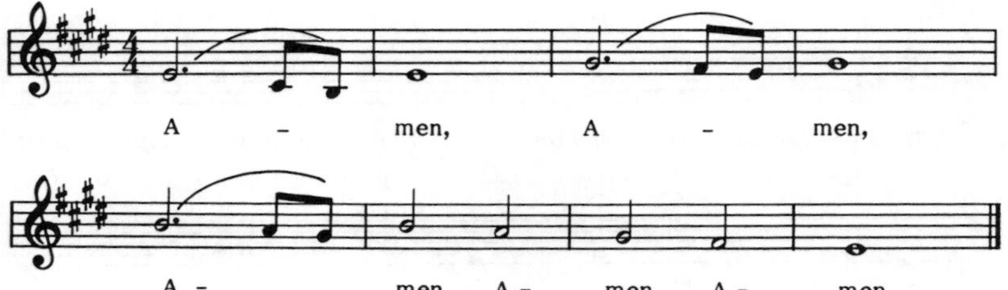
A - men, A - men,
A - men, A - men, A - men.

452 Communion Song 3

Paul Inwood

G Am7 Dsus4 D Em Bm7 Am7 Dsus4 D
C(Am) G(Em7) Am(F) Em(C) C(Am6) G(Emaj)
3
Hear our prayer, have merc–y; hear our prayer, have merc – y; give us your peace.

Capo 5 chords in brackets are for last time only.

GENERAL

1. Jesus, Lamb of God and source of life:
   Jesus, loving bearer of our sins:
2. Jesus, Son of God and Son of Man:
   Jesus, true redeemer of the world:

*3. Jesus Christ, our Way, our Truth, our Life:
   Jesus Christ, our living Cornerstone:

4. Jesus, Lord of life and Lord of light:
   Jesus, here in form of bread and wine:

ADVENT

5. = 1
6. Jesus, coming near to bring us joy:
   Jesus, Son of God, Emmanuel:
7. Jesus, bringing hope to all who fear:
   Jesus, bringing strength to all who mourn:

*8. Jesus, Saviour heralded by John:
   Jesus, son of David's house and line:

*9. = 4

CHRISTMAS

10. Jesus, Lamb of God, the Word made flesh:
    Jesus, Son of God come down on earth:
11. Jesus, King of glory, Prince of Peace:
    Jesus, shining in our darkened world:
12. Jesus, King of angels, Lord of joy:
    Jesus, born to save the world from sin:
13. = 4

LENT

14. Jesus, source of everlasting life:
    Jesus, source of reconciling love:
15. Jesus, by whose suffering we are healed:
    Jesus, man of sorrows, friend of grief:
16. Jesus, crucified, transcending time:
    Jesus, Saviour, by whose death we live:

EUCHARISTIC *(Maundy Thursday, Corpus Christi)*

17. Jesus, Lamb of God and bread of life:
    Jesus, blood that cleanses us from sin:
18. Jesus, showing how we ought to serve:
    Jesus, teaching how we ought to love:

*19. Jesus Christ, our true, eternal priest:
    Jesus, food and drink that makes us one:

20. = 4

EASTER

21. Jesus, risen Lord, triumphant King:
    Jesus, true redeemer of the world:
22. Jesus, Morning Star which never sets:
    Jesus, Paschal Lamb and sacrifice:
23. Jesus, bursting from the shattered tomb:
    Jesus, mighty Victor over death:
24. = 4

PENTECOST *(Spirit, healing ...)*

25. Jesus, glorious brightness, flame of love:
    Jesus, filling hearts and minds with life:
26. Jesus, healing strength, redeeming power:
    Jesus, burning out the mark of sin:
27. Jesus, by whose truth we are inspired:
    Jesus, present here among us now:
28. = 4

453 Jesus, Lamb of God (Farrell)

Bernadette Farrell

VERSE 1: Cantor/Choir
Jesus, Lamb of God, bearer of our sin; Jesus, Saviour:

REFRAIN: All

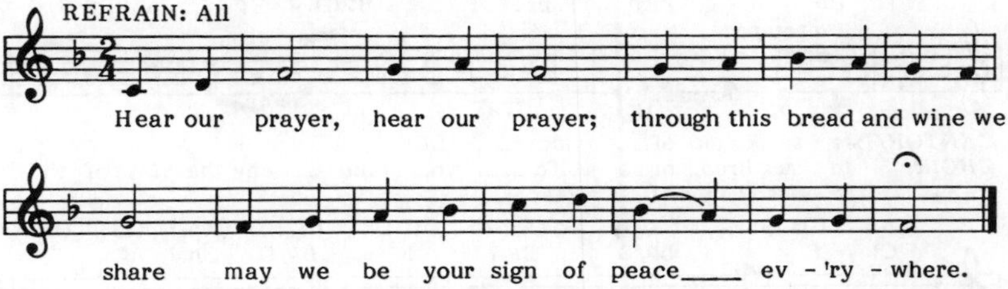

Hear our prayer, hear our prayer; through this bread and wine we share may we be your sign of peace___ ev - 'ry - where.

454 Gathering Mass – Jesus, Lamb of God

Paul Inwood

Je - sus, Lamb of God,
1 Bread of Life for us;
2 Source of u - ni - ty;
3 Bread that makes us one;
4 Food for hearts and minds;
5 Build - ing up your Church;

Je - sus, Lamb of God,
1 Wine of Joy for us;
2 Pre - cious cor - ner - stone;
3 Wine that heals our minds;
4 Giv - ing strength to all;
5 Source of light and love;

Je - sus, Lamb of God bear-ing all our sin: have mer-cy on us, give us your peace. *Hmm,___, Hmm,___

Hmm,___ Hmm,___ Hmm,___

Hmm,___ Hmm,___ *Fine*

* *Following the breaking of bread all hum the melody. This continues through the distribution of communion while the Cantor sings verses,or solo instrument plays instrumental descants.*

455 Jesus, Lamb of God (Haugen)

Marty Haugen

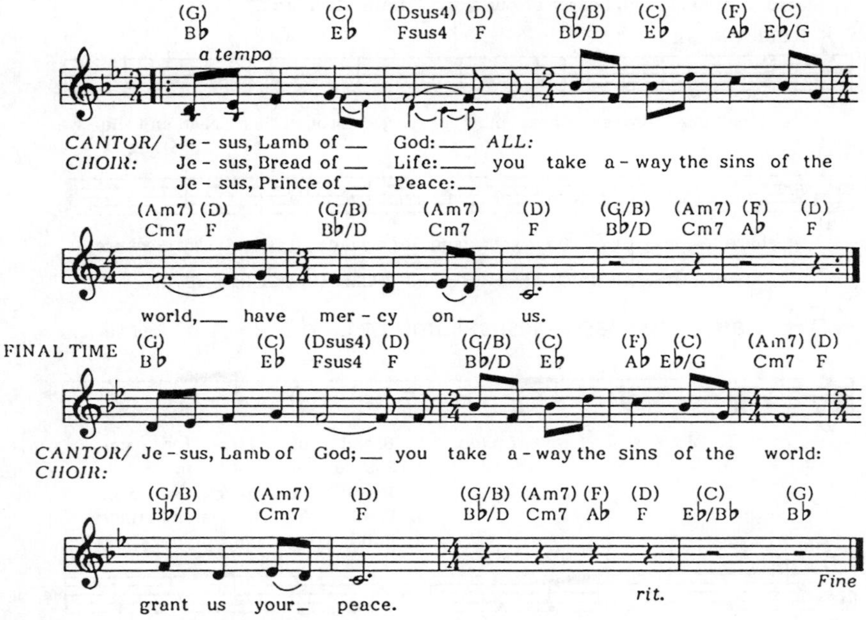

(G) B♭ (C) E♭ (Dsus4) (D) Fsus4 F (G/B) B♭/D (C) E♭ (F) A♭ (C) E♭/G

a tempo

CANTOR/ CHOIR: Je - sus, Lamb of ___ God: ___ *ALL:*
Je - sus, Bread of ___ Life: ___ you take a - way the sins of the
Je - sus, Prince of ___ Peace: ___

(Am7) (D) Cm7 F (G/B) B♭/D (Am7) Cm7 (D) F (G/B) B♭/D (Am7) Cm7 (F) A♭ (D) F

world, ___ have mer - cy on ___ us.

FINAL TIME (G) B♭ (C) E♭ (Dsus4) (D) Fsus4 F (G/B) B♭/D (C) E♭ (F) A♭ (C) E♭/G (Am7) (D) Cm7 F

CANTOR/ CHOIR: Je - sus, Lamb of God; ___ you take a - way the sins of the world:

(G/B) B♭/D (Am7) Cm7 (D) F (G/B) B♭/D (Am7) Cm7 (F) A♭ (D) F (C) E♭/B♭ (G) B♭

grant us your ___ peace. *rit.* *Fine*

Additional Verses:
Jesus, Word of God . . .
Jesus, Tree of Life . . .
Jesus, Ancient Cup . . .
Jesus, Lord of Lords . . .
Jesus, King of Kings . . .
Jesus, Cup of Life . . .
Jesus, Fire of Love . . .
Jesus, Bread of Peace . . .
Jesus, Hope for all . . .

456 Lamb of God (Mass of Peace)

Seoirse Bodley

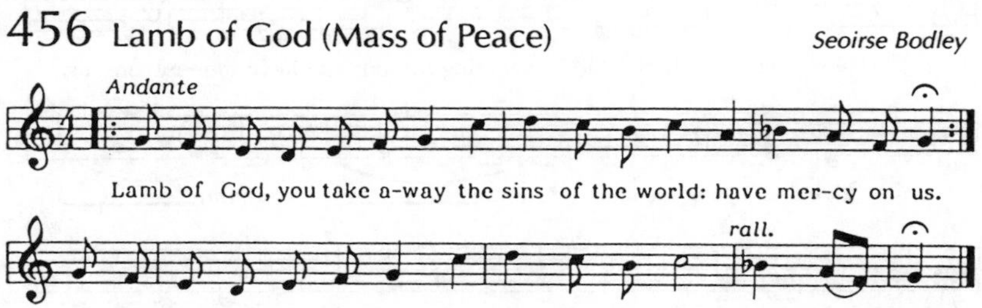
Andante
Lamb of God, you take a-way the sins of the world: have mer-cy on us.
rall.
Lamb of God you take a - way the sins of the world: grant us ___ peace.

457 Holy Name Communion Song

Ernest Sands

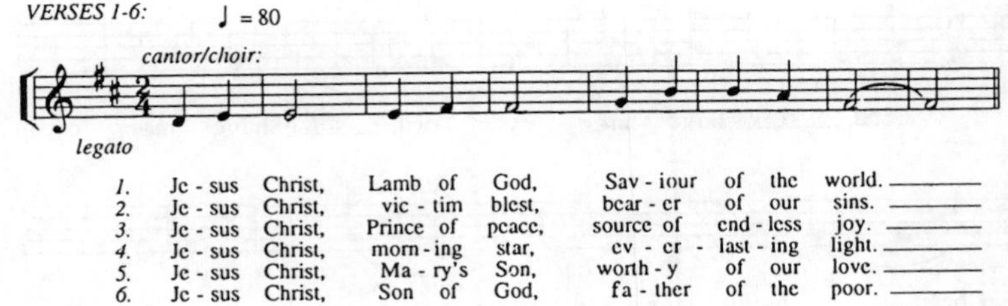
VERSES 1-6:
♩ = 80
cantor/choir:
legato
1. Je - sus Christ, Lamb of God, Sav - iour of the world.
2. Je - sus Christ, vic - tim blest, bear - er of our sins.
3. Je - sus Christ, Prince of peace, source of end - less joy.
4. Je - sus Christ, morn - ing star, ev - er - last - ing light.
5. Je - sus Christ, Ma - ry's Son, worth - y of our love.
6. Je - sus Christ, Son of God, fa - ther of the poor.

RESPONSE: all/choir
Fine
Hear our pray'r, Lamb of God. Grant us peace.

Verses 7–12:

7 Jesus Christ, heav'nly king, glory of our race.

8 Jesus Christ, Word made flesh, author of all life.

9 Jesus Christ, bread of life, food and drink for us.

10 Jesus Christ, mighty God, crown of all the Saints.

11 Jesus Christ, crucified, broken for our sins.

12 Jesus Christ, risen Lord, present in our midst.

Ernest Sands

458 May God bless and keep you

Christopher Walker

RESPONSE:
May God bless and keep you, may God's face shine on you:
(us) (us)
May God be kind to you and give you peace
(us) (us)

459 Lord, have mercy

A Gregory Murray, OSB 1905–1992

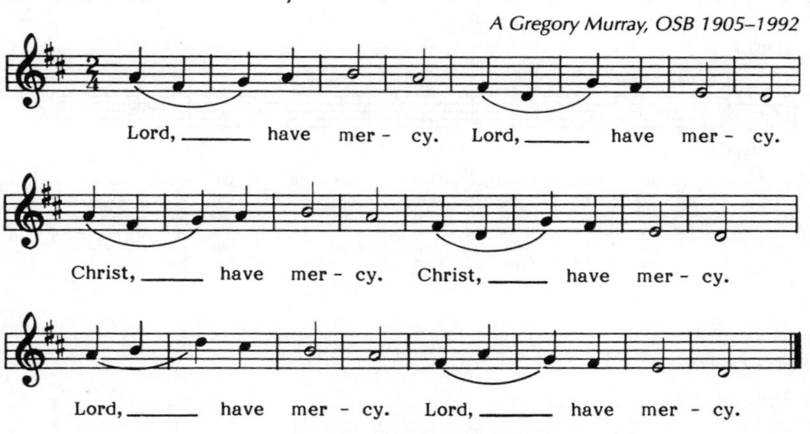
Lord, ___ have mer - cy. Lord, ___ have mer - cy.
Christ, ___ have mer - cy. Christ, ___ have mer - cy.
Lord, ___ have mer - cy. Lord, ___ have mer - cy.

460 Glory to God

A Gregory Murray, OSB 1905–1992

Glo - ry to God in the high - est, ___ and peace to his

peo-ple on earth. ___ Lord God, hea - ven-ly King, ___ al -

migh - ty God and ___ Fa - ther, ___ we wor - ship you, we

give you thanks, we praise you ___ for your glo - ry.

Lord Je - sus Christ, on - ly Son of the Fa - ther,

Lord God, Lamb of ___ God, you take a - way the sin of the
world, ___ have mer - cy on us; ___ you are sea- ted at the
right hand of the ___ Fa - ther, re - ceive our ___ pray'r. ___
___ For you a - lone are the Ho - ly One, you a -
lone are the Lord, you a - lone are the Most High,
Je ___ sus Christ, with the ___ Ho -ly Spi - rit
in the glo - ry of God the Fa - ther. A ___ men.

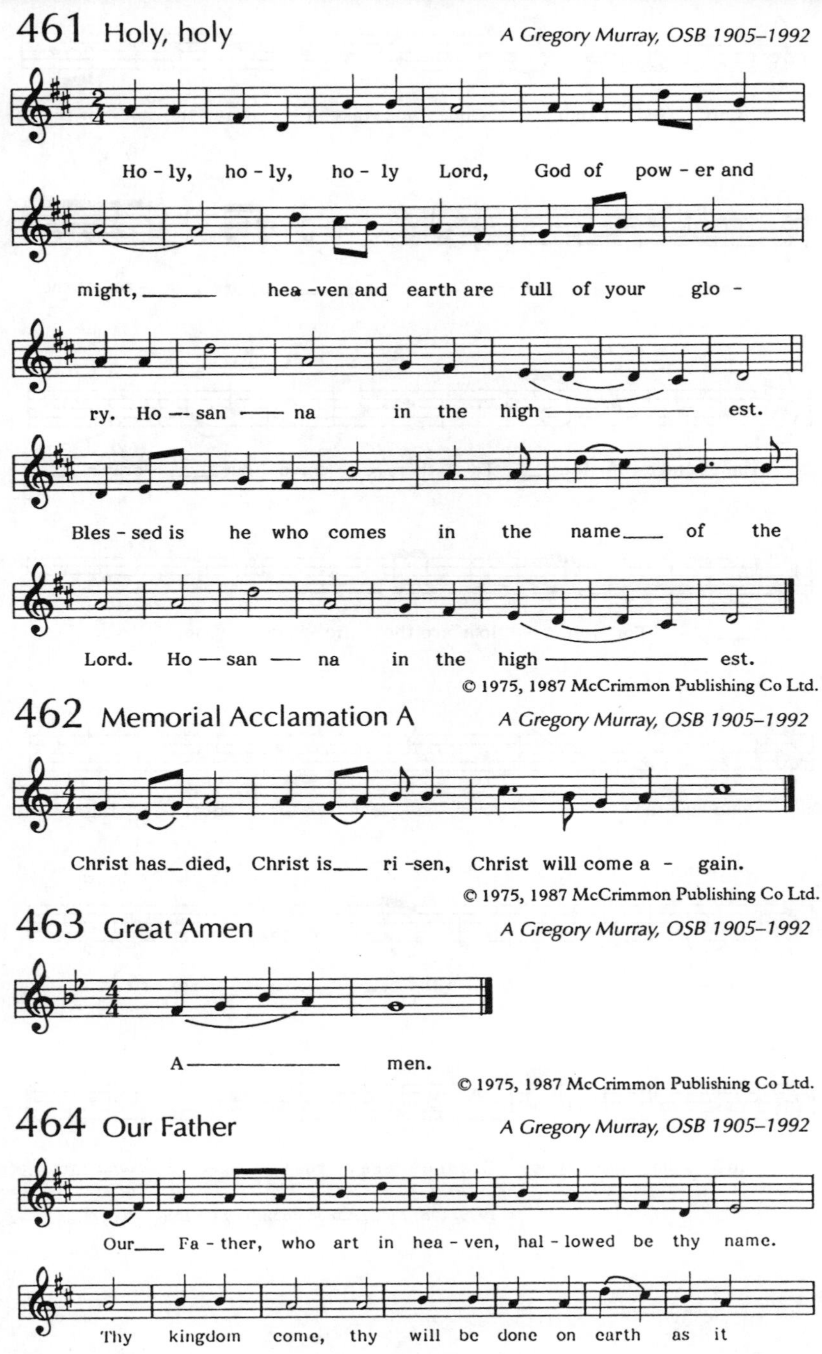
461 Holy, holy
A Gregory Murray, OSB 1905–1992
Ho - ly, ho - ly, ho - ly Lord, God of pow - er and
might, ___ hea -ven and earth are full of your glo -
ry. Ho — san — na in the high ——— est.
Bles - sed is he who comes in the name ___ of the
Lord. Ho — san — na in the high ——— est.
© 1975, 1987 McCrimmon Publishing Co Ltd.
462 Memorial Acclamation A
A Gregory Murray, OSB 1905–1992
Christ has ___ died, Christ is ___ ri -sen, Christ will come a - gain.
© 1975, 1987 McCrimmon Publishing Co Ltd.
463 Great Amen
A Gregory Murray, OSB 1905–1992
A ——— men.
© 1975, 1987 McCrimmon Publishing Co Ltd.
464 Our Father
A Gregory Murray, OSB 1905–1992
Our ___ Fa - ther, who art in hea - ven, hal - lowed be thy name.
Thy kingdom come, thy will be done on earth as it

is in heav - en. Give us this day our dai - ly bread, and for -
give us our tres - pas - ses, as we for - give those who tres -
pass a - gainst us, and lead us not in - to temp - ta - tion,
but de - li - ver us from e - vil. A ---------- men.
© 1975, 1987 McCrimmon Publishing Co Ltd.
465 For the kingdom
A Gregory Murray, OSB 1905–1992
For the king - dom the pow-er and the glo - ry are yours,
now and for - ev- er.
© 1975, 1987 McCrimmon Publishing Co Ltd.
466 Lamb of God
A Gregory Murray, OSB 1905–1992
Lamb of God, you take a - way the sins of the world,
have mer- cy on us.
Lamb of God, you take a - way the sins of the world,
grant us peace.
© 1975, 1987 McCrimmon Publishing Co Ltd.

467 Missa de Angelis

Plainchant

Kyrie Elesion

Ky-ri - e, e - le-i-son.

3 Chri- ste, e - le-i-son.

5 Ky-ri-e, - - - - e - le-i-son.

7 Ky-ri-e, - - - - e - le-i-son.

Gloria

Glo-ri-a in ex-cel-sis De-o. Et in ter-ra pax ho-mi-ni-bus

3 bo-nae vo-lun-ta-tis. Lau-da - mus te. Be-ne-di-ci- mus-te. -

6 -A do-ra - mus - te. Glo-ri - fi - ca-mus-te.

8 Gra-ti-as a-gi- mus - ti - bi pro-pter mag-nam glo-ri-am tu - am.

10 Do-mi-ne De-us, Rex cae-le-stis, De-us__ Pa-ter__ o__ mni-po-tens.

12 Do-mi-ne Fi-li u-ni-ge-ni-te Je__ su__ Chri-ste.

14
Do-mi-ne De- us, - A-gnus De - i, Fi - li - us___ Pa___ tris.

16
Qui tol-lis pec-ca-ta mun___ di,___ mi-se-re___ re___ no-bis.

18
Qui tol- lis pec - ca - ta mun - di, su - sci - pe de - pre - ca - ti -

20
o- nem___ no___ stram. - Qui se-des ad dex-te-ram Pa - tris,

22
mi - se - re - re no - bis. Quo - ni - am tu so - lus san - ctus.

24
Tu so- lus___ Do___ min___ nus. Tu so-lus Al___ tis___ si- mus,___

26
Je - su - Chri - ste. Cum San- cto___ Spi - ri - tu,

28
in glo-ri - a De-i Pa___ tris.___ A___ men.___

Sanctus

San___ ctus, San___ ctus - San___ ctus,___
4
Do___ mi - nus De - us___ Sa___ ba___ oth.
6
Ple - ni - sunt cae___ li et___ ter___ ra___

7
glo-ri - a tu a. Ho- san - na in ex cel sis.
9
Be- ne - di ctus qui - ve nit in no-mi-ne Do - mi- ni.
10
Ho- san na in ex - cel sis.
Pater Noster
Pa-ter nos- ter, qui es in cae- lis, san-cti-fi-ce- tur no men tu um.
3
Ad ve ni atre gnumtu um. Fi atvo lun tastu- a,si cutincae lo, et in ter- ra.
5
Pa-nem nos-trum quo - ti - di - a - num da no - bis ho - di - e.
6
Et - di - mit - te no - bis de - bi - ta nos - tra
7
si - cut et nos di - mit - ti - mus de - bi - to - ri - bus nos- tris.
8
Et ne nos in-du-cas in ten-ta - ti - o - nem: sed li - be-ra nos a ma - lo.
Agnus Dei
A gnus De i qui tol lis pec-ca-ta mun di,
3
mi-se - re-re no bis. A- gnus- De i,

5
qui tol - lis pec-ca-ta mun di, mi-se-re-re no - bis.
7
A - gnus De - i, qui tol - lis pec-ca-ta mun - di,
9
do - na no - bis pa - cem.

Dismissal

I - te mis-sa est.
De-o gra - ti - as.

468 Kyrie eleison (Orbis factor)

Plainchant

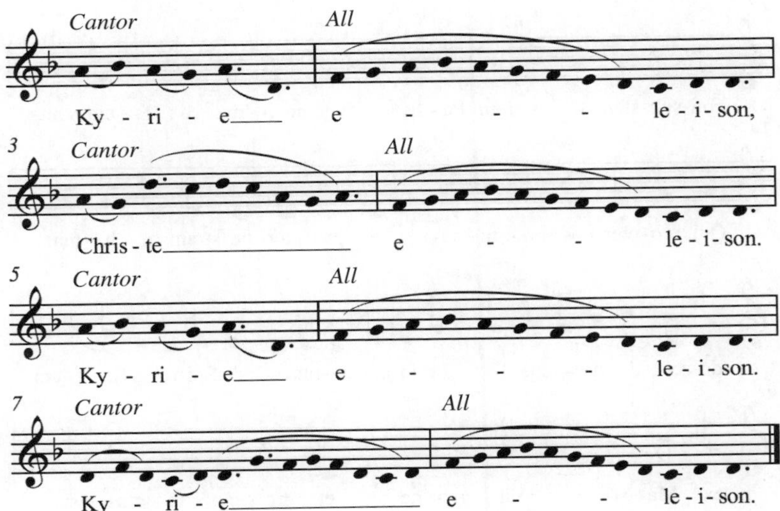
Cantor
All
Ky - ri - e e - - - le - i - son,
3
Cantor
All
Chris - te e - - le - i - son.
5
Cantor
All
Ky - ri - e e - - - le - i - son.
7
Cantor
All
Ky - ri - e e - - le - i - son.

469 Credo III

Plainchant

Cre-do in u-num De - um. Pa - trem o-mni-po-ten-tem,

3 fac-to-rem cae-li et ter-rae, vi-si-bi-li-um o - mni-um,

5 et in-vi-si-bi - li-um. Et in u-num Do-mi-num Je-su Chri-stum,

7 Fi-li-um De-i-u-ni-ge-ni-tum. Et ex Pa-tre na - tum

9 an-te o-mni-a sae - cu-la. De-um de De-o, lu-men de lu-mi-ne,

11 De-um ve-rum de De-o ve-ro. Ge-ni-tum non fa - ctum,

13 con-sub-stan-ti-a-lem Pa-tri: per quem o-mni-a fa-cta sunt.

14 Qui pro-pter nos ho-mi-nes, et pro-pter no-stram sa-lu-tem

16 de-scen-dit de - cae-lis. Et in-car-na-tus est de Spi-ri-tu San - cto

18 ex Ma-ri-a Vir-gi-ne: et ho-mo-fa-ctus est.

20
Cru-ci - fi - xus e-ti-am pro no - bis: sub Pon-ti-o Pi-la-to
22
pas-sus, et se- pul - tus est. Et re-sur-re-xit ter-ti-a di-e,
24
se-cun-dum Scri-ptu-ras. Et a scen - dit in cae - lum:
26
se-det ad dex-te-ram Pa - tris. Et i-te-rum ven-tu-rus est cum glo-ri-a,
28
ju-di-ca-re vi-vos et mor-tu-os: cu-jus re-gni non e-rit fi-nis.
30
Et in Spi-ri-tum San-ctum, Do-mi-num, et vi-vi-fi-can-tem:
32
qui ex Pa-tre Fi-li-o-que pro - ce-dit. Qui cum Pa-tre et Fi-li-o
34
si-mul a-do-ra-tur, et con-glo-ri-fi-ca-tur:
36
qui-lo-cu-tus est per Pro-phe-tas. Et u-nam san-ctam ca-tho-li-cam
38
et a-po-sto-li-cam Ec-cle-si-am. Con-fi-te-or u-num bap - ti-sma

40
in re mis si-o nempec ca to rum. Et ex spe ctore sur re cti o nemmor tu-o rum.
42
Et vi - tam ven-tu-ri sae-cu-li. A - - - men.

470 Sanctus XVIII *Plainchant*

Sanc- tus, - Sanc- tus, - Sanc-tus Do-mi-nus De-us Sa - ba-oth.
5
Ple - ni sunt coe - li et ter - ra glo - ri - a tu - a
6
Ho - san - na in ex - cel - sis. Be - ne - dic - tus qui ve - nit in
8
no - mi - ne Do - mi - ni. Ho - san - na in ex - cel - sis. -

471 Mortem tuam (Memorial Acclamation) *Plainchant*

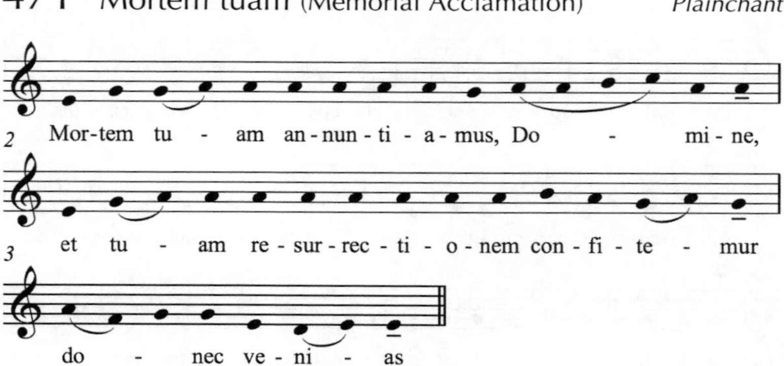
Mor-tem tu - am an - nun - ti - a - mus, Do - mi - ne,
2
et tu - am re - sur - rec - ti - o - nem con - fi - te - mur
3
do - nec ve - ni - as

472 Great Amen

Plainchant

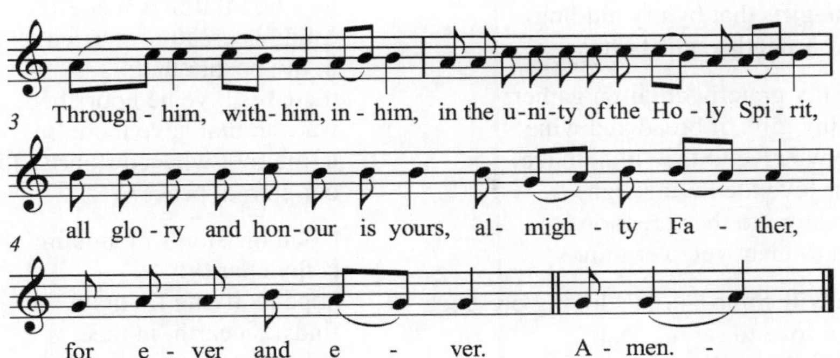
Through - him, with - him, in - him, in the u - ni - ty of the Ho - ly Spi - rit,
all glo - ry and hon - our is yours, al - migh - ty Fa - ther,
for e - ver and e - ver. A - men. -

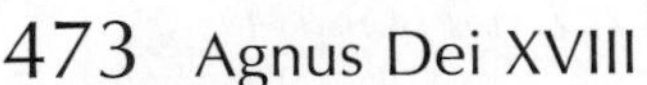

473 Agnus Dei XVIII

Plainchant

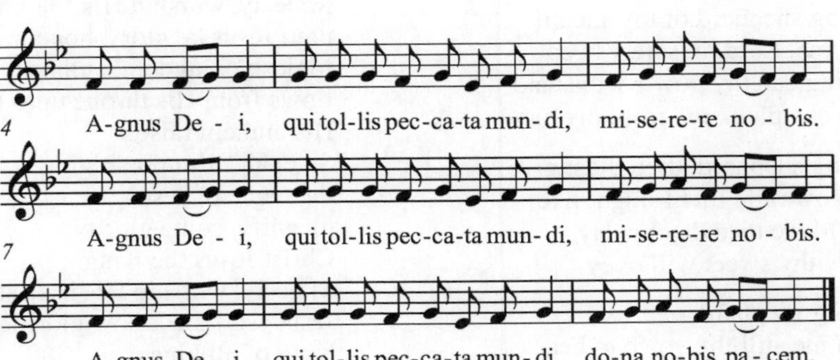
A-gnus De - i, qui tol - lis pec - ca - ta mun - di, mi - se - re - re no - bis.
A-gnus De - i, qui tol - lis pec - ca - ta mun - di, mi - se - re - re no - bis.
A-gnus De - i, qui tol - lis pec - ca - ta mun - di, do - na no - bis pa - cem.

474 *James Quinn, SJ*

1 Loving Father, from thy bounty
choicest gifts unnumbered flow:
all the blessings of salvation,
which to Christ thy Son we owe,
all the gifts that by thy bidding
nature's hands on us bestow!

2 Here thy grateful children gather,
offering gifts of bread and wine;
these we give to thee in homage,
of our love the loving sign,
and restore to thee creation,
given to man, yet ever thine!

3 Soon will come Christ's loving presence
on our love to set his seal!
Body broken, Blood shed for us,
bread and wine will then reveal!
Bread and wine, though these no longer,
flesh and blood will yet conceal!

475 *Jane E. Leeson (1809–91)*

1 Loving shepherd of thy sheep,
keep me, Lord, in safety keep;
nothing can thy pow'r withstand,
none can pluck me from thy hand.

2 Loving shepherd, thou didst give
thine own life that I might live;
may I love thee day by day,
gladly thy sweet will obey.

3 Loving shepherd, ever near,
teach me still thy voice to hear;
suffer not my steps to stray
from the strait and narrow way.

4 Where thou leadest may I go,
walking in thy steps below;
then before thy Father's throne,
Jesu, claim me for thine own.

476 *Dante Alighieri (1265–1321), tr. R.A. Knox (1888–1957)*

1 Maiden yet a mother,
daughter of thy Son,
high beyond all other,
lowlier is none;
thou the consummation
planned by God's decree,
when our lost creation
nobler rose in thee!

2 Thus his place preparèd,
he who all things made
'mid his creatures tarried,
in thy bosom laid;
there his love he nourished,
warmth that gave increase
to the root whence flourished
our eternal peace.

3 Noon on Sion's mountain
is thy charity;
hope its living fountain
finds, on earth, in thee:
lady, such thy power,
he, who grace would buy
not as of thy dower,
without wings would fly.

477 *Jack W. Hayford*

Majesty, worship His Majesty;
unto Jesus be glory, honour and praise.
Majesty, kingdom, authority,
flows from His throne unto His own,
His anthem raise.
So exalt, lift upon high,
the name of Jesus,
magnify, come glorify,
Christ Jesus the King.
Majesty, worship His Majesty,
Jesus who died, now glorified,
King of all kings.

478 *Sebastian Temple*

1 Make me a channel of your peace.
Where there is hatred, let me bring your love.
Where there is injury your pardon, Lord.
And where there's doubt true faith in you.

2 Make me a channel of your peace.
Where there's despair in life, let me bring hope.
Where there is darkness only light,
and where there's sadness ever joy.

3 Oh, Master, grant that I may never seek
so much to be consoled as to console,
to be understood as to understand,
to be loved, as to love,
with all my soul.

4 Make me a channel of your peace.
It is in pardoning that we are pardoned,
in giving to all that we receive,
and in dying that we're born to eternal
life.

Second tune only:
Make me a channel of your peace (Repeat)

479 *Graham Kendrick*

1 Make way, make way,
for Christ the King in splendour arrives.
Fling wide the gates
and welcome Him into your lives.

Make way! Make way!
for the King of kings.
Make way! Make way!
And let His kingdom in.

2 He comes the broken hearts to heal
The prisoners to free.
The deaf shall hear, the lame shall dance,
The blind shall see.

3 And those who mourn with heavy hearts.
Who weep and sigh;
With laughter, joy and royal crown
He'll beautify.

4 We call you now to worship Him
As Lord of all.
To have no gods before Him
Their thrones must fall!

480 *Estelle White*

1 Man of Galilee
will you come and stand by me
through the length of each working day?
Bless, O Lord, my efforts, I pray.

2 Man who healed the blind
open up the eyes of my mind
to the needs of my fellow man.
Help me give with open hands.

3 Man of bread and of wine
show me by the means of this sign
that I share your life and your light
with the neighbour here at my side.

4 Man of Calvary
give me strength and will to be free
of the weight of self–pity's chains,
then my trials will be but gains.

5 Man at God's right hand,
will you help me understand
that in you, when my breath is stilled,
all my longings will be fulfilled?

481 *De unitate ecclesiae, Cyprian of Carthage (252AD), tr. Anders Frostenson*

1 Many are the lightbeams from the one
light.
Our one light is Jesus.
Many are the lightbeams from the one
light;
we are one in Christ.

2 Many are the branches of the one tree.
Our one tree is Jesus.
Many are the branches of the one tree;
we are one in Christ.

3 Many are the gifts giv'n, love is all one.
Love's the gift of Jesus.
Many are the gifts giv'n, love is all one;
we are one in Christ.

4 Many ways to serve God, the Spirit is one;
servant spirit of Jesus.
Many ways to serve God, the Spirit is one;
we are one in Christ.

5 Many are the members, the body is one;
members all of Jesus.
Many are the members, the body is one;
we are one in Christ.

482 *Stanbrook Abbey*

1 Mary, crowned with living light,
temple of the Lord,
place of peace and holiness,
shelter of the Word.

2 Mystery of sinless life
in our fallen race,
free from shadow, you reflect
plenitude of grace.

3 Virgin–Mother of our God,
lift us when we fall,
Jesus named you on the Cross
Mother of us all.

4 Father, Son and Holy Ghost,
heaven sings your praise,
Mary magnifies your name
through eternal days.

483 *F.W. Weatherell*

1 Mary immaculate, star of the morning,
chosen before the creation began,
chosen to bring, for thy bridal adorning,
rescue to woman and rescue to man.

2 Here, in an orbit of shadow and sadness
veiling thy splendour, thy course thou
hast run;
now thou art throned in all glory and
gladness,
crowned by the hand of thy saviour and Son.

3 Sinners, we honour thy sinless perfection,
fallen and weak, for thy pity we plead;
grant us the shield of thy sovereign
protection,
measure thine aid by the depth of our need.

4 Frail is our nature, and strict our probation,
watchful the foe that would lure us to
wrong,
succour our souls in the hour of temptation,
Mary immaculate tender and strong.

5 Bend from thy throne at the voice of our
crying;
bend to this earth which thy footsteps
have trod;
stretch out thine arms to us living and dying,
Mary immaculate, mother of God.

484 *David Mowbray*

1 May Christ, the Lord of Cana's feast,
who made the water wine,
be welcomed as the honoured guest,
our risen Master now confessed,
God's messenger and sign: (2)

2 What God has joined, we hear him say,
let no–one tear apart!
With his two servants here today
may Christ's own love for ever stay,
true bond of mind and heart; (2)

3 Whatever joys or sorrows come,
may steadfastness be theirs!
God's truth and kindness grace their home,
his presence fill the humblest room,
his Spirit stir their prayers; (2)

4 With brightened eyes of faith
we'll see God's plan for them made plain:
so shall our hearts together
be uplifted in the Trinity
and echo the Amen; (2)

485 *Ernest Sands*

May the choirs of angels come to greet you.
May they speed you to paradise.
May the Lord enfold you in his mercy.
May you find eternal life.

1 The Lord is my light and my help;
it is he who protects me from harm.
The Lord is the strength of my days;
before whom should I tremble with fear?

2 There is one thing I ask of the Lord;
that he grant me my heartfelt desire.
To dwell in the courts of our God
ev'ry day of my life in his presence.

3 O Lord, hear my voice when I cry;
have mercy on me and give answer.
Do not cast me away in your anger,
for you are the God of my help.

4 I am sure I shall see the Lord's goodness;
I shall dwell in the land of the living.
Hope in God, stand firm and take heart,
for place all your trust in the Lord.

486 *Kevin Mayhew*

May the peace of Christ be with you today,
may the peace of Christ be with you today,
may the love of Christ, the joy of Christ,
may the peace of Christ be yours.

487 *Graham Kendrick*

1 Meekness and majesty, manhood and deity,
in perfect harmony, the Man who is God.
Lord of eternity dwells in humanity,
kneels in humility and washes our feet.

O what a mystery, meekness and majesty,
Bow down and worship for this is your God,
this is your God.

2 Father's pure radiance, perfect in innocence,
yet learns obedience to death on a cross.
Suffering to give us life, conquering
through sacrifice,
and as they crucify prays: 'Father forgive.'

3 Wisdom unsearchable, God the invisible,
love indestructible in frailty appears.
Lord of infinity, stooping so tenderly,
lifts our humanity to the heights of His
throne.

488 *Julia Ward Howe (1819–1910)*

1 Mine eyes have seen the glory of the
coming of the Lord.
He is trampling out the vintage
where the grapes of wrath are stored.
He has loosed the fateful lightning of his
terrible swift sword.
His truth is marching on.

Glory, glory hallelujah! (3)
His truth is marching on.

2 I have seen him in the watchfires of a
hundred circling camps.
They have gilded him an altar in the
evening dews and damps.
I can read his righteous sentence by the
dim and flaring lamps.
His day is marching on.

3 He has sounded forth the trumpet that
shall never sound retreat.
He is sifting out the hearts of all before
his judgement seat.
O, be swift my soul to answer him, be
jubilant my feet!
Our God is marching on.

4 In the beauty of the lilies Christ was born
across the sea
with a glory in his bosom that
transfigures you and me.
As he died to make us holy, let us make
all people free.
Whilst God is marching on.

489 *From Psalm 88 (89) Taizé chant*

Misercordias Domini in aeternum cantabo.

1 From age to age through all generations,
my mouth shall proclaim your truth,
O Lord.

2 Who, O God, who in the universe
can compare with you?

3 Blest be the Lord for ever,
throughout eternity. Amen! Amen!

490 *Eleanor Farjeon (1881–1965)*

1 Morning has broken like the first
morning,
blackbird has spoken like the first bird.
Praise for the singing! Praise for the
morning!
Praise for them, springing fresh from the
Word!

2 Sweet the rain's new fall sunlit from
heaven,
like the first dew–fall on the first grass.
Praise for the sweetness of the wet
garden,
sprung in completeness where his feet
pass.

3 Mine is the sunlight! Mine is the morning
born of the one light Eden saw play!
Praise with elation, praise ev'ry morning,
God's re–creation of the new day!

491 *Estelle White*

1 'Moses I know you're the man,'
the Lord said.
'You're going to work out my plan,'
the Lord said.
'Lead all the Israelites out of slavery.
And I shall make them a wandering race
called the people of God.'

So ev'ry day we're on our way,
for we're a travelling, wandering race
called the people of God.

2 'Don't get too set in your ways,'
the Lord said.
'Each step is only a phase,' the Lord said.
'I'll go before you and I shall be a sign
to guide my travelling, wandering race.
You're the people of God.'

3 'No matter what you may do,'
the Lord said,
'I shall be faithful and true,' the Lord said.
'My love will strengthen you as you go
along,
for you're my travelling, wandering race.
You're the people of God.'

4 'Look at the birds in the air,'
the Lord said,
'They fly unhampered by care,' the Lord
said.
'You will move easier if you're travelling
light,
for you're a wandering vagabond race.
You're the people of God.'

5 'Foxes have places to go,' the Lord said.
'But I've no home here below,' the Lord
said.
'So if you want to be with me all your days,
keep up the moving and travelling on.
You're the people of God.'

492 *Frederick William Faber (1814–63)*

1 Most ancient of all mysteries,
before thy throne we lie;
have mercy now, most merciful,
most Holy Trinity.

2 When heaven and earth were yet unmade,
when time was yet unknown,
thou, in thy bliss and majesty,
didst live and love alone.

3 Thou wert not born; there was no fount,
from which thy being flowed;
there is no end which thou canst reach:
but thou art simply God.

4 How wonderful creation is,
the work that thou didst bless;
and oh, what then must thou be like,
Eternal Loveliness!

5 Most ancient of all mysteries,
still at thy throne we lie;
have mercy now, most merciful,
most Holy Trinity.

493 *John Glynn (English version)*

1 Mother of our Lord, we greet you;
we have come to pray and be with you.
All our hopes and dreams we bring you;
with our burdened hearts entrust you.

Look on us with love, console us,
lay your gentle hands upon us.
Lead us to your Son, our Brother,
Mary Queen of Peace, our Mother.

2 Mother of the church, we seek you;
in these final times our evening star;
purify our hearts, embrace us,
faithful to God's Word, sustain us.

3 Mother of the world, we praise you
here upon the earth you show your face:
holy is the place we find you,
joyfully in song proclaim you.

4 Mother of our lives, we thank you,
You bestow your love on each of us.
Faithful we will be to Jesus,
Mary, full of grace, stay with us.

494 *Paschal Jordan, OSB*

Mould us, Lord, as the potter's clay.
Fire us, Lord, with your Spirit today.
Shape us, Lord, in the likeness of Jesus,
your Son,
so we, his flock, may continue
what the Great Shepherd has begun.

1 Set us apart as your priesthood and praise
once again, in your might.
Call us anew, out of darkness,
to walk in your light.

2 Wake us each morning to listen to you
as we stand in the breach.
When we reply to the wearied,
provide us with speech.

3 When in the heat of the battle, Lord,
hold high our limp arms in prayer.
Alone on the lake of our terror,
we find you are there.

4 Fill us, renew us, restore us, release us
all over the land,
with boldness and power, yet docile
as clay in your hand.

495 *Matthew Bridges (1800–94)*

1 My God, accept my heart this day,
and make it wholly thine,
that I from thee no more may stray,
no more from thee decline.

2 Before the cross of him who died,
behold, I prostrate fall;
let every sin be crucified,
and Christ be all in all.

3 Anoint me with thy heavenly grace,
and seal me for thine own,
that I may see thy glorious face,
and worship at thy throne.

4 Let every thought, and work and word
to thee be ever given,
then life shall be thy service, Lord,
and Death the gate of heaven.

5 All glory to the Father be,
all glory to the Son,
all glory, Holy Ghost, to thee,
while endless ages run.

496 *Philip Doddridge (1702–51)*

1 My God, and is thy table spread,
and does thy cup with love o'er–flow?
Thither be all thy children led,
and let them all thy sweetness know.

2 Hail, sacred feast, which Jesus makes!
Rich banquet of his flesh and blood!
Thrice happy those, who here partake
that sacred stream, that heavenly food.

3 O let thy table honoured be,
and furnished well with joyful guests;
and may each soul salvation see,
that here its sacred pledges tastes.

497 *Frederick William Faber (1814–63)*

1 My God, how wonderful thou art,
thy majesty how bright,
how beautiful thy mercy–seat
in depths of burning light.

2 How dread are thine eternal years,
O everlasting Lord!
by prostrate spirits day and night
incessantly adored.

3 How wonderful, how beautiful
the sight of thee must be,
thine endless wisdom, boundless power
and aweful purity!

4 Oh, how, I fear thee, living God!
with deepest, tenderest fears,
and worship thee with trembling hope
and penitential tears.

5 Yet I may love thee too, O Lord,
almighty as thou art,
for thou hast stooped to ask of me
the love of my poor heart.

6 No earthly father loves like thee,
no mother e'er so mild
bears and forbears as thou hast done
with me thy sinful child.

7 Father of Jesus, love's reward,
what rapture will it be
prostrate before thy throne to lie,
and gaze and gaze on thee!

498 *17th century, tr. Edward Caswall (1814–78)*

1 My God I love thee, not because
I hope for heav'n thereby;
nor yet that those who love thee not
are lost eternally.

2 Thou, O my Jesus, thou didst me
upon the cross embrace;
for me didst bear the nails and spear
and manifold disgrace,

3 And griefs and torments numberless
and sweat of agony;
e'en death itself – and all for one
who was thine enemy.

4 Then why, O Blessed Jesu Christ,
should I not love thee well;
not for the sake of winning heaven,
or of escaping hell;

5 Not with the hope of gaining aught;
not seeking a reward,
but, as thyself hast lovèd me,
O ever–loving Lord?

6 E'en so I love thee, and will love,
and in thy praise will sing;
solely because thou art my God
and my eternal king.

499 *Verse 1 Anonymous, Verses 2-5 Sandra Joan Billington*

1 My God loves me.
His love will never end.
He rests within my heart
for my God loves me.

2 His gentle hand
he stretches over me.
Though storm–clouds threaten the day
he will set me free.

3 He comes to me
in sharing bread and wine.
He brings me life that will reach
past the end of time.

4 My God loves me,
his faithful love endures.
And I will live like a child
held in love secure.

5 The joys of love
as offerings now we bring.
The pains of love will be lost
in the praise we sing.

500 *Graham Kendrick*

1 My Lord, what love is this,
that pays so dearly,
that I, the guilty one,
may go free!

Amazing love, O what sacrifice,
the Son of God giv'n for me.
My debt He pays, and my death He dies,
that I might live.

2 And so they watched Him die,
despised, rejected;
but oh, the blood He shed
flowed for me!

3 And now this love of Christ
shall flow like rivers:
come wash your guilt away,
live again!

501 *Anthony Sharpe*

My people, I hear you calling,
I will forgive you your sin, if you believe.
My people, you know my love outlasts all time,
so constant, forgiving, my love will set you free.

1 You who search in the desert,
you who find my pardon there,
you have found salvation,
your God has come to you from afar.

2 All of you who are blind and lame,
all who are my scattered sheep,
you, I will bring back to me,
my hand will gather you, from every land.

3 You who once turned away from me,
you who show regret and shame,
you will now rejoice again;
you are forgiven, give thanks and praise!

502 *The Grail*

My shepherd is the Lord, nothing
indeed shall I want.

or

His goodness shall follow me always to
the end of my days.

or

The Lord himself will give me repose.

1 The Lord is my shepherd,
there is nothing I shall want.
Fresh and green are the pastures
where he gives me repose,
near restful waters he leads me,
to revive my drooping spirit.

2 He guides me along the right path:
he is true to his name.
If I should walk in the valley of darkness
no evil would I fear.
You are there with your crook and your
staff,
with these you give me comfort.

3 You have prepared a banquet for me
in the sight of my foes.
My head you have anointed with oil;
my cup is overflowing.

4 Surely goodness and kindness shall
follow me
all the days of my life.
In the Lord's own house shall I dwell
for ever and ever.

5 (To the Father and Son give glory,
give glory to the Spirit.
To God who is, who was, and who will be
for ever and ever.)

503 *Samuel Crossman (c.1624–83)*

1 My song is love unknown,
my Saviour's love for me,
love to the loveless shown,
that they might lovely be.
O who am I, that for my sake,
my Lord should take frail flesh and die?

2 He came from his blest throne,
salvation to bestow;
but men made strange, and none
the longed–for Christ would know,
but O my friend, my friend indeed,
who at my need his life did spend!

3 Sometimes they strew his way,
and his sweet praises sing;
resounding all the day
hosannas to their King;
then 'Crucify!' is all their breath,
and for his death they thirst and cry.

4 Why, what hath my Lord done?
What makes this rage and spite?
He made the lame to run,
he gave the blind their sight.
Sweet injuries! Yet they at these
themselves displease, and 'gainst him rise.

5 They rise, and needs will have
my dear Lord made away;
a murderer they save,
the Prince of Life they slay.
Yet cheerful he to suffering goes,
that he his foes from thence might free.

6 In life, no house, no home
my Lord on earth might have:
in death no friendly tomb
but what a stranger gave.
What may I say? Heaven was his home;
but mine the tomb wherein he lay.

7 Here might I stay and sing,
no story so divine,
never was love, dear King,
never was grief like thine.
This is my Friend, in whose sweet praise
I all my days could gladly spend.

504 *Anthony Sharpe*

1 My soul cannot be still,
my heart cries in pain.
Is now a plea to heaven in vain?
Our land is empty now,
our towns laid waste:
God's anger the people have faced.

Lord, show us your mercy,
O Lord, hear our prayer;
O Lord, renew our hearts and minds
with your all–healing love.

2 We look to the mountains,
we see their fear:
the anger of your presence is near.
The land is a wilderness,
the trees are dead.
The birds of heaven have fled.

3 O turn to your people, Lord,
and we shall be healed,
to live in your covenant resealed.
O praise to the God of hope
set high on his throne;
we trust in your promise to relent.

505 *Lucien Deiss*

My soul is longing for your peace,
near to you, my God.

1 Lord, you know that my heart is not proud,
and my eyes are not lifted from earth.

2 Lofty thoughts have never filled my mind,
far beyond my sight all ambitious deeds.

3 In your peace I have maintained my soul,
I have kept my heart in your quiet peace.

4 As a child rests on a mother's knee,
so I place my soul in your loving care.

5 Israel, put all your hope in God,
place your trust in God, now and evermore.

506 *Owen Alstott*

My soul rejoices in God, my Saviour.
My spirit finds its joy in God,
the living God.

1 My soul proclaims his mighty deeds.
My spirit sings the greatness of his name.

2 His mercy flows throughout the land
and ev'ry generation knows his love.

3 He casts the mighty from their thrones
and raises up the poor and lowly to new life.

4 He fills the hungry with good things.
With empty hands he sends the rich away.

5 Just as he promised Abraham,
he comes to free his people, Israel.

507 *Valerie Helen Van Hove*

1 My strength comes from the Lord, my God,
who guides me with his staff and rod.
He knows my sorrow, he shares my pain,
He gives me comfort and life again.
For Him I'll carry my cross each day,
for Him, I'll walk in his light and way.

2 My faith comes from the Lord, my God,
who shows me where his feet have trod.
The path is there, the road is clear
and I can walk and have no fear;
for Christ himself once walked that way
that I might know my God one day.

3 My hope comes from the Lord, my God,
who gives me clothes and keeps me shod.
He lifts me up that I may nest
in gentle arms where there is rest.
For how could I go it alone
and come before the Father's throne?

4 My love comes from the Lord, my God,
whose love breathes life like Aaron's rod.
He gave us all his last decree
that love would lead us to the key
of life eternal, God supreme,
in Christ portrayed, the living stream.

5 My life comes from the Lord, my God,
my faith, my hope, my strength, my God.
In joy I feel his love around,
his gifts to me each day abound.
He knows my needs, he fills my cup.
In his abode he takes me up.

508 *St. Bede the Venerable (673–735) tr. R. A. Knox (1888–1957)*

1 New praises be given to Christ newly crowned,
who back to his heaven a new way hath found;
God's blessedness sharing before us he goes,
what mansions preparing, what endless repose!

2 His glory still praising on thrice holy ground
the apostles stood gazing, his mother around;
with hearts that beat faster, with eyes full of love,
they watched while their master ascended above.

3 'No star can disclose him', the bright angels said;
'Eternity knows him, your conquering head;
those high habitations he leaves not again,
till, judging all nations, on earth he shall reign.'

4 Thus spoke they and straightway, where legions defend
heaven's glittering gateway, their Lord they attend,
and cry, looking thither, 'Your portals let down
for him who rides hither in peace and renown.'

5 They asked, who keep sentry in that blessed town,
'Who thus claimeth entry, a king of renown?'
'The Lord of all valiance', that herald replied,
'Who Satan's battalions laid low in their pride.'

6 Grant, Lord, that our longing may follow thee there,
on earth who are thronging thy temples with prayer;
and unto thee gather, Redeemer, thine own,
where thou with thy Father dost sit on the throne.

509 *Erik Routley (1917–82)*

1 New songs of celebration render
to him who has great wonders done;
awed by his power his foes surrender
and fall before the Mighty One.
He has made known his great salvation
which all his friends with joy confess;
he has revealed to every nation
his everlasting righteousness.

2 Joyfully, heartily resounding,
let every instrument and voice
peal out the praise of grace abounding,
calling the whole world to rejoice.
Trumpets and organs set in motion
such sounds as make the heavens ring:
all things that live in earth and ocean
make music for your mighty King.

3 Rivers and seas and torrents roaring
honour the Lord with wild acclaim;
mountains and stones look up adoring
and find a voice to praise his name.
Righteous, commanding, ever glorious,
praises be his that never cease:
just is our God, whose truth victorious
establishes the world in peace.

510 *Michael Cockett*

1 Now come to me all you who seek
and place your trust in me.
For I have comfort for the weak,
the strength to set you free.
And, just as gentle blades of grass
can crack the hardened earth,
creation will be yours at last
when love is brought to birth.

2 Now come to me all you who seek
and place your trust in me.
For I will comfort those who mourn
and make the blind to see.
However dark the stormy night,
the sun will raise the dawn,
and you will live beneath the light
of love in darkness born.

3 Now come to me all you who seek
and place your trust in me.
For I bring peace to those at war
and set the captives free.
Just as in cutting sun–ripe wheat
we count the summer's worth,
so shall all those who justice seek
be there at love's new birth.

511 *Marty Haugen*

Now in this banquet, Christ is our bread;
here shall all hungers be fed.
Bread that is broken, wine that is poured,
love is the Sign of our Lord.

1 You who have touched us and graced us with love,
make us your people of goodness and light.

2 Let our hearts burn with the fire of your love;
open our eyes to the glory of God.

3 God who makes the blind to see,
God who makes the lame to walk,
bring us dancing into day,
lead your people in your way.

4 Hope for the hopeless, light for the blind,
'Strong' is your name, Lord, 'Gentle' and 'Kind'.

5 Call us to be your light, call us to be your love,
make us your people again.

5 Come, O Spirit! Renew our hearts!
We shall arise to be children of light.

Alternative texts for refrain:

God of our journeys, daybreak to night;
lead us to justice and light.
Grant us compassion, strength for the day,
wisdom to walk in your way.

Lord, you can open hearts that are stone;
live in our flesh and our bone;
lead us to wonder, mystery and grace,
one in your loving embrace.

512 *Martin Rinkart (1586–1649), tr. Catherine Winkworth*

1 Now thank we all our God,
with heart and hands and voices,
who wondrous things hath done,
in whom this world rejoices;
who from our mother's arms
hath blessed us on our way
with countless gifts of love,
and still is ours today.

2 O may this bounteous God
through all our life be near us,
with ever joyful hearts
and blessed peace to cheer us;
and keep us in his grace,
and guide us when perplexed,
and free us from all ills
in this world and the next.

3 All praise and thanks to God
the Father now be given,
the Son, and him who reigns
with them in highest heaven,
the one Eternal God,
whom earth and heaven adore;
for thus it was, is now,
and shall be evermore.

513 *J. M. C. Crum*

1 Now the green blade riseth from the buried grain,
wheat that in the dark earth many days has lain;
love lives again, that with the dead has been:
love is come again like wheat that springeth green.

2 In the grave they laid him, Love whom men had slain,
thinking that never he would wake again,
laid in the earth like grain that sleeps unseen:
love is come again like wheat that springeth green.

3 Forth he came at Easter, like the risen grain,
he that for three days in the grave had lain,
quick from the dead my risen Lord is seen:
love is come again like wheat that
springeth green.

4 When our hearts are wintry, grieving or
in pain,
thy touch can call us back to life again,
fields of our hearts that dead and bare
have been:
love is come again like wheat that
springeth green.

514 *Willard F. Jabusch*

1 Now watch for God's coming, be patient
till then;
like sunshine he'll brighten all women
and men;
who hope in the Lord will possess fertile
land;
the poor he will welcome and grasp by
the hand.

2 Our steps are directed, God watches our
path;
he guides us and holds us and saves us
from wrath,
and though we may fall we will not go
headlong,
for God gives sound footing and keeps us
from wrong.

3 So wait for his coming, be patient till then;
the wicked are armed and would kill
honest men.
Their arms shall be broken, no refuge
they'll see,
but saved are the needy by God's own
decree.

4 Now those who do evil will wither like
grass,
like green of the springtime they fade
and they pass,
so trust in the Lord and to him give your
life,
he'll bring heart's desires and peace in
our strife.

515 *Te lucis ante terminum, tr. Sebastian Bullough*

1 Now with the fading light of day,
Maker of all, to thee we pray
that with thy wonted care and love,
thou guard and protect us from above.

2 Take far away each hideous dream,
things in the night that monstrous seem,
wiles of our old arch–foe restrain
lest faltering flesh contract a stain.

3 Father almighty, grace afford,
grant it through Jesus Christ our Lord,
who with the Holy Ghost and thee
is reigning for all eternity.

516 *7th century, tr. Edward Caswall (1814–78)*

1 Now with the fast–departing light,
maker of all! we ask of thee,
of thy great mercy, through the night
our guardian and defence to be.

2 Far off let idle visions fly:
no phantom of the night molest:
curb thou our raging enemy,
that we in chaste repose may rest.

3 Father of mercies! hear our cry:
hear us, O sole–begotten Son!
Who, with the Holy Ghost most high,
reignest while endless ages run.

517 *St Alphonsus Liguori (1696–1787), tr. Edmund Vaughan (1827–1908)*

1 O bread of heaven, beneath this veil
thou dost my very God conceal;
my Jesus, dearest treasure, hail;
I love thee and adoring kneel;
each loving soul by thee is fed
with thine own self in form of bread.

2 O food of life, thou who dost give
the pledge of immortality;
I live; no, 'tis not I that live;
God gives me life, God lives in me:
he feeds my soul, he guides my ways,
and every grief with joy repays.

3 O bond of love, that dost unite
the servant to his living Lord;
could I dare live, and not requite
such love, then death were meet reward:
I cannot live unless to prove
some love for such unmeasured love.

4 Belovèd Lord in heaven above,
there, Jesus, thou awaitest me;
to gaze on thee with changeless love,
yes, thus I hope, thus shall it be:
for how can he deny me heaven
who here on earth himself hath given?

5 In broken bread, in wine out–poured,
your new and living way
proclaim to us, O risen Lord,
O Christ of this our day.

6 O changeless Christ, till life is past
your blessing still be given;
then bring us home, to taste at last
the timeless joys of heaven.

518 *Timothy Dudley–Smith*

1 O changeless Christ, for ever new,
who walked our earthly ways,
still draw our hearts as once you drew
the hearts of other days.

2 As once you spoke by plain and hill
or taught by shore and sea,
so be today our teacher still,
O Christ of Galilee.

3 As wind and storm their master heard
and his command fulfilled,
may troubled hearts receive your word,
the tempest–tossed be stilled.

4 And as of old to all who prayed
your healing hand was shown,
so be your touch upon us laid,
unseen but not unknown.

520 *18th century, tr. Frederick Oakeley (1802–80)*

1 O come, all ye faithful,
joyful and triumphant.
O come ye, O come ye to Bethlehem;
come and behold him,
born the king of angels:
O come, let us adore him, (3)
Christ the Lord.

2 God of God,
light of light,
lo! he abhors not the virgin's womb;
very God,
begotten not created:

3 Sing, choirs of angels,
sing in exultation,
sing all ye citizens of heaven above;
glory to God
in the highest:

*4 Yea, Lord, we greet thee,
born this happy morning,
Jesu, to thee be glory given;
word of the Father,
now in flesh appearing:

**This verse is not sung until Christmas Day.*

519 *Taizé chant*

Verses from Psalms 22 (23), 24 (25), 33 (34), 84 (85) or 129 (130) may be sung by the Cantor.

♩ = 60
fine
O Chris-te Do-mi-ne Je-su, O Chris-te Do-mi-ne Je-su! O

521 *Frederick William Faber (1814–63) altered*

1 O come and mourn with me awhile;
see, Mary calls us to her side;
O come and let us mourn with her;

Jesus our love, Jesus our love,
is crucified.

2 Have we no tears to shed for him,
while soldiers scoff and men deride?
Ah! look how patiently he hangs;

3 How fast his feet and hands are nailed;
his blessed tongue with thirst is tied;
his failing eyes are blind with blood;

4 Seven times he spoke, seven words of love,
and all three hours his silence cried
for mercy on humanity;

5 O love of God! O human sin!
In this dread act your strength is tried;
and victory remains with love;

522 *From the 'Great O Antiphons' (12th–13th century), tr. John Mason Neale (1818–66)*

1 O come, O come, Emmanuel,
and ransom captive Israel,
that mourns in lonely exile here
until the Son of God appear:

Rejoice, rejoice! Emmanuel
shall come to thee, O Israel.

2 O come, thou Rod of Jesse, free
thine own from Satan's tyranny;
from depths of hell thy people save,
and give them vict'ry o'er the grave:

3 O come, thou dayspring, come and cheer
our spirits by thine advent here;
disperse the gloomy clouds of night,
and death's dark shadows put to flight:

4 O come, thou key of David, come
and open wide our heavenly home;
make safe the way that leads on high,
and close the path to misery.

5 O come, O come, thou Lord of might,
who to thy tribes, on Sinai's height
in ancient times, didst give the law
in cloud and majesty and awe:

523 *Paraphrased by Chrysogonus Waddell*

1 O comfort my people
and calm all their fear,
and tell them the time of
salvation draws near.
O tell them I come
to remove all their shame.
Then they will forever
give praise to my name.

2 Proclaim to the cities
of Juda my word:
that gentle yet strong is
the hand of the Lord.
I rescue the captives,
my people defend
and bring them to justice
and joy without end.

3 All mountains and hills shall
become as a plain
for vanished are mourning
and hunger and pain.
And never again shall
these war against you.
Behold I come quickly
to make all things new.

524 *James Quinn, SJ*

1 O Father, take in sign of love
these gifts of bread and wine!
With them we give our very selves,
to be for ever thine!

2 These gifts another gift will be,
thy Son in very deed,
for us a willing victim made,
the Lamb on whom we feed!

3 These are the gifts thy Son did bless
the night before he died,
by which he showed himself a priest
and victim crucified!

4 He now has given us as our own
his offering made to thee:
his Body broken, Blood outpoured,
for us on Calvary!

5 This bread his Body will become,
this wine his Blood will be!
Our humble gifts will be the gift
that is most dear to thee!

6 This perfect gift thou wilt restore
to greatest and to least,
to make all one in love and joy
in thy communion–feast!

525 *Maintzisch Gesangbuch, 1661, tr. Walter H. Shewring and others*

1 O food of travellers, angels' bread,
manna wherewith the blest are fed,
come nigh, and with thy sweetness fill
the hungry hearts that seek thee still.

2 O fount of love, O well unpriced,
outpouring from the heart of Christ,
give us to drink of very thee,
and all we pray shall answered be.

3 O Jesus Christ, we pray to thee
that this thy presence which we see,
though now in form of bread concealed,
to us may be in heaven revealed.

526 *South African traditional*

1 O freedom. O freedom. O freedom.
O yes, I know. O yes, I know. O yes, I know.

2 O Jesus, O Jesus. O Jesus, Jesus is coming.
O yes, I know. O yes, I know.

527 *G. K. Chesterton (1874–1936)*

1 O God of earth and altar,
bow down and hear our cry,
our earthly rulers falter,
our people drift and die;
the walls of gold entomb us,
the swords of scorn divide,
take not thy thunder from us,
but take away our pride.

2 From all that terror teaches,
from lies of tongue and pen,
from all the easy speeches
that comfort cruel men,
from sale and profanation
of honour and the sword,
from sleep and from damnation,
deliver us, good Lord!

3 Tie in a living tether
the prince and priest and thrall,
bind all our lives together,
smite us and save us all;
in ire and exultation
aflame with faith, and free,
lift up a living nation,
a single sword to thee.

528 *Isaac Watts (1674–1748)*

1 O God, our help in ages past,
our hope for years to come,
our shelter from the stormy blast,
and our eternal home:

2 Beneath the shadow of thy throne,
thy saints have dwelt secure;
sufficient is thine arm alone,
and our defence is sure.

3 Before the hills in order stood,
or earth received her frame,
from everlasting thou art God,
to endless years the same.

4 A thousand ages in thy sight
are like an evening gone;
short as the watch that ends the night
before the rising sun.

5 Time, like an ever–rolling stream,
bears all its sons away;
they fly forgotten, as a dream
dies at the opening day.

6 O God, our help in ages past,
our hope for years to come,
be thou our guard while troubles last,
and our eternal home.

529 *Anthony Nye*

1 O God, thy people gather,
obedient to thy word,
around thy holy altar,
to praise thy name, O Lord;
for all thy living kindness
our grateful hearts we raise;
but pardon first the blindness
of all our sinful ways.

2 Thou art our loving Father,
thou art our holiest Lord,
but we have sinned against thee,
by thought and deed and word.
Before the court of heaven
we stand and humbly pray
our sins may be forgiven,
our faults be washed away.

3 Though sinful, we implore thee
to turn and make us live,
that so we may adore thee,
and our due offering give,
and may the prayers and voices
of thy glad people rise,
as thy whole Church rejoices
in this great sacrifice.

530 *Anthony Nye*

1 O God, we give ourselves today
with bread and wine to thee,
the selfsame gift which thy dear Son
gave once on Calvary.

2 Entire and whole, our life and love
with heart and soul and mind,
for all our sins and faults and needs,
thy Church and humankind.

3 With humble and with contrite heart
this bread and wine we give
because thy Son once gave himself
and died that we might live.

4 Though lowly now, soon by thy word
those offered gifts will be
the very body of our Lord,
his soul and deity.

5 His very body, offered up,
a gift beyond all price,
he gives to us, that we may give
in loving sacrifice.

6 O Lord, who took our human life,
as water mixed with wine,
grant through this sacrifice that we
may share thy life divine.

531 *St. Thomas Aquinas (1227–74), tr. Edward Caswall (1814–78)*

1 O Godhead hid, devoutly I adore thee,
who truly art within the forms before me;
to thee my heart I bow with bended knee,
as failing quite in contemplating thee.

2 Sight, touch, and taste in thee are each
deceived,
the ear alone most safely is believed:
I believe all the Son of God has spoken;
than truth's own word there is no truer
token.

3 God only on the cross lay hid from view;
but here lies hid at once the manhood too:
and I, in both professing my belief,
make the same prayer as the repentant
thief.

4 Thy wounds, as Thomas saw, I do not see;
yet thee confess my Lord and God to be;
make me believe thee ever more and more,
in thee my hope, in thee my love to store.

5 O thou memorial of our Lord's own dying!
O bread that living art and vivifying!
Make ever thou my soul on thee to live:
ever a taste of heavenly sweetness give.

6 O loving Pelican! O Jesus, Lord!
Unclean I am, but cleanse me in thy blood;
of which a single drop, for sinners spilt,
is ransom for a world's entire guilt.

7 Jesus, whom for the present veiled I see,
what I so thirst for, oh, vouchsafe to me:
that I may see thy countenance unfolding,
and may be blest thy glory in beholding.

532 *Archbishop Francis Mostyn of Cardiff (1860–1939)*

1 O Great Saint David, still we hear thee call us,
unto a life that knows no fear of death;
Yea, down the ages, will thy words enthral us,
strong happy words: 'Be joyful, keep the faith.'

On Cambria's sons stretch out thy hands in blessing;
For our dear land thy help we now implore.
Lead us to God, with humble hearts confessing
Jesus, Lord and King for evermore.

2 Christ was the centre rock of all thy teaching,
God's holy will – the splendour of its theme.
His grace informed, his love inflamed thy preaching;
Christ's sway on earth, the substance of thy dream.

On Cambria's sons …

3 In early childhood, choosing Jesus only,
thy fervour showed his yoke was light and sweet!
And thus for thee, life's journey was not lonely –
the path made plain by prints of wounded feet.

On Cambria's sons …

4 O glorious saint, we wander in the dark;
with thee we seek our trusted guide in Rome.
Help him to steer on earth Saint Peter's barque,
that we may safely reach our heavenly home.

On Cambria's sons …

533 *Owen Alstott*

O holy Dwelling Place of God,
O holy Temple of the Word.
O holy Mary, holy Mother of God.

1 O radiant star of heaven, illuminating the night;
reflection of the Son, our source of life and light.

2 O blest beyond all others, of ev'ry land and race,
possessing in your soul the fullness of God's grace.

3 From heav'n the angel Gabriel announced the ancient plan
and humbly you accepted to bear the God made man.

4 With joy beyond all measure you cared for God's own son
and pondered in your heart the new age now begun.

5 Exquisite was your sorrow, unequalled was the loss
you suffered when your son was raised upon the cross.

6 All praise and adoration we sing now to your son
who reigns in highest heaven and has the vict'ry won.

534 *Randall DeBruyn*

O how lovely is your dwelling place,
dwelling of the Lord of hosts!
How we long for your house, O Lord,
singing out a song of joy to the living God!

1 Even sparrows find a home with you,
and swallows lay their young to rest.
Blessed are those who dwell in you
and sing your praise, O God!

2 Bless'd are those who find their strength in you,
whose hearts are highways for your will.
Bringing joy to those around them,
they go from strength to strength.

3 Hear our prayer, O Lord God of hosts;
receive our life into your hands!
Look into the hearts of those you love
and grant us all we need!

4 For one day within your house exceeds
a thousand spent away from you.
We would rather serve within your house
than wealth and power receive.

5 For our God protects us from all harm;
he gives his favour and his love.
All good things will come to those
who love
the Lord, and walk with him.

535 *Edward Caswall (1814–78)*

1 O Jesus Christ, remember,
when thou shalt come again,
upon the clouds of heaven,
with all thy shining train;
when every eye shall see thee
in deity revealed,
who now upon this altar
in silence art concealed.

2 Remember then, O Saviour,
I supplicate of thee,
that here I bowed before thee
upon my bended knee;
that here I owned thy presence,
and did not thee deny,
and glorified thy greatness
though hid from human eye.

3 Accept, divine Redeemer,
the homage of my praise;
be thou the light and honour
and glory of my days.
Be thou my consolation
when death is drawing nigh:
be thou my only treasure
through all eternity.

536 *J.E. Bode*

1 O Jesus, I have promised
to serve thee to the end;
be thou for ever near me,
my Master and my Friend;
I shall not fear the battle
if thou art by my side,
nor wander from the pathway
if thou wilt be my guide.

2 O let me feel thee near me:
the world is ever near;
I see the sights that dazzle,
the tempting sounds I hear;
my foes are ever near me,
around me and within;
but, Jesus, draw thou nearer,
and shield my soul from sin.

3 O let me hear thee speaking
in accents clear and still,
above the storms of passion,
the murmurs of self-will;
O speak to reassure me,
to hasten or control;
O speak, and make me listen,
thou guardian of my soul.

4 O Jesus, thou hast promised
to all who follow thee,
that where thou art in glory
there shall thy servant be;
and, Jesus, I have promised
to serve thee to the end:
O give me grace to follow,
my Master and my Friend.

5 O let me see thy foot–marks,
and in them plant mine own;
my hope to follow duly
is in thy strength alone:
O guide me, call me, draw me,
uphold me to the end;
and then in heaven receive me,
my Saviour and my Friend.

537 *A. Gregory Murray, OSB (1905–1992)*

1 O king of might and splendour,
creator most adored,
this sacrifice we render
to thee as sov'reign Lord.
May these, our gifts, be pleasing
unto thy majesty;
from sin, O Lord, release us,
who have offended thee.

2 Thy body thou hast given,
thy blood thou hast outpoured,
that sin might be forgiven,
O Jesus, loving Lord.
As now with love most tender
thy death we celebrate,
our lives in self–surrender
to thee we consecrate.

538 *Estelle White*

1 O lady, full of God's own grace,
whose caring hands the child embraced,
who listened to the Spirit's word,
believed and trusted in the Lord.

O virgin fair, star of the sea,
my dearest mother, pray for me. (2)

2 O lady, who felt daily joy
in caring for the holy boy,
whose home was plain and shorn of wealth,
yet was enriched by God's own breath.

3 O lady, who bore living's pain
but still believed that love would reign,
who on a hill watched Jesus die
as on the cross they raised him high.

4 O lady, who, on Easter day,
had all your sorrow wiped away
as God the Father's will was done
when from death's hold he freed your Son.

539 *Denis E. Hurley*

1 O light forever dawning
beyond the darkest night;
O comfort of the mourning,
our strength and our delight;
receive our humble pleading
for those whose course is run,
lest pardon they be needing
for any evil done.

2 To him who like the eagle
arose on conqu'ring wing,
the cross his banner regal,
O death, where is your sting?
There's surely no rejection
for those who share his strife,
but hope and resurrection
and everlasting life.

540 *Phillips Brooks (1835–93)*

1 O little town of Bethlehem,
how still we see thee lie!
Above thy deep and dreamless sleep
the silent stars go by.
Yet, in thy dark streets shineth
the everlasting light;
the hopes and fears of all the years
are met in thee tonight.

2 O morning stars, together
proclaim the holy birth,
and praises sing to God the King,
and peace to men on earth;
for Christ is born of Mary;
and, gathered all above,
while mortals sleep, the angels keep
their watch of wondering love.

3 How silently, how silently,
the wondrous gift is given!
So God imparts to human hearts
the blessings of his heaven.
No ear may hear his coming;
but in this world of sin,
where meek souls will receive him, still
the dear Christ enters in.

4 Where children pure and happy
pray to the blessèd Child,
where misery cries out to thee,
son of the mother mild;
where charity stands watching
and faith holds wide the door,
the dark night waits, the glory breaks,
and Christmas comes once more.

5 O holy child of Bethlehem,
descend to us, we pray;
cast out our sin, and enter in,
be born in us today.
We hear the Christmas angels
the great glad tidings tell:
O come to us, abide with us,
our Lord Emmanuel.

541 *Lucien Deiss*

O Lord, be not mindful of our guilt and our sins;
O Lord, do not judge us for our faults and offences.
May your merciful love be upon us.

1 Help your people, Lord,
O God our Saviour,
deliver us for the glory of your name!

2 Pardon us, O Lord,
all our sins,
deliver us for the glory of your name!

3 Praise to you, O Lord,
through all the ages without end,
deliver us for the glory of your name!

542 *Taizé chant*

O Lord hear my pray'r, O Lord hear my pray'r; when I call,
an - swer me. O Lord hear my pray'r, O Lord hear my pray'r.
Come and li - sten to me. O

543 Refrain by Paul Inwood

O Lord, you are the centre of my life:
I will always praise you,
I will always serve you,
I will always keep you in my sight.

1 Keep me safe, O God, I take refuge in you.
I say to the Lord: 'You are my God.
My happiness lies in you alone;
my happiness lies in you alone.'

2 I will bless the Lord who gives me counsel,
who even at night directs my heart.
I keep the Lord ever in my sight:
since he is at my right hand, I shall stand firm.

3 And so my heart rejoices, my soul is glad;
even in safety shall my body rest.
For you will not leave my soul among the dead,
nor let your beloved know decay.

4 You will show me the path of life,
the fullness of joy in your presence,
at your right hand, at your right hand
happiness for ever.

544 St. Alphonsus Liguori (1699–1787), tr. Edmund Vaughan (1827–1908)

1 O Mother blest, whom God bestows
on sinners and on just,
what joy, what hope thou givest those
who in thy mercy trust.

Thou art clement, thou art chaste,
Mary, thou art fair;
of all mothers sweetest, best;
none with thee compare.

2 O heavenly mother, mistress sweet!
It never yet was told
that suppliant sinner left thy feet
unpitied, unconsoled.

3 O mother pitiful and mild,
cease not to pray for me;
for I do love thee as a child,
and sigh for love of thee.

4 Most powerful mother, we all know
thy Son denies thee nought;
thou askest, wishest it, and lo!
His power thy will hath wrought.

5 O mother blest, for me obtain
ungrateful though I be,
to love that God who first could deign
to show such love for me.

545 Estelle White

1 O my Lord, within my heart
pride will have no home,
every talent that I have
comes from you alone.

And like a child at rest
close to its mother's breast,
safe in your arms
my soul is calmed.

2 Lord, my eyes do not look high
nor my thoughts take wings,
for I can find treasures in
ordinary things.

3 Great affairs are not for me,
deeds beyond my scope,
in the simple things I do
I find joy and hope.

546 Dorothy Francis Gurney (1858–1932)

1 O perfect love, all human thought transcending,
lowly we kneel in prayer before thy throne.
That theirs may be the love which knows no ending,
whom thou for evermore dost join in one.

2 O perfect life, be thou their full assurance
of tender charity and steadfast faith,
of patient hope, and quiet, brave endurance,
with childlike trust that fears nor pain nor death.

3 Grant them the joy which brightens earthly sorrow,
grant them the peace which calms all earthly strife;
and to life's day the glorious unknown morrow
that dawns upon eternal love and life.

547 *Henry Williams Baker (1821–77)*

1 O praise ye the Lord! Praise him in the height;
rejoice in his word, ye angels of light;
ye heavens, adore him, by whom ye were made,
and worship before him, in brightness arrayed.

2 O praise ye the Lord! praise him upon earth,
in tuneful accord, ye sons of new birth.
Praise him who hath brought you his grace from above,
praise him who hath taught you to sing of his love.

3 O praise ye the Lord, all things that give sound;
each jubilant chord re–echo around;
loud organs, his glory forth tell in deep tone,
and, sweet harp, the story of what he hath done.

4 O praise ye the Lord! Thanksgiving and song
to him be outpoured all ages along;
for love in creation, for heaven restored,
for grace of salvation, O praise ye the Lord! (Amen.)

548 *H. Auber (1773–1862)*

1 O praise our great and gracious Lord
and call upon his name;
to strains of joy tune every chord,
his mighty acts proclaim;
tell how he led his chosen race
to Canaan's promised land;
tell how his covenant of grace
unchanged shall ever stand.

2 He gave the shadowing cloud by day,
the moving fire by night;
to guide his Israel on their way,
he made their darkness light;
and have not we a sure retreat,
a Saviour ever nigh,
the same clear light to guide our feet,
the dayspring from on high?

3 We, too, have manna from above,
the bread that came from heaven;
to us the same kind hand of love
hath living waters given.
A rock we have, from whence the spring
in rich abundance flows;
that rock is Christ, our priest, our king,
who life and health bestows.

4 O let us prize this blessèd food,
and trust our heavenly guide;
so shall we find death's fearful flood
serene as Jordan's tide,
and safely reach that happy shore,
the land of peace and rest,
where angels worship and adore,
in God's own presence blest.

549 *St Thomas Aquinas (1227–74), tr. James Quinn, SJ*

1 O Priest and Victim, Lord of life,
throw wide the gates of paradise!
We face our foes in mortal strife;
thou art our strength: O heed our cries!

2 To Father, Son and Spirit blest,
one only God, be ceaseless praise!
May he in goodness grant us rest
in heav'n, our home, for endless days!

550 *Frederick William Faber (1814–63)*

1 O purest of creatures!
Sweet mother, sweet maid;
the one spotless womb
wherein Jesus was laid.
Dark night hath come down
on us, mother, and we
look out for thy shining,
sweet star of the sea.

2 Deep night hath come down on
this rough–spoken world,
and the banners of darkness
are boldly unfurled;
and the tempest–tossed Church,
all her eyes are on thee,
they look to thy shining,
sweet star of the sea.

3 He gazed on thy soul,
it was spotless and fair;
for the empire of sin,
it had never been there;
none ever had owned thee,
dear mother, but he,
and he blessed thy clear shining,
sweet star of the sea.

4 Earth gave him one lodging;
'twas deep in thy breast,
and God found a home where
the sinner finds rest,
his home and his hiding–place,
both were in thee;
he was won by thy shining,
sweet star of the sea.

5 Oh, blissful and calm
was the wonderful rest
that thou gavest thy God
in thy virginal breast;
for the heaven he left
he found heaven in thee,
and he shone in thy shining,
sweet star of the sea.

551 *Ralph Wright, OSB*

1 O raise your eyes on high and see
there stands our sovereign Lord,
his glory is this day revealed,
his Word a two–edged sword.

2 We glimpse the splendour and the power
of him who conquered death,
the Christ in whom the universe
knows God's creating breath.

3 Of every creed and nation King
in him all strife is stilled;
the promise made to Abraham
in him has been fulfilled.

4 The prophets stand and with great joy
give witness as they gaze;
the Father with a sign has sealed
our trust, our hope, our praise.

5 This glory that today our eyes
have glimpsed of God's own Son
will help us ever sing with love
of Three who are but One.

552 *Paulus Gerhardt (1607–76), tr. Robert Bridges (1844–1930)*

1 O sacred head sore wounded,
defiled and put to scorn;
O kingly head surrounded
with mocking crown of thorn:
what sorrow mars thy grandeur?
can death thy bloom deflower?
O countenance whose splendour
the hosts of heaven adore.

2 Thy beauty, long–desirèd,
hath vanished from our sight;
thy power is all expirèd,
and quenched the light of light.
Ah me! for whom thou diest,
hide not so far thy grace:
show me, O love most highest,
the brightness of thy face.

3 I pray thee, Jesu, own me,
me, shepherd good, for thine;
who to thy fold hast won me,
and fed with truth divine.
Me guilty, me refuse not;
incline thy face to me,
this comfort that I lose not
on earth to comfort thee.

4 In thy most bitter passion
my heart to share doth cry,
with thee for my salvation
upon the cross to die.
Ah, keep my heart thus movèd
to stand thy cross beneath,
to mourn thee, well–belovèd,
yet thank thee for thy death.

5 My days are few, O fail not,
with thine immortal power,
to hold me that I quail not
in death's most fearful hour:
that I may fight befriended,
and see in my last strife
to me thine arms extended
upon the cross of life.

553 *Francis Stanfield (1835–1914)*

1 O Sacred Heart,
our home lies deep in thee;
on earth thou art an exile's rest,
in heav'n the glory of the blest,
O Sacred Heart.

2 O Sacred Heart,
thou fount of contrite tears;
where'er those living waters flow,
new life to sinners they bestow,
O Sacred Heart.

3 O Sacred Heart,
our trust is all in thee,
for though earth's night be dark and drear,
thou breathest rest where thou art near,
O Sacred Heart.

4 O Sacred Heart,
when shades of death shall fall,
receive us 'neath thy gentle care,
and save us from the tempter's snare,
O Sacred Heart.

5 O Sacred Heart,
lead exiled children home,
where we may ever rest near thee,
in peace and joy eternally,
O Sacred Heart.

554 *St Thomas Aquinas (1227–74)*

1 O salutaris hostia,
Quae caeli pandis ostium,
Bella premunt hostilia,
Da robur, fer auxilium.

2 Uni trinoque Domino
Sit sempiterna gloria,
Qui vitam sine termino
Nobis donet in patria. Amen.

555 *Response and v.1 from the Grail Psalter. Vv 2-3 adapted by Chris O'Hara.*

O that today you would listen to his voice:
'Harden not your hearts.'

1 Come, ring out our joy to the Lord;
hail the rock, hail the rock who saves us.
Let us come before him giving thanks,
with songs let us hail the Lord.

2 Come in, let us bow and bend low;
let us kneel to the God who made us;
like a flock he leads us by his hand
to pasture he guides us on.

3 'At Meribah you harden your hearts
and at Massah you seek to test me.'
Let us trust our God and hope in him;
today let us seek his voice.

556 *William Harry Turton (1856–1938)*

1 O thou, who at
thy Eucharist didst pray
that all thy Church
might be for ever one,
grant us at every
Eucharist to say,
with longing heart and soul,
'Thy will be done'.
O may we all one bread, one body be,
one through this sacrament of unity.

2 For all thy Church,
O Lord, we intercede;
make thou our sad
divisions soon to cease;
draw us the nearer
each to each, we plead,
by drawing all to thee,
O Prince of peace;
thus may we all one bread, one body be,
one through this sacrament of unity.

3 We pray thee too
for wanderers from thy fold,
O bring them back,
good shepherd of the sheep,
back to the faith which
saints believed of old,
back to the Church which still
that faith doth keep;
soon may we all one bread, one body be,
one through this sacrament of unity.

4 So, Lord, at length
when sacraments shall cease,
may we be one
with all thy Church above,
one with thy saints in one
unbroken peace,
one with thy saints in one
unbounded love:
more blessèd still, in peace and love to be
one with the Trinity in unity.

557 *Charles Wesley (1707–88)*

1 O thou who camest from above
the fire celestial to impart,
kindle a flame of sacred love
on the mean altar of my heart!

2 There let it for thy glory burn
with inextinguishable blaze,
and, trembling, to its source return
in humble prayer and fervent praise.

3 Jesus, confirm my heart's desire
to work and speak and think for thee;
still let me guard the holy fire
and still stir up the gift in me.

4 Still let me prove thy perfect will,
my acts of faith, and love repeat;
till death thy endless mercies seal,
and make the sacrifice complete.

558 *Chris O'Hara*

O wash me in the water of redeeming love:
living water from the fountain of salvation.

1 The water of life renews the soul:
your gift to us all the source of life.
O cleanse us! Cleanse us Lord and
refresh us!
Renew the spring of your spirit in us.

2 Creator of life, of all we are:
forgive us our weakness and our fear.
Deliver us from the darkness of evil;
from danger free us body and soul.

3 You stretched out your hand to calm the sea:
the people of Israel you set free.
O freedom! Lead your people to freedom!
And liberty, through the water of life.

559 *Robert Grant (1779–1838)*

1 O worship the King all glorious above;
O gratefully sing his power and his love:
our shield and defender, the ancient of days,
pavilioned in splendour, and girded with
praise.

2 O tell of his might, O sing of his grace,
whose robe is the light, whose canopy space.
His chariots of wrath, the deep thunder
clouds form,
and dark is his path on the wings of the
storm.

3 This earth, with its store of wonders untold,
almighty, thy power hath founded of old;
hath stablished it fast by a changeless
decree;
and round it hath cast, like a mantle, the sea.

4 Thy bountiful care what tongue can
recite?
It breathes in the air, it shines in the light;
it streams from the hills, it descends to
the plain,
and sweetly distils in the dew and the rain.

5 Frail children of dust, and feeble as frail,
in thee do we trust, nor find thee to fail;
thy mercies how tender! How firm to the
end!
Our maker, defender, redeemer, and friend.

6 O measureless might, ineffable love,
while angels delight to hymn thee above,
thy humbler creation, though feeble their
lays,
with true adoration shall sing to thy praise.

560 *J.S. Monsell (1811–75)*

1 O worship the Lord in the beauty of
holiness!
Bow down before him, his glory proclaim;
with gold of obedience, and incense of
lowliness,
kneel and adore him, the Lord is his name!

2 Low at his feet lay thy burden of
carefulness,
high on his heart he will bear it for thee,
comfort thy sorrows, and answer thy
prayerfulness,
guiding thy steps as may best for thee be.

3 Fear not to enter his courts in the
slenderness
of the poor wealth thou wouldst reckon
as thine:
truth in its beauty, and love in its tenderness,
these are the offerings to lay on his shrine.

4 These, though we bring them in
trembling and fearfulness,
he will accept for the name that is dear;
mornings of joy give for evenings of
tearfulness,
trust for our trembling and hope for our fear.

5 O worship the Lord in the beauty of
holiness!
Bow down before him, his glory proclaim;
with gold of obedience, and incense of
lowliness,
kneel and adore him, the Lord is his name!

561 *Anonymous: medieval*

1 Of one that is so fair and bright,
velut maris stella,
brighter than the day is light,
parens et puella;
I cry to thee to turn to me,
Lady, pray thy Son for me,
tam pia,
that I may come to thee,
Maria.

2 In sorrow, counsel thou art best,
felix fecundata:
for all the weary thou art rest,
mater honorata:
beseech him in thy mildest mood,
who for us did shed his blood
in cruce,
that we may come to him
in luce.

3 All this world was forlorn,
Eva peccatrice,
till our Saviour Lord was born
de te genetrice;
with thy ave sin went away,
dark night went and in came day
salutis.
The well of healing sprang from thee,
virtutis.

4 Lady, flower of everything,
rosa sine spina,
thou bore Jesus, heaven's king,
gratia divina.
Of all I say thou bore the prize,
Lady, Queen of Paradise,
electa;
maiden mild, Mother
es effecta.

562 *Aurelius C. Prudentius (348–413) tr. J.M. Neale (1818–66), H.W. Baker (1823–77), and others*

1 Of the Father's love begotten,
ere the worlds began to be,
he is Alpha and Omega,
he the source, the ending he,
of all things that are and have been
and that future years shall see:
Evermore and evermore.

2 By his word was all created;
he commanded, it was done:
heaven and earth and depth of ocean,
universe of three in one,
all that grows beneath the shining
of the light of moon and sun:
Evermore and evermore.

3 Blessed was the day for ever
when the virgin, full of grace,
by the Holy Ghost conceiving,
bore the Saviour of our race,
and the child, the world's Redeemer,
first revealed his sacred face:
Evermore and evermore.

4 O, ye heights of heaven, adore him,
angels and archangels sing!
Every creature bow before him
singing praise to God our King;
let no earthly tongue be silent,
all the world with homage ring:
Evermore and evermore.

5 He, by prophets sung, is here now,
promised since the world began,
now on earth in flesh descended
to atone for sins of man.
All creation praise its Master,
see fulfilment of his plan:
Evermore and evermore.

6 Glory be to God the Father,
glory be to God the Son,
glory to the Holy Spirit,
persons three, yet Godhead one.
Glory be from all creation
while eternal ages run:
Evermore and evermore.

563

St. Thomas Aquinas (1227–74),
tr. J. M. Neale, (1818–66)
E. Caswall (1814–78), and others

1 Of the glorious body telling,
O my tongue, its myst'ries sing,
and the blood, all price excelling,
which the world's eternal king,
in a noble womb once dwelling,
shed for this world's ransoming.

2 Giv'n for us, for us descending,
of a virgin to proceed,
man with man in converse blending,
scattered he the gospel seed,
'till his sojourn drew to ending,
which he closed in wondrous deed.

3 At the last great supper lying,
circled by his brethren's band,
meekly with the law complying,
first, he finished its command.
Then, immortal food supplying,
gave himself with his own hand.

4 Word made flesh, by word he maketh
very bread his flesh to be;
man in wine Christ's blood partaketh,
and if senses fail to see,
faith alone the true heart waketh,
to behold the mystery.

5 Therefore, we before him bending,
this great sacrament revere;
types and shadows have their ending,
for the newer rite is here;
faith, our outward sense befriending,
makes the inward vision clear.

6 Glory let us give, and blessing,
to the Father and the Son;
honour, might and praise addressing,
while eternal ages run;
ever too his love confessing,
who from both, with both is one.

564

Marty Haugen

Oh God, I seek You,
my soul thirsts for You,
Your love is finer than life.

1 As a dry and weary desert land,
so my soul is thirsting for my God,
and my flesh is faint for the God I seek,
for Your love is more to me than life.

2 I think of You when at night I rest,
I reflect upon Your steadfast love.
I will cling to You, oh Lord my God,
in the shadow of Your wings I sing.

3 I will bless Your name all the days I live,
I will raise my hands and call on You.
My joyful lips shall sing Your praise,
You alone have filled my hungry soul.

565 *Fred Hellerman and Fran Minkoff*

Repeat each line after the leader.

1 Oh healing river,
send down your waters,
send down your waters
upon this land.
O healing river
send down your waters,
and wash the blood
from off the sand.

2 This land is parching,
this land is burning,
no seed is growing
in the barren ground.
O healing river
send down your waters,
O healing river
send your waters down.

3 Let the seed of freedom
awake and flourish,
let the deep roots nourish,
let the tall stalks rise.
O healing river
send down your waters
O healing river
from out of the skies.

566 *Sr Virginia Vissing, SSMN*

Oh living water, refresh my soul.
Oh living water, refresh my soul.
Spirit of joy, Lord of creation.
Spirit of hope, Spirit of peace.

1 Spirit of God. (2)

2 Oh set us free. (2)

3 Come, pray in us. (2)

567 *Patrick Appleford*

1 Oh Lord, all the world belongs to you,
and you are always making all things new.
What is wrong you forgive,
and the new life you give
is what's turning the world upside down.

2 The world's only loving to its friends,
but you have brought us love that never
ends;
loving enemies too,
and this loving with you
is what's turning the world upside down.

3 This world lives divided and apart.
You draw all men together and we start
in your body to see
that in fellowship we
can be turning the world upside down.

4 The world wants the wealth to live in state,
but you show us a new way to be great;
like a servant you came,
and if we do the same,
we'll be turning the world upside down.

5 Oh Lord all the world belongs to you,
and you are always making all things new.
Send your Spirit on all
in your Church whom you call
to be turning the world upside down.

568 *Carl Boberg (1850–1940) tr. Stuart K. Hine*

1 O Lord, my God, when I in awesome
wonder,
consider all the worlds thy hand hast made,
I see the stars, I hear the rolling thunder,
thy power throughout the universe
displayed.

Then sings my soul, my Saviour God to thee:
How great thou art, how great thou art. (2)

2 When through the woods and forest
glades I wander
and hear the birds sing sweetly in the
trees;
when I look down from lofty mountaind
grandeur,
and hear the brook, and feel the gentle
breeze.

3 And when I think that God, his Son not sparing,
sent him to die, I scarce can take it in
that on the cross, my burden gladly bearing,
he bled and died to take away my sin.

Then sings my soul, my Saviour God to thee:
How great thou art, how great thou art. (2)

4 When Christ shall come with shout of acclamation
and take me home, what joy shall fill my heart;
when I shall bow in humble adoration,
and there proclaim; my God, how great thou art.

569 *Traditional*

1 Oh, the Lord looked down from his window in the sky,
said: 'I created man but I can't remember why!
Nothing but fighting since creation day.
I'll send a little water and wash them all away.'
Oh, the Lord came down and looked around a spell.
There was Mister Noah behaving mighty well.
And that is the reason the Scriptures record
Noah found grace in the eyes of the Lord.

Noah found grace in the eyes of the Lord, (3)
and he left him high and dry.

2 The Lord said: 'Noah, there's going to be a flood,
there's going to be some water, there's going to be some mud,
so take off your hat, Noah, take off your coat,
get Sham, Ham and Japhat and build yourself a boat.'
Noah said: 'Lord, I don't believe I could.'
The Lord said: 'Noah, get yourself some wood.
You never know what you can do till you try.
Build it fifty cubits wide and thirty cubits high.'

3 Noah said: 'There she is, there she is Lord!'
The Lord said: 'Noah, it's time to get aboard.
Take of each creature a he and a she
and of course take Mrs Noah and the whole family.'
Noah said: 'Lord, it's getting mighty dark,'
The Lord said: 'Noah, get those creatures in the ark.'
Noah said: 'Lord, it's beginning to pour.'
The Lord said: 'Noah, hurry up and close the door.'

4 The ark rose up on the bosom of the deep.
After forty days Mr Noah took a peep.
He said: 'We're not moving, Lord, where are we at?'
The Lord said: 'You're sitting right on Mount Ararat.'
Noah said: 'Lord, it's getting nice and dry.'
The Lord said: 'Noah, see my rainbow in the sky.
Take all your creatures and people the earth
and be sure that you're not more trouble than you're worth.'

570 *Estelle White*

1 Oh, the love of my Lord is the essence
of all that I love here on earth.
All the beauty I see
he has given to me
and his giving is gentle as silence.

2 Every day, every hour, every moment
have been blessed by the strength of his love.
At the turn of each tide
he is there at my side,
and his touch is as gentle as silence.

3 There've been times when I've turned from his presence,
and I've walked other paths, other ways.
But I've called on his name
in the dark of my shame,
and his mercy was gentle as silence.

571 *Traditional*

1 Oh when the saints go marching in. (2)
I want to be in that number,
when the saints go marching in.

2 Oh when the drums begin to bang …

3 Oh when the stars fall from the sky …

4 Oh when the moon turns into blood …

5 Oh when the sun turns into fire …

6 Oh when the fires begin to blaze …

7 Oh when the Lord calls out the names …

572 *Damian Lundy*

Oh the word of my Lord, deep within my being,
oh the word of my Lord, you have filled my mind.

1 Before I formed you in the womb
I knew you through and through,
I chose you to be mine.
Before you left your mother's side
I called to you, my child, to be my sign.

2 I know that you are very young,
but I will make you strong
– I'll fill you with my word;
and you will travel through the land,
fulfilling my command which you have heard.

3 And ev'rywhere you are to go
my hand will follow you;
you will not be alone.
In all the danger that you fear
you'll find me very near, your words my own.

4 With all my strength you will be filled:
you will destroy and build,
for that is my design.
You will create and overthrow,
reap harvests I will sow – your word is mine.

573 *George Bennard (1873–1960)*

1 On a hill far away
stood an old rugged cross,
the emblem of suff'ring and shame;
and I loved that old cross
where the dearest and best
for a world of lost sinners was slain.

So I'll cherish the old rugged cross
'till my trophies at last I lay down;
I will cling to the old rugged cross
and exchange it someday for a crown.

2 Oh that old rugged cross,
so despised by the world,
has a wondrous attraction for me:
for the dear Lamb of God
left his glory above
to bear it to dark Calvary.

3 In the old rugged cross,
stained with blood so divine,
a wondrous beauty I see.
For 'twas on that old cross
Jesus suffered and died
to pardon and sanctify me.

4 To the old rugged cross
I will ever be true,
its shame and reproach gladly bear.
Then he'll call me some day
to my home far away
there his glory for ever I'll share.

574 *Traditional*

1 On Christmas night all Christians sing,
to hear the news the angels bring, (2)
news of great joy, news of great mirth,
news of our merciful King's birth.

2 Then why should men on earth be so sad,
since our Redeemer made us glad? (2)
When from our sin he set us free,
all for to gain our liberty?

3 When sin departs before his grace,
then life and health come in its place; (2)
angels and men with joy may sing,
all for to see the new–born King.

4 All out of darkness we have light,
which made the angels sing this night: (2)
'Glory to God and peace to men,
now and for evermore. Amen.'

575 *C. Coffin (1676–1749), tr. J. Chandler (1808–76)*

1 On Jordan's bank the Baptist's cry
announces that the Lord is nigh;
come then and hearken, for he brings
glad tidings from the King of kings.

2 Then cleansed be every Christian breast,
and furnished for so great a guest!
Yea, let us each our heart prepare,
for Christ to come and enter there.

3 For thou art our salvation, Lord,
our refuge and our great reward;
without thy grace our souls must fade,
and wither like a flower decayed.

4 Stretch forth thy hand to heal our sore,
and make us rise, to fall no more;
once more upon thy people shine,
and fill the world with love divine.

5 All praise, eternal Son, to thee
whose advent sets thy people free,
whom, with the Father, we adore,
and Holy Ghost, for evermore.

576 *Sister M. Pereira*

1 On this house your blessing, Lord;
on this house your grace bestow.
On this house your blessing, Lord;
may it come and never go.
Bringing peace and joy and happiness,
bringing love that knows no end.
On this house your blessing, Lord;
on this house your blessing send.

2 On this house your loving, Lord;
may it overflow each day.
On this house your loving, Lord;
may it come and with us stay.
Drawing us in love and unity
by the love received from you.
On this house your loving, Lord;
may it come each day anew.

3 On this house your giving, Lord;
may it turn and ever flow.
On this house your giving, Lord;
on this house your wealth bestow.
Filling all our hopes and wishes, Lord,
in the way you know is best.
On this house your giving, Lord;
may it come and with us rest.

4 On this house your calling, Lord;
may it come to us each day.
On this house your calling, Lord;
may it come to lead the way.
Filling us with nobler yearnings, Lord,
calling us to live in you.
On this house your calling, Lord;
may it come each day anew.

577 *Cecil Francis Alexander (1818–95)*

1 Once in royal David's city
stood a lowly cattle shed,
where a mother laid her baby
in a manger for his bed;
Mary was that Mother mild,
Jesus Christ her little child.

2 He came down to earth from heaven,
who is God and Lord of all,
and his shelter was a stable
and his cradle was a stall;
with the poor, and mean, and lowly,
lived on earth our Saviour holy.

3 And through all his wondrous childhood
he would honour and obey,
love, and watch the lowly maiden
in whose gentle arms he lay;
Christian children all must be
mild, obedient, good as he.

4 For he is our childhood's pattern,
day by day like us he grew;
he was little, weak and helpless,
tears and smiles like us he knew;
and he feeleth for our sadness,
and he shareth in our gladness.

5 And our eyes at last shall see him
through his own redeeming love,

for that child so dear and gentle
is our Lord in heaven above;
and he leads his children on
to the place where he is gone.

6 Not in that poor lowly stable,
with the oxen standing by,
we shall see him; but in heaven,
set at God's right hand on high;
when like stars his children crowned
all in white shall wait around.

578 *John B Foley, SJ*

One bread, one body, one Lord of all,
one cup of blessing which we bless.
And we, though many, throughout the earth,
we are one body in this one Lord.

1 Gentile or Jew, servant or free,
woman or man, no more.

2 Many the gifts, many the works,
one in the Lord of all.

3 Grain for the fields,
scattered and grown, gathered to one, for all.

579 *Ronald Gokool*

1 One day will come
when this world which we roam
will cease to produce sorrows
from seeds which we have sown;
that day there'll be such rejoicing,
joy will banish all tears.
One day when love conquers all our fears.

That day a glow will surround us,
evil will be no more;
no wars, nor hatred around us
peace on earth will be sure.
One day when man's heart
returns to God;
the day when all men acclaim him
all pow'rful Lord;
with radiant gowns he'll adorn us.
'My true children', he'll say,
one day when love teaches us how to pray.
One day when love teaches us how to pray.

2 Some day we'll learn
how to control our lives.
It's only then we'll be able
to open our eyes
to see the beauty around us,
which God meant us to share.
One day when love teaches us how to care.

580 *Graham Kendrick*

1 One shall tell another,
and he shall tell his friends:
husbands, wives and children
shall come following on.
From house to house in families
shall more be gathered in;
and lights will shine in every street,
so warm and welcoming.

Come on in and taste the new wine,
the wine of the kingdom,
the wine of the kingdom of God:
here is healing and forgiveness,
the wine of the kingdom,
the wine of the kingdom of God.

2 Compassion of the Father
is ready now to flow;
through acts of love and mercy
we must let it show.
He turns now from his anger
to show a smiling face,
and longs that we should stand beneath
the fountain of his grace.

Come on in and taste the new wine,
the wine of the kingdom,
the wine of the kingdom of God:
here is healing and forgiveness,
the wine of the kingdom,
the wine of the kingdom of God.

3 He longs to do much more
than our faith has yet allowed,
to thrill us and surprise us
with his sovereign power.
Where darkness has been darkest,
the brightest light will shine;
his invitation comes to us,
it's yours and it is mine.

581 *S. Baring–Gould (1834–1924)*

1 Onward, Christian soldiers,
marching as to war,
with the Cross of Jesus
going on before.
Christ the royal Master
leads against the foe;
forward into battle,
see, his banners go!

Onward, Christian soldiers,
marching as to war,
with the Cross of Jesus
going on before.

2 At the sign of triumph
Satan's legions flee;
on then, Christian soldiers,
on to victory.
Hell's foundations quiver
at the shout of praise;
we shall lift our voices,
loud our anthem raise.

3 Like a mighty army
moves the Church of God.
Humbly, we are treading
where the Saints have trod;
we are not divided,
all one body we,
one in hope and doctrine,
one in charity.

4 Crowns and thrones may perish,
kingdoms rise and wane,
but the Church of Jesus
constant will remain;
gates of hell can never
'gainst that Church prevail;
we have Christ's own promise,
and that cannot fail.

5 Onward, then, ye people,
join our happy throng,
blend with ours your voices
in the triumph song;
glory, laud, and honour
unto Christ the King;
this through countless ages
saints and angels sing.

582 *Willard F. Jabusch*

1 Open your ears, O Christian people,
open your ears and hear Good News.
Open your hearts O royal priesthood
God has come to you.

God has spoken to his people, alleluia.
And his words are words of wisdom,
alleluia.

2 Israel comes to greet the Saviour,
Judah is glad to see his day.
From East and West the people travel,
he will show the way.

Verse 3 on next page

---

583 *Taizé chant*

Principal Canon
A
B
Os-ten-de no-bis Do-mi-ne, mi-se-ri-cor-di-am tu-
C
D
1,2,3 ...
Fine
am. A-men! A-men! Ma-ra-na-tha! Ma-ra-na-tha! Os-ten-de. -tha.
A Dm Gm A A
Guitar

3 Those who have ears to hear his message;
those who have ears, then let them hear.
Those who would learn the way of wisdom,
let them hear God's words.

584 *Traditional Caribbean*

1 Our Father, who art in heaven,
hallowed be thy name.
Thy kingdom come, thy will be done,
hallowed be thy name. (2)

2 On earth as it is in heaven.
Give us this day our daily bread.

3 Forgive us our trespasses,
as we forgive those who trespass against us.

4 And lead us not into temptation,
but deliver us from all that is evil.

5 For thine is the kingdom, the power and the glory,
for ever, and for ever and ever.

6 Amen, amen, it shall be so.
Amen, amen, it shall be so.

585 *Estelle White*

1 Our Father, who art in heaven,
hallowed be thy name.
Thy kingdom come,thy will be done,
on earth as it is in heaven.
Give us this day our daily bread
and forgive us our trespasses,
as we forgive those who trespass against us.
And lead us not into temptation,
but deliver us from evil.

586 THE LORD'S PRAYER

Our Father, who art in heaven;
hallowed be thy name;
Thy kingdom come,
Thy will be done
on earth as it is in heaven;
give us this day our daily bread,
and forgive us our trespasses,
as we forgive those who trespass against us;
and lead us not into temptation,
but deliver us from evil. Amen.

587 *Kevin Nichols*

1 Our Father, we have wandered
and hidden from your face,
in foolishness have squandered
your legacy of grace.
But now, in exile dwelling,
we rise with fear and shame,
as distant but compelling,
we hear you call our name.

2 And now at length discerning
the evil that we do,
behold us Lord, returning
with hope and trust to you.
In haste you come to meet us
and home rejoicing bring.
In gladness there to greet us
with calf and robe and ring.

3 O Lord of all the living,
both banished and restored,
compassionate, forgiving
and ever caring Lord,
grant now that our transgressing,
our faithlessness may cease.
Stretch out your hand in blessing
in pardon and in peace.

588 *Estelle White*

1 Our Saviour Jesus Christ proclaimed
that when we gather in his name
he would be there to love and guide,
lead us towards the Father's side.

Our hearts are longing for you, Lord,
give us the faith to trust your word.

2 He told us, 'Ask, you will receive,
seek and you'll find if you believe.
Knock at the door of love and truth
and we shall open it for you.'

3 His hands brought healing to the blind,
his words brought ease to troubled minds.
He said his friends could do the same
by invocation of his name.

4 He came to earth in form of man
to give to us his Father's plan.
We are the branches, he the vine,
we too can share his life divine.

589 Isaiah 53, Anthony Sharpe

1 Ours were the sins you bore,
ours were the blows received.
You never said a word
though treated harshly.
To be killed like a lamb,
like a sheep to be sheared.
You never said a word
as you died for us.

2 It was the Father's will
that you should suffer
your death, a sacrifice
to bring forgiveness.
You will again know joy,
you did not die in vain:
it is for your sake
we will be forgiven.

590 Francesca Leftley

Ours were the sufferings he bore
ours were the sorrows he carried.
He bears a punishment that brings us peace
and through his wounds we are healed.

1 Come, Lord and heal us,
O Lamb of God, O Lamb of God. *(2)*

2 Come, Lord and heal us,
You died for us, you died for us. *(2)*

3 Come, Lord and heal us,
Grant us your peace, grant us your peace. *(2)*

591 Christopher Walker

Out of darkness God has called us,
claimed by Christ as God's own people.
Holy nation, royal priesthood,
walking in God's marv'lous light.

1 Let us take the words you give,
strong and faithful words to live.
Words that in our hearts are sown;
words that bind us as your own.

2 Let us take the Christ you give.
Broken Body, Christ we live.
Christ the risen from the tomb;
Christ who calls us as your own.

3 Let us take the love you give,
that the way of love we live.
Love to bring your people home;
love to make us all your own.

592 Fred Kaan

1 Out of deep unordered water
God created land and life;
world of beast and bird and later
twosome people, man and wife.

There is water in the river
bringing life to tree and plant.
Let creation praise its giver:
there is water in the font.

2 Water on the human forehead,
birthmark of the love of God,
in the sign of death and rising,
through the sea there runs a road.

3 Standing round the font reminds us
of the Hebrew's climb ashore.
Life is hallowed by the knowledge
God has been this way before.

593 St Thomas Aquinas (1227–74)

1 Pange, lingua, gloriosi
corporis mysterium,
sanguinisque pretiosi,
quem in mundi pretium
fructus ventris generosi
Rex effudit gentium.

2 Nobis datus, nobis natus
ex intacta Virgine;
et in mundo conversatus,
sparso verbi semine,
sui moras incolatus
miro clausit ordine.

3 In supremae nocte coenae
recumbens cum fratribus,
observata lege plene
cibis in legalibus:
cibum turbae duodenae
se dat suis manibus.

4 Verbum caro, panem verum
verbo carnem efficit:
fitque sanguis Christi merum;
et si sensus deficit,
ad firmandum cor sincerum
sola fides sufficit.

5 Tantum ergo Sacramentum
veneremur cernui:
et antiquum documentum
novo cedat ritui:
præstet fides supplementum
sensuum defectui.

6 Genitori, genitoque
laus, et jubilatio,
salus, honor, virtus quoque
sit et benedictio:
procedenti ab utroque
compar sit laudatio. Amen.

594 *Anthony Sharpe*

1 Peace I give to you, my friends.
peace the world can never know,
given you now to share with each other,
peace I give to you, my friends.

2 Love I give …

3 Joy I give …

595 *Anonymous*

1 Peace is flowing like a river,
flowing out through you and me,
spreading out into the desert,
setting all the captives free.

2 Love is flowing like a river …

3 Joy is flowing like a river …

4 Hope is flowing like a river …

596 *John Glynn*

1 Peace is the gift of heaven to earth,
softly enfolding our fears.
Peace is the gift of Christ to the world,
given for us.
He is the Lamb who bore the pain of peace.

2 Peace is the gift of Christ to his Church,
wound of the lance of his love.
Love is the pain he suffered for all,
offered to us:
Oh, to accept the wound that brings us peace!

3 Joy is the gift the Spirit imparts,
born of the heavens and earth.
We are his children, children of joy,
people of God:
He is our Lord, our peace, our love, our joy!

597 *Kevin Mayhew*

1 Peace, perfect peace, is the gift of Christ
our Lord.
Peace, perfect peace, is the gift of Christ
our Lord.
Thus, says the Lord, will the world know
my friends.
Peace, perfect peace, is the gift of Christ
our Lord.

2 Love, perfect love …

3 Faith, perfect faith …

4 Hope, perfect hope …

5 Joy, perfect joy …

598 *E.H. Bickersteth (1823–1906), altered*

1 Peace, perfect peace, in this dark world of sin?
The blood of Jesus whispers peace within.

2 Peace, perfect peace, by thronging duties pressed?
To do the will of Jesus, this is rest.

3 Peace, perfect peace, with sorrows surging round?
In Jesus' care will nought but calm be found.

4 Peace, perfect peace, with loved ones far away?
In Jesus' keeping we are safe, and they.

5 Peace, perfect peace, our future all unknown?
Jesus we know, and he is on his throne.

6 Peace, perfect peace, death shadowing us and ours?
Jesus has vanquished death and all its powers.

7 It is enough; earth's troubles soon shall cease,
and Jesus calls us to heaven's perfect peace.

599 *Malcolm Campbell-Carr*

Peacemakers to be called the sons of God. (2)

1 Seeing the crowd,
Jesus went up to the hill.
There he sat down
and was joined by his friends.
Then he began to speak to them,
and this is what he said:
You must be …

2 Happy the gentle,
for I give to them the earth.
Happy the mourners,
I will comfort their distress.
Happy are those who thirst and
hunger after what is right.
They shall be …

600 *John Kennett*

Praise Him on the trumpet, the psaltery and harp,
praise Him on the timbrel and the dance,
praise Him with stringed instruments too.
Praise Him on the loud cymbals,
praise Him on the loud cymbals,
let ev'rything that has breath praise the Lord.

Hallelujah, praise the Lord,
Hallelujah, praise the Lord,
let ev'rything that has breath praise the Lord. (2)

601 *Anonymous*

1 Praise him praise him,
praise him in the morning,
praise him in the noontime.
Praise him, praise him,
praise him when the sun goes down

2 Love him, …

3 Trust him, …

4 Serve him, …

5 Jesus, …

602 *Henry Francis Lyte (1793–1847)*

1 Praise, my soul, the king of heaven!
To his feet thy tribute bring.
Ransomed, healed, restored, forgiven,
who like me his praise should sing?
Praise him! Praise him! (2)
Praise the everlasting king!

2 Praise him for his grace and favour
to our fathers in distress;
praise him still the same for ever,
slow to chide and swift to bless.
Praise him! Praise him! (2)
Glorious in his faithfulness!

3 Father–like he tends and spares us;
well our feeble frame he knows;
in his hands he gently bears us,
rescues us from all our foes.

Praise him! Praise him! (2)
Widely as his mercy flows!

4 Angels, help us to adore him;
ye behold him face to face;
sun and moon bow down before him,
dwellers all in time and space.
Praise him! Praise him! (2)
Praise with us the God of grace!

603 *C.J. Marivoet*

1 Praise now your God, every tongue, ev'ry nation,
tell the good news to the next generation:
Christ, the Redeemer, who rose from the dead,
stays with his people as life–giving Bread.

Alleluia, God is great! Alleluia, God is good!

2 Christ gave his word at the multiplication.
Bread and sweet wine are now Christ our oblation.
Cross and Last Supper are with us today.
Life now abounds, and God's will we obey.

3 Here is your Saviour, give deep adoration,
sing of his glory in glad celebration.
Come, for his manna is food for the road,
strength for the journey, our glory foreshowed.

604 *Gerald O'Mahony*

Praise the Lord, and sing hallelujah,
hallelujah, hallelujah. (2)

1 Praise him for the sun and
for the stars above,
hallelujah, hallelujah.
Praise him everybody
for he is the God of love,
hallelujah, hallelujah.

2 Praise him when you're happy,
praise him when you're sad,
hallelujah, hallelujah.
He's the God who saves us
and his message makes us glad,
hallelujah, hallelujah.

3 Praise him in the morning,
praise him in the night,
hallelujah, hallelujah.
Praise him in the thunder
for he is the God of might,
hallelujah, hallelujah.

605 *Verses 1-2 from the Foundling Hospital Collection (1796); verse 3 by E. Osler (1798–1863)*

1 Praise the Lord! ye heavens adore him;
praise him, angels, in the height;
sun and moon, rejoice before him,
praise him, all ye stars of light.
Praise the Lord! For he hath spoken;
worlds his mighty voice obeyed:
laws, which never shall be broken,
for their guidance he hath made.

2 Praise the Lord! for he is glorious;
never shall his promise fail:
God hath made his saints victorious;
sin and death shall not prevail.
Praise the God of our salvation;
hosts on high, his power proclaim;
heaven and earth and all creation,
laud and magnify his name!

3 Worship, honour, glory, blessing,
Lord, we offer to thy name;
young and old, thy praise expressing,
join their Saviour to proclaim.
As the saints in heaven adore thee,
we would bow before thy throne;
as thine angels serve before thee,
so on earth thy will be done.

606 *John Henry Newman (1801–90)*

1 Praise to the Holiest in the height,
and in the depth be praise,
in all his words most wonderful,
most sure in all his ways.

2 O loving wisdom of our God!
When all was sin and shame,
a second Adam to the fight,
and to the rescue came.

3 O wisest love! That flesh and blood
which did in Adam fail,
should strive afresh against the foe,
should strive and should prevail;

4 And that a higher gift than grace
should flesh and blood refine,
God's presence and his very self,
and Essence all divine.

5 O generous love! That he who smote
in man for man the foe,
the double agony in man
for man should undergo,

6 And in the garden secretly
and on the Cross on high,
should teach his brethren, and inspire
to suffer and to die.

7 Praise to the Holiest in the height,
and in the depth be praise,
in all his words most wonderful,
most sure in all his ways.

607 *Estelle White*

Praise to the Lord our God,
let us sing together,
lifting our hearts and our voices
to sing with joy and gladness.
Come along, along, along,
and sing with …

608 *Joachim Neander (1650–80), tr. C. Winkworth (1827–78), and others*

1 Praise to the Lord, the Almighty,
the King of creation!
O my soul, praise him,
for he is your health and salvation.
All you who hear, now to his altar draw near,
join in profound adoration.

2 Praise to the Lord, let us offer
our gifts at his altar;
let not our sins and transgressions
now cause us to falter.
Christ, the High Priest,
bids us all join in his feast,
gathered with him at the altar.

3 Praise to the Lord, who will
prosper our work and defend us;
surely his goodness and mercy
here daily attend us;
ponder anew all the Almighty can do,
he who with love will befriend us.

4 Praise to the Lord, oh, let all that
is in us adore him!
All that has life and breath,
come now in praises before him.
Let the Amen sound from
his people again,
now as we worship before him.

609 *David McRoberts*

1 Praise we now the Lord our God,
voices joined in chorus;
ceaselessly let seraphim,
angels, pow'rs and cherubim
sing with joy their praise of him,
holy, Lord of Sabaoth.

2 All the earth and sea and sky,
glorify their maker:
blessed martyrs, prophets grand,
Christ's beloved apostle–band,
holy Church in every land
sing his praise for ever.

3 Hail thou king of glory, Christ,
born before all ages!
Born of Mary, Virgin pure,
thou didst us from death secure,
opening wide for evermore
stores of heavenly treasure.

4 Seated now at God's right hand,
bless thy chosen people;
rule o'er us, dear Lord, we pray,
keep us free from sin this day,
save us, Lord, without delay,
lest we be confounded.

5 In the solemn day of doom,
we shall hear thy judgement;
but remember, Lord, we cry,
in that day when we shall die,
how thy blood on us did lie,
signing us thy people.

6 Praise we yet the Lord our God,
throned in triune splendour;
praise the Father, Lord of might,
praise the Son, redeemer bright,
praise the Spirit, source of light,
through eternal ages.

610 *Frederick Oakeley (1802–80), and others*

1 Praise we our God with joy
and gladness never ending;
angels and saints with us
their grateful voices blending.
He is our Father dear,
o'er filled with parent's love;
mercies unsought, unknown,
he showers from above.

2 He is our shepherd true;
with watchful care unsleeping,
on us, his erring sheep
an eye of pity keeping;
he with a mighty arm
the bonds of sin doth break,
and to our burden'd hearts
in words of peace doth speak.

3 Graces in copious stream
from that pure fount are welling,
where, in our heart of hearts,
our God hath set his dwelling.
His word our lantern is;
his peace our comfort still;
his sweetness all our rest;
our law, our life, his will.

611 *Steuart Wilson (1889–1966)*

1 Praise we the Lord, who made all beauty
for all our senses to enjoy;
give we our humble thanks and duty
that simple pleasures never cloy;
praise we the Lord, who made all beauty
for all our senses to enjoy.

2 Praise him who makes our life a pleasure
sending us things which glad our eyes;
thank him who gives us welcome leisure,
that in our heart sweet thoughts may rise:
praise him who makes our life a pleasure
sending us things which glad our eyes.

3 Praise him who, by a simple flower,
lifts up our hearts to things above;
thank him who gives to each one power
to find a friend to know and love;
praise him who, by a simple flower,
lifts up our hearts to things above.

4 Praise we the Lord, who made all beauty
for all our senses to enjoy;
give we our humble thanks and duty
that simple pleasures never cloy;
praise we the Lord, who made all beauty
for all our senses to enjoy.

612 *Stephen Dean*

Prepare ye the way of the Lord!
Make straight his paths!
Fill in the valleys, lay the hills low,
smooth the rough places where he will go,
and all the earth shall see
the saving power of God!

1 Repent, for the Kingdom of God is at hand,
the light which the darkness can never
withstand.

2 Cry out with a voice that is strong and sure:
'The flower will fade, but my word will
endure!'

3 Get up the high mountain and shout the
Good News:
'Fear not, for the Lord God Almighty rules!'

4 Like a shepherd he shelters his flock
from harm;
and tenderly leads the young lambs with
his arm.

613 *Roger Ruston, based on a Jewish Passover Song*

1 Promised Lord, and Christ is he,
may we soon his kingdom see.

Come, O Lord, quickly come,
come in glory, come in glory,
come in glory, quickly come.

2 Teaching, healing once was he,
may we soon his kingdom see.

3 Dead and buried once was he,
may we soon his kingdom see.

4 Risen from the dead is he,
may we soon his kingdom see.

5 Soon to come again is he,
may we soon his kingdom see.

Come, O Lord, quickly come,
in our lifetime, in our lifetime,
in our lifetime may it be.

614 *Taizé chant from Psalm 97 (98)*

♩ = 88 Without rushing
A
Psa-lli-te Do-mi-no in vo-ce psal-mi. Can-ta-te Do-mi-no can-ti cum no-vum.

B
Psa-lli-te Do-mi-no in vo-ce psal-mi. Can-ta-te Do-mi-no can-ti-cum no-vum.

Exsultate! Exsultate!
Cantate alleluia! Cantate alleluia!

Sing! Sing! Sing a new song!
Sing! Sing! Sing to the Lord!

All the ends of the earth have seen
the salvation of our God.
Shout to the Lord all the earth,
ring out your joy, alleluia!

---

615 *Peter Icarus*

1 Reap me the earth as a harvest to God,
gather and bring it again,
all that is his, to the Maker of all.
Lift it and offer it high.

Bring bread, bring wine,
give glory to the Lord;
whose is the earth but God's,
whose is the praise but his?

2 Go with your song and your music with joy,
go to the altar of God.
Carry your offerings, fruits of the earth,
work of your labouring hands.

3 Gladness and pity and passion and pain,
all that is mortal in man,
lay all before him, return him his gift,
God, to whom all shall go home.

616 *Author unknown (11th century)*

Regina cæli, lætare, alleluia,
quia quem meruisti portare, alleluia,
resurrexit sicut dixit, alleluia.
Ora pro nobis Deum, alleluia.

617 *From Scripture*

1 Rejoice in the Lord always,
and again I say rejoice.
Rejoice in the Lord always,
and again I say rejoice.
2 Rejoice, rejoice,
and again I say rejoice.
Rejoice, rejoice,
and again I say rejoice.

618 *Graham Kendrick*

Rejoice! Rejoice! Christ is in you,
the hope of glory in our hearts.
He lives! He lives!
His breath is in you.
Arise! A mighty army, we arise!

1 Now is the time for us
to march upon the land,
into our hands
He will give the ground we claim.
He rides in majesty
to lead us into victory,
the world shall see that Christ is Lord!

2 God is at work in us
His purpose to perform,
building a kingdom
of power not of words,
where things impossible
by faith shall be made possible;
let's give the glory
to Him now.

3 Though we are weak, His grace
is everything we need;
we're made of clay
but this treasure is within.
He turns our weaknesses
into His opportunities,
so that the glory
goes to Him.

619 *Charles Wesley (1707–88)*

1 Rejoice! The Lord is King!
Your Lord and King adore;
mortals, give thanks and sing,
and triumph evermore:

Lift up your heart, lift up your voice;
rejoice, again I say, rejoice.

2 Jesus the Saviour reigns,
the God of truth and love;
when he had purged our stains,
he took his seat above:

3 His kingdom cannot fail;
he rules o'er earth and heaven;
the keys of death and hell
are to our Jesus given:

4 He sits at God's right hand
till all his foes submit,
and bow to his command,
and fall beneath his feet:

620 *H. W. Baker (1821–77)*

1 Rejoice today with one accord,
sing out with exultation:
rejoice and praise our mighty Lord,
whose arm hath brought salvation;
his works of love proclaim
the greatness of his name:
for he is God alone
who hath his mercy shown;
let all the saints in heaven adore him!

2 When in distress to him we cried,
he heard our sad complaining;
O trust in him, whate'er betide,
his love is all–sustaining;
triumphant songs of praise
to him our hearts shall raise;
now ev'ry voice shall say,
'O praise our God alway';
let all his saints adore him!

621 *Response: Paul Inwood, Verses: The Grail*

Remember, remember your mercy Lord. (2)
Hear your people's prayer as they call to you:
remember, remember your mercy Lord

1 Lord, make me know your ways.
Lord, teach me your paths.
Make me walk in your truth, and teach me:
for you are God my Saviour.

2 Remember your mercy, Lord,
and the love you have shown from of old.
Do not remember the sins of my youth.
In your love, remember me,
in your love remember me,
because of your goodness, O Lord.

3 The Lord is good and upright.
He shows the path to all who stray,
he guides the humble in the right path;
he teaches his way to the poor.

622 *ICEL*

Receive his soul, receive his soul
and present him to God, the Most High.
Receive his soul, receive his soul
and present him to God, the Most High.

1 Saints of God, come to his aid!
Hasten to meet him, angels of the Lord.

2 May Christ, who called you, take you to himself,
may angels lead you to Abraham's side.

3 Eternal rest give unto him, O Lord,
and let perpetual light shine upon them.

Footnote: 'her' may be substituted for 'him' and 'his' as required.

623 *H. H. Milman (1791–1868)*

1 Ride on! Ride on in majesty!
Hark, all the tribes hosanna cry;
thy humble beast pursues his road
with palms and scattered garments strowed.

2 Ride on! Ride on in majesty!
In lowly pomp ride on to die;
O Christ, thy triumphs now begin
o'er captive death and conquered sin.

3 Ride on! Ride on in majesty!
The wingèd squadrons of the sky
look down with sad and wondering eyes,
to see the approaching sacrifice.

4 Ride on! Ride on in majesty!
Thy last and fiercest strife is nigh;
the Father, on his sapphire throne,
expects his own anointed Son.

5 Ride on! Ride on in majesty!
In lowly pomp ride on to die;
bow thy meek head to mortal pain,
then take, O God, thy power, and reign.

624 *A. M. Toplady (1740–1778)*

1 Rock of ages, cleft for me,
let me hide myself in thee;
let the water and the blood,
from thy riven side which flowed,
be of sin the double cure:
cleanse me from its guilt and power.

2 Not the labours of my hands
can fulfil thy law's demands;
could my zeal no respite know,
could my tears for ever flow,
all for sin could not atone:
thou must save, and thou alone.

3 Nothing in my hand I bring,
simply to thy Cross I cling;
naked, come to thee for dress;
helpless, look to thee for grace;
foul, I to the fountain fly;
wash me, Saviour, or I die.

4 While I draw this fleeting breath,
when my eyelids close in death,
when I soar through tracts unknown,
see thee on thy judgement throne;
rock of ages, cleft for me,
let me hide myself in thee.

625 *W. Romanis*

1 Round me falls the night,
Saviour be my light;
through the hours in darkness shrouded
let me see thy face unclouded.
Let thy glory shine
in this heart of mine.

2 Earthly work is done,
earthly sounds are none;
rest in sleep and silence seeking,
let me hear thee softly speaking;
in my spirit's ear
whisper: 'I am near'.

3 Blessed heav'nly light
shining through earth's night;
voice that oft of love has told me,
arms, so strong, to clasp and hold me;
thou thy watch will keep.
Saviour o'er my sleep.

626 *Timothy Dudley-Smith*

1 Safe in the shadow of the Lord,
beneath his hand and power,
I trust in him, I trust in him,
my fortress and my tower.

2 My hope is set on God alone
though Satan spreads his snare;
I trust in him, I trust in him
to keep me in his care.

3 From fears and phantoms of the night,
from foes about my way,
I trust in him, I trust in him
by darkness as by day.

4 His holy angels keep my feet
secure from every stone;
I trust in him, I trust in him
and unafraid go on.

5 Strong in the everlasting name,
and in my Father's care,
I trust in him, I trust in him
who hears and answers prayer.

6 Safe in the shadow of the Lord,
possessed by love divine,
I trust in him, I trust in him
and meet his love with mine.

627 *James J .Donohue*

1 Saint Joseph, God has chosen you,
to keep his Church from harm.
So hold the Church as once you held
the Christ child on your arm.

2 Saint Joseph, God has given you
all workers for your own.
Teach them to do the best they can
with steel and wood and stone.

3 Saint Joseph, when you pray for me,
pray to the Three-in-One;
but talk in human words with him
who let you call him Son.

628 *Author unknown (11th century)*

Salve Regina, Mater misericordiæ
vita dulcedo, et spes nostra, salve.
Ad te clamamus, exules filii hevæ.
Ad te suspiramus, gementes et flentes,
in hac lacrimarum vale.
Eja ergo, Advocata nostra,
illos tuos misericordes oculos
ad nos converte.
Et Jesum benedictum fructum ventris tui,
nobis post hoc exsilium ostende.
O clemens, O pia, O dulcis Virgo Maria.

629 *Michael Cockett*

1 Seasons come, seasons go,
moon-struck tides will ebb and flow;
when I forget my constant one
he draws me back, he brings me home.
O love, my love, I hear you faraway,
a distant storm that will refresh the day.

2 Seasons come seasons go,
petals fall though flowers grow;
and when I doubt love lifts a hand
and scatters stars like grains of sand.
Oh love, my love, I see you passing by
like birds that fearlessly possess the sky.

3 Seasons come, seasons go,
times to reap and times to sow;
but you are love, a fruitful vine,
in ev'ry season yielding wine.
I hear my love in laughter and in song,
no day too short, no winter night too long.

630 *Edward Caswall (1814–78)*

1 See, amid the winter's snow,
born for us on earth below,
see, the tender lamb appears,
promised from eternal years.

Hail, thou ever-blessèd morn,
hail, redemption's happy dawn!
Sing through all Jerusalem,
Christ is born in Bethlehem.

2 Lo, within a manger lies
he who built the starry skies;
he who, throned in heights sublime,
sits amid the cherubim.

3 Say, ye holy shepherds, say,
what your joyful news today?
Wherefore have ye left your sheep
on the lonely mountain steep?

4 'As we watched at dead of night,
lo, we saw a wondrous light;
angels, singing peace on earth,
told us of the Saviour's birth.'

5 Sacred infant, all divine,
what a tender love was thine,
thus to come from highest bliss,
down to such a world as this!

6 Virgin mother, Mary blest,
by the joys that fill thy breast,
pray for us, that we may prove
worthy of the Saviour's love.

631 *John Greally*

1 See us, Lord, about thine altar;
though so many, we are one;
many souls by love united
in the heart of Christ thy Son.

2 Hear our prayers, O loving Father,
hear in them thy Son, our Lord;
hear him speak our love and worship,
as we sing with one accord.

3 Once were seen the blood and water;
now he seems but bread and wine;
then in human form he suffered,
now his form is but a sign.

4 Wheat and grape contain the meaning;
food and drink he is to all;
one in him, we kneel adoring,
gathered by his loving call.

5 Hear us yet; so much is needful
in our frail, disordered life;
stay with us and tend our weakness
till that day of no more strife.

6 Members of his mystic body,
now we know our prayer is heard,
heard by thee, because thy children
have received th' eternal word.

632 *Dan Feiten*

Seed, scattered and sown,
wheat, gathered and grown,
bread, broken and shared as one,
the Living Bread of God.
Vine, fruit of the land,
wine, work of our hands.
One cup that is shared by all;
the Living Cup, the Living Bread of God.

1 Is not the bread we break
a sharing in our Lord?
Is not the cup we bless
the blood of Christ outpoured?

2 The seed which falls on rock
will wither and will die.
The seed within good ground
will flower and have life.

3 As wheat upon the hills
was gathered and was grown,
so may the church of God
be gathered into one.

633 *Karen Lafferty*

1 Seek ye first the Kingdom of God,
and his righteousness,
and all these things shall be added unto
you;
allelu, alleluia.

Alleluia, alleluia, alleluia,
allelu, alleluia.

2 Ask and it shall be given unto you,
seek and ye shall find;
knock and it shall be opened unto you;
allelu, alleluia.

634 Denis E. Hurley

1 Send forth your Spirit, God our Father,
as you have sent him in the past:
at Gabriel's word, by Jordan's water,
as Jesus went to pray and fast.

2 In this same Spirit he proclaimed you
on Juda's hills, by Galilee,
he called us to your heav'nly kingdom,
he died and rose triumphantly.

3 And now though seen by us no longer
he rests not from the task begun,
but breathes the Spirit of his sonship,
on men of ev'ry race and tongue.

4 May he be with us at this moment
and give us of your Spirit still,
that we may do the work that waits us
and strive your purpose to fulfil.

At confirmation:

5 May all who come for confirmation
be richly with your Spirit sealed:
to love and serve you in their brothers,
until your glory is revealed.

635 Garfield Rochard

Send forth your Spirit, O Lord.
Send forth your Spirit
on these your chosen ones.
Send forth your Spirit of love.

1 To show the love of the Father,
to show the love of the Son.
To show the love of Jesus for all;
this is his new commandment.

Send forth your Spirit, O Lord.
Send forth your Spirit
on these your chosen ones.
Send forth your Spirit of truth.

2 To know the will of the Father,
to know the will of the Son,
to know the Gospel of Jesus the Lord,
to proclaim to everyone.

Send forth your Spirit, O Lord.
Send forth your Spirit
on these your chosen ones.
Send them to cast your fire on earth.

Sung by Confirmation candidates:

3 Come upon us, O Spirit of the living God!
Come upon us, O Spirit of truth!
Come upon us, O Spirit of love and life!
Send us to cast your fire on earth!

Send forth your Spirit, O Lord.
Send forth your Spirit
on these your chosen ones.
Send forth your Spirit of love.

636 Author unknown

1 Send me Jesus, send me Jesus,
Send me Jesus, send me Lord.

2 Send me Jesus, …

3 Lead me Jesus, …

4 Fill me Jesus, …

637 Christopher Walker

Send us as your blessing, Lord,
send us in the pow'r of your Spirit,
to live the Good News.
Proclaiming your gospel of peace;
that all the world will come to believe;
salvation and glory,
and wisdom and power are yours, are yours.
Salvation and glory
and wisdom and power are yours,
now and for evermore!

1 Bless the lips of those
proclaiming your Holy Word,
with a voice of truth
revealing your glory.
That the sound of your Word
will be a blessing for all.

2 Bless the ears of all
who wait for your Saving Word,
may your voice be heard
by those you have chosen.
Make them strong in faith
and hope to face the unknown.

3 Be with those whose hands
are blessed with your healing pow'r.
Through their touch
awaken those in depression,
from their darkness
lead them into your light.

4 Bless all those who suffer
hours of sickness and pain,
may they feel your caring hand
is upon them,
through their suffering
reveal your crucified Son.

5 Bless all those in prison
for their belief in you.
Be with them and help their lives
be your witness.
Let their faith in you
grow stronger hour by hour.

6 Bless us all, the music–makers
who sing your praise.
In our songs and music speak
to your people;
that the music of heav'n
will sound out here on the earth.

638 *Nicaraguan traditional, tr. Jorge Maldonado*

Sent by the Lord am I;
my hands are ready now
to make the earth the place
in which the kingdom comes.
Sent by the Lord am I;
my hands are ready now
to make the earth the place
in which the kingdom comes.

The angels cannot change
a world of hurt and pain
into a world of love,
of justice and of peace.
The task is mine to do,
to set it really free.
Oh, help me to obey;
help me to do your will.

639 *Steven Jones*

Shalom, my friend,
shalom my friend, shalom, shalom.
May peace and joy be with you today,
shalom, shalom.

640 *John L. Bell and Graham Maule*

1 She sits like a bird, brooding on the waters,
hovering on the chaos of the world's first day;
she sighs and she sings, mothering creation,
waiting to give birth to all the Word will say.

2 She wings over earth, resting where she wishes,
lighting close at hand or soaring through the skies;
she nests in the womb, welcoming each wonder,
nourishing potential hidden to our eyes.

3 She dances in fire, startling her spectators,
walking tongues of ecstasy where dumbness reigned;
she weans and inspires all whose hearts are open,
nor can she be captured, silenced or restrained.

4 For she is the Spirit, one with God in essence,
gifted by the Saviour in eternal love;
she is the key opening the scriptures,
enemy of apathy and heavenly dove.

641 *J. Clifford Evans*

1 Shepherd of souls, in love come feed us.
Life–giving bread for hungry hearts.
To those refreshing waters lead us
where dwells that grace your peace imparts.
May we, the wayward in your fold,
by your forgiveness rest consoled.

2 Life–giving vine, come, feed and nourish,
strengthen each branch with life divine.
Ever in you O may we flourish,
fruitful the branches of the vine.
Lord, may our souls be purified
so that in Christ we may abide.

3 Sinful are we who stand before you
worthy of you is Christ alone.
So in Christ's name do we implore you;
rich are mercies you have shown.
Say but the word, O Lord divine,
then are our hearts made pure like thine.

4 Following you, O Lord, who led them,
multitudes thronged the mountainside;
filled with compassion, Lord, you fed them,
fed them with loaves you multiplied.
Come, feed us now, O Lord, we pray:
life–giving bread give us this day.

5 Help us, dear Lord, prepare a dwelling
worthy of you who made us all;
cleanse thou our hearts, our guilt dispelling,
purify us who heed your call.
'Take this and eat' were words you said,
so we have gathered for this bread.

642 *Sebastian Temple*

1 Show me your ways that I may follow you,
lead me, O master, on my way.
Guide me in all the things that I must do,
direct my steps that I don't go astray.

In you I place my confidence and trust,
O Lord, have your way with me for I am yours.

2 Guard me when temptation calls on me to sin.
Protect me when the enemy is near.
Strengthen me to turn to you that I may win,
and bless me, Jesus, that I persevere.

Alternative Response:
The spirit's willing but the flesh is weak, O Lord.
But your support is all I'll ever need.

3 Show me your ways that I may follow you,
lead me, O Master, on my way.
Guide me in all the things that I must do,
direct my steps that I don't go astray.

643 *Joseph Mohr (1792–1848), tr. J. Young*

1 Silent night, holy night,
all is calm all is bright,
round yon virgin mother and child;
holy infant, so tender and mild:
sleep in heavenly peace, (2)

2 Silent night, holy night.
Shepherds quake at the sight,
glories stream from heaven afar,
heavenly hosts sing alleluia;
Christ, the Saviour is born, (2)

3 Silent night, holy night.
Son of God, love's pure light
radiant beams from thy holy face,
with the dawn of redeeming grace:
Jesus, Lord, at thy birth, (2)

644 *Dan Schutte*

Sing a new song unto the Lord;
let your song be sung from mountains high.
Sing a new song unto the Lord,
singing alleluia.

1 Yahweh's people dance for joy.
O come before the Lord
and play for him on glad tambourines,
and let your trumpet sound.

2 Rise, O children, from your sleep;
your Saviour now has come.
He has turned your sorrow to joy,
and filled your soul with song.

3 Glad my soul for I have seen
the glory of the Lord.
The trumpet sounds; the dead shall be raised.
I know my Saviour lives.

645 *Versified by Timothy Dudley–Smith*

1 Sing a new song to the Lord,
he to whom wonders belong!
Rejoice in his triumph and tell of his power.
O sing to the Lord a new song!

2 Now to the ends of the earth
see his salvation is shown;
and still he remembers his mercy and truth
unchanging in love to his own.

3 Sing a new song and rejoice,
publish his praises abroad!
Let voices in chorus, and trumpet and horn,
resound for the joy of the Lord!

4 Join with the hills and the sea
thunders of praise to prolong!
In judgement and justice he comes to the earth,
O sing to the Lord a new song!

646 *James Quinn, SJ*

1 Sing, all creation, sing to God in gladness!
Joyously serve him, singing hymns of homage!
Chanting his praises, come before his presence!
Praise the Almighty!

2 Know that our God is Lord of all the ages!
He is our maker, we are all his creatures,
people he fashioned, sheep he leads to pasture!
Praise the Almighty!

3 Enter his temple, ringing out his praises!
Sing in thanksgiving as you come before him!
Blessing his bounty, glorify his greatness!
Praise the Almighty!

4 Great in his goodness is the Lord we worship;
steadfast his kindness, love that knows no ending!
Faithful his word is, changeless, everlasting!
Praise the Almighty!

647 *Linda Stassen*

1 Sing alleluia to the Lord.
2 Sing alleluia to the Lord.
1 Sing alleluia to the Lord.
2 Sing alleluia.
1 Sing alleluia, sing alleluia,
2 Alleluia.
1&2 Sing alleluia to the Lord.

648 *Mike Anderson*

Sing it in the valleys,
shout it from the mountain tops;
Jesus came to save us,
and his saving never stops.
He is King of Kings,
and new life he brings,
sing it in the valleys,
shout it from the mountain tops, (Oh!)
shout it from the mountain tops.

1 Jesus you are by my side,
you take all my fears.
If I only come to you,
you will heal the pain of years.

2 You have not deserted me,
though I go astray.
Jesus take me in your arms,
help me walk with you today.

3 Jesus, you are living now,
Jesus, I believe.
Jesus, take me, heart and soul,
Yours alone I want to be.

649 *Michael Cockett*

Sing, my soul. Sing, my soul.
Sing, my soul, of his mercy. (2)

1 The Lord is good to me.
His light will shine on me.
When city lights would blind my eyes.
He hears my silent call.
His hands help when I fall.
His gentle voice stills my sighs.

2 The Lord is good to me.
His word will set me free
when some would tie me to the ground.
He mocks my foolish ways
with love that never fails.
When I'm most lost then I'm found.

3 The Lord is good to me.
I hear him speak to me.
His voice is in the rain that falls.
He whispers in the air
of his unending care.
If I will hear, then he calls.

650 *Venantius Fortunatus (530–609), tr. J. M. Neale (1818–66), and others*

1 Sing, my tongue, the glorious battle,
sing the last, the dread affray;
o'er the cross, the victor's trophy,
sound the high triumphal lay:
how, the pains of death enduring,
earth's redeemer won the day.

2 Faithful cross! above all other,
one and only noble tree!
None in foliage, none in blossom,
none in fruit thy peer may be;
sweetest wood and sweetest iron!
sweetest weight is hung on thee.

3 Bend, O lofty tree, thy branches,
thy too rigid sinews bend;
and awhile the stubborn hardness,
which thy birth bestowed, suspend;
and the limbs of heaven's high monarch
gently on thine arms extend.

4 Thou alone wast counted worthy
this world's ransom to sustain,
that by thee a wrecked creation
might its ark and haven gain,
with the sacred blood anointed
of the Lamb that hath been slain.

5 Praise and honour to the Father,
praise and honour to the Son,
praise and honour to the Spirit,
ever three and ever one,
one in might and one in glory,
while eternal ages run.

651 *William Josiah Irons (1812–83)*

1 Sing of Christ, proclaim his glory,
sing the resurrection song!
Death and sorrow, earth's dark story,
to the former days belong.
All around the clouds are breaking,
soon the storms of time shall cease;
in God's likeness, people, waking,
know the everlasting peace.

2 O what glory, far exceeding
all that eye has yet perceived!
Holiest hearts for ages pleading
never that full joy conceived.
God has promised, Christ prepares it,
there on high our welcome waits;
ev'ry humble spirit shares it,
Christ has passed th'eternal gates.

3 Life eternal! Heaven rejoices:
Jesus lives who once was dead:
shout with joy, O deathless voices!
Child of God, lift up your head!
Patriarchs from distant ages,
saints all longing for their heaven,
prophets, psalmists, seers and sages,
all await the glory giv'n.

4 Life eternal! O what wonders
crowd on faith, what joy unknown,
when, amid earth's closing thunders,
saints shall stand before the throne!
O to enter that bright portal,
see that glowing firmament,
know, with you, O God immortal,
Jesus Christ whom you have sent!

652 *Roland F. Palmer, SSJE*

1 Sing of Mary, pure and lowly,
virgin mother undefiled.
Sing of God's own Son most holy,
who became her little child.
Fairest child of fairest mother,
God, the Lord, who came to earth,
Word made flesh, our very brother,
takes our nature by his birth.

2 Sing of Jesus, son of Mary,
in the home at Nazareth.
Toil and labour cannot weary
love enduring unto death.
Constant was the love he gave her,
though he went forth from her side,
forth to preach and heal and suffer,
till on Calvary he died.

3 Glory be to God the Father,
glory be to God the Son;
glory be to God the Spirit,
glory to the three in one.
From the heart of blessed Mary,
from all saints the song ascends
and the Church the strain re-echoes
unto earth's remotest ends.

653 *Michael Cockett*

1 Sing of the bride and sing of the groom,
and the wine that was flowing free,
when the Lord was a guest at the
wedding feast
in a town in Galilee.

Fill the pots with water and raise the
glasses high,
for the Lord has come to Cana
and changed water into wine.

2 Sing of the bride and sing of the groom,
and the feasting all night and day,
with the wine running short at the
wedding feast
to the steward's sad dismay.

3 'Please will you help, they have no more
wine,'
said a mother to her only son.
He said: 'Woman, don't you know you
can't turn to me,
for my time has not yet come.'

4 'Wait till the day and wait till the time
for the cross and for Calvary,
but until that time here's a fine new wine
with a taste that's fine and free.'

5 Drink to the bride and drink to the groom
at the wedding in Galilee,
and drink to the life that is like new wine
to all those who wish to be free.

654 *Ernest Sands*

1 Sing of the Lord's goodness,
Father of all wisdom,
come to him and bless his name.
Mercy he has shown us, his love is for ever,
faithful to the end of days.

Come then all you nations,
sing of your Lord's goodness,,
melodies of praise and thanks to God.
Ring out the Lord's glory,
praise him with your music,
worship him and bless his name.

2 Power he has wielded,
honour is his garment,
risen from the snares of death.
His word he has spoken,
one bread he has broken,
new life he now gives to all.

3 Courage in our darkness,
comfort in our sorrow,
Spirit of our God most high;
solace for the weary,
pardon for the sinner,
splendour of the living God.

4 Praise him with your singing,
praise him with the trumpet,
praise God with the lute and harp;
praise him with the cymbals,
praise him with your dancing,
praise God till the end of days.

655 *Sebastian Temple*

1 Sing praises to the living God,
glory, hallelujah.
Come, adore the living God,
glory, hallelujah.
Though sun and moon may pass away
his words will ever stay.
His power is for evermore,
glory, hallelujah.

Glory to the Trinity.
The undivided Unity,
the Father, Son and Spirit one,
from whom all life and greatness come.

2 And to the living God we sing,
glory, hallelujah.
Let our love and praises ring,
glory, hallelujah.
To all his sons he always gives
his mercy and his love.
So praise him now for evermore,
glory, hallelujah.

3 And to the God who cannot die,
glory hallelujah.
To the living God we cry,
glory hallelujah.
He promised to be with us and
he lives in ev'ry one.
We love him now for evermore,
glory hallelujah.

656 *Aniceto Nazareth*

Sing to the Bride, sing to the Groom,
for they love one another in Jesus the Lord.
Sing to the Bride, sing to the Groom,
sing to Jesus Christ.

1 Yahweh has brought you to the bone of your bones,
has joined you to the flesh of your flesh.

2 You are the sign of the New Jerusalem,
come down, out of heaven from our God.

3 Love one another, for love is of God,
the person who loves is born of God.

4 Faith, hope and love be with you unto the end,
the greatest of these is surely love.

5 Vain is your labour, all your planning, your dreams
unless the Lord builds your home.

6 May God protect you all the days of your life
may peace and prosperity be yours.

657 *Bob Dufford, SJ.*

Sing to the mountains, sing to the sea.
Raise your voices, lift your hearts.
This is the day the Lord has made.
Let all the earth rejoice.

1 I will give thanks to you, my Lord.
You have answered my plea.
You have saved my soul from death.
You are my strength and my song.

2 Holy, holy, holy Lord.
Heaven and earth are full of your glory.

3 This is the day that the Lord has made.
Let us be glad and rejoice.
He has turned all death to life.
Sing of the glory of God.

658 *Patrick Lee*

1 Sing to the world of Christ our sov'reign Lord;
tell of his birth which brought new life to all.
Speak of his life, his love, his holy word;
let ev'ry nation hear and know his call.
Sing to the world of Christ our Sov'reign Lord.

2 Sing to the world of Christ the Prince of peace,
showing to me the Father's loving care,
pleading that love should reign and wars might cease,
teaching we need the love of God to share.
Sing to the world of Christ the Prince of peace.

3 Sing to the world of Christ our steadfast friend,
off'ring himself to live the constant sign;
food for our souls until we meet life's end,
gives us his flesh for bread, his blood for wine.
Sing to the world of Christ our steadfast friend.

4 Sing to the world of Christ our Saviour King,
born that his death the world's release should win;
hung from a cross, forgiveness he could bring;
buried, he rose to conquer death and sin.
Sing to the world of Christ our Saviour King.

5 Sing to the world of Christ at God's right hand,
praise to the Spirit both have sent to me,
living in us till earth shall reach its span,
time be no more, and Christ shall come again.
Sing to the world of Christ at God's right hand.

659 *G. B. Timms*

1 Sing we of the blessèd Mother
who received the angel's word,
and obedient to his summons
bore in love the infant Lord;
sing we of the joys of Mary
at whose breast that child was fed
who is Son of God eternal
and the everlasting Bread.

2 Sing we, too, of Mary's sorrows,
of the sword that pierced her through,
when beneath the cross of Jesus
she his weight of suffering knew,
looked upon her Son and Saviour
reigning high on Calvary's tree,
saw the price of man's redemption
paid to set the sinner free.

3 Sing again the joys of Mary
when she saw the risen Lord,
and in prayer with Christ's apostles,
waited on his promised word:
from on high the blazing glory
of the Spirit's presence came,
heavenly breath of God's own being,
manifest through wind and flame.

4 Sing the chiefest joy of Mary
when on earth her work was done,
and the Lord of all creation
brought her to his heavenly home:
virgin Mother, Mary blessèd,
raised on high and crowned with grace,
may your Son, the world's redeemer,
grant us all to see his face.

660 *Edward Caswall (1814–78)*

1 Sleep, holy babe,
upon thy mother's breast;
great Lord of earth and sea and sky,
how sweet it is to see thee lie
in such a place of rest.

2 Sleep, holy babe;
thine angels watch around,
all bending low, with folded wings,
before th'incarnate King of kings,
in reverent awe profound.

3 Sleep, holy babe,
while I with Mary gaze
in joy upon that face awhile,
upon the loving infant smile,
which there divinely plays.

4 Sleep, holy babe,
ah, take thy brief repose,
too quickly will thy slumbers break,
and thou to lengthen'd pains awake,
that death alone shall close.

5 O lady blest,
sweet Virgin, hear my cry;
forgive the wrong that I have done
to thee, in causing thy dear Son
upon the cross to die.

661 *Christopher Wordsworth (1807–85)*

1 Songs of thankfulness and praise,
Jesus, Lord to thee we raise,
manifested by the star
to the sages from afar;
branch of royal David's stem,
in thy birth at Bethlehem;
anthems be to thee addressed;
God in man made manifest.

2 Manifest at Jordan's streams,
prophet, Priest and King supreme,
and at Cana wedding–guest,
in thy Godhead manifest,
manifest in power divine,
changing water into wine;
anthems be to thee addressed;
God in man made manifest.

3 Manifest in making whole,
palsied limbs and fainting soul,
manifest in valiant fight,
quelling all the devil's might,
manifest in gracious will,
ever bringing good from ill;
anthems be to thee addressed;
God in man made manifest.

4 Sun and moon shall darkened be,
stars shall fall, the heavens shall flee.
Christ will then like lightning shine.
All will see his glorious sign.
All will see the judge appear;
all will then the trumpet hear;
thou by all wilt be confessed;
God in man made manifest.

5 Grant us grace to see thee, Lord,
mirrored in thy holy word;
may we imitate thee now
and be pure, as pure art thou;
that we like to thee may be
at thy great Epiphany,
and may praise thee, ever blest,
God in man made manifest.

662 *James Theim*

Sons of God, hear his holy Word!
Gather round the table of the Lord!
Eat his Body, drink his Blood,
and we'll sing a song of love.
Allelu, allelu, allelu, alleluia.

1 Brothers, sisters, we are one,
and our life has just begun.
In the Spirit we are young.
We can live for ever.

2 Shout together to the Lord
who has promised our reward:
happiness a hundredfold,
and we'll live forever.

3 Jesus gave a new command
that we love each other, then
we will reach the promised land,
where we'll live forever.

4 If we want to live with him;
we must also die with him;
die to selfishness and sin,
and we'll rise forever.

5 Make the world a family,
gather all in unity
till we meet the Trinity
and live with them forever.

6 With the Church we celebrate;
Jesus' coming we await,
so we make a holiday,
so we'll live forever.

663 *Ascribed to John XXII (1249–1334), tr. Anonymous*

1 Soul of my Saviour, sanctify my breast;
Body of Christ, be thou my saving guest;
Blood of my Saviour, bathe me in thy
tide,
wash me with water flowing from thy
side.

2 Strength and protection may thy
Passion be;
O Blessed Jesus hear and answer me;
deep in thy wounds, Lord, hide and
shelter me;
so shall I never, never part from thee.

3 Guard and defend me from the foe malign;
in death's dread moments make me only
thine;
call me, and bid me come to thee on high,
when I may praise thee with thy saints
for aye.

664 *Sr. Miriam Thérèse Winter*

1 Spirit of God in the clear running water,
blowing to greatness the trees on the hill.
Spirit of God in the finger of morning,
fill the earth, bring it to birth and blow
where you will.

*Blow, blow, blow till I be but breath of
the Spirit blowing in me.*

2 Down in the meadow the willows are
moaning,
sheep in the pasture–land cannot lie still.
Spirit of God, creation is groaning,
fill the earth, bring it to birth and blow
where you will.
Blow …

3 I saw the scar of a year that lay dying,
heard the lament of a lone whippoorwill.
Spirit of God, see that cloud crying,
fill the earth, bring it to birth and blow
where you will.
Blow …

4 Spirit of God, every man's heart is lonely,
watching and waiting and hungry until,
Spirit of God, man longs that you only
fulfil the earth, bring it to birth and blow
where you will.
Blow …

665 *Timothy Dudley–Smith*

1 Spirit of God within me,
possess my human frame.
Fan the dull embers of my heart,
stir up the living flame.
Strive till that image Adam lost,
new minted and restored,
in shining splendour brightly bears
the likeness of the Lord.

2 Spirit of truth within me,
possess my thought and mind;
lighten anew the inward eye
by Satan rendered blind;
shine on the words that wisdom speaks
and grant me pow'r to see
the truth made known to all in Christ
and in that truth be free.

3 Spirit of love within me,
possess my hands and heart;
break through the bonds of self–concern
that seeks to stand apart:
grant me the love that suffers long,
that hopes, believes and bears,
the love fulfilled in sacrifice
that cares as Jesus cares.

4 Spirit of life within me,
possess this life of mine;
come as the wind of heaven's breath,
come as the fire divine!
Spirit of Christ, the living Lord,
reign in this house of clay,
till from its dust with Christ I rise
to everlasting day.

666 *Daniel Iverson*

Spirit of the living God, fall afresh on me.
Spirit of the living God, fall afresh on me.
Break me, melt me, mould me, fill me.
Spirit of the living God, fall afresh on me.

667 *Huub Oosterhuis, tr. Tony Barr*

[1]Stand and stare not at what used to be
[2]and remain not in the past. For
[3]I, says he, make new beginnings. Look,
[4]all things are new now, do you not see?

668 *9th century, tr. R. A. Knox (1888–1957)*

1 Star of ocean, lead us;
God for mother claims thee,
ever Virgin names thee;
gate of heaven, speed us.

2 Ave to thee crying
Gabriel went before us;
peace do thou restore us,
Eva's knot untying.

3 Loose the bonds that chain us,
darkened eyes enlighten,
clouded prospects brighten,
heavenly mercies gain us.

4 For thy sons thou carest;
offer Christ our praying –
still thy word obeying –
whom on earth thou barest.

5 Purer, kinder maiden
God did never fashion;
pureness and compassion
grant to hearts sin–laden.

6 From that sin release us,
shield us, heavenward faring,
heaven, that is but sharing
in thy joy with Jesus.

7 Honour, praise and merit
to our God address we;
Three in One confess we,
Father, Son and Spirit.

669 *Afro–American Spiritual*

Steal away, steal away,
steal away to Jesus.
Steal away, steal away home.
I ain't got long to stay here.

1 My Lord, he calls me.
He calls me by the thunder.
The trumpet sounds within my soul;
I ain't got long to stay here.

2 Green trees are bending,
the sinner stands a–trembling.
The trumpet sounds within my soul;
I ain't got long to stay here.

3 My Lord, he calls me,
he calls me by the lightning.
The trumpet sounds within my soul;
I ain't got long to stay here.

670 *Philip Green*

Suffer little children to come unto me,
for theirs is the kingdom of heaven.
Suffer little children to come unto me,
for theirs is the kingdom of the Lord.

1 There came unto him
children, little children,
that he might lay his hands upon them,
pray for and bless them,
children, little children,
gathered round our Lord.

2 The disciples said:
'Children, little children,
leave the Master to his prayer.
Begone and stay not,
children, little children,
gathered round our Lord.'

3 But Jesus said:
'Children, little children,
stay my blessing to receive.
Forbid you not that
children, little children,
shall gather round the Lord.'

4 'For you must be like
children, little children,
humble, simple, pure in heart.
For it is to these
children, little children,
the kingdom of heav'n belongs.'

671 *Delores Dufner, OSB*

1 Summoned by the God who made us
rich in our diversity,
gathered in the name of Jesus,
richer still in unity:

Let us bring the gifts that differ
and, in splendid, varied ways,
sing a new church into being
one in faith and love and praise.

2 Radiant risen from the water,
robed in holiness and light,
male and female in God's image,
male and female, God's delight:

3 Trust the goodness of creation;
trust the Spirit strong within.
Dare to dream the vision promised
sprung from seed of what has been.

4 Bring the hopes of ev'ry nation;
bring the art of ev'ry race.
Weave a song of peace and justice;
let it sound through time and space.
Let us bring the gifts that differ
and, in splendid, varied ways,
sing a new church into being
one in faith and love and praise.

5 Draw together at one table
all the human family;
shape a circle ever wider
and a people ever free.

672 *Taizé chant Psalm verses from the Grail version*

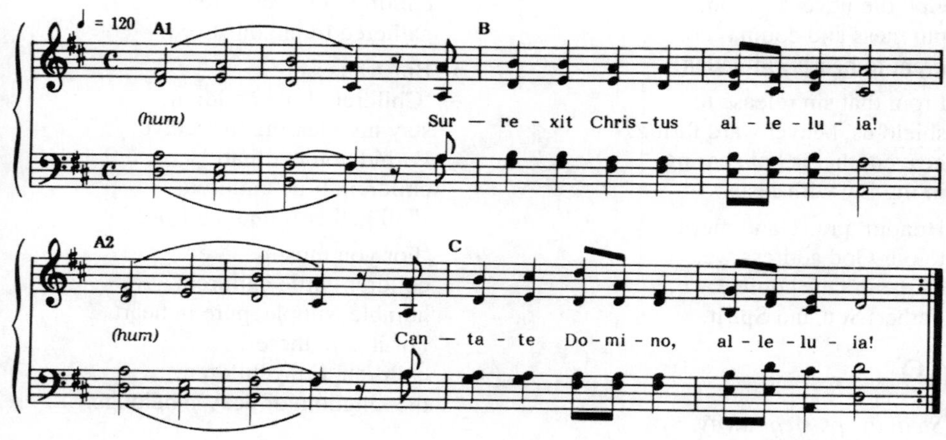

♩ = 120
A1
B
(hum)
Sur — re - xit Chris - tus al - le - lu - ia!
A2
C
(hum)
Can — ta - te Do - mi - no, al - le - lu - ia!

From Psalm 117 (118):

1 Give thanks to the Lord for he is good,
for his love has no end.

2 The Lord is my strength, the Lord is my song,
he has been my Saviour.

3 I shall not die, I shall live,
I shall live and recount his deeds.

From Daniel 3:

1 All you heavens, bless the Lord.
Stars of the heavens, bless the Lord.

2 Sun and moon, bless the Lord.
And you, night and day, bless the Lord.

3 Frost and cold, bless the Lord.
Ice and snow, bless the Lord.

4 Fire and heat, bless the Lord.
And you, light and darkness, bless the Lord.

5 Spirits and souls of the just, bless the Lord.
Saints and the humble hearted, bless the Lord.

---

673 *Traditional*

1 Sweet heart of Jesus, fount of love and mercy,
today we come, thy blessing to implore;
O touch our hearts, so cold and so ungrateful,
and make them, Lord, thine own for evermore.

Sweet heart of Jesus, we implore,
O make us love thee more and more.

2 Sweet heart of Jesus, make us know and love thee,
unfold to us the treasures of thy grace;
that so our hearts, from things of earth uplifted,
may long alone to gaze upon thy face.

3 Sweet heart of Jesus, make us pure and gentle,
and teach us how to do thy blessed will;
to follow close the print of thy dear footsteps,
and when we fall – sweet heart, oh, love us still.

4 Sweet heart of Jesus, bless all hearts that love thee,
and may thine own heart ever blessed be,
bless us, dear Lord, and bless the friends we cherish,
and keep us true to Mary and to thee.

674 *Francis Stanfield (1835–1914)*

1 Sweet sacrament divine,
hid in thy earthly home,
lo! Round thy lowly shrine,
with suppliant hearts we come;
Jesus, to thee our voice we raise,
in songs of love and heartfelt praise,
sweet sacrament divine.

2 Sweet sacrament of peace,
dear home of every heart,
where restless yearnings cease,
and sorrows all depart,
there in thine ear all trustfully
we tell our tale of misery,
sweet sacrament of peace.

3 Sweet sacrament of rest,
Ark from the ocean's roar,
within thy shelter blest
soon may we reach the shore,
save us, for still the tempest raves;
save, lest we sink beneath the waves
sweet sacrament of rest.

4 Sweet sacrament divine,
earth's light and jubilee,
in thy far depths doth shine
thy Godhead's majesty;
sweet light, so shine on us, we pray,
that earthly joys may fade away,
sweet sacrament divine.

675 *Frederick William Faber (1814–63)*

1 Sweet Saviour, bless us ere we go,
thy word into our minds instil;
and make our lukewarm hearts to glow
with lowly love and fervent will.

Through life's long day
and death's dark night,
O gentle Jesus, be our light.

2 The day is done; its hours have run,
and thou hast taken count of all,
the scanty triumphs grace has won,
the broken vow, the frequent fall.

3 Grant us, dear Lord, from evil ways,
true absolution and release;
and bless us more than in past days
with purity and inward peace.

4 Do more than pardon; give us joy,
sweet fear and sober liberty,
and loving hearts without alloy,
that only long to be like thee.

5 Labour is sweet, for thou hast toiled,
and care is light, for thou hast cared;
let not our works with self be soiled.
Nor in unsimple ways ensnared.

6 For all we love – the poor, the sad,
the sinful – unto thee we call;
oh let thy mercy make us glad,
thou art our Jesus and our all.

676 *Sebastian Temple*

1 Take my hands and make them as your own,
and use them for your Kingdom here on earth.
Consecrate them to your care,
anoint them for your service where
you may need your gospel to be sown.

2 Take my hands. They speak now for my heart,
and by their actions they will show their love.
Guard them on their daily course,
be their strength and guiding force
to ever serve the Trinity above.

3 Take my hands. I give them to you, Lord.
Prepare them for the service of your name.
Open them to human need
and by their love they'll sow your seed
so all may know the love and hope you give.

677 Frances R. Havergal (1836–79)

1 Take my life, and let it be
consecrated, Lord, to thee;
take my moments and my days,
let them flow in ceaseless praise.

2 Take my hands, and let them move
at the impulse of thy love.
Take my feet, and let them be
swift and purposeful for thee.

3 Take my voice, and let me sing
always, only, for my King.
Take my intellect, and use
every power as thou shalt choose.

4 Take my will, and make it thine:
it shall be no longer mine.
Take my heart; it is thine own:
it shall be thy royal throne.

5 Take my love; my Lord, I pour
at thy feet its treasure–store.
Take myself, and I will be
ever, only, all for thee.

678 Joseph Wise

Take our bread, we ask you,
take our hearts, we love you,
take our lives, oh Father,
we are yours, we are yours.

1 Yours as we stand at the table you set,
yours as we eat the bread our hearts can't forget.
We are the signs of your life with us yet;
we are yours, we are yours.

2 Your holy people stand washed in your blood,
Spirit filled, yet hungry, we await your food.
Poor though we are, we have brought ourselves to you:
we are yours, we are yours.

679 James Harrison

1 Take the word of God with you as you go.
Take the seeds of God's word and make them grow.

Go in peace to serve the world,
in peace to serve the world.
Take the love of God, the love of God
with you as you go.

2 Take the peace of God with you as you go.
Take the seeds of God's peace and make them grow.

3 Take the joy of God with you as you go.
Take the seeds of God's joy and make them grow.

4 Take the love* of God with you as you go.
Take the seeds of God's love and make them grow.

** Add other words if needed, such as 'faith', 'hope' …*

680 John L. Bell and Graham Maule

1 Take this moment, sign and space;
take my friends around;
here among us make the place
where your love is found.

2 Take the time to call my name,
take the time to mend
who I am and what I've been,
all I've failed to tend.

3 Take the tiredness of my days,
take my past regret,
letting your forgiveness touch
all I can't forget.

4 Take the little child in me,
scared of growing old;
help him/her here to find his/her worth
made in Christ's own mould.

5 Take my talents, take my skills,
take what's yet to be;
let my life be yours, and yet,
let it still be me.

681 *St Thomas Aquinas (1227–74)*

1 Tantum ergo Sacramentum
veneremur cernui:
et antiquum documentum
novo cedat ritui:
praestet fides supplementum
sensuum defectui.

2 Genitori, genitoque
laus et jubilatio,
salus, honor, virtus quoque
sit et benedictio;
procedenti ab utroque
compar sit laudatio. Amen.

682 *Stephen Dean*

Taste and see,
taste and see that the Lord is good,
the Lord is good.

1 I will bless the Lord at all times,
his praise always on my lips.
The Lord shall be the glory of my soul;
the humble shall hear and be glad.

2 Glorify the Lord with me,
together let us praise his name.
I sought the Lord: he answered me;
he set me free from all my fear.

3 Look upon the Lord and be radiant,
hide not your face from the Lord.
He heard the cry of the poor;
he rescued them from all their woes.

4 The angel of the Lord is with his people
to rescue those who trust in him.
Taste and see the goodness of the Lord;
seek refuge in him and be glad.

5 Saints of the Lord, revere him;
those who fear him lack nothing.
Lions suffer want and go hungry,
but those who seek him lack no blessing.

6 Children of the Lord come and hear;
and learn the fear of the Lord.
Who is he who longs for life,
whose only love is for his wealth?

7 Keep evil words from your tongue,
your lips from speaking deceit.
Turn aside from evil and do good;
seek and strive after peace.

683 *Te Deum Laudamus, Author unknown (4th century)*

Te Deum laudamus: te Dominum
confitemur.
Te æternum Patrem omnis terra
veneratur.
Tibi omnes Angeli, tibi cæli et universæ
potestates:
tibi Cherubimet Seraphim incessabili
voce proclamant:
Sanctus: Sanctus: Sanctus Dominus Deus
Sabaoth.
Pleni sunt cæli et terra majestatis gloriæ
tuæ.
Te gloriosus Apostolorum chorus:
Te Prophetarum laudabilis numerus:
Te Martyrum candidatus laudat exercitus.
Te per orbem terrarum sancta confitetur
Ecclesia:
Patrem immensæ majestatis:
Venerandum tuum verum et unicum
Filium:
Sanctum quoque Paraclitum Spiritum.
Tu Rex gloriæ, Christe.
Tu Patris sempiternus es Filius.
Tu ad liberandum suscepturus hominem,
non horruisti Virginis uterum.
Tu devicto mortis aculeo,
aperuisti credentibus regna cælorum.
Tu ad dexteram Dei sedes, in gloria
Patris.
Judex crederis esse venturus.
Te ergo quæsumus, tuis famulis subveni,
quos pretioso sanguine redemisti.
Æterna fac cum sanctis tuis in gloria
numerari.
Salvum fac populum tuum Domine,
et benedic hæreditati tuæ.
Et rege eos, et extolle illos usque in
æternum.
Per singulos dies, benedicimus te.
Et laudamus nomen tuum in sæculum, et
in sæculum sæculi.

Dignare Domine die isto
sine peccato nos custodire.
Miserere nostri Domine, miserere nostri.
Fiat misericordia tua Domine super nos,
quemadmodum speravimus in te.
In te Domine speravi:
non confundar in æternum.

684 *Timothy Dudley-Smith*

1 Tell out, my soul, the greatness of the Lord!
Unnumbered blessings, give my spirit voice;
tender to me the promise of his word;
in God my Saviour shall my heart rejoice.

2 Tell out, my soul, the greatness of his name!
Make known his might, the deeds his arm has done;
his mercy sure, from age to age the same;
his holy name – the Lord, the Mighty One.

3 Tell out, my soul, the greatness of his might!
Powers and dominions lay their glory by.
Proud hearts and stubborn wills are put to flight,
the hungry fed, the humble lifted high.

4 Tell out, my soul, the glories of his word!
Firm is his promise, and his mercy sure.
Tell out, my soul, the greatness of the Lord
to children's children and for evermore!

685 *Walter van der Haas and Peter-Paul van Lelyveld*

1 Thank you for giving me the morning.
Thank you for ev'ry day that's new.
Thank you that I can know my worries
can be cast on you.

2 Thank you for all my friends and brothers.
Thank you for all the men that live.
Thank you for even greatest enemies
I can forgive.

3 Thank you, I have my occupation.
Thank you for ev'ry pleasure small.
Thank you for music, light and gladness.
Thank you for them all.

4 Thank you for many little sorrows.
Thank you for ev'ry kindly word.
Thank you for ev'rywhere your guidance
reaches ev'ry land.

5 Thank you, I see your Word has meaning.
Thank you, I know your Spirit here.
Thank you because you love all people,
those both far and near.

6 Thank you, O Lord, you spoke unto us.
Thank you that for our words you care.
Thank you, O Lord, you came among us,
bread and wine to share.

7 Thank you, O Lord, your love is boundless.
Thank you that I am full of you.
Thank you, you made me feel so glad
and thankful as I do.

686 *Basque carol paraphrased by Sabine Baring-Gould (1834–1924)*

1 The angel Gabriel from heaven came,
his wings as drifted snow, his eyes as flame;
'All hail,' said he, 'thou lowly maiden Mary,
most highly favoured lady.' *Gloria!*

2 'For know, a blessed Mother thou shalt be,
all generations laud and honour thee,
thy Son shall be Emmanuel, by seers foretold;
most highly favoured lady.' *Gloria!*

3 Then gently Mary meekly bowed her head,
'To me be as it pleaseth God,' she said.
'My soul shall laud and magnify his holy name';
most highly favoured lady. *Gloria!*

4 Of her, Emmanuel, the Christ was born
in Bethlehem, all on a Christmas morn,
and Christian folk throughout the world will ever say
'most highly favoured lady.' *Gloria!*

687 *Hubert Richards*

1 The bakerwoman in her humble lodge
received a grain of wheat from God.
For nine whole months the grain she stored.
Behold the handmaid of the Lord.
Make us the bread, Mary, Mary.
Make us the bread, we need to be fed.

2 The bakerwoman took the road which led
to Bethlehem, the house of bread.
To knead the bread she laboured through
the night,
and brought it forth about midnight.
Bake us the bread, Mary, Mary.
Bake us the bread, we need to be fed.

3 She baked the bread for thirty years
by the fire of her love and the salt of her
tears,
by the warmth of a heart so tender and
bright,
and the bread was golden brown and white.
Bring us the bread, Mary, Mary.
Bring us the bread, we need to be fed.

4 After thirty years the bread was done.
It was taken to town by her only son;
the soft white bread to be given free
to the hungry people of Galilee.
Give us the bread, Mary, Mary.
Give us the bread, we need to be fed.

5 For thirty coins the bread was sold,
and a thousand teeth so cold, so cold,
tore it to pieces on a Friday noon
when the sun turned black and red the
moon.
Break us the bread, Mary, Mary.
Break us the bread, we need to be fed.

6 And when she saw the bread so white,
the living bread she had made at night,
devoured as wolves might devour a sheep,
the bakerwoman began to weep.
Weep for the bread, Mary, Mary.
Weep for the bread, we need to be fed.

7 But the bakerwoman's only son
appeared to his friends when three days
had run
on the road which to Emmaus led,
and they knew him in the breaking of bread.
Lift up your head, Mary, Mary.
Lift up your head, for now we've been fed.

688 *S. J. Stone (1830–1900)*

1 The Church's one foundation
is Jesus Christ, her Lord;
she is his new creation
by water and the Word;
from heav'n he came and sought her
to be his holy bride,
with his own blood he bought her,
and for her life he died.

2 Elect from every nation,
yet one o'er all the earth,
her charter of salvation
one Lord, one faith, one birth;
one holy name she blesses,
partakes one holy food,
and to one hope she presses,
with every grace endued.

3 'Mid toil, and tribulation,
and tumult of her war,
she waits the consummation
of peace for evermore;
till with the vision glorious
her longing eyes are blest,
and the great Church victorious
shall be the Church at rest.

4 Yet she on earth hath union
with God the Three in One,
and mystic sweet communion
with those whose rest is won:
O happy ones and holy!
Lord, give us grace that we,
like them, the meek and lowly,
on high may dwell with thee.

689 *Charles Coffin (1676–1749), tr. R. Campbell (1814–68)*

1 The coming of our God
our thoughts must now employ;
then let us meet him on the road
with songs of holy joy.

2 The co–eternal Son,
a maiden's offspring see;
a servant's form Christ putteth on
to set his people free.

3 Daughter of Sion, rise
to greet thine infant king,
nor let thy stubborn heart despise
the pardon he doth bring.

4 In glory from his throne
again will Christ descend,
and summon all that are his own
to joys that never end.

5 Let deeds of darkness fly
before the approaching morn,
for unto sin 'tis ours to die,
and serve the virgin–born.

6 Our joyful praises sing
to Christ, that sets us free;
like tribute to the Father bring,
and, Holy Ghost, to thee.

690 *St. John Damascene (c. 750), tr. J. M. Neale (1818–66)*

1 The day of resurrection!
earth, tell it out abroad;
the Passover of gladness,
the Passover of God!
From death to life eternal,
from earth unto the sky,
our Christ hath brought us over
with hymns of victory.

2 Our hearts be pure from evil,
that we may see aright
the Lord in rays eternal
of resurrection–light;
and listening to his accents,
may hear so calm and plain
his own 'All hail' and, hearing,
may raise the victor strain.

3 Now let the heavens be joyful,
and earth her song begin,
the round world keep high triumph,
and all that is therein;
let all things seen and unseen
their notes of gladness blend,
for Christ the Lord hath risen,
our joy that hath no end.

691 *John Ellerton (1826–93)*

1 The day thou gavest, Lord, is ended:
the darkness falls at thy behest;
to thee our morning hymns ascended;
thy praise shall sanctify our rest.

2 We thank thee that thy Church unsleeping,
while earth rolls onward into light,
through all the world her watch is keeping,
and rests not now by day or night.

3 As o'er each continent and island
the dawn leads on another day,
the voice of prayer is never silent,
nor dies the strain of praise away.

4 The sun that bids us rest is waking
our brethren 'neath the western sky
and hour by hour fresh lips are making
thy wondrous doings heard on high.

5 So be it, Lord; thy throne shall never,
like earth's proud empire, pass away;
thy kingdom stands, and grows for ever,
till all thy creatures own thy sway.

692 *Traditional Old English*

1 The first Nowell the angel did say
was to certain poor shepherds in fields as
they lay;
in fields where they lay keeping their sheep,
on a cold winter's night that was so deep.

Nowell, Nowell, Nowell, Nowell,
born is the King of Israel!

2 They lookèd up and saw a star,
shining in the east, beyond them far,
and to the earth it gave great light,
and so it continued both day and night.

Nowell, Nowell, Nowell, Nowell,
born is the King of Israel!

3 And by the light of that same star,
three wise men came from country far.
To seek for a king was their intent,
and to follow the star wherever it went.

4 This star drew nigh to the north–west,
o'er Bethlehem it took its rest,
and there it did both stop and stay
right over the place where Jesus lay.

5 Then entered in those wise men three,
full reverently upon their knee,
and offered there in his presence,
their gold and myrrh and frankincense.

6 Then let us all with one accord
sing praises to our heavenly Lord,
that hath made heaven and earth of nought,
and with his blood mankind hath bought.

693 *Sr. Katherine Boschetti, MSC*

1 The gift of the Holy Spirit
is the gift of God's great love.
To us comes the touch of healing
from the God of heaven above;
joy and strength for our daily living,
trust and love for the work of giving,
and the spirit of true forgiving each one.

2 Anointed, we are Christ's witness
in the walk of life each day,
a comfort and light to others
whom we meet along the way.
We will cherish your life within us,
show the mercy you show to sinners,
by your suffering, you chose to win us
from death.

3 Thanksgiving we bring, and honour,
to the Father and the Son
and, with them, the Holy Spirit,
God for ever, Three in One.
Praise and glory we give and blessing,
one faith, one in truth confessing,
one in love in your all–embracing design.

694 *Ascribed to Venantius Fortunatus (530–609), tr. J. M. Neale (1818–66)*

1 The God whom earth, and sea, and sky,
adore and laud and magnify,
who o'er their threefold fabric reigns,
the Virgin's spotless womb contains.

2 The God whose will by moon and sun,
and all things in due course is done,
is borne upon a maiden's breast
by fullest heavenly grace possessed.

3 How blest that mother, in whose shrine
the great Artificer divine,
whose hand contains the earth and sky,
vouchsafed, as in his ark, to lie!

4 Blest, in the message Gabriel brought;
blest, by the work the Spirit wrought;
from whom the great desire of earth,
took human flesh and human birth.

5 All honour, laud and glory be,
O Jesus, virgin–born, to thee!
All glory, as is ever meet
to Father and to Paraclete.

695 *Luke Connaughton (1919–79)*

1 The green life rises from the earth,
the life of sun and rain and soil,
in seed and shoot, in grain and grape,
in food and drink for men.

Praise be to God for all his gifts,
praise for the bread and wine.

2 The Lord of Spring, the Lord of Life,
made bread his body, wine his blood.
The life of earth, the life of God,
becomes the life of man.

3 We take in hand the bread and wine,
reminder of the dying Lord.
This food, this drink, this feast of joy
gives Christ's own life to us.

4 'The Son of Man must die,' said he,
'my death will raise you all to life.
No blade is born, no harvest reaped,
until the seed has died.'

5 'These are the signs of death and life,
the bread you break, the cup you share:
my dying gift in which I live,
my death is life to you.'

6 Give praise to God who gave this gift,
his very Son, to bring us life.
The Father's life in him is ours,
his Spirit breathes in us.

696 *Thomas Kelly (1769–1854)*

1 The head that once was crowned with thorns
is crowned with glory now:
a royal diadem adorns
the mighty victor's brow.

2 The highest place that heaven affords
is his, is his by right.
The King of kings and Lord of lords,
and heaven's eternal light;

3 The joy of all who dwell above,
the joy of all below,
to whom he manifests his love,
and grants his name to know.

4 To them the cross, with all its shame
with all its grace is given;
their name an everlasting name,
their joy the joy of heaven.

5 They suffer with their Lord below,
they reign with him above,
their profit and their joy to know
the mystery of his love.

6 The cross he bore is life and health,
though shame and death to him;
his people's hope, his people's wealth,
their everlasting theme.

697 *St. Thomas Aquinas (1227–74), tr. J. M. Neale (1818–66)*

1 The heav'nly Word, proceeding forth
yet leaving not the Father's side,
accomplishing his work on earth
had reached at length life's eventide.

2 By false disciple to be giv'n
to foemen for his life athirst,
himself, the very bread of heav'n,
he gave to his disciples first.

3 He gave himself in either kind,
he gave his flesh, he gave his blood;
in love's own fullness thus designed,
to be, for humankind, the food.

4 O saving victim, opening wide
the gate of heav'n to all below,
our foes press on from every side;
thine aid supply, thy strength bestow.

5 To thy great name be endless praise,
Immortal Godhead, one in three:
O grant us endless length of days
in our true native land with thee.

698 *W. F. Jabusch*

*The King of glory comes the nation rejoices
open the gates before him, lift up your
voices.*

1 Who is the King of glory
how shall we call him?
He is Emmanuel,
the promised of ages.

2 In all of Galilee,
in city and village,
he goes among his people,
curing their illness.

3 Sing then of David's Son,
our Saviour and brother;
in all of Galilee
was never another.

4 He gave his life for us,
the pledge of salvation.
He took upon himself
the sins of the nation.

5 He conquered sin and death;
he truly has risen.
And he will share with us
his heavenly vision.

699 *Henry Williams Baker (1821–77)*

1 The King of love my shepherd is,
whose goodness faileth never;
I nothing lack if I am his
and he is mine for ever.

2 Where streams of living water flow
my ransomed soul he leadeth,
and where the verdant pastures grow
with food celestial feedeth.

3 Perverse and foolish oft I strayed
but yet in love he sought me,
and on his shoulder gently laid,
and home, rejoicing, brought me.

4 In death's dark vale I fear no ill
with thee, dear Lord, beside me;
thy rod and staff my comfort still,
thy cross before to guide me.

5 Thou spread'st a table in my sight,
thy unction grace bestoweth:
and O what transport of delight
from thy pure chalice floweth!

6 And so through all the length of days
thy goodness faileth never;
good Shepherd, may I sing thy praise
within thy house for ever.

700 *John Brownlie (1859–1925)*

1 The King shall come when morning dawns
and light triumphant breaks,
when beauty gilds the eastern hills
and life to joy awakes.

2 Not as of old a little child,
to bear and fight and die,
but crowned with glory like the sun
that lights the morning sky.

3 O brighter than the rising morn
when he, victorious, rose,
and left the lonesome place of death,
despite the rage of foes.

4 O brighter than the glorious morn
shall this fair morning be,
when Christ our King in beauty comes,
and we his face shall see!

5 The King shall come when morning dawns
and light and beauty brings;
'Hail, Christ the Lord!' your people pray,
'Come quickly, King of kings!'

701 *Bryn Rees (1911–83)*

1 The kingdom of God is justice and joy;
for Jesus restores what sin would destroy.
God's power and glory in Jesus we know;
and here and hereafter the kingdom shall grow.

2 The kingdom of God is mercy and grace;
the captives are freed, the sinners find place,
the outcast are welcomed God's banquet to share;
and hope is awakened in place of despair.

3 The kingdom of God is challenge and choice:
believe the good news, repent and rejoice!
His love for us sinners brought Christ to his cross:
our crisis of judgement for gain or for loss.

4 God's kingdom is come, the gift and the goal;
In Jesus begun, in heaven made whole.
The heirs of the kingdom shall answer his call;
and all things cry 'Glory!' to God all in all.

702 *The Beatitudes, Mike Anderson*

The Kingdom of Heaven
the Kingdom of Heaven is yours.
A new world in Jesus,
a new world in Jesus is yours.

1 Blessed are you in sorrow and grief:
for you shall all be consoled.
Blessed are you the gentle in heart;
you shall inherit the earth.

2 Blessed are you who hunger for right:
for you shall be satisfied.
Blessed are you the merciful ones:
for you shall be pardoned too.

3 Blessed are you whose hearts are pure:
your eyes shall gaze on the Lord.
Blessed are you who strive after peace:
the Lord will call you His own.

4 Blessed are you who suffer for right:
the Heavenly Kingdom is yours.
Blessed are you who suffer for me:
for you shall reap your reward.

703 *Donald Fishel*

The light of Christ has come into the world (2)

1 We must all be born again
to see the kingdom of God;
the water and the Spirit
bring new life in God's love.

2 God gave up his only Son
out of love for the world
so that ev'ryone who believes in him
will live for ever.

3 The Light of God has come to us
so that we might have salvation,
from the darkness of our sins, we walk
into glory with Christ Jesus.

704 *John B. Foley, SJ*

*The Lord hears the cry of the poor,
blessed be the Lord.*

1 I will bless the Lord at all times,
his praise ever in my mouth.
Let my soul glory in the Lord,
for he hears the cry of the poor.

2 Let the lowly hear and be glad:
the Lord listens to their pleas;
and to hearts broken he is near,
for he hears the cry of the poor.

3 Ev'ry spirit crushed he will save;
will be ransom for their lives;
will be safe shelter for their fears,
for he hears the cry of the poor.

4 We proclaim the greatness of God,
his praise ever in our mouth;
ev'ry face brightened in his light,
for he hears the cry of the poor.

705 *Hubert Richards*

1 The Lord is my shepherd.
He provides all I need
in the rich grassland,
where he lets me feed.
He brings me to water
my life to renew.
He guides me on true paths
because he is true.

2 I walk through the darkness,
with nothing to fear;
his right hand protects me
when danger is near.
He lays me a table
in sight of my foes.
He fills me with gladness,
my cup overflows.

3 Each day he is goodness,
each day he's my song.
I live in his household
the whole of life long.
The Lord is my shepherd.
He provides all I need
in the rich grassland,
where he lets me feed.

706 *Paraphrased from Psalm 22 (23) in the Scottish Psalter 1650*

1 The Lord's my shepherd, I'll not want,
he makes me down to lie
in pastures green. He leadeth me
the quiet waters by.

2 My soul he doth restore again,
and me to walk doth make
within the paths of righteousness,
e'en for his own name's sake.

3 Yea, though I walk in death's dark vale,
yet will I fear none ill.
For thou art with me, and thy rod
and staff me comfort still.

4 My table thou hast furnishèd
in presence of my foes,
my head thou dost with oil anoint,
and my cup overflows.

5 Goodness and mercy all my life
shall surely follow me.
And in God's house for evermore
my dwelling–place shall be.

707 *The Magnificat, The Grail*

The Lord has done marvels for me,
holy is his name.

1 My soul glorifies the Lord,
my spirit rejoices in God, my Saviour.

2 He looks on his servant in her
nothingness;
henceforth all ages will call me blessed.

3 The Almighty works marvels for me.
Holy his name!

4 His mercy is from age to age,
on those who fear him.

5 He puts forth his arm in strength
and scatters the proud–hearted.

6. He casts the mighty from their thrones
and raises the lowly.

7 He fills the starving with good things,
sends the rich away empty.

8 He protects Israel, his servant,
remembering his mercy.

9 The mercy promised to our fathers,
for Abraham and his sons for ever.

10 (Praise the Father, the Son, and Holy Spirit,
both now and for ever, world without end.)

708 *Sebastian Temple*

1 The Mass is ended, all go in peace.
We must diminish, and Christ increase.
We take him with us where'er we go
that through our actions his life may show.

2 We witness his love to ev'ryone
by our communion with Christ the Son.
We take the Mass to all those we meet,
so Christ may shine forth for all to see.

3 Thanks to the Father who shows the way.
His life within us throughout each day.
Let all our living and loving be
to praise and honour the Trinity.

4 The Mass is ended, all go in peace.
We must diminish and Christ increase.
We take him with us where'er we go
that through our actions his life may show.

709 *Ralph Finn*

1 The Master came to bring good news,
the news of love and freedom,
to heal the sick and seek the poor,
to build the peaceful kingdom.

Father, forgive us!
Through Jesus hear us!
As we forgive one another!

2 The Law's fulfilled through Jesus Christ,
the man who lived for others,
the law of Christ is: Serve in love
our sisters and our brothers.

3 To seek the sinners Jesus came,
to live among the friendless,
to show them love that they might share
the kingdom that is endless.

4 Forgive us, Lord, as we forgive
and seek to help each other.
Forgive us, Lord, and we shall live
to pray and work together.

710 *Luke Connaughton (1919–79)*

1 The prophet in his hunger asked for bread.
He asked the poor and famine was their guest.
They saw starvation walking in the street,
the doomed who thought to eat their last and die.

2 It is the Lord who lights the blinded eye,
who lends the poor his wealth, the weak his strength,
who feeds us with his everlasting love,
and pours for us his justice like strong wine.

3 Because the widow offered of her last,
and opened to his need her empty hand,
Elijah promised her: 'You shall not want.
Your larder never shall be clean of food.'

4 The widow and the orphan are his care;
whom none will else defend, he will defend:
he puts the strutting pride of tyrants down,
and raises up the lowly from the dust.

5 See, in the temple, how with gestures wide,
the rich men cast their casual gold to God,
the widow offers all her dwindling purse,
the pence of poverty – a richer gift.

711 *John Morison (1749–98)*

1 The race that long in darkness pined
has seen a glorious light:
the people dwell in day, who dwelt
in death's surrounding night.

2 To hail thy rise, thou better sun,
the gathering nations come,
joyous as when the reapers bear
the harvest treasures home.

3 To us a child of hope is born,
to us a Son is given;
him shall the tribes of earth obey,
him all the hosts of heaven.

4 His name shall be the Prince of Peace,
for evermore adored,
the Wonderful, the Counsellor,
the great and mighty Lord.

5 His power increasing still shall spread,
his reign no end shall know;
justice shall guard his throne above,
and peace abound below.

712 *Venantius Fortunatus (530–609), tr. J. M. Neale (1818–66), and others*

1 The royal banners forward go,
the cross shines forth in mystic glow,
where he in flesh, our flesh who made,
our sentence bore, our ransom paid.

2 There whilst he hung, his sacred side
by soldier's spear was open'd wide,
to cleanse us in the precious flood
of water mingled with his blood.

3 Fulfill'd is now what David told
in true prophetic song of old,
how God the heathen's king should be;
for God is reigning from the tree.

4 O tree of glory, tree most fair,
ordain'd those holy limbs to bear,
how bright in purple robe it stood,
the purple of a saviour's blood!

5 Upon its arms, like balance true,
he weigh'd the price for sinners due,
the price which none but he could pay:
and spoil'd the spoiler of his prey.

6 To thee, eternal Three in One,
let homage meet by all be done,
as by the cross thou dost restore,
so rule and guide us evermore. Amen.

713 *Traditional Irish, tr. James Quinn, SJ*

The seed is Christ's, the harvest his:
may we be stored within God's barn.
The sea is Christ's, the fish are his:
may we be caught within God's net.
From birth to age, from age to death,
enfold us, Christ, within your arms.
Until the end, the great re–birth, Christ,
be our joy in Paradise.

714 *Carey Landry*

The Spirit is moving all over,
all over this land.

1 People are gathering, the Church is born;
the Spirit is blowing on a world reborn.

2 Doors are opening as the Spirit comes;
his fire is burning in his people now.

3 Filled with his Spirit we are sent to serve;
we are called out as brothers, we are called to work.

4 The world, born once, is born again;
we recreate it in love and joy.

5 Old men are dreaming dreams;
and young men see the light.

6 Old walls are falling down;
and people are speaking with each other.

7 The Spirit fills us with his power
to be his witnesses to all we meet.

8 The Spirit urges us to travel light,
to be people of courage who spread his fire.

9 God has poured out his Spirit
on all; on all creation.

715 *Stephen Dean*

1 Thanks be to God whose love has gathered us today.
Thanks be to God who helps and guides us on our way;
thanks be to God who gives us voice, that we may thank him:

Deo gratias, Deo gratias, thanks be to God most high.

2 Thanks be to God for all the gifts of life and light;
thanks be to God whose care protects us, day and night;
thanks be to God who keeps in mind us who forget him:

3 Thanks be to God who knows our secret joys and fears;
thanks be to God who when we call him, always hears;
thanks be to God our rock and strength, ever sustaining:

4 Thanks be to God who never turns his face away;
thanks be to God who heals and pardons all who stray;
thanks be to God who welcomes us into the Kingdom:

5 Thanks be to God who made our world and all we see;
thanks be to God who gave his Son to set us free;
thanks be to God whose Spirit brings warmth and rejoicing:

716 *Anonymous*

The Spirit of the Lord is now upon me
to heal the broken heart and set the captives free,
to open prison doors and make the blind to see.
The Spirit of the Lord is now on me.

717 *Traditional West Indian*

1 The Virgin Mary had a baby boy, (3)
and they said that his name was Jesus.

He came from the glory,
he came from the glorious kingdom.
Oh yes, believer. Oh yes, believer.
He came from the glory,
he came from the glorious kingdom.

2 The angels sang when the baby was born (3)
and proclaimed him the Saviour Jesus.

3 The wise men saw where the baby was born (3)
and they saw that his name was Jesus.

718 *Luke Connaughton (1919–79)*

1 The voice of God goes out to all the world:
his glory speaks across the universe.
The Great King's herald cries from star to star;
with power, with justice, he will walk his way.

2 Give glory to the mystery revealed,
the voice of God, his image and his Word:
his word of peace, the image of his grace: …

3 The Lord has said: Receive my messenger,
my promise to the world, my pledge made flesh,
a lamp to every nation, light from light: …

4 The broken reed he will not trample down,
nor set his heel upon the dying flame.
He binds the wounds, and health is in his hand: …

5 Anointed with the Spirit and with power,
he comes to crown with comfort all the weak,
to show the face of justice to the poor: …

6 His touch will bless the eyes that darkness held,
the lame shall run, the halting tongue shall sing,
and prisoners laugh in light and liberty: …

719 *J. Smith*

1 The wandering flock of Israel
is scattered and far from home and hope;
the Shepherd alone, with crook and staff,
can find them and lead and keep them safe.

He made and upheld us, granted grace;
his smile is our peace, his word our hope.

2 I walk on the heights, I climb and cling,
the terror beneath, the ice aloft.
I look for his tracks, await his hand
to help and to hold, to guide and save.

3 I thirst for his word as grass in drought,
dry, brittle and barren, parched and brown;
no shower can fall, no sap rise green
no hope, if the Lord should send no rain.

4 Creator of all, your craftsman's care
with fashioning hand caressed our clay;
this vine is the work your hands have wrought,
your love is the sun, our soil of growth.

720 *Adapted by Chris O'Hara*

The word of God is more desired than gold;
the word of God is sweeter than honey.
Light to our eyes, the Lord's command is clear;
greater than gold: the message of eternal life.

1 The law of God is perfect,
gives the soul new life.
The Lord's decree is to be trusted,
fills the simple heart with wisdom.

2 The precepts of the Lord
fill our hearts with joy.
The Lord's command is clear and truthful;
giving light for the eyes.

3 Much more desired than gold,
more than finest gold;
the word of God is so much sweeter,
sweeter than the honeycomb.

721 *Cecil Frances Alexander (1818–95)*

1 There is a green hill far away,
without a city wall,
where the dear Lord was crucified
who died to save us all.

2 We may not know, we cannot tell,
what pains he had to bear,
but we believe it was for us
he hung and suffered there.

3 He died that we might be forgiven,
he died to make us good;
that we might go at last to heaven,
saved by his precious blood.

4 There was no other good enough
to pay the price of sin;
he only could unlock the gate
of heaven, and let us in.

5 O, dearly, dearly has he loved,
and we must love him too,
and trust in his redeeming blood,
and try his works to do.

722 *Verse 1 traditional; verses 2-5 Robert B. Kelly*

1 There is a river that flows from God above;
there is a fountain that's filled with his great love.

Come to the waters; there is a great supply;
there is a river that never shall run dry.

2 Wash me with water, and then I shall be clean;
white as the new snow, if you remove my sin.

3 Plunged in the water, the tomb of our rebirth,
so may we rise up to share in Christ's new life.

4 All who are thirsty, now hear God as he calls;
come to the Lord's side, his life pours out for all.

5 Safe in the new Ark, the Church of Christ our Lord,
praise God for water, his sign to save the world.

723 *Estelle White*

1 There is a world where people come and go
about their ways and never care to know
that ev'ry step they take is placed on roads
made out of men who had to carry loads
too hard to bear.

'That world's not ours,' that's what we always say.
'We'll build a new one but some other day.'
When will we wake from comfort and from ease,
and strive together to create a world of love and peace?

2 There is a world where people walk alone,
and have around them men with hearts of stone,
who would not spare one second of their day,
or spend their breath in order just to say:
'Your pain is mine.'

3 There is a world where brothers cannot meet
with one another, where the tramp of feet
brings men of ice, men who would force apart
friends of all races having but one heart,
a heart of love.

724 *Chris O'Hara*

There is one thing I ask of the Lord,
there is one thing I ask of the Lord,
for this I long,
to live in the house of God
each day of my life, each day of my life.

1 The Lord is my light, my help
whom shall I fear with you beside me?
The Lord is the stronghold of my life;
I shall not be afraid.

2 To live in the house of God
through all the days of my life!
To dwell in the beauty of the Lord,
to rejoice in God's temple!

3 I know I shall surely see,
shall see God's goodness in my life.
Be strong! Let courage fill your heart:
rest your hope in the Lord.

725 *A. Pinnock*

1 There lived a man who walked by Galilee.
There lived a man who longed for harmony.
And the things he said were beautiful,
and the things he did were wonderful,
and he wanted us to follow in his way.

The heavens rang with his cry
high on Calvary's hill,
although they left him to die,
he lives still!

2 There lived a man who knew his destiny.
There lived a man who gave his best for me.
And the things he said were beautiful,
and the things he did were wonderful,
and he wanted us to follow in his way.

3 There lives a man whose light now leads the way.
There lives a man whose voice still speaks today.
For the things he says are beautiful,
and the things he does are wonderful,
and he wants us all to follow in his way.

726 *Chris O'Hara*

1 There will be signs upon the sun;
the moon and stars will share Earth's agony,
and ev'ry nation will be fearful of the sound:
the ocean's roar, the raging sea;
then they will see the son of man
riding the clouds with pow'r and glory;
hold up your heads, your liberation is at hand:
your destiny, your destiny.

O stay awake, do not fear the night;
the dawn will break with the Saviour's light,
your liberation is at hand; O stay awake!

2 The time is near, we must arise,
no longer living in the dark of night.
So arm yourselves as people
living in the way of truthfulness, integrity,
and hold a dream of days to come
when we will reach God's holy mountain
and change all weapons into instruments
of peace to sow the seed of justice.

727 *Spiritual*

1 They hung him on a cross, they hung him on a cross,
they hung him on a cross for me.
One day when I was lost, they hung him on a cross,
they hung him on a cross for me.

2 They whipped him up the hill, …

3 They speared him in the side, …

4 The blood came streaming down, …

5 He hung his head and died, …

6 He's coming back again, …

728 *Edmond Louis Budry (1854–1932), tr. Richard Birch Hoyle (1875–1939)*

1 Thine be the glory, risen conquering Son,
endless is the victory thou o'er death hast won;
angels in bright raiment rolled the stone away,
kept the folded grave–clothes, where thy body lay.

Thine be the glory, risen, conquering Son,
endless is the victory thou o'er death hast won.

2 Lo, Jesus meets us risen from the tomb;
lovingly he greets us, scatters fear and gloom;
let the church with gladness hymns of triumph sing,
for her Lord is living, death has lost its sting.

3 No more we doubt thee, glorious Prince of life;
life is nought without thee; aid us in our strife;
make us more than conquerors, through thy deathless love;
bring us safe through Jordan to thy home above.

729 *Adapted from St Patrick's Breastplate, by James Quinn, SJ*

1 This day God gives me
strength of high heaven,
sun and moon shining, flame in my hearth,
flashing of lightning, wind in its swiftness,
deeps of the ocean, firmness of earth.

2 This day God sends me
strength as my steersman,
might to uphold me, wisdom as guide.
Your eyes are watchful,
your ears are listening,
your lips are speaking, friend at my side.

3 God's way is my way,
God's shield is round me,
God's host defends me, saving from ill.
Angels of heaven, drive from me always
all that would harm me, stand by me still.

4 Rising, I thank you, mighty and strong One,
King of creation, giver of rest,
firmly confessing Threeness of Persons,
Oneness of Godhead, Trinity blest.

730 *Verses 1 and 2 Jimmy Owens; verses 3–5 Damian Lundy*

1 This is my body, broken for you,
bringing you wholeness, making you free.
Take it and eat it, and when you do,
do it in love for me.

2 This is my blood poured out for you,
bringing forgiveness, making you free.
Take it and drink it, and when you do,
do it in love for me.

3 Back to my Father soon I shall go.
Do not forget me; then you will see
I am still with you, and you will know
you're very close to me.

4 Filled with my Spirit, how you will grow!
You are my branches; I am the tree.
If you are faithful, others will know
you are alive in me.

5 Love one another – I have loved you,
and I have shown you how to be free;
serve one another, and when you do,
do it in love for me.

731 *Leslie Garrett*

1 This is the day (2)
that the Lord has made. (2)
We will rejoice, (2)
and be glad in it. (2)
This is the day
that the Lord has made.
We will rejoice
and be glad in it.
This is the day (2)
that the Lord has made.

2 This is the day
when he rose again …

3 This is the day
when the Spirit came …

732 *James Quinn, SJ*

1 This is my will, my one command,
that love should dwell among you all.
This is my will, that you should love
as I have shown that I love you.

2 No greater love a man can have
than that he die to save his friends.
You are my friends if you obey
all I command that you should do.

3 I call you now no longer slaves;
no slave knows all his master does.
I call you friends, for all I hear
my Father say you hear from me.

4 You chose not me, but I chose you,
that you should go and bear much fruit.
I called you out that you in me
should bear much fruit that will abide.

5 All that you ask my Father dear
for my name's sake you shall receive.
This is my will, my one command,
that love should dwell in each, in all.

733 *Edward Caswall (1814-78)*

1 This is the image of the Queen
who reigns in bliss above;
of her who is the hope of men,
whom men and angels love.
Most holy Mary, at thy feet
I bend a suppliant knee;
in this thy own sweet month of May,
do thou remember me.

2 The homage offered at the feet
of Mary's image here
to Mary's self at once ascends
above the starry sphere.
Most holy Mary, at thy feet
I bend a suppliant knee;
in all my joy, in all my pain,
do thou remember me.

3 How fair so ever be the form
which here your eyes behold,
its beauty is by Mary's self
excell'd a thousandfold.
Most holy Mary, at thy feet,
I bend a suppliant knee;
in my temptations each and all,
do thou remember me.

4 Sweet are the flow'rets we have culled,
this image to adorn;
but sweeter far is Mary's self,
that rose without a thorn.
most holy Mary, at thy feet
I bend a suppliant knee;
when on the bed of death I lie,
do thou remember me.

5 O lady, by the stars that make
a glory round thy head;
and by the pure uplifted hands,
that for thy children plead;
when at the judgement–seat I stand,
and my dread saviour see;
when waves of night around me roll
O then remember me.

734 *Mary McGann, RSCJ*

This is what Yahweh asks of you, only this:
that you act justly, that you love tenderly,
that you walk humbly, with your God.

1 'My children, I am with you such a little while,
and where I go now you cannot come;
a new commandment I give to you:
as I have loved you, so love each other.'

2 'Do not let your hearts be troubled;
trust in God now, and trust in me.
I go to prepare a place for you,
and I shall come again to take you home.'

3 'Peace is the gift I leave with you,
a peace the world can never give.
If you keep my word, my Father will love you,
and we will come to you to make our home.'

735 *George Ratcliffe Woodward (1849–1934)*

1 This joyful Eastertide,
away with sin and sorrow,
my love, the Crucified,
hath sprung to life this morrow:

Had Christ, that once was slain,
ne'er burst his three–day prison,
our faith had been in vain:
but now hath Christ arisen.

2 My flesh in hope shall rest,
and for a season slumber:
till trump from east to west
shall wake the dead in number:

3 Death's flood hath lost his chill,
since Jesus crossed the river:
lover of souls, from ill
my passing soul deliver:

736 *Traditional*

This little light of mine,
I'm gonna let it shine. (3)
let it shine, let it shine, let it shine.

1 This light that shines is the light of love,
lights the darkness from above.
It shines on me and it shines on you,
and shows what the power of love can do.
I'm gonna shine my light both far and near,
I'm gonna shine my light both bright and clear.
Where there's a dark corner in this land
I'm gonna let my little light shine.

2 On Monday he gave me the gift of love,
Tuesday peace came from above.
On Wednesday he told me to have more faith,
on Thursday he gave me a little more grace.
Friday he told me just to watch and pray,
Saturday he told me just what to say.
On Sunday he gave me the power divine
to let my little light shine.

737 Martin Willett

1 Those who were in the dark
are thankful for the sunlight;
we who live, we who die
are grateful for his gift,
thankful for his love.

Behold, behold the Lamb of God.
All who eat, all who drink shall live;
and all, all who dwell in God
shall come to know his glory.

2 Peaceful now, those whose hearts
are blessed with understanding.
Of the wheat, of the wine
united with his word
and the love we share.

3 Gentle one, Child of God,
join with us at this table.
Bless our lives; nourish all
who hunger for this feast;
shelter them with peace.

4 Lord of all, give us light.
Deliver us from evil.
Make us one; be our shield.
Make still the winds that blow;
cradle us with love.

738 J Marriott (1780–1825)

1 Thou whose almighty Word
chaos and darkness heard,
and took their flight;
hear us, we humbly pray,
and where the Gospel–day
sheds not its glorious ray
let there be light!

2 Thou who didst come to bring
on thy redeeming wing
healing and sight,
health to the sick in mind,
sight to the inly blind,
ah! now to all mankind
let there be light.

3 Spirit of truth and love,
life–giving, holy dove,
speed forth thy flight!
Move on the water's face,
bearing the lamp of grace,
and in earth's darkest place
let there be light!

4 Blessed and holy Three,
glorious Trinity,
wisdom, love, might;
boundless as ocean tide
rolling in fullest pride,
through the world far and wide
let there be light!

739 Daniel L. Schutte, SJ

Though the mountains may fall, and the hills turn to dust,
yet the love of the Lord will stand
as a shelter for all who will call on his name.
Sing the praise and glory of God.

1 Could the Lord ever leave you?
Could the Lord forget his love?
Though the Mother forsake her child,
he will not abandon you.

2 Should you turn and forsake him,
he will gently call your name.
Should you wander away from him,
he will always take you back.

3 Go to him when you're weary;
he will give you eagle's wings.
You will run, never tire,
for your God will be your strength.

4 As he swore to your Fathers,
when the flood destroyed the land.
He will never forsake you;
he will swear to you again.

740 *Psalm 34 in Tate and Brady's 'New Version' (1696)*

1 Through all the changing scenes of life,
in trouble and in joy,
the praises of my God shall still
my heart and tongue employ.

2 Of his deliverance I will boast,
till all that are distressed,
when learning this, will comfort take
and charm their griefs to rest.

3 O magnify the Lord with me,
with me exalt his name;
when in distress to him I called
he to my rescue came.

4 The hosts of God encamp around
the dwellings of the just;
deliverance he affords to all
who on his succour trust.

5 O make but trial of his love;
experience will decide
how blest are they, and only they,
who in his truth confide.

6 Fear him, ye saints, and you will then
having nothing else to fear;
make you his service your delight,
your wants shall be his care.

7 To Father, Son, and Holy Ghost,
the God whom we adore,
be glory, as it was, is now,
and shall be evermore.

741 *E.H. Plumptre (1821–91)*

1 Thy hand, O God, has guided
thy flock from age to age;
the wondrous tale is written,
full clear, on ev'ry page;
our fathers owned thy goodness,
and we their deeds record;
and both of this bear witness:
one Church, one Faith, one Lord.

2 Thy heralds brought glad tidings
to greatest, as to least;
they bade men rise, and hasten
to share the great king's feast;
and this was all their teaching,
in every deed and word,
to all alike proclaiming
one Church, one Faith, one Lord.

3 When shadows thick were falling,
and all seemed sunk in night,
thou, Lord, didst send thy servants,
thy chosen sons of light.
On them and on thy people
thy plenteous grace was poured,
and this was still their message:
one Church, one Faith, one Lord.

4 Through many a day of darkness,
through many a scene of strife,
the faithful few fought bravely,
to guard the nation's life.
Their gospel of redemption,
sin pardoned, man restored,
was all in this enfolded:
one Church, one Faith, one Lord.

5 And we, shall we be faithless?
Shall hearts fail, hands hang down?
Shall we evade the conflict,
and cast away our crown?
Not so: in God's deep counsels
some better thing is stored;
we will maintain, unflinching,
one Church, one Faith, one Lord.

6 Thy mercy will not fail us,
nor leave thy work undone;
with thy right hand to help us
the vict'ry shall be won;
and then, by earth and heaven
thy name shall be adored.
And this shall be their anthem:
one Church, one Faith, one Lord.

742 *Clyde Harvey*

To be the body of the Lord in this world,
to have his Spirit coursing through my soul,
to know the passion of my Jesus
in his love for ev'ryone,
to show his mercy in the shadows of this
land.

1 Come, walk with me; come, share my life,
you must know the shadows
if you would know the light.

2 No eyes have I, no ears to hear,
you must be my Body and show
my Father's care.

3 Open your eyes, see what I see.
For this world how I suffer.
Share my destiny.

4 I am the vine, branches are you.
Life from me eternal to make
your world anew.

5 One bread, one cup; one heart and mind.
One great human people
in fellowship divine.

743 *Roman Breviary, tr. W.H. Shewring*

1 To Christ the Lord of worlds we sing,
the nations' universal king.
Hail, conqu'ring Christ, whose reign alone
over our hearts and souls we own.

2 Christ, who art known the prince of peace,
bid all rebellious tumults cease;
call home thy straying sheep, and hold
for ever in one faithful fold.

3 For this, thine arms, on Calvary,
were stretched across th'empurpled tree,
and the sharp spear that through thee ran
laid bare the heart that burned for man.

4 For this, in forms of bread and wine
lies hid the plenitude divine,
and from thy wounded body runs
the stream of life to all thy sons.

5 May those who rule o'er men below
thee for their greater sovereign know,
and human wisdom, arts, and laws,
in thee repose as in their cause.

6 Let kingly signs of pomp and state
unto thy name be dedicate,
city and hearth and household be
under thy gentle sceptre free.

7 Praise be to Christ, whose name and throne
o'er every throne and name we own;
and equal praises still repeat
to Father and to Paraclete.

744 *Catholicum Hymnologium Germanicum (1587) tr. E. Caswall (1814–78)*

1 To Christ, the Prince of peace,
and Son of God most high,
the father of the world to come,
sing we with holy joy.

2 Deep in his heart for us
the wound of love he bore:
that love wherewith he still inflames
the hearts that him adore.

3 O Jesu, victim blest,
what else but love divine
could thee constrain to open thus
that sacred heart of thine?

4 O fount of endless life,
O spring of water clear,
O flame celestial, cleansing all
who unto thee draw near!

5 Hide us in thy dear heart,
for thither we do fly;
there seek thy grace through life, in death
thine immortality.

6 Praise to the Father be,
and sole–begotten Son;
praise, holy Paraclete, to thee
while endless ages run.

745 *Fanny Crosby (née Frances J. van Alstyne 1820–1915)*

1 To God be the glory, great things he has done!
So loved he the world that he gave us his Son.
Who yielded his life in atonement for sin,
and opened the life–gate that all may go in.

Praise the Lord! Praise the Lord!
Let the earth hear his voice!
Praise the Lord! Praise the Lord!
Let the people rejoice!
O come to the Father through Jesus his Son;
and give him the glory, great things he has done!

2 O perfect redemption, the purchase of blood,
to every believer the promise of God!
And every offender who truly believes,
that moment from Jesus a pardon receives

Praise the Lord! Praise the Lord!
Let the earth hear his voice!
Praise the Lord! Praise the Lord!
Let the people rejoice!
O come to the Father through Jesus his Son;
and give him the glory, great things he has done!.

3 Great things he has taught us, great things he has done,
and great our rejoicing through Jesus the Son;
but purer, and higher, and greater will be
our wonder, our rapture, when Jesus we see.

746 *James Quinn, SJ*

1 To God with gladness sing
your Rock and Saviour bless
within your temple bring
your songs of thankfulness!
O God of might, to you we sing,
enthroned as King on heaven's height!

2 He cradles in his hand
the heights and depths of earth;
he made the sea and land
he brought the world to birth!
O God most high, we are your sheep,
on us you keep your shepherd's eye.

3 Your heav'nly Father praise,
acclaim his only Son,
your voice in homage raise
to him who makes all one!
O dove of peace, on us descend
that strife may end and joy increase!

747 *Martin B.Hellriegel (1891–1981) alt.*

1 To Jesus Christ, our sovereign King,
who is the world's salvation,
all praise and homage do we bring
and thanks and adoration.

Christ Jesus, Victor!
Christ Jesus, Ruler!
Christ Jesus, Lord and Redeemer!

2 Your reign extend, O King benign,
to every land and nation;
for in your Kingdom, Lord divine,
alone we find salvation.

3 To you, and to your church, great king,
we pledge our heart's oblation;
until before your throne we sing
in endless jubilation.

748 *Aloys Schlör (1805–52), tr. A.J. Christie (1817–1891)*

1 To Jesus' Heart, all burning
with fervent love for all,
my heart with fondest yearning
shall raise its joyful call.

While ages course along,
blest be with loudest song
the sacred heart of Jesus
by ev'ry heart and tongue.
The sacred heart of Jesus
by ev'ry heart and tongue.

2 O Heart, for me on fire
with love no–one can speak,
my yet untold desire
God gives me for thy sake. (Refrain)

3 Too true, I have forsaken
thy love for wilful sin;
yet now let me be taken
back by thy grace again. (Refrain)

4 As thou are meek and lowly,
and ever pure of heart,
so may my heart be wholly
of thine the counterpart. (Refrain)

5 When life away is flying,
and earth's false glare is done;
still, Sacred Heart, in dying
I'll say I'm all thine own. (Refrain)

749 *15th century, tr. J.M. Neale (1818–66)*

1 To the name that brings salvation
honour, worship, laud we pay:
that for many a generation
hid in God's foreknowledge lay;
but to ev'ry tongue and nation
Holy Church proclaims today.

2 Name of gladness, name of pleasure,
by the tongue ineffable,
name of sweetness passing measure,
to the ear delectable;
'tis our safeguard and our treasure,
'tis our help 'gainst sin and hell.

3 'Tis the name of adoration,
'tis the name of victory;
'tis the name for meditation
in the vale of misery;
'tis the name for veneration
by the citizens on high.

4 'Tis the name by right exalted
over every other name:
that when we are sore assaulted
puts our enemies to shame:
strength to them that else had halted,
eyes to blind, and feet to lame.

5 Jesu, we thy name adoring,
long to see thee as thou art:
of thy clemency imploring
so to write it in our heart,
that hereafter, upward soaring,
we with angels may have part.

750 *Robert F. O'Connor, SJ*

Trust in the Lord; you shall not tire.
Serve you the Lord; you shall not weaken.
For the Lord's own strength will uphold you.
You shall renew your life and live.

1 The Lord is our eternal God.
He neither faints nor grows weary.
Our hearts he probes from afar,
knowing our ways, knowing our ways.

2 Young hearts may grow faint and weak.
Youths may collapse, stumble and fall.
They that hope in the Lord will renew their courage.
They'll soar with eagle's might.

3 Old men shall dream new dreams;
young men will find wisdom in visions.
The Lord will speak in our lifetime,
show his face to those who wait.

751 *Estelle White*

1 Trust is in the eyes of a tiny babe
leaning on his mother's breast.
In the eager beat of a young bird's wings
on the day it leaves the nest.

It is the living Spirit
filling the earth, bringing to birth
a world of love and laughter,
joy in the light of the Lord.

2 Hope is in the rain that makes crystal streams
tumble down a mountain side,
and in every man who repairs his nets,
waiting for the rising tide.

3 Love is in the hearts of all those who seek
freedom for the human race.
Love is in the touch of the hand that heals,
and the smile that lights a face.

4 Strength is in the wind as it bends the trees,
warmth is in the bright red flame,
light is in the sun and the candle–glow,
cleansing are the ocean's waves.

752 *John Foley, SJ*

Turn to me, O turn, and be saved,
says the Lord, for I am God
there is no other, none beside me.
I call your name.

1 I am God who comforts you;
who are you to be afraid,
of flesh that fades,
is made like the grass of the field soon to wither.

2 Listen to me, my people;
give ear to me, my nation:
a law will go forth from me,
and my justice for a light to the people.

3 Lift up your eyes to the heavens,
and look at the earth down below.
The heavens will vanish like smoke,
and the earth will wear out like a garment.

753 *Dominique Ombrie, tr. Fred Kaan*

Unite us, Lord, in peace,
and uphold us with your love.

1 Our faults divide and hinder;
your grace can make us one;
we wonder at your rising,
your light is like the sun.

2 You are our expectation
in loneliness and pain;
your healing and your pardon
are greater than our sin.

3 Lord, look upon the starving
and set the captive free.
Share out among each other
the bread of unity.

4 How happy are the people
who strive to be at one,
who learn to live as brothers,
who lay their hatred down.

5 O Lord, whose silent spirit
enlightens and endows,
make us in faith receptive
and help us love your house.

6 Your cross will draw together
the love of humankind;
in you shall all the people
their true communion find.

7 Death can no longer hurt us,
triumphant is your word.
Let life now grow and blossom,
O Jesus, risen Lord!

754 *Versified by Bernadette Farrell*

Unless a grain of wheat shall fall
upon the ground and die,
it remains but a single grain
with no life.

1 If we have died with him then we shall
live with him;
if we hold firm we shall reign with him.

2 If anyone serves me then they must
follow me;
wherever I am my servants will be.

3 Make your home in me as I make mine
in you;
those who remain in me bear much fruit.

4 If you remain in me and my word lives in
you;
then you will be my disciples.

5 Those who love me are loved by my
Father;
we shall be with them and dwell in them.

6 Peace I leave with you, my peace I give
to you;
peace which the world cannot give is my
gift.

755 *15th century, tr. G.R. Woodward*

1 Unto us is born a Son,
King of quires supernal;
see on earth his life begun,
of lords the Lord eternal, (2)

2 Christ, from heav'n descending low,
comes on earth a stranger:
ox and ass their owner know
becradled in a manger, (2)

3 This did Herod sore affray,
and grievously bewilder:
so he gave the word to slay,
and slew the little childer, (2)

4 Of his love and mercy mild
this the Christmas story,
and O that Mary's gentle Child
might lead us up to glory! (2)

5 O and A and A and O
cum cantibus in choro,
let the merry organ go,
Benedicamus Domino, (2)

756 *M.F.C. Willson (1884–1944)*

1 Upon thy table, Lord we place
these symbols of our work and thine,
life's food won only by thy grace,
who giv'st to all the bread and wine.

2 Within these simple things there lie
the height and depth of human life,
the thoughts we own, our tears and toil,
our hopes and fears, our joy and strife.

3 Accept them, Lord; from thee they come;
we take them humbly at thy hand.
These gifts of thine for higher use
we offer, as thou dost command.

757 *Author unknown*

1 Vaster far than any ocean,
deeper than the deepest sea
is the love of Christ my Saviour,
reaching through eternity.

2 But my sins are truly many,
is God's grace so vast, so deep?
Yes, there's grace o'er sin abounding,
grace to pardon, grace to keep.

3 Can he quench my thirst for ever?
Will his Spirit strength impart?
Yes, he gives me living water
springing up within my heart.

758 *Veni, Creator Spiritus* *Attributed to Rabanus Maurus (766–856)*

1 Veni, Creator Spiritus,
mentes tuorum visita,
imple superna gratia,
quae tu creasti pectora.

2 Qui diceris Paraclitus,
Altissimi donum Dei,
fons vivus, ignis, caritas,
et spiritalis unctio.

3 Tu septiformis munere,
digitus paternae dexterae,
tu rite promissum Patris,
sermone ditans guttura.

4 Accende lumen sensibus,
infunde amorem cordibus,
infirma nostri corporis
virtute firmans perpeti.

5 Hostem repellas longius,
pacemque dones protinus:
ductore sic te praevio,
vitemus omne noxium.

6 Per te sciamus, da, Patrem,
noscamus atque Filium,
teque utriusque Spiritum
credamus omni tempore. Amen.

759 *Attrib. to Stephen Langton (c.1160–1228), altered by Christopher Walker from the translation by Edward Caswall (1814–1878)*

Veni Sancte Spiritus (4)

Some or all of these verses may be sung by a soloist.

1 Holy Spirit Lord of light,
radiance give from celestial height.
Come thou Father of the poor,
come now with treasures that endure:
Light of all who live.

2 Thou of all consolers the best.
Thou the soul's delightful guest;
refreshing peace bestow.
Thou in toil my comfort sweet,
thou coolness in the heat.
Thou my solace in time of woe.

3 Light immortal, light divine;
fire of love, our hearts refine,
our inmost being fill.
Take thy grace away
and nothing pure in us will stay,
all our good is turned to ill.

4 Heal our wounds, our strength renew,
on our dryness pour thy dew;
wash guilt away, bend the stubborn heart
melt the frozen, warm the chill
and guide the steps that go astray.

5 Sevenfold gifts on us be pleased to pour,
who thee confess and thee adore;
bring us thy comfort when we die;
give us life with thee on high;
give us joys, give us joys that never end.

760 *Victimae paschali laudes*
Attributed to Wipo of Burgundy (10th century)

Victimae paschali laudes
immolent Christiani.
Agnus redemit oves:
Christus innocens Patri
reconciliavit peccatores.
Mors et vita duello conflixere mirando:
dux vitae mortuus regnat vivus.

Dic nobis Maria quid vidisti in via?
Sepulchrum Christi viventis
et gloriam vidi resurgentis:
Angelicos testes sudarium et vestes.

Surrexit Christus spes mea:
praecedit suos in Galilaeam.
Scimus Christum surrexisse a mortuis vere:
tu nobis, victor Rex, miserere.
Amen. (Alleluia.)

761 *St. Ephrem Syrus (c. 307-373), tr. J.W. Atkinson (1866–1921)*

1 Virgin, wholly marvellous,
who didst bear God's Son for us,
worthless is my tongue and weak
of thy purity to speak.

2 Who can praise thee as they ought?
Gifts, with every blessing fraught,
gifts that bring the eternal life,
thou didst grant us, Maiden–Wife.

3 God became thy lowly Son,
made himself thy little one,
raising us to tell thy worth
high in heav'n as here on earth.

4 Heav'n and earth, and all that is
thrill today with ecstasies,
chanting glory unto thee,
singing praise with festal glee.

5 Cherubim with fourfold face,
are no peers of thine in grace;
and the six–wing'd seraphim
shine, amid thy splendour, dim.

6 Purer art thou than are all
heav'nly hosts angelical,
who delight with pomp and state
on thy beauteous Child to wait.

762 *Taizé chant*

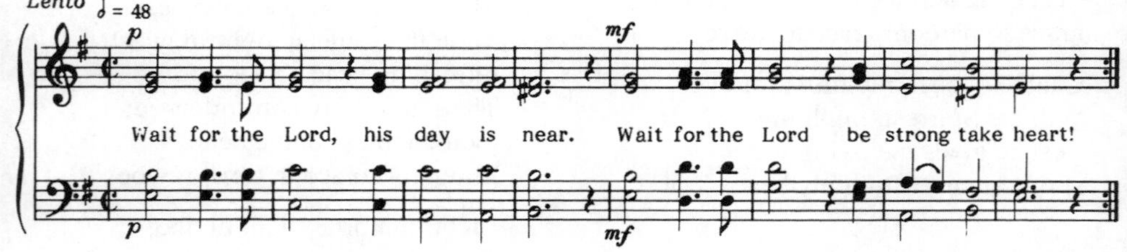
Lento ♩ = 48
p
mf
Wait for the Lord, his day is near. Wait for the Lord be strong take heart!

1 Prepare the way for the Lord.
Make a straight path for Him.

2 The glory of the Lord shall be revealed.

3 All the earth will see the Lord.

4 Rejoice in the Lord always. He is at hand.

5 Seek first the kingdom of God,
seek and you shall find.

6 Joy and gladness
for all who seek the Lord.

7 I waited for the Lord; He heard my cry.

8 Our eyes are fixed on the Lord our God.

9 O Lord, show us your way.
Guide us in your truth.

10 Prepare the way for the Lord.

763 *Philipp Nicolai (1556–1608) tr F. C. Burkitt (1864–1935) alt*

1 Wake, O wake! with tidings thrilling
the watchers all the air are filling,
Arise, Jerusalem, arise!
Midnight strikes! no more delaying
'The hour has come!' we hear them saying
Where are ye all, ye virgins wise?
The Bridegroom comes in sight,
Raise high your torches bright!
Alleluia!
The wedding song swells loud and strong:
Go forth and join the festal throng

2 Sion hears the watchers shouting,
her heart leaps up with joy undoubting,
she stands and waits with eager eyes.
See her Friend from heaven descending,
adorned with truth and grace unending!
Her light burns clear, her star doth rise.
Now come thou precious Crown
Lord Jesus, God's own Son!
Sing hosanna!
Let us prepare to follow there
where in thy supper we may share.

3 Every soul in thee rejoices;
all mankind and angel voices
give glory to our God alone.
Now the gates of pearl receive us
thy presence never more shall leave us,
we stand with angels round thy throne.
Earth cannot give below
the joy thou dost bestow.
Alleluia!
Grant us to raise through all our days
the triumph–chorus of thy praise.

764 *Luke Connaughton (1919–79)*

Wake up! The dawn is near;
no time for sleeping, this:
our God is sending us his gift,
his Son, the Lord of bliss.

1 Come, Lord of all the world,
creation's source and sum;
break through these barren wintry skies
and show your mercy – come!

2 Our sins are multiplied,
yet yours alone we stand –
you shaped us as the clay is shaped
beneath the potter's hand.

3 See how we stray from you,
so deeply have we sinned,
swept on by wickedness; like leaves
before the autumn wind.

4 Yet still we trust your word,
your pardon precious–priced,
your wisdom sweetly ruling all,
the chosen one, your Christ.

765 *Estelle White*

Walk with me, oh my Lord,
through the darkest night and brightest day.
Be at my side, oh Lord,
hold my hand and guide me on my way.

1 Sometimes the road seems long,
my energy is spent.
Then, Lord, I think of you
and I am given strength.

2 Stones often bar my path
and there are times I fall,
but you are always there
to help me when I call.

3 Just as you calmed the wind
and walked upon the sea,
conquer, my living Lord,
the storms that threaten me.

4 Help me to pierce the mists
that cloud my heart and mind,
so that I shall not fear
the steepest mountain–side.

5 As once you helped the lame
and gave sight to the blind,
help me when I'm downcast
to hold my head up high.

766 *Paraphrased by John C. Ylvisaker*

We are bound for the promised land,
we're bound for the promised land;
Oh, who will come and go with us?
We are bound for the promised land.

1 We seek you, Lord, and all your strength
your presence constantly,
rememb'ring all your marv'lous works,
and all that you can be:

2 You are the Lord, you are the God
whose judgements fill this earth;
you're mindful of your covenant;
we can trust you at your Word.

3 To Abraham you made a vow,
a promise to his son:
'I'll give to you the promised land!
Your inheritance is won.'

4 Give glory to the Father, Son,
and Spirit, One in Three;
as it was in the beginning,
it shall forever be.

767 *Anonymous*

1 We are gathering together unto him.
We are gathering together unto him.
Unto him shall the gath'ring of the
people be.
We are gathering together unto him.

2 We are offering together unto him …

3 We are singing together unto him …

4 We are praying together unto him …

768 *Traditional Bantu song*

We are marching in the light of God,
we are marching in the light of God. *(2)*
We are marching, oh,
we are marching in the light of God. *(2)*

769 *Peter Scholtes*

1 We are one in the Spirit,
we are one in the Lord, *(2)*
and we pray that all unity
may one day be restored.

And they'll know we are Christians
by our love, by our love,
yes, they'll know we are Christians
by our love.

2 We will walk with each other,
we will walk hand in hand, *(2)*
And together we'll spread the news
that God is in our land.

3 We will work with each other,
we will work side by side. *(2)*
And we'll guard each man's dignity
and save each man's pride.

4 All praise to the Father
from whom all things come,
and all praise to Christ Jesus,
his only Son,
and all praise to the Spirit
who makes us one.

770 *Brian A. Wren*

1 We are your people:
Lord, by your grace,
you dare to make us
Christ to our neighbours,
of every nation and race.

2 How can we demonstrate
your love and care?
Speaking or listening?
Battling or serving?
Help us to know when and where.

3 Called to portray you,
help us to live
closer than neighbours,
open to strangers,
able to clash and forgive.

4 Glad of tradition,
help us to see
in all life's changing
where you are leading,
where our best efforts should be.

5 Joined in community,
breaking your bread,
may we discover
gifts in each other,
willing to lead and be led.

6 Lord, as we minister
in diff'rent ways,
may all we're doing
show that you're living,
meeting your love with our praise.

771 *Graham Kendrick*

We believe in God the Father,
maker of the universe,
and in Christ His Son our saviour,
come to us by virgin birth.
We believe He died to save us,
bore our sins, was crucified.
Then from death He rose victorious,
ascended to the Father's side.

Jesus, Lord of all, Lord of all, (4)
Name above all names. (3)

We believe He sends His Spirit
on His church with gifts of power.
God His word of truth affirming,
sends us to the nations now.
He will come again in glory,
judge the living and the dead,
every knee shall bow before Him,
then must every tongue confess.

772 *John L. Bell and Graham Maule*

1 We cannot measure how you heal
or answer every sufferer's prayer,
yet we believe your grace responds
where faith and doubt unite to care.
Your hands, though bloodied on the cross,
survive to hold and heal and warn,
to carry all through death to life
and cradle children yet unborn.

2 The pain that will not go away,
the guilt that clings from things long past,
the fear of what the future holds,
are present as if meant to last.
But present too is love which tends
the hurt we never hoped to find,
the private agonies inside,
the memories that haunt the mind.

3 So some have come who need your help
and some have come to make amends,
as hands which shaped and saved the world
are present in the touch of friends.
Lord, let your Spirit meet us here
to mend the body, mind and soul,
to disentangle peace from pain
and make your broken people whole.

773 *Willard F. Jabusch*

1 We celebrate this festive day
with pray'r and joyful song.
Our Father's house is home to us,
we know that we belong.

The bread is broken, wine is poured,
a feast to lift us up!
Then thank the Lord who gives himself
as food and saving cup!

2 The door is open, enter in
and take your place by right.
For you've been chosen as his guest
to share his love and light.

3 We came together as the twelve
came to the Upper Room.
Our host is Jesus Christ the Lord,
now risen from the tomb.

4 Who travel need both food and drink
to help them on their way.
Refreshed and strong we'll journey on
and face another day.

5 Who share this meal receive the Lord
who live, though they were dead.
So death can hold no terrors now
for those who eat this bread.

774 *David Haas*

We come to share our story,
we come to break the bread,
we come to know our rising
from the dead.

1 We come as your people,
we come as your own,
united with each other,
love finds a home.

2 We are called to heal the broken,
to be hope for the poor,
we are called to feed the hungry
at our door.

3 Bread of life and cup of promise,
in this meal we all are one.
In our dying and our rising,
may your kingdom come.

4 You will lead and we shall follow,
you will be the breath of life;
living water, we are thirsting
for your light.

5 We will live and sing your praises,
'Alleluia' is our song.
May we live in love and peace
our whole life long.

775 *Mimi Farra*

We cry 'Hosanna, Lord,
yes, 'Hosanna, Lord,'
yes, 'Hosanna, Lord' to you. (2)

1 Behold, our Saviour comes.
Behold, the Son of our God.
He offers himself and he comes among us,
a lowly servant to all.

2 Children wave their palms
as the King of all kings rides by.
Should we forget to praise our God,
the very stones would sing.

3 He comes to set us free.
He gives us liberty.
His vict'ry over death is
th'eternal sign of God's love for us.

776 *Willard F. Jabusch*

1 We gather together
as brothers and sisters
for Jesus our Lord truly lives.
He's risen in glory;
the full gospel story,
what freedom and courage it gives.

He binds up the wounded and the broken.
He gives the poor his chalice and his bread.
The Father has raised him,
together we'll raise him,
and march with the Lord at our head.

2 For mother and father,
for sister and brother,
for children and husband and wife,
his Word spreads like flame,
for all people came,
bringing peace and the seeds of new life.

3 God takes what is foolish,
he chooses the weakest
to put wise and strong both to shame.
Give thanks to the Father,
we live in Christ Jesus,
bow low and sing sweetly his name.

777 *Michael Perry*

1 We give God thanks for those who knew
the touch of Jesus' healing love;
they trusted him to make them whole,
to give them peace, their guilt remove.

2 We offer prayer for all who go
relying on his grace and power,
to help the anxious and the ill,
to heal their wounds, their lives restore.

3 We dedicate our skills and time
to those who suffer where we live,
to bring such comfort as we can
to meet their need, their pain relieve.

4 So Jesus' touch of healing grace
lives on within our willing care;
by thought and prayer and gift we prove
his mercy still, his love we share.

778 *Edward J. Burns*

1 We have a gospel to proclaim,
good news for men in all the earth;
the gospel of a saviour's name:
we sing his glory, tell his worth.

2 Tell of his birth at Bethlehem,
not in a royal house or hall
but in a stable dark and dim:
the Word made flesh, a light for all.

3 Tell of his death at Calvary,
hated by those he came to save;
in lonely suffering on the cross
for all he loved, his life he gave.

4 Tell of that glorious Easter morn:
empty the tomb, for he was free;
he broke the power of death and hell
that we might share his victory.

5 Tell of his reign at God's right hand,
by all creation glorified;
he sends his Spirit on his church
to live for him, the lamb who died.

6 Now we rejoice to name him king;
Jesus is Lord of all the earth;
the gospel–message we proclaim:
we sing his glory, tell his worth.

779 *David Haas*

We have been told, we've seen his face,
and heard his voice alive in our hearts;
'Live in my love with all your heart,
as the Father has loved me,
so I have loved you.'

1 'I am the vine, you are the branches,
and all who live in me will bear great fruit.'

2 'You are my friends, if you keep my commands,
no longer slaves, I call you friends.'

3 'No greater love is there than this:
to lay down one's life for a friend.'

780 *John B. Foley, SJ*

Antiphon:
We hold a treasure, not made of gold,
in earthen vessels, wealth untold;
one treasure only: the Lord, the Christ,
in earthen vessels.

1 Light has shone in our darkness;
God has shone in our heart,
with the light of the glory of Jesus, the Lord.

2 He has chosen the lowly,
who are small in this world;
in his weakness is glory, in Jesus, the Lord.

781 *David Haas*

We hold the death of the Lord deep in our hearts.
Living, now we remain with Jesus, the Christ.

1 Once we were people afraid,
lost in the night.
Then by your cross we were saved;
dead became living, life from your giving.

2 Something which we have known,
something we've touched,
what we have seen with our eyes:
this we have heard; life–giving Word.

3 He chose to give of himself,
became our bread.
Broken that we might live.
Love beyond love, pain for our pain.

4 We are the presence of God;
this is our call.
Now to become bread and wine:
food for the hungry, life for the weary,
for to live with the Lord, we must die with the Lord.

782 M. Claudius (1740–1815), tr. J.M. Campbell

1 We plough the fields and scatter
the good seed on the land,
but it is fed and watered
by God's almighty hand;
he sends the snow in winter,
the warmth to swell the grain,
the breezes and the sunshine,
and soft refreshing rain.

All good gifts around us
are sent from heav'n above,
then thank the Lord,
O thank the Lord, for all his love.

2 He only is the maker
of all things near and far;
he paints the wayside flower,
he lights the ev'ning star.
The winds and waves obey him,
by him the birds are fed:
much more to us his children,
he gives our daily bread.

3 We thank thee then, O Father,
for all things bright and good:
the seed–time and the harvest,
our life, our health, our food.
No gifts have we to offer
for all thy love imparts,
but that which thou desirest,
our humble, thankful hearts.

783 Donal Murray

1 We praise you and thank you, our Father above,
who offers us peace in your kingdom of love.
Your people are saved by the death of your Son
who leads us to glory where all will be one.
Accepting this Gospel we honour Saint Patrick,
who taught in our land what your kindness has done.

2 Your Word has revealed what our future will be,
'Raised up from earth I draw all men to me.'
May we, like Saint Patrick, bear witness to you,
reflecting your love in whatever we do.
He came to our country which once had enslaved him,
to preach the good news that God makes all things new.

784 The Benedictine Nuns of West Malling

1 We praise you, Father, for your gifts
of dusk and nightfall over earth,
foreshadowing the mystery
of death that leads to endless birth.

2 Within your hands we rest secure;
in quiet sleep our strength renew;
yet give your people hearts that wake
in love to you, unsleeping Lord.

3 Your glory may we ever seek
in rest, as in activity,
until its fullness is revealed,
O source of life, O Trinity.

785 Te Deum laudamus, tr. James Quinn, SJ

1 We praise you, God, confessing you as Lord!
Eternal Father, all earth worships you!
Angelic choirs, high heavens, celestial powers,
cherubs and seraphs praise you ceaselessly:
'All–holy Lord, O God of heavenly hosts,
your glorious majesty fills heaven and earth.'

2 Blessed apostles join in praise of you
with prophets famed and martyrs clothed in white,
singing with holy Church throughout the earth:
'Father, we praise your boundless majesty!
We praise your glorious, true and only Son!
We praise you, Holy Spirit, Paraclete!'

3 You are the King of glory, Jesus Christ!
You are the Father's everlasting Son!
Born for mankind from lowly Virgin's
womb,
death you have conquered, opening
heaven to faith;
throned now in glory at the Father's side
you shall return in glory as our judge.

4 We pray you, therefore, give your
servants aid,
whom you have ransomed with your
precious blood,
let them be ranked in glory with your
saints;
save, Lord, the people who are wholly
yours,
bless them, for they are your inheritance,
and, as their ruler, ever raise them up.

5 Throughout each single day, we bless
you Lord,
for all eternity we praise your name.
Keep us this day, Lord, free from every sin;
have mercy on us, Lord; have mercy, Lord;
show us your love, as we have hoped in
you!
You are my hope, Lord; you shall fail me
not!

786 *Traditional*

1 We shall overcome, we shall overcome,
we shall overcome some day.
Oh, deep in my heart I do believe
that we shall overcome some day.

2 We'll walk hand in hand …

3 We shall live in peace …

4 We shall live with him …

787 *Paul Inwood*

We shall draw water joyfully,
singing joyfully, singing joyfully,
We shall draw water joyfully
from the wellsprings of salvation.

1 Truly God is our salvation;
we trust, we shall not fear.
For the Lord is our strength, our song;
he became our saviour.

2 Give thanks, O give thanks to the Lord;
give praise to his holy name!
make his mighty deeds known
to all of the nations,
proclaim his greatness.

3 Sing a psalm, sing a psalm to the Lord
for he has done glorious deeds.
Make known his works to all of the earth;
people of Zion, sing for joy,
for great in your midst, great in your midst
is the Holy One of Israel.

788 *John Henry Hopkins (1822–1900)*

1 We three Kings of Orient are;
bearing gifts we traverse afar,
field and fountain, moor and mountain,
following yonder star.

O Star of wonder, star of night,
star with royal beauty bright,
westward leading, still proceeding,
guide us to thy perfect light.

2 Born a King on Bethlehem plain,
gold I bring, to crown him again,
King for ever, ceasing never,
over us all to reign.

3 Frankincense to offer have I,
Incense owns a Deity nigh.
Prayer and praising, all are raising,
worship him, God most high.

4 Myrrh is mine, its bitter perfume
breathes a life of gathering gloom;
sorrowing, sighing, bleeding, dying,
sealed in the stone–cold tomb.

5 Glorious now behold him arise,
King and God and sacrifice.
'Alleluia, alleluia!'
earth to heaven replies.

789 *Henry Alford (1810–71) alt.*

1 We walk by faith, and not by sight:
no gracious words we hear
of him who spoke as none e'er spoke,
but we believe him near.

2 We may not touch his hands and side,
nor follow where he trod;
yet in his promise we rejoice,
and cry 'My Lord and God!'

3 Help then, O Lord, our unbelief,
and may our faith abound;
to call on you when you are near,
and seek where you are found:

4 That when our life and faith is done
in realms of clearer light
we may behold you as you are
in full and endless sight.

5 We walk by faith, and not by sight:
no gracious words we hear
of him who spoke as none e'er spoke,
but we believe him near.

790 *Michael Cockett*

1 We will walk through the valley in the shadow of death.
We will walk through the darkness without fear.
Though the night may be long, the dark enclosing,
we know Jesus, our morning light is near.

2 He has walked through the valley of the shadow of death,
he has walked through the night of fear alone.
Though the darkness had gathered to destroy him
he was there at the rising of the sun.

3 We will walk in the glory of the bright morning sun,
we will walk in the light that guides our way.
For with Jesus the lord of light beside us
we will walk in the glory of the day.

791 *Afro-American Spiritual*

1 Were you there when they crucified my Lord?
Were you there when they crucified my Lord?
Oh sometimes it causes me to tremble, tremble, tremble.
Were you there when they crucified my Lord?

2 Were you there when they nailed him to a tree? …

3 Were you there when they pierced him in the side? …

4 Were you there when the sun refused to shine? …

5 Were you there when they laid him in the tomb? …

6 Were you there when he rose from out the tomb? …

792 *Robert J. Stamp*

1 Welcome all ye noble saints of old,
as now before your very eyes unfold
the wonders all so long ago foretold.

God and man at table are sat down. (2)

2 Elders, martyrs, all are falling down,
prophets, patriarchs are gath'ring round;
what angels longed to see, now we have found.

3 Who is this who spreads the vict'ry feast?
Who is this who makes our warning cease?
Jesus risen, Saviour, Prince of Peace.

4 Beggars lame, and harlots also here;
repentant publicans are drawing near;
wayward sons come home without a fear.

5 Worship in the presence of the Lord
with joyful songs, and hearts in one accord,
and let our host at table be adored.

6 When at last this earth shall pass away,
when Jesus and his bride are one to stay,
the feast of love is just begun that day.

793 *Tom Shelley*

1 What can we offer you, Lord our God?
How can we worship you as you deserve?
We can only offer what our lips do
proclaim.
We can only offer you humble acts of praise.
But we offer this with Jesus our brother,
Jesus your Son.
We join with him, glory to you, O God! (2)

2 What can we offer you, Lord our God?
How can we thank you for all that you've
done?
We can only say it, Lord God, we thank
you so.
We can only try to live grateful lives,
O Lord.
But we offer this with Jesus, our brother,
Jesus your Son.
We join with him, our thanks to you,
O God. (2)

3 What can we offer you, Lord our God?
How do we prove we are truly sorry, Lord?
We can say it often, God, sorry that we are.
We can try to prove it, Lord, by the way
we live.
And we offer this with Jesus, our brother,
Jesus, your Son.
We join with him, forgive our sins,
O God. (2)

4 What can we offer you, Lord our God?
Dare we present you with another call for
help?
We just have to say it, Lord God, we
need you so.
We just have to beg you, Lord, take us by
the hand.
And we offer this with Jesus, our brother,
Jesus, your Son.
We join with him, Lord, we need you so. (2)

794 *W. C. Dix*

1 What child is this, who, laid to rest,
on Mary's lap is sleeping?
Whom angels greet
with anthems sweet,
while shepherds watch are keeping?
This, this is Christ the King,
whom shepherds guard and angels sing:
come, greet the infant Lord,
the Babe, the Son of Mary!

2 Why lies he in such mean estate,
where ox and ass are feeding?
Good Christians, fear:
for sinners here
the silent Word is pleading.
Nails, spear, shall pierce him through,
the cross be born for me, for you:
hail, hail the Word made flesh,
the Babe, the Son of Mary!

3 So bring him incense, gold and myrrh,
come peasants, king, to own him.
The King of kings
salvation brings,
let loving hearts enthrone him.
Raise, raise the song on high,
the Virgin sings her lullaby:
joy, joy for Christ is born,
the Babe, the Son of Mary!

795 *Sr. Donna Marie Cargill, OSM*

1 What do you want of me, Lord?
Where do you want me to serve you?
Where can I sing your praises?
I am your song.
Jesus, Jesus, you are the Lord.
Jesus, Jesus, you are the way.

2 I hear you call my name, Lord,
and I am moved within me.
Your Spirit stirs my deepest self.
Sing your songs in me.
Jesus, Jesus, you are my Lord.
Jesus, Jesus, you are the way.

3 Above, below and around me,
Before, behind, and all through me,
your Spirit burns deep within me.
Fire my life with your love.
Jesus, Jesus, be warmth of my heart.
Jesus, Jesus, you are the way.

4 You are the light in my darkness.
You are my strength when I'm weary.
You give me sight when I'm blinded.
Come, see for me.
Jesus, Jesus, you are my Light.
Jesus, Jesus, you are the way.

5 I am your song and servant,
singing your praise like Mary.
Surrendered to your Spirit,
'Let it be done to me.'
Jesus, Jesus, 'Let it be done to me.'
Jesus, Jesus, you are the way.

796 *Albert F.Bayly (1901–84)*

1 What does the Lord require
for praise and offering?
What sacrifice, desire
or tribute bid you bring?
Do justly; love mercy;
walk humbly with your God.

2 Rulers of earth, give ear!
should you not justice know?
Will God your pleading hear,
while crime and cruelty grow?
Do justly; love mercy;
walk humbly with your God.

3 Masters of wealth and trade,
all you for whom men toil,
think not to win God's aid
if lies your commerce soil.
Do justly; love mercy;
walk humbly with your God.

4 Still down the ages ring
the prophet's stern commands:
to merchant, worker, king,
he brings God's high demands:
Do justly; love mercy;
walk humbly with your God.

5 How shall our life fulfil
God's law so hard and high?
Let Christ endue our will
with grace to fortify.
Then justly, love mercy;
walk humbly with your God.

797 *Huub Oosterhuis, tr. Tony Barr (after David Smith)*

1 What is this place where we are meeting?
Only a room, the earth a floor.
Walls and a roof, refuge for people,
windows for eyes, an open door.
House which becomes a body that lives
when we are gathered here,
and know God is near.

2 Words from afar, stars that are falling,
sparks sown among us long ago.
Names for our God, dreams, signs and
wonders
voicing the world's relentless flow.
We are but dust who see and who hear,
who speak what we have heard:
God's free resplendent word.

3 Table for one, bread that is broken,
cup to be shared, one bread, one wine.
Wonder of God: peace among people,
ancient yet new this hidden sign.
Breaking and sharing, how can this be,
impossible come true?
From death comes life anew.

798 *Rev. Alexander Means (1801–1853)*

1 What wondrous love is this,
O my soul, O my soul?
What wondrous love is this, O my soul?
What wondrous love is this
that caused the Lord of bliss
to bear the dreadful curse for my soul,
for my soul;
to bear the dreadful curse for my soul?

2 To God and to the Lamb
I will sing, I will sing;
to God and to the Lamb I will sing;
to God and to the Lamb

who is the great I am,
while millions join the theme,
I will sing, I will sing;
while millions join the theme, I will sing.

3 And when from death I'm free,
I'll sing on, I'll sing on;
and when from death I'm free, I'll sing on;
and when from death I'm free,
I'll sing and joyful be,
and through eternity
I'll sing on, I'll sing on!
And through eternity, I'll sing on!

799 *W. F. Jabusch*

Whatsoever you do
to the least of my brothers,
that you do unto me.
Whatsoever you do
to the least of my sisters,
that you do unto me.

1 When I was hungry you gave me to eat.
When I was thirsty you gave me to drink.
Now enter into the home of my Father.

2 When I was homeless you opened your door.
When I was naked you gave me your coat.
Now enter into the home of my Father.

3 When I was weary you helped me find rest.
When I was anxious you calmed all my fears.
Now enter into the home of my Father.

4 When in a prison you came to my cell.
When on a sick bed you cared for my needs.
Now enter into the home of my Father.

5 Hurt in a battle you bound up my wounds.
Searching for kindness you held out your hands.
Now enter into the home of my Father.

6 When I was Black, or Chinese or White,
mocked and insulted, you carried my cross.
Now enter into the home of my Father.

7 When I was aged you bothered to smile.
When I was restless you listened and cared.
Now enter into the home of my Father.

8 When I was laughed at you stood by my side.
When I was happy you shared my joy.
Now enter into the home of my Father.

800 *Sydney Carter*

1 When I needed a neighbour were you there were you there?
When I needed a neighbour were you there?
And the creed and the colour and the
name won't matter were you there?

2 I was hungry and thirsty, …

3 I was cold, I was naked, …

4 When I needed a shelter, …

5 When I needed a healer, …

6 Wherever you travel, I'll be there I'll be there.
Wherever you travel, I'll be there.
And the creed and the colour and the
name won't matter I'll be there.

801 *Isaac Watts (1674–1748)*

1 When I survey the wondrous cross
on which the Prince of Glory died,
my richest gain I count but loss,
and pour contempt on all my pride.

2 Forbid it, Lord, that I should boast,
save in the death of Christ, my God:
all the vain things that charm me most,
I sacrifice them to his blood.

3 See from his head, his hands, his feet,
sorrow and love flow mingled down;
did e'er such love and sorrow meet,
or thorns compose so rich a crown?

4 Were the whole realm of nature mine,
that were an offering far too small;
love so amazing, so divine,
demands my soul, my life, my all.

802 *Fred Pratt Green*

1 When, in our music, God is glorified,
and adoration leaves no room for pride,
it is as though the whole creation cried:
Alleluia!

2 How often, making music, we have found
a new dimension in the world of sound,
as worship moved us to a more profound:
Alleluia!

3 So has the Church, in liturgy and song,
in faith and love, through centuries of
wrong,
borne witness to the truth in every tongue:
Alleluia!

4 And did not Jesus sing a psalm that night
when utmost evil strove against the Light?
then let us sing, for whom he won the fight:
Alleluia!

5 Let every instrument be tuned for praise!
Let all rejoice who have a voice to raise!
and may God give us faith to sing always:
Alleluia! (Amen.)

803 *Afro–American Spiritual*

1 When Israel was in Egypt's land,
let my people go,
oppressed so hard they could not stand,
let my people go.

Go down, Moses,
way down in Egypt's land.
Tell old Pharaoh
to let my people go.

2 The Lord told Moses what to do,
let my people go,
to lead the children of Israel through,
let my people go.

3 Your foes shall not before you stand,
let my people go,
and you'll possess fair Canaan's land,
let my people go.

4 O let us all from bondage flee,
let my people go,
and let us all in Christ be free,
let my people go.

5 I do believe without a doubt,
let my people go,
a Christian has a right to shout,
let my people go.

804 *Timothy Dudley–Smith*

1 When John baptised by Jordan's river
in faith and hope the people came,
that John and Jordan might deliver
their troubled souls from sin and shame.
They came to seek a new beginning,
the human spirit's ageless quest,
repentance, and an end of sinning,
renouncing every wrong confessed.

2 There as the Lord, baptised and praying,
rose from the stream, the sinless one,
a voice was heard from heaven saying,
'This is my own beloved Son.'
There as the Father's word was spoken,
not in the power of wind and flame,
but of his love and peace the token,
seen as a dove, the Spirit came.

3 O Son of Man, our nature sharing,
in whose obedience all are blest,
Saviour, our sins and sorrows bearing,
hear us and grant us this request:
daily to grow, by grace defended,
filled with the Spirit from above;
in Christ baptised, beloved, befriended,
children of God in peace and love.

805 *19th century, tr. E. Caswall (1814–78)*

1 When morning gilds the skies,
my heart awakening cries,
may Jesus Christ be praised:
alike at work and prayer
to Jesus I repair:
may Jesus Christ be praised!

2 To God, the word on high,
the hosts of angels cry:
may Jesus Christ be praised!
Let mortals, too, upraise

their voice in hymns of praise:
may Jesus Christ be praised!

3 Let earth's wide circle round
in joyful notes resound:
May Jesus Christ be praised!
Let air, and sea, and sky,
from depth to height, reply:
may Jesus Christ be praised!

4 Does sadness fill my mind?
A solace here I find,
may Jesus Christ be praised:
or fades my earthly bliss?
My comfort still is this,
may Jesus Christ be praised.

5 The night becomes as day,
when from the heart we say,
may Jesus Christ be praised:
the powers of darkness fear,
when this sweet chant they hear,
may Jesus Christ be praised.

6 Be this, while life is mine,
my canticle divine,
may Jesus Christ be praised:
be this the eternal song
through ages all along,
may Jesus Christ be praised.

806 *Christopher Idle*

1 When the King shall come again
all his power revealing,
splendour shall announce his reign,
life and joy and healing:
earth no longer in decay,
hope no more frustrated;
this is God's redemption day
longingly awaited.

2 In the desert trees take root
fresh from his creation;
plants and flowers and sweetest fruit
join the celebration:
rivers spring up from the earth,
barren lands adorning;
valleys, this is your new birth,
mountains, greet the morning!

3 Strengthen feeble hands and knees,
fainting hearts, be cheerful!
God who comes for such as these
seeks and saves the fearful:
now the deaf can hear the dumb
sing away their weeping;
blind eyes see the injured come
walking, running, leaping.

4 There God's highway shall be seen
where no roaring lion,
nothing evil or unclean
walks the road to Zion:
ransomed people homeward bound
all your praises voicing,
see your Lord with glory crowned,
share in his rejoicing!

807 *Michael Scouarnec, tr. Margaret Daly*

1 When the time came to stretch out his
arms,
and to lay down his life for his friends,
God's only Son, in breaking the bread,
gave us the food of heaven to eat, *(2)*

2 This is my body; take it and eat.
This is my blood; come, take it and
drink.
And, to proclaim my death for your sake,
this must you do until I return, *(2)*

3 Hunger and thirst no longer we fear;
Christ's holy bread becomes now our food.
And, when we raise his chalice to drink,
joy overflows; our hope is renewed, *(2)*

4 O Bread of life, O Banquet Divine,
sign of the love that makes us all one,
we who now share this gift from above
surely have seen the goodness of God, *(2)*

5 Through Jesus Christ, our perfect High
Priest,
and in the Spirit, pledge of his love,
for this great feast which you have
prepared,
Father in heaven, praised be your name! *(2)*

808 *John Glynn*

Where are you bound, Mary, Mary?
Where are you bound, Mother of God?

1 Beauty is a dove sitting on a sunlit bough,
beauty is a pray'r without the need of words.
Words are more than sounds falling off
an empty tongue:
let it be according to his word.

2 Mary heard the word spoken in her
inmost heart;
Mary bore the Word and held him in her
arms.
Sorrow she has known, seeing him upon
the cross
– greater joy to see him rise again.

3 Where are we all bound, carrying the
Word of God?
Time and place are ours to make his
glory known.
Mary bore him first, we will tell the
whole wide world;
let it be according to his word.

809 *From the Office of the Mandatum, tr. R. A. Knox (1888–1957)*

1 Where is love and loving–kindness,
God is fain to dwell.
Flock of Christ, who loved us,
in one fold containèd,
joy and mirth be ours, for mirth
and joy he giveth,
fear we still and love the God who
ever liveth,
each to other joined by charity unfeignèd.

2 Where is love and loving–kindness,
God is fain to dwell.
Therefore, when we meet,
the flock of Christ, so loving,
take we heed lest bitterness be
there engendered;
all our spiteful thoughts and
quarrels be surrendered,
seeing Christ is there, divine among us
moving.

3 Where is love and loving-kindness,
God is fain to dwell.
So may we be gathered once
again, beholding
glorified the glory, Christ, of thy unveiling,
there, where never ending joy, and never
failing
age succeeds to age eternally unfolding.

810 *Nahum Tate (1652–1715)*

1 While shepherds watched
their flocks by night,
all seated on the ground,
the angel of the Lord came down,
and glory shone around.

2 'Fear not,' said he,
(for mighty dread
had seized their troubled mind)
'Glad tidings of great joy I bring
to you and all mankind.'

3 'To you in David's
town this day
is born of David's line
a Saviour, who is Christ the Lord;
and this shall be the sign:

4 'The heavenly Babe
you there shall find
to human view displayed,
all meanly wrapped in swathing bands,
and in a manger laid.'

5 Thus spoke the Seraph;
and forthwith
appeared a shining throng
of Angels praising God, who thus
addressed their joyful song:

6 'All glory be
to God on high,
and on the earth be peace,
goodwill henceforth from heaven to men
begin and never cease.'

811 *After John Bunyan (1628–1688), by Michael Saward*

1 Who honours courage here,
who fights the devil?
Who boldly faces fear,
who conquers evil?
We're not afraid to fight!
We'll score the devil's spite:
Christ gives to us the right
to be his pilgrims.

2 Some may be terrified
by Satan's testing,
but faith is verified
when we're resisting.
There's no discouragement
shall cause us to relent
our firm declared intent
to be his pilgrims.

3 Though evil powers intend
to break our spirit
we know we at the end
shall life inherit.
So, fantasies, away!
Why fear what others say?
We'll labour night and day
to be his pilgrims.

812 *John L. Bell and Graham Maule*

1 Will you come and follow me
if I but call your name?
Will you go where you don't know
and never be the same?
Will you let my love be shown,
will you let my name be known,
will you let my life be grown
in you and you in me?

2 Will you leave yourself behind
if I but call your name?
Will you care for cruel and kind
and never be the same?
Will you risk the hostile stare
should your life attract or scare?
Will you let me answer prayer
in you and you in me?

3 Will you let the blinded see
if I but call your name?
Will you set the prisoners free
and never be the same?
Will you kiss the leper clean,
and do such as this unseen,
and admit to what I mean
in you and you in me?

4 Will you love the 'you' you hide
if I but call your name?
Will you quell the fear inside
and never be the same?
Will you use the faith you've found
to reshape the world around,
through my sight and touch and sound
in you and you in me?

5 Lord, your summons echoes true
when you but call my name.
Let me turn and follow you
and never be the same.
In your company I'll go
where your love and footsteps show.
Thus I'll move and live and grow
in you and you in me.

813 *Richard Gillard*

1 Will you let me be your servant,
let me be as Christ to you?
Pray that I may have the grace to
let you be my servant too.

2 We are pilgrims on a journey,
we are trav'llers on the road;
we are here to help each other
walk the mile and bear the load.

3 I will hold the Christ–light for you
in the night–time of your fear;
I will hold my hand out to you,
speak the peace you long to hear.

4 I will weep when you are weeping;
when you laugh I'll laugh with you.
I will share your joy and sorrow
till we've seen this journey through.

5 When we sing to God in heaven
we shall find such harmony,
born of all we've known together
of Christ's love and agony.

6 Will you let me be your servant,
let me be as Christ to you?
Pray that I may have the grace to
let you be my servant too.

814 Estelle White

*With a song in our hearts we shall go on
our way,
to bring God's love to ev'ryone we meet
today.*

Love, love, love is his name.
Love, love, love is his name.
Great, great, great is his name.
Great, great, great is his name.
(Repeat Refrain)

815 Aidan Whelan

*With open hands we come before you
offering to you, Lord, gifts from your
creation.
With loving hearts as one before you
grant us, O Lord, your peace and your
salvation.*

1 Blest are you, Lord, God of creation
through your goodness there is bread
here for us,
fruit of the earth and work of human hands;
it will become the bread of life.

2 Blest are you, Lord, God of creation
through your goodness there is wine here
for us,
fruit of the vine and work of human hands;
it will become your precious blood.

3 Oh Father, hear our prayer,
use us for your glory.

816 Daniel L. Schutte, SJ

*Yahweh, I know you are near,
standing always at my side.
You guard me from the foe
and you lead me in ways everlasting.*

1 Lord, you have searched my heart
and you know when I sit and when I stand.
Your hand is upon me, protecting me
from death,
keeping me from harm.

2 When can I run from your love?
If I climb to the heavens, you are there.
If I fly to the sunrise or sail beyond the sea
still I'd find you there.

3 You know my heart and its ways,
you who formed me before I was born,
in secret of darkness, before I saw the sun,
in my mother's womb.

4 Marvellous to me are your works;
how profound are your thoughts my Lord!
Even if I could count them, they number
as the stars,
you would still be there.

817 Estelle White

*Yahweh, you are my strength and salvation.
Yahweh, you are my rock and my shield.*

1 When foes inside my soul assailed me,
he heard my cry for help and came to my
aid.

2 He bent the heav'ns and came in thunder.
He flew to me and soared on wings of
the wind.

3 The depths within my mind he showed me,
the hidden thoughts that I did not know
were there.

4 His arm stretched from on high and held me.
He drew me from the deep, wild waters
of self.

5 He is the lamp who lights the darkness.
he guides me as I leap the ramparts of life.

6 I raise my voice and sing his glory.
With all my heart I praise the God of my joy.

818 *St. Fulbert of Chartres (c. 1000), tr. R. Campbell (1814–68)*

1 Ye choirs of new Jerusalem,
your sweetest notes employ,
the Paschal victory to hymn
in strains of holy joy.

2 How Judah's Lion burst his chains,
and crushed the serpent's head;
and brought with him, from death's domain,
the long–imprisoned dead.

3 From hell's devouring jaws the prey
alone our leader bore;
his ransomed hosts pursue their way
where he hath gone before.

4 Triumphant in his glory now
his sceptre ruleth all:
earth, heaven, and hell before him bow
and at his footstool fall.

5 While joyful thus his praise we sing,
his mercy we implore,
into his palace bright to bring,
and keep us evermore.

6 All glory to the Father be,
all glory to the Son,
all glory, Holy Ghost, to thee,
while endless ages run.

819 *Charles Wesley (1707–88)*

1 Ye servants of God, your master proclaim
and publish abroad his wonderful name;
the name all–victorious of Jesus extol;
his kingdom is glorious, and rules over all.

2 God ruleth on high, almighty to save;
and still he is nigh, his presence we have;
the great congregation his triumph shall
sing,
ascribing salvation to Jesus our King.

3 'Salvation to God who sits on the throne!'
let all cry aloud, and honour the Son;
the praises of Jesus the angels proclaim,
fall down on their faces, and worship the
Lamb.

4 Then let us adore, and give him his right:
all glory and power, all wisdom and might,
all honour and blessing, with angels above,
and thanks never–ceasing, and infinite
love.
Amen.

820 *17th century, tr. E. Caswall (1814–78)*

1 Ye sons and daughters of the Lord!
the king of glory, king adored,
this day himself from death restored.

Alleluia! (3)

2 All in the early morning grey
went holy women on their way
to see the tomb where Jesus lay.

3 Of spices pure a precious store
in their pure hands those women bore,
to anoint the sacred body o'er.

4 Then straightway one in white they see,
who saith, 'Ye seek the Lord; but he
is risen, and gone to Galilee.'

5 This told they Peter, told they John:
who forthwith to the tomb are gone,
but Peter is by John outrun.

6 That self–same night, while out of fear
the doors were shut, their Lord most dear
to his apostles did appear.

7 But Thomas, when of this he heard,
was doubtful of his brethren's word:
wherefore again there comes the Lord.

8 'Thomas, behold my side.' saith he:
'My hands, my feet, my body see,
and doubt not, but believe in me.'

9 When Thomas saw that wounded side,
the truth no longer he denied:
'Thou art my Lord and God!' he cried.

10 Now let us praise the Lord most high,
and strive his name to magnify
on this great day, through earth and sky.

11 Whose mercy ever runneth o'er,
whom saints and angel hosts adore;
to him be glory evermore.

821 *Marty Haugen*

1 You are salt for the earth, O people:
salt for the Kingdom of God!
Share the flavour of life, O people:
life in the Kingdom of God!

Bring forth the Kingdom of mercy,
bring forth the Kingdom of peace;
bring forth the Kingdom of justice,
bring forth the City of God!

2 You are a light on the hill, O people:
light for the city of God!
Shine so holy and bright, O people:
shine for the Kingdom of God!

3 You are a seed of the Word, O people:
bring forth the Kingdom of God!
Seeds of mercy and seeds of justice,
grow in the Kingdom of God!

4 We are a blest and a pilgrim people:
bound for the Kingdom of God!
Love our journey and love our homeland:
love is the Kingdom of God!

822 *V1. Mavis Ford; vv2–3 by Loxley & Mavis Ford*

1 You are the King of glory,
you are the Prince of Peace,
you are the Lord of heaven and earth,
you're the sun of righteousness,
angels bow down before You,
worship and adore – for
you have the words of eternal life;
you are Jesus Christ, the Lord.

Hosanna to the Son of David!
Hosanna to the King of Kings!
Glory in the highest heaven,
for Jesus the Messiah reigns.

2 You are the one who conquered,
sin and death and pain.
You triumphed over Satan's power
you rose to life again.
Now Lord You reign in glory
every knee shall bow – for
you have the name above all names,
you are Jesus Christ the Lord.

3 You are the King of Glory,
you are God's chosen Son,
you are the heir of everything,
you're the Ever Living One.
Now we bow down before You
worship and adore – for
you are exalted to God's right hand,
you are Jesus Christ the Lord.

823 *Randall DeBruyn*

1 You are the Lord, you are the Lord,
you are the Lord of creation,
you are the Lord.
You are master of ocean and sky,
and all earth bow in adoration.

O Lord, as we gather before you
to adore you and your mercy proclaim,
we give thanks, Lord,
for the love that you show us,
for you know us,
you have called us by name.

2 You are the light, you are the light,
you are light for the nations,
you are the light,
shining brightly throughout every land
to end the darkness of sin and suffering.

3 You, who are love and compassion,
you who are love and compassion,
in your likeness we have all been made.
Help us to carry each other's burdens.

4 You are the hope, you are the hope,
you are the hope of your people,
you are the hope,
for your word holds the promise of peace
for all who follow the path of justice.

824 Chris O'Hara

You are the vine, we are the branches,
together we are one;
without your word love has no meaning
so let your will be done.

1 The fruit of the vine
will become the true wine;
through joy and sorrow
our love will grow to be a sign;
be a sign of the Kingdom
giving hope to light our way,
with love that forms us
as the potter moulds the clay.

2 Together you stand,
divided you fall,
but those who listen
receive my word and hear my call.
Make your home here within me
and you'll find I'll be with you,
with you forever
making life forever new.

825 Refrain from the Rite of Baptism; Verses from Scripture, adapted by Stephen Dean

You have put on Christ,
in him you have been baptised,
alleluia, alleluia, alleluia!

1 We who were dead are now reborn;
we who were buried now are raised.
We who were dwelling in the dark now
see light.

2 For though in Adam all have sinned,
in Jesus Christ are all made clean;
the grace abounding of his death sets us
free.

3 One Lord we serve who died for us;
one faith we hold, in life to come;
one God and Father of us all we proclaim.

4 And this we know, that nothing ill,
no price nor power, nor death nor sin,
can separate us from God's love in Christ.

826 Tom Colvin, based on a Tumbuka hymn by N.Z. Tembo

1 You, Israel, return now;

return to God, your Father,
your only great Creator;
return to God, your Father.

2 You won't be disappointed;

3 Although you have offended;

4 Although your sins are many;

5 He's sure to listen to you;

6 For he is calling to you;

7 Now seek your Lord's forgiveness;

8 He calls you all to hear him;

9 And give yourselves to him now;

10 For he is your redeemer;

11 The people's liberator;

12 Return now, O return now;

13 You lonely and you lost ones;

14 Now pray to him his people;

15 And he will quickly answer;

16 So come now all you people;

827 Chris O'Hara

You lead us O Lord from our bondage:
as we sow with our tears
we shall sing when we reap.
Your people rejoice at your wonder,
our words touched with laughter,
our lips filled with song.

1 See what the Lord has done!
Freedom He brings to His people!
Children of Zion arise,
for our Saviour will come
like a dream in the night,
we will follow His song
leading into the light of His love.

You lead us O Lord from our bondage:
as we sow with our tears
we shall sing when we reap.
Your people rejoice at your wonder,
our words touched with laughter,
our lips filled with song.

2 We are streams in dry land:
you are the living water.
Those who go out full of tears
carry seed for the earth
when they reap they will sing,
tell a song of rebirth
tell a song of rebirth and new life.

828 *Carol Gordon*

1 You must cry out the Word of the Lord! (2)
For you can heal a wounded man
or make a widow rich,
if you sing out the Word of the Lord!

2 You are called to the Word of the Lord! (2)
For the Lord has come in power;
if you believe, he lives in you,
you must breathe out the Word of the Lord!

3 O my people, don't wait any longer! (2)
For my children are starving
for my living water,
you must cry out the Word of the Lord!

4 You must cry out the Word of the Lord! (2)
For you can heal a wounded man,
or make a widow rich,
if you give out the Word of the Lord!

829 *Mark Altrogge*

You sat down at the right hand of the
Father in majesty.
You sat down at the right hand of the
Father in majesty.
You are crown'd Lord of all,
You are faithful and righteous and true,
You're my Master, You're my Owner,
and I love serving You.

830 *Robert J Dufford, SJ*

1 You shall cross the barren desert,
but you shall not die of thirst.
You shall wander far in safety
though you do not know the way.
You shall speak your words to foreign men
and they will understand.
You shall see the face of God and live.

Be not afraid, I go before you always.
Come, follow me, and I will give you rest.

2 If you pass through raging waters in the
sea,
you shall not drown.
If you walk amid the burning flames,
you shall not be harmed.
If you stand before the pow'r of hell
and death is at your side,
know that I am with you through it all.

3 Blessed are your poor,
for the kingdom shall be theirs.
Blest are you that weep and mourn,
for one day you shall laugh.
And if wicked men insult and hate you
all because of me,
blessed, blessed are you!

831 *Stuart Dauermann*

1 You shall go out with joy
and be led forth with peace.
The mountains and the hills will
break forth before you;
there'll be shouts of joy,
and all the trees of the field
will clap, will clap their hands.

2 And all the trees of the field
will clap their hands,
the trees of the field
will clap their hands.
The trees of the field
will clap their hands
while you go out with joy.

Repeat You shall go out …

832 *Michael Joncas*

1 You who dwell in the shelter of the Lord,
who abide in his shadow for life,
say to the Lord:
'My refuge, my Rock in whom I trust!'

And he will raise you up on eagle's wings,
bear you on the breath of dawn,
make you to shine like the sun,
and hold you in the palm of his hand.

2 The snare of the fowler will never capture you,
and famine will bring you no fear:
under his wings your refuge
his faithfulness your shield.

3 You need not fear the terror of the night,
nor the arrow that flies by day;
though thousands fall about you,
near you it shall not come.

4 For to his angels he's given a command
to guard you in all of your ways;
upon their hands they will bear you up,
lest you dash your foot against a stone.

And he will raise you up on eagle's wings,
bear you on the breath of dawn,
make you to shine like the sun,
and hold you in the palm of his hand.
And hold you, hold you in the palm of his hand.

833 *British National Anthem*

1 God save our gracious Queen,
long live our noble Queen,
God save our Queen.
Send her victorious,
happy and glorious,
long to reign over us:
God save the Queen.

2 Thy choicest gifts in store
on her be pleased to pour,
long may she reign.
May she defend our laws,
and ever give us cause
to sing with heart and voice,
God save the Queen.

THE PRAYER OF THE CHURCH

The Prayer of the Church (also known as *The Liturgy of the Hours* or *The Divine Office*) has for many years been the preserve of the clergy and religious communities. In recent years, it has resumed its place at the heart of the liturgy of the whole church.

The Prayer of the Church is presented here in a form which has been based upon the *Liturgy of the Hours*, but adapted to promote its fullest use in parishes.

The psalms and canticles are at the heart of this liturgy. Both are intended to be sung, and it is important to find ways of helping people join in. It may be helpful to sing the same setting for several weeks, or for a season. The refrain alone could be sung by everyone, and the verses recited by a reader or sung by a cantor. In several places songs or hymns based on an appropriate psalm or canticle, and found elsewhere in this book, are listed as alternatives to the setting provided here.

834 Invitatory

All make the sign of the cross on their lips.

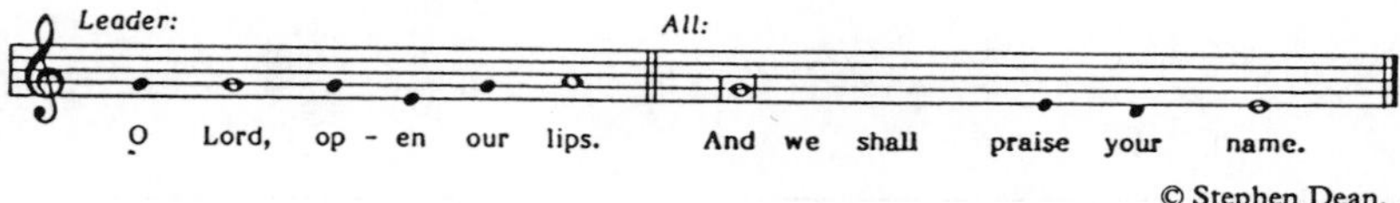
Leader:
O Lord, op - en our lips.
All:
And we shall praise your name.
© Stephen Dean.

835 Invitatory Psalm

Psalm 95 (94) is sung with optional refrain as follows:

SD
A might - y God is the Lord, come, let us a — dore him!

Tone 1
© McCrimmon Publishing Co Ltd
omit in 5 - line s.
Gelineau Tone
omit in 4-line stanzas

Come, ríng out your jóy to the Lórd;
háil the róck who sáves us.
Let us cóme befóre him, gíving thanks,
with sóngs let us háil the Lórd.

A míghty Gód is the Lórd,/
a gréat king abóve all góds.
In his hánd are the dépths of the éarth;/
the héights of the móuntains are hís.
To hím belongs the séa, fór he máde it,
and the dry land shápéd by his hánds.

Come ín; let us bów and bend lów;
let us knéel before the Gód who máde us
for hé is our Gód and wé/
the péople who belóng to his pásture,
the flóck that is léd by his hánd.

O that todáy you would lísten to his vóice!
Hárden not your héarts as at Meríbah,/
as on that dáy at Mássah in the désert
when your fáthers pút me to the tést;
when they tríed me, thóugh they sáw my wórk.

For forty yéars I was wéaried of these péople/
and I sáid: 'Their heárts are astráy,
these péople do not knów my wáys.'
Thén I took an oáth in my ánger:
'Néver shall they énter my rést.'

Give glóry to the Fáther Almíghty,
to his Són, Jesus Chríst, the Lórd,
to the Spírit who dwélls in our héarts,
both nów and for éver. Amén.

• Alternatives:

No. 555 *O that today you would listen*
No. 746 *To God with gladness sing*

836 Introduction *Omitted if the invitatory has been sung*

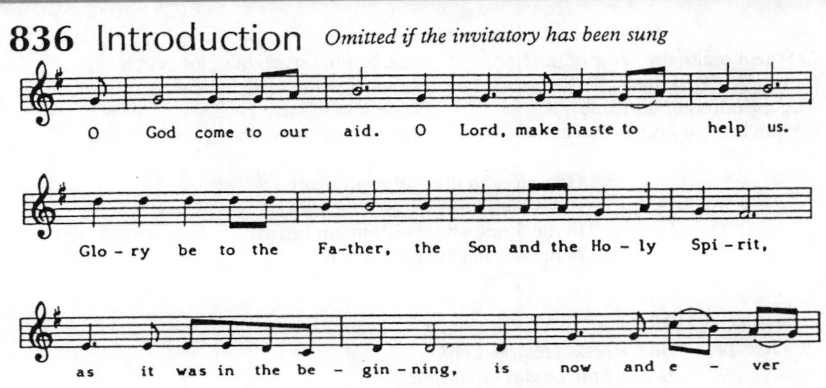
O God come to our aid. O Lord, make haste to help us.
Glo-ry be to the Fa-ther, the Son and the Ho-ly Spi-rit,
as it was in the be-gin-ning, is now and e-ver
shall be world without end, A-men.
Except in Lent
Al-le-lu-ia.

Hymn

see GATHERING *or* MORNING *in Topical Index*

837 Psalm 148

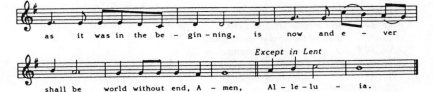

Tone 1
LB
Gelineau Tone

Práise the Lórd from the héavens,
práise him in the héights.
Práise him, all his ángels,
práise him, áll his hósts.

Práise him, sún and móon,
práise him, shining stárs.
Práise him, highest héavens
and the wáters abóve the héavens.

Let them práise the náme of the Lórd.
He commánded: they were máde.
He fixed them for éver,
gave a láw which shall nót pass awáy.

Práise the Lórd from the éarth,
séa creatures and all óceans,
fire and háil, snow and míst,
stormy winds that obéy his wórd;

áll móuntains and hílls,
all frúit trees and cédars,
béasts, wild and táme,
réptiles and bírds on the wíng;

áll earth's kings and péoples,
earth's prínces and rúlers;
yóung men and máidens,
old men togéther with chíldren.

Let them práise the náme of the Lórd
for he alóne is exálted.
The spléndour of his náme
réaches beyond héaven and éarth.

He exálts the stréngth of his péople.
He is the práise of all his sáints,
of the sóns of Israel,
of the péople to whóm he comes clóse.

Give glóry to the Fáther almíghty,
to his Són, Jesus Christ, the Lórd,
to the Spírit who dwélls in our héarts,
both nów and for ever, Amén.

• Alternatives

- *No. 14* — *All Creation bless the Lord*
- *No. 77* — *Because the Lord is my shepherd*
- *No. 543* — *O Lord, you are the centre of my life*
- *No. 614* — *Psallite Domino*
- *No. 644* — *Sing a new song to the Lord*
- *No. 645* — *Sing a new song unto the Lord*
- *No. 672* — *Surrexit Christus*

See also Scriptural Index

Scripture Reading

from the Liturgy of the Hours *or ad libitum*

838 Response to the Word of God

Refrain
G Am C D7 Bm Am SD
We praise you, Lord; we hear your word, be here a — mong us this
D G Am C D7 G C D G
day. O - pen our ears, o - pen our hearts, and may your word be our way.
VERSE (Cantor)
G Em Am D
1. Advent: Let us see, O Lord, your mercy; and give us your sa - ving help. R.
1. Christmas: The Word was made flesh, and lived among us. R.
1. Lent: A pure heart create for me, O Lord, put a steadfast spi - rit with - in me. R.
1. Easter: This day was made by the Lord, we rejoice and are glad. R.
1. General: Your words are spirit, Lord, and they are life; you have the message of e-ter - nal life. R.
2. Glory be to the Father, and to the Son; and to the Ho - ly Spirit. R.

• Alternatives

No. 81 *Bless the Lord, my soul*
No. 137 *Confitemini Domino*
No. 416 *Praise to you, O Christ, our Saviour* (Refrain only)
No. 519 *O Christe Domine Jesu*
No. 614 *Psallite Domino*

Benedictus

See No. 86

839 Intercessions

A response such as the following is made:

Em
Am
Em
S D
Have mer–cy on us, Lord, and hear our prayer.

Music © Stephen Dean.

• Alternatives

During the last Sundays in Ordinary time and throughout Advent
No. 418 *Come, Lord Jesus, Maranatha*
At other times:
No. 308 *In the Lord I'll be ever thankful*
No. 419 *Lord, in your mercy, hear our prayer*
No. 421 *Through our lives*
No. 420 *In our need, we pray to the Lord*
No. 542 *O Lord, hear my prayer*
No. 850 *Lord, in your mercy, hear our prayer*

The Lord's Prayer

is said or sung
See Nos. 584, 585 and 586

Concluding Prayer

The concluding prayer, taken from the Liturgy of the Hours *(or other suitable source), is said by the leader.*

Blessing

A priest or deacon uses the usual form of blessing.
A lay–person says:
The Lord bless us and keep us from all evil, and bring us to everlasting life.

• Alternative

For a sung blessing see
No. 458 *May God bless and keep you*

No blessing is said or sung on Good Friday or Holy Saturday.

Evening Prayer may begin as Morning Prayer, or with a Service of Light (Lucernarium).

Either

840 Introduction

O God come to our aid. O Lord, make haste to ___ help us.
Glo - ry be to the Fa-ther, the Son and the Ho - ly Spi - rit,
as it was in the be - gin - ning, is now and e - ver___
shall be world without end, A - men,
Except in Lent
Al - le - lu - ia.

Hymn

See GATHERING *or* EVENING *in Topical Index*
or as appropriate for the season (see Liturgical Index)

After the hymn, turn to No. 845 Psalm 114 (113a)

Or

Service of Light (Lucernarium)

841 Greeting

Leader: Jesus Christ is the light of the world.
All: A light the darkness cannot o - ver - power.

842 Hymn

1 O gracious Light, Lord Jesus Christ,
in you the Father's glory shone.
Immortal, holy, blest is he,
and blest are you, his only Son.

2 Now sunset comes, but light shines forth,
the lamps are lit to pierce the night.
Praise Father, Son and Spirit: God
who dwells in the eternal light.

3 Worthy are you of endless praise,
O Son of God, Life-giving Lord;
wherefore you are through all the earth
and in the highest heaven adored.

2nd century, tr. F. Bland Tucker

843 Evening Thanksgiving

Leader: Let us give thanks to God the Father always and for everything.
All: In the name of our Lord Je - sus Christ.

We give you thanks, O Lord,
through your Son Jesus Christ,
through whom you have enlightened us
and shown us the light which can never be extinguished.
Now we have come to the end of the day and night is falling.
Through the day you have shone on us the light
which you created for our need,
and now, through your grace, we do not lack the light of evening;
and so we praise you and glorify you
through your son, Jesus Christ our Lord,
through whom, with the Holy Spirit,
are glory and power and honour
now and for ever and to endless ages.
Amen.

From Hyppolytus (d. 215)

844 Incense Psalm

Incense may be used as a symbol of prayer, during which Psalm 141 (140) is sung as follows:

O Lord, let my prayer rise be - fore you like in - cense, — the
raising of my hands like an e — vening sa - cri — fice.

I have cálled to you, Lórd, hásten to hélp me!
Héar my vóice when I cry to yóu.
Let my práyer aríse befóre you like íncense,
the ráising of my hánds like an évening oblátion.

Sét, O Lord, a guard óver my móuth;
keep wátch, O Lórd, at the dóor of my líps!
Do not túrn my héart to thíngs that are wróng,
to évil déeds with mén who are sínners.

Néver allów me to sháre in their féasting.
If a góod man stríkes or repróves me it is kíndness;
but let the óil of the wícked not anóint my héad.
Let my práyer be éver agáinst their málice.

To yóu, Lord Gód, my éyes are túrned:
in yóu I take réfuge; spáre my sóul!
From the tráp they have láid for me kéep me sáfe:
kéep me from the snáres of thóse who do évil.

Give glóry to the Fáther, the Són and Holy Spírit,
both nów and for éver, wórld withóut end.

Either

Outside the season of Lent, Nos. 828 and 829 may be used on alternate weeks.

845 Psalm 114 (113a)

This psalm is not used during Lent.

Refrain
The earth trem - bled be - fore the Lord

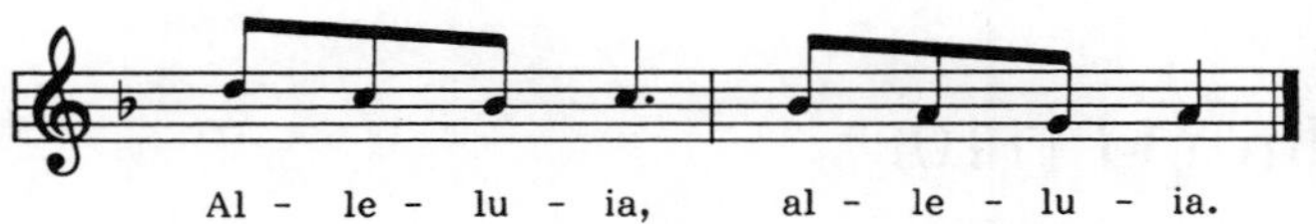
Al - le - lu - ia, al - le - lu - ia.

Tone:

The verses may be sung or read alternately by a cantor (A) and all (B).

A When Israel came forth from Egypt,
Jacob's sons from an alien people,
Judah became the Lord's temple,
Israel became his kingdom. *(Refrain)*

B The sea fled at the sight:
the Jordan turned back on its course,
the mountains leapt like rams
and the hills like yearling sheep. *(Refrain)*

A Why was it, sea, that you fled,
that you turned back, Jordan, on your course?
Mountains, that you leapt like rams,
hills, like yearling sheep? *(Refrain)*

B Tremble, O earth, before the Lord,
in the presence of the God of Jacob,
who turns the rock into a pool
and flint into a spring of water. *Refrain)*

A&B Glory be to the Father, and to the Son
and to the Holy Spirit,
as it was in the beginning, is now and ever shall be,
world without end, Amen. *(Refrain)*

After the psalm turn to No. 847 Canticle

Or

846 Psalm 111 (110)

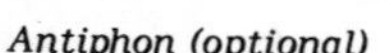
Antiphon (optional)

Lord our God, mer-ci - ful and lo - ving, won-drous things you have done.

1. I will thank the Lord with all my heart, in the meet - ing of the just and their as - sem- bly.

Great are the works_of the Lord, to be pon-dered by all who__ love him.

2 Glorious in majesty his work
and his justice stands firm for ever.
His mighty deeds will be remembered;
Yes, our Lord is compassion and love.

3 He gives food to all those who fear him,
keep his covenant ever in mind.
He has shown his might to the poeple,
he has given them the land of the nations.

4 All his works are done in truth and justice,
and his laws and commandments are sure.
They will stand for ever and for ever,
they were made in uprightness and truth.

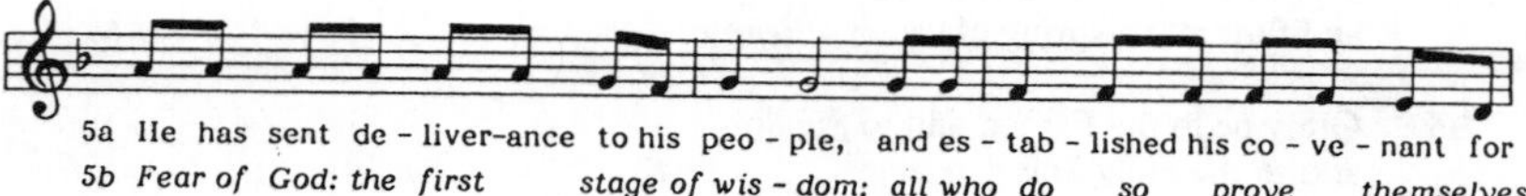
5a He has sent de - liver-ance to his peo - ple, and es - tab - lished his co - ve - nant for
5b Fear of God: the first stage of wis - dom; all who do so prove themselves

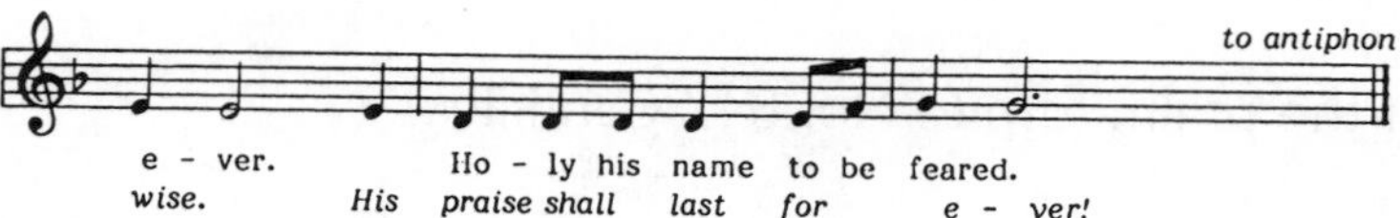
to antiphon
e - ver. Ho - ly his name to be feared.
wise. His praise shall last for e - ver!

6 *(first tune)*
Glory to our Father and Creator,
To his Son, Jesus Christ, our Lord.
Glory to the Spirit and life–giver
as it was, is now and ever shall be.

• Alternatives

No. 53 *As the deer longs*
No. 370 *Like as the deer*
No. 505 *My soul is longing for your peace*

See also Scriptural Index

After the psalm turn to either No. 847 Canticle (during the year) or No. 848 Canticle (during Lent).

Either

847 Canticle (outside Lent)

Refrain

Cantor sings and all repeat. Cantor sings verses and all join in Alleluias
Refrain is repeated after verse 2 and verse 4

A E A/CH E7 A Bm
The Lord is King our God, the Al - migh - ty.
C♯m F♯m Bm E A E A
al - le - lu - ia!
A D A F♯m E
1 Salvation and glory and power be - long to our God. AL-LE-LU-IA!
2 Praise our God, all you his servants.
3 The Lord our God, the al - migh-ty reigns.
4 The marriage feast of the Lamb has come.
F♯m B E
1 His judgements are true and just.
2 You who fear him, small and great.
3 Let us rejoice, and exult, and give him the glory.
4 And his bride has made herself ready.
E F♯m A D E A D.S.
AL - LE - LU -IA, AL - LE - LU - IA! The
Repeat Antiphon after verse 2 and verse 4

After the canticle, turn to the Scripture Reading (No. 853)

Or

848 Canticle (during Lent)

Canticle of Christ the Servant of God (1 Peter 2:21-24)

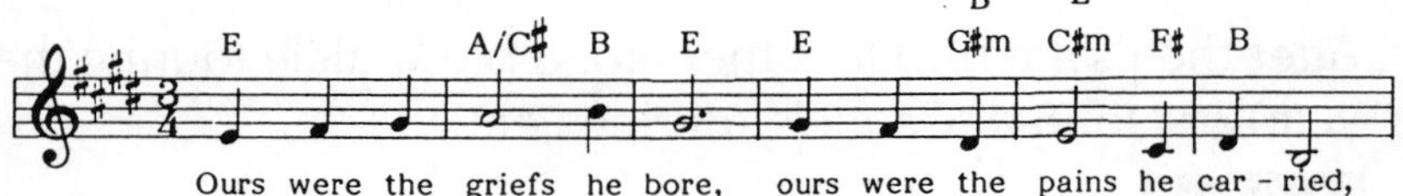
E
A/C♯
B
E
E
B
G♯m
E
C♯m
F♯
B
Ours were the griefs he bore, ours were the pains he car - ried,

E
A
B
C♯m
A
E/G♯
ours were the sins he took on him; and by — his

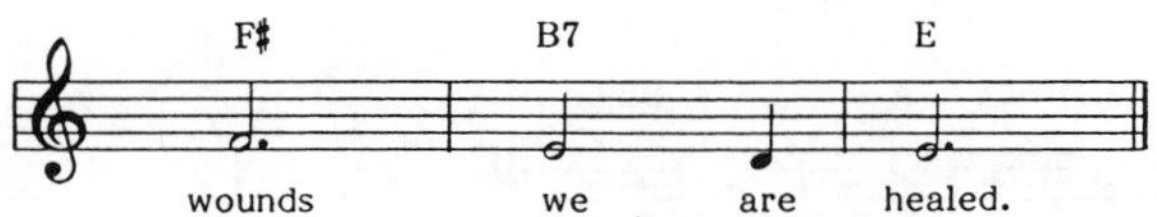
F♯
B7
E
wounds we are healed.

The response is sung after the cantor, and between verses.
The verses are recited by the cantor or reader.

Verses

1 Christ suffered for you
leaving you an example
that you should follow in his steps.
He committed no sin
no guile was found on his lips.
When he was reviled,
he did not revile in return. *(Refrain)*

2 When he suffered.
He did not threaten;
but he trusted to him
who judges justly.
He himself bore our sins
in his body on the tree,
that we might die to sin
and live to righteousness. *(Refrain)*

3 *(All)*
Give glory to the Father Almighty,
to his Son Jesus Christ the Lord,
to the Spirit who dwells in our hearts
both now and for ever, Amen. *(Refrain)*

• Alternative

No. 590 Ours were the sufferings

Scripture Reading

from the Liturgy of the Hours *or ad libitum*

Response to the Reading

A silence may follow the reading or a chant may be sung for example -

No. 81	*Bless the Lord, my soul*
No. 137	*Confitemini Domino*
No. 416	*Praise to you, O Christ, our Saviour* (Refrain only)
No. 519	*O Christe Domine Jesu*
No. 614	*Psallite Domino*

849 Magnificat

Refrain My soul glo- ri -fies the Lord, my
Spi- rit___ re- joi - ces in God my___ Sav -iour. He
looks on his ser-vant in her noth-ing-ness hence -
to verses
forth all a - ges___ will call me___ bless-ed ___
last time
fine
bless- ed _______
verses
1. The al - migh-ty works mar-vels for me. Ho - ly his
name. His mer-cy is from age to
D.S.
age on those___ who ___ fear him ___ My

2 He puts forth his arm in strength
and scatters the proud-hearted.
He casts the mighty from their thrones
and raises the lowly.
My soul glorifies the Lord,
my spirit rejoices in God, my Saviour.
He looks on his servant in her nothingness;
henceforth all ages will call me blessed.

3 He fills the starving with good things,
and sends the rich away empty.
He fills the starving with good things,
sends the rich away empty.
Chorus

4 He protects Israel, his servant,
remembering his mercy,
the mercy promised to our fathers,
for Abraham for ever.
Chorus

5 Give glory to the Father almighty,
to his Son, Jesus Christ, the Lord:
to the Spirit who dwells in our hearts,
for ever and ever.
Chorus

Words: Luke 1: 46b–55 (Grail translation)
Music: Ken Belasco

• Alternatives

No. 213 *God has gladdened my heart with joy*
No. 231 *Great is the Lord*
No. 506 *My soul rejoices*
No. 684 *Tell out my soul*
No. 707 *The Magnificat*

850 Intercessions

The following or a similar response is made:

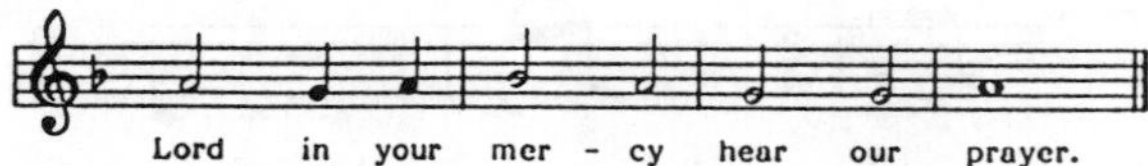
Lord in your mer - cy hear our prayer.

• Alternatives

During the last Sundays in Ordinary time and throughout Advent

No. 418 *Come, Lord Jesus, Maranatha*

At other times:

No. 308 *In the Lord I'll be ever thankful*
No. 419 *Lord, in your mercy, hear our prayer*
No. 421 *Through our lives*
No. 420 *In our need, we pray to the Lord*
No. 542 *O Lord, hear my prayer*
No. 839 *Have mercy on us, Lord and hear our prayer*

The Lord's Prayer

is said or sung.

See Nos. 584, 585 and 586

Concluding Prayer

The concluding prayer, taken from the Liturgy of the Hours *(or other suitable source), is said by the leader.*

Blessing

A priest or deacon uses the usual form of blessing.
A lay–person says:

The Lord bless us and keep us from all evil, and bring us to everlasting life.

• Alternative

For a sung blessing see

No. 458 May God bless and keep you

No blessing is said or sung on Good Friday or Holy Saturday.

NIGHT PRAYER

851 Introduction

O God come to our aid. O Lord, make haste to— help us.

Glo – ry be to the Fa–ther, the Son and the Ho – ly Spi – rit,

as it was in the be – gin – ning, is now and e – ver—

Except in Lent
shall be world without end, A – men, Al – le – lu – ia.

Examination of Conscience

An examination of conscience is recommended.
In a common celebration this may be included in a penitential act using the formulas given in the missal.

Hymn

No. 138 *Creator of the stars of night* (especially in Advent)
No. 142 *Day is done but night unfailing*
No. 205 *God be in my head*
No. 348 *Lead, kindly light*
No. 386 *Lord of all hopefulness*
No. 691 *The day thou gavest*
No. 784 *We praise you, Father for your gift*

See also EVENING *in Topical Index*

852 Psalm 4

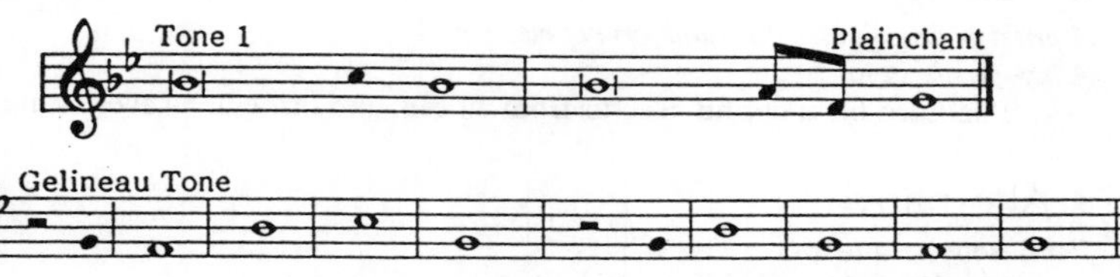
Tone 1
Plainchant
Gelineau Tone

When I cáll, ánswer me, O Gód of jústice;
from ánguish you reléased me, have mércy and héar me.

O mén, how lóng will your héarts be clósed,
will you lóve what is fútile and séek what is fálse?

It is the Lórd who grant fávours to thóse whom he lóves;
the Lórd hears me whenéver I cáll him.

Fear him; do not sín; pónder on your béd and be stíll;
make jústice your sácrifice and trúst in the Lórd.

'Whát can bring us háppiness?' mány sáy;
let the líght of your fáce shíne on us, O Lórd.

You have pút into my héart a gréater jóy
than they have from abúndance of córn and new wíne.

I will líe down in péace and sléep comes at ónce
for yóu alone, Lórd, make me dwéll in sáfety.

Glory bé to the Fáther, the Són, and Holy Spírit
both nów and for éver, wórld without énd.

853 Psalm 134 (133)

Tone 1
SD

1 O come, bless the Lord,
all yóu who sérve the Lórd,
who stand in the house of the Lord,
in the cóurts of the hóuse of our Gód.

2 Lift up your hands to the holy place
and bléss the Lórd through the níght.
May the Lord bless you from Sion,
he who máde both heáven and éarth.

3 Give glory to the Father Almighty,
to his Són, Jesus Chríst, our Lórd,
to the Spirit who dwélls in our hearts
both nów and for éver, Amén.

Tone 2
AGM

- Alternatives

No. 76 *Be with me, Lord (Joncas)*
No. 91 *Blest be the Lord*
No. 250 *Hear my cry, O God*
No. 816 *Yahweh, I know you are near*
No. 832 *You who dwell in the shelter of the Lord*

Scripture Reading

Deuteronomy 6:4–7

Hear, O Israel: the Lord our God is one Lord; and you shall love the Lord your God with all your heart, and with all your soul, and with all your might. And these words which I command you this day shall be upon your heart; and you shall teach them diligently to your children, and shall talk of them when you sit in your house, and when you walk by the way, and when you lie down, and when you rise.

854/855 Response to the Word of God

Words in brackets are omitted during Lent.

Response
fine
1. In - to your hands, O Lord, I commend my Spi-rit. (Al-le-lu - ia, al-le - lu — ia).
Verse
D.C.
1. You have re-deemed us Lord, God of Truth. 2. Glo-ry be to the Fa-ther, and to the
Son, and to the Ho-ly Spi-rit. D.C.

856 Nunc Dimittis

Antiphon text © The Bishops' Conference of England and Wales.
Music © Stephen Dean.
Antiphon
SD
Save us, Lord, while we are a — wake, pro - tect us while — we
sleep, that we may keep watch with Christ, and rest here in peace.
Tone 1
omit in 1st stanza
© McCrimmon Publishing Co Ltd.

At lást, all pówerful Máster,
you give léave to your sérvant to gó
in péace, accórding to your prómise.

For my éyes have séen your salvátion
which yóu have prepáred for all nátions,
the líght to enlíghten the Géntiles,
and give glóry to Israel, your péople.

Give práise to the Fáther Almíghty,
to his Són, Jesus Christ, the Lórd,
to the Spírit who dwélls in our héarts
both nów and for éver, Amén.

- Alternative

  No. 56 *At last all powerful Master*

Concluding Prayer

The concluding prayer, taken from the Liturgy of the Hours *(or other suitable source) is said by the leader.*

Blessing

The Lord grant us a quiet night and a perfect end. Amen.

Anthem to Our Lady

During Eastertide:

No. 616 *Regina Caeli*

At other times:

No. 225 *God, who made the earth and sky*
No. 482 *Mary, crowned with living light*
No. 533 *O holy Dwelling Place*
No. 628 *Salve Regina*

SUPPLEMENT
857 – 1009

857 *John F Wade c1711-86*

1 Adeste fideles, laeti triumphantes,
Venite, venite in Bethlehem;
Natum videte, Regem angelorum.
Venite adoremus, venite adoremus,
Venite adoremus, Dominum.

2 Deum de Deo, Lumen de Lumine,
Gestant puellae viscera.
Deum verum, genitum non factum.
Venite adoremus, venite adoremus,
Venite adoremus, Dominum.

3 Cantet nunc io, chorus angelorum,
Cantet nunc aula caelestium.
Gloria, gloria in excelsis Deo.
Venite adoremus, venite adoremus,
Venite adoremus, Dominum.

4 Ergo qui natus die hodierna,
Jesu, tibi sit gloria.
Patris aeternae Verbum caro factum.
Venite adoremus, venite adoremus,
Venite adoremus, Dominum.

858 *Roy Turner*

1 All over the world
the Spirit is moving,
All over the world
as the prophet said it would be;
All over the world
there's a mighty revelation
Of the glory of the Lord,
as the waters cover the sea.

2 All over His church
God's Spirit is moving,
All over His church
as the prophet said it would be;
All over His church
there's a mighty revelation
Of the glory of the Lord,
as the waters cover the sea.

3 Right here in this place
the Spirit is moving,
Right here in this place
as the prophet said it would be;
Right here in this place
there's a mighty revelation
Of the glory of the Lord,
as the waters cover the sea.

859 *Maria Parkinson*

1 As I kneel before you,
as I bow my head in prayer,
take this day, make it yours
and fill me with your love.

Ave Maria, gratia plena,
Dominus tecum, benedicta tu.

2 All I have I give you
ev'ry dream and wish are yours.
Mother of Christ, Mother of mine,
present them to my Lord.

3 As I kneel before you,
and I see your smiling face,
ev'ry thought, ev'ry word
is lost in your embrace.

859A *Joanne Boyce & Mike Stanley*

1 Behold the Lamb of God.
Behold the body of my Lord.
Behold the greatest sacrifice made
for all time.
We come to be made new
to eat from the table of the Lord.
Only by grace is our worthiness restored
and we behold.

Behold the Lamb, behold the Lamb,
behold the Lamb of God.
Behold the Lamb, behold the Lamb
behold the Lamb of God.

2 Father, let your glory shine,
in this Eucharist: for us a sign
of heaven's mercy, poured out
in Jesus your Son.
Jesus, Saviour of the world,
by your dying you destroyed our death
by rising you have restored us to life
and we behold.

Jesus, body of my Lord
Jesus, Saviour of the world
Jesus, blood for us outpoured
Jesus, Saviour of the world.

860 *Owen Alstott, based on Luke 1: 68-79*

1 Blest be the Lord, the God of Israel,
who brings the dawn and darkest night
dispels,
who raises up a mighty saviour from
the earth,
of David's line, a son of royal birth.

2 The prophets tell a story just begun
of vanquished foe and glorious
vict'ry won,
of promise made to all who keep the law
as guide:
God's faithful love and mercy will abide.

3 This is the oath once sworn to Abraham:
all shall be free to dwell upon the land,
free now to praise, unharmed by the
oppressor's rod,
holy and righteous in the sight of God.

4 And you, my child, this day you shall
be called
the promised one, the prophet of
our God,
for you will go before the Lord to clear
the way,
and shepherd all into the light of day.

5 The tender love God promised from
our birth
is soon to dawn upon this shadowed
earth,
to shine on those whose sorrows seem to
never cease,
to guide our feet into the path of peace.

861 *Christopher Walker*

Lord, we share in this one true bread,
by this sign of love may our souls be fed,
Gift of your Son, making us one.

1 Lord, we bring you our doubt:
for not trusting you,
for not hearing you,
in your mercy forgive.
When we've gone astray
from your gentle way,
in your mercy forgive.

Lord, we share in this wine of grace,
in the sign of love may we see your face,
Gift of your Son, making us one.

2 Lord, we bring you our strength:
in the work we do,
may we follow you,
to the praise of your name.
Father, make me strong
though the work be long,
to the praise of your name.

3 Lord, we bring you our faith:
through the gift of prayer
may we learn to share
in the love you have giv'n;
make us steadfast,
'til we come at last
to your kingdom in heav'n.

Original refrain for use during the Preparation of the Gifts:

Bread we bring to the God of Love
as an offering at your table laid,
bread of the earth, work of our hands.

Wine we bring to the God of Love
as an offering at your table laid,
fruit of the vine, work of our hands.

862 *Jo Boyce and Mike Stanley*

Bread of Life,
Truth eternal,
broken now to set us free.
The risen Christ,
his saving power,
is here in bread and wine for me.

1 Lord, I know I am not worthy to receive
you.
You speak the words and I am healed.
Here at your table, love's mystery,
one bread, one cup, one family.

2 Lord, by your cross you reconciled us to
the Father.
We have only to believe.
Your sacrifice, our victory;
now by your blood we are redeemed.

3 Lord, you gave your people manna in
the desert;
still you fulfil our every need.
Lord when we hunger, Lord when
we thirst,
we come to you and we receive the
(*Bread…*)

863 *Janet Lunt*

Broken for me, broken for you,
the body of Jesus broken for you.

1 He offered His body, He poured out
His soul,
Jesus was broken that we might
be whole:
Broken for me…

2 Come to My table and with Me dine,
eat of My bread and drink of My wine:
Broken for me…

3 This is My body given for you,
eat it remembering I died for you:
Broken for me…

4 This is My blood I shed for you,
for your forgiveness, making you new:
Broken for me…

864 *Christopher Walker*

Children of God in one family,
loved by God in one family.
And no matter what we do
God loves me and God loves you.

1 Jesus teaches us to love.
Sometimes we get it wrong.
But God forgives us every time
for we belong to the…

2 Jesus wants us to forgive.
Sometimes we get it wrong.
But God forgives us every time
for we belong to the…

3 Jesus wants us to be kind.
Sometimes we get it wrong.
But God forgives us every time
for we belong to the…

4 Jesus wants us to be truthful.
Sometimes we get it wrong.
But God forgives us every time
for we belong to the…

5 Jesus wants us to be sorry.
Sometimes we get it wrong.
But God forgives us every time
for we belong to the…

865 *Mike Stanley*

*Come, let us go, up to the mountain of
the Lord,
to the temple of his Holy Spirit.
Come, let us go, up to the mountain of
the Lord,
and glorify his Holy Name.*

1 Through noise and confusion,
our witness shall be heard.
We raise our voices,
to proclaim your holy Word.

2 Heavenly Father,
Receive my brokeness.
Change me, re-arrange me,
Restore my worthiness.

3 With banners lifted
We approach His glorious throne.
By graces gifted,
His power shall be known.

4 Zion, holy mountain,
We turn our eyes to you,
Lead us ever closer
In spirit and in truth.

866 *Daniel L. Schutte*

*Come to the feast of heaven and earth!
Come to the table of plenty!
God will provide for all that we need,
here at the table of plenty.*

1 O come and sit at my table
where saints and sinners are friends.
I wait to welcome the lost and lonely
to share the cup of my love.

2 O come and eat without money;
come to drink without price.
My feast of gladness will feed your spirit
with faith and fullness of life.

3 My bread will ever sustain you
through days of sorrow and woe.
My wine will flow like a sea of gladness
to flood the depths of your soul.

4 Your friends will flower in fullness;
your homes will flourish in peace.
For I, the giver of home and harvest,
will send my rain on the soil.

867 *Brian Doerksen*

Faithful One so unchanging,
Ageless One you're my rock of peace.
Lord of all I depend on you,
I call out to You, again and again.
I call out to You, again and again.
You are my rock in times of trouble.
You lift me up when I fall down.
All through the storm Your love is
the anchor,
my hope is in You alone.

868 *Ian Smale*

Father God, I wonder how I managed
to exist without the knowledge
of Your parenthood and Your loving care.
But now I am Your son,
I am adopted in Your family,
and I can never be alone 'cause,
Father God, You're there beside me.
I will sing Your praises,
I will sing Your praises,
I will sing Your praises for ever more.

869 *Mike Stanley*

1 Father, I know that your love for me
knows no bounds.
When darkness has fallen your voice
from the heavens resounds;
saying "trust and believe,
come and walk on my road to its end."
Take me home Father, Spirit and Son,
my master and friend.

2 Spirit, I know that your truth
is spoken each day.
But power and greed change the creed
leaving truth to decay.
So let the heavens resound
with 'Hosannas' to you, Holy One,
For in you, Father, Spirit and Son
the battle is won.

3 Jesus, I know that your love
for me has no end.
My faith growing stronger each day
that on you I depend.
When my doubting subsides,
when I'm finally brought to my knees;
Through my prayers, Father, Spirit
and Son
Your grace is revealed.

870 *Christine McCann*

1 Gifts of bread and wine, gifts we've
offered,
fruits of labour, fruits of love,
taken, offered, sanctified,
blessed and broken; words of one
who died.
Take my body, take my saving blood.
Gifts of bread and wine: Christ our Lord.

2 Christ our Saviour, living presence here,
as he promised while on earth:
I am with you for all time,
I am with you in this bread and wine.
Take my body, take my saving blood.
Gifts of bread and wine: Christ our Lord.

3 Through the Father, with the Spirit,
one in union with the Son,
for God's people, joined in prayer
faith is strengthened by the food
we share.
Take my body, take my saving blood.
Gifts of bread and wine: Christ our Lord.

871 *John L. Bell*

God to enfold you, Christ to uphold you,
Spirit to keep you in heaven's sight;
so may God grace you, heal and
embrace you,
lead you through darkness into the light.

872 *William Arms Fisher*

1 Going home, going home,
I'm a-going home.
Quiet like, some still day,
I'm just going home.
It's not far, just close by,
through an open door.
Work all done, care laid by,
going to fear no more.
Mother's there expecting me,
father's waiting too.
Lots of folk gathered there,
all the friends I knew,
all the friends I knew.

2 Morning star lights the way,
restless dreams all done.
Shadows gone, break of day,
real life just begun.
There's no break, there's no end,
just a living on,
wide awake with a smile,
going on and on.
Going home, going home,
I'm just going home.
It's not far, just close by,
through an open door.
I'm just going home.

Traditional Spiritual

873 *Chris Bowater*

1 Holy Spirit, we welcome You,
Holy Spirit, we welcome You!
Move among us with holy fire
as we lay aside all earthly desire,
hands reach out and our hearts aspire.
Holy Spirit, Holy Spirit,
Holy Spirit, we welcome You!

2 Holy Spirit, we welcome You,
Holy Spirit, we welcome You!
Let the breeze of Your presence blow
that Your children here might truly know
how to move in the Spirit's flow.
Holy Spirit, Holy Spirit,
Holy Spirit, we welcome You!

3 Holy Spirit, we welcome You,
Holy Spirit, we welcome You!
Please accomplish in us today
some new work of loving grace, we pray
– unreservedly – have Your way.
Holy Spirit, Holy Spirit,
Holy Spirit, we welcome You!

874 *William Young Fullerton (1857-1932)*

1 I cannot tell why He, whom angels
worship,
should set His love upon the sons of men,
or why, as Shepherd, He should seek
the wanderers,
to bring them back, they know not how
or when.
But this I know, that He was born of
Mary
when Bethl'em's manger was His
only home,
and that He lived at Nazareth
and laboured,
and so the Saviour, Saviour of the world,
is come.

2 I cannot tell how silently He suffered,
as with His peace He graced this place
of tears,
or how His heart upon the cross
was broken,
the crown of pain to three and
thirty years.
But this I know, He heals the
broken-hearted,
and stays our sin, and calms our
lurking fear,
and lifts the burden from the heavy laden,
for yet the Saviour, Saviour of the world,
is here.

3 I cannot tell how He will win the nations,
how He will claim His earthly heritage,
how satisfy the needs and aspirations,
of east and west, of sinner and of sage.
But this I know, all flesh shall see
His Glory,
and He shall reap the harvest He
has sown,
and some glad day His sun shall shine
in splendour,
when He the Saviour, Saviour of the
world, is known.

4 I cannot tell how all the lands shall
worship,
when, at His bidding, every storm is
stilled,
or who can say how great the jubilation
when all the hearts of men with love
are filled.
But this I know, the skies will fill with
rapture,
and myriad, myriad human voices sing,
and earth to heaven, and heaven to earth,
will answer:
At last the Saviour, Saviour of the world,
is King!

875 *Stephen Dean*

I know that my Redeemer lives
and on the last day I will rise again;
I know that my Redeemer lives
and on the last day I will rise again.

1 With my own eyes I shall gaze on my God,
face to face.
It is my Saviour who calls me:
I trust in his grace.

I know that my Redeemer lives
and on the last day I will rise again;
I know that my Redeemer lives
and on the last day I will rise again.

2 And this one hope I will cherish,
this promise he gives:
that though this body will perish,
in Christ I will live.

3 And nothing evil can touch us,
no danger befall;
God watches over his people,
and answers their call.

4 And though we go into darkness,
all hidden from sight,
God's arms are open to welcome
and lead us to light.

876 *Ernest Sands*

I will call upon the Lord and bless
his name
for he is good and forgiving.
He is for us a merciful God
and his tender love lasts from age to age.

1 In you, O Lord, I take refuge,
let me never be put to shame.
In your justice rescue me, free me;
pay heed to me and save me.

2 O Lord, hear my voice when I call.
Have mercy on me and answer.
Do not send me away in anger
for you are the God of my help.

3 I am sure I shall see the Lord's goodness
which he promised to us from of old.
Hope in him, hold firm and take heart,
place all your trust in the Lord.

877 *Michael O'Shields*

I will call upon the Lord,
who is worthy to be praised.
So shall I be saved from mine enemies.
The Lord liveth,
and blessed be my Rock
and may the God of my salvation
be exalted.

878 *Traditional, Spanish. Translated by Deborah L. Schmitz*

1 If we are living, we are in the Lord,
and if we die, we are in the Lord,
for if we live or if we die
we belong to God, we belong to God.

2 Throughout our lives we have fruit
to bear.
All of our good works are for us
to share.
Whether we give, or we receive
we belong to God, we belong to God.

3 When there is sadness, when there is pain,
in Christ the Lord, we have love to gain.
Whether we suffer, or we rejoice,
we belong to God, we belong to God.

4 And in this world we will always find
those who are weeping, sick in heart
and mind.
They need our help, they need our care.
We belong to God, we belong to God.

879 *Stephen Dean*

1 In God's good time our eyes will open,
we'll see great signs and marvels,
and know the day has come;
Yes, in God's good time we will hear
glad music,
and angels and archangels will call
us home.
Who can tell when these wonders
will happen?
We know not the second, the minute,
the hour

but the day will come when our chains
will break
and our tears will dry away in God's
good time.

2 In God's good time the poor will prosper,
the hungry will be sated,
the sick will be made whole;
Yes, in God's good time things we dare
not dream of,
will fill our deepest longings of heart
and soul.
None can tell when such marvels will
happen;
it may be tomorrow, it may be today
but the day will come when the clouds
will burst;
and the night will turn to day in God's
good time.

3 In God's good time all war will vanish,
old hates will be forgotten,
old enemies forgive;
and all hearts will stir, and all swords
will shatter,
what's hidden will be open, what's dead
will live.
Come, Lord Jesus, and change us for
ever,
we're getting impatient, so hasten the day
when the world will sing and a great
hosanna
will arise from earth to heav'n in God's
good time.

880 *Stephen Dean*

1 Into the family of God we welcome
this child.
Into the family of God we welcome
this child.
Child of the promise, child of grace,
come to the Spirit's dwelling place,
come to Christ's own loving embrace,
come to the Lord.

2 Set on a journey of faith with the people
of God;
led into paths that the saints before you
have trod:
oil of rejoicing grace your head,
at the Lord's feast may you be fed
Christ's own life in wine and bread:
strength for the way.

* For children:

3 God who created us all,
we give thanks for this child;
Help us to cherish what Christ
by blood reconciled.
help us to teach what he has taught,
train for the fight which he has fought,
seek the life his victory bought,
teach us to strive.

4. Into the family of God we welcome
this child;
into the family of God we welcome
this child;
risen with Christ and dead to sin,
after new birth, new life begin,
Christ the Saviour welcomes you in,
come to the Lord!

* *For adult initiation:*

3 God who created us all,
we give thanks for this day.
Help us to cherish new friends
now sharing our way.
Help us to teach what Christ has taught,
strengthen the faith which they
have sought,
live the life Christ's victory bought,
teach us to strive.

4. Into the family of God we welcome
you now;
Into the family of God we welcome
you now;
risen with Christ and dead to sin,
after new birth, new life begin,
Christ the Saviour welcomes you in,
come to the Lord!

881 *Michael Frye*

1 Jesus, be the centre,
be my source,
be my light,
Jesus.

Be the fire in my heart,
be the wind in these sails;
be the reason that I live,
Jesus, Jesus.

2 Jesus, be the centre,
be my hope,
be my song,
Jesus.

3 Jesus, be my vision,
be my path,
be my guide,
Jesus.

4 Jesus, be the centre,
be my source,
be my light,
Jesus.

882 *John Barnett*

Jesus, Jesus
holy and anointed One, Jesus.
Jesus, Jesus
risen and exalted One, Jesus.
Your name is like honey on my lips,
Your Spirit like water to my soul.
Your word is a lamp unto my feet.
Jesus, I love You, I love You.
Jesus, Jesus
holy and anointed One, Jesus.
Jesus, Jesus
risen and exalted One, Jesus.

883 *Nadia Hearn*

Jesus, Name above all names,
beautiful Saviour, glorious Lord,
Emmanuel, God is with us,
blessed Redeemer, living Word.

884 *Graham Kendrick*

1 Jesus put this song into our hearts,
Jesus put this song into our hearts.
It's a song of joy no-one can take away
Jesus put this song into our hearts.

2 Jesus taught us how to live in harmony,
Jesus taught us how to live in harmony.
Different faces, different races, He made
us one,
Jesus taught us how to live in harmony.

3 Jesus taught us how to be a family,
Jesus taught us how to be a family.
Loving one another with the love that
He gives,
Jesus taught us how to be a family.

4 Jesus turned our sorrow into dancing,
Jesus turned our sorrow into dancing.
Changed our tears of sadness into rivers
of joy,
Jesus turned our sorrow into dancing.

885 *Christopher Walker*

Laudate, laudate Dominum,
omnes gentes, laudate Dominum.
Exultate, jubilate
per annos Domini, omnes gentes.
Laudate, laudate Dominum,
omnes gentes, laudate Dominum.
Exultate, jubilate
per annos Domini, omnes gentes.

1 In the faith of Christ we walk hand
in hand,
light before our path as the Lord has
planned;
shining the torch of faith in our land:
in the name of Christ Jesus.

2 In the name of Christ we will spread
the seed;
share the Word of God with those
in need,
faithful in thought and word and deed:
in the name of Christ Jesus.

3 In the power of Christ we proclaim
one Lord.

All who put on Christ are by faith restored;
sharing new life, salvation's reward.
in the name of Christ Jesus.

4 In the name of Christ, through the blood he shed,
we are justified and by him are fed,
nourished by word and living bread:
in the name of Christ Jesus.

5 In the Church of God we are unified,
by the Spirit's power we are sanctified,
temples of grace, where God may abide.
by the power of the Spirit.

6 Praise to God the Father while ages run.
Praise to Christ the Saviour, God's only Son,
praise to the Holy Spirit be sung:
omnes gentes, laudate.

Extra verses for ordination

1 In the Church we answer the Saviour's call,
serving, as he showed us, both great and small,
sharing the Lord's compassion for all:
in the name of Christ Jesus.

2 In the name of Christ we baptize and teach,
truth upon our lips in the way we preach,
raising the cup of blessing for each:
in the name of Christ Jesus.

886

S.S.Wesley.
Arranged by John Rombaut

Lead me Lord,
Lead me in your righteousness.
Make your way plain
Before my face.
Lead me Lord,
Lead me in your righteousness.
Make your way plain
Before my face.
For it is you, Lord,
You Lord only
That makest me dwell in
Safety.

887

Teresa Brown

Let us go forth in the
peace of Christ,
take his love to the
world outside.
Go forth in the
peace of Christ,
to love and to serve,
proclaim to the world
that Jesus Christ is
Lord.

1 For here in this holy place,
we all rejoice;
together now heaven and
earth share one voice.
With angels and saints,
and with all souls we sing
in praise of your glory
Christ Jesus our King.

2 O Lord God of power and
might, we now pray
that your Holy Spirit will
guide us today.
Come shine in our hearts
for all people to see
the hope of salvation
that sets us all free.

3 The harvest is plenty but
labourers are few;
if we remain silent then
who spreads Good News?
We pray for the courage to
speak out God's words,
with wisdom and strength
in the joy of the Lord.

4 So thanks be to God for this
grace we've received
in Word and in sacrament;
we have been healed,
and now in the pow'r
of the Spirit we go
to lighten the darkness
God's glory to show.

888 *John Watson*

1 Let Your living water flow over my soul.
Let Your Holy Spirit come and take control
of ev'ry situation that has troubled my mind.
All my cares and burdens on to You I roll.
Jesus, Jesus, Jesus.

2 Come now Holy Spirit and take control.
Hold me in Your loving arms and make me whole.
Wipe away all doubt and fear and take my pride.
Draw me to Your love and keep me by Your side.
Father, Father, Father.

3 Give your life to Jesus, let Him fill your soul.
Let Him take you in His arms and make you whole.
As you give your life to Him He'll set you free.
You will live and reign with Him eternally.
Spirit, Spirit, Spirit.

4 Let Your living water flow over my soul.
Let Your Holy Spirit come and take control
of ev'ry situation that has troubled my mind.
All my cares and burdens on to You I roll.
Jesus, Jesus, Jesus.

889 *David Haas*

1 Like a shepherd I will feed you;
I will gather you with care.
I will lead you and hold you
close to my heart.

We will run and not grow weary,
for our God will be our strength,
and we will fly like the eagle,
we will rise again.

2 I am strength to the weary;
to the weak I am new life.
Though the young may grow weary,
I will be their hope.

3 Lift up your eyes,
and see who made the stars.
I lead you and I know you,
I call you each by name.

4 Fear not, I am with you;
I am your God.
I will strengthen you, and help you;
uphold you with my hand.

Isaiah 40:11, 26, 29-30; Isaiah 41:10

890 *Aniceto Nazareth*

Listen, let your heart keep seeking;
listen to his constant speaking;
listen to the Spirit calling you.
Listen to his inspiration;
listen to his invitation;
listen to the Spirit calling you.

1 He's in the sound of the thunder,
in the whisper of the breeze.
He's in the might of the whirlwind,
in the roaring of the seas.

2 He's in the laughter of children,
in the patter of the rain.
Hear him in cries of the suff'ring,
in their moaning and their pain.

3 He's in the noise of the city,
in the singing of the birds.
And in the night-time the stillness
helps you listen to his word.

891 *Bernadette Farrell*

1 Longing for light, we wait in darkness.
Longing for truth, we turn to you.
Make us your own, your holy people,
light for the world to see.

Christ be our light! Shine in our hearts.
Shine through the darkness
Christ be our light!
Shine in your church gathered today.

2 Longing for peace, our world is troubled.
Longing for hope, many despair.
Your word alone has power to save us.
Make us your living voice.

3 Longing for food, many are hungry.
Longing for water, many still thirst.
Make us your bread, broken for others,
shared until all are fed.

4 Longing for shelter, many are homeless.
Longing for warmth, many are cold.
Make us your building, sheltering others,
walls made of living stone.

5 Many the gifts, many the people,
many the hearts that yearn to belong.
Let us be servants to one another,
helping your kingdom come.

892 *Chris Rolinson, Mike Stanley*

1 Lord of all creation,
Master of the sea.
Ruler of the universe,
Word of life to me,
Word of life to me.

Let us turn our eyes again
and focus on the One
Send your spirit Lord of love
Reveal to us Your Son,
Reveal to us Your Son.

2 Power in the heavens,
Mover through the deep,
God of all who walk this land,
Friend of all who sleep,
Friend of all who sleep.

3 Son of God and Son of Man,
The one who was to come,
Human and divine in one,
The Father's will was done,
The Father's will was done.

893 *Catherine Walker*

1 Lord of life, we come to you;
Lord of all, our Saviour be;
come to bless and to heal
with the light of your love.

2 Through the days of doubt and toil,
in our joy and in our pain,
guide our steps in your way,
make us one in your love.

894 *James Quinn*

1 May God the Father look on you
with love,
and call you to himself in bliss above.
May God the Son, good Shepherd of
his sheep,
stretch out his hand and waken you
from sleep.
May God the Spirit breathe on you
his peace,
where joys beyond all knowing
never cease.

2 May flights of angels lead you on
your way
to paradise, and heaven's eternal day!
May martyrs greet you after death's
dark night,
and bid you enter into Zion's light!
May choirs of angels sing you to
your rest,
with once poor Laz'rus, now for
ever blest.

In paradisum, tr. James Quinn, S.J.

895 *Darlene Zschech*

My Jesus, my Saviour,
Lord, there is none like You.
All of my days I want to praise
the wonders of Your mighty love.

My comfort, my shelter,
tower of refuge and strength,
let ev'ry breath, all that I am,
never cease to worship You.

Shout to the Lord all the earth
let us sing power and majesty,
praise to the King.
Mountains bow down
and the seas will roar
at the sound of Your name.

I sing for joy
at the work of Your hands.
Forever I'll love You,
forever I'll stand.
Nothing compares to the
promise I have in You.

Psalm 92:4; 98:4

896 *S. Adams*

1 Nearer my God to thee, Nearer to thee,
E'en though it be a cross that raiseth me:
Still all my song shall be nearer my God
to thee,
Nearer my God to thee, Nearer to thee.

2 Though like the wanderer, the sun
gone down,
Darkness be over me, my rest a stone:
Yet in my dreams I'd be nearer my God
to thee,
Nearer my God to thee, Nearer to thee.

3 There let the way appear steps unto
heav'n:
All that thou sendest me in mercy giv'n:
Angels to beckon me nearer my God
to thee,
Nearer my God to thee, Nearer to thee.

4 Deep in thy sacred heart let me abide,
Thou who hast come for me, suffered
and died.
Sweet shall my weeping be, grief surely
leading me,
Nearer my God to thee, Nearer to thee.

Arranger Rombaut for McCrimmons Publishing

897 *Ruth M. Duck*

1 Now let your servant go in peace;
for praise and blessing here increase;
for in our midst word is done
and you have sent your Promised One.

2 Before the peoples you prepare
your way of life which all may share,
your saving power now made known;
among the nations love is shown.

3 Child, you are chosen as a sign
to test the human heart and mind;
for secrets hiding in the night
shall be revealed in piercing light.

4 Now let us sing our Saviour's praise,
and tell God's goodness all our days,
while breath is ours, let praise be heard
for God's own faithful, saving word.

Luke 2:22-28;

898 *Bernadette Farrell from Psalm 139*

1 O God, you search me and you
know me.
All my thoughts lie open to your gaze.
When I walk or lie down you are
before me:
ever the maker and keeper of my days.

2 You know my resting and my rising.
You discern my purpose from afar,
and with love everlasting you
besiege me:
in ev'ry moment of life and death,
you are.

3 Before a word is on my tongue, Lord,
you have known its meaning through
and through.
You are with me, beyond my
understanding:
God of my present, my past and future,
too.

4 Although your Spirit is upon me,
still I search for shelter from your light.
There is nowhere on earth I can
escape you:
even the darkness is radiant in your sight.

5 For you created me and shaped me,
gave me life within my mother's womb.
For the wonder of who I am,
I praise you:
safe in your hands, all creation is
made new.

899 *John Wimber*

1 O let the Son of God enfold you
with His Spirit and His love,
let Him fill your heart and satisfy
your soul.
O let Him have the things that hold you,
and His Spirit like a dove
will descend upon your life and make
you whole.

Jesus, O Jesus, come and fill Your lambs.
Jesus, O Jesus, come and fill Your lambs.

2 O come and sing this song with gladness
As your hearts are filled with joy,
Lift your hands in sweet surrender to
His name.
O give Him all your tears and sadness,
Give Him all your years of pain,
And you'll enter into life in Jesus' name.

Jesus, O Jesus, come and fill Your lambs.
Jesus, O Jesus, come and fill Your lambs.

900 *Graham Kendrick*

O Lord, Your tenderness,
melting all my bitterness,
O Lord, I receive Your love.
O Lord, Your loveliness,
changing all my ugliness,
O Lord, I receive Your love.
O Lord, I receive Your love.
O Lord, I receive Your love.

901 *Sydney Carter*

1 One more step along the world I go,
one more step along the world I go,
from the old things to the new
keep me travelling along with You.

And it's from the old I travel to the new,
keep me travelling along with You.

2 Round the corner of the world I turn,
more and more about the world I learn.
All the new things that I see
you'll be looking at along with me.

And it's from the old I travel to the new,
keep me travelling along with You.

3 As I travel through the bad and good
keep me travelling the way I should.
Where I see no way to go
you'll be telling me the way, I know.

4 Give me courage when the world
is rough,
keep me loving though the world
is tough.
Leap and sing in all I do,
keep me travelling along with You.

5 You are older than the world can be,
You are younger than the life in me,
Ever old and ever new,
keep me travelling along with You.

902 *Gerrit Gustafson*

Only by grace can we enter,
Only by grace can we stand,
not by our human endeavour,
but by the blood of the lamb.

Into your presence you call us,
you call us to come.
Into your presence you draw us,
and now by your grace we come,
now by your grace we come.

Lord, if you mark our transgressions,
who would stand?
Thanks to your grace we are cleansed
by the blood of the lamb.
Lord, if you mark our transgressions,
who would stand?
Thanks to your grace we are cleansed
by the blood of the lamb.

903 *Brenton Brown*

1 Over all the earth, you reign on high,
every mountain stream, every sunset sky.
But my one request, Lord, my only aim
is that you'd reign in me again.

Lord, reign in me, reign in your power;
over all my dreams, in my darkest hour.
You are the Lord of all I am,
so won't you reign in me again.

2 Over every thought, over every word,
may my life reflect the beauty of
my Lord;
'cause you mean more to me than any
earthly thing.
So won't you reign in me again.

904 *Christopher Walker*

Prepare the way for the coming of God.
Make a straight path for the coming
of God.
Prepare the way for the coming of God.
Make a straight path for the coming
of God.

1 Ev'ry valley: fill it in.
Ev'ry mountain: make it small.
Ev'ry valley: fill it in.
Ev'ry mountain: make it small.

2 Crooked pathways: make them straight.
All the rough land: make it smooth.
Crooked pathways: make them straight.
All the rough land: make it smooth.

3 All will see: God's power strong.
God has promised: glory comes.
All will see: God's power strong.
God has promised: glory comes.

905 *Marty Haugen*

Return to God with all your heart,
the source of grace and mercy:
come, seek the tender faithfulness of God.

1 Now the time of grace has come,
the day of salvation:
come and learn now the way of our God.

2 I will take your heart of stone
and place a heart within you,
a heart of compassion and love.

3 If you break the chains of oppression,
if you set the pris'ner free;
if you share your bread with the hungry,
give protection to the lost;
give a shelter to the homeless,
clothe the naked in your midst,
then your light shall break forth like
the dawn.

Joel 2:12, Ezekiel 36:26; Isaiah 58:9-14

906 *Traditional arr. E.J. Hume*

Rise, and shine,
and give God his glory, glory.
Rise, and shine,
and give God his glory, glory.
Rise, and shine,
and give God his glory, glory,
children of the Lord.

1 The Lord said to Noah:
'There's gonna be a floody, floody.'
Lord said to Noah:
'There's gonna be a floody, floody.
Get those children
out of the muddy, muddy,
children of the Lord.'

2 The Lord told Noah
to build him an arky, arky,
The Lord told Noah
to build him an arky, arky,
Build it out of
gopher barky, barky,
children of the Lord.

3 The animals, the animals,
they came on, by twosies, twosies,
The animals, the animals,
they came on, by twosies, twosies,
Elephants and
kangaroosies, 'roosies,
children of the Lord.

4 It rained and poured
for forty daysies, daysies,
It rained and poured
for forty daysies, daysies,
Almost drove those
animals crazies, crazies,
children of the Lord.

5 The sun came out and
dried up the landy, landy,
The sun came out and
dried up the landy, landy,
Everything was
fine and dandy, dandy,
children of the Lord.

907 *Michael Perry,*

1 See Him lying on a bed of straw:
A draughty stable with an open door;
Mary cradling the babe she bore
The Prince of glory is His name.

O now carry me to Bethlehem
To see the Lord appear to men!
Just as poor as was the stable then,
The Prince of glory when He came.

2 Star of silver, sweep across the skies,
Show where Jesus in the manger lies;
Shepherds swiftly from your stupor rise
To see the Saviour of the World!

3 Angels, sing the song that you began,
Bring God's glory to the heart of man;
Sing that Beth'lem's little baby can
Be salvation to the soul.

4 Mine are riches, from Your poverty,
From Your innocence, eternity;
Mine forgiveness by Your death for me,
Child of sorrow for my joy.

908 *Bernadette Farrell*

1 Share the light of Jesus.
Share the light that shows the way.
Share the light of Jesus.
Share God's spirit today.
Share God's spirit today.

2 Share the word of Jesus.
Share the word that shows the way.
Share the word of Jesus.
Share God's spirit today.
Share God's spirit today.

3 Share the love of Jesus.
Share the love that shows the way.
Share the love of Jesus.
Share God's spirit today.
Share God's spirit today.

4 Share the smile of Jesus.
Share the smile that shows the way.
Share the smile of Jesus.
Share God's spirit today.
Share God's spirit today.

909 Bernadette Farrell

Spirit of God, rest on your people:
waken your song deep in our hearts.

1 Spirit of the quiet earth,
Spirit breathing hope to birth:
sustain in us
the fire of your love.

2 Spirit blowing through creation,
love that cannot be contained:
bring forth for us
the wonders you proclaim.

3 Song that echoes through our story,
music of our restless souls:
resound with joy
in those you call your own.

4 Spirit moving through our lives
work in our mem'ries
healing and restoring, teaching
and revealing.
strenghtening and bringing to life.

5 Spirit breaking through our selfhood,
Spirit tearing down our walls:
challenge and disturb us;
be the voice that questions and calls.

910 Graham Kendrick

1 Such love, pure as the whitest snow;
such love weeps for the shame I know;
such love, paying the debt I owe;
O Jesus, such love.

2 Such love, stilling my restlessness;
such love, filling my emptiness;
such love, showing me holiness;
O Jesus, such love.

3 Such love, springs from eternity;
such love, streaming through history;
such love, fountain of life to me;
O Jesus, such love.

911 Francesca Leftley

1 Take me, Lord,
use my life in the way you wish to do.
Fill me, Lord,
touch my heart till it always thinks of you.
Take me now,
as I am, this is all I can offer.
Here today I,
the clay, will be moulded by my Lord.

2 Lord, I pray
that each day I will listen to your will.
Many times
I have failed but I know you love me still.
Teach me now,
guide me, Lord, keep me close to you
always.
Here today
I, the clay, will be moulded by my Lord.

3 I am weak,
fill me now with your strength and set
me free.
Make me whole,
fashion me so that you will live in me.
Hold me now
in your hands, form me now with
your Spirit.
Here today
I, the clay, will be moulded by my Lord.

912 Marty Haugen

The heavens are telling the glory of God,
And all creation is shouting for joy.
Come, dance in the forest,
Come, play in the field,
And sing, sing the glory of the Lord.
Sing, sing the glory of the Lord.

1 Praise for the sun,
the bringer of day,
He carries the light of the
Lord in his rays;
The moon and the stars
who light up the way
Unto your throne.

2 Praise for the wind that
blows through the trees,
The seas mighty storms,
the gentlest breeze;
They blow where they will,
they blow where they please
To please the Lord.

3 Praise for the rain that
waters our fields,
And blesses our crops so
all the earth yields;
From death unto life
her myst'ry revealed
Springs forth in joy.

4 Praise for the fire who
gives us his light,
The warmth of the sun to
brighten our night;
He dances with joy,
his spirit so bright,
He sings of you.

5 Praise for the earth who
makes life to grow,
The creatures you made to
let your life show;
The flowers and the trees
that help us to know
The heart of love.

6 Praise for the death that
makes our life real,
The knowledge of loss that
helps us to feel;
The gift of yourself,
your presence revealed
To lead us home.

913 *Bro James Bain*

1 The Lord's my shepherd, I'll not want,
he makes me down to lie
in pastures green. He leadeth me
the quiet waters by.

2 My soul he doth restore again,
and me to walk doth make
within the paths of righteousness,
e'en for his own name's sake.

3 Yea, though I walk in death's dark vale,
yet will I fear none ill.
For thou art with me, and thy rod
and staff me comfort still.

4 My table thou hast furnished,
in presence of my foes
my head thou dost with oil anoint,
and my cup overflows.

5 Goodness and mercy all my life,
shall surely follow me.
And in God's house for evermore
my dwelling-place shall be.

914 *Damian Lundy*

1 The Spirit lives to set us free,
walk, walk in the light.
He binds us all in unity,
walk, walk in the light.

Walk in the light,
walk in the light,
walk in the light,
walk in the light of the Lord.

2 Jesus promised life to all,
walk, walk in the light.
The dead were wakened by his call,
walk, walk in the light.

3 He died in pain on Calvary,
walk, walk in the light.
To save the lost like you and me,
walk, walk in the light.

4 We know his death was not the end,
walk, walk in the light.
He gave his Spirit to be our friend,
walk, walk in the light.

5 By Jesus' love our wounds are healed,
walk, walk in the light.
The Father's kindness is revealed,
walk, walk in the light.

6 The Spirit lives in you and me,
walk, walk in the light.
His light will shine for all to see,
walk, walk in the light.

915 *Anne Quigley*

There is a longing in our hearts, O Lord,
for you to reveal yourself to us.
There is a longing in our hearts for love
we only find in you, our God.

1 For justice, for freedom,
for mercy: hear our prayer.
In sorrow, in grief: be near,
hear our prayer, O God.

2 For wisdom, for courage,
for comfort: hear our prayer.
In weakness, in fear: be near,
hear our prayer, O God.

3 For healing, for wholeness,
for new life: hear our prayer.
In sickness, in death: be near,
hear our prayer, O God.

4 Lord save us, take pity,
light in our darkness.
We call you, we wait: be near,
hear our prayer, O God.

916 *Bernadette Farrell*

1 We are young, we are old,
in your world our lives unfold.
All around us earth's abundance
brings more than our hands can hold.
Set us free. Make us see
what our stewardship must be:
all the gifts of your creation
shared out equally.

2 For the sake of the poor
Jesus came and gladly bore
condemnation and derision
from those who enshrined 'the law'.
He proclaimed endlessly
laws of love and jubilee,
breaking chains of debt and empire
setting nations free.

3 All the land, soil and seed,
can provide for ev'ry need,
yet God's children thirst and hunger,
divided by human greed.
Let the earth, sea and sky,
now reflect and glorify
God, whose tenderness and mercy
lift the lowly high.

4 Christ Jesus, yesterday
and tomorrow and today,
through all times and through all ages,
your word is our living way.
That the world be made new,
keep your gospel people true.
Let us once again with courage
rise and follow you!

Let the trumpet sound to announce
the year.
Let it tell God's people that their time
is here.
Like a living stream, let mercy flow.
Like a mountain high, let justice grow.
Let the reign of God from sea to sea
set captives free.
Cry 'Jubilee!'

917 *Paul Inwood*

1 We bring you this bread and wine,
a symbol of our hearts and minds:
our grains of thought can become
your life
if you will take them to yourself.

2 We bring you this bread and wine,
a symbol of our hearts and minds:
our grapes of love can become your truth
if you will take them to yourself.

3 In you we find our source of strength,
in you we see our path set forth;
we sense your power and your
loving care
in everything we come to share.

4 So we will thank you for these gifts,
and hold them dear as you hold us.
Your life and truth now make manifest
within our prayer of eucharist.

**Verse 3 may be omitted if desired.*

918 *Stephen Dean*

1 What shall we give to the child in
the manger?
What shall we give him that he
will enjoy?
Milk and wild honey for this
little stranger,
Food to give strength to a new little boy.

2 What shall we give to the first-born
of Mary;
Things that will nourish a new life
begun?
Fruits of the forest and figs from the
fig tree
Nurtured in soil and ripened by sun.

3 This Child must grow to inherit a
kingdom,
Blossom and ripen like fields of
good corn,
Bearing a seed that will fall and
lie buried,
Springing up new in the bright
Easter morn..

4 What shall we give to the child in
the manger?
What shall we give him that he will
enjoy?
Give of the best to the one who will
save us,
Food to give strength to this Man still
a boy.

919 *Christopher Walker*

1 When my mind is still and my heart
is open,
your word springs fresh to my ear,
and I hear your voice speaking softly,
softly,
purging all my fear;
and I hear you Lord, calling softly
over the noise of the crowd in the street
and I hold your word ever closer, closer
guiding my wayward feet.

2 When my heart is proud and I say I don't
need you,
your word cuts into my pride,
and I hear your voice speaking firmly,
firmly,
taking me to your side;
and I hear you Lord, calling softly
over the noise of the crowd in the street
and I hold your word ever closer, closer
guiding my wayward feet.

3 When the daylight dies and I look
for slumber,
your word is there with me still,
and I hear your voice speaking gently,
gently,
keeping me from ill;
and I hear you Lord, calling softly
over the noise of the crowd in the street
and I hold your word ever closer, closer
guiding my wayward feet.

4 Your word is truth, your word is living,
it fills my mind with its light,
and the word is "love" falling softly,
softly,
leading me from the night;
and I hear you Lord, calling softly
over the noise of the crowd in the street
and I hold your word ever closer, closer
guiding my wayward feet.

920 Kyrie Eleison I

Jacques Berthier

REFRAIN
All

Ky - ri - e, Ky - ri - e, e - le - i - son.
(Chri - ste, Chri - ste, e - le - i - son.)

921 Jesus Lord have mercy on us

Bill Tamblyn

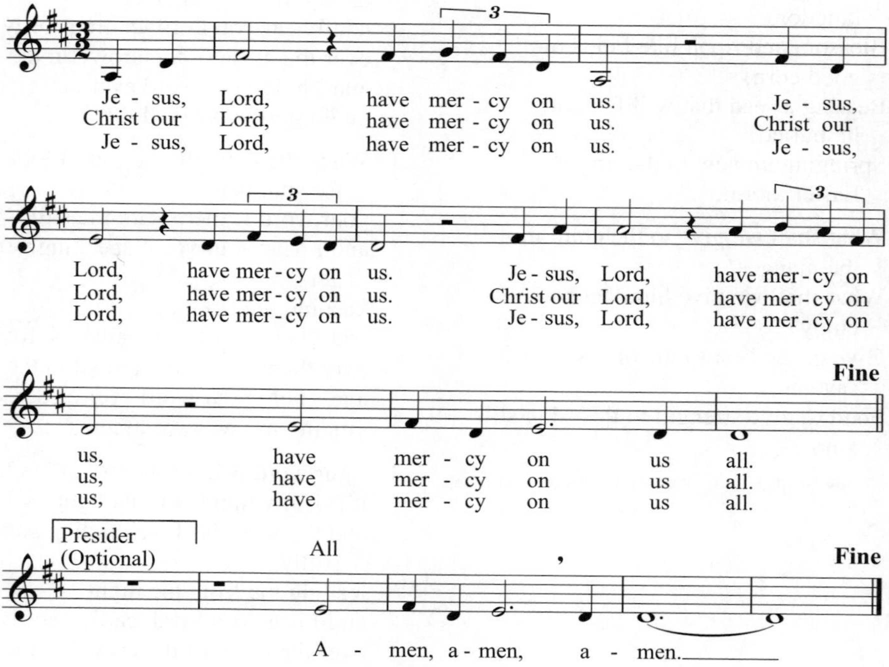

Je - sus, Lord, have mer - cy on us. Je - sus, Lord, have mer - cy on us. Je - sus, Lord, have mer - cy on us, have mer - cy on us all.
Christ our Lord, have mer - cy on us. Christ our Lord, have mer - cy on us. Christ our Lord, have mer - cy on us, have mer - cy on us all.
Je - sus, Lord, have mer - cy on us. Je - sus, Lord, have mer - cy on us. Je - sus, Lord, have mer - cy on us, have mer - cy on us all.

Fine

Presider (Optional)

All

A - men, a - men, a - men.

Fine

922 Penitential Paraphrase

Christopher Walker

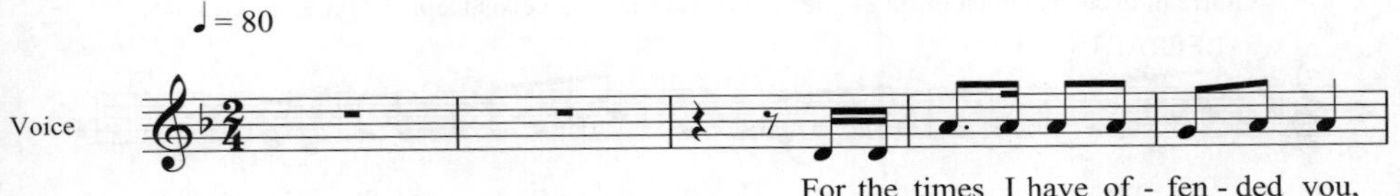
♩ = 80
Voice
For the times I have of - fen - ded you,

Lord have mer - cy. For the times I have not fol - lowed you, Lord, have mer - cy.
A - men. A - men.

For the people I have hurt this day, Christ have mercy.
When I shut my ears to what you say, Christ have mercy.

For the things I have failed to do, Lord have mercy.
For the things I've done in hurting you, Lord have mercy.

May almighty God forgive our sins, Amen,
and bring us to eternal life, Amen.

923 Kyrie Eleison

Anon Russian

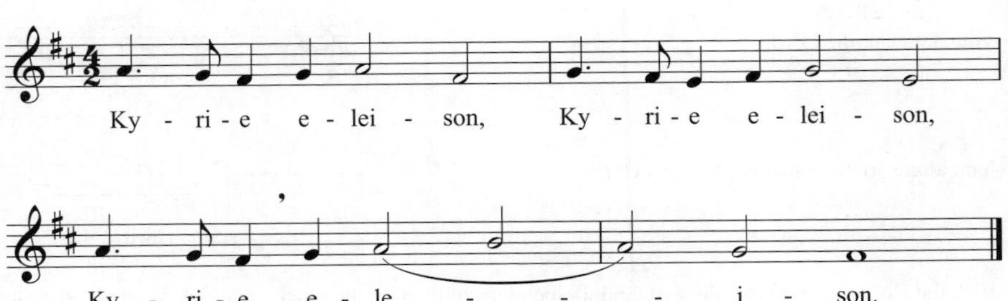
Ky - ri - e e - lei - son, Ky - ri - e e - lei - son,
Ky - ri - e e - le - - - i - son.

924 Millennium Gloria

Paul Inwood

Choir/cantor
Gloria in excelsis Deo, Gloria et interra pax; Gloria in excelsis Deo, Gloria et in terra pax.

REFRAIN: (All)

Glo - ri - a___ in ex - cel - sis___ De - o, Glo - ri - a,___ et in ter - ra pax;
Glo - ri - a___ in ex - cel - sis___ De - o, Glo - ri - a___ et in ter - ra pax.

Choir/cantor
Lord God, heavenly King, almighty God and Father,
we worship you, we give you thanks, we praise you for your glory! Refrain: (All)

Choir/cantor
Lord Jesus Christ, Lord Jesus Christ, only Son of the Father,
Lord God, Lord God, Lamb of God. Refrain: (All)

Choir/cantor
You take away the sin of the world: have mercy on us,

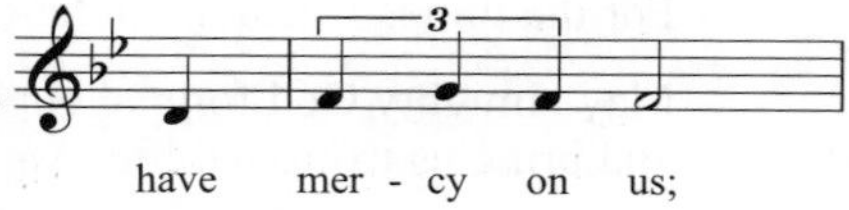

have mer - cy on us;

You are seated at the right hand of the Father:
receive our prayer,

re - ceive___ our prayer;

For you alone are the Holy One,

Ho - ly One,

you alone are the Lord,

Lord,___

You alone are the Most High, Jesus Christ,

Je - sus Christ,

with the Holy Spirit, in the glory of God, in the glory of God, in the glory of God the Father. Refrain: (All)

Cantor/choir:
All:
A - men, A - men, A - men, A - men,

925 Glory to God

Anne Ward

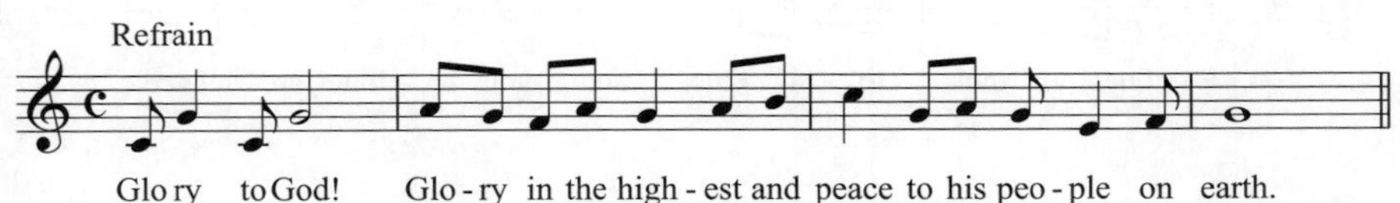
Refrain
Glo ry to God! Glo - ry in the high - est and peace to his peo - ple on earth.

Glo - ry to God! Glo - ry in the high - est and peace to his peo - ple on earth.

Verse
1. Lord God, heav - en - ly King, al - migh - ty God_ and_ Fa - ther,

we wor - ship you, we give_ you thanks, we praise you for your glo - ry.

Refrain
to verses
Glo - ry to God! Glo - ry in the high - est and peace to his peo - ple on earth.

Verse
2. Lord Je - sus Christ_ on - ly Son of the Fa - ther,_ Lord God Lamb_ of_

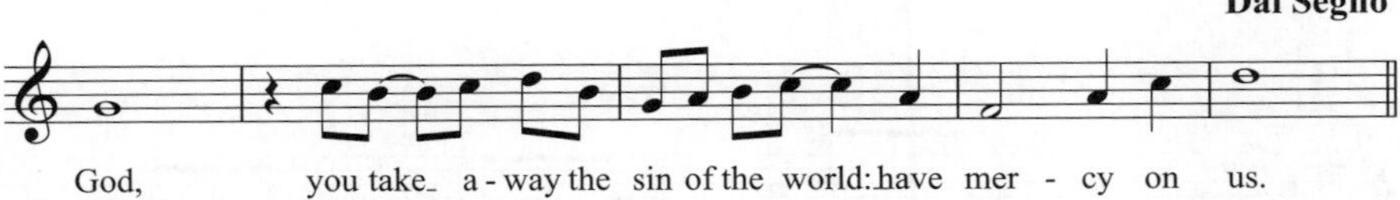
Dal Segno
God, you take_ a - way the sin of the world: have mer - cy on us.

Verse
3. You are seat - ed at the right hand of the Fa - ther: re - ceive_ our_ prayer.

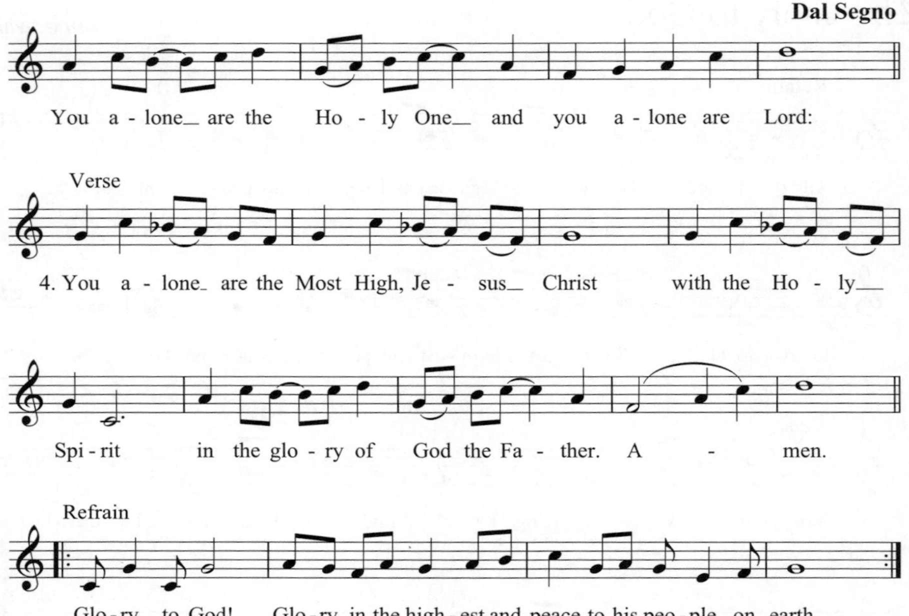
Dal Segno
You a - lone_ are the Ho - ly One_ and you a - lone are Lord:
Verse
4. You a - lone_ are the Most High, Je - sus_ Christ with the Ho - ly_
Spi - rit in the glo - ry of God the Fa - ther. A - men.
Refrain
Glo - ry to God! Glo - ry in the high - est and peace to his peo - ple on earth._

926 Gloria III

Jacques Berthier

This setting may be sung as a canon with the entries as indicated.

1
2
Glo - ri - a, glo - ri - a, in ex - cel - sis De - o!
3
4
Glo - ri - a, glo - ri - a, al - le - lu - ia, al - le - lu - ia!

927 Shrewsbury Gloria

Paul Inwood

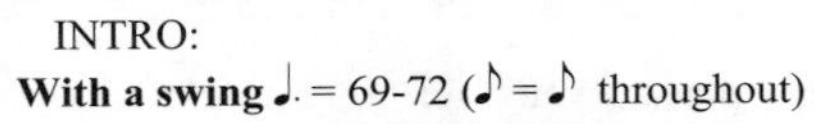
INTRO:
With a swing ♩. = 69-72 (♪♪ = ♪ throughout)

Cantor/choir
Glo - ry, glo - ry to God, glo - ry to God in the high - est;

Glo - ry, glo - ry to God, glo - ry to God in the high - est; and

peace to his peo - ple on earth, and peace to his peo - ple on earth.

A All
Glo - ry, glo - ry to God, glo - ry to God in the high - est;

B
Glo - ry, glo - ry to God, glo - ry to God in the high - est.

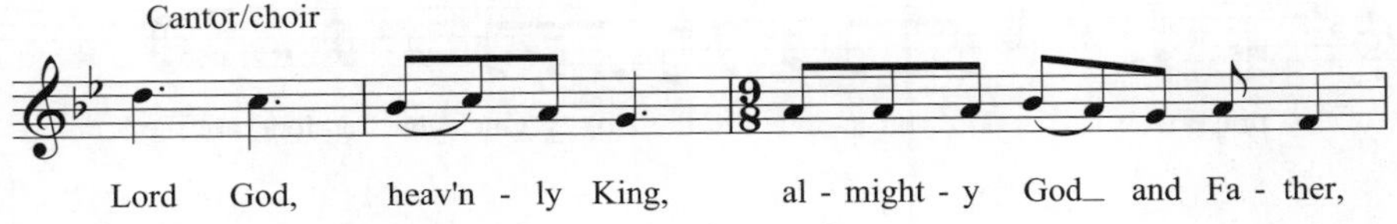
Cantor/choir
Lord God, heav'n - ly King, al - might - y God_ and Fa - ther,

al - might - y God_ and Fa - ther, we wor - ship you, we give you thanks, we

praise you for your glo - ry, we praise you for your glo - ry.

Repeat A to B
Cantor/choir
Lord Je - sus Christ, Lord Je - sus Christ,

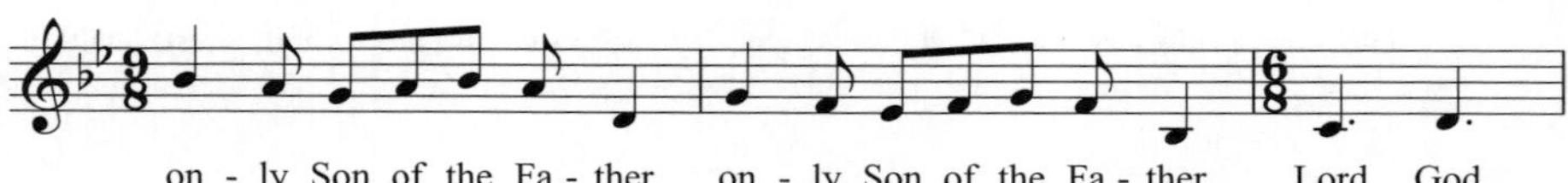
on - ly Son of the Fa - ther, on - ly Son of the Fa - ther, Lord God,

a little slower
Lamb of God, you take a-way the sin of the world: have mer - cy, mer - cy on

us; you are seat - ed at the right hand of the Fa - ther: re - ceive, re-ceive our

Repeat A to B
Cantor/choir
prayer. For you a - lone are the Ho - ly One, you a - lone are the Lord,

you a - lone are the Most High, Je - sus Christ, with the Ho - ly

to C
Spi - rit, in the glo - ry of God the Fa - ther.
C All
Glo - ry, glo - ry to God, glo - ry to God in the high - est;
rit.
Glo - ry, glo - ry to God, glo - ry to God in the high - est.
English text ©1970, International Consultation on English texts (ICET)
Music © 1985, Paul Inwood. All rights reserved. Reproduced by permission of Magnificat Music
928 Gospel Greeting
Bernadette Farrell
REFRAIN: 1st time: Cantor/Choir; each time thereafter: All
Al - le - lu - ia! Your words, O Lord, are spi - rit and life.
to verses
Al - le lu - ia! O - pen our hearts to your word.
VERSES: Cantor/Choir
(Advent) 1. Pre - pare a way for the Lord. Make God's
(Christmas) 2. To - day a Sa - viour is born who is
(Easter) 3. Re - joice and sing, all the earth, for the
path - way straight, and all the earth shall
Christ the Lord. God's Word is with us and
night is gone! Our God has raised us
D.S.
see the sav - ing love of God.
lives a - mong us with - in our world.
up from death in Christ Je - sus the Son.

929 Millennium Alleluia

Paul Inwood

REFRAIN:
Al - le - lu - ia, al - le - lu - ia, al - le - lu - ia, al - le - lu - ia.
to verses
Final
Al - le - lu - ia, al - le - lu - ia, al - le - lu - ia! ia!
VERSES:
D.C.
1. O - pen our hearts, o - pen our hearts so that we may hear the words of your Son.

Alleluia, alleluia, alleluia.
Alleluia, alleluia, alleluia!

1 Open our hearts, open our hearts
so that we may hear the words of your Son.

2 Come to us, Lord; do not delay!
for your people long to greet you with joy.

3 This is the day, made by the Lord:
all the nations rejoice and are glad.

4 I know my sheep; my sheep know me
and they follow me to life without end.

5 Blessed are you, you who are poor,
for the kingdom of heaven is yours!

6 I am the light, the light of the world
giving life to all who walk in my light.

7 You do not know the day or the hour:
stay awake and stand ready for me.

8 Come, Holy Spirit, kindle our hearts
and renew in us the fire of your love.

930 Song of Welcome for the Word

Christopher Walker

Joyfully ♩. = 60
(Flute)
Leader/All
All
L/A
1. Sing prais - es to the Lord, Al - le - lu - ia, Sing
All
L/A
praise to greet his word: Al - le - lu - ia. His word is a sign of his
All
wis - dom and love: Al - le - lu - ia, Al - le - lu - ia.

1 Sing praises to the Lord, Alleluia,
Sing praise to greet the word: Alleluia.
The word is a sign of God's
wisdom and love:
Alleluia, Alleluia.

2 God's truth can set us free: Alleluia,
Christ Jesus is the key, Alleluia.
Our ears hear the word but it
lives in our hearts:
Alleluia, Alleluia.

3 We listen for your voice, Alleluia,
We praise you and rejoice, Alleluia.
Your Spirit is with us,
She breathes in your word:
Alleluia, Alleluia.

4 Sing praises to the Lord, Alleluia,
Sing praise to greet the word: Alleluia.
Creator and Son with the
Spirit be adored:
Alleluia, Alleluia.

931 Alleluia Gaudete

Christopher Walker

Cantor/Choir
All
Al - le - lu - ia, al - le - lu - ia, Al - le - lu - ia, al - le - lu - ia,
Cantor
All
Al - le - lu - ia, al - le - lu - ia, Al - le - lu - ia,
Cantor/Choir
al - le - lu - ia, Al - le - lu - ia, al - le - lu - ia,
Descant
Al - le - lu - ia, Al - le, al - le - lu - ia,
All
Al - le - lu - ia, al - le - lu - ia,
Cantor/Choir
Verses
If anyone loves me he will keep my word.
I bring you news of great joy:
May the peace of Christ reign in your hearts;
Go, make dis - ciples of the nations;
Speak, Lord, your servant is listening;
Your word is truth, O Lord;
Open our heart, O Lord;
And my father will love him, and we shall come to him.
today a Saviour has been born to us, Christ the Lord.
let the message of Christ find a home with you.
I am with you always, yes, to the end of time.
you have the message of e - ter - nal life.
consecrate us in the truth.
to accept the words of your Son.

932 Halle, Halle, Halle

Trad. Caribbean
arr. John Bell

lively tempo
G D G D Em C Am7
Hal - le, hal - le, hal - le - lu - jah! Hal - le, hal - le, hal - le -
D7 G D G D Em
lu - jah! Hal - le, hal - le, hal - le - lu - jah! Hal - le -
Am G/D D7 G G
1. Final
lu - jah! Hal - le - lu - jah! jah!

933 Alleluia the Christ

Peter Jones

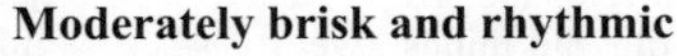
Moderately brisk and rhythmic

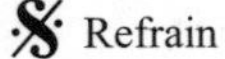
Refrain

mf
Al - le - lu - ia, Al - le - lu - ia! Al - le - lu - ia, Al - le - lu - ia! Al-

le - lu - ia, Al - le - lu - ia! Al - le - lu - ia, Al - le - lu - ia!

1. Here in our midst the Word of God; Je - sus the Christ, the
2. Here in our midst the Son of God; Je - sus the Christ, the

D.S.

Way of Life; Al - le - lu - ia! Al - le - lu - ia!
Truth of Life; Al - le - lu - ia! Al - le - lu - ia!

934 We believe in God the Father

Christopher Walker

REFRAIN

We be - lieve in God the Fa - ther, we be - lieve in God the Son,

we be - lieve in God the Spi - rit; God is three,

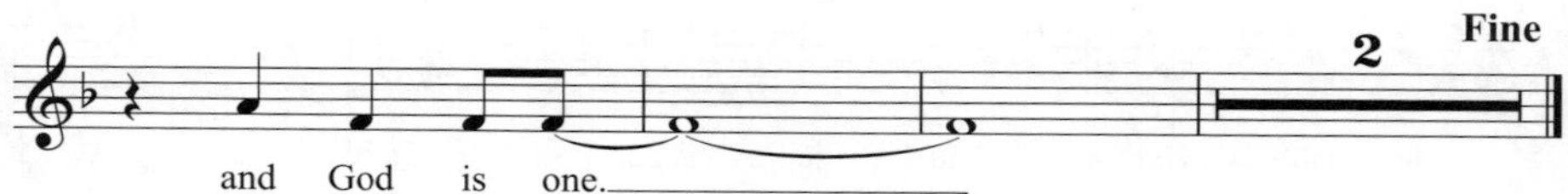
and God is one.
2
Fine

VERSES

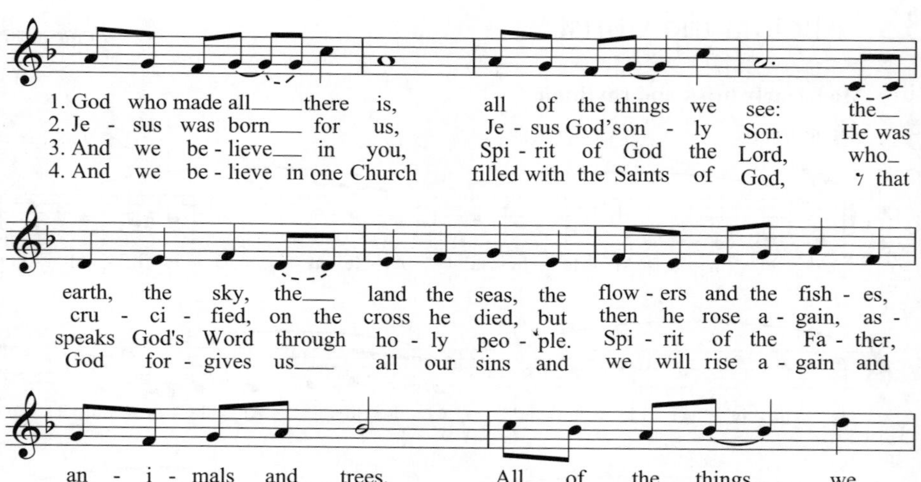
1. God who made all there is, all of the things we see: the earth, the sky, the land the seas, the flow - ers and the fish - es, an - i - mals and trees. All of the things we
2. Je - sus was born for us, Je - sus God's on - ly Son. He was cru - ci - fied, on the cross he died, but then he rose a - gain, as - cend - ed in - to heav'n. Je - sus God's on - ly
3. And we be - lieve in you, Spi - rit of God the Lord, who speaks God's Word through ho - ly peo - ple. Spi - rit of the Fa - ther, Spi - rit of the Son, Spi - rit of God the
4. And we be - lieve in one Church filled with the Saints of God, that God for - gives us all our sins and we will rise a - gain and live for e - ver - more. God, we be - lieve in

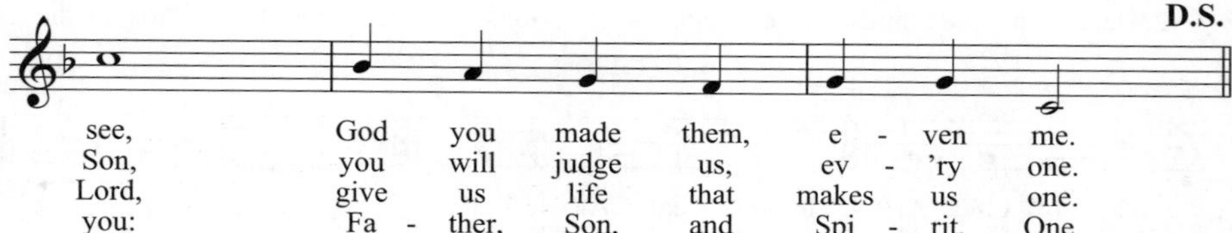
D.S.
see, God you made them, e - ven me.
Son, you will judge us, ev - 'ry one.
Lord, give us life that makes us one.
you: Fa - ther, Son, and Spi - rit, One.

935 Hear our prayer

Ernest Sands

REFRAIN: 1st time: Cantor; 2nd time: All
♩ = 63
mp
Hear our pray'r, an - swer in our need, let our cry come un - to you!
INTERCESSIONS: Choir
Hmm
Hmm
FINAL REFRAIN: All
Hear our pray'r, an - swer in our need, let our cry come un - to you!

Millennium Mass

936 Sanctus

Paul Inwood

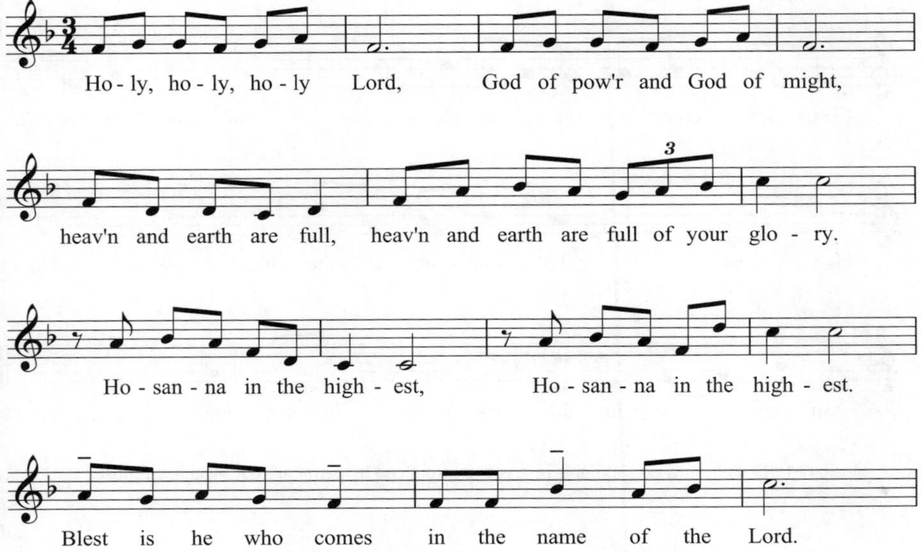
Ho - ly, ho - ly, ho - ly Lord, God of pow'r and God of might,
heav'n and earth are full, heav'n and earth are full of your glo - ry.
3
Ho - san - na in the high - est, Ho - san - na in the high - est.
Blest is he who comes in the name of the Lord.

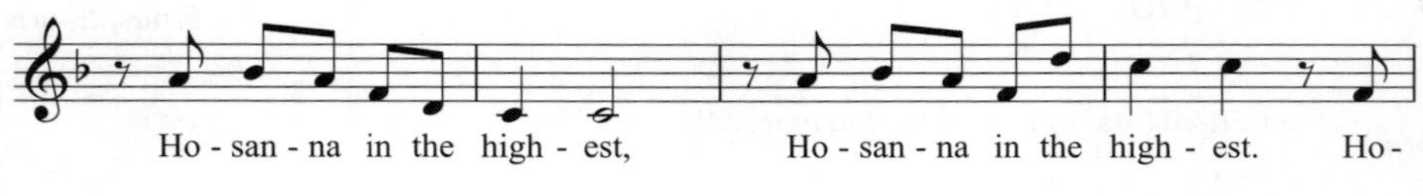
Ho - san - na in the high - est,
Ho - san - na in the high - est.
Ho-

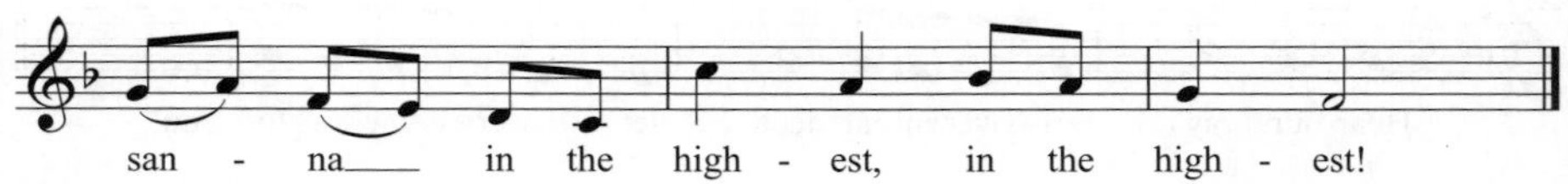
san - na___ in the high - est, in the high - est!

Millennium Mass

937 Memorial Acclamation A

Paul Inwood

PRESIDER/DEACON/CANTOR: (INTRO)

Let us proclaim the myster- y of faith: Christ has died Christ is

ri - sen, Christ has died,_ Christ is ri - sen, Christ will come a - gain,

Christ will come a - gain_ in glo - ry. Ho - san - na in the

high - est, ho - san - na in the high - est, Ho -

san - na - in the high - est in the high - est.

Memorial Acclamation B

Paul Inwood

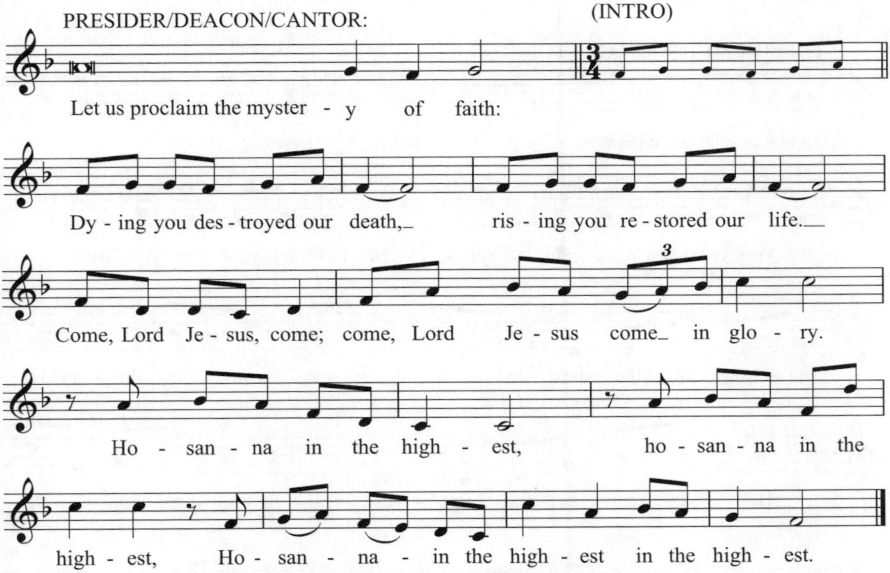

PRESIDER/DEACON/CANTOR: (INTRO)

Let us proclaim the myster - y of faith:

Dy - ing you des - troyed our death,_ ris - ing you re - stored our life._

Come, Lord Je - sus, come; come, Lord Je - sus come_ in glo - ry.

Ho - san - na in the high - est, ho - san - na in the

high - est, Ho - san - na - in the high - est in the high - est.

Memorial Acclamation C

Paul Inwood

PRESIDER/DEACON/CANTOR: (INTRO)

Let us proclaim the myster - y of faith:
When we eat this liv - ing bread,_ when we drink this sav - ing cup,_
we pro - claim your death un - til you come_ in glo - ry.
Ho - san - na in the high - est, ho - san - na in the
high - est, Ho - san - na - in the high - est in the high - est.

Memorial Acclamation D

Paul Inwood

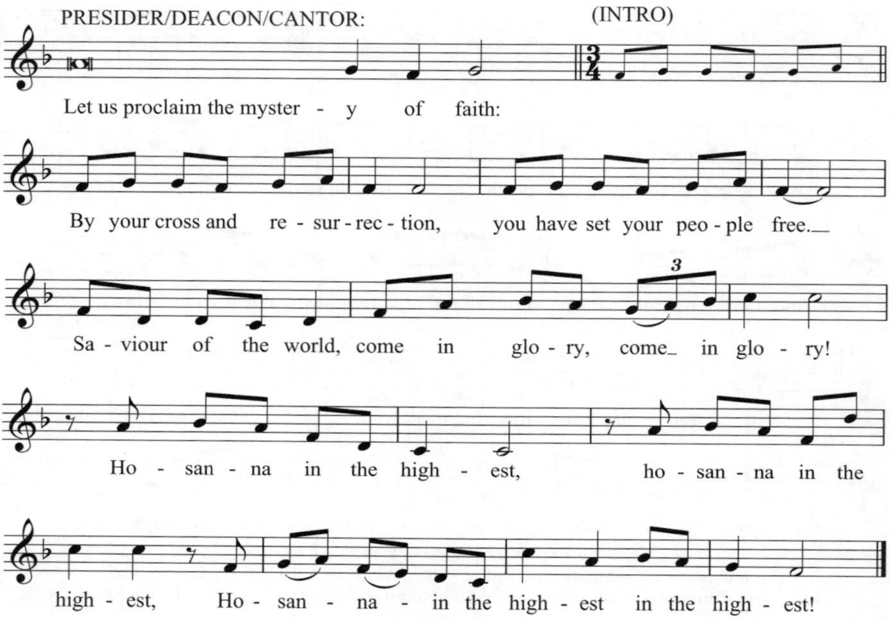

PRESIDER/DEACON/CANTOR: (INTRO)

Let us proclaim the myster - y of faith:

By your cross and re - sur - rec - tion, you have set your peo - ple free.

Sa - viour of the world, come in glo - ry, come in glo - ry!

Ho - san - na in the high - est, ho - san - na in the high - est, Ho - san - na - in the high - est in the high - est!

MILLENNIUM MASS

938 Amen

Paul Inwood

PRESIDER/DEACON/CANTOR:

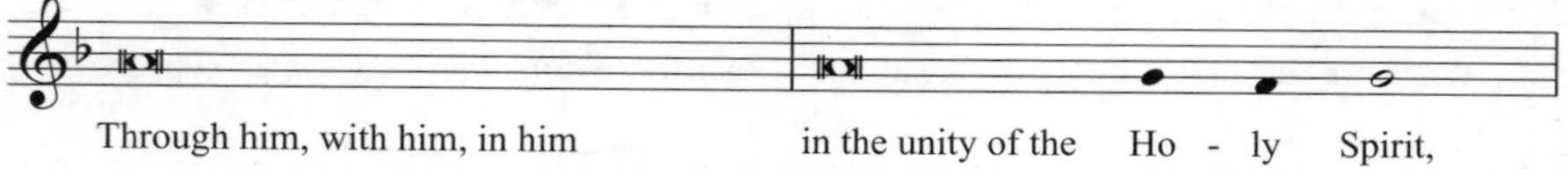
Through him, with him, in him
in the unity of the Ho - ly Spirit,

all glory and honour is yours al - might - y Father,
for e - ver and ever.

ALL:

A - men, A - men.

939 Holy Holy

Paul Inwood

Cantor(s)
All repeat
Ho - ly, ho - ly, ho - ly Lord, Ho - ly, ho - ly, ho - ly Lord,

Cantor(s)
All repeat
God of pow'r and God of might, God of pow'r and God of might,

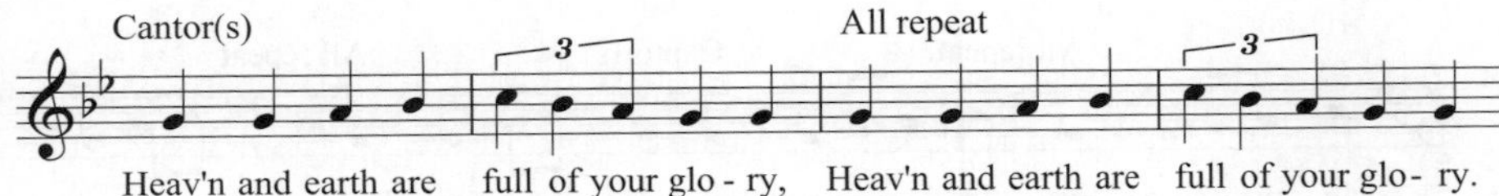
Cantor(s)
All repeat
3
Heav'n and earth are full of your glo - ry, Heav'n and earth are full of your glo - ry.

Cantor(s)
All repeat
Ho - san - na in the high - est, Ho - san - na in the high - est,

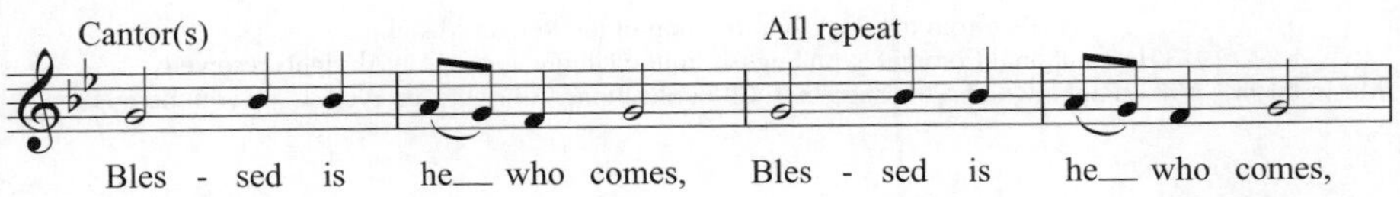
Cantor(s)
All repeat
Bles - sed is he__ who comes, Bles - sed is he__ who comes,

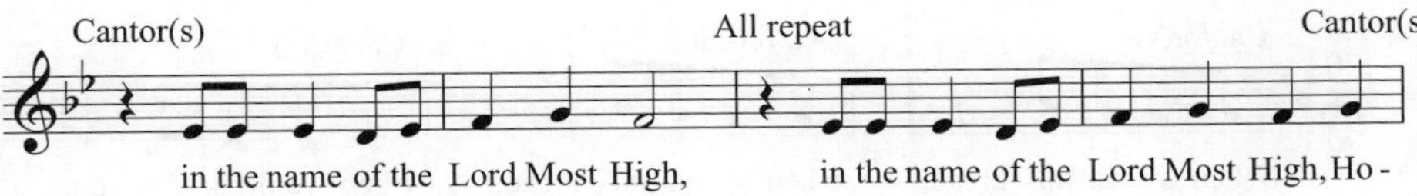
Cantor(s)
All repeat
Cantor(s)
in the name of the Lord Most High, in the name of the Lord Most High, Ho -

All repeat
Cantor(s)
All repeat
san - na, Ho - san - na, Ho - san - na, Ho - san - na,

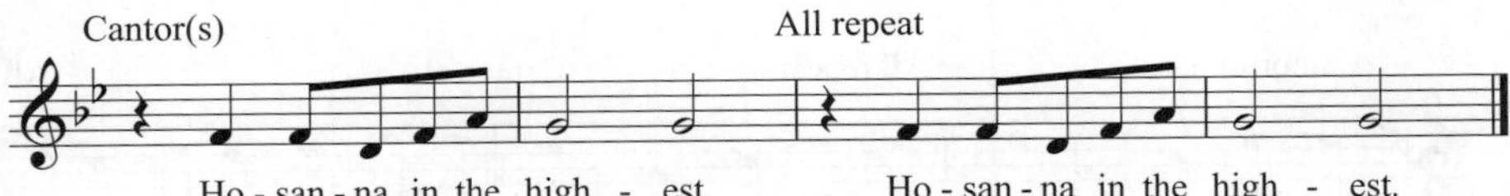
Cantor(s)
All repeat
Ho - san - na in the high - est, Ho - san - na in the high - est.

940 B Dying

Paul Inwood

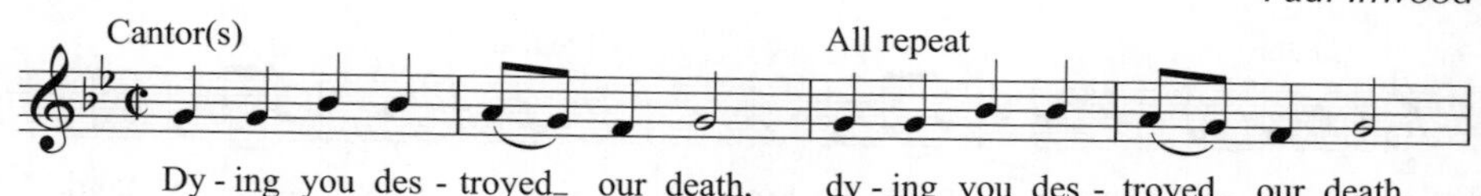
Cantor(s)
All repeat
Dy - ing you des - troyed_ our death, dy - ing you des - troyed_ our death,

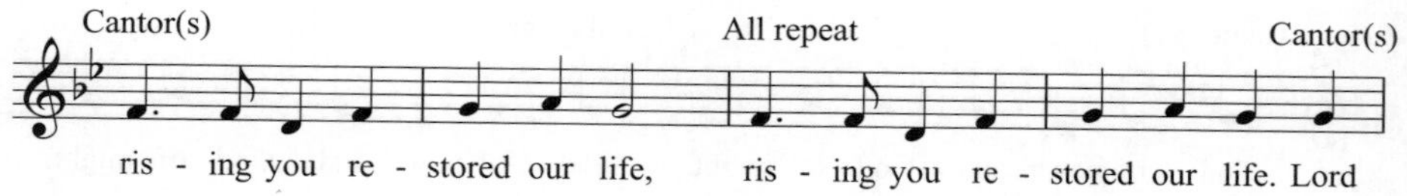
Cantor(s)
All repeat
Cantor(s)
ris - ing you re - stored our life, ris - ing you re - stored our life. Lord

All repeat
Cantor(s)
All repeat
Je - sus_ come, Lord Je - sus_ come, Lord Je - sus_ come, Lord Je - sus_ come,

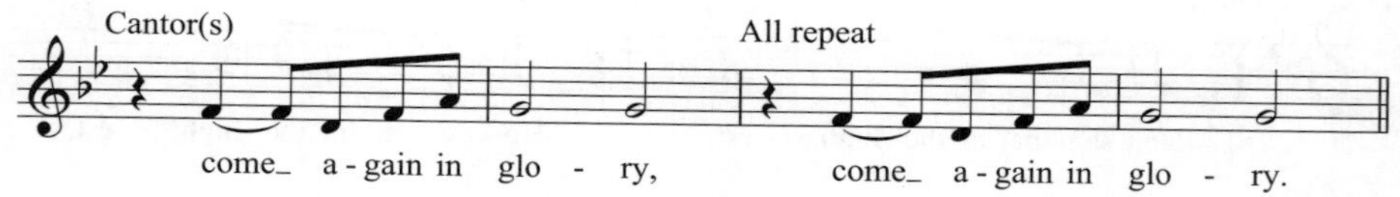
Cantor(s)
All repeat
come_ a - gain in glo - ry, come_ a - gain in glo - ry.

C When we eat

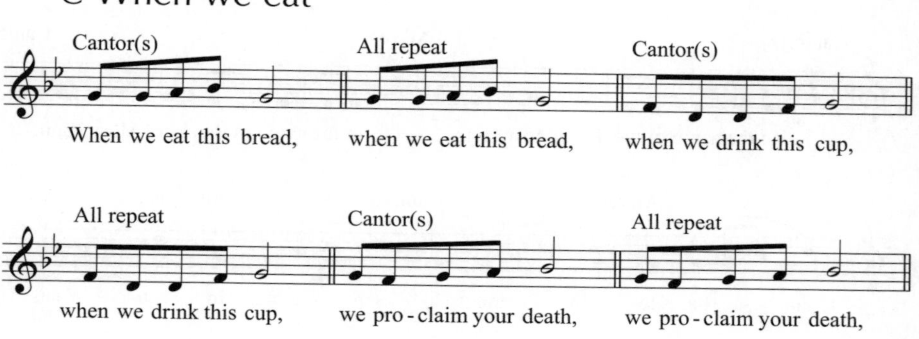
Cantor(s)
All repeat
Cantor(s)
When we eat this bread, when we eat this bread, when we drink this cup,
All repeat
Cantor(s)
All repeat
when we drink this cup, we pro - claim your death, we pro - claim your death,

Cantor(s)
All repeat
Cantor(s)
All
Lord, Je - sus Christ, Lord, Je - sus Christ, un - til you come in glo - ry, un-

repeat
Cantor(s)
All repeat
Cantor(s)
til you come in glo - ry, un - til you come in glo - ry, un - til you come in glo - ry, un-

All repeat
til you come in glo - ry, un - til you come in glo - ry,

Cantor(s)
All repeat
Lord, Je - sus Christ, Lord, Je - sus Christ.

941 Amen

Cantor(s)
All repeat
A - men, A - men, A - men, A - men,

942 Holy Holy

Christopher Walker

Cantor
All
Ho - ly, ho - ly, ho - ly Lord,
Ho - ly, ho - ly, ho - ly Lord,
God of pow - er, God of might,
God of pow - er, God of might.
Heav - en and earth are full of your glo - ry,
Heav - en and earth are full of your glo - ry.
Ho - san - na in the high - est,
Ho - san - na in the high - est,
Bles - sed, bles - sed is he,
Bles - sed, bles - sed is he,
he who comes in the Lord's name,
he who comes in the Lord's name,
Ho - san - na in the high - est,
Ho - san - na in the high - est,
Ho - san - na in the high - est,
Ho - san - na in the high - est,
Ho - san - na!
Ho - san - na!

GLASTONBURY ACCLAMATIONS

943 Christ has died

Christopher Walker

Cantor
All
Christ has died, Christ has died,
Cantor
All
Christ is ris - en, Christ is ris - en,
Cantor
All
Christ will come a - gain, Christ will come a - gain!

Text: English Translation from the Roman Missal

GLASTONBURY ACCLAMATIONS

944 Amen

Christopher Walker

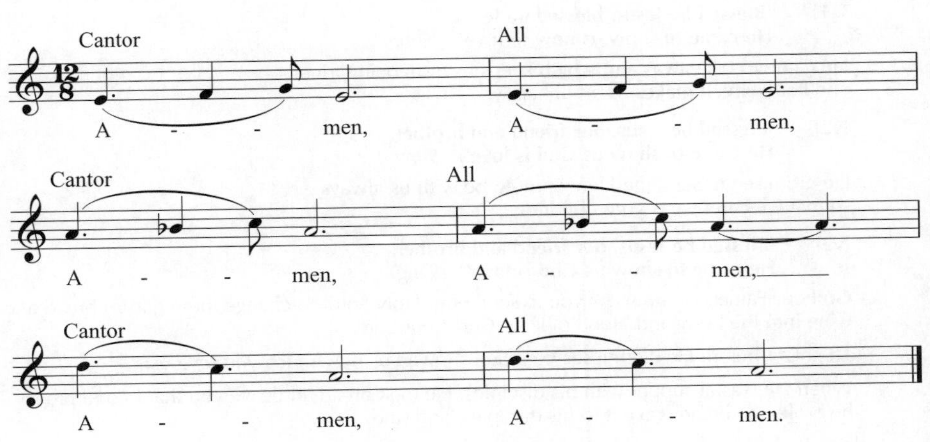
Cantor
All
A - - men, A - - men,
Cantor
All
A - - men, A - - men,
Cantor
All
A - - men, A - - men.

Childrens Eucharistic Acclamations

Suggested use with Eucharistic Prayer for Children II

The Lord be with you.	**And also with you.**
Lift up your hearts.	**We lift them up to the Lord.**
Let us give thanks to the Lord our God.	**It is right to give him thanks and praise.**

945A [1] **'We sing your glory, Sing your praise'.** *(Sung)*

God our loving Father, we are glad to give you thanks and praise, because you love us.
With Jesus we sing your praise.

[2] **'We sing your glory, Sing your praise'.** *(Sung)*

Because you love us, you gave us this beautiful world.
With Jesus we sing your praise.

[3] **'We sing your glory, we sing your glory'.** *(Sung)*

Because you love us, you sent Jesus your Son to bring us to you and to gather us around him as the children of one family.
With Jesus we sing your praise.

[4] **'Glory, glory and praise.'** *(Sung)*

For such great love we thank you with the angels and saints as they praise you and sing

945B **'We sing hosanna, sing your praise, we sing hosanna,**
sing yor praise, we sing hosanna, we sing hosanna,
glory, glory and praise'. *(Sung)*

Blessed be Jesus, whom you sent to be the friend of children and of the poor.

946 [v1] **'Blessed be Jesus, blessed be Jesus,**
He came to show us how to love'. *(Sung)*

He came to show us how we can love you Father, by loving one another.

[v1] **'Blessed be Jesus, blessed be Jesus,**
He came to show us how to love'. *(Sung)*

He came to take away sin, which keeps us from being friends,
and hate, which makes us all unhappy.

[v2] **'Blessed be Jesus, our friend and brother,**
He came to show us God is love'. *(Sung)*

He promised to send the Holy Spirit to be with us always,
so that we can live as your children.

[v2] **'Blessed be Jesus, our friend and brother,**
He came to show us God is love'. *(Sung)*

God our Father, we now ask you to send your Holy Spirit to change these gifts of bread and wine into the body and blood of Jesus Christ our Lord.

The night before He died, Jesus your Son showed us how much you love us.

When He was at supper with his disciples, He took bread and gave you thanks and praise. Then he broke the bread, gave it to his disciples, and said:

'Take this all of you and eat it;
this is my body which will be given up for you.'

946 *(cont.)* [v3] **'Though we are many, we are one family, we are one body in your love'.** *(Sung)*

When supper was ended, Jesus took the cup that was filled with wine.
He thanked you, gave it to his friends, and said:

'Take this all of you and drink from it:
this is the cup of my blood,
the blood of the new and everlasting covenant.
It will be shed for you and for all
so that sins may be forgiven.'

[v3] **'Though we are many, we are one family, we are one body in your love'.** *(Sung)*

Then he said to them:

'Do this in memory of me.'

[v4] **'Make us your people, people of Jesus, make us your people, called by love'.** *(Sung)*

And so, loving Father, we remember that Jesus died and rose again to save the world. He put himself into our hands to be the sacrifice we offer You.

946(B) **'Make us a sign of love to all in the world'.** *(Sung)*

Lord our God, listen to our prayer.
Send the Holy Spirit to all of us who share in this meal.
May this Spirit bring us close together in the family of the Church, with John Paul our Pope, N…, our Bishop, all other bishops, and all who serve your people.

'Make us a sign of love to all in the world'. *(Sung)*

Remember, Father, our families and friends,
and all those we do not love as we should.
Remember those who have died.
Bring them to you to be with you for ever.

'Make us a sign of love to all in the world'. *(Sung)*

Gather us all together into your kingdom.
There we shall be happy for ever,
with the Virgin Mary, Mother of God and our Mother.

'Make us a sign of love to all in the world'. *(Sung)*

There all the friends of Jesus the Lord will sing a song of joy.

'Make us a sign of love to all in the world'. *(Sung)*

947 Through Jesus Christ our Lord, with Him and in Him,
in the unity of the Spirit, almighty Father,
all glory and honour is yours,
for ever and ever.

Amen, Amen, Amen, Amen.

945B **'We sing hosanna, sing your praise,** *(Sung)*
we sing hosanna, sing your praise,
we sing hosanna, we sing hosanna,
glory, glory and praise,
Amen, Amen, Amen, Amen.

945A We sing Your glory (Preface)

Bernadette Farrell

1
2
3
4
We sing your glo- ry,
sing your praise,
We sing your glo- ry,
sing your praise,
We sing your glo - ry,
We sing your glo - ry,
Glo - ry,
glo - ry, and praise!

May be sung in 2 bar phrases, repeated after a Cantor.

Also may be sung as a round with entries as shown.

945B We sing hosanna (Sanctus)

Bernadette Farrell

1
2
We sing ho - san - na, sing your praise, We sing ho - san - na,
3
sing your praise, We sing ho - san - na,
4
We sing ho - san - na, Glo - ry, glo - ry, and praise!

Note: Amen may be added after the Cantor's lead, if the refrain is repeated at the end of the Eucharistic Prayer

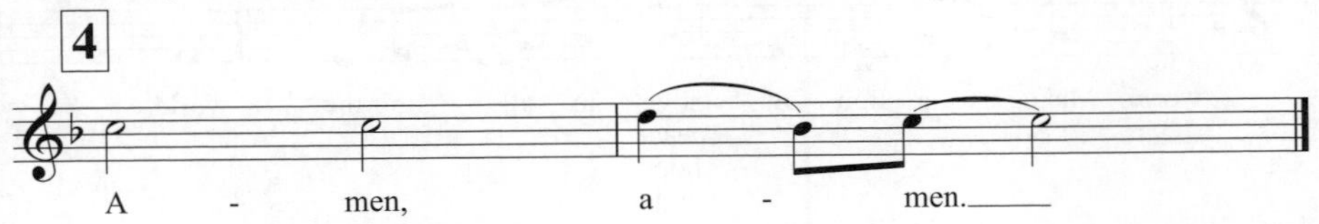
4
A - men, a - men.

May be sung as a round with entries as shown.

946 Blessed be Jesus - Make us a sign

Bernadette Farrell

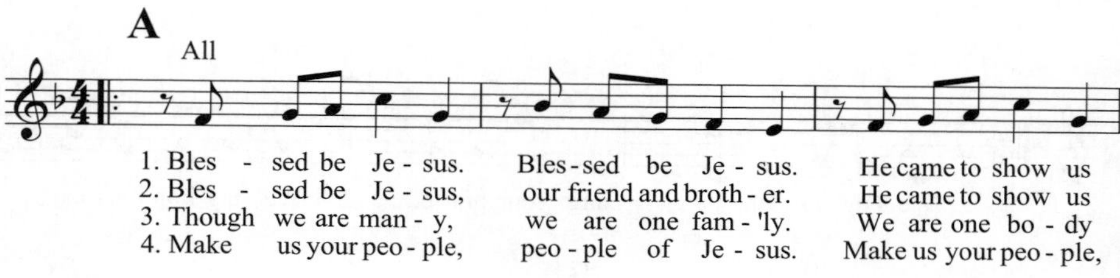
A
All
1. Bles - sed be Je - sus. Bles - sed be Je - sus. He came to show us
2. Bles - sed be Je - sus, our friend and broth - er. He came to show us
3. Though we are man - y, we are one fam - 'ly. We are one bo - dy
4. Make us your peo - ple, peo - ple of Je - sus. Make us your peo - ple,

repeat 3x
B
Cantor/Choir
how to love.
God is love.
in your love.
called by love.
(world.) Make us a sign of love to all in the
peace
hope
light
Christ

All
repeat 4x
world. Make us a sign of love to all in the world.
peace
hope
light
Christ

947 Doxology and Amen

Bernadette Farrell

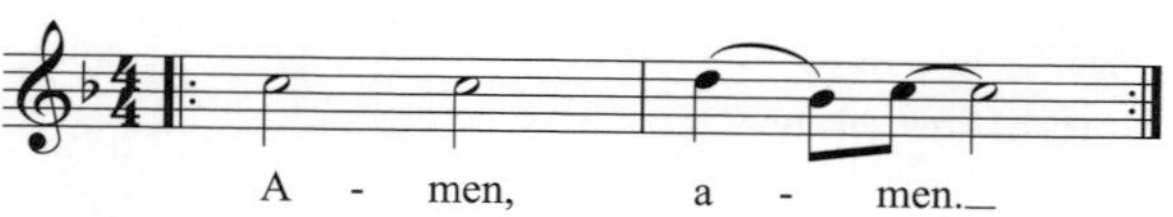
A - men, a - men.

Through Jesus Christ our Lord,
with him and in him,
in the unity of the Spirit,
almighty Father,
all glory and honour is yours
for ever and ever and ever.
Amen, amen.

Note: Repeat Amens after Cantor. 89B may be sung at this point, perhaps as a 4 part round, with Amens coming in instead of Glory, glory and praise.

948 Christ has died

Joe Wise

Christ has died, al-le-lu-ia. Christ is ri-sen, al-le-lu-ia.

Christ will come a-gain, al-le-lu-ia, al-le-lu-ia.

949 When we eat this bread

Traditional Irish

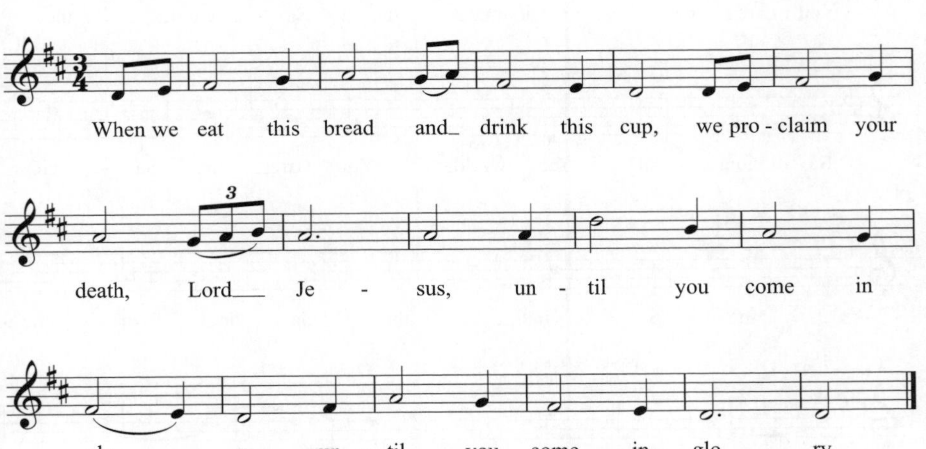
When we eat this bread and drink this cup, we pro-claim your
death, Lord Je-sus, un-til you come in
glo-ry, un-til you come in glo-ry.

950 Lord by your Cross

Chris Rolinson

With expression and feeling
Lord, by your cross and re - sur - rec - tion, you set us free,
you set us free.
Lord, by your cross and re - sur -
rec - tion, you set us free,
you set us free.
You are the Sa - viour, the Sa - viour, the
Sa - viour of the world. You are the Sa - viour,
the Sa - viour, the Sa - viour of the
world,
Sa - viour of the world!

951 Russian Our Father

Attributed to Rimsky-Korsakov

Our Fa - ther, who art in heav'n, hal - lowed be thy name, thy king dom come, thy

will be done, on earth as it is in heav'n. Give us this day our dai - ly bread,

and for - give us our tres - pas - ses, as we for - give those who tres - pass a - gainst us;

and lead us not in - to temp - ta - tion, but de - li - ver us from e - vil.

The Priest continues: Deliver us O Lord from every evil…
… as we wait in joyful hope for the coming of our Saviour, Jesus Christ.

For the king - dom, the power, and the glo - ry are yours, now and for e - ver.

952 Our Father (Celtic Mass)

Christopher Walker

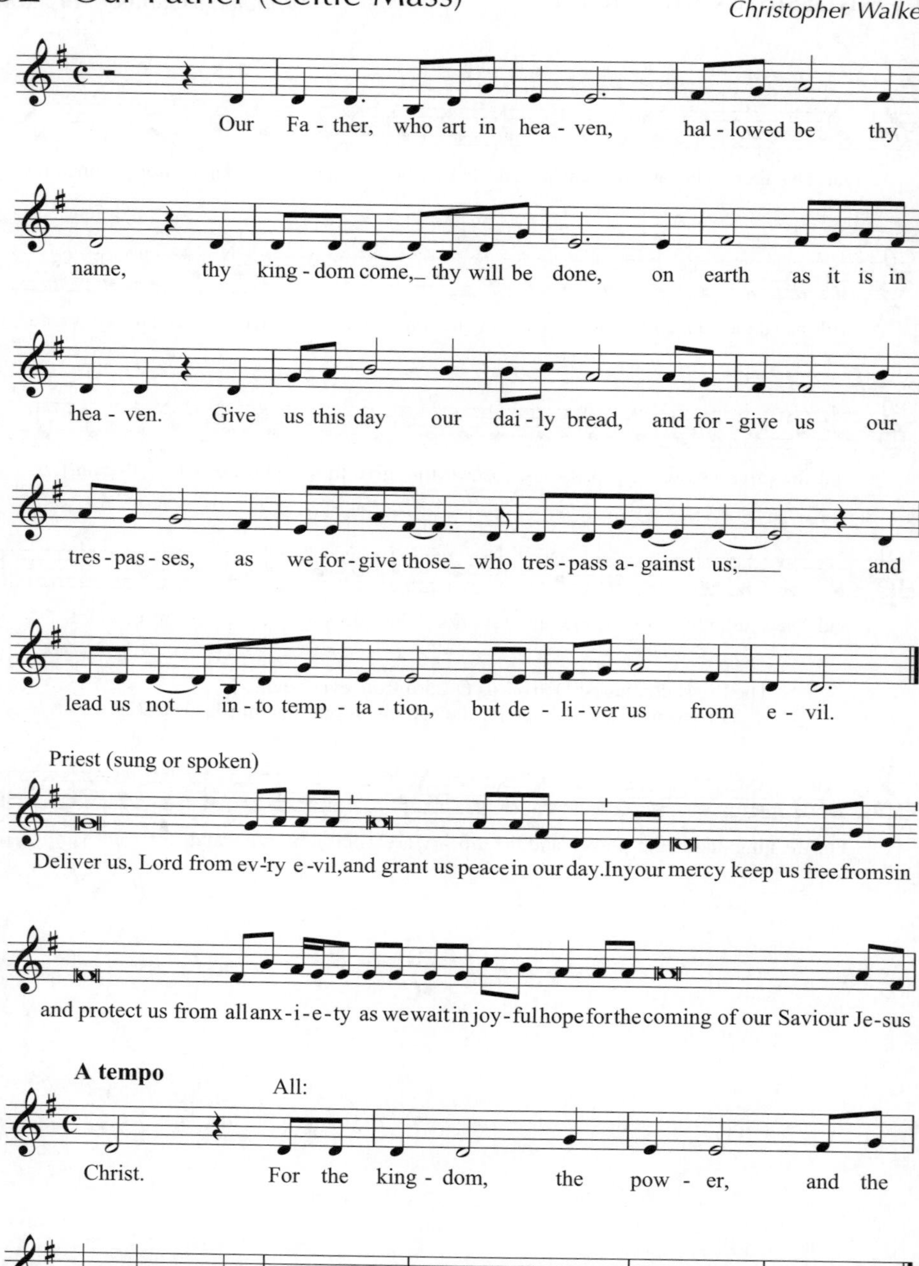
Our Fa - ther, who art in hea - ven, hal - lowed be thy
name, thy king - dom come,_ thy will be done, on earth as it is in
hea - ven. Give us this day our dai - ly bread, and for - give us our
tres - pas - ses, as we for - give those_ who tres - pass a - gainst us;___ and
lead us not___ in - to temp - ta - tion, but de - li - ver us from e - vil.
Priest (sung or spoken)
Deliver us, Lord from ev'ry e - vil, and grant us peace in our day. In your mercy keep us free from sin
and protect us from all anx - i - e - ty as we wait in joy - ful hope for the coming of our Saviour Je - sus
A tempo
All:
Christ. For the king - dom, the pow - er, and the
glo - ry are yours, now and for e - ver.

953 Breaking of Bread – Millennium Mass

Paul Inwood

Je - sus, Lamb of God, Je - sus, Lamb of God, Je - sus,
Sa - viour, have mer - cy on us. Je - sus, bear - ing all our sin,
Je - sus, bear - ing all our sin, Je - sus, Sa - viour, have
mer - cy on us. Je - sus, Re - deem - er of the world, Je - sus, Re-
deem - er of the world, Je - sus, Sa - viour, O give us your peace.

954 Peace Song/Agnus Dei

Peter McGrail

Largo (♩ = 60)
Cantor/Choir
All
1. Lov - ing Sa - viour, bread of life: Come and bring your peace.

Cantor/Choir
All
Gen - tle Mas - ter, heal - ing Lord: Come and bring your Peace. Je - sus, Lord, be

mer - ci - ful to us. Je - sus, Lamb of God, Fill us with your Love.

1 Loving Saviour, bread of Life:
All. Come and bring your Peace.
Gentle Master, healing Lord:
All. Come and bring your Peace.
Jesus, Lord, be merciful to us.
Jesus, Lamb of God, fill us with
your Love.

2 Lord who calmed the stormy seas:
All. Come and bring your Peace.
Lord, you hear the ones who call:
All. Come and bring your Peace.
Jesus, Lord, be merciful to us.
Jesus, Lamb of God, fill us with
your Love.

3 To our homes and families:
All. Come and bring your Peace.
To our friends and dear ones:
All. Come and bring your Peace.
Jesus, Lord, be merciful to us.
Jesus, Lamb of God, fill us with
your Love.

4 Lord, you know our deepest needs:
All. Come and bring your Peace.
Lord, you hear our darkest fears:
All. Come and bring your Peace.
Jesus, Lord, be merciful to us.
Jesus, Lamb of God, fill us with
your Love.

5 Show to us your tenderness:
All. Come and bring your Peace.
Gentle Master, healing Lord:
All. Heal us with your gentle Love.
Jesus, Lord, be merciful to us.
Jesus, Lamb of God, fill us with
your Love.

955 Communion Song 4

Paul Inwood

Solo
All
Je - sus, Lamb of God, have mer - cy on us. Je - sus, Lamb of
Solo or Choir
God, have mer - cy on us. Je - sus, Word made flesh, bear - er of our
All
sins: Je - sus, Lamb of God, have mer - cy on us.
Solo
All
Je - sus, Bread of Life, have mer - cy on us. Je - sus, Bread of
Solo or Choir
Life, have mer - cy on us. Je - sus, Morn - ing Star; Je - sus, Prince of
All
Peace: Je - sus, bread of Life, have mer - cy on us.
Solo
All
Je - sus, Lamb of God, have mer - cy on us. Je - sus, Lamb of
Solo or Choir
God, have mer - cy on us. Je - sus, King of kings; Je - sus, Lord of
All
all: Je - sus, Lamb of God, give us your peace.

956 Jesus, Lamb of God

Martin Hall

Largo ♩ = 58
p
Je - sus, Lamb of God, have mer - cy on us,
People
p
have mer - cy on us,
Cantor
mf
Je - sus, bear - er of our sins, have mer - cy on us,
People
mf
have mer - cy on us.
Cantor
f dim.
Je - sus,
People
f dim.
Cantor
mf
Je - sus, Re - deem - er of the world,
People
mf
Re - deem - er of the world,
Cantor
f
Give us your peace,
mf
give us your peace,
rit.
p dim. pp
give us your peace.
People
f
Give us your peace,
mp
give us your
p dim. pp
peace.

MASS FOR ALL SAINTS

957 Lord have mercy

Joan McCrimmon

KYRIE

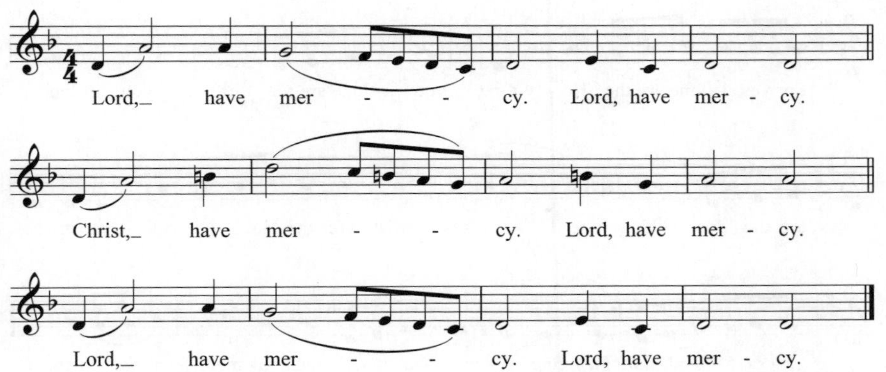
Lord,_ have mer - - cy. Lord, have mer - cy.
Christ,_ have mer - - cy. Lord, have mer - cy.
Lord,_ have mer - - cy. Lord, have mer - cy.

Words: anonymous

MASS FOR ALL SAINTS

958 Glory to God

Joan McCrimmon

GLORIA

Glo - ry to God in the high - est, and peace to his peo - ple on earth. Lord God,
heav - en - ly King, al - might - y God and Fa - ther, we wor - ship you, we give you thanks, we
praise you for_ your glo - ry. Lord Je - sus Christ, on - ly Son of the Fa - ther.
Lord God, Lamb of God, you take a - way_ the sin of the world: have mer - cy on
us,___ have mer - cy on us; you are seat - ed at the right hand of the

Fa - - ther; re - ceive our pray'r,_ re - ceive our pray'r.
For you a - lone are the Ho - ly One, you a - lone are the Lord, you a - lone
are the Most High, Je - sus Christ, with the Ho - ly Spi - rit, in the
glo - ry of God_ the Fa - ther. A - men, a - men, a - men, a - men.

MASS FOR ALL SAINTS

959 Holy Holy

Joan McCrimmon

SANCTUS

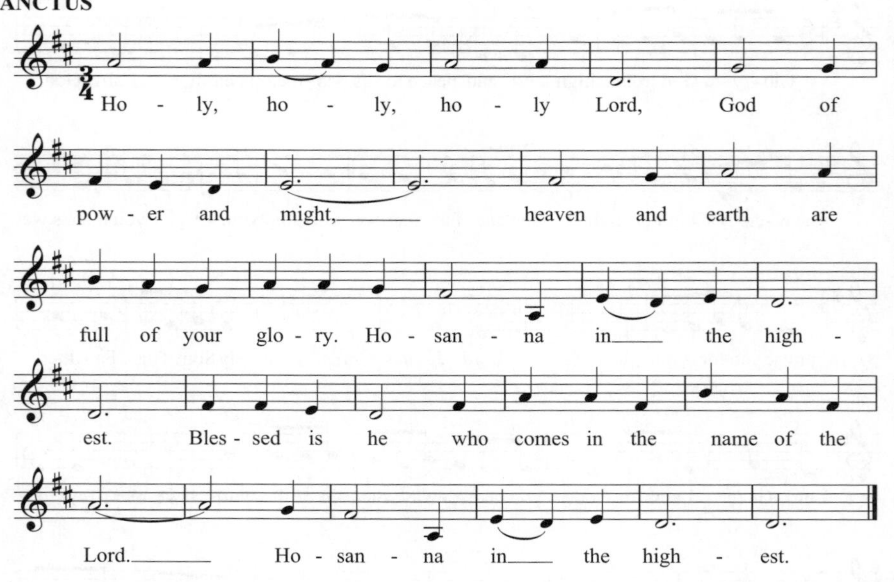
3
4
Ho - ly, ho - ly, ho - ly Lord, God of
pow - er and might,_ heaven and earth are
full of your glo - ry. Ho - san - na in_ the high -
est. Bles - sed is he who comes in the name of the
Lord._ Ho - san - na in_ the high - est.

MASS FOR ALL SAINTS

960 Christ has died

Joan McCrimmon

ACCLAMATION

Christ has_ died. Christ is___ ri - sen. Christ will come a - gain.

Words: anonymous

MASS FOR ALL SAINTS

961 Amen

Joan McCrimmon

GREAT AMEN

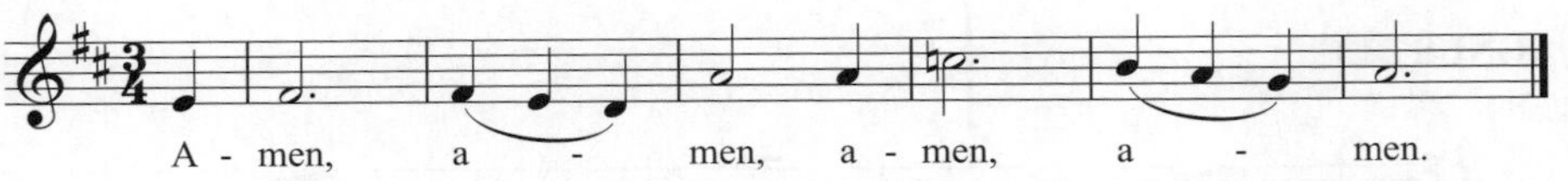
A - men, a - men, a - men, a - men.

Words: anonymous

MASS FOR ALL SAINTS

962 The Lord's Prayer

Joan McCrimmon

THE LORD'S PRAYER

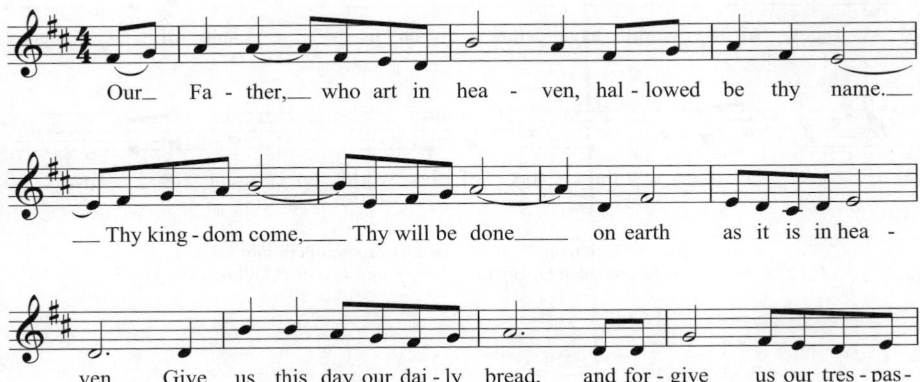
Our_ Fa - ther,_ who art in hea - ven, hal - lowed be thy name.__
__ Thy king - dom come,____ Thy will be done_____ on earth as it is in hea -
ven. Give us this day our dai - ly bread, and for - give us our tres - pas -

ses, as we for - give those who tres - pass a - gainst us. And

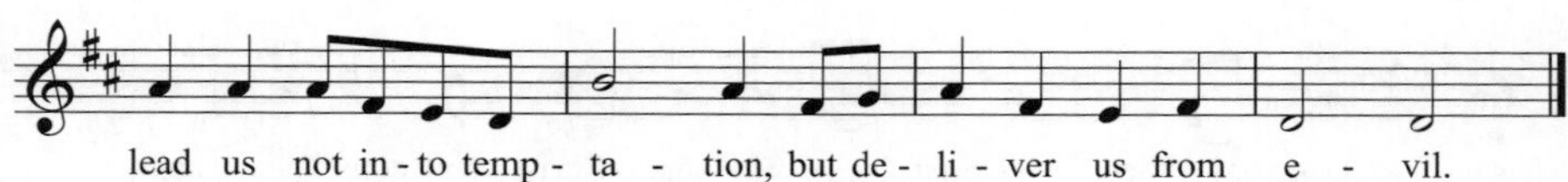
lead us not in - to temp - ta - tion, but de - li - ver us from e - vil.

Music: © Joan McCrimmon. Published by McCrimmon Publishing Co. Ltd.
Words: anonymous

MASS FOR ALL SAINTS

963 Lamb of God

Joan McCrimmon

AGNUS DEI

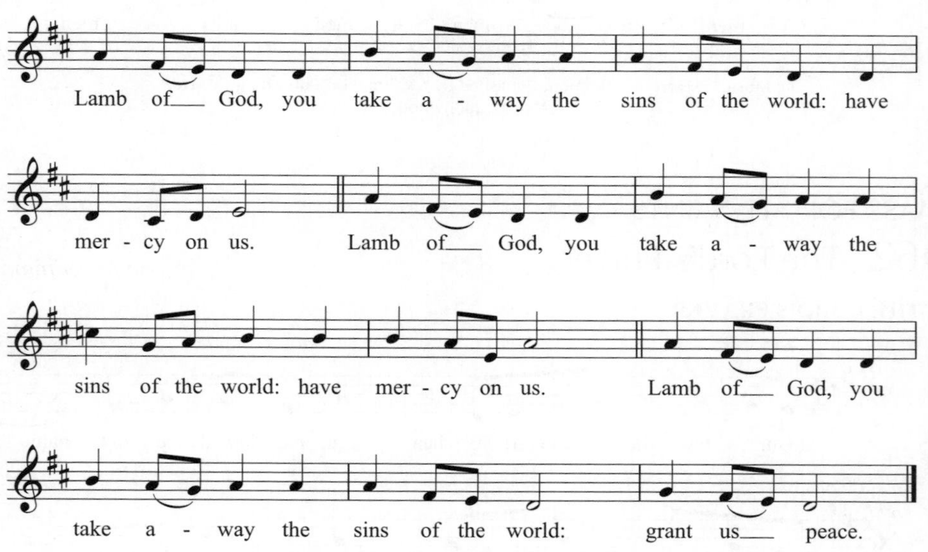
Lamb of God, you take a - way the sins of the world: have
mer - cy on us. Lamb of God, you take a - way the
sins of the world: have mer - cy on us. Lamb of God, you
take a - way the sins of the world: grant us peace.

Music: © Joan McCrimmon. Published by McCrimmon Publishin Co. Ltd.

964 Lord have mercy

James MacMillan

KYRIE

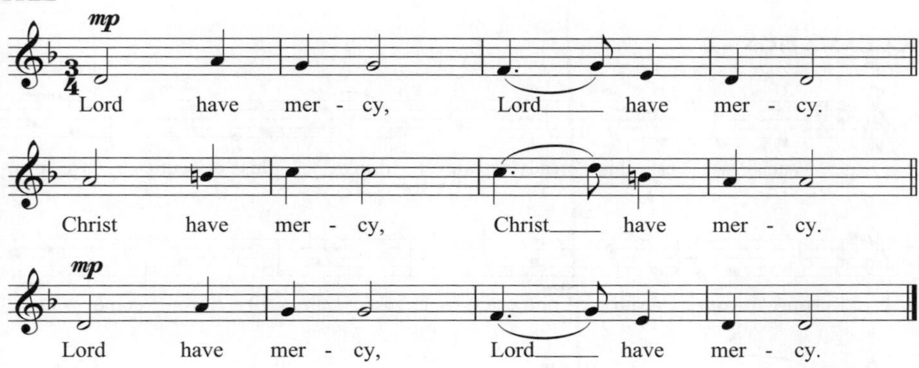
mp
Lord have mer - cy, Lord___ have mer - cy.
Christ have mer - cy, Christ___ have mer - cy.
mp
Lord have mer - cy, Lord___ have mer - cy.

ST. ANNE'S MASS

965 Holy Holy

James MacMillan

Sanctus and Benedictus

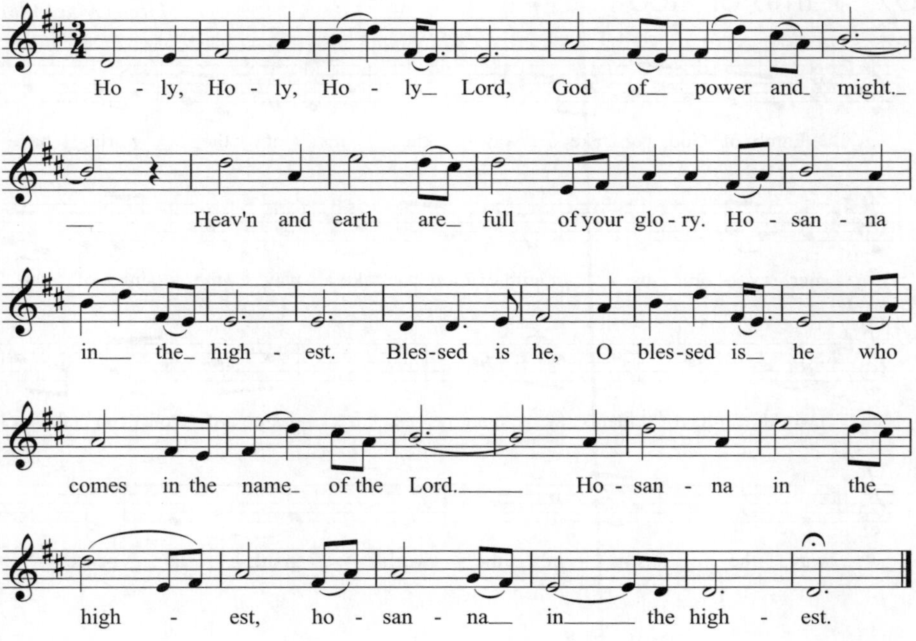

Ho - ly, Ho - ly, Ho - ly_ Lord, God of_ power and_ might._
___ Heav'n and earth are_ full of your glo - ry. Ho - san - na
in___ the_ high - est. Bles-sed is he, O bles-sed is_ he who
comes in the name_ of the Lord.______ Ho - san - na in the_
high - est, ho - san - na_ in______ the high - est.

ST. ANNE'S MASS

966 When we eat

James MacMillan

ACCLAMATION

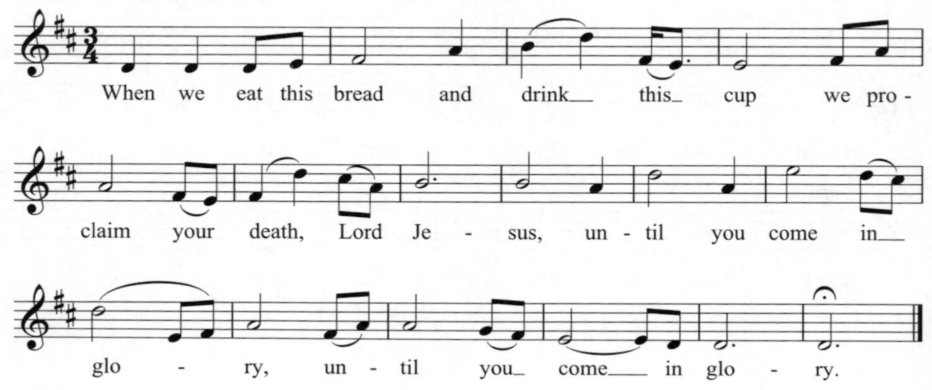
When we eat this bread and drink this cup we proclaim your death, Lord Jesus, until you come in glory, until you come in glory.

ST. ANNE'S MASS

967 Lamb of God

James MacMillan

Lamb of God, you take away the sins of the world, have mercy on us. Lamb of God, you take away the sins of the world, have mercy on us. Lamb of God, you take away the sins of the world, grant us peace.

The Psalms

For each Psalm we indicate the Sunday(s) or Feast when it is the Psalm for the day using abbreviations e.g.

7A	*means the 7th Sunday of Ordinary time in Year A;*
Easter 3B	*means the 3rd Sunday of Easter in Year B;*
Lent 4C	*means the 4th Sunday of Lent in Year C* and so on.

The Common Psalms which can be used instead of the Psalm of the Day in a particular Season are shown thus: Common Psalm for Lent, Advent, Easter or Ordinary Time (as the case may be.)
A complete list of Common Psalms appears at the end of the book.

968 Psalm 16(15) Keep me safe, O God

13C, Easter 3A, 33B, Easter Vigil 1st

Paul Inwood

REFRAIN: 1st time: Cantor; each time thereafter: All.

Keep me safe, O God, I take re - fuge in you.

Keep me safe, O God, I take re - fuge in you.

Cantor

1 O Lord, it is you who are my portion and cup;
it is you yourself who are my prize.
I keep the Lord ever in my sight:
since he is at my right hand I shall stand firm. *(to Refrain)*

2 And so my heart rejoices, my soul is glad;
even my body shall rest in safety.
For you will not leave my soul among the dead,
nor let your beloved know decay. *(to Refrain)*

3 You will show me the path of life,
the fullness of joy in your presence,
at your right hand, at your right hand
happiness for ever. *(to Refrain)*

969 Psalm 19(18) You, Lord, have the Message

26B, 3C, Lent 3B, Easter Vigil 6
Common Psalm for ordinary time

Paul Inwood

REFRAIN

1
2
Fine
You, Lord, have the mes - sage of e - ter - nal life.

1 The law of the Lord is perfect, it revives the soul.
The rule of the Lord is to be trusted, it gives wisdom to the simple. *Refrain*

2 The precepts of the Lord are right, they gladden the heart.
The command of the Lord is clear, it gives light to the eyes. *Refrain*

3 The fear of the Lord is holy, abiding forever.
The decrees of the Lord are truth, and all of them just. *Refrain*

4 Your decrees are more to be desired than gold, the purest of gold,
and sweeter are they than honey, than honey from the comb. *Refrain*

970 Psalm 23(22) — Shepherd me, O God

28A, Christ the King A, Easter 4A, Lent 4A, 16B

Marty Haugen

REFRAIN

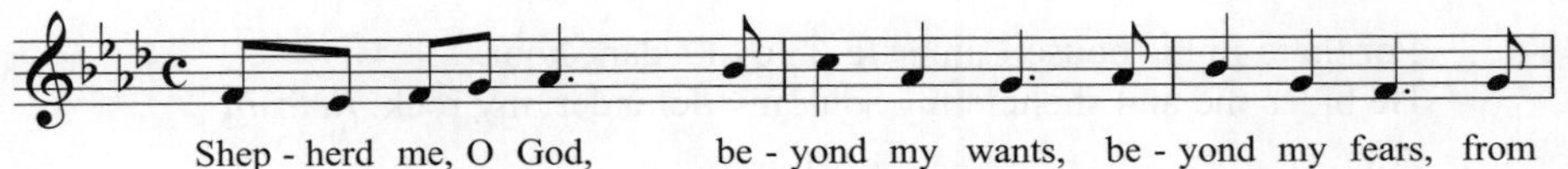
Shep - herd me, O God, be - yond my wants, be - yond my fears, from

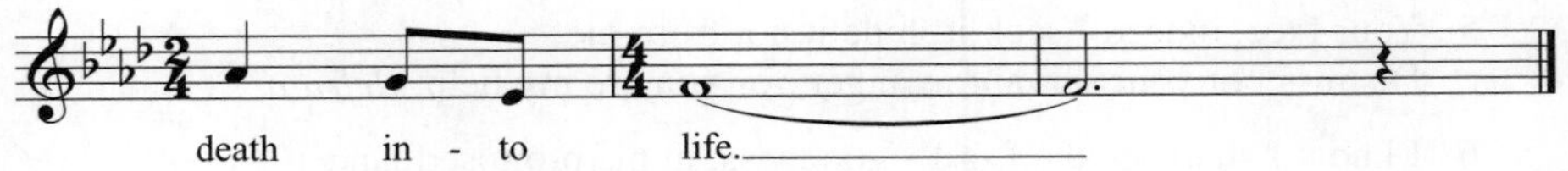
death in - to life.

1 God is my shepherd, so nothing shall I want,
I rest in the meadows of faithfulness and love,
I walk by the quiet waters of peace.

2 Gently you raise me and heal my weary soul,
you lead me by pathways of righteousness and truth,
my spirit shall sing the music of your name.

3 Though I should wander the valley of death,
I fear no evil, for you are at my side,
your rod and your staff, my comfort and my hope.

971 Psalm 27(26) One thing I ask

3A, Lent 2C, Easter 3A
Common Psalm for ordinary time

Stephen Dean

REFRAIN: Cantor/All

One thing I ask of the Lord, for this I long, to

live in the house of the Lord all the days of my life.

1 The Lord is my light and my help. Whom shall I fear?
The Lord is the stronghold of my life, before whom shall I shrink? *Refrain*

2 Though armies do battle against me, my heart will not fear.
Though war and destruction break forth, even then would I trust. *Refrain*

3 For there in his house I am safe, in evil's dark hour.
He hides me and shelters my soul, my defender, my rock. *Refrain*

4 O Lord, hear my voice when I call; have mercy and answer;
Of you my heart has spoken: "Seek his face." *Refrain*

5 Your face, indeed I seek it; hide it not from me.
Dismiss not your servant in anger, for you are my help. *Refrain*

6 I know I shall see the Lord's goodness, in his promised land.
Take heart and stand firm. O my soul, put your hope in the Lord! *Refrain*

972 Psalm 33(32 May your love be upon us O Lord

Lent 2A, 29B, Trinity B, 19C, Easter 5A, Easter Vigil 1

Anne Ward

May your love be up - on us, O Lord, as we place all our hope in you.

1 The Word of the Lord is faithful,
and all his works to be trusted.
The Lord loves justice and right
and fills the earth with his love.

2 By his word the heavens were made,
by the breath of his mouth all the stars.
He collects the waves of the ocean;
he stores up the depths of the sea.

3 They are happy whose God is the Lord:
the people he chose as his own.
From the heavens the Lord looks forth,
he sees all the children of men.

4 Our soul is waiting for the Lord.
The Lord is our help and our shield.
May your love be upon us, O Lord,
as we place all our hope in you.

973 Psalm 51(50)

Give me a new heart

Ash Wednesday, Lent 1A, 24C, Lent 5B, Easter Vigil 7th,
Common Psalm for Lent

Christopher Walker

REFRAIN
Give me a new heart, O God. Put your Spi - rit in me. Keep me
with you, give me joy. Give me a new heart, O God.
VERSES
1. God, in your love, have mer - cy on me.
2. All of my faults, I know them so well.
3. Truth in the heart you love most of all.
4. Give me a - gain the joy of your help.
5. You do not want a sa - cri - fice made.
6. O spare my life and save me, O God.
1. In your com - pas - sion cleanse me.
2. All of my sins, I know them.
3. Now fill my mind with wis - dom.
4. Put a new spi - rit in me,
5. You would re - fuse burnt off' - rings.
6. I will pro - claim your good - ness.
1. All of my guilt, wash it a - way.
2. For a - gainst you a - lone have I sinned.
3. Wash me from sin and I shall be clean;
4. that I may teach sin - ners your ways,
5. My spi - rit is hum - ble, of - fered to you.
6. O - pen my lips and help me to speak
To Refrain
1. Lord make me clean from my sin.
2. E - vil in your sight have I done.
3. I shall be pure as the snow.
4. that they will turn back to you.
5. You will not sourn my hum - ble heart.
6. and I will praise you with joy.

974 Psalm 63(62)

O Lord, I will sing

22A, 32A, 12C, Common Psalm for ordinary time

Christopher Walker

Refrain:
O Lord, I will sing of your con - stant love and your faith - ful ness will I

al - ways pro - claim. O Lord, I will sing of your

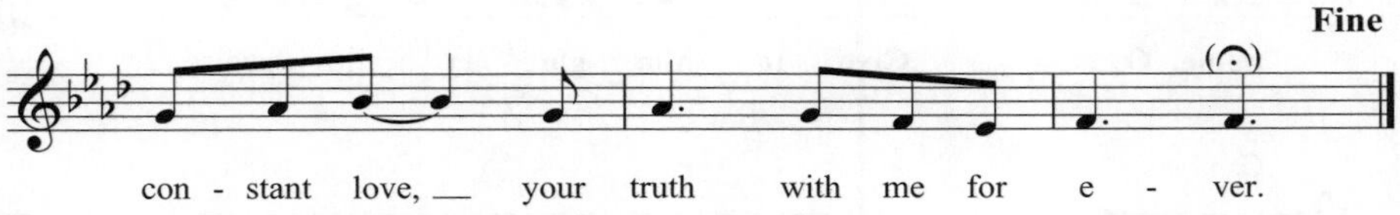

Fine
con - stant love, your truth with me for e - ver.

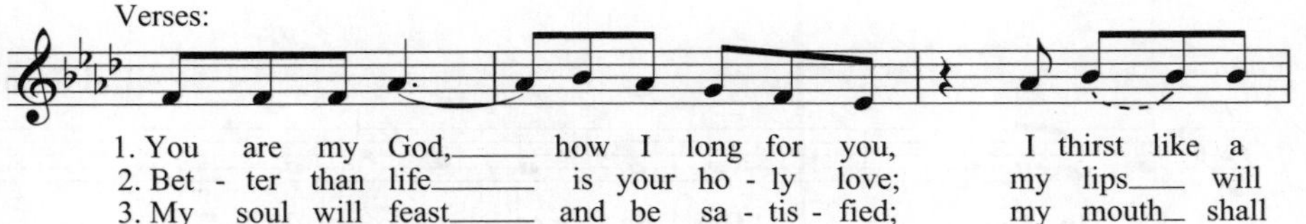

Verses:
1. You are my God, how I long for you, I thirst like a
2. Bet - ter than life is your ho - ly love; my lips will
3. My soul will feast and be sa - tis - fied; my mouth shall

dry wea - ry land. I gaze on you in your ho - ly place to
speak of your praise. I bless you my God for all of my life and
praise you with joy. At night I re - mem - ber you are my help. I

To Refrain
see how migh - ty and glor - ious you are. O
in your name I will lift up my hands. O
sing for joy for your hand keeps me safe. O

975 Psalm 66(65)

Cry out with joy to God

14C, Easter 6A, Common Psalm Easter

Chris O'Hara

Cantor
All
v.1. Cry out with Joy to God all the earth,
Cry out with Joy to God all the earth,

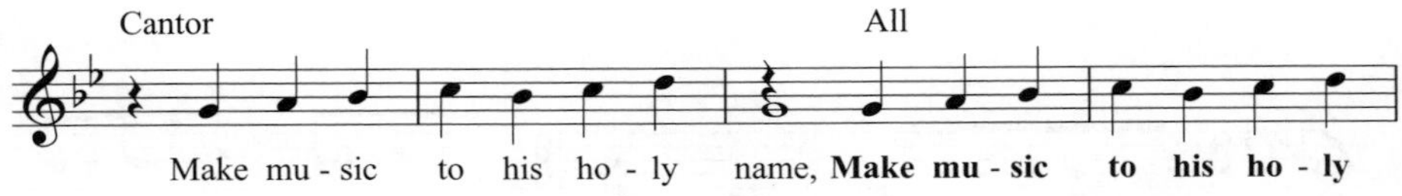
Cantor
All
Make mu - sic to his ho - ly name,
Make mu - sic to his ho - ly

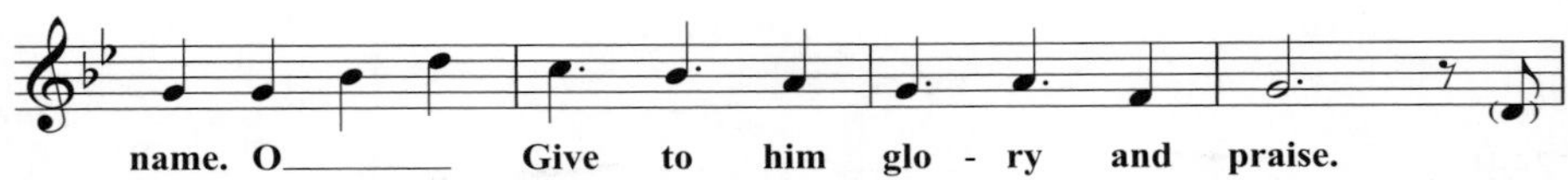
name. O
Give to him glo - ry and praise.

Cantor
Say to God
"How im - mense are your deeds."

All
Dal Segno
Say to God
"How im - mense are your deeds."

2 Before you all the earth shall bow; (All repeat)
with songs of praise shall sing your name! (All repeat)
O come see the wonders of God,
tremendous are His deeds among men. (All repeat)

3 He turned the sea into dry land (All repeat)
and theough the river led them home. (All repeat)
O let us rejoice in His name,
forever He rules in His might. (All repeat)

4 Come listen all who fear the Lord, (All repeat)
and I will tell His wond'rous deeds. (All repeat)
O blessed the mercy of God,
blessed His love is for me. (All repeat)

Note: In this psalm setting, the people respond by repeating lines 1, 2 & 4 after the Cantor, and by joining in line 3.

976 Psalm 85(84) — Let us see, O Lord, your mercy

19A, 15B, Advent 2B, Common Psalm Advent

Elsie Wright

Response

Let us see, O Lord, your mer - cy, and give us your sav - ing help.

1 I will hear what the Lord God has to say,
a voice that speaks of peace, peace for his people.
His help is near for those who fear him
and his glory will dwell in our land.

2 Mercy and faithfulness have met;
justice and peace have embraced.
Faithfulness shall spring from the earth
and justice look down from heaven.

3 The Lord will make us prosper
and our earth shall yield its fruit.
Justice shall march before him
and peace shall follow his steps.

977 Psalm 85(84) — Give us your saving help

19A, 15B, Advent 2B, Common Psalm Advent

Chris O'Hara

ANTIPHON

Show to us your love and mer - cy,

Give us your sav - ing help. Show to us your love and

mer - cy, Give us your sav - ing help.

1 Let us listen and hear the voice of God Speaking
peace deep within our hearts.
When we turn and repent, his help is near
then his Glory will live
then his glory will live in our land. *To Antiphon*

2 See your faithfulness and your love
now meet;
peace and justice now embrace.
From the land a steadfast faith will grow
and his justice look down,
and his justice look down from the
heavens.

3 With the help of the Lord we live
and grow,
and the blossom will yield its fruit.
Love and justice shall march before his
name;
peace will follow the steps,
peace will follow the steps of our Lord.

978 Psalm 85(84)

Let us see your kindness

Common Psalm for Advent, 19A, 15B, Advent 2B

Marty Haugen

Lord, let us see your kind - ness;
Lord, let us see your kind - ness.

1 Let us hear what our God proclaims:
Peace to the people of God,
salvation is near to the ones who fear him.

2 Kindness and truth, justice and peace;
truth shall spring up as the water from the earth,
justice shall rain from the heavens.

3 The Lord will come and you shall know his love,
justice shall walk in his pathways,
salvation the gift that he brings.

979 Psalm 91(90) Be with me Lord

Lent 1C, Common Psalm for Lent

Chris O'Hara

ANTIPHON
Be with me Lord in my dis - tress,
in my dis - tress.

1 He who lives in the shelter, the shelter of God;
He who lives in the shadow of the Lord,
sings to his God, my refuge.
In your strength and love I put my trust.

2 No evil can touch you, no terror of night,
and where you live no ill can dwell;
for you his angels watching over
and guiding your steps along the way.

3 Loving hands reaching to you to carry
you safe,
lest you dash your foot against a stone.
In your distress I shall answer:
reveal my salvation and my glory.

980 Psalm 92(91) It is good to give thanks to You

11B, 8C

Christopher Walker

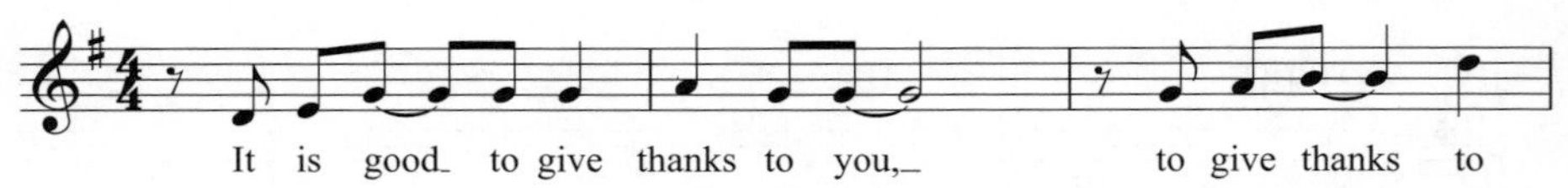
It is good to give thanks to you, to give thanks to

you, our God. It is good. It is good.

1 It is good to give thanks to the Lord,
to make music to your name, O Most High,
to proclaim your love in the morning light,
and your truth in the watches of the night.

2 And the just like the palm tree will grow,
they will flourish like a Lebanon cedar,
and planted deep in the house of God,
they will thrive in the temple of our God.

3 They bear fruit even when they are old;
in old age they will stay fresh and green
to proclaim to all that our God is just.
In our Rock no injustice can be found.

Note: This Response and the music for the verses are also suitable for the other psalms printed below.

Psalm 67(66) / 20A, Easter 6C

1 O be gracious and bless us, O Lord,
let your face shine out upon your people;
so all your ways will be known on earth,
and your help will save all of humankind.

2 Let the nations be glad and exult.
Let them sing, because you rule
with justice,
and all your judgements are fair and true,
for you guide all the nations of the earth.

3 Let the peoples give praise to our God.
O let all the people praise your name,
that your blessing still will be on us all
till the ends of the earth revere
your name.

Psalm 68(67) / 22C

1 This I pray for your goodness to me:
come with love and help that never fails.
O Lord, answer me, for your love is kind;
in your love and compassion turn to me.

2 As for me, in my poverty and pain,
O my Saviour, you will lift me up.
I will praise God's name with a
joyful song.
I will thank and give glory to my God.

3 And the poor will be glad when they see;
those who seek the Lord will come to life,
for the Lord will listen to all in need
and will turn to the servants in their chains

Psalm 1 / 6C

1 They are blest who reject wicked talk,
nor sit with those who have no use
for God;
but whose one delight is the law of God,
and who think of God's law by day
and night.

2 All who hope in the Lord will be blest,
like the tree that grows by living waters,
that yields good fruit and whose leaves
don't fade;
all they do shall be prosperous and good.

3 But the wicked are not like the good!
They're like chaff that's blown away by the wind.
For the Lord will guide and protect the good,
but the way of the wicked leads to doom.

Psalm 96(95) / 29A, 2C

1 Sing to God, sing a song that is new.
Sing out loud, all people, bless
God's name.
Day by day God helps us; tell all the
world
of our joy in the wonders God has done.

2 God is great and is worthy of praise,
to be feared above all other gods;
for the heathen gods have no pow'r at all:
it was God, our God, who made
the heav'ns.

3 Give the Lord, all you peoples of earth,
all you families, give power to God,
and give glory now to the name of God
and proclaim all the wonders God
has done.

4 In God's temple give worship and praise.
Tremble, earth, before the Lord your God.
Now tell all the nations that God is King,
and with truth God gives justice to
the earth.

Psalm 107(106) / 12B

1 People sailed to the ocean in ships,
come to trade upon the mighty seas.
All these people see what the Lord
can do,
and the wonders God has done upon
the deep.

2 For God spoke and the storm wind
arose;
the wind stirred up all the waves of
the sea.
They were flung to heaven and down to
the deep;
in their fear they lost courage in
their hearts.

3 Then they cried to the Lord in their need,
and God rescued them from all their
distress,
and stilled the storm to a whisper soft;
they were hushed, all the waves of
the sea.

4 They rejoiced, they were glad in the
calm.
To their port God led them safely home.
So let all give thanks for God's love
for us,
and give thanks for the wonders God
has done.

981 Psalm 95(94) If today you hear His voice

23A, 4B, 18C, 27C, Common Psalm for ordinary time

David Haas

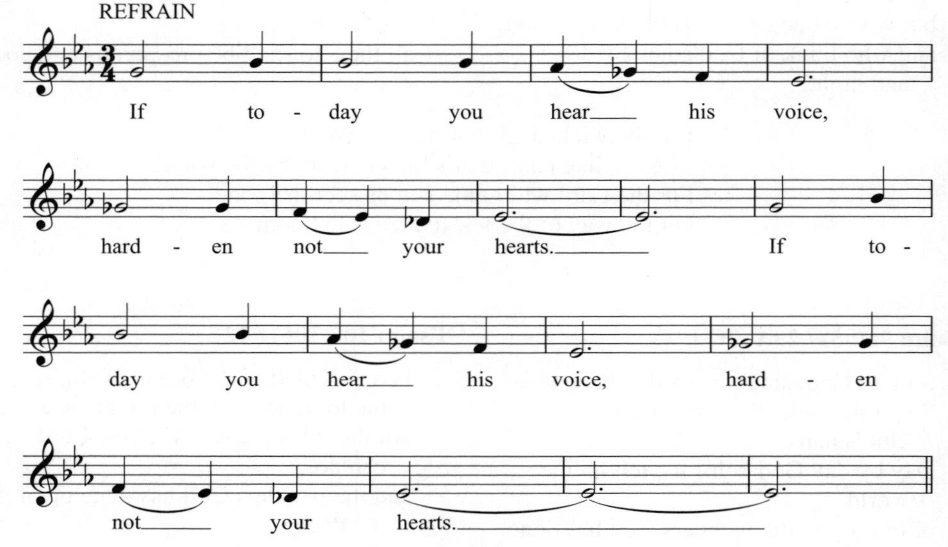
REFRAIN
If to - day you hear his voice,
hard - en not your hearts. If to -
day you hear his voice, hard - en
not your hearts.

1 Come, ring out our joy to the Lord,
Hail the Rock who saves us,
Let us come now before him,
with songs let us hail the Lord.

2 Come, let us bow and bend low,
let us kneel before him who made us,
For he is our God; we his people,
the flock that is led by his hand.

3 O that today you would hear his voice,
"Harden not your hearts,
as on that day in the desert,
when your parents put me to the test."

982 Psalm 96(95) Today a Saviour has been born to us

Christmas

Joan McCrimmon

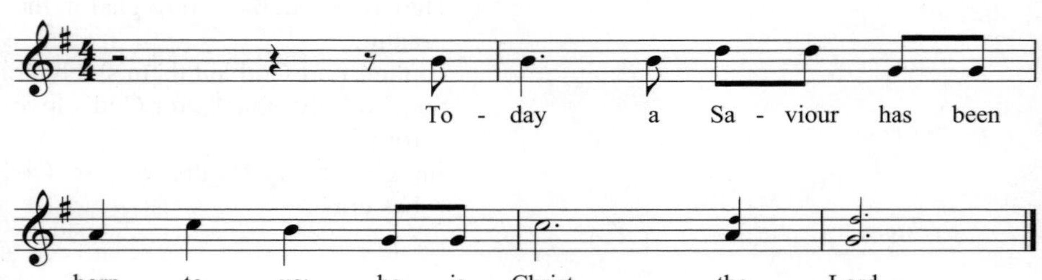
To - day a Sa - viour has been
born to us; he is Christ the Lord.

1 O sing a new song to the Lord,
sing to the Lord all the earth.
O sing to the Lord, bless his name.

2 Proclaim God's help day by day,
tell among the nations his glory
and his wonders among all the peoples.

3 Let the heavens rejoice and earth be glad,/
let the sea and all within it thunder praise,
let the land and all it bears rejoice,
all the trees of the wood shout for joy/
at the presence of the Lord who comes,
who comes to rule the earth.

4 With justice he will rule the world,
and will judge the peoples with truth.

983 Psalm 100(99) — We are His people

11A, Easter 4C, Common Psalm for Ordinary Time

Michael Coy

RESPONSE

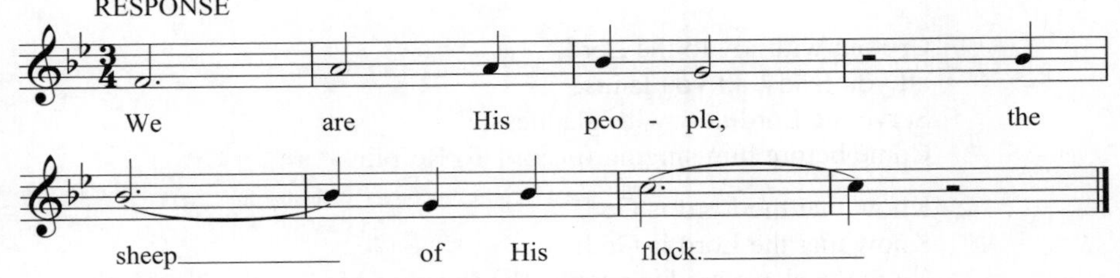
We are His peo - ple, the
sheep of His flock.

A. Gregory Murray

ALTERNATIVE RESPONSE, 4 Easter C

Al - le - lu - ia, al - le - lu - ia, al - le - lu - ia!

PSALM-TONE

1 Cry out with joy to the Lord, all the earth.
Serve the Lord with gladness.
Come before him, singing for joy.

2 Know that He the Lord is God.
He made us, we be-long to Him,
We are His people, the sheep of His flock.

3 Indeed, how good is the Lord,
eternal His merciful love.
He is faithful from age to age.

984 Psalm 100(99) We are His people

11A, Easter 4C, Common Psalm for Ordinary Time

David Haas

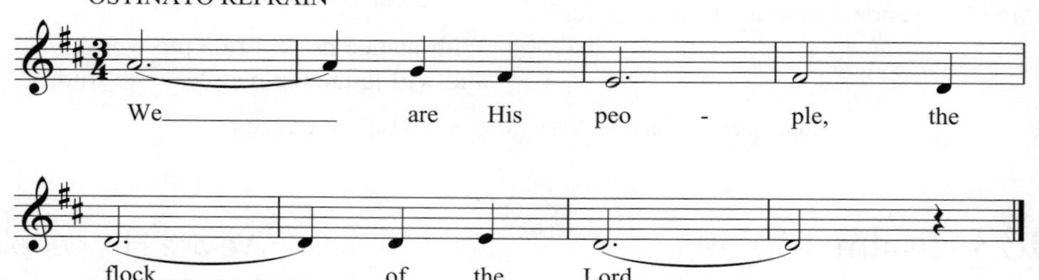

OSTINATO REFRAIN
We are His peo - ple, the
flock of the Lord.

1 Cry out with joy to the Lord,
all you lands, all you lands.
Serve the Lord now with gladness,
Come before him singing for joy! To Refrain

2 Know that the Lord is God!
Know that the Lord is God!
He made us we are his people, the sheep of his flock! *To refrain*

3 Go, now within his gates
giving thanks, giving thanks.
Enter his courts singing praise,
give him thanks and bless his name! *To refrain*

4 Indeed, how good is the Lord,
his mercy endures forever,
For the Lord he is faithful,
he is faithful from age to age! *To refrain*

985 Psalm 103(102) The Lord is compassion and love

7A, 8B, 7C, Easter Vigil 1st, Common Psalm for Ordinary Time

Geoffrey Boulton Smith

RESPONSE
1.
2.
The Lord is com - pas - sion and love.
- pas - sion and love.

1 My soul, give thanks to the Lord,
all my being, bless his holy name.
My soul, give thanks to the Lord
and never forget all his blessings.

2 It is He who forgives all your guilt,
who heals every one of your ills,
who redeems your life from the grave,
who crowns you with love and compassion.

3 The Lord is com-passion and love,
slow to anger and rich in mercy.
He does not treat us according to our sins
nor repay us according to our faults.

4 As far as the east is from the west
so far does he remove our sins.
As a father has compassion on his sons,
the Lord has pity on those who fear him.

986 Psalm 104(103)

Send forth Your Spirit, O Lord

Pentecost, Easter Vigil 1st Psalm

REFRAIN
Fine
Send forth your Spi - rit, O Lord, and re - new the face of the earth.

VERSE 1
1. Bless the Lord, O my soul, O Lord how great you are! How

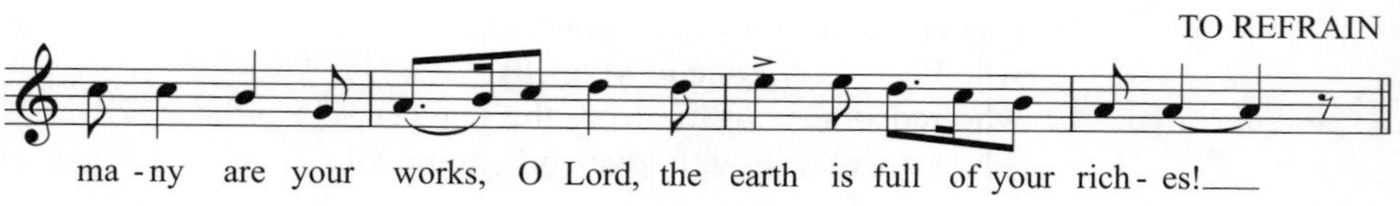
TO REFRAIN
ma - ny are your works, O Lord, the earth is full of your rich - es!

VERSE 2
2. You take back your Spi - rit, they die, back to the dust from which they came; you

TO REFRAIN
send forth your Spi - rit, they are cre - a - ted, the whole earth is re - newed!

VERSE 3
3. Your glo - ry will last for ev - er, may you re - joice in all your works.

TO REFRAIN
May my thoughts be pleas - ing to you, I find my joy in you, Lord.

Verses for the Easter Vigil

1 Bless the Lord O my soul,
O Lord how great you are!
With glory and with majesty clothed;
you are covered with light!

2 Foundation of earth you made sure,
standing firm from age to age.
You placed the ocean like a robe,
the waters covered the hills.

3 The valleys are flowing with springs;
rivers run between the hills;
the birds of heaven dwell on their banks,
they make their nests as they sing.

4 You send down your rain on the hills.
All your blessings fill the earth.
You give the cattle grass for their food,
and plants for crops to be grown.

5 In wisdom you made all these things,
Lord, they are numberless.
Your riches fill the whole of the earth.
Bless the Lord, O my soul!

987 Psalm 116(115) — Our blessing cup

Maundy Thursday, Corpus Christi B

Bob Hurd

REFRAIN

Our bless - ing cup is a com - mu - nion with the
blood of Christ; and the bread we break, it is a

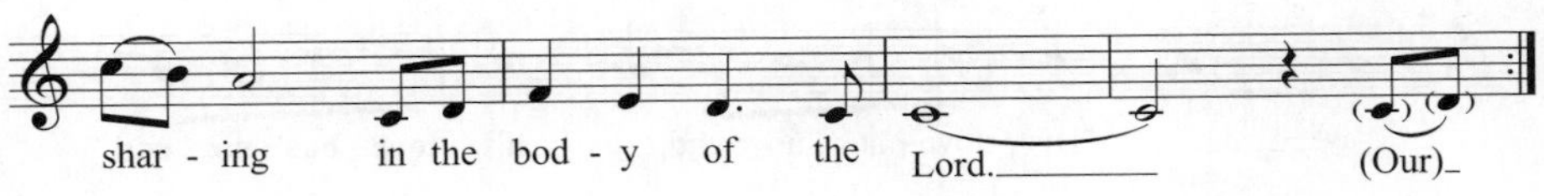
shar - ing in the bod - y of the Lord. (Our)

1 How can we make a return
for all the goodness God has shown?
We will take the cup of life,
and call upon God's name.

2 Precious indeed in your sight
the life and death of those you love.
We are you servants,
for you have set us free.

3 Gracious and merciful God,
we give you thanks and bless your name:
with all your people,
praise and glory to your name.

4 For you have heard my voice,
for you have heard my pleading.
Though death surrounded me,
you heard and answered me.

988 Psalm 118(117)

Easter Alleluia Psalm

Easter Vigil and Sunday, 2 Easter, Easter 4B, Common Psalm for Easter

Paul Inwood

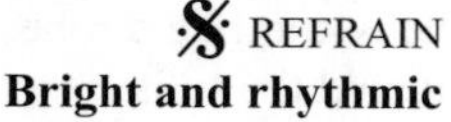
REFRAIN
Bright and rhythmic

♩ = 126
Cantor:
All:
Cantor:
Al - le - lu - ia, al - le - lu - ia, al - le -

All:
Fine
lu - - ia, al - le - lu - - - ia!

VERSE 1

Cantor:
1. Give thanks to the Lord for he is good, for his

All:
Cantor:
3
love has no end, for his love has no end. Let the sons of Is - ra - el

All:
D.S.
say: "His love has no end, his love has no end."

VERSE 2

Cantor:
2. The Lord's right hand has tri - umphed: his

All:
Cantor:
right hand raised me up, his right hand raised me up. I shall not die, I shall

D.S.
All:
live and re - count his deeds, and re - count his deeds.

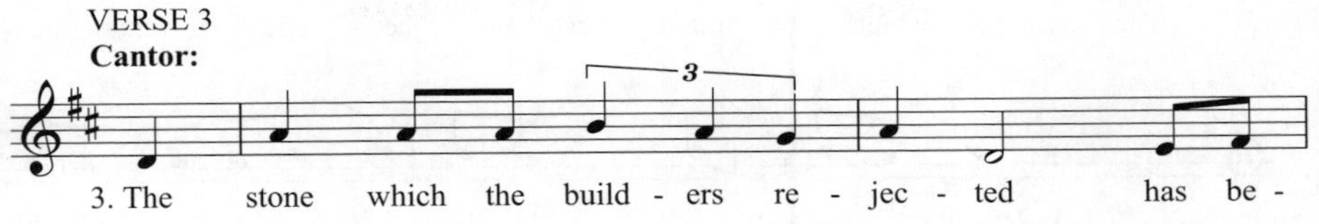
VERSE 3
Cantor:
3
3. The stone which the build - ers re - jec - ted has be -

All:
Cantor:
3
come the corn - er - stone, has be - come the corn - er - stone. This is the work of the

D.S.
All:
Lord, a mar - vel in our eyes, a mar - vel in our eyes.

989 Psalm 118(117) The stone which the builders rejected

Easter Vigil and Sunday, 2 Easter, Easter 4B, Common Psalm for Easter

Bernadette Farrell

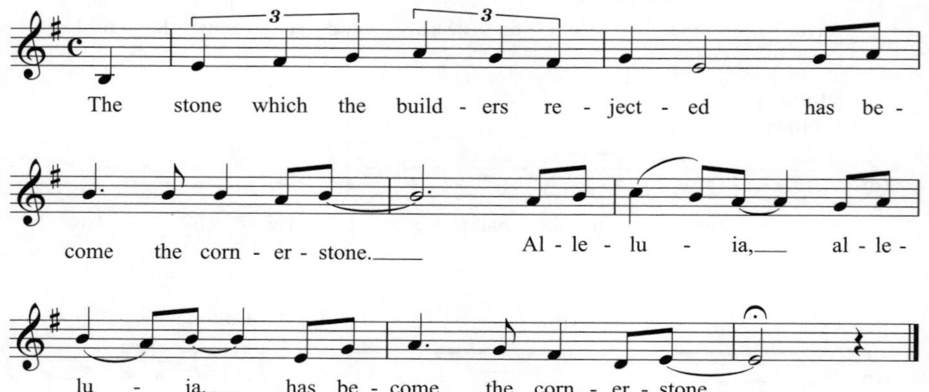
Refrain: 1st time: Cantor; each time thereafter: All
3
3
The stone which the build - ers re - ject - ed has be -
come the corn - er - stone.
Al - le - lu - ia, al - le -
lu - ia, has be - come the corn - er - stone.

Cantor/Choir

1 Let the family of Israel say:
"God's love has no end, God's love has no end."
Let the family of Aaron say:
"God's love has no end, God's love has no end."
And let all who fear God, and let all who fear God
say his love is without end.
Alleluia, alleluia, say his love is without end. *(to Refrain)*

2 I called to the Lord in my distress,
he answered me and set me free.
God is at my side, God is at my side,
God is here to help me now.
Alleluia, alleluia, God is here to help me now. *(to Refrain)*

3 Open to me the gates of holiness;
I will enter and give thanks.
This is the Lord's own gate,
the gate where the just may enter in.
I will thank you, Lord, I will thank you, Lord,
for you hear and answer me.
Alleluia, alleluia, for you hear and answer me. *(to Refrain)*

4 Go forward with branches, go forward processing,
go to the altar of the Lord
and give thanks to God, and give thanks to God
for his love is without end.
Alleluia, alleluia, for his love is without end. *(to Refrain)*

990 Psalm 128(127) — O blessed are those

Holy Family 33A, 27B

Paul Inwood

REFRAIN
O blessed are those who fear the Lord and walk in his ways. O
blessed are those who fear the Lord and walk in his ways.
VERSES
1. O blessed are those who fear the Lord and walk in his ways! By the la - bour of your hands you shall eat. You will be hap - py and pros - per. O
2. Your wife like a fruit - ful vine in the heart of your house; your child - ren like shoots of the o - live a - round your ta - ble. O
3. In - deed thus shall be blest all those who fear the Lord. May the Lord bless you from Zi - on all the days of your life! O
3
D.S.

991 Psalm 130(129) Come to me and I shall give you rest

10B, Lent 5A

Noel Donnelly

RESPONSE

Come to me and I shall give you rest.

1 From the depths I call to you.
Listen, Lord, and hear my pleading.

2 Love and mercy flow from you,
Lord of life and kind redeemer.

3 In the dark I hope for you,
you are light of new day dawning.

4 Weak and frail we come to you,
God of love and new beginning.

992 Psalm 131(130) Like a child rests

31A

Christopher Walker

REFRAIN:

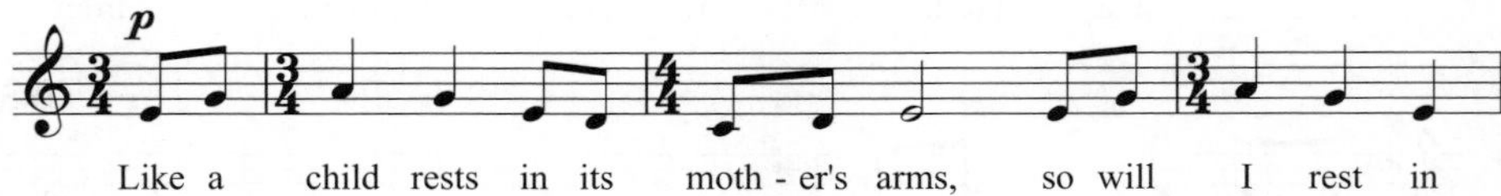
p
Like a child rests in its moth - er's arms, so will I rest in

Fine
you, Like a child rests in its moth - er's arms, so will I rest in you.

VERSES 1-3: Solo Voice

to Refrain
1. My God, I am not proud. I do not look for things too great.
2. My God, I trust in you. You care for me, you give me peace.
3. O Is - ra - el, trust in God, now and al - ways trust in God.

993 Psalm 136(135)

Vespers

O give thanks to the Lord

Joseph Gelineau

1 O give thanks to the Lord who is good,

Great is God's love, love without end; (RESPONSE)

2 Who alone has wrought marvellous works,
3 It was God who made the great lights,
4 The first-born of the Egyptians God smote,
5 God divided the Red Sea in two,
6 Through the desert the people God led,
7 God let Israel inherit their land,
8 And God snatched us away from our foes,

Great is God's love, love with - out end;

1 Give thanks to the God of gods,
2 whose wisdom it was made the skies,
3 the sun to rule in the day,
4 and brought Israel out from their midst,
5 and made Israel pass through the midst,
6 Nations in their greatness God struck,
7 the heritage of Israel, God's servant;
8 God gives food to all living things,

Great is God's love, love with - out end;

1 Give thanks to the Lord of lords,
2 who fixed the earth firmly on the seas,
3 the moon and stars in the night,
4 arm outstretched, with powerful hand,
5 and made Israel pass through the midst,
6 Kings in their splendour God slew,
7 God remembered us in our distress,
8 to the God of heaven give thanks.

Great is God's love, love with - out end.

994 Psalm 138(137)

21A, 5C, 17C

The fragrance of Christ

David Haas

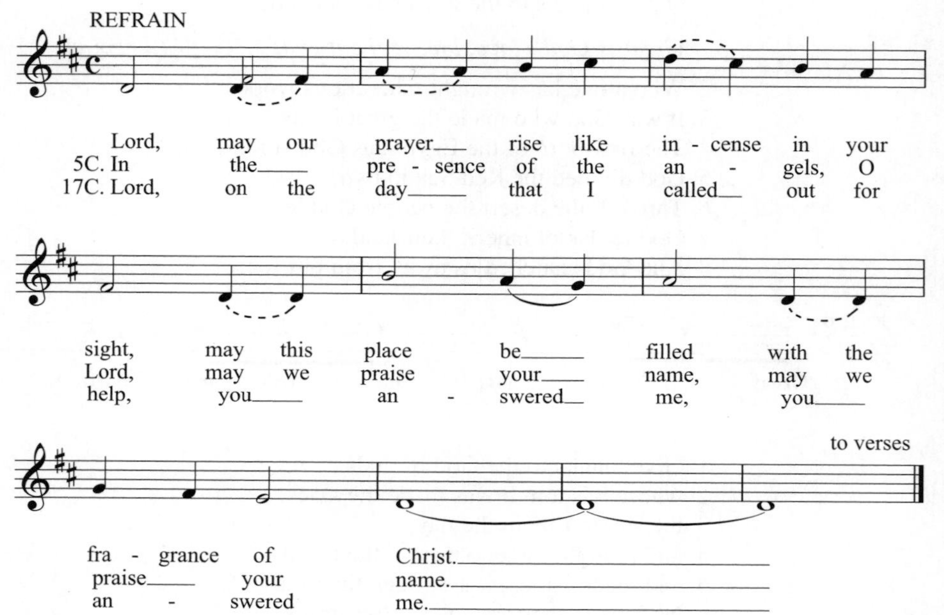
REFRAIN
Lord, may our prayer rise like in - cense in your sight, may this place be filled with the fra - grance of Christ.
5C. In the pre - sence of the an - gels, O Lord, may we praise your name, may we praise your name.
17C. Lord, on the day that I called out for help, you an - swered me, you an - swered me.
to verses

1 I will thank you, Lord, with all of my heart,
you have heard the words of my mouth.
In the presence of the angels I will bless you,
I will adore before your holy temple.

2 I will thank you, Lord, for your faithfulness
and love beyond all my hopes and dreams.
On the day that I called you answered;
you gave life to the strength of my soul.

3 All who live on earth shall give you thanks
when they hear the words of your voice.
And all shall sing of your ways:
'How great is the glory of God!'

995 Psalm 141(140)

Evening Prayer

O Lord, let my prayer rise

Paul Inwood

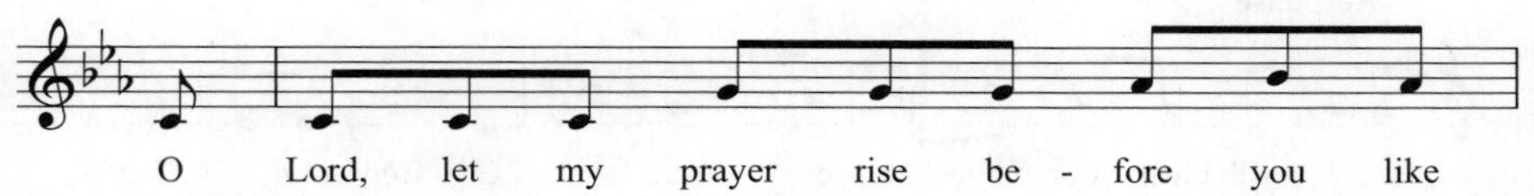
O Lord, let my prayer rise be - fore you like

in - cense, my hands like an eve - ning of - fer - ing.

1 Lord, I am calling: hasten to help me.
Listen to me as I cry to you.
Let my prayer rise before you like incense,
my hands like an evening offering.

2 Lord, set a guard at my mouth,
keep watch at the gate of my lips.
Let my heart not turn to things that are wrong,
to sharing the evil deeds done by the sinful.
No, I will never taste their delights.

3 The good may reprove me,
in kindness chastise me,
but the wicked shall never anoint my head:
every day I counter their malice with prayer.

4 To you, Lord my God, my eyes are turned:
in you I take refuge - do not forsake me.
Keep me safe from the traps they have set for me,
from the snares of those who do evil.

5 Praise to the Father, praise to the Son,
all praise to the life-giving Spirit,
as it was, is now and shall always be
for ages unending. Amen.

996 Psalm 145(144) — I will bless Your name for ever

14A, 31C, Easter 5C, 18A, 17B

Martin Hall

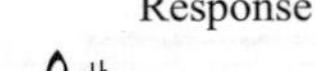
Response

I will bless your name for - ev - er, O God my King.
18A, 17B You o - pen wide your hand O Lord, You grant our de - sires.

Psalm Tone

1 I will give you glory, O God my King,
I will bless your name for ever.
I will bless you day after day
and praise your name for ever.

2 The Lord is kind and full of com-passion,
slow to anger, abounding in love.
How good is the Lord to all,
compassionate to all his creatures.

3 All your creatures shall thank you,
O Lord,
and your friends shall repeat their
blessing.
They shall speak of the glory of your reign
and declare your might, O God.

4 The Lord is faithful in all his words
and loving in all his deeds.
The Lord supports all who fall
and raises all who are bowed down.

5 To make known to men your mighty
deeds,
And the glorious splendour of your reign.
Yours is an everlasting kingdom.
Your rule lasts from age to age.

6 The eyes of all creatures look to you,
and you give them their food in good
time.
You open wide your hand,
grant the desires of all who live.

Key to verses:- 14A, 31C verses 1, 2, 3 & 4
Easter 5C verses 2, 3 & 5
18A verses 2, 6 & 4
17B verses 3, 6 & 4

997 Psalm 145(144) — I will give you glory

14A, 31C, Common Psalm for Ordinary Time

Chris O'Hara

1 I will give you glory, O God my King.
Giving praise to God for ever.
Each day I turn to you: sing your praise
and bless your name for ever.

2 The Lord is full of compassion
with a heart abounding in love.
To every creature the Lord is good,
compassionate to his people.

3 Yes! Every creature gives praise to God:
the world resounds to their blessing.
The Lord gives help to those who fall
and raises up the lowly.

Chorus

The prom - i - ses of the Lord are true and lov - ing are all his

deeds. I will give you glo - ry, O God my King and praise your name for

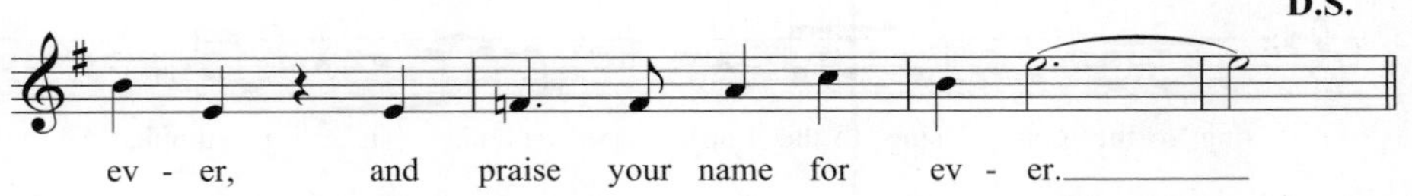
D.S.
ev - er, and praise your name for ev - er.

998 Psalm 147 — O praise the Lord Jerusalem

2nd Christmas; Corpus Christi A

Tony Charlier

(2nd Christmas) The word was made flesh and lived a - mong us.
(Corpus Christi) O praise the Lord Je - ru - sa - lem.

1 O praise the Lord Jerusalem;
Zion praise your God.
He has strengthened the bars of your gates;
He has blessed the children within you.

2 He established peace on your borders;
He feeds you with finest wheat.
He sends out his word to the earth;
and swiftly runs his command.

3 He makes his word known to Jacob;
to Israel his laws and decrees.
He has not dealt thus with other nations;
He has not taught them his decrees.

For Psalms 1, 67(66), 69(67), 96(95) and 107(106)
– *see Psalm 92(91)*

999 Canticle of Moses

Easter Vigil
Based on Exodus 15: 1-6, 17-18

John Gibbons

Refrain: All
I will sing to the Lord, sing to the Lord, glo-ri-ous_ in_ tri-umph._ I will

sing to the Lord, sing to the Lord, glo-ri-ous_ in_ tri-umph._

1 Horse and rider thrown to the sea!
The Lord is my strength, my song, my salvation.
This is my God, whom I exalt,
Praise to my ancestors' God. *(to Refrain)*

2 The Lord is a warrior, great his name.
The chariots of Pharoah hurled to the sea.
The might of his army drowned in the sea.
Waves hide them, they sank like a stone. *(to Refrain)*

3 Your right hand, Lord, is full of might;
Your right hand, Lord, has shattered the enemy.
Through the greatness of your glory
You crushed the foe. *(to Refrain)*

4 You will guide your people up to your mountain,
The place, O Lord, where you make your home.
The shelter, Lord, your hands have made.
You will reign for ever and ever. *(to Refrain)*

1000 Blessed be the God and Father

Evening Prayer
Ephesians 1:3-10

Tony Charlier

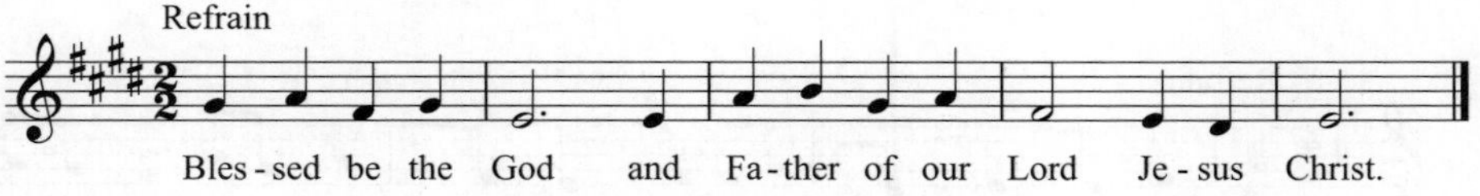
Refrain
Bles-sed be the God and Fa-ther of our Lord Je-sus Christ.

1 Who blest us in Christ
with every blessing from heaven
as he chose us in him
before the world was born,
that we shall be holy
and blameless before him,
and called us to be sons and daughters
through Jesus Christ.

2 He promised us his grace
through his beloved son,
we are redeemed through his blood
and our sins forgiv'n,
because of the riches
of his glorious grace,
for he has opened to us
the mystery of his will.

3 According to his purpose
which he set forth in Christ
as a plan for the fullness
of time to come,
that all things should be
united in him,
all things in the heavens
and all things on earth.

1001 Give thanks to the Father

Evening Prayer
Colossians 1:12-20

Tony Charlier

Refrain
Give thanks to the Fa - ther_ for let- ting_ us share with the saints the re - ward he's pre-
pared for us there; to share the joy of his glo - rious light.

1 He has delivered us
from the dominion of darkness,
and has transferred us
to the kingdom of his beloved son.

2 In him we have redemption,
the forgiveness of sins,
the image of the unseen God,
the first born of creation.

3 For in him was all created
in heaven and earth,
invisible and visible,
thrones and dominations,
all was made by and for him.

4 He is before all things
and all things hold together in him,
the head of the church, his body,
the first born from the dead
pre-eminent in all.

5. For in him God was pleased to dwell
in all his fullness,
and through him
to reconcile all to himself,
making peace
by the blood of his cross.

1002 Before Heaven and Earth were made

Philippians 2:6-11
Tune: Narenza SM

Melody from
Catholicum Hymnologium Germanicum,
J.Leisentritt (1584),

adapted by W.H.Havergal (1793-1870)

1. Be - fore the heaven and earth were made by God's de - cree, the

Son of God all glo - rious dwelt in God's e - ter - ni - ty.

1 Before the heaven and earth
were made by God's decree,
the Son of God all glorious dwelt
in God's eternity.

2 Though in the form of God
and rich beyond compare,
he did not stop to grasp his prize;
nor did he linger there.

3 From heights of heaven he came
to this world full of sin,
to meet with hunger, hatred, hell,
our life, our love to win.

4 The Son became true man
and took a servant's role:
with lowliness and selfless love,
he came, to make us whole.

5 Obedient to his death
that death upon the cross,
no son had ever shown such love,
nor father known such loss.

6 To him enthroned on high,
by angel hosts adored,
all knees shall bow, and tongues confess
that Jesus Christ is Lord.

1003 Great indeed is the Mystery

Praise the Lord all you nations

Evening Prayer, Epiphany & Transfiguration
1 Timothy 3:16

Tony Charlier

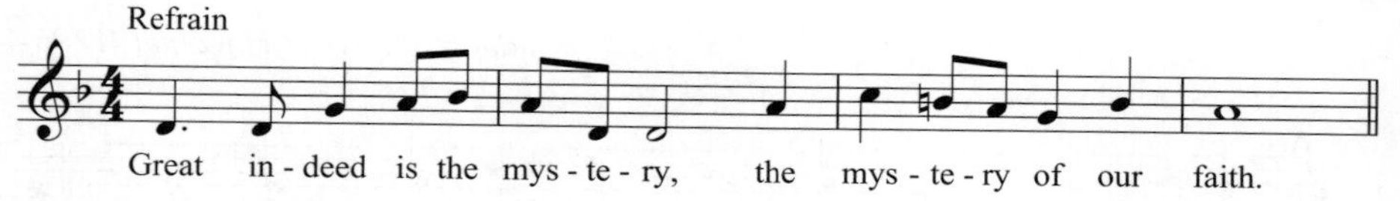
Refrain
Great in - deed is the mys - te - ry, the mys - te - ry of our faith.

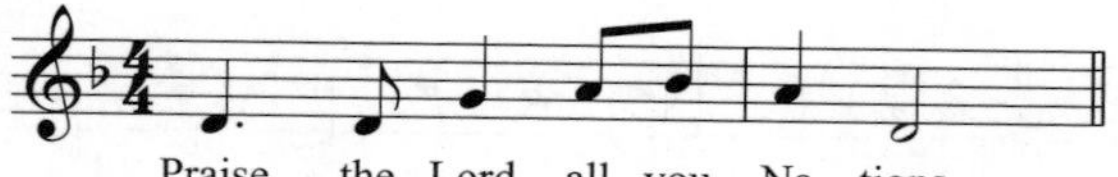
Alternative Refrain for Evening Prayer
Praise the Lord all you Na - tions.

He was manifested in the flesh,
vindicated in the Spirit,
seen by angels,
preached among the nations,
believed on in the world,
taken up in glory.

1004 Worthy are you our Lord and God

Evening Prayer & Eastertide
Revelation 4:11, 5:9, 10, 12

Tony Charlier

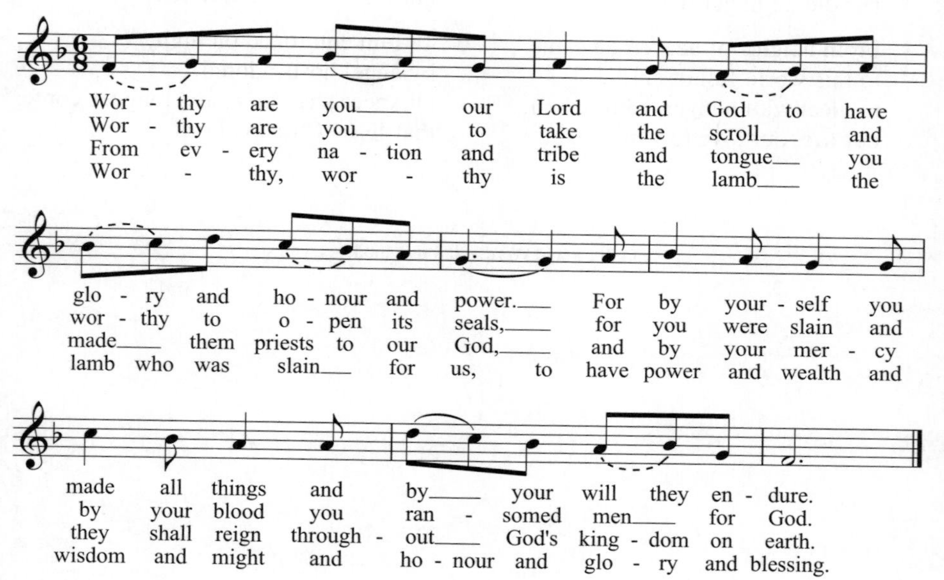
Wor - thy are you our Lord and God to have glo - ry and ho - nour and power. For by your - self you made all things and by your will they en - dure.
Wor - thy are you to take the scroll and wor - thy to o - pen its seals, for you were slain and by your blood you ran - somed men for God.
From ev - ery na - tion and tribe and tongue you made them priests to our God, and by your mer - cy they shall reign through - out God's king - dom on earth.
Wor - thy, wor - thy is the lamb the lamb who was slain for us, to have power and wealth and wisdom and might and ho - nour and glo - ry and blessing.

1005 We give thanks to you Lord

Evening Prayer & Eastertide
Revelation 11:17-18; 12:10b-12a

Tony Charlier

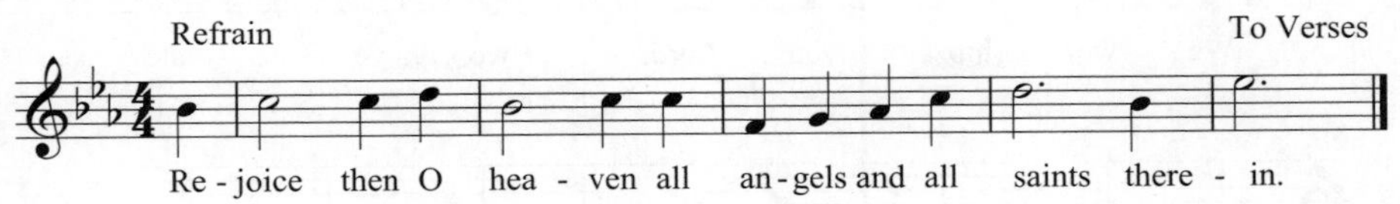
Refrain
To Verses
Re - joice then O hea - ven all an - gels and all saints there - in.

1 We give thanks to you Lord,
almighty and ever living God,
that you have taken your great and
wonderful power
and begun to reign. *To Refrain*

2 The nations all raged,
but your wrath came
and the time for the dead to be judged,
for rewarding your servants
the prophets and saints,
and those who fear your name
both small and great,
and for destroying the destroyers
of the earth. *To Refrain*

3 Now is come the salvation
and the power and the kingdom of God,
and the authority of Christ,
who has thrown down the one
who day and night accuses
the brethren standing before their God.
To Refrain

4 They have conquered him
by the blood of the lamb,
and by the word of their testimony,
for they loved not their lives even unto
death. *To Refrain*

1006 Great and wonderful are your deeds

Canticle for Morning or Evening Prayer
Revelation 15:3-4

Tony Charlier

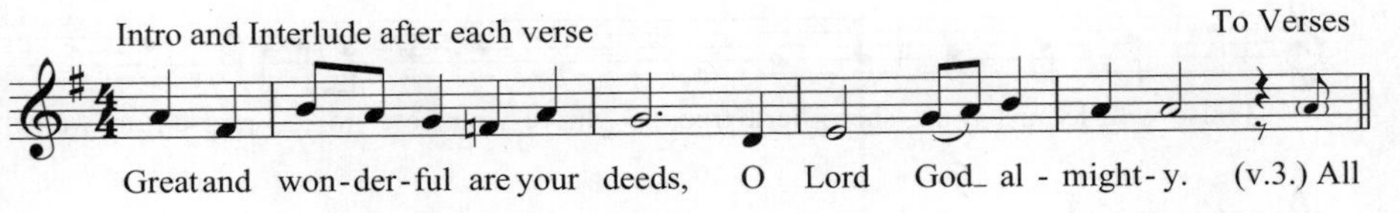
Intro and Interlude after each verse
To Verses
Great and won - der - ful are your deeds, O Lord God_ al - might - y. (v.3.) All

1 Just and true are your ways,
O King of the ages.

2 Who shall not fear and glorify your name O Lord?
For you alone are holy.

3 All nations shall come and worship you,
for your judgements have been revealed.

1007 We worship you Lord

Good Friday Antiphon

Tony Charlier

We wor - ship you Lord, we ve - ne - rate your
cross, we praise your re - sur - rec - tion. Through the
cross you brought joy to the world.

May God be gracious
and bless us;
and let his face
shed its light upon us.

1008 Sion lift your voice and sing (Lauda Sion)

Sequence for Corpus Christi

Samuel Webbe (1740-1816)

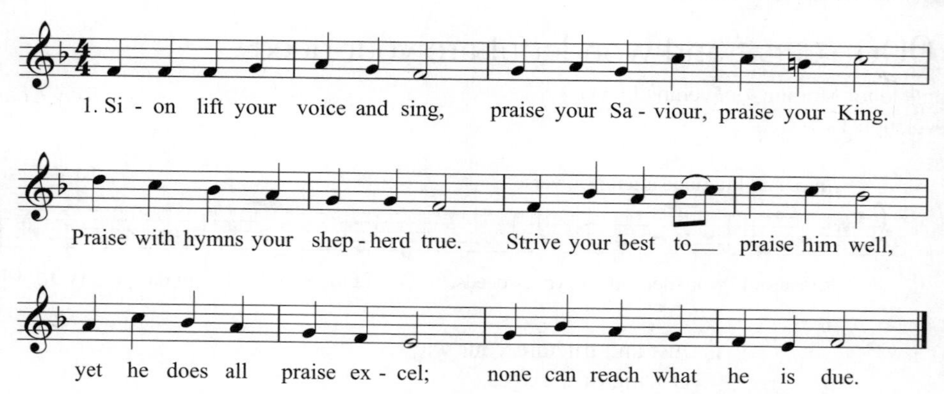
1. Si - on lift your voice and sing, praise your Sa - viour, praise your King.
Praise with hymns your shep - herd true. Strive your best to praise him well,
yet he does all praise ex - cel; none can reach what he is due.

1 Sion lift your voice and sing,
praise your Saviour, praise your King;
praise with hymns your shepherd true.
Strive your best to praise him well,
yet he does all praise excel;
none can reach what he is due.

2 See today before us laid
living and life-giving bread,
theme for praise and joy profound;
bread which at the sacred board
was, by our incarnate Lord,
giv'n to his apostles round.

3 Let the praise be loud and high;
sweet and rev'rent be the joy
felt today in every breast;
on this festival divine,
which records the origin
of the glorious Eucharist.

4 On the new king's table here,
this the new law's paschal fare
brings to end the ancient rite.
Here for empty shadows fled,
Is reality instead;
Here instead of darkness light.

5 What he did at supper seated,
Christ ordained to be repeated
in his memory divine.
Therefore we with adoration,
Thus the host of our salvation
Consecrate from bread and wine.

6 Taught by Christ the church maintains,
that the bread his flesh becomes,
and the wine becomes his blood.
Does it pass your comprehending?
Faith the law of sight transcending,
Leaps to things not understood.

7 Here beneath these signs are hidden
priceless things to sense forbidden;
signs, not things, are all we see.
Flesh from bread and blood from wine,
yet is Christ in either sign,
all entire proclaimed to be.

8 They too who of him partake,
Sever not, nor rend, nor break,
But entire their Lord receive.
Whether one or thousands eat,
All receive the self-same meat,
Nor the less for others leave.

9 Lo, the wicked with the good
Eat of this celestial food.
Yet with ends how opposite.
Life to these, but death to those,
see how from like taking flows
difference truly infinite.

10 When the host is broke in twain,
doubt not that each part contains
what was in the whole before.
Sign alone has changed its form,
while what's signified is one
and the same for evermore.

11 Hid upon the altar lies
bread of angels from the skies,
made the food of mortal man.
In old types foresignified,
in the manna heav'n supplied,
Isaac and the Paschal Lamb.

12 Jesus, shepherd, bread indeed,
You take pity on our need;
lead us to the land of grace.
Grant that at thy feast of love
sitting with the saints above,
we may see thee face to face.

1009 Processional Litany of the Saints

(Including optional Saints of England and Wales)

James Walsh

A cantor, or choir, or schola sing the response in unison. It is immediately repeateed by all, preceded by the one bar introduction.

Strong and steady
Saints of God, come to our aid! Pray for us, O

pray for us all. Saints of God come to our aid. Hear us when we call.

Then a cantor declaims the names of each group of saints, over a gentle background of sustained organ chords; other saints' names can replace those in this list.
After each section, all join in singing the response, which is sung once only each time.

Verses (spoken)

Verse 1

Holy Mary, Mother of God
Saint Michael
Holy angels of God
St. John the Baptist
St. Joseph
St. Peter and St. Paul
St. Andrew
St. John

To 𝄋

General	England and Wales
Verse 2	*Verse 2*
St. Mary Magdalene St. Stephen St. Ignatius St. Lawrence St. Perpetua and St. Felicity St. Agnes	St. Eleutherius St. Celestine St. Gregory To 𝄋
Verse 3	*Verse 3*
St. Gregory St. Augustine St. Basil St. Martin St. Benedict	St. George St. David St. Austin St. Columba St. Aidan St. Paulinus To 𝄋
Verse 4	*Verse 4*
St. Francis St. Dominic St. Francis Xavier St. John Vianney St. Catherine St. Teresa All holy men and women	St. Alban St. Julius and St. Aaron St. Thomas of Canterbury St. John Fisher St. Thomas More St. Cuthbert Mayne St. John Houghton St. Edmund Campion St. John Boste St. John Jones St. Edmund Arrowsmith St. Ambrose Barlow St. John Southworth St. Richard Gwynn St. Philip Howard St. John Rigby St. Margaret Clitheroe St. Margaret Ward All holy martyrs of England and Wales To 𝄋

Verse 5		*Verse 5*
Lord be merciful.	R. Lord save your people	St. Bede
From all evil.	R. Lord save your people	St. Anselm
From every sin.	R. Lord save your people	St. Patrick
From everlasting death.	R. Lord save your people	St. Willibrord
		St. Boniface
		To 𝄋

Verse 6		*Verse 6*
By your coming as man	R. Lord save your people	St. Deiniol
By your death and rising to new life	R. Lord save your people	St. Chad
By your gift of the Holy Spirit	R. Lord save your people	St. Cuthbert
		St. Wilfrid
		St. Edward
		St. William
		St. Hugh
		St. Edmund
		All holy pastors and confessors
		To 𝄋

Verse 7		Verse 7
Be merciful to us sinners	R. Lord hear our prayer	St. Aelred
(For Easter Vigil)		St. Simon Stock
Give new life to those chosen ones		St. Winifred
by the grace of baptism	R. Lord hear our prayer	St. Ethelburga
Jesus Son of the living God	R. Lord hear our prayer	St. Etheldreda
Christ hear us	R. Christ hear us	St. Hilda
Lord Jesus hear our prayer	R. Lord Jesus hear our prayer	St. Walburga
		All holy virgins and widows
		All holy men and women
		To 𝄋

The following are, as far as can be ascertained, the copyright holders or their administrators.
While every effort has been made to make this list as accurate as possible, it may be that some errors or omissions have occurred, for which we apologise. These will be corrected in future editions.
A list of addresses is given at the end of the section

1 © 1971 The Benedictine Foundation of the State of Vermont, Inc.
2 © 1980 International Committee on English in the Liturgy, Inc (ICEL)
3 © Honor Mary Thwaites, Campbell, ACT 2601, Australia.
5 © Faber Music Ltd, 3 Queen Square, London WC1N 3AU
6 © 1980 Geoffrey Chapman (a division of Cassell plc).
7 © 1977 Carey Landry and North American Liturgy Resources (NALR). Administered by OCP Publications.
8 © 1974 Shalom Community, 1504 Polk, Wichita Falls, Texas 76309 USA.
10 © The Archdiocese of Durban, South Africa, 408 Innes Rd, Durban 4001, South Africa.
11 © Ateliers et Presses de Taizé.
14 © Josef Weinberger.
15 © Robertson Publications (for J. Curwen & Sons Ltd), Stockley Close, Stockley Rd, West Drayton, Middx UB7 9BE.
16 © Novello & Co. Ltd.
18 © 1987 Thankyou Music/Admin. By worshiptogether.com songs. Used by permission.
20 © 1987 Thankyou Music/Admin. By worshiptogether.com songs. Used by permission.
23 © 1967 OCP Publications All rights reserved. Used with permission.
24 © 1965 World Library Publications, Inc, a division of J.S. Paluch Company Inc.
25 © 1983 GIA Publications Inc.
26 © McCrimmon Publishing Co. Ltd.
28 © 1966 Oregon Catholic Press Publications (OCP).
30 © 1965 World Library Publications, a division of J.S. Paluch Company Inc.
32 © 1973 Word of God Music. Administered by Copycare. Used by permission.
33 © McCrimmon Publishing Co. Ltd.
34 © 1976 Gerry Fitzpatrick, St Leo's the Great, 5 Beech Avenue, Dumbreck, Glasgow G41 5BY.
35 © Christopher Walker, 948 Sixteenth St, Apartment B, Santa Monica, CA 90403–3263 USA. Published by Clifton Music.
38 © 1986 GIA Publications, Inc.
39 © United Reform Church, 86 Tavistock Place, London WC1H 9RT.
42 © 1974 Stainer & Bell Ltd.
46 © 1969 Geoffrey Chapman (a division of Cassell plc).
49 © 1989 Wild Goose Resource Group/Iona Community, Pearce Institute, 840 Govan Road, Glasgow G51 3UU, Scotland.
50 © 1984 GIA Publications Inc.
51 © 1994 McCrimmon Publishing Co. Ltd.
52 © 1989 Wild Goose Resource Group/The Iona Community.
53 © 1988 New Dawn Music.
54 © 1983 Restoration Music Ltd. Administered by Sovereign Music UK.
56 © 1963 The Grail (England). Used by permission of A.P. Watt Ltd
60 © Rev Roger Ruston, OP, c/o St Dominic's Priory, Southampton Rd, Haverstock Hill, London NW5 4LB.
61 © McCrimmon Publishing Co. Ltd.
63 © 1983 GIA Publications Inc.
64 © Mrs Mildred Peacey, 10 Park Cottages, Manor Rd, Hurstpierpoint, West Sussex.
65 © 1981 Daniel L. Schutte and New Dawn Music.
67 © 1981 Michael Saward/Jubilate Hymns.
68 © Search Press Ltd (a division of Burns & Oates).
69 © Anne Scott (née Conway).
72 © 1986 Thankyou Music/Adm. By worshiptogether.com songs. Used by permission.
75 © Oxford University Press.
76 © 1981, 1990 Michael Joncas and Co-operative Ministries. OCP Publications.
77 © 1985 Christopher Walker. Published by OCP Publications.
80 © 1977 Thankyou Music/Adm. By worshioptogether.com songs. Used by permission.
81 © Ateliers et Presses de Taizé.
82 © 1983 Word Music Inc. Administered by Copycare. Used by permission
85 © 1988 GIA Publications Inc.
86 © The Grail (England). Used by permission of A.P. Watt Ltd.
89 © 1986 GIA Publications Inc.
90 © 1984 Kevin Mayhew Ltd. Reproduced by permission from Hymns Old & New.
91 © 1976 Daniel L. Schutte, SJ and New Dawn Music.
92 © 1991 Bernadette Farrell. Published by OCP Publications
93 © 1991 OCP Publications.
94 © 1981 Christopher Walker. Published by OCP Publications.
95 © 1982, 1987 New Dawn Music.
102 © Famous Music Corporation (Chappell Music Ltd), 129 Park St, London W1Y 3FA.
103 © 1979 Coronation Music Publishing/Kingsway Music. (ex. N. America, S.Africa, Europe outside of the UK & Australia). Used by permission.
104 © 1979 James G. Johnston, Joliet Lutheran Parish, Box 956, Red Lodge, Montana 59068 USA.
106 © 1969 Geoffrey Chapman (a division of Cassell plc).
107 © Pamela Stotter, 2 Fergus Drive, Shannon, Co Claire, Eire.
108 © The Trustees of the Diocese of Westminster.
110 © McCrimmon Publishing Co. Ltd.
111 © 1969 Stainer & Bell Ltd.
113 © Michael Saward/Jubilate Hymns.
114 © Christopher Idle/Jubilate Hymns.
115 © 1989 Wild Goose Resource Group/Iona Community.
118 © 1974 Thankyou Music/Adm. by worshiptogther.com songs excl. UK & Europe, adm. by Kingsway Music. Used by permission.
119 © 1969 Geoffrey Chapman (a division of Cassell plc).
120 © 1985 GIA Publications Inc.
122 © 1972, from the recording Listen, The Bendictine Foundation of the State of Vermont, Inc.
123 © McCrimmon Publishing Co. Ltd.
127 © 1988 GIA Publications Inc.
128 © Kevin Mayhew Ltd.
130 © 1985 GIA Publications Inc.
131 © 1969 Geoffrey Chapman (a division of Cassell plc).
132 English words © McCrimmon Publishing Co. Ltd.
134 © 1971, from the recording Locusts and Wild Honey, The Benedictine Foundation of the State of Vermont, Inc.
135 © 1982 OCP Publications.
137 © Ateliers et Presses de Taizé.
141 © Pamela Stotter.
142 © 1969 Geoffrey Chapman (a division of Cassell plc).
144 © 1980 Geoffrey Chapman (a division of Cassell plc).
145 © 1987 GIA Publications Inc.
146 © SPCK, Holy Trinity Church, Marylebone Rd, London NW1 4DU.
147 © 1978 Kevin Mayhew Ltd. Reproduced by permission from Hymns Old & New.
148 © 1967 OCP Publications.
151 © Ateliers et Presses de Taizé.
153 © 1961, 1974 Stainer & Bell Ltd.
154 © 1982 GIA Publications Inc.
155 © 1986 OCP Publications.
159 © 1975 Thankyou Music/Adm. by worshiptogether.com songs excl. UK & Europe, adm. by Kingsway Music. Used by permission.
160 © Chevalier Press, PO Box 13, Kensington, NSW 2033, Australia.
161 © Stewart Cross, Ribchester Rd, Blackburn BB1 9EF.
162 © Christopher Alston.
164 © 1972 CCCM Music/Maranatha! Music. Administered by Copycare. Used by permission
165 © 1985 Anthony Sharpe, 13 Meadow Rise, High Crompton, Shaw, Oldham, Lancs.

340 © 1965 World Library Publications Inc, a division of J.S. Paluch Company Inc.
341 The Trustees of the Diocese of Westminster
345 © 1988 Lifestyle Music Ltd. Administered by Sovereign Music UK.
346 © Ateliers et Presses de Taizé.
347 © 1983 North American Liturgy Resources (NALR). Admin. by OCP Publications.
349 © McCrimmon Publishing Co. Ltd.
350 © 1985 GIA Publications Inc.
353 © 1976 Timothy Manion and New Dawn Music.
354 © Willard F. Jabusch. Admin. by OCP Publications.
358 © 1979 Thankyou Music/Adm. by worshiptogether.com songs excl. UK & Europe, adm. by Kingsway Music. Used by permission.
360 © McCrimmon Publishing Co. Ltd.
361 © 1975 Agape, Carol Stream, Illinois 60188 USA.
363 © Hymns Ancient & Modern Ltd.
365 © Richard Connolly.
366 © 1975 The Missionary Society of St Paul the Apostle in the State of New York, 1865 Broadway, NY USA.
367 © Michael Perry/Jubilate Hymns.
368 © Kevin Mayhew Ltd.
369 © 1976 Robert J. Dufford, SJ and New Dawn Music.
370 Translation © Charles Watson, OSB, Prinknash Abbey, Cranham, Gloucester GL4 8EX.
372 © Oxford University Press. Reproduced from the Oxford Book of Carols by permission of OUP.
374 © McCrimmon Publishing Co. Ltd.
375 © Stainer & Bell Ltd.
376 © 1976 Celebration/Kingsway Music. Europe & Commonwealth (excl. Canada, Australasia & Africa). Used by permission.
377 © Sr M. Teresine, OSF.
378 © 1978 Patrick Lee.
381 © 1979 Josef Weinberger Ltd.
382 © 1988 Wild Goose Resource Group/Iona Community.
383 © 1979 Josef Weinberger Ltd.
385 © McCrimmon Publishing Co. Ltd.
386 © Oxford University Press.
387 © 1982 Averil Norton.
388 © 1987 Kingsway's Thankyou Music.
389 © The Archdiocese of Durban, South Africa.
391 © 1967 OCP Publications.
393 © 1986 Thankyou Music/Adm. by worshiptogether.com songs excl. UK & Europe, adm. by Kingsway Music. Used by permission.
394 © 1978 Hope Publishing Co.
395 © 1987 Robert C. Trupia. Published by OCP Publications
396 © 1992 Stephen Dean. Published by OCP Publications.
399 © McCrimmon Publishing Co. Ltd.
400 © 1965,1966,1968,1973 World Library Publications, a division of J.S. Paluch Co. Inc. All rights reserved. Used with permission.
401 © 1980 Stephen Dean. Published by OCP Publications. All rights reserved.
402 © Paul Inwood. Published by OCP Publications.
403 © 1993 David Ogden. Published by Clifton Music.
404 © 1981 Seoirse Bodley.
405 © 1981 Seoirse Bodley.
406 Translation, keyboard & choral harmony © 1993 Paul Inwood. Published by OCP Publications. All rights reserved. Used with permission. Music © 1984 George Salazar.
407 © 1981,1982 Peter Jones. Published by OCP Publications.
408 © 1983 Mike Anderson 83 Denholme, Up Holland, Skelmersdale. Lancs. WN8 0AX
409 © Francis Duffy.
410 © 1985 Fintan P. O' Carroll and Christopher Walker. Published by OCP Publications. All rights reserved. Used with permission.
411 © GIA Publications Inc. All rights reserved.
412 © 1988,1992 Christopher Walker. Published by OCP Publications. All rights reserved. Used with permission.
413 © Ateliers de Presses de Taizé.
414 –
415 Music © James Walsh.
416 Words & Melody © 1984 Bernadette Farrell.Published by OCP Publications. All rights reserved. Used with permission.
417 English translation from the Roman Missal © 1973 International Committee on English in the Liturgy, Inc. (ICEL) Music © 1983,198y Christopher Walker. All rights reserved. Used with permission.
418 © 1986 Christopher Walker. Published by OCP Publications. All rights reserved. Used with permission.
419 © Paul Inwood. Published by OCP Publications.
420 © 1985 Patrick Geary. Published by Clifton Music.
421 Music © 1987 Wild Goose Resource Group/Iona Community.
422 © 1982 Christopher Walker.
423 © 1982 Christopher Walker.
424 © 1982 Christopher Walker.
425 © 1982 Paul Inwood. Published by OCP.
426 © 1982 Paul Inwood. Published by OCP.
427 © 1982 Paul Inwood. Published by OCP.
428 © 1985 Bernadette Farrell. Published by OCP.
429 English translation from the Roman Missal © 1973 International Committee on English in the Liturgy, Inc (ICEL) Music © 1986 Bernadette Farrell. Published by OCP.
430 English translation from the Roman Missal © 1973 International Committee on English in the Liturgy, Inc (ICEL) Music © 1986 Bernadette Farrell. Published by OCP.
431 English translation from the Roman Missal © 1973 International Committee on English in the Liturgy, Inc (ICEL) Music © 1985 Bernadette Farrell. Published by OCP.
432 © 1985 Bernadette Farrell. Published by OCP.
433 English translation from the Roman Missal © 1973 International Committee on English in the Liturgy, Inc (ICEL) Music © 1988 Paul Inwood. Published by OCP.
434 English translation from the Roman Missal © 1973 International Committee on English in the Liturgy, Inc (ICEL) Music © 1988 Paul Inwood. Published by OCP.
435 English translation from the Roman Missal © 1973 International Committee on English in the Liturgy, Inc (ICEL) Music © 1988 Paul Inwood. Published by OCP.
436 English translation from the Roman Missal © 1973 International Committee on English in the Liturgy, Inc (ICEL) Music © 1988 Paul Inwood. Published by OCP.
437 English translation from the Roman Missal © 1973 International Committee on English in the Liturgy, Inc (ICEL) Music © 1988 Paul Inwood. Published by OCP.
438 English translation from the Roman Missal © 1973 International Committee on English in the Liturgy, Inc (ICEL) Music © 1988 Paul Inwood. Published by OCP.
439 © 1984 GIA Publications Inc. All rights reserved. Used with permission
440 © 1984 GIA Publications Inc. All rights reserved. Used with permission.
441 © 1984 GIA Publications Inc. All rights reserved. Used with permission.
442 © 1981 Seoirse Bodley.
443 © 1981 Seoirse Bodley.
444 © 1987 Stephen Dean
445 © 1987 Stephen Dean
446 © 1987 Stephen Dean
447 © 1987 Stephen Dean
448 © 1987 Stephen Dean
449 © 1987 Stephen Dean
450 English translation from the Roman Missal © 1973 International Committee on English in the Liturgy, Inc (ICEL). Music © 1984, 1985 Chris O'Hara and McCrimmon Publishing Co. Ltd.
451 –
452 © 1983 Paul Inwood. Published by OCP Publications.
453 © Bernadette Farrell. Published by OCP Publications.
454 © 1988 Paul Inwood. Published by OCP Publications.
455 © 1983 GIA Publications Inc. All rights reserved. Used with permission.

456 © 1981 Seoirse Bodley.
457 © 1983,1989 Ernest Sands. Published by OCP Publications.
458 © 1988,1989 Christopher Walker. Published by OCP Publications. All rights reserved. Used with permission.
459 © 1975,1987 McCrimmon Publishing Co Ltd.
460 © 1975,1987 McCrimmon Publishing Co Ltd.
461 © 1975,1987 McCrimmon Publishing Co Ltd.
462 © 1975,1987 McCrimmon Publishing Co Ltd.
463 © 1975,1987 McCrimmon Publishing Co Ltd.
464 © 1975,1987 McCrimmon Publishing Co Ltd.
465 © 1975,1987 McCrimmon Publishing Co Ltd.
466 © 1975,1987 McCrimmon Publishing Co Ltd.
467 © McCrimmon Publishing Co. Ltd.
468 © McCrimmon Publishing Co. Ltd.
469 © McCrimmon Publishing Co. Ltd.
470 –
471 –
472 English translation from the Roman Missal © 1973 International Committee on English in the Liturgy, Inc (ICEL) Music © 1988 Paul Inwood. Published by OCP Publications.
473 –
474 © 1969 Geoffrey Chapman (a division of Cassell plc).
477 © 1976 Rocksmith Music. Administered by Leo Song Copyright Service Ltd for UK and Eire, 7-8 Greenland Place, London NW1 0AT.
478 Dedicated to Mrs Frances Tracy. © 1967 OCP Publications.
479 © 1986 Thankyou Music/Adm. by worshiptogether.com songs excl. UK & Europe, adm. by Kingsway Music. Used by permission.
480 © McCrimmon Publishing Co. Ltd.
481 Translation © Verbum Forlong AB, Sweden.
482 © 1974 Stanbrook Abbey (England).
483 Source unknown.
484 © David Mowbray and Jubilate Hymns.
485 © 1990 Ernest Sands. Published by OCP Publications.
486 © Kevin Mayhew Ltd.
487 © 1986 Thankyou Music/Adm. by worshiptogether.com songs excl. UK & Europe, adm. by Kingsway Music. Used by permission.
489 © Ateliers et Presses de Taizé.
490 © David Higham Associates Ltd, 5-8 Lower John St, Golden Square, London W1R 4HA.
491 © McCrimmon Publishing Co. Ltd.
493 English translation © John Glynn.
494 © Paschal Jordan, OSB.
499 vv2-5 © Kevin Mayhew Ltd.
500 © 1989 Make Way Music, PO Box 263, Croydon, Surrey CR9 5AP.
501 © 1986 Anthony Sharpe.
502 Psalm & Response 1 © The Grail (England) Ltd. Used by permission of A.P. Watt Ltd. Response 2 © McCrimmon Publishing Co. Ltd.
504 © Anthony Sharpe.
505 © 1965 World Library Publications Inc, a division of J.S Paluch Company Inc.
506 © 1984 New Dawn Music.
507 © 1994 McCrimmon Publishing Co. Ltd.
508 © The Trustees of the Diocese of Westminster.
509 © 1974 Hope Publishing Company. Administered by Copycare.
510 © McCrimmon Publishing Co. Ltd.
511 © 1986 GIA Publications Inc.
513 © Oxford University Press. Reproduced from the Oxford Book of Carols by permission of OUP.
514 © OCP Publications.
515 © Novello & Co. Ltd.
518 © Timothy Dudley-Smith.
519 © Ateliers et Presses de Taizé.
523 © Chrysogonus Waddell and Mount St Joseph's Abbey, Mount St Joseph's Abbey, Roscreen, Co. Tipperary, Eire.
524 © 1969 Geoffrey Chapman (a division of Cassell plc).
526 © 1984 Utryck. Administered by Walton Music Corporation.
527 © Oxford University Press.
529 © The Trustees of Rev Clifford Howell, SJ.
530 © The Trustees of Rev Clifford Howell, SJ.
533 © 1984 Owen Alstott and New Dawn Music.
534 © 1982 Randall DeBruyn and OCP Publications.
537 © The Executor of A. Gregory Murray, OSB, Dom Andrew Moore, Downside Abbey, Stratton-on-the-Fosse, Bath.
538 © Kevin Mayhew Ltd.
539 © The Archdiocese of Durban, South Africa.
541 © 1965, 1966 World Library Publications, a division of J.S. Paluch Company Inc.
542 © Ateliers et Presses de Taizé
543 Text of the response copyright © 1985 OCP. Verses from The Psalms: A New Translation © The Grail (England) Ltd. Used by permission of A.P. Watt Ltd.
545 © McCrimmon Publishing Co. Ltd.
549 © 1969 Geoffrey Chapman (a division of Cassell plc).
551 © Ampleforth Abbey Trustees, York YO6 4EN.
555 © 1984, 1985 Chris O'Hara and McCrimmon Publishing Co. Ltd.
557 Source unknown.
558 © 1985 Chris O'Hara and McCrimmon Publishing Co. Ltd.
564 © 1982 GIA Publications Inc.
565 © 1964 Appleseed Music Inc, sub-published by Harmony Music Ltd, 1A Farm Place, London W8 7SX.
566 © 1974, 1994 Sisters of St Mary of Namur, 909 West Shaw, Ft. Worth, Texas 76110. All rights reserved.
567 © 1979 Josef Weinberger Ltd.
568 © 1953 Stuart K. Hine/The Stuart Hine Trust/Published by Kingsway Music. Worldwide excl. North and South America. Used by permission.
570 © McCrimmon Publishing Co. Ltd.
572 © 1978 Kevin Mayhew Ltd. Reproduced by permission from Hymns Old & New.
573 © 1941 The Rodeheaver Company. Administered by Copycare. Used by permission.
576 © McCrimmon Publishing Co. Ltd.
578 © 1978 John B. Foley, SJ and New Dawn Music.
579 © McCrimmon Publishing Co. Ltd.
580 © 1981 Thankyou Music/Adm. by worshiptogether. com songs excl. UK & Europe, adm. by Kingsway Music. Used by permission.
582 © OCP Publications.
583 © Ateliers et Presses de Taizé.
585 © McCrimmon Publishing Co. Ltd.
587 © 1981 ICEL.
588 © McCrimmon Publishing Co. Ltd.
589 © 1983 Anthony Sharpe.
590 © 1985, 1994 Francesca Leftley, 25 Fairmead Avenue, Westcliff-on-sea, Essex SS0 9RY. Published by Clifton Music.
591 © 1989 Christopher Walker. Published by OCP Publications.
592 © 1968 Stainer & Bell Ltd.
594 © 1987 Anthony Sharpe.
596 © McCrimmon Publishing Co. Ltd.
597 © Kevin Mayhew Ltd.
598 © McCrimmon Publishing Co. Ltd.
599 © McCrimmon Publishing Co. Ltd.
600 © 1981 Thankyou Music/Adm. by worshiptogether.com songs excl. UK & Europe, adm. by Kingsway Music. Used by permission.
603 Original words © L. de Vocht. Translation © C.J. Marivoet.
604 © McCrimmon Publishing Co. Ltd.
607 © McCrimmon Publishing Co. Ltd.
608 © Rt Rev Mgr David McRoberts.
611 © Oxford University Press. Reproduced from the Oxford Book of Carols by permission of OUP.
612 © 1984 Stephen Dean. Published by OCP Publications.
613 © Rev Roger Ruston, OP.
614 © Ateliers et Presses de Taizé.
615 © McCrimmon Publishing Co. Ltd.
617 © 1967 Sacred Songs. Admin. by Copycare.Used by permission.
618 © 1983 Thankyou Music/Adm. by worshiptogether.com songs excl. UK & Europe, adm. by Kingsway Music.Used by permission.
621 Verses © 1963 The Grail (England) Ltd. Used by permission of A.P. Watt Ltd. Refrain © 1981 OCP.

622 © 1985 ICEL.
626 © Timothy Dudley-Smith.
627 © James J. Donahue.
629 © Kevin Mayhew Ltd.
631 © The Trustees of Revd Clifford Howell, SJ.
632 © 1987 Ekklesia Music, Inc, PO Box 22967, Denver, Colorado 80222 USA.
633 © 1972 CCCM Music/Maranatha! Music. Administered by Copycare. Used by permission.
634 © The Archdiocese of Durban, South Africa.
635 © McCrimmon Publishing Co. Ltd.
636 © 1984 Utryck. Administered by Walton Music Corporation.
637 © 1987 Christopher Walker. Published by OCP Publications.
638 From the oral tradition © 1991 Jorge Maldona do, 40 CH des Coudriers, 1209 Geneva, Switzerland.
639 © McCrimmon Publishing Co. Ltd.
640 © 1988 Wild Goose Resource Group/Iona Community.
641 © World Library Publications, a division of J.S. Paluch Company Inc.
642 © McCrimmon Publishing Co. Ltd.
644 © Timothy Dudley-Smith.
645 © 1972 Daniel L. Schutte and New Dawn Music.
646 © 1969 Geoffrey Chapman (a division of Cassell plc).
647 © 1974 Linda Stassen/New Song Ministries, PO Box 11662, Costa Mesa, California 92626, USA.
648 © 1983 Michael J. Anderson.
649 © McCrimmon Publishing Co. Ltd.
652 © Roland F. Palmer, SSJE
653 © Vanguard Music Corporation.
654 © 1981 OCP Publications.
655 © 1984, 1985 Sebastian Temple. Admin by OCP Publications.
656 © 1994 Aniceto Nazareth. Text only may be reprinted for one-time use at Nuptial Mass.
657 © 1975 Robert J. Dufford, SJ and New Dawn Music.
658 © 1978 Patrick Lee.
659 © Oxford University Press.
662 © 1966 FEL Publications. Administered by The Lorenz Corporation, 501 East Third St, PO Box 802, Dayton, Ohio 45401–0802 USA.
664 © 1976, 1980 Medical Mission Sisters.
665 © 1988 Timothy Dudley-Smith.
666 © Daniel Iverson. Birdwing Music/Alliance Media Ltd. Admin. by Copycare.
667 Translation of Oosterhuis texts by Tony Barr © OCP Publications.
668 © The Trustees of the Diocese of Westminster.
670 © Belwyn Mills Music Ltd, 250 Purley Way, Croydon CR9 4QD.
671 © 1993 Delores Dufner. Published by OCP Publications.
672 © Ateliers et Presses de Taizé.
676 © 1967 OCP Publications.
678 © World Library Publications, a division of J.S. Paluch Company Inc.
679 © 1991 Christopher Walker and James Harrison. Published by OCP Publications.
680 © 1989 Wild Goose Resource Group/Iona Community.
682 © 1981 Stephen Dean. Published by OCP Publications.
684 © Timothy Dudley-Smith.
685 © Bosworth & Co. Ltd, 1418 Heddon St, London W1R 8DP.
687 © Vanguard Music Corporation, Radio City Station, PO Box 673, New York, NY 10101 USA.
693 © Diocesan Liturgical Centre of Melbourne Commission for the Liturgy, 406 Albert Square, East Melbourne, Victoria 3002, Australia.
695 © McCrimmon Publishing Co. Ltd.
698 © 1966, 1982 Willard F. Jabusch. Admin. by OCP Publications.
701 © Mrs Morfydd E. Rees, St Benedict's Abbey, Charlbury Grove, Ealing, London W5 2DY.
702 © 1983 Mike Anderson. 11a Rampit Close, Penny Lane, Haydock, Merseyside WA11 0YH.
703 © 1974 The Word of God Music. Administered by Copycare. Used by permission.
704 © John B. Foley, SJ and New Dawn Music.
705 © McCrimmon Publishing Co. Ltd.
707 © 1963 The Grail (England) Ltd. Used by permission of A.P. Watt Ltd.
708 © 1967 OCP Publications.
709 © 1965 GIA Publications Inc.
710 © McCrimmon Publishing Co. Ltd.
713 © 1980 Geoffrey Chapman (a division of Cassell plc).
714 © 1969 Rev Carey Landry and NALR. Admin. by OCP Publications.
715 © 1994 Stephen Dean. Published by Decani Music.
718 © McCrimmon Publishing Co. Ltd.
719 © McCrimmon Publishing Co. Ltd.
720 © 1984 Chris O'Hara and McCrimmon Publishing Co. Ltd.
722 © McCrimmon Publishing Co. Ltd.
723 © McCrimmon Publishing Co. Ltd.
724 © 1984, 1985 Chris O'Hara and McCrimmon Publishing Co. Ltd.
725 © High-Fye Music, 8-9 Frith Street, London W1V 5TZ.
726 © 1991 Chris O'Hara/Kalajodo Music, 53 Pikes Lane, Glossop SK13 8ED.
729 © 1969 Geoffrey Chapman (a division of Cassell plc).
730 © 1978 Bud John Songs/Alliance Media Ltd. Administered by Copycare.
731 © Kingsway/Thankyou Music.
732 © 1969 Geoffrey Chapman (a division of Cassell plc).
734 © 1974 Ephpheta House, c/o Mary McGann, 3330 Adams Road, Auburn Heights, Michigan 48057, USA.
737 © 1984 OCP Publications.
739 © 1975 Daniel L. Schutte and New Dawn Music.
742 © McCrimmon Publishing Co. Ltd.
743 © The Trustees of the Diocese of Westminster.
746 © 1966, 1987 Geoffrey Chapman (a division of Cassell plc).
747 © 1941 Irene C. Mueller.
750 © 1976 Robert F. O'Connor and New Dawn Music.
751 © McCrimmon Publishing Co. Ltd.
752 © 1975 John B. Foley, SJ and New Dawn Music.
753 English translation © Fred Kaan, Spencer St, Leamington Spa, Worcs CV31 3NE. French original © SEFIM
754 © 1983 Bernadette Farrell. Published by OCP Publications
755 © A.R. Mowbray & Co. (a division of Cassell plc).
759 Translation © Christopher Walker. Published by OCP Publications.
762 © Ateliers et Presses de Taizé.
764 © McCrimmon Publishing Co. Ltd.
765 © McCrimmon Publishing Co. Ltd.
766 © 1979 John C. Ylvisaker, 1568 Eustis St, St Paul, Minnesota 55108, USA.
768 © Wild Goose/ Iona Community.
769 © 1966 FEL Publications. Administered by The Lorenz Corporation.
770 © Stainer & Bell.
771 © 1986 Thankyou Music/Adm. by worshiptogether.com songs excl. UK & Europe, adm. by Kingsway Music. Used by permission.
772 © 1989 Wild Goose Resource Group/Iona Community.
773 © 1974m 1982 Willard F. Jabusch. Admin. by OCP Publications.
774 © 1989 GIA Publications Inc.
775 © 1975 Celebration/Kingsway Music. Europe & Commonwealth (excl. Canada, Australasia & Africa). Used by permission.
776 © 1975 Willard F. Jabusch. Admin. by OCP Publications.
777 © Michael Perry/Jubilate Hymns.
778 © Dr E.J. Burns, Christ Church Vicarage, 6 Watling Street Rd, Fulwood, Preston, Lancs PR2 4DY.
779 © 1983 GIA Publications Inc.
780 © 1975, 1978 John B. Foley, SJ and New Dawn Music.
781 © 1983 GIA Publications Inc.
783 © Donal Murray, St Kevin's, St Agnes' Rd, Curmlin, Dublin 12, Eire.
784 © St Mary's Abbey, West Malling, Kent ME19 6JX.
785 © 1969 Geoffrey Chapman (a division of Cassell plc).
786 © 1960, 1963 Ludlow Music Inc. Assigned to Tro Essex Music Ltd, 85 Gower St, London WC1E 6HJ.
787 © 1988 Paul Inwood. Published by OCP Publications.
789 © 1984 GIA Publications Inc.
790 © McCrimmon Publishing Co. Ltd.
792 © Dawntreader Music/Copycare.
793 © 1977 Alba House Communications, Canfield, Ohio 44406 USA.
795 © 1984 Sr. Donna Marie McGargill, OSM and OCP Publications.
796 © Oxford University Press.
797 © 1967 Gooi en Sticht, bv Baarn, The Netherlands. OCP

798 © 1981 ICEL.
799 © 1966, 1982 Willard F. Jabusch. Admin. by OCP Publications.
800 © 1965, 1969 Stainer & Bell Ltd.
802 © Stainer & Bell Ltd.
804 © Timothy Dudley-Smith.
806 © Christopher Idle/Jubilate Hymns.
807 French original © SEFIM. English translation © 1978, 1994 Margaret Daly, 7 Reuben Avenue, South Circular Road, Dublin 8, Eire.
808 © McCrimmon Publishing Co. Ltd.
809 © The Trustees of the Diocese of Westminster.
811 © Michael Saward and Jubilate Hymns.
812 © 1987 Wild Goose Resource Group/Iona Community.
813 © 1977 Scripture in Song. Administered by Copycare.
814 © McCrimmon Publishing Co. Ltd.
815 © Aidan Whelan, Flat 1, 5 Saville Terrace, Seville Park Rd, Halifax, Yorks HX1 3DN.
816 © 1971 Daniel L. Schutte, SJ and New Dawn Music.
817 © McCrimmon Publishing Co. Ltd.
821 © 1986 GIA Publications Inc.
822 © 1978 Springtide. Administered by Copycare.
823 © 1984 Randal Debruyn. Published by OCP Publications.
824 © 1985 Chris O'Hara and McCrimmon Publishing Co. Ltd.
825 © 1993 OCP Publications.
826 © 1976 Agape.
827 © 1991 Chris O'Hara/Kalajodo Music.
828 © McCrimmon Publishing Co. Ltd.
829 © 1987 Integrity's Hosanna Music!/People of Destiny Int. Administered by Kingsway's Thankyou Music.
830 © 1975, 1978 Robert J. Dufford, SJ and New Dawn Music.
831 © Lillenas Publishing Co., Box 527, Kansas City, Missouri 64141 USA.
832 © 1979 Michael Joncas and New Dawn Music.
833 –
834 © Stephen Dean
835 Music © McCrimmon Publishing Co. Ltd.Words © he Grail (England) Ltd Used by permission of A.P. Watt Ltd.
836 Words © The Bishops' Conference of England and Wales. Music © Stephen Dean
837 –
838 © Stephen Dean
839 Music © Stephen Dean. Words © The Bishops' Conference of England and Wales
840 Words © The Bishops' Conference of England and Wales. Music © Stephen Dean
841 –
842 © Church Pension Fund
843 © Stephen Dean
844 © Stephen Dean
845 © Stephen Dean
846 © Stephen Dean
847 © Stephen Dean
848 © Stephen Dean
849 Words © The Grail (England) Ltd. Used by permission of A.P. Watt Ltd. Music © Ken Belasco
850 © Stephen Dean
851 Words © The Bishops' Conference of England and Wales. Music © Stephen Dean
852 © The Grail (England) Ltd. Used by permission of A.P. Watt td.
853 © McCrimmon Publishing Co. Ltd.
854 © The Bishops' Conference of England and Wales. Music © Stephen Dean
855 © The Bishops' Conference of England and Wales. Music © Stephen Dean
856 –
857 –
858 © 1984 Thankyou Music/Adm by worshiptogether.com songs excl. UK & Europe, adm. by Kingsway Music. Used by permission.
859 © 1978 Kevin Mayhew Ltd.
860 Text © 1991, Owen Alstott. Published by OCP Publications. All rights reserved. Used with permission.
861 © 1982, Christopher Walker. Published by OCP Publications. All rights reserved. Used with permission.
862 © 1995 CJM Music Ltd. www.cjmmusic.com
863 © 1978 Sovereign Music UK.
864 © 1991, Christopher Walker. Published by OCP Publications. All rights reserved. Used with permission.
865 © CJM Music Ltd.
866 © 1992, Daniel L. Schutte. Published by OCP Publications. All rights reserved. Used with permission.
867 © 1989 Vineyard Songs Canada. Administered by Copycare. Used by permission.
868 © CJM Music Ltd.
869 © 1984 Thankyou Music/Adm. by worshiptogether.com songs excl. UK & Europe, adm. by Kingsway Music. Used by permission.
870 © Kevin Mayhew Ltd.
871 © 1997, WGRG, Iona Community, G2 3DH
872 –
873 © Sovereign Lifestyle Music
874 © Arrangement 1998 McCrimmon Publishing Co Ltd
875 © 1989, Stephen Dean. Published by OCP Publications. All rights reserved. Used with permission.
876 © 1989, Ernest Sands. Published by OCP Publications. All rights reserved. Used with permission.
877 © 1981 Sound III Incorporated, USA. Universal/MA Music Ltd. Used by permission of Music Sales Ltd. All rights reserved. International copyright reserved.
878 © 1984 GIA Publications Inc.* All Right Reserved
879 Music and text © 1999, Stephen Dean. Published by OCP Publications. All rights reserved. Used with permission.
880 © 1993, Stephen Dean. Published by OCP Publications. All rights reserved. Used with permission.
881 © 1999 Vineyard Songs UK. Administered by Copycare. Used by permission.
882 © 1988 Mercy/Vineyard Publishing. Administered by Copycare. Used by permission.
883 © 1974 Scripture in Song (a division of Integrity Music)/Sovereign Music UK.
884 © 1986 Thankyou Music/Adm. by worshiptogether.com songs excl. UK & Europe, adm. by Kingsway Music. Used by permission.
885 © 1997 Christopher Walker. Published by OCP Publications. All rights reserved. Used with permission.
886 © Arrangement 1998 McCrimmon Publishing Co Ltd.
887 © 1996 Teresa Brown/Devine Music, 21 Main St. Thurning, Nr. Oundle,Peterborough PE8 5RB
888 © 1979 Mercy/Vineyard Songs UK. Administered by Copycare. Used by permission.
889 © 1985, David Haas. Published by OCP Publications. All rights reserved. Used with permission.
890 © 1984 Kevin Mayhew Ltd.
891 © 1994, Bernadette Farrell. Published by OCP Publications. All rights reserved. Used with permission.
892 © 1996 CJM Music Ltd.
893 © St Mungo's Music, St. Leo's, 5 Beech Ave., Glasgow. G41 5BY
894 © James Quinn
895 © 1993 Darlene Zschech/Hillsong Publishing/Kingsway Music.
896 © McCrimmon Publishing Co. Ltd.
897 © 1992 GIA Publications Inc.*All Rights Reserved
898 © 1992, Bernadette Farrell. Published by OCP Publications. All rights reserved. Used with permission.
899 © 1979 Vineyard Songs UK. Administered by Copycare. Used by permission.
900 © 1986 Thankyou Music/Adm. by worshiptogether.com songs excl. UK & Europe, adm. by Kingsway Music. Used by permission.
901 © Stainer and Bell Ltd
902 © 1990 Intergrity's Hosanna! Music/Sovereign Music UK
903 © 1998 Vineyard Songs UK. Administered by Copycare. Used by permission.
904 © 1991, Christopher Walker Publised by OCP Publications. All rights reserved. Used with permission.

905 © 1990 GIA Publications Inc.*All Rights Reserved
906 –
907 © Mrs B Perry/Jubilate Hymns, 4 Thorne Park, Torquay TQ2 6RX
908 © 1999, Bernadette Farrell. Published by OCP Publications. All rights reserved. Used with permission
909 © 1991, Bernadette Farrell. Published by OCP Publications. All rights reserved. Used with permission.
910 © 1988 Make Way Music. PO Box 263, Croydon. C9 5AP UK
911 © Kevin Mayhew Ltd.
912 © 1980 GIA Publication Inc.*All Rights Reserved
913 © Arrangement 2004 Tony Charlier
914 © Kevin Mayhew Ltd.
915 © 1992, Anne Quigley. Published by OCP Publications. All rights reserved. Used with permission.
916 © 1999, Bernadette Farrell. Published by OCP Publications. All rights reserved. Used with permission.
917 © Paul Inwood/Magnificat Music
918 © 1996, Stephen Dean. Published by OCP Publications. All rights reserved. Used with permission.
919 © 1982 Christopher Walker. Published by OCP Publications. All rights reserved. Used with permission.
920 © Ateliers et Presses de Taizé.
921 © Bill Tamblyn. Published by OCP Publications. All rights reserved. Used with permission.
922 © Christopher Walker. Published by OCP Publications. All rights reserved Used with permission.
923 –
924 English text © 1970, International Consultation on English Text (ICET) Music © 1997, Paul Inwood. All rights reserved. Reproduced by permission of Magnificat Music.
925 © Anne Ward 2 Goodacres, Arundel Rd, Fontwell, West Sussex. BN18 0SF.
926 © Ateliers et Presses de Taizé
927 English text © 1970, International Consultation on English Text (ICET) Music © 1997, Paul Inwood. All rights reserved. Reproduced by permission of Magnificat Music.
928 © 1993, Bernadette Farrell. Published by OCP Publications. All rights reserved. Used with permission.
929 Text and Music © Paul Inwood. All rights reserved. Reproduced by permission of Magnificat Music.
930 © 1985, Christopher Walker. Published by OCP Publications. All rights reserved. Used with permission.
931 © Christopher Walker. Published by OCP Publications. All rights reserved. Used with permission.
932 © 1990, WGRG, Iona Community, G2 3DH
933 © 1994, Peter Jones. Administered by OCP Publications. All rights reserved. Used with permission.
934 © 1988, Christopher Walker. Published by OCP Publications. All rights reserved. Used with permission. Verse text © ICEL
935 © 1984, 1991, Ernest Sands. Published by OCP Publications. All rights reserved. Used with permission.
936 English text © 1970, International Consultation on English Text (ICET) Music © 1997, Paul Inwood. All rights reserved. Reproduced by permission of Magnificat Music.
937(A) Text Public Domain. Music © 1997, Paul Inwood. All rights reserved. Reproduced by permission of Magnificat Music.
(B-D) Text from the English translation of the Roman Missal, copyright © 1973, International Committee on English in the Liturgy, Inc (ICEL) All rights reserved. Music copyright © 1997, Paul Inwood. All rights reserved. Reproduced by permission of Magnificat Music.
938 Text of the doxology from the English translation of the Roman Missal, copyright © 1973, International Committee on English int the Liturgy, Inc. (ICEL) All rights reserved. Music copyright © 1997, Paul Inwood. All rights reserved. Reproduced by permission of Magnificat Music.
939 English text copyright © 1970, International Consultation on English Texts (ICET) Music copyright © 1981,1983,Paul Inwood. All rights reserved. Published by OCP Publications.
940 Text from the English translation of the Roman Missall, copyright © 1973, International Committee on English in the Liturgy, Inc. (ICEL) All rights reserved. Music copyright © 1981,1983, Paul Inwood. All rights reserved. Published by OCP Publications.
941 Music copyright © 1981,1983, Paul Inwood. All rights reserved. Published by OCP Publications.
942 © 1985, 1989, Christopher Walker. Published by OCP Publications. All rights reserved. Used with permission.
943 English translation from the Roman Missal © 1973, International committee on English in the Liturgy. All rights reserved. Music © 1685, 1989, Christopher Walker. Published by OCP Publications. All rights reserved. Used with permission.
944 © 1985, 1989, Christopher Walker. Published by OCP Publications. All rights reserved. Used with permission.
945 © 1999, Bernadette Farrell. Published by OCP Publications. All rights reserved. Used with permission.
946 © 1999, Bernadette Farrell. Published by OCP Publications. All rights reserved. Used with permission.
947 Text of Doxology © 1973, International Committee on English in the Liturgy, Inc. All rights reserved. Music © 1985, Bernadette Farrell. Published by OCP Publications.
948 © GIA Publications, Inc. *All Rights Reserved.
949 –
950 © CJM Music Ltd. www.cjmmusic.com
951 –
952 © 1996, Christopher Walker. Published by OCP Publications. All rights reserved. Used with permission.
953 Text and music copyright © 1682, Paul Inwood. All rights reserved. Reproduced by permission of Magnificat Music.
954 –
955 Text and Music copyright © 1982, Paul Inwood. All rights reserved. Published by OCP Publications.
956 © Martin Hall 70 Bexley Rd, Erith, DA8 3SP.
957 © McCrimmon Publishing Co. Ltd.
958 © McCrimmon Publishing Co. Ltd.
959 © McCrimmon Publishing Co. Ltd.
960 © McCrimmon Publishing Co. Ltd.
961 © McCrimmon Publishing Co. Ltd.
962 © McCrimmon Publishing Co. Ltd.
963 © McCrimmon Publishing Co. Ltd.
964 © 1997 by Boosey and Hawkes Publishers Ltd. Reproduced by permission of Boosey and Hawkes Music Publishers Ltd. Words © ICEL.
965 © 1997 by Boosey and Hawkes Publishers Ltd. Reproduced by permission of Boosey and Hawkes Music Publishers Ltd. Words © ICEL.
966 © 1997 by Boosey and Hawkes Publishers Ltd. Reproduced by permission of Boosey and Hawkes Music Publishers Ltd. Words © ICEL.
967 © 1997 by Boosey and Hawkes Publishers Ltd. Reproduced by permission of Boosey and Hawkes Music Publishers Ltd. Words © ICEL.
968 Verses text © 1963, The Grail (England). Music & refrain text © 1985, Paul Inwood. All rights reserved. Published by OCP Publications.
969 Verses text copyright © 1963, The Grail (England). Music and refrain text copyright © 1985, Paul Inwood. All rights reserved. Published by OCP Publications.
970 Copyright © 1986 GIA Publications, Inc.* All Rights Reserved.
971 Music © 1987, Stephen Dean. Published by OCP Publications. All rights reserved. Used with permission. Words © Reprinted by permission of HarperCollins Publishers Ltd.
972 Music © Anne Ward 2 Goodacres, Arundel Rd. Fontwell, West Sussex. BN18 0SF. Text © 1963, 1994 Reprinted by permission of HarperCollins Publishers Ltd.
973 © 1988, 1989, Christopher Walker. Published by OCP Publications. All rights reserved. Used with permission.
974 © 1989, Christopher Walker. Published by OCP Publications. All rights reserved. Used with permission.
975 Words and music copyright © 1984, 1985 Chris O' Hara and McCrimmon Publishing Co. Ltd.
976 Music © Elsie Wright. Text © Reprinted by permission of HarperCollins Publishers Ltd.

977 Words and music copyright © 1984,1985 Chris O' Hara and McCrimmon Publishing Co. Ltd.
978 Copyright © 1983 GIA Publications, Inc. *All Right Reserved.
979 Words and music copyright © 1984,1985 Chris O' Hara and McCrimmon Publishing Co. Ltd.
980 © 1992, Christopher Walker. Published by OCP Publications. All rights reserved. Used with permission.
981 Copyright © 1983 GIA Publications, Inc.* All Rights Reserved.
982 © McCrimmon Publishing Co. Ltd.
983 © Michael Coy. Reprinted by permission of HarperCollins Publishers Ltd.
984 Copyright © 1983 GIA Publications, Inc.* All Rights Reserved.
985 © Geoffrey Boulton Smith
986 © 1984, 1985, Christopher Walker. Published by OCP Publications. All rights reserved. Used with permission.
987 © 1988 Bob Hurd. Published by OCP Publications. All rights reserved. Used with permission.
988 Verses text copyright © 1963, Reprinted by permission of HarperCollins Publishers Ltd. Music and refrain text copyright © 1984, Paul Inwood. All rights reserved. Published by OCP Publications.
989 Refrain text © 1963, Reprinted by permission of HarperCollins Publishers Ltd. Verse text and music © 1990, Bernadette Farrell. Published by OCP Publications. All rights reserved. Used with permission.
990 Verses text copyright © 1963, The Grail (England). Music and refrain text copyright © 1981, Paul Inwood. All rights reserved. Published by OCP Publications.
991 Copyright © Noel S Donnelly. Used by permission.
992 © 1988, 1989, Christopher Walker. Published by OCP Publications. All rights reserved. Used with permission.
993 Music Joseph Gelineau S.J. © 1963,1994. Reprinted by permission of HarperCollins Publishers Ltd. Words © Reprinted by permission of HarperCollins Publishers Ltd.
994 Copyright © 1989 GIA Publications, Inc. *All Rights Reserved.
995 Text and music copyright © 1984, Paul Inwood. All rights reserved. Published by OCP Publications.
996 Copyright © Martin Hall 70 Bexley Rd, Erith. DA8 3SP.
997 Words and music copyright © 1984,1985 Chris O' Hara and McCrimmon Publishing Co. Ltd.
998 Copyright Music © Tony Charlier. Words © Reprinted by permission of HarperCollins Publishers Ltd.
999 Copyright © John Gibbons 1988, 1992.
1000 Copyright © Tony Charlier.
1001 Copyright © Tony Charlier.
1002 Words © Brain Black & Jubilate Hymns.
1003 Copyright © Tony Charlier 2004
1004 Copyright © Tony Charlier 2004
1005 Copyright © Tony Charlier 2004
1006 Copyright © Tony Charlier 2004
1007 Copyright © Tony Charlier 2004
1008 –
1009 –

Addresses of main copyright holders

ANICETO NAZARETH,
St Pius College, Goregaon East, Bombay 400063, India.

ATELIERS ET PRESSES DE TAIZÉ,
71250 Taizé Community, France.

THE BENEDICTINE FOUNDATION OF THE STATE OF VERMONT, INC,
Weston Priory, 58 Priory Hill Rd, West, Vermont 05161 USA.

BOOSEY & HAWKES MUSIC PUBLISHERS LTD
Aldwych House, 71-91 Aldwych, London. WC2B 4HN Tel: 0207 054 7215 Fax: 0207 054 7294

CASSELL PLC, Villiers House, 41/47 Strand, London WC2N 5JE.

CJM MUSIC LTD. Don Bosco House, Coventry Rd, Coleshill, West Midlands B46 3EA. www.cjmmusic.com

COPYCARE LTD,
PO Box 77, Hailsham, East Sussex BN27 3EF. Tel: 01323 840942 Fax: 01323 849355 Email: music@copycare.com

GIA PUBLICATIONS INC,
7404 South Mason Avenue, Chicago, Illinois 60638 USA.

HARPERCOLLINS PUBLISHERS
77-85 Fulham Palace Rd., Hammersmith, London W6 8JB

HOPE PUBLISHING CO.,
380 South Main Place, Carol Stream, Illinois 60188 USA.

HYMNS ANCIENT & MODERN LTD,
St Mary's Words, St Mary's Plain, Norwich, Norfolk NR3 3BH.

INTERNATIONAL COMMITTEE ON ENGLISH IN THE LITURGY (ICEL),
1275 K. Street NW, Suite 1202, Washington DC 20005-4097 USA

JOSEF WEINBERGER LTD, 12–14 Mortimer St, London W1N 8EL.

JUBILATE HYMNS, 4 Thorne Park Rd. Chelston Torquay. TQ2 6RX
Tel: 01803 607754 Fax: 01803 605682
Email: enquiries@jubilate.co.uk

KEVIN MAYHEW LTD, Buxhall, Stowmarket, Suffolk IP14 3BW.

KINGSWAY COMMUNICATIONS LTD.,
26-28 Lottbridge Drove, Eastbourne. East Sussex BN23 6NT. UK.
Tel: 01323 437700 Fax: 01323 411970
Tym@kingsway.co.uk

MAGNIFICAT MUSIC
Park Place Pastoral Centre, Winchester Road, Wickham, Fareham, Hampshire PO17 5HA Tel: 01329-835521

MCCRIMMON PUBLISHING CO. LTD.,
10-12 High Street, Great Wakering, Essex SS3 0EQ
Tel: 01702-218956

NEW DAWN MUSIC,
PO Box 13248, Portland, Oregon 97213–0248, USA.

NOVELLO & CO. LTD, 8/9 Frith St, London W1V 5TZ.

OCP PUBLICATIONS,
5536 NE Hassalo, Portland, Oregon 97213 USA.

OXFORD UNIVERSITY PRESS,
3 Park Rd, London NW1 6XN.

SEFIM, 13 Avenue Savornin, 94240 L'Hay-les-Roses, France

SOVEREIGN MUSIC UK,
P.O.Box 356, Leighton Buzzard, LU7 3WP
Tel: 01525 385578 Fax: 01525 372743
Email: Sovereign@aol.com

STAINER & BELL LTD,
PO Box 110, Victoria House, 23 Gruneisen Road, London N3 1DZ.

STEPHEN DEAN
Decani Music, Oak House, 70 High Street, Brandon, Suffolk IP27 0AU

TONY CHARLIER,
28 Harestone Valley Rd, Caterham, Surrey, CR3 6HD

A.P. WATT LTD (THE GRAIL, (ENGLAND) LTD),
20 John St, London WC1N 2DR.

WILD GOOSE RESOURCE GROUP/IONA COMMUNITY,
4th Floor Savoy House 140 Sauchiehall St., Glasgow G2 3DH

WORLD LIBRARY PUBLICATIONS, INC,
a division of J.S. Paluch Company Inc,
3815 North Willow Rd, Schiller Park,
Illinois 60176 USA.

An extra note on copyright

You are not allowed to make copies of copyright hymns without permission.
A hymn written by someone who is still alive, or who died less than 50 years ago, can be assumed to be copyright.

If you want to make copies of a hymn in this book:

- o first find out if it is copyright – the information is in the acknowledgement section.

Then:

- o If it isn't copyright you can make copies freely (though there is one extra catch – you can't actually photocopy the page without permission because of what is called 'graphical copyright' – the publisher has invested money in having the pages typeset and laid out, and has the right to stop people copying them. This lasts for 25 years from publication date. Find a book older than this and you can make as many copies as you like; or type the words out yourself).

- o If it is copyright, apply to the copyright holder. You can telephone at first but they will probably ask you to apply in writing. The copyright holder will normally give permission and charge a fee.

Do you have to write to America?

- o Some overseas (particularly US) publishers have agents in this country so you don't need to write several letters abroad. Calamus (address below) is the agent for the following:

- OREGON CATHOLIC PRESS (OCP): composers include: Bernadette Farrell, Paul Inwood, Christopher Walker, Ernest Sands, James Walsh, Stephen Dean.

- GIA PUBLICATIONS INC: composers include: Marty Haugen, David Haas and Michael Joncas.

- WESTON PRIORY.

  There are other US publishers represented in Celebration Hymnal for Everyone and it is not possible to give all their British agents. The Churches' Copyright Directory (Stainer & Bell, 1992) is a good source for addresses, but a phone call to Calamus (number below) will often provide the information as they are always willing to help.

  Taizé is administered by HarperCollins Religious; Iona copyright are administered by Wild Goose Publications. Contact the other publishers direct.

Annual Licences

These are something slightly different from one-off permissions. Calamus also issue an Annual Licence which includes, as well as the people on this list, McCrimmons, James Quinn SJ, Worth Abbey Music and Clifton Music.

The other main annual licence scheme is the Church Copyright Licence which covers Oxford University Press, Kevin Mayhew Publications and most of the 'evangelical' music including Thankyou Music, Make Way Music, and Jubilate Hymns. Stainer & Bell operate their own annual licence scheme.

Addresses

CALAMUS, Oak House, 70 High Street,
Brandon, Suffolk IP27 0AU
(Tel: 01842-819830,
Fax: 01842-819832).

CHRISTIAN COPYRIGHT LICENSING LTD,
26 Gildredge Road, Eastbourne,
East Sussex BN21 4SA
(Tel: 01323 417711, Fax: 01323 417722).

STAINER & BELL, PO Box 110,
Victoria House, 23 Gruneisen Road,
London N3 1DZ
(Tel: 0181 343 3303, Fax: 0181 343 3024).

SEASONS AND FEASTS

ADVENT

*Hymns marked * are not sung before 17th Dec.*

First Sunday of Advent (A)

Stand ready because the Son of Man is coming.

Isaiah 2:1-5; Ps 121(122); Rom 13:11-14; MATTHEW 24:37-44

First Sunday of Advent (B)

Give us life that we may call upon your name.

Isaiah 63:16-17; 64:1, 3-8; Ps 79(80); 1 Cor 1:3-9; MARK 13:33-37

241 Hail to the Lord's anointed
368 Like a sea without a shore
376 Look around you
494 Mould us now, as the potter's clay
535 O Jesus Christ remember
613 Promised Lord and Christ is he
905 Return to God
763 Wake, O wake! with tidings thrilling
764 Wake up the dawn is near

First Sunday of Advent (C)

See, the days are coming.

Jeremiah 33:14-16; Ps 24(25); 1 Thess 3:12-4:2; LUKE 21:25-28, 34-36

64 Awake, awake, fling off the night
118 Colours of day
400 Grant to us, O Lord, a heart renewed
255 Hills of the north, rejoice
535 O Jesus Christ remember
621 Remember, remember your mercy, Lord
908 Share the light of Jesus
726 Stay awake
726 There will be signs upon the sun
762 Wait for the Lord

Second Sunday of Advent (A)

Prepare a way for the Lord, make his paths straight and all mankind shall see the salvation of God.

Isaiah 11:1-10; Ps 71(72); Rom 15:4-9; MATTHEW 3:1-12

10 Across the years there echoes
253 Gather us in
217 God is working his purpose outt
241 Hail to the Lord's anointed
255 Hills of the north rejoice
879 In God's good time
376 Look around you
575 On Jordan's bank, the Baptist's cry
268 Our God reigns
904 Prepare the way
612 Prepare ye the way
804 When John baptised by Jordan's river

Second Sunday of Advent (B)

Prepare a way for the Lord!

Isaiah 40:1-5, 9-11; Ps 84(84); 2 Peter 3:8-14; MARK 1:1-8

10 Across the years there echoes
133 Come, thou long–expected Jesus
243 Hark! a herald voice is calling
369 Like a shepherd
373 Lo, he comes with clouds descending
523 O comfort my people
575 On Jordan's bank, the Baptist's cry
763 Wake, O wake with tidings thrilling
904 Prepare the way
804 When John baptised by Jordan's river

Second Sunday of Advent (C)

Arise, Jerusalem, stand on the heights.

Baruch 5:1-9; Ps 125(126); Phil 1:4-6, 8-11; LUKE 3:1-6

10 Across the years there echoes
253 Gather us in
253 Here in this place
575 On Jordan's bank, the Baptist's cry
904 Prepare the way
612 Prepare ye the way
718 The voice of God
804 When John baptised by Jordan's river

Third Sunday of Advent (A)

The eyes of the blind shall be opened.

Isaiah 35:1-6, 10; Ps 145; James 5:7-10; MATTHEW 11:2-6

860 Blest be the Lord
110 Christ is our King
128 Come Lord Jesus
132 Come, Saviour, come like dew
133 Come thou long expected Jesus
368 Like a sea without a shore
511 Now in this banquet (God of our journeys)
591 Out of darkness
718 The voice of God
762 Wait for the Lord
806 When the King shall come again

Third Sunday of Advent (B)

Good news to the poor.

Isaiah 61:1-2, 10-11; Luke 1:46-50, 53-4; 1 Thess 5:16-24; JOHN 1:6-8, 19-28

10 Across the years there echoes
29 All who claim the faith of Jesus
860 Blest be the Lord
227 Go, tell everyone
888 Let your living water flow
479 Make way, make way, for Christ the King
575 On Jordan's bank, the Baptist's cry
804 When John baptised by Jordan's river
716 The Spirit of the Lord

See also settings of the Magnificat: 213, 231, 506, 684 , 707, 849

Third Sunday of Advent (C)

The Lord is very near.

Zephaniah 3:14-18; Isaiah 12:2-6; Phil 4:4-7; LUKE 3:10-18

10 Across the years there echoes
64 Awake awake fling off the night
241 Hail to the Lord's anointed
880 Into the family of God
368 Like a sea without a shore
575 On Jordan's bank, the Baptist's cry
613 Promised Lord and Christ is he
617 Rejoice in the Lord always
644 Sing a new song to the Lord
718 The voice of God
787 We shall draw water joyfully
804 When John baptised by Jordan's river
831 You shall go out with joy

Fourth Sunday of Advent (A)

The virgin will conceive and give birth to a son.

Isaiah 7:10-14; Ps 23:1-6; Romans 1:1-7; MATTHEW 1:18-24

5 A noble flower of Judah
6 A sign is seen in heaven
86 Benedictus
86 Blessed be the Lord
860 Blest be the Lord
129 Come O divine Messiah
186 Freely I give to you

241 Hail to the Lord's anointed
522 O come, O come Emmanuel
533 O holy Dwelling Place
533 O Holy Mary
686 The Angel Gabriel

Fourth Sunday of Advent (B)

Listen! you are to conceive and bear a son.

2 Sam 7:1-5, 8-12, 14, 16; Ps 88(89); Romans 16:25-27; LUKE 1:26-38

6 A sign is seen in heaven
29 All who claim the faith of Jesus
129 Come, O divine Messiah
181 For you, O Lord
187 From heaven you came
231 Great is the Lord, my soul proclaims
263 Holy Virgin, by God's decree
373 Lo, he comes with clouds descending
181 My soul in stillness waits
522 O come, O come Emmanuel
686 The Angel Gabriel
689 The coming of our God
187 The Servant King

Fourth Sunday of Advent (C)

Out of you will be born the one who is to rule over Israel.

Micah 5:1-4; Ps 79(80); Hebrews 10:5-10; LUKE 1-38

6 A sign is seen in heaven
29 All who claim the faith of Jesus
860 Blest be the Lord
129 Come O divine Messiah
133 Come, thou long–expected Jesus
236 Hail Mary full of grace
373 Lo, he comes with clouds descending
375 Long ago, prophets knew
511 Now in this banquet (God of our journeys)
522 O come, O come Emmanuel
561 Of one that is so fair and bright
591 Out of darkness
686 The Angel Gabriel
689 The coming of our God

CHRISTMAS

Midnight Mass:

Isaiah 9:1-7; Ps 95(96); Titus 2:11-14; LUKE 2:1-14

Dawn Mass:

Isaiah 62:11-12; Ps 96(97); Titus 3:4-7; LUKE 2:15-20

Day Mass:

Isaiah 52:7-10; Ps 97(98) (several settings to choose from); Hebrews 1:1-6; JOHN 1:1-18 (or 1-5, 9-14)

1 A child is born for us today
2 A child is born in Bethlehem
857 Adeste fidelis
25 All the ends of the earth
46 Angel voices richly blending
47 Angels we have heard in heaven
48 Angels we have heard on high
55 As with gladness men of old
63 Awake, awake and greet the new morn
64 Away in a manger
79 Bethlehem of noblest cities
94 Bread for the world broken (Christmas)
96 Bread of life, hope of the world (Christmas)
99 Brightest and best
105 Child in the manger
124 Come, come, come to the manger
146 Ding dong! merrily on high
180 For unto us a child is born
202 Go, tell it on the mountain
223 God rest you merry gentlemen
229 Good Christians all, rejoice
241 Hail to the Lord's anointed
244 Hark! the herald angels sing
245 He became poor
266 How brightly beams the morning star
267 How dark was the stable
292 I wonder, as I wander
310 Infant holy, infant lowly
314 It came upon the midnight clear
331 Jesus the Word has lived among us
335 Joy to the world
374 Long ago, in Bethlehem
397 Love came down at Christmas
520 O come, all ye faithful
533 O holy Dwelling Place
533 O Holy Mary
540 O little town of Bethlehem
560 O worship the Lord
562 Of the Father's love begotten
574 On Christmas night all Christians sing
577 Once in royal David's city
63 Rejoice, rejoice
630 See, amid the winter's snow
907 See him lying on a bed of straw
660 Sleep, holy babe
661 Songs of thankfulness and praise
643 Silent night
692 The first Nowell
711 The race that long in darkness
788 We three kings of Orient are
918 What shall we give?
810 While shepherds watched their flocks

Holy Family (A)

Help us to live as the Holy Family, united in respect and love.

Ecclus 3:2-6, 12-14; Ps 127(128); Col 3:12-21; MATTHEW 2:13-15, 19-23

47 Angels we have heard
859 As I kneel before you
864 Children of God
245 He became poor
507 I saw a star
305 In the bleak midwinter
310 Infant holy, infant lowly
383 Lord Jesus Christ
540 O little town of Bethlehem
577 Once in royal David's city
576 On this house
755 Unto us is born a Son
788 We three kings of Orient are
794 What child is this?

Holy Family (B)

The Lord remembers his covenant forever.

Optional Readings for Year B: Genesis 15:1-6; 21:1-3; Ps 104(105); Heb 11:8, 11-12, 17-19; LUKE 2:22-40 (or 22, 39-40)

56 At last all powerful master
96 Bread of life, hope of the world (Christmas)
897 Now let your servant go in peace
703 The light of Christ
56 Nunc Dimittis

See also Year A

Holy Family (C)

My dear people, we are already the children of God.

1 Sam 1:20-22, 24-28; Ps 83(84); 1 John 3:1-2, 21-24; LUKE 2:41-52

29 All who claim the faith of Jesus
897 Now let your servant
534 O how lovely is your dwelling place

See also Year A

Mary, Mother of God

When the appointed time came, God sent his Son, born of a woman.

Numbers 6:22-27; Ps 66(67); Gal 4:4-7; LUKE 2:16-21

859 As I kneel before you
51 As we come before you now
482 Mary, crowned with living light
458 May God bless and keep you
533 O holy Dwelling Place
533 O Holy Mary

See also under Christmas, and under Mary in Topical Index

Second Sunday after Christmas

The word was made flesh, and dwelt among us.

Ecclus 24:1-2,8-12; Ps 147; Eph 1:3-6, 15-18; JOHN 1:1-18 (or 1-5, 9-14)

215 God is love, his the care
871 God to enfold you
225 God, who made the earth and sky
221 God who made the earth, the sky
266 How brightly beams the morning star

See also under Christmas above

Epiphany

The nations come to your light and kings to your dawning brightness.

Isaiah 60:1-6; Ps 71(72); Eph 3:2-3, 5-6; MATTHEW 2:1-12

55 As with gladness men of old
79 Bethlehem of noblest cities
99 Brightest and best
245 He became poor
282 I saw a star up high
560 O worship the Lord
661 Songs of thankfulness and praise
692 The first Nowell
711 The race that long in darkness
788 We three kings of Orient are

Baptism of the Lord (A)

This is my beloved Son; my favour rests on him.

Isaiah 42:1-4, 6-7; Ps 28(29); Acts 10:34-38; MATTHEW 3:13-17

241 Hail to the Lord's anointed
880 Into the family of God
331 Jesus the Word has lived among us
661 Songs of thankfulness and praise
319 The spirit of the Lord
718 The voice of God goes out
401 Water of life, cleanse and refresh us
804 When John baptised by Jordan's river

Baptism of the Lord (B)

Come to the water.

Isaiah 55:1-11; Isaiah 12:2-6; 1 John 5:1-9; MARK 1:7-11

221 God, our fountain of salvation
331 Jesus the Word has lived among us
582 Open your ears, O Christian people
661 Songs of thankfulness and praise
787 We shall draw water joyfully
804 When John baptised by Jordan's river

Baptism of the Lord (C)

Here is the Lord coming with power.

Isaiah 40:1-5, 9-11; Ps 103(104); Titus 2:11-14; 3:4-7; LUKE 3:15-16, 21-22

331 Jesus the Word has lived among us
582 Open your ears, O Christian people
612 Prepare ye the way
634 Send forth your Spirit, God our Father
661 Songs of thankfulness and praise
804 When John baptised by Jordan's river

LENT

835 A mighty God is the Lord
10 Across the years there echoes
13 Ah, holy Jesus, how hast thou offended
21 All my hope on God is founded
299 All that is hidden
494 As the potter's clay
57 At the cross her station keeping
59 At the name of Jesus
60 Attend and keep this happy fast
251 Attende Domine
64 Awake, awake, fling off the night
120 Be light for our eyes
830 Be not afraid
70 Be still and know that I am God (Iona)
74 Be thou my vision
75 Be thou my vision (anacrusic version)
76 Be with me, Lord
77 Because the Lord is my shepherd
81 Bless the Lord my soul (Taizé)
85 Blessed be God! O blessed be God
88 Blest are the pure in heart
91 Blest be the Lord
821 Bring forth the kingdom
863 Broken for me
104 Called to be servants
109 Christ is made the sure foundation

812 Will you come and follow me
813 Will you let me be your servant
821 You are salt for the earth
826 You, Israel, return now
830 You shall cross the barren desert
832 You who dwell in the shelter of the Lord

First Sunday of Lent (A)

We do not live on bread alone.

Genesis 2:7-9; 3:1-7; Ps 50(51); Rom 5:12-9 (or 12:17-9); MATTHEW 4:1-11

830 Be not afraid
78 Behold the Lamb of God (Iona)
185 Forty days and forty nights
[illegible] I am the bread of life 272
341 Keep we the fast our ancestors learned
886 Lead me Lord
351 Lead us, heavenly Father, lead us
750 Trust in the Lord
830 You shall cross the barren desert

First Sunday of Lent (B)

Repent, and believe the Good News.

Genesis 9:8-15; Ps 24(25); 1 Peter 3:18-22; MARK 1:12-15

60 Attend and keep this happy fast
830 Be not afraid
185 Forty days and forty nights
341 Keep we the fast our ancestors learned
351 Lead us, heavenly Father, lead us
529 O God, thy people gather
911 Take me Lord
830 You shall cross the barren desert

First Sunday of Lent (C)

Everyone who calls on the name of the Lord will be saved.

Deuteronomy 26:4-10; Ps 90(91); Rom 10:8-13; LUKE 4:1-13

60 Attend and keep this happy fast
830 Be not afraid
76 Be with me, Lord
91 Blest be the Lord
185 Forty days and forty nights
341 Keep we the fast our ancestors learned
351 Lead us, heavenly Father, lead us
893 Lord of life
832 On eagle's wings
830 You shall cross the barren desert
832 You who dwell in the shelter of the Lord

Second Sunday of Lent (A)

Lord, it is wonderful for us to be here.

Genesis 12:1-4; Ps 32(33); 2 Tim 1:8-10; MATTHEW 17:1-9

At the name of Jesus
74 Be thou my vision
111 Christ is the world's light
154 Eye has not seen
869 Father God I wonder
226 God, your glory we have seen
301 Immortal, invisible
388 Lord, the light of your love is shining
908 Share the light of Jesus
388 Shine, Jesus, Shine

Second Sunday of Lent (B)

Tell no one what you have seen, until after the Son of Man has risen from the dead.

Gen 22:1-2, 9-13, 15-18; Ps 115(116); Rom 8:31-34; MARK 9:2-10

111 Christ is the world's light
154 Eye has not seen
285 Here I am, Lord
295 If God is for us, who can be against
301 Immortal, invisible
881 Jesus be the centre
890 Listen
388 Lord, the light of your love is shining
548 O praise our great and gracious Lord
388 Shine, Jesus, Shine

Second Sunday of Lent (C)

They saw his glory.

Genesis 15:5-12, 17-18; Ps 26(27); Phil 3:17-4:1 (or 3:20 – 4:1): LUKE 9:28-36

59 At the name of Jesus
111 Christ is the world's light
154 Eye has not seen
166 Father we come to you
226 God your glory we have seen
301 Immortal, invisible
890 Listen, let your heart keep seeking
388 Lord, the light of your love is shining
497 My God how wonderful thou art
388 Shine, Jesus, Shine

Third Sunday of Lent (A)

A spring of water welling up to eternal life.

Exodus 17:3-7; Ps 94(95); Rom 5:1-2, 5-8; JOHN 4:5-42 (or 5-15, 19-26, 39-42)

A mighty God is the Lord
7 Abba, Abba Father
543 Centre of my life
221 God, our fountain of salvation
233 Guide me O thou great Redeemer
307 In the land there is a hunger
889 Like a shepherd
542 O Lord hear my prayer
555 O that today you would listen
566 Oh living water
602 Praise my soul the King of heaven
624 Rock of ages
754 Unless a grain of wheat
401 Water of life, cleanse and refresh us
816 Yahweh, I know you are near
830 You shall cross the barren desert

See also Water in Topical Index

Third Sunday of Lent (B)

In three days I will raise up this sanctuary.

Ex 20:1-17 (or 1-3, 7-8, 12-17); Ps 18(19); 1 Cor 1:22-25; JOHN 2:13-25

21 All my hope on God is founded
861 Bread we bring
(Lord we share in this one true bread)
109 Christ is made the sure foundation

113 Christ triumphant
886 Lead me Lord
356 Let all that is within me
380 Lord for tomorrow
383 Lord Jesus Christ
390 Lord thy word abideth
720 More desired than gold
567 Oh Lord, all the world belongs to you
720 The word of God is more desired than gold

Third Sunday of Lent (C)

It is he who forgives all your guilt.

Exodus 3:1-8, 13-15; Ps 102(103); 1 Cor 10:1-6, 10-12; LUKE 13:1-9

863 Broken for me
188 From the depths of sin and sadness
209 God forgave my sin
400 Grant to us, O Lord, a heart renewed
529 O God, thy people gather
568 O Lord my God
602 Praise my soul the king of heaven
905 Return toGod
752 Turn to me
803 When Israel was in Egypt's land
826 You, Israel, return now

Fourth Sunday of Lent (A)

I am the light of the world.

1 Sam 16:1,6-7, 10-13; Ps 22(23); Eph 5:8-14; JOHN 9:1-41 (or 1:6-9, 13-17, 34-38)

64 Awake, awake, fling off the night
120 Be light for our eyes
74 Be thou my vision
75 Be thou my vision (anacrusic version)
77 Because the Lord is my shepherd
891 Longing for light (Christ be our light)
120 Come and be light for our eyes
253 Gather us in
212 God has chosen me
253 Here in this place
881 Jesus be the centre
591 Out of darkness
908 Share the light
703 The light of Christ
706 The Lord's my shepherd
913 The Lord's my shepherd

Fourth Sunday of Lent (B)

God so loved the world that he sent his only Son.

2 Chron 36:14-16, 19-23; Ps 136(137); Eph 2:4-10; JOHN 3:14-21

64 Awake, awake, fling off the night
113 Christ triumphant
215 God is love, his the care
340 Keep in mind that Jesus Christ
891 Longing for light (Christ be our light)
396 Lord, your love has drawn us near
895 My Jesus my Saviour
568 Oh Lord my God
591 Out of darkness
678 Take our bread
703 The light of Christ
757 Vaster far than any ocean

Fourth Sunday of Lent (C)

This man welcomes sinners.

Joshua 5:9-12; Ps 33(34); 2Cor 5:17-21; LUKE 15:1-3, 11-32

Day for the Second Scrutiny: Year A readings may be used instead.

10 Across the years
81 Bless the Lord my soul (Taizé)
863 Broken for me
182 Forgive our sins, as we forgive
209 Freely, freely
209 God forgave my sin
280 I received the living Lord
309 In the land there is a hunger
399 Love is his word
511 Now in this banquet
905 Return to God
678 Take our bread we ask you
682 Taste and see

Fifth Sunday of Lent (A)

I am the resurrection and the life.

Ezekiel 37:12-14; Ps 129(130); Romans 8:8-11; JOHN 11:1-45 (or 3-7, 17-20, 33-45)

81 Bless the Lord my soul (Taizé)
861 Bread we bring
(Lord we share in this one true bread)
862 Bread of life
188 From the depths of sin and sadness
400 Grant to us, O Lord, a heart renewed
272 I am the bread of life (Toolan)
883 Jesus name above all names
605 Praise the Lord ye heavens adore him
754 Unless a grain of wheat
917 We bring to you this bread and wine

Fifth Sunday of Lent (B)

If anyone serves me, they must follow me.

Jeremiah 31:31-34; Ps 50(51); Hebrews 5:7-9; JOHN 12:20-23

145 Deep within I will plant my law
167 Father, we love you
175 Follow me
400 Grant to us, O Lord, a heart renewed
226 God, your glory we have seen
363 Lift high the cross
663 Soul of my Saviour
744 To Christ the Prince of peace
754 Unless a grain of wheat

Fifth Sunday of Lent (C)

Go, and don't sin any more.

Isaiah 43:16-21; Ps 125(126); Phil 3:8-14; JOHN 8:1-11

Day for the Third Scrutiny: Year A readings may be used instead.

81 Bless the Lord my soul (Taizé)
209 Freely, freely
196 Glory and praise to our God
209 God forgave my sin
871 God to enfold you
398 Love divine, all loves excelling
602 Praise my soul the King of heaven
745 To God be the glory

EASTER

Second Sunday of Easter (ABC)

(A) Thomas acknowledges the risen Jesus.
Acts 2:42-47; Ps 117(118); 1 Peter 1:3-9; JOHN 20:19-31

(B) Thomas acknowledges the risen Jesus.
Acts 4:32-35; Ps 117(118); 1 John 5:1-6; JOHN 20:19-31

(C) Happy are those who have not seen and yet believe.
Acts 5:12-16; Ps 117(118); Apoc 1:9-13, 17-19; JOHN 20:19-31

Third Sunday of Easter (A)

They recognised him in the breaking of bread.

Acts 2:14, 22-33; Ps 15(16); 1 Peter 1:17-21; LUKE 24:13-35

737 Behold the Lamb of God
862 Bread of life, truth eternal
543 Centre of my life
307 In the land there is a hunger
893 Lord of life
737 Those who were in the dark
543 O Lord, you are the centre of my life
773 We celebrate this festive day
919 When my mind is still

Third Sunday of Easter (B)

It is written that Christ would suffer, and rise on the third day.

Acts 3:13-15, 17-19; Ps 4: 1 John 2:1-5; Luke 24:35-48

120 Be light for our eyes
891 Christ be our light
108 Christ is King
120 Come and be light for our eyes
881 Jesus be the centre
379 Lord, enthroned in heavenly splendour
728 Thine be the glory
745 To God be the glory

Third Sunday of Easter (C)

Feed my sheep. Follow me.

Acts 5:27-32, 40,41; Psalm 29(30); Apoc 5:11-14; JOHN 21:1-19 (or 1-14)

18 All hail the Lamb
20 All heaven declares
32 Alleluia, alleluia give thanks
170 Feed my lambs
175 Follow me, follow me
183 Forth in the peace of Christ
289 I will be with you
379 Lord, enthroned in heavenly splendour
903 Over all the earth
648 Sing it in the valleys
654 Sing of the Lord's goodness
728 Thine be the glory

Fourth Sunday of Easter (A)

I am the gate of the sheepfold.

Acts 2:14, 36-41; Ps 22(23); 1 Peter 2:20-25; JOHN 10:1-10

77 Because the Lord is my shepherd
369 Like a shepherd
889 Like a shepherd (We will rise again)
475 Loving shepherd of thy sheep
502 My Shepherd is the Lord
519 O Christi Domine Jesu
900 O Lord your tenderness
848 Ours were the griefs he bore
648 Sing it in the valleys
706 The Lord's my shepherd

Fourth Sunday of Easter (B)

The Good Shepherd lays down his life for his sheep.

Acts 4:8-12; Ps 117(118); 1 John 3:1-2; JOHN 10:11-18

22 All people that on earth do dwell
58 At the lamb's high feast
59 At the name of Jesus
154 Eye has not seen
239 Hail Redeemer, King divine
877 Iwill call upon the Lord
641 Shepherd of souls
648 Sing it in the valleys
699 The King of love my shepherd is
706 The Lord's my shepherd

Fourth Sunday of Easter (C)

We are his people, the sheep of his flock.

Acts 13:14, 43-52; Ps 99(100); Apoc 7:9, 14-17; JOHN 10:27-30

22 All people that on earth do dwell
24 All the earth proclaim the Lord
77 Because the Lord is my shepherd
869 Father God I wonder
903 Over all the earth
699 The King of love my shepherd is
706 The Lord's my shepherd
913 The Lord's my shepherd
357 Let all the world in every corner sing
678 Take our bread, we ask you

See also settings of Psalm 100(99) at nos 336, 338, 646

Fifth Sunday of Easter (A)

I am the Way, the Truth and the Life.

Acts 6:1-7; Ps 32(33); 1 Peter 2:4-9; JOHN 14:1-12

862 Bread of life, truth eternal
891 Christ be our light
111 Christ is the world's light
159 Father I place into your hands
876 I will call upon the Lord
280 I received the living God
333 Jesus, you are Lord
579 One day will come
591 Out of darkness
903 Over all the earth
906 Rise and shine
908 Share the light

Fifth Sunday of Easter (B)

I am the vine, you are the branches.

Acts 9:26-31; Ps 21(22); 1 John 3:18-24; JOHN 15:1-8

107 Christ is alive, with joy we sing
273 I am the vine, you are the branches
893 Lord of life
547 Oh praise ye the Lord
695 The green life rises
732 This is my will
754 Unless a grain of wheat
779 We have been told
824 You are the vine

Fifth Sunday of Easter (C)

How good is the Lord to all, compassionate to all his creatures.

Acts 14:21-27; Ps 144(145); Apoc 21:1-5; JOHN 13:31-35

4 A new commandment I give unto you
864 Children of God
113 Christ triumphant
195 Glorious things of you are spoken
226 God your glory we have seen
312 Into one we all are gathered

399 Love is his word, love is his way
898 O God you search me
732 This is my will, my one command

Sixth Sunday of Easter (A)

If you love me, keep my commandments.

Acts 8:5-8, 14-17; Ps 65(66); 1 Peter 3:15-18; JOHN 14:23

30 All you nations sing your joy
37 Alleluia, sing to Jesus
69 Be still and know I am with you
862 Bread of life
273 I am the vine
505 My soul is longing for your peace
900 O Lord your tenderness
596 Peace is the gift
597 Peace perfect peace
905 Return to God
910 Such love
915 There is a longing
730 This is my body, broken for you
742 To be the body of the Lord
754 Unless a grain of wheat

Sixth Sunday of Easter (B)

Greater love has no man than to lay down his life.

Acts 10:25-26, 34-35, 44-48; Ps 97(98); 1 John 4:7-10; JOHN 15:9-17

215 God is love, his the care
871 God to enfold you
513 Now the green blade riseth
902 Only be grace
644 Sing a new song to the Lord
915 There is a longing
730 This is my body, broken for you
779 We have been told

Sixth Sunday of Easter (C)

A peace the world cannot give.

Acts 15:1-2, 22-29; Ps 66(67); Apoc 21:10-14, 22-23; JOHN 14:23-29

8 Abba Father send your Spirit
273 I am the vine
399 Love is his word, love is his way
505 My soul is longing for your peace
902 Only by grace
596 Peace is the gift
597 Peace perfect peace
734 This is what Yahweh asks of you
754 Unless a grain of wheat
818 Ye choirs of new Jerusalem

Ascension of the Lord (ABC)

Jesus at the right hand of God.

A: Acts 1:1-11; Ps 46(47); Eph 1:17-23; MATTHEW 28:16-20

B: Acts 1:1-11; Ps 46(47); Eph 4:1-13 (or 1-7, 11-13); MARK 16:15-20

C: Acts 1:1-11; Ps 46(47); Hebrews 9:24-28; 10:19-23; LUKE 24:46-53

37 Alleluia, sing to Jesus
59 At the name of Jesus
113 Christ triumphant
201 Envoi Round
869 Father God I wonder
201 Go out to the whole world
226 God your glory we have seen
240 Hail the day that sees him rise
246 He is Lord
289 I will be with you
326 Jesus is Lord
333 Join in the dance
379 Lord, enthroned in heavenly splendour
508 New praises be given
619 Rejoice! the Lord is King
667 Stand and stare not
914 Walk in the light

Seventh Sunday of Easter (A)

Father, the hour has come: glorify your Son, so that your Son may glorify you.

Acts 1:12-14; Ps 26(27); 1 Peter 4:13-16; JOHN 17:1-11

37 Alleluia, sing to Jesus
69 Be still and know I am with you
866 Come to the feast
869 Father God I wonder
874 I cannot tell
893 Lord of life
477 Majesty
724 There is one thing I ask
754 Unless a grain of wheat
914 Walk in the light

See also Ascension of the Lord

Seventh Sunday of Easter (B)

Consecrate them in the truth.

Acts 1:15-17, 20-26; Ps 102(103); 1 John 4:11-16; JOHN 17:11-19

7 Abba, Abba Father
37 Alleluia, sing to Jesus
81 Bless the Lord my soul (Taizé)
82 Bless the Lord, O my soul (E Walker)
312 Into one we all are gathered
379 Lord enthroned in heavenly splendour
394 Lord, you give the great commission
395 Lord you have come to the lakeside
602 Praise my soul the King of heaven
908 Share the light of Jesus

Seventh Sunday of Easter (C)

He saw the glory of God and Jesus standing at his right hand.

Acts 7:55-56; Psalm 96(97); Apoc 22:12-14, 16-17, 20; JOHN 17:20-26

7 Abba,Abba Father
37 Alleluia, sing to Jesus
240 Hail the day that sees him rise
326 Jesus is Lord
882 Jesus, Jesus
883 Jesus name above all names
333 Jesus, you are Lord
508 New praises be given
556 O thou, who at thy Eucharist
774 Song of the Body of Christ
696 The head that once was crowned
774 We come to share our story
778 We have a gospel to proclaim

Sacred Heart (B)
God is love.

Hosea 11:1, 3-4, 8-9; Isaiah 12:2-6; Eph 3:8-12, 14-19; JOHN 19:31-37

58 At the Lamb's high feast
215 God is love
216 God is love his the care
319 Jesu lover of my soul
553 O Sacred Heart
519 Oh Christi Domine Jesu
570 Oh the love of my Lord
663 Soul of my Saviour
673 Sweet heart of Jesus
744 To Christ the Prince of peace
748 To Jesus, heart all–burning
787 We shall draw water joyfully

Sacred Heart (C)
I have found my sheep that was lost.

Ezekiel 34:11-16; Ps 22(23); Romans 5:5-11; LUKE 15:3-7

11 Adoramus te Domine
77 Because the Lord is my shepherd
553 O Sacred Heart
570 Oh the love of my Lord
905 Return to God
663 Soul of my Saviour
673 Sweet heart of Jesus
699 The King of love
706 The Lord's my shepherd
748 To Jesus, heart all–burning

SOLEMNITIES & FEASTS

Presentation of the Lord (2 February)
A light to enlighten the Gentiles.

Malachi 3:1-4; Ps 23(24); Hebrews 2:14-18; LUKE 2:22-40 (or 22-32)

212 God has chosen me
364 Lift up your heads, ye mighty gates
56 At last all powerful master
56 Nunc Dimittis

See also Light in Topical Index

St David (1 March)
821 Bring forth the kingdom
253 Gather us in
253 Here in this place
736 This little light of mine
532 O great Saint David
821 You are salt for the earth

St Patrick (17 March)
131 Come, praise the Lord, the Almighty
137 Confitemini Domino
234 Hail glorious Saint Patrick
572 Oh the word of my Lord
572 Song of a young prophet
783 We praise you and thank you

St Joseph (19 March)
11 Adoramus te, Domine
235 Hail, holy Joseph, hail!
627 Saint Joseph, God has chosen you
785 Te Deum
683 Te Deum laudamus
785 We praise you God, confessing you as Lord

Annunciation of the Lord (25 March)
186 Freely I give to you
207 God, beyond all names
533 O holy Dwelling Place
533 O Holy Mary
686 The Angel Gabriel
698 The King of Glory comes

Birth of John the Baptist (24 June – vigil)
What will this child turn out to be?

Vigil readings: Jer 1:4-10; Ps 70(71); 1 Peter 1:8-12; LUKE 1:5-17

10 Across the years there echoes
183 Forth in the peace of Christ
572 Oh the word of my Lord
612 Prepare ye the way
572 Song of a young prophet
804 When John baptised by Jordan's river
816 Yahweh, I know you are near

Birth of John the Baptist (24 June)
What will this child turn out to be?

Day mass readings: Is 49:1-6; Ps 138(139); Acts 13:22-26; LUKE 1:57-66, 80

85 Blessed be God! O blessed be God
860 Blest be
86 Benedictus
127 Come! live in the light
592 Out of deep, unordered water
127 We are called
85 Who calls you by name
816 Yahweh, I know you are near
816 You are Near

See also the hymns for the Vigil

Ss Peter and Paul (29 June – Vigil)
I have fought the good fight to the end.

Vigil readings: Acts 3:1-10; Ps 18(19); Gal 1:11-20; JOHN 21:15-19

780 Earthen Vessels
170 Feed my lambs, my son
289 I will be with you
720 More desired than gold
720 The word of God is more desired than gold
780 We hold a treasure

Ss Peter and Paul (29 June)
I have fought the good fight to the end.

Day mass readings: Acts 12:1-11; Ps 33(34); 2 Tim 4:6-8, 17-18; MATTHEW 16:13-19

143 Dear Lord and Father
176 For all the saints
116 Christus vincit
156 Faith of our fathers

170 Feed my lambs
395 Lord you have come to the lakeside
741 Thy hand O God has guided
581 Onward Christian soldiers
704 The Cry of the Poor
704 The Lord hears the cry of the poor

Transfiguration of the Lord (ABC) (6 August)

They saw his glory.

Daniel 7:9-10, 13-14; Ps 96(97); 2 Peter 1:16-19;

Year A: MATTHEW 17:1-9; Year B: MARK 9:2-10; Year C: Luke 9:28-36

59 At the name of Jesus
74 Be thou my vision
88 Blest are thepoor in heart
301 Immortal, invisible
388 Lord, the light of your love is shining
559 O worship the king
388 Shine, Jesus, Shine
741 Thy hand O God has guided

Assumption (15 August & vigil)

The Almighty has done great things for me: he has exalted the lowly.

Vigil readings: 1 Chron 15:3-4, 15-16; 16:1-2; Ps 131(132); 1 Cor 15:54-57; LUKE 11:27-28.
Day mass readings: Apoc 11:19; 12:1-6, 10; Ps 44(45); 1 Cor 15:20-27; LUKE 1:39-56

6 A sign is seen in heaven
236 Hail Mary, full of grace
238 Hail Queen of heaven
482 Mary, crowned with living light
651 Sing of Christ, proclaim his glory
684 Tell out my soul
707 The magnificat

Also settings of the Magnificat: 213, 231, 506, 684, 707, 849
See also Mary in Topical Index

Triumph of the Cross (14 September)

The Son of Man must be lifted up.

Numbers 21:4-9; Ps 77(78); Phil 2:6-11; JOHN 3:13-17

109 Christ is made the sure foundation
111 Christ is the world's light
113 Christ triumphant
279 I met you at the cross
330 Jesus, the holy Lamb of God
363 Lift high the cross
383 Lord Jesus Christ
573 On a hill far away
650 Sing, my tongue, the glorious battle
712 The royal banners forward go
801 When I survey

See also Cross in Topical Index

All Saints (1 November)

Theirs is the kingdom of heaven.

Apoc 7:2-4, 9-14; Ps 23(24); 1 John 3:1-3; MATTHEW 5:1-12

83 Beatitudes
83 Blessed are they
860 Blest be the Lord
176 For all the saints
248 He who would valiant be
295 If God is for us, who can be against
651 Sing of Christ, proclaim his glory
741 Thy hand O God has guided
811 Who honours courage here
819 Ye servants of God, your Master proclaim

Commemoration of the Faithful Departed – Year A – All Souls (2 November)

I Hope in him, hold firm and take heart.

Isaiah 25:6-9; Choice of Psalms includes 22(23) and 26(27); Romans 5:5-11; MATTHEW 11:25-30

31 All ye who seek a comfort sure
134 Come to me, all who labour
369 Like a shepherd
889 Like a shepherd
510 Now come to me, all you who seek
528 O God our help in ages past
724 There is one thing I ask

Commemoration of the Faithful Departed – Year B – All Souls (2 November)

I Hope in him, hold firm and take heart.

Isaiah 25:6-9; Choice of Psalms includes 22(23) and 26(27); Romans 5:5-11; MARK 15:33-39; 16:1-6

31 All ye who seek a comfort sure
513 Now the green blade riseth
724 There is one thing I ask
789 We walk by faith

Commemoration of the Faithful Departed – Year C – All Souls (2 November)

I Hope in him, hold firm and take heart.

Isaiah 25:6-9; Choice of Psalms includes 22(23) and 26(27); Romans 5:5-11; LUKE 7:11-17

31 All ye who seek a comfort sure
77 Because the Lord is my shepherd
272 I am the bread of life (Toolan)
724 There is one thing I ask

Dedication of the Lateran (9 November)

You are God's temple.

Ezekiel 47:1-2, 8-9,12; Ps 45(46); 1 Cor 3:9-11, 16-17; JOHN 2:13-22

See Dedication of a Church

Remembrance Sunday

See All Souls

St Andrew (30 November)

175 Follow me, follow me
232 Great Saint Andrew
269 How shall they hear the word of God
326 Jesus is Lord
812 The Summons
812 Will you come and follow me

Exposition of the Eucharistic Sacrament

See also Communion above and Adoration in Topical Index

Funerals

– RECEPTION OF THE BODY

– FUNERAL SERVICE

– FUNERAL – COMMUNION

– SONG OF FAREWELL

Marriage

Mass

See Eucharist

Ordination & Religious Profession

See also Mission, Ministry and Holy Spirit in Topical Index

Pastoral Care of the Sick

69 Be still and know I am with you
71 Be still and know that I am God (Anon)
72 Be still, for the presence of the Lord
73 Be still my soul
159 Father, I place into your hands
155 Flow river flow
871 God to enfold you
626 Safe in the shadow of the Lord
915 There is a longing
816 Yahweh, I know you are near
817 Yahweh, you are my strength
816 You are Near

See also Blessing, Comfort, and Healing in Topical Index

Reconciliation (Penance)

See Blessing, Forgiveness – God's, Forgiveness of others and Repentance in Topical Index

Religious Profession

See Ordination and Religious Profession above

SUNDAYS IN ORDINARY TIME

Baptism of the Lord

See Seasons and Feasts

Second Sunday of the Year (A)

Look, there is the Lamb of God.

Isaiah 49:3, 56; Ps 39(40); 1 Cor 1:1-3; JOHN 1:29-34

28 All this world belongs to Jesus
59 At the name of Jesus
78 Behold the Lamb of God (Iona)
111 Christ is the world's light
183 Forth in the peace of Christ
285 Here I am, Lord
881 Jesus be the centre
737 Behold the Lamb of God (Willett)
268 Our God reigns
658 Sing to the world of Christ our sov'reign Lord
737 Those who were in the dark
738 Thou whose almighty Word
919 When my mind is still

Second Sunday of the Year (B)

Speak, Lord, your servant is listening.

1 Sam 3:3-10, 19; Ps 39(40); 1 Cor 6:13-15, 17-20; JOHN 1:35-42

78 Behold the Lamb of God (Iona)
737 Behold the Lamb of God (Willett)
543 Centre of my life
210 God gives his people strength
871 God to enfold you
285 Here I am, Lord
285 I, the Lord of sea and sky
879 In God's good time
890 Listen
572 Oh the word of my Lord
910 Such love
676 Take my hands
915 There is a longing
732 This is my will
737 Those who were in the dark

Second Sunday of the Year (C)

A wedding at Cana: Jesus let his glory be seen.

Isaiah 62:1-5; Ps 95(96); 1 Cor 12:4-11; JOHN 2:1-11

509 New songs of celebration
511 Now in this banquet
580 One shall tell another
653 Sing of the bride
661 Songs of thankfulness and praise
773 We celebrate this festive day

Third Sunday of the Year (A)

The people that lived in darkness have seen a great light.

Isaiah 8:23-9:3; Ps 26(27); 1 Cor 1:10-13, 17; MATTHEW 4:12-23 (or 12-17)

299 All that is hidden
891 Christ be our light
111 Christ is the world's light
110 Christ is our King
118 Colours of day
157 Father and life-giver
253 Gather us in
218 God of day and God of darkness
226 God your glory we have seen
241 Hail to the Lord's anointed
253 Here in this place
299 If you would follow me
881 Jesus be the centre
395 Lord you have come to the lakeside
591 Out of darkness
608 Praise to the Lord, the almighty
698 The King of glory comes
773 We celebrate this festive day

Third Sunday of the Year (B)

He called them at once and they went after him.

Jonah 3:1-5, 10; Ps 24(25); 1 Cor 7:29-31; MARK 1:14-20

128 Come Lord Jesus come
866 Come to the feast
143 Dear Lord and Father of mankind
175 Follow me, follow me
248 He who would valiant be
279 I met you at the cross
886 Lead me Lord
536 O Jesus, I have promised
901 One more step
618 Rejoice, rejoice (Kendrick)
621 Remember, remember your mercy, Lord
621 Remember your mercy, Lord
703 The light of Christ
919 When my mind is still
811 Who honours courage here

Third Sunday of the Year (C)

This text is being fulfilled today even as you listen.

Nehemiah 8:2-6, 8-10; Ps 18(19); 1 Cor 12:12-30 (or 12-14, 27); LUKE 1:1-4; 4:14-21

110 Christ is our King
227 Go, tell everyone
227 God's spirit is in my heart
241 Hail to the Lord's anointed
879 In God's good time
890 Listen
879 In God's good time
720 More desired than gold
268 Our God reigns
416 Praise to you, O Christ
716 The Spirit of the Lord
718 The voice of God goes out to all the world
720 The word of God is more desired than gold
730 This is my body
919 When my mind is still

Fourth Sunday of the Year (A)

Blessed are the poor in spirit.

Zeph 2:3; 3:12-13; Ps 145; 1 Cor 1:26-31; MATTHEW 5:1-12

50 As a tree planted
83 Beatitudes
83 Blessed are they
88 Blest are the pure in heart
89 Blest are they, the poor in spirit
98 Breathe on me, breath of God
184 Forth in thy name
212 God has chosen me
242 Happy the man who wanders with the Lord
248 He who would valiant be
887 Let us go forth in the peace of Christ
527 O God of earth and altar
599 Peacemakers
916 We are young

Fourth Sunday of the Year (B)

His teaching made a deep impression because he taught with authority.

Deut 18:15-20; Ps 94(95); 1 Cor 7:32-35; MARK 1:21-28

3 A mighty stronghold is our God
59 At the name of Jesus
323 Jesus Christ is waiting
886 Lead me Lord
365 Light of our darkness
898 O God you search me
555 O that today you would listen
903 Over all the earth
645 Sing a new song to the Lord
658 Sing to the world of Christ
703 The light of Christ
738 Thou whose almighty word

Fourth Sunday of the Year (C)

I have appointed you prophet. No prophet is accepted in his own country.

Jeremiah 1:4-5, 17-19; Ps 70(71); 1 Cor 12:31 – 13:13 (or 13:4-13); LUKE 4:21-30

3 A mighty stronghold is our God
194 Glorious God, King of creation
203 Go the Mass is ended
871 God to enfold you
211 God who made the earth
213 God Alone
269 How shall they hear the word of God
312 Into one we all are gathered
881 Jesus be the centre
398 Love divine all loves excelling
543 O Lord, you are the centre
572 Oh the word of my Lord
572 Song of a young prophet
679 Take the word of God with you
698 The king of glory comes
265 Walk with my, O my Lord

Fifth Sunday of the Year (A)

Seeing your good works, they may give praise to your Father.

Isaiah 58:7-10; Ps 111(112); 1 Cor 2:1-5; MATTHEW 5:13-16

92 Bread for the world, a world of hunger
821 Bring forth the kingdom
127 Come! live in the light
128 Come, Lord Jesus come
183 Forth in the peace of Christ
888 Let your living water flow
591 Out of darkness
595 Peace is flowing like a river
633 Seek ye first the kingdom of God
693 The gift of the Holy Spirit
127 We are called
821 You are salt for the earth

Fifth Sunday of the Year (B)

He went all through Galilee, preaching and casting out devils.

Job 7:1-4, 6-7; Ps 146; 1 Cor 9:16-19, 22-23

33 Alleluia, I will praise the Father
110 Christ is our King
128 Come Lord Jesus come
253 Gather us in
871 God to enfold you
248 He who would valiant be
253 Here in this place
288 I watch the sunrise
311 Jesus the Word
347 Lay your hands gently upon us
480 Man of Galilee
511 Now in this banquet
570 Oh the love of my Lord
559 O worship the king
637 Send us as your blessing, Lord
915 There is a longing

Fifth Sunday of the Year (C)

I am a sinful man, Lord. Do not be afraid; you will be a fisher of men.

Isaiah 6:1-8; Psalm 137(138); 1 Cor 15:1-11 (or 15:3-8,11)

299 All that is hidden
143 Dear Lord and Father of mankind
147 Do not be afraid
175 Follow me, follow me
184 Forth in thy name
259 Holy, holy, holy! Lord God almighty

285 I the Lord of sea and sky
299 If you would follow me
395 Lord, you have come to the lakeside
636 Send me, Jesus
676 Take my hands
693 The gift of the Holy Spirit
812 The Summons
636 Thuma mina
812 Will you come and follow me

Sixth Sunday of the Year (A)

They are happy who follow God's law.

Ecclus 15:15-20; Ps 118(119); 1 Cor 2:6-10; MATTHEW 5:17-37 (or 20-22, 27-28, 33-34, 37)

88 Blest are the pure in heart
145 Deep within I will plant my law
182 Forgive our sins
380 Lord for tomorrow
390 Lord thy word abideth
529 O God, thy people gather
720 More desired than gold
495 My God accept my heart this day
642 Show me your ways
720 The word of God is more desired
769 We are one in the Spirit
796 What does the Lord require

Sixth Sunday of the Year (B)

Happy the man whose offence is forgiven. If you want, you can cure me.

Lev 13:1-2, 44-46; Ps 31(32); 1 Cor 10:31-11:1; MARK 1:40-45

40 Amazing grace
88 Blest are the pure in heart
92 Bread for the world, a world of hunger
862 Bread of life, truth eternal
166 Father we come to you
182 Forgive our sins
242 Happy the man
319 Jesu lover of my soul
347 Lay your hands
380 Lord for tomorrow
390 Lord thy word abideth
602 Praise my soul the King of heaven
654 Sing of the Lord's goodness
662 Sons of God
912 Take me Lord
757 Vaster far than any ocean
772 We cannot measure

Sixth Sunday of the Year (C)

Happy are those who place their trust in the Lord.

Jeremiah 17:5-8; Psalm 1; 1 Cor 15:12, 16-20; LUKE 6:17, 20-26

33 Alleluia, alleluia! I will praise the Father
40 Amazing grace
50 As a tree planted
69 Be still and know I am with you
74 Be thou my vision
75 Be thou my vision (anacrusic version)
83 Beatitudes
83 Blessed are they
89 Blest are they, the poor in spirit
862 Bread of life, truth eternal

867 Faithful one
242 Happy the man
280 I received the living Lord
876 I will call upon the Lord
886 Lead me Lord
567 Oh Lord, all the world belongs to you
751 Trust is in the eyes of a tiny babe

Seventh Sunday of the Year (A)

You have learnt how it was said... But I say to you...

Lev 19:1-2, 17-18; Ps 102(103); 1 Cor 3:16-23; MATTHEW 5:38-48

4 A new commandment
103 And be like your father
82 Bless the Lord, O my soul (E Walker)
862 Bread of life, truth eternal
103 But I say unto you
869 Father God I wonder
182 Forgive our sins, as we forgive
210 God gives his people strength
303 In Christ there is no east or west
312 Into one we all are gathered
478 Make me a channel of your peace
567 Oh Lord all the world belongs to you
602 Praise my soul the King of heaven
693 The gift of the Holy Spirit
732 This is my will
770 We are your people

Seventh Sunday of the Year (B)

Who can forgive sins but God?

Isaiah 43:18-19, 21-22, 24-25; Ps 40(41); 2 Cor 1:18-22; MARK 2:1-2

334 Bread blessed and broken
863 Broken for me
209 Freely, freely
209 God forgave my sin
275 I danced in the morning
275 Lord of the Dance
541 O Lord, be not mindful
902 Only by grace
693 The gift of the Holy Spirit
709 The Master came to bring good news

Seventh Sunday of the Year (C)

Treat others as you would like them to treat you.

1 Sam 26:2, 7-9, 12-13, 22-23; Ps 102(103); 1 Cor 15:45-49; LUKE 6:27-38

103 And be like your father
82 Bless the Lord, O my soul (E Walker)
103 But I say unto you
209 God forgave my sin
210 God gives his people strength
312 Into one we all are gathered
318 Jesu, Jesu, fill us with your love
380 Lord for tomorrow and his needs
602 Praise my soul the King of heaven
813 The Servant Song
723 There is a world
732 This is my will my one command
813 Will you let me be your servant

Eighth Sunday of the Year (A)
Do not worry about tomorrow.
Isaiah 49:14-15; Ps 61(62); 1 Cor 4:1-5; MATTHEW 6:24-34

148 Do not worry over what to eat
172 Fill my house unto the fullest
233 Guide my O thou great Redeemer
307 In the land there is a hunger
347 Lay your hands
348 Lead kindly light
386 Lord of all hopefulness
505 My soul is longing for your peace
633 Seek ye first the kingdom of God
676 Take my hands
739 Though the mountains may fall
817 Yahweh you are my strength

Eighth Sunday of the Year (B)
Rejoice while the bridegroom is with you.
Hosea 2:16-17, 21-2; Ps 102(103); 2 Cor 3:1-6; MARK 2:18-22

81 Bless the Lord my soul (Taizé)
122 Come back to me
172 Fill my house unto the fullest
253 Gather us in
870 Gifts of bread and wine
215 God is love his the care
253 Here in this place
343 King of glory, king of peace
496 My God and is thy table spread
610 Praise we our God with joy
617 Rejoice in the Lord always
917 We bring to you this bread and wine
792 Welcome, all ye noble saints

Eighth Sunday of the Year (C)
By their fruits you shall know them.
Ecclus 27:4-7; Ps 91(92); 1 Cor 15:54-58; LUKE 6:39-45

50 As a tree planted
74 Be thou my vision
120 Be light for our eyes
88 Blest are the pure in heart
98 Breathe on me breath of God
543 Centre of my life
120 Come and be light for our eyes
242 Happy the man who wanders with the Lord
315 It is good to give thanks
351 Lead us, heavenly Father, lead us
365 Light of our darkness
368 Like a sea without a shore
478 Make me a channel of your peace
633 Seek ye first the kingdom of God

Ninth Sunday of the Year (A)
A house built on rock.
Deut 11:18, 26-28, 32; Ps 30(31); Rom 3:21-25, 28; MATTHEW 7:21-27

21 All my hope on God is founded
33 Alleluia, alleluia! I will praise the Father
74 Be thou my vision
106 Christ be beside me
109 Christ is made the sure foundation
654 Sing of the Lord's goodness
648 Sing it in the valleys
210 God gives his people strength
319 Jesu lover of my soul
884 Jesus put this song into our hearts
507 My strength comes from the Lord
528 O God our help in ages past
624 Rock of ages

Ninth Sunday of the Year (B)
The Son of Man is Lord even of the Sabbath.
Deut 5:12-15; Ps 80(81); 2 Cor 4:6-11; MARK 2:23 – 3:6 (or 2:23-28)

858 All over the world
22 All people that on earth do dwell
28 All this world belongs to Jesus
253 Gather us in
326 Jesus is Lord! creations voice proclaims it
275 I danced in the morning
315 It is good to give thanks
326 Jesus is Lord
605 Praise the Lord, ye heavens adore him
709 The Master came to bring good news

Ninth Sunday of the Year (C)
Proclaim the Good News.
1 Kings 8:41-43; Ps 116(117); Gal 1:1-2, 6-10; LUKE 7:1-10

19 All hail the power of Jesus' name
110 Christ is our King
118 Colours of day
201 Envoi Round
183 Forth in the peace of Christ
184 Forth in thy name
201 Go out to the whole world
203 Go the Mass is ended
303 In Christ there is no east or west
709 The Master came to bring good news
778 We have a gospel to proclaim
789 We walk by faith
828 You must cry out the word of the Lord

Tenth Sunday of the Year (A)
I did not come to call the virtuous, but sinners.
Hosea 6:3-6; Ps 49(50); Rom 4:18-25; MATTHEW 9:9-13

128 Come Lord Jesus come
143 Dear Lord and Father of mankind
175 Follow me, follow me
211 God who made the earth
279 I met you at the cross
285 I the Lord of sea and sky
876 I will call upon the Lord
339 Just as I am
886 Lead me Lord
383 Living Lord
383 Lord Jesus Christ, you have come to us
905 Return to God
701 The kingdom of God
745 To God be the glory

Tenth Sunday of the Year (B)
All men's sins will be forgiven... anyone who does the will of God is my brother and sister and mother.
Genesis 3:9-15; Ps 129(130); 2 Cor 4:13 – 5:1; MARK 3:20-35

37 Alleluia, sing to Jesus
3 A mighty stronghold is our God

188 From the depths of sin and sadness
209 God forgave my sin
248 He who would valiant be
326 Jesus is Lord
886 Lead me Lord
351 Lead us heavenly Father, lead us
895 My Jesus, my Saviour
720 More desired than gold
587 Our Father we have wandered
605 Praise the Lord, ye heavens
633 Seek ye first
720 The word of God is more desired than gold
811 Who honours courage here

Tenth Sunday of the Year (C)

O Lord, you have raised my soul from the dead.

1 Kings 17:17-24; Ps 29(30); Gal 1:11-19; LUKE 7:11-17

12 Again the Lord's own day is here
31 All ye who seek a comfort sure
37 Alleluia, sing to Jesus
135 Come to set us free
208 God everlasting,wonderful and holy
879 In God's good time
347 Lay your hands
511 Now in this banquet
528 O God our hel in ages past
610 Praise we our God with joy
648 Sing it in the valleys
715 The Spirit lives to set us free
715 Walk in the light
776 We gather together
822 You are the King of Glory

Eleventh Sunday of the Year (A)

He made us, we belong to him.

Exodus 19:2-6; Ps 99(100); Rom 5:6-11; MATTHEW 9:36 – 10:8

22 All people that on earth do dwell
118 Colours of day
201 Envoi Round
183 Forth in the peace of Christ
201 Go out to the whole world
227 Go, tell everyone
203 Go the Mass is ended
227 God's spirit is in my heart
226 God, your glory we have seen
289 I will be with you
528 O God, our help in ages past
899 O let the Son of God
832 On eagle's wings
615 Reap me the earth
637 Send us as your blessing, Lord
911 Take me Lord
676 Take my hands

Eleventh Sunday of the Year (B)

What can we say the Kingdom of Heaven is like?

Ezekiel 17:22-24; Ps 91(92); 2 Cor 5:6-10; MARK 4:26-34

50 As a tree planted
108 Christ is King of earth and heaven
169 Fear not rejoice and be glad
226 God, your glory we have seen
242 Happy the man
306 In the earth
315 It is good to give thanks
912 The heavens are telling
695 The green life rises
724 There is one thing I ask
903 Over all the earth
738 Thou whose almighty Word
754 Unless a grain of wheat

Eleventh Sunday of the Year (C)

The one who is forgiven much, shows much love.

2 Sam 12:7-10, 13; Ps 31(1-2, 5, 7,11)

10 Across the years ther echoes still
40 Amazing grace
163 Father of heaven, whose love profound
168 Father we praise you
182 Forgive our sins
304 In the abundance of your compassion
319 Jesu, lover of my soul
332 Jesus, thou art coming
380 Lord for tomorrow
529 O God, thy people gather
899 O let the Son of God
587 Our Father, we have wandered
654 Sing of the Lord's goodness
910 Such love
401 Water of life, cleanse and refresh us

Twelfth Sunday of the Year (A)

Do not be afraid of those who kill the body but cannot kill the soul...

Jeremiah 20:10-13; Ps 68(69); Rom 5:12-15; MATTHEW 10:26-33

299 All that is hidden
830 Be not afraid
147 Do not be afraid
158 Father hear theprayer
160 Father in my life I see
327 Jesus, lead the way
295 If God is for us
878 If we are living
299 If you would follow me
334 Jesus, you're the one I love
348 Lead, kindly light
542 Oh Lord hear my prayer
626 Safe in the shadow
911 Take me Lord
830 You shall cross the barren desert

Twelfth Sunday of the Year (B)

Who can this be? Even the wind and the sea obey him.

Job 38:1, 8-11; Ps 106(107); 2 Cor 5:14-17; MARK 4:35-41

69 Be still and know
70 Be still and know that I am God
72 Be still for the presence of the Lord
73 Be still my soul
152 Eternal Father, strong to save
210 God gives his people strength
285 Here I am, Lord
249 He's got the whole world in his hands
289 I will be with you
326 Jesus is Lord!
351 Lead us, heavenly Father lead us
383 Lord Jesus Christ, you have come to us
559 O worship the King

605 Praise the Lord! ye heavens adore him
674 Sweet sacrament divine
688 The Church's one foundation
765 Walk with me, O my Lord
830 You shall cross the barren desert

Twelfth Sunday of the Year (C)

Who do you say I am? Peter spoke up: The Christ of God.

Zech 12:10-11; 13:1; Ps 62(63); Gal 3:26-29; LUKE 9:18-24

59 At the name of Jesus
862 Bread of life truth eternal
111 Christ is the world's light
113 Christ triumphant
173 Firmly I believe and truly
216 God is my great desire
285 Here I am Lord
279 I met you at the cross
326 Jesus is Lord
495 My God accept my heart
564 Oh God, I seek you
903 Over all the earth
754 Unless a grain of wheat
801 When I survey the wondrous cross
564 Your love is Finer than Life

Thirteenth Sunday of the Year (A)

Anyone who welcomes my disciple, welcomes me.

2 Kings 4:8-11, 14-16; Ps 88(89); Rom 6:3-4, 8-11; MATTHEW 10:37-42

543 Centre of my life
113 Christ triumphant
171 Fight the good fight
172 Fill my house
871 God to enfold you
880 Into the family of God
376 Look around you
572 O the word of my Lord
741 Thy hand O God has guided
754 Unless a grain of wheat
401 Water of life
799 Whatsoever you do
800 When I needed a neighbour
812 Will you come and follow me

Thirteenth Sunday of the Year (B)

O Lord, you have raised my soul from the dead.

Wisdom 1:13-5; 2:23-4; Ps 29(30); 2 Cor 8:7, 9, 13-15; MARK 5:21-43 (or 21-4, 35-43)

8 Abba Father send your Spirit
543 Centre of my life
110 Christ is our King
179 For the healing of the nations
199 Glory to thee, Lord God
301 Immortal invisible, God only wise
879 In God's good time
368 Like a sea without a shore
895 My Jesus my Saviour
507 My strength comes from the Lord
512 Now thank we all our God
649 Sing my soul
655 Sing praises to the living God
790 We will walk through the valley

Thirteenth Sunday of the Year (C)

No one who looks back is fit for the kingdom.

1 Kings 19:16, 19-21; Ps 15(16); Gal 5:1, 13-18; LUKE 9:51-62

543 Centre of my life
172 Fill my house
175 Follow me, follow me
203 Go the Mass is ended
233 Guide me, O thou great Redeemer
289 I will be with you
892 Lord of all creation
543 O Lord, you are the centre of my life
795 Servant Song
248 He who would valiant be
491 Moses I know you're the man
676 Take my hands
693 The gift of the holy Spirit
741 Thy hand, O God, has guided
795 What do you want of me

Fourteenth Sunday of the Year (A)

Come to me all you who labour... I am gentle and humble of heart.

Zech 9:9-10; Ps 144(145); Rom 8:9, 11-13; MATTHEW 11:25-30

31 All ye who seek a comfort sure
780 Earthen Vessels
226 God your glory we have seen
319 Jesu lover of my soul
320 Jesu, meek and lowly
325 Jesus, gentlest Saviour
381 Lord in everything I do
900 O Lord your tenderness
570 O the love of my Lord
588 Our Saviour, Jesus Christ, proclaimed
649 Sing my soul
654 Sing of the Lord's goodness
677 Take my life
780 We hold a treasure

Fourteenth Sunday of the Year (B)

All too full is our soul with the proud man's disdain.

Ezekiel 2:2-5; Ps 122(123); 2 Corinthians 12:7-10; MARK 6:1-6

33 Alleluia, alleluia! I will praise the Father
74 Be thou my vision
75 Be thou my vision (anacrusic version)
91 Blest be the Lord
860 Blest be the Lord
147 Do not be afraid
166 Father we come to you
171 Fight the good fight
183 Forth in the peace of Christ
242 Happy the man
248 He who would valiant be
285 Here I am Lord
269 How shall they hear the word of God
750 Trust in the Lord
771 We believe in God the Father

Fourteenth Sunday of the Year (C)

Go out and say: Peace be to this house. The Kingdom is very near to you.

Isaiah 66:10-14; Ps 65(66); Gal 6:14-18; LUKE 10:1-12, 17-20 (or 10:1-9)

Fifteenth Sunday of the Year (A)

The Word that I speak does not return to me empty.

Isaiah 55:10-11; Ps 64(65); Rom 8:18-23; MATTHEW 13:1-23 (or 1-9)

Fifteenth Sunday of the Year (B)

Go, prophesy to my people.

Amos 7:12-15; Ps 84(85); Eph 1:3-14 (or 3-10); MARK 6:7-13

Fifteenth Sunday of the Year (C)

You must love the Lord your God... and your neighbour as yourself.

Deut 30:10-14; Ps 68(69) or 18(19); Col 1:15-20; LUKE 10:25-37

Sixteenth Sunday of the Year (A)

O Lord, slow to anger, abounding in love.

Wisdom 12:13, 16-19; Ps 85(86); Rom 8:26-27; MATTHEW 13:24-43 (or 24-30)

Sixteenth Sunday of the Year (B)

I will gather my flock.

Jeremiah 23:1-6; Ps 22(23); Eph 2:13-18; MARK 6:30-34

Sixteenth Sunday of the Year (C)

Abraham welcomes the Lord; Martha welcomes Jesus.

Genesis 18:1-10; Ps 14(15); Col 1:24-28; LUKE 10:38-42

22 All people that on earth do dwell
69 Be still and know
88 Blest are the pure in heart
543 Centre of my life
106 Christ be beside me
280 I received the living God
331 Jesus the Word has lived among us
368 Like a sea without a shore
386 Lord of all hopefulness
543 O Lord, you are the centre of my life
570 Oh the love of my Lord
724 There is one thing I ask
770 We are your people
796 What does the Lord require
813 Will you let me be your servant

Seventeenth Sunday of the Year (A)

Choose the real treasure.

1 Kings 3:5, 7-12; Ps 118(119); Rom 8:28-30; MATTHEW 13:44-52 (or 44-46)

16 All for Jesus
74 Be thou my vision
106 Christ be beside me
780 Earthen Vessels
309 In your love remember me
886 Lead me Lord
386 Lord of all hopefulness
720 More desired than gold
895 My Jesus my Saviour
900 O Lord your tenderness
633 Seek ye first the kingdom of God
642 Show me your ways
701 The kingdom of God
720 The word of God is more desired than gold
780 We hold a treasure

Seventeenth Sunday of the Year (B)

You give us our food in due time.

Kings 2:42-44; Ps 144(145); Eph 4:1-6; JOHN 6:1-15

39 Almighty Father Lord most high
862 Bread of life, truth eternal
172 Fill my house
253 Gather us in
208 God everlasting
214 God is love, his the care
362 Let us with a gladsome mind
511 Now in this banquet
525 O food of travellers
548 O praise our great and gracious Lord
654 Sing of the Lord's goodness
684 Tell out my soul
747 To Jesus Christ, our sovereign King
792 Welcome all ye noble saints

Seventeenth Sunday of the Year (C)

Lord, teach us to pray… Ask and you will receive.

Genesis 18:2-32; Ps 137(138); Col 2:12-14; LUKE 11:1-13

31 All ye who seek a comfort sure
39 Almighty Father, Lord most high
148 Do not worry over what to eat
159 Father, I place into your hands
166 Father, we come to you
192 Give me yourself
208 God everlasting, wonderful and holy
272 I am the bread of life
307 In the land there is a hunger
351 Lead us heavenly Father lead us
362 Let us with a gladsome mind
196 Glory and praise to our God
556 O thou who at thy Eucharist
608 Praise to the Lord, the Almighty
633 Seek ye first the kingdom of God
654 Sing of the Lord's goodness

See also Our Father nos 464, 584–586

Eighteenth Sunday of the Year (A)

A God who feeds us.

Isaiah 55:1-3; Ps 144(145); Rom 8:35, 37-39; MATTHEW 14:13-21

37 Alleluia, sing to Jesus
90 Blest are you Lord God
92 Bread for the world, a world of hunger
93 Bread for the world broken (standard)
95 Bread of life, hope of the world (standard)
862 Bread of life, truth eternal
870 Gifts of bread and wine
192 Give me yourself
271 I am the bread of life
272 I am the bread of life
280 I received the living God
355 Let all mortal flesh keep silence
496 My God and is thy table spread
511 Now in this banquet

Eighteenth Sunday of the Year (B)

Do not work for bread that cannot last. I am the bread of life.

Exodus 16:2-4, 12-15; Ps 77(78); Eph 4:17, 20-24; JOHN 6:24-35

37 Alleluia sing to Jesus
334 Bread, blessed and broken for us all
271 I am the bread of life (Konstant)
272 I am the bread of life (Toolan)
875 God to enfold you
334 Jesus, you're the one I love
377 Lord accept the gifts we offer
496 My God and is thy table spread
895 My Jesus my Saviour
511 Now in ths banquet
603 Praise now your God, every tongue
641 Shepherd of souls, in love come feed us
773 We celebrate this festive day

Eighteenth Sunday of the Year (C)

Do not store up treasure for yourself on earth.

Eccles 1:2; 2:21-23; Ps 89(90) or 94(95); Col 3:1-5, 9-11; LUKE 12:13-21

21 All my hope on God is founded
74 Be thou my vision
88 Blest are the pure in heart
125 Come down O love divine
143 Dear Lord and Father of mankind

148 Do not worry over what to eat
154 Eye has not seen
170 Feed my lambs
301 Immortal, invisible
307 In the land there is a hunger
355 Let all mortal flesh keep silence
505 My soul is longing for your peace
511 Now in this banquet
528 O God our help in ages past
555 O that today you would listen

Nineteenth Sunday of the Year (A)

Give us your saving help. Calm the sea.

1 Kings 19:9, 11-13; Ps 84(85); Rom 9:1-5; MATTHEW 14:22-23

59 At the name of Jesus
543 Centre of my life
70 Be still and know
73 Be still my soul
143 Dear Lord and Father of mankind
147 Do not be afraid
152 Eternal Father strong to save
249 He's got the whole world in his hands
289 I will be with you
351 Lead us heavenly Father lead us
889 Like a shepherd
528 O God, our help in ages past
559 O worship the king
901 One more step
626 Safe in the shadow of the Lord
648 Sing it in the valleys
913 The Lord's my shepherd

Nineteenth Sunday of the Year (B)

Anyone who eats this bread will live for ever.

1 Kings 19:4-8; Ps 33(34); Eph 4:30-5:2; JOHN 6:41-51

861 Bread we bring
862 Bread of life, truth eternal
97 Bread of the world
157 Father and life-giver
271 I am the bread of life (Konstant)
272 I am the bread of life (Toolan)
280 I received the living God
355 Let all mortal flesh
399 Love is his word, love is his way
548 O praise our great and gracious Lord
912 The heavens are telling
742 To be the body
754 Unless a grain of wheat

Nineteenth Sunday of the Year (C)

Happy the people the Lord has chosen as his own.

Wis 18:6-9; Psalm 32(33); Heb 11:1-2, 8-19 (or 1-2, 8-12); LUKE 12:32-48 (or 35-40)

22 All people that on earth do dwell
65 Awake from your slumber
65 City of God
242 Happy the man
118 Colours of day
867 Faithful one
386 Lord of all hopefulness
395 Lord you have come to the lakeside
398 Love divine, all loves excelling
568 Oh Lord my God

535 O Jesus Christ remember
688 The Church's one foundation
763 Wake, O wake! with tidings thrilling
789 We walk by faith
806 When the King shall come again

Twentieth Sunday of the Year (A)

My house is a house of prayer for all peoples.

Isaiah 56:1, 6-7; Ps 66(67); Rom 11:13-15, 29-32; MATTHEW 15:21-28

22 All people that on earth do dwell
25 All the ends of the earth
30 All you nations
131 Come praise the Lord the Almighty
109 Christ is made the sure foundation
184 Forth in the name
326 Jesus is Lord! creations voice proclaims it
883 Jesus name above all names
509 New songs of celebration
903 Over all the earth
644 Sing a new song to the Lord
703 The light of Christ
822 You are the King of Glory

Twentieth Sunday of the Year (B)

Anyone who eats this bread, I will raise upon the last day.

Proverbs 9:1-6; Ps 33(34); Eph 5:15-20; JOHN 6:51-58

866 Come to the feast
151 Eat this bread (Taizé)
870 Gifts of bread and wine
271 I am the bread of life (Konstant)
272 I am the bread of life (Toolan)
280 I received the living God
383 Lord Jesus Christ
531 O Godhead hid
662 Sons of God, hear his holy word
682 Taste and see
730 This is my body
754 Unless a grain of wheat

Twentieth Sunday of the Year (C)

God's word can make people take sides.

Jer 38:4-6, 8-10; Ps 39(40); Heb 12:1-4; LUKE 12:49-53

31 All ye who seek a comfort sure
73 Be still my soul
147 Do not be afraid
319 Jesu lover of my soul
160 Father in my life I see
210 God gives his people strength
233 Guide me, O thou great Redeemer
320 Jsus meek and lowly
348 Lead kindly light
350 Lead us from death to life
351 Lead us heavenly Father lead us
390 Lord thy word abideth
527 O God of earth and altar
350 World peace prayer
817 Yahweh, you are my strength

Twenty–First Sunday of the Year (A)
On this rock I will build my church.
Isaiah 22:19-23; Ps 137(138); Rom 11:33-36; MATTHEW 16:13-20

21 All my hope on God is founded
114 Christ's church shall glory in his power
869 Father God I wonder
170 Feed my lambs
173 Firmly I believe and truly
246 He is Lord
326 Jesus is Lord
356 Let all that is within me
395 Lord you have come t the lakeside
688 The Church's one foundation
417 We believe (Walker)
771 We believe in God the Father
789 We walk by faith

Twenty–First Sunday of the Year (B)
Lord, to whom shall we go?
Joshua 24:1-2, 15-18; Ps 33(34); Eph 5:21-32; JOHN 6:60-69

119 Come adore this wondrous presence
173 Firmly I believe and truly
280 I received the living God
893 Lord of life
537 O King of might and splendour
658 Sing to the world
663 Soul of my Saviour
682 Taste and see
701 The kingdom of God
754 Unless a grain of wheat

Twenty–First Sunday of the Year (C)
1 am coming to gather the nations into the kingdom.
Isaiah 66:18-21; Ps 116(117); Heb 12:5-7,11-13; LUKE 13:22-30

37 Alleluia sing to Jesus
118 Colours of day
865 Come let us go
866 Come to the feast
201 Envoi Round
253 Gather us in
201 Go out to the whole world
253 Here in this place
303 In Christ there is no east or west
312 Into one we all are gathered
536 O Jesus, I have promised
684 Tell out my soul
741 Thy hand, O God, has guided

Twenty–Second Sunday of the Year (A)
Anyone who loses his life for my sake will find it.
Jer 20:7-9; Ps 62(63); Rom 12:1-2; MATTHEW 16:21-27

74 Be thou my vision
88 Blest are the pure in heart
113 Christ triumphant
175 Follow me follow me
248 He who would valiant be
876 I will call upon the Lord
878 If we are living
495 My God accept my heart this day
564 Oh God, I seek you
812 The Summons
754 Unless a grain of wheat
801 When I survey the wondrous cross
811 Who honours courage here
812 Will you come and follow me
564 Your love is Finer than Life

Twenty–Second Sunday of the Year (B)
True intentions come from the heart.
Deut 4:1-2, 6-8; Ps 14(15); James 1:17-18, 21-22, 27; MARK 7:1-8, 14-15, 21-23

33 Alleluia, alleluia! I will praise the Father
50 As a tree planted
72 Be still for the presence of the Lord
88 Blest are the pure in heart
98 Breathe on me breath of God
543 Centre of my life
143 Dear Lord and Father of mankind
190 Give me joy in my heart
242 Happy the man who wanders with the Lord
890 Listen let your heart keep seeking
720 More desired than gold
309 In your love, remember me
543 O Lord, you are the centre of my life
633 Seek ye first the kingdom of God
720 The word of God is more desired than gold

Twenty–Second Sunday of the Year (C)
The one who humbles himself will be exalted.
Ecclus 3:17-20, 28-29; Ps 67(68); Heb 12:18-19, 22-24; LUKE 14:1, 7-14

50 As a tree planted
74 Be thou my vision
88 Blest are the pure in heart
110 Christ is our King
179 For the healing of the nations
253 Gather us in
253 Here in this place
399 Love is his word
474 Loving Father from thy bounty
480 Man of Galilee
631 See us Lord about thine altar
684 Tell out my soul
915 There is a longing
770 We are your people
792 Welcome, all ye noble saints

Twenty–Third Sunday of the Year (A)
Our duty to win people back to the right path.
Ezekiel 33:7-9; Ps 94(95); Rom 13:8-10; MATTHEW 18:15-20

103 And be like your father
103 But I say unto you
161 Father Lord of all creation
179 For the healing of the nations
182 Forgive our sins, as we forgive
885 Laudate, laudate Dominum
350 Lead us from death to life
887 Let us go forth in the peace of Christ
555 O that today you would listen
905 Return to God
730 This is my body
769 We are one in the Spirit
800 When I needed a neighbour

Twenty–Third Sunday of the Year (B)

The deaf hear and the dumb speak.

Isaiah 35:4-7; Ps 145(146); James 2:1-5; MARK 7:31-37

110 Christ is our King
269 How shall they hear the word of God
347 Lay your hands
886 Lead me Lord
480 Man of Galilee
511 Now in this banquet
518 O changeless Christ
588 Our Saviour, Jesus Christ, proclaimed
602 Praise my soul the King of heaven
698 The King of glory comes
915 There is a longing
725 There lived a man
776 We gather together
822 You are the King of Glory

Twenty–Third Sunday of the Year (C)

Who can divine the will of the Lord? 'Anyone who does not carry his cross cannot be my disciple'

Wisdom 9:13-18; Ps 89(90); Philemon 9-10, 12-17; LUKE 14:25-33

21 All my hope on God is founded
23 All that I am
74 Be thou my vision
98 Breathe on me breath of God
158 Father hear the prayer we offer
171 Fight the good fight
279 I met you at the cross
350 Lead us from death to life
893 Lord of life
896 Nearer my God to thee
528 O God, our help in ages past
729 This day God gives me
752 Turn to me
754 Unless a grain of wheat
801 When I survey the wondrous cross
350 World peace prayer

Twenty–Fourth Sunday of the Year (A)

God does not repay us according to our faults; neither should we.

Ecclus 27:30 – 28:7; Ps 102(103); Rom 14:7-9; MATTHEW 18:21-35

10 Across the years there echoes
82 Bless the Lord, O my soul (E Walker)
863 Broken for me
103 But I say unto you
182 Forgive our sins, as we forgive
209 God forgave my sin in Jesus name
215 God is love, his the care
895 My Jesus my Saviour
567 Oh Lord, all the world belongs to you
633 Seek ye first the kingdom
908 Share the light
678 Take our bread, we ask you
693 The gift of the holy Spirit

Twenty–Fourth Sunday of the Year (B)

Who do you say I am? You are the Christ.

Isaiah 50:5-9; Ps 114(115); James 2:14-18; MARK 8:27-35

16 All for Jesus
59 At the name of Jesus
109 Christ is made the sure foundation
113 Christ triumphant
197 Glory be to Jesus
248 He who would valiant be
874 I cannot tell
279 I met you at the cross
326 Jesus is Lord
330 Jesus, the holy Lamb of God
355 Let all mortal flesh
895 My Jesus my Saviour
503 My song is love unknown
568 Oh Lord my God when I in awesome wonder
658 Sing to the world of Christ

Twenty–Fourth Sunday of the Year (C)

This son of mine was dead and has come back to life.

Exodus 32:7-11, 13-14; Ps 50(51); 1 Tim 1:12-17; LUKE 15:1-32 (or 1-10) – The Prodigal Son

10 Across the years
40 Amazing grace
162 Father most holy
166 Father we come to you
209 God forgave my sin
339 Just as I am
570 Oh the love of my Lord
587 Our Father, we have wandered
602 Praise my soul the King of heaven
621 Remember, remember your mercy, Lord
621 Remember your mercy, Lord
654 Sing of the Lord's goodness
757 Vaster far than any ocean
792 Welcome all ye noble saints

Twenty–Fifth Sunday of the Year (A)

God is close to those who call: but he rewards us as he decides.

Isaiah 55:6-9; Ps 144(145); Phil 1:2-24, 27; MATTHEW 20:1-6

81 Bless the Lord my soul
869 Father God I wonder
215 God is love his the care
289 I will be with you
301 Immortal invisible, God only wise
302 In bread we bring you Lord
362 Let us with a gladsome mind
567 Oh Lord, all the world belongs to you
587 Our Father, we have wandered
606 Praise to the holiest in the height
684 Tell out my soul

Twenty–Fifth Sunday of the Year (B)

The Lord upholds my life.

Wisdom 2:12, 17-20; Ps 53(54); James 3:16 – 4:3; MARK 9:30-37

3 A mighty stronghold
31 All ye who seek a comfort sure
128 Come Lord Jesus come
295 If God is for us, who can be against
881 Jesus be the centre

325 Jesus gentlest Saviour
327 Jesus, lead the way
528 Oh God our help in ages past
624 Rock of ages
913 The Lord's my shepherd
739 Though the mountains may fall
308 In the Lord I'll be ever thankful
Whatsoever you do
817 Yahweh you are my strength

Twenty–Fifth Sunday of the Year (C)

If you cannot be trusted with money, that tainted thing, who will trust you with genuine riches?

Amos 8:4-7; Ps 112(113); 1 Tim 2:1-8; LUKE 16:1-13 (or 10-13)

74 Be thou my vision
103 But I say unto you
147 Do not worry over what to eat
178 For the fruits of his creation
182 Forgive our sins
242 Happy the man
479 Make way, make way, for Christ the King
567 Oh Lord all the world belongs to you
902 Only by grace
633 Seek ye first
704 The Cry of the Poor
704 The Lord hears the cry of the poor
819 Ye servants of God, your Master proclaim

Twenty–Sixth Sunday of the Year (A)

He shows the path to those who stray.

Ezekiel 18:25-28; Ps 24(25); Phil 2:1-11 (or 1-5); MATTHEW 21:28-32

299 All that is hidden
40 Amazing grace
59 At the name of Jesus
88 Blest are the pure in heart
210 God gives his people strength
209 God forgave my sin
226 God your glory we have seen
245 He became poor
299 If you would follow me
902 Only by grace
621 Remember, remember your mercy, Lord
621 Remember your mercy, Lord
911 Take me Lord
915 There is a longing
792 Welcome, all ye noble saints

Twenty–Sixth Sunday of the Year (B)

Anyone who is not against us is for us.

Numbers 11:25-29; Ps 18(19); James 5:1-6; MARK 9:38-43, 45, 47-48

88 Blest are the pure in heart
166 Father, we come to you
183 Forth in the peace of Christ
201 Go out to the whole world
212 God has chosen me
269 How shall they hear the word of God
887 Let us go forth in the peace of Christ
901 One more step
693 The gift of the Holy Spirit
732 This is my will, my one command
769 We are one in the Spirit

828 You must cry out the word of the Lord

Twenty–Sixth Sunday of the Year (C)

It is the Lord who keeps faith forever, who is just to those who are oppressed.

Amos 6:1, 4-7; Ps 145(146); 1 Tim 6:11-16; LUKE 16:19-31

115 A Touching Place
115 Christ's is the world in which we move
179 For the healing of the nations
253 Gather us in
218 God of day and God of darkness
253 Here in this place
301 Immortal invisible
886 Lead me Lord
567 Oh Lord all the world belongs to you
706 The Lord's my shepherd
710 The prophet in his hunger
718 The voice of God
799 Whatsoever you do
800 When I needed a neighbour

Twenty–Seventh Sunday of the Year (A)

The vineyard of the Lord.

Isaiah 5:1-7; Ps 79(80); Phil 4:6-9; MATTHEW 21:33-43

113 Christ triumphant
866 Come to the feast
136 Come ye thankful people come
197 Glory be to Jesus
285 Here I am, Lord
285 I, the Lord of sea and sky
398 Love divine, all loves excelling
503 My song is love unknown
615 Reap me the earth
742 To be the body of the Lord
745 To God be the glory
824 You are the vine
807 When the time came to stretch out his arms

Twenty–Seventh Sunday of the Year (B)

They become one body.

Genesis 2:18-24; Ps 127(128); Hebrews 2:9-11; MARK 10:2-16 (or 2-12)

80 Bind us together Lord
177 For the beauty of the earth
220 God of tender mercy, God of love
303 In Christ there is no east or west
312 Into one we all are gathered
399 Love is his word
220 Love Which Never Ends
546 O perfect love
576 On this house your blessing Lord
578 One bread, one body
776 We gather together as brothers and sisters
769 We are one in the spirit

Twenty–Seventh Sunday of the Year (C)

We are servants; we have done no more than our duty.

Hab 1:2-3; 2:2-4; Ps 94(95); 2 Tim 1:6-8, 13-14; LUKE 17:5-10

21 All my hope on God is founded
555 O that today you would listen
158 Father hear the prayer we offer
159 Father, I place into your hands
210 God gives his people strength

257 Holy God we praise thy name
309 In your love remember me
348 Lead, kindly light
886 Lead me Lord
395 Lord you have come to the lakeside
676 Take my hands
741 Thy hand, O God, has guided
765 Walk with me Oh my Lord
817 Yahweh, you are my strength

Twenty–Eighth Sunday of the Year (A)

The wedding feast of the Lord.

Isaiah 25:6-10; Ps 22(23); Phil 4:12-14, 19-20; MATTHEW 22:1-14 (or 1-10)

77 Because the Lord is my shepherd
862 Bread of life, truth eternal
866 Come to the feast
157 Father and life–giver
253 Here in this place
272 I am the bread of life
511 Now in this banquet
534 O how lovely is your dwelling place
603 Praise now your God, every tongue
774 Song of the Body of Christ
688 The Church's one foundaton
699 The king of love
917 We bring to you this bread and wine
774 We come to share our story

Twenty–Eighth Sunday of the Year (B)

That we may gain wisdom of heart.

Wisdom 7:7-11; Ps 89(90); Hebrews 4:12-13; MARK 10:17-30 (or 17-27)

21 All my hope on God is founded
23 All that I am
74 Be thou my vision
75 Be thou my vision (anacrusic version)
88 Blest are the pure in heart
98 Breathe on me breath of God
543 Centre of my life
106 Christ be beside me
780 Earthen Vessels
175 Follow me
183 Forth in the peace of Christ
543 O Lord, you are the centre of my life
582 Open your ears, O Christian people
780 We hold a treasure

Twenty–Eighth Sunday of the Year (C)

Finding himself cured, one of them praised God at the top of his voice.

2 Kings 5:14-17; Ps 97(98); 2 Tim 2:8-13; LUKE 17:11-19

25 All the ends of the earth
40 Amazing grace
81 Bless the Lord my soul
869 Father God I wonder
208 God everlasting wonderful and holy
215 God is love, his the care
877 I will call upon the Lord
362 Let us with a gladsome mind
509 New songs of celebration
512 Now thank we all our God
547 Oh praise ye the Lord
602 Praise my soul the King of heaven
617 Rejoice in the Lord always
644 Sing a new song to the Lord
745 To God be the glory

Twenty–Ninth Sunday of the Year (A)

There is no other God besides me.

Isaiah 45:1, 4-6; Ps 95(96); 1 Thess 1:1-5; MATTHEW 22:15-21

21 All my hope on God is founded
22 All people that on earth do dwell
59 At the name of Jesus
74 Be thou my vision
111 Christ is the world's light
194 Glorious God, King of creation
246 He is Lord, he is Lord
257 Holy God we praise thy name
301 Immortal invisible, God only wise
882 Jesus, Jesus
883 Jesus, name above all names
333 Jesus, you are Lord
477 Majesty
895 My Jesus, my Saviour
615 Reap me the earth
388 Shine Jesus shine
654 Sing of the Lord's goodness
658 Sing to the world of Christ
752 Turn to me

Twenty–Ninth Sunday of the Year (B)

Can you drink the cup that I must drink?

Isaiah 53:10-11; Ps 32(33); Hebrews 4:14-16; MARK 10:35-45 (or 42-45)

113 Christ triumphant
226 God your glory we have seen
340 Keep in mind that Jesus Christ
893 Lord of life
524 O Father take in sign of love
537 O King of might and splendour
568 Oh Lord my God
590 Ours were the sufferings
648 Sing it in the valleys
654 Sing of the Lord's goodness
911 Take me Lord
697 The heavenly Word, proceeding forth
701 The kingdom of God
754 Unless a grain of wheat

Twenty–Ninth Sunday of the Year (C)

God will see justice done for those who call to him.

Exodus 17:8-13; Ps 120(121); 2 Tim 3:14 – 4:2; LUKE 18:1-8

21 All my hope on God is founded
31 All ye who seek a comfort sure
91 Blest be the Lord
865 Come let us go
158 Father, hear the prayer we offer
179 For the healing of the nations
210 God gives his people strength
218 God of day and God of darkness
876 I will call upon the Lord
380 Lord for tomorrow
528 O God our help in ages past
588 Our Saviour, Jesus Christ, proclaimed
739 Though the mountains may fall

Thirtieth Sunday of the Year (A)

The greatest commandment of all.

Exodus 22:20-26; Ps 17(18); 1 Thess 1:5-10; MATTHEW 22:34-40

4 A new commandment
161 Father, Lord of all creation
179 For the healing of the nations
259 Holy holy
312 Into one we all are gathered
318 Jesu, Jesu, fill us with your love
343 King of glory, king of peace
350 Lead us from death to life
399 Love is his word
478 Make me a channel of your peace
564 Oh God, I seek you
900 O Lord your tenderness
911 Take me Lord
732 This is my will
564 Your love is Finer than Life

Thirtieth Sunday of the Year (B)

I will gather them all: the blind and the lame.

Jeremiah 31:7-9; Ps 125(126); Hebrews 5:1-6; MARK 10:46-52

64 Awake, awake, fling off the night
74 Be thou my vision
110 Christ is our King
118 Colours of day
253 Gather us in
283 I saw the grass
288 I watch the sunrise
297 If God should lead us home
347 Lay your hands
480 Man of Galilee
511 Now in this banquet
602 Praise my soul the King of heaven
703 The light of Christ
738 Thou whose almighty Word
822 You are the King of glory

Thirtieth Sunday of the Year (C)

The one who humbles himself will be exalted.

Ecclus 35:12-14, 16-19; Ps 33(34); 2 Tim 4:6-8, 16-18

115 A Touching Place
500 Amazing grace
863 Broken for me
115 Christ's is the world in which we move
182 Forgive our sins
316 It's me O Lord
332 Jesus thou art coming
505 My soul is longing for your peace
527 O God of earth and altar
529 O God, thy people gather
902 Only by grace
587 Our Father we have wandered
704 The Cry of the Poor
704 The Lord hears the cry of the poor
915 There is a longing
757 Vaster far than any ocean

Thirty–First Sunday of the Year (A)

The greatest among you must be your servant.

Malachi 1:14 – 2:2, 8-10; Ps 130(131); 1 Thess 2:7-9, 13; MATTHEW 23:1-12

39 Almighty Father God most high
50 As a tree planted
143 Dear Lord and Father of mankind
309 In your love, remember me
505 My soul is longing for your peace
527 O God of earth and altar
545 O my Lord, within my heart
911 Take me Lord
734 This is what Yahweh asks
753 Unite us, Lord, in peace

Thirty–First Sunday of the Year (B)

What is the greatest of the commandments?

Deut 6:2-6; Ps 17(18); Hebrews 7:23-28; MARK 12:28-34

4 A new commandment I give unto you
302 In bread we bring you, Lord
312 Into one we all are gathered
321 Jesu the very thought of thee
343 King of glory, King of peace
900 O God your tenderness
665 Spirit of God within me
730 This is my body, broken for you
732 This is my will
919 When my mind is still
809 Where is love and loving kindness

Thirty–First Sunday of the Year (C)

The Son of Man has come to seek out and save what was lost.

Wisdom 11:22 – 12:2; Ps 144(145); 2 Thess 1:11-2:2; LUKE 19:1-10

23 All that I am
40 Amazing grace
863 Broken for me
108 Christ is king of earth and heaven
209 Freely, freely
209 God forgave my sin
495 My God, accept my heart this day
602 Praise my soul the king of heaven
654 Sing of the Lord's goodness
676 Take my hands
739 Though the mountains may fall
745 To God be the glory

Thirty–Second Sunday of the Year (A)

Watch and wait.

Wisdom 6:12-16; Ps 62(63); 1 Thess 4:13-18 (or 13-14); MATTHEW 25:1-13

53 As the deer longs for running streams
54 As the deer pants
64 Awake, awake, fling off the night
74 Be thou my vision
284 I sing a song to you Lord
307 In the land there is a hunger
332 Jesus thou art coming
398 Love divine all loves excelling
535 O Jesus Christ remember
268 Our God reigns

Thirty–Second Sunday of the Year (B)

The poor are more generous than the rich.

1 Kings 17:10-16; Ps 145(146); Hebrews 9:24-28; MARK 12:38-44 (or 41-44)

Thirty–Second Sunday of the Year (C)

God not of the dead, but of the living.

2 Macc 7:1-2, 9-14; Ps 16(17); 2 Thess 2:16-3:5; LUKE 20:27-38 (or 27:34-38)

Thirty–Third Sunday of the Year (A)

Well done, good and faithful servant.

Prov 31:10-13, 19-20, 30-31; Ps 127(128); 1 Thess 5:1-6; MATTHEW 25:14-30 (or 14-15, 19-21)

Thirty–Third Sunday of the Year (B)

In those days... they will see the Son of Man coming with great power and glory.

Daniel 12:1-3; Ps 15(16); Hebrews 10:11-14, 18; MARK 13:24-32

Thirty–Third Sunday of the Year (C)

Your endurance will win you your lives.

Malachi 3:19-20; Ps 97(98); 2 Thess 3:7-12; LUKE 21:5-19

Our Lord Jesus Christ, Universal King (A)

Come, you blessed of my Father.

Ezekiel 34:11-12, 15-17; Ps 22(23); 1 Cor 15:20-26, 28; MATTHEW 25:31-46

See also Kingdom of God and Majesty and Power in Topical Index

Our Lord Jesus Christ, Universal King (B)

Mine is not a kingdom of this world.

Daniel 7:13-14; Ps 92(93); Apocalypse 1:5-8; JOHN 18:33-37

15 All creatures of our God and King
25 All the ends of the earth
108 Christ is king of earth and heaven
110 Christ is our King
113 Christ triumphant
139 Crown him with many crowns
239 Hail redeemer King divine
326 Jesus is Lord! creations voice proclaims it
373 Lo, he comes with clouds descending
477 Majesty, worship his majesty
559 O worship the king
619 Rejoice the Lord is King
747 To Jesus Christ our sovereign King

See also Kingdom of God and Majesty and Power in Topical Index

Our Lord Jesus Christ, Universal King (C)

I rejoiced when I heard them say: Let us go to God's house.

2 Sam 5:1-3; Ps 121(122); Col 1:11-20; LUKE 23:35-43

139 Crown him with many crowns
184 Forth in thy name
239 Hail redeemer King divine
257 Holy God we praise thy name
279 I met you at the cross
281 I rejoiced when I heard them say
477 Majesty, worship his majesty
503 My song is love unknown
619 Rejoice! the Lord is King
648 Sing it in the valleys
696 The head that once was crowned
712 The royal banners forward go
747 To Jesus Christ our sovereign King

See also Kingdom of God and Majesty and Power in Topical Index

Adoration

Blessing

Celebration

Children's hymns

Christian life

Christian unity

Church

Comfort

Community

Creation

Creativity

Cross

Discipleship

Eternal life

Evening

Faith

Faithfulness of God

Fasting

Fear

Forgiveness – God's

Forgiveness for others

Gathering

God the Father (Creator)

God's wisdom

Going forth

Grace

Guidance

Harvest

Healing

Holy Spirit

Hope and trust

Jesus' ministry

Jesus the Redeemer

Justice

Kingdom of God

Law of God

Life

Light

138 Creator of the stars of night
142 Day is done, but love unfailing
181 For you, O Lord
196 Glory and praise to our God
414 Glory and praise to you
212 God has chosen me
215 God is love, his the care
218 God of day and God of darkness
253 Here in this place
256 Holy Father, God of might
266 How brightly beams the morning star
283 I saw the grass
285 I, the Lord of sea and sky
288 I watch the sunrise
299 If you would follow me
301 Immortal, invisible
881 Jesus be the centre
348 Lead, kindly light
365 Light of our darkness
366 Light the Advent candle one
891 Longing for light (Christ be our Light)
388 Lord, the light of your love is shining
416 Praise to you, O Christ, our Saviour
481 Many are the light beams
494 Mould us now, as the potter's clay
511 Now in this banquet
539 O light forever dawning
591 Out of darkness
908 Share the light of Jesus
665 Spirit of God within me
682 Taste and see
690 The day of resurrection
703 The light of Christ
711 The race that long in darkness
914 The Spirit lives (Walk in the Light)
724 There is one thing I ask
736 This little light of mine
737 Those who were in the dark
738 Thou whose almighty Word
759 Veni Sancte Spiritus
763 Wake, O wake! with tidings thrilling
768 We are marching
790 We will walk through the valley
813 Will you let me be your servant
821 You are salt for the earth
822 You are the King of Glory
823 You are the Lord

Love of God for us

4 A new commandment I give unto you
27 All things bright and beautiful
33 Alleluia, alleluia! I will praise the Father
43 And can it be
58 At the Lamb's high feast we sing
63 Awake, awake and greet the new morn
70 Be still and know that I am God (Iona)
77 Because the Lord is my shepherd
82 Bless the Lord, O my soul (E Walker)
86 Blessed be the Lord
93 Bread for the world broken (standard)
94 Bread for the world broken (Christmas)
100 Bring, all ye dear–bought nations, bring
102 Brother Sun and Sister Moon
864 Children of God
109 Christ is made the sure foundation
118 Colours of day
123 Come Christian people
124 Come, come, come to the manger
125 Come down, O love divine
131 Come, praise the Lord, the Almighty
137 Confitemini Domino
142 Day is done, but love unfailing
144 Dear love of my heart
145 Deep within I will plant my law
868 Father God I wonder
163 Father of heaven, whose love profound
177 For the beauty of the earth
178 For the fruits of his creation
207 God, beyond all names
210 God gives his people strength
211 God who made the earth
215 God is love, his the care
224 God the creator, you in love made me
226 God, your glory we have seen
230 Good Christians all, rejoice and sing
245 He became poor
273 I am the vine, you are the branches
276 I have loved you with an everlasting love
285 I, the Lord of sea and sky
289 I will be with you
290 I will never forget you
295 If God is for us, who can be against
296 If God is our defender
298 If I were a butterfly
878 If we are living
318 Jesu, Jesu, fill us with your love
319 Jesu, lover of my soul
886 Lead me Lord
353 Leaping the mountains
369 Like a shepherd he feeds his flock
889 Like a shepherd (We will rise again)
893 Lord of life
393 Lord, you are so precious to me
396 Lord, your love has drawn us near
397 Love came down at Christmas
398 Love divine, all loves excelling
399 Love is his word, love is his way
475 Loving shepherd of thy sheep
498 My God, I love thee not because
499 My God loves me
895 My Jesus, my Saviour
500 My Lord, what love is this
501 My people, I hear you calling
503 My song is love unknown
511 Now in this banquet
512 Now thank we all our God
513 Now the green blade riseth
517 O bread of heaven
898 O God, you search me
900 O Lord your tenderness
564 Oh God, I seek you
567 Oh Lord, all the world belongs to you
570 Oh the love of my Lord
591 Out of darkness
595 Peace is flowing like a river

Love for God

Love for others

Majesty and power

Mary

Mercy

Ministry

See also: Music Ministry

Mission

Morning

Music ministry

National

Peace

Petition

Praise

Priesthood of all believers

Repentance

Saints and angels

Salvation

Second coming

Self-offering

Strength and courage

Suffering

Thanksgiving

Truth

Victory over sin and death

Water

Way, truth and life

Word of God

Work

THE SCRIPTURE INDEX OF PSALMS INCLUDES: RESPONSONIAL PSALMS (see supplement settings) AND ALTERNATIVE TRANSLATIONS AND SONGS BASED ON THE APPROPRIATE PSALM.

Proverbs

Song of Songs

Wisdom

Ecclesiaticus (Sirach)

Isaiah

Jeremiah

Lamentations

Ezekiel

Daniel

John

Acts

Romans

1 Corinthians

2 Corinthians

NOTE

The numbering of some psalms in the Septuagint differs from that of the Hebrew Old Testament. Until now, most Roman Catholic liturgical books have followed the Septuagint numbering. Since the Hebrew numbering is now becoming standard, this is the system followed here. However, where the Septuagint number differs, it has been given in parenthesis.

A

B

C

G

H

T

Y

* * *

THE PRAYER OF THE CHURCH

Morning Prayer

Evening Prayer

Night Prayer

SERVICE MUSIC

Children's Eucharistic Acclamations

The Lord's Prayer

Breaking of Bread

Blessing

Plainchant settings

Complete settings

A NEW PEOPLE'S MASS

MASS FOR ALL SAINTS

ST. ANNE'S MASS

Psalm no.		*Supplement no.*	*Main no.*
ADVENT			
25/24	Remember, Remember – Paul Inwood		621
	In your love remember – Chris O'Hara		309
85/84	Let us see your kindness – Marty Haugen	S122	978
	Let us see O Lord – Elsie Wright	S120	976
	Give us your saving help – Chris O'Hara	S121	977
LENT			
51/50	Give me a new heart – Christopher Walker	S117	970
91/90	On eagles wings – Michael Joncas		832
	Be with me O Lord – Chris O'Hara	S123	979
130/129	Come to me and I will give you rest – Noel Donnelly	S135	991
EASTER			
118/117	Easter Alleluia Psalm Paul Inwood	S132	988
	The stone which the builders rejected – Bernadette Farrell	S133	989
66/65	It is good to give thanks – Christopher Walker	S124	980
	Cry out with joy to God – Chris O'Hara	S119	975
ORDINARY TIME			
19/18	You Lord have the message – Paul Inwood	S113	969
	More desired than gold – Chris O'Hara		720
27/26	One thing I ask – Stephen Dean	S115	971
	There is one thing I ask – Chris O'Hara		724
34/33	Taste and see – Stephen Dean		682
63/62	Your love is finer than life – Marty Haugen		564
	O Lord I will sing – Christopher Walker	S118	974
95/94	O that today you would – Chris O'Hara		555
	If today you hear – David Haas	S125	981
100/99	We are his people – David Haas	S128	984
	We are his people – Michael Coy	S127	983
103/102	Bless the Lord my soul – Taizé		81
	The Lord is compassion and love – G. BoultonSmith/Gelineau	S129	985
145/144	I will bless your name for ever – Martin Hall	S140	996
	I will give you glory – Chris O'Hara	S141	997

	Psalm	Title	Year A	Year B	Year C
972	33/32	May your love be upon us O Lord	2nd Sun of Lent 5th Sun of Easter	29th Sun in OT	
989	118/7	The stone which the builder rejected		4th Sun of Easter	
975	66/65	Cry out with joy to God	6th Sun of Easter		14th Sun in OT
977	85/84	Give us your saving help		15th Sun in OT 2nd Sun of Advent	
979	91/90	Be with me Lord in my distress			1st Sun of Lent
981	95/94	If today you hear his voice	3rd Sun of Lent 23rd Sun in OT	4th Sun in OT	18th Sun in OT
997	145/4	I will give you glory	14th Sun in OT		
973	51/50	Give me a new heart	Ash Wednesday ——————	Common /Lent	——————
974	63/62	O Lord I will sing	32nd Sun in OT		
980	92/91	It is good to give thanks		11th Sun in OT	8th Sun in OT
986	104/3	Send forth your Spirit	—————— The Easter Vigil	Pentecost	——————
992	131/30	Like a child rests in his mother's arms	31st Sun in OT		
983	100/99	We are his people	11th Sun in OT	Common	4th Sun of Easter
991	130/29	Come to me and I shall give you rest		10th Sun in OT	
976	85/84	Let us see O Lord your mercy	19th Sun in OT	2nd Sun of Advent 15th Sun in OT	
985	103/2	The Lord is compassion and love	Common		3rd Sun of Lent
993	136/5	O give thanks to the Lord who is good	Common		
984	100/99	We are his people	11th Sun in OT		4th Sun of Easter
994	138/7	The fragrance of Christ	21st Sun in OT		5th Sun in OT 17th Sun in OT
987	116/5	Our blessing cup is a communion	——————	Holy Thursday	——————
982	96/95	Today a saviour has been born to us	——————	Christmas Midnight Mass	——————
996	145/4	I will bless your name for ever	14th Sun in OT		5th Sun of Easter
970	23/22	Shepherd me O God	Common 28th Sun in OT 4th Sun of Lent 4th Sun of Easter		
978	85/84	Let us see your kindness	19th Sun in OT	2nd Sun of Advent 15th Sun in OT	
968	16/15	Keep me safe O Lord	3rd Sun of Easter	33rd Sun of OT	13th Sun in OT
969	19/18	You Lord have the message	Easter Vigil		
988	118/7	Alleluia Psalm	——————	Easter Sunday	——————
990	128/7	O blessed are those who fear the Lord	The Holy Family 33rd Sun in OT	The Holy Family 27th Sun in OT	
995	141/0	O Lord let my prayer rise like incense	Prayer		
971	27/26	One thing I ask of the Lord	7th Sun of Easter 3rd Sun in OT		2nd Sun of Lent
998	147	The Word was made flesh and lived among us (O Praise the Lord Jerusalem)	2nd Sun after Christmas